2d Edition

OFFICE AUTOMATION

A SYSTEMS APPROACH

Dr. Charles Ray
Department of Administrative
  Office Systems
Western Kentucky University
Bowling Green, Kentucky

Dr. Janet Palmer
Lehman College of the
  City University of New York
Bronx, New York

Amy D. Wohl
The Wohl Associates
555 City Lane Avenue
Bala Cynwyd, PA

WE50BA
PUBLISHED BY
SOUTH-WESTERN PUBLISHING CO.
CINCINNATI, OH   DALLAS, TX   LIVERMORE, CA

OSRA
Office Systems Research Assoc.
Model Curriculum Series

Inset cover photo © Jon Feingresh/The Stock Market

Copyright © 1991
by South-Western Publishing Co.
Cincinnati, Ohio

Library of Congress Cataloging-in-Publication Data

Ray, Charles M.
    Office automation : a systems approach / Charles Ray, Janet
Palmer, Amy D. Woh. — 2nd ed.
        p.   cm.
    ISBN 0–538–70036–X :
        1. Office practice—Automation.   I. Palmer, Janet (Janet J.)
II. Wohl, Amy D.   III. Title.
HF5548.R35   1991   89–26184
651.7—dc20   CIP

    2 3 4 5 6 7 8 9 D 7 6 5 4 3 2 1 0

Printed in the United States of America

PREFACE

OFFICE AUTOMATION: A SYSTEMS APPROACH, second edition introduces the interaction of people, processes, and technologies that form office information systems within contemporary organizations. The office environment has become critical to the profitability of business enterprises and to the efficiency and effectiveness of profit- and nonprofit-making organizations. Information and communication systems are major ingredients in the strategic plans of today's organizations. Office systems will provide a major influence upon the productivity of the world's more than 400 million information workers as we prepare for the beginning of a new century.

A systems approach—both in the study of office automation and in the application of its concepts to organizations—is used because all elements of an organization must function harmoniously if the organization is to succeed. Therefore, this text continues to stress both the social factors and the technological factors of contemporary office systems. It explores key concepts related to people, organizations, and technologies as they relate to the implementation of office automation. Systems that enhance the productivity of information workers (technology users) at all levels—professional, managerial, technical, and administrative support—are analyzed.

OFFICE AUTOMATION: A SYSTEMS APPROACH, second edition is an introductory text for college and university students, business and management professionals, information systems professionals, or participants in management training programs for these professional areas. It requires no previous study of information processing.

OSRA AND PSI ENDORSEMENTS

This second edition carries the endorsement of the Office Systems Research Association for the first course (OS1—Office Systems and Technologies) in that association's *Model Curriculum in Office Systems.* This text has also been endorsed by Professional Secretaries, International for the course Office Systems and Technology Management for that association's *Model Curriculum in Office Technologies.* The content is also appropriate for the Advanced Office Systems (CIS-9) course in the Data Processing Management Association (DPMA) *Model Curriculum for Undergraduate Computer Information Systems Education.*

NEW FEATURES IN THE SECOND EDITION

Among the features new to the second edition are expanded coverage and additional support. Specifically, this edition includes the new features described below.

FOUR NEW CHAPTERS

Chapter 6, entitled "Desktop Publishing and Reprographics Systems," has been added. The chapter "Implementing Office Systems" in the first edition has been expanded to a three-chapter series in the second edition. They are

Chapter 11: "Strategic Planning for Office Systems";
Chapter 12: "Office Systems Analysis and Design"; and
Chapter 13: "Office Systems Implementation."

Chapter 17, "Human Factors in the Office," has also been added. In addition to these new chapters, the "Careers in Office Systems" chapter has been moved to Chapter 3 and the coverage of ergonomics has been expanded in Chapter 10. All chapters in Part II, beginning with Chapter 4, have been expanded to include career implications for the described content area.

WOHL'S BUSINESS PERSPECTIVE

Amy Wohl, an office systems and information systems consultant to major firms throughout the United States and many foreign countries, joins this second edition as the author of "Wohl's Business Perspective," a new feature in each chapter. She provides for the student a real-world perspective of the material covered in each chapter.

DECISION ASSISTANT SOFTWARE

Colleges, universities, and corporate training centers adopting OFFICE AUTOMATION: A SYSTEMS APPROACH will be provided free software for student/trainee use in solving the six special cases at the end of the text. The Decision Assistant section is a collection of five problem-solving tools designed to guide learner thinking in situations related to office systems decisions.

OVERVIEW

Part I, "Introduction to Office Automation," approaches the study of office systems by examining its typical environment. Organizational dynamics and office technologies provide the basic foundations upon which office automation builds. The concept of *integrated office systems* is introduced. This concept is expected to influence the manner in which future generations of office personnel will process, distribute, and retrieve information. So that students may associate the systems being studied with real-world situations, Chapter 3 presents a discussion of office systems careers.

Part II, "Office Systems and Technologies," introduces major office systems technologies and the technologies associated with information resources management. It also encompasses all forms of communication and the use of technology to support business and professional communication. This part concludes with an examination of administrative support—both human and technical support.

Part III, "Management Strategies for Office Automation," concentrates on management decisions and personnel considerations necessitated by office automation. Ergonomics, the science of the working environment, is applied to the management of people in office environments. Critical management and analysis activities involved with implementation of office systems are explored, including strategic planning for the entire organization and planning for specific user groups. Current systems analysis, future systems design, staff selection and training, and hardware-software selection are covered.

Part IV, "Changes and Challenges of Office Automation," examines critical human factors currently at the forefront of office systems planning and identifies emerging technologies that are likely to influence office systems as these technologies mature. It introduces probable trends in society, organizations, and technology.

ACKNOWLEDGMENTS

We are grateful to the information systems professionals and educators who reviewed the manuscript and suggested improvements. We thank Dr. William E. Worth, Georgia State University, Atlanta, GA who served as a contributing author. In addition, we owe a significant debt of gratitude to the following persons who served as reviewers: Dr. Joyce L. Arntson, Irvine Valley College,

Irvine Valley, California; Dr. Ernest J. Bourgeois, Jr., Castleton State College, Castleton, Utah; Dr. Kay Durden, The University of Tennessee at Martin, Martin, Tennessee; Dr. Eleanor J. Flanigan, Ashton-Tat Corporation and Monclair State College, Upper Montclair, New Jersey; Dr. Maxine Hart, Baylor University, Waco, Texas; Dr. Joel D. Levy, J L Management, Rochester, New York; and Dr. Connie M. Masson, Unisys Corporation, Dallas, Texas. To students in our office systems classes at Western Kentucky University and Lehman College of The City University of New York and students and faculty members at other schools throughout the country, we offer a special thanks for suggestions and reactions to the first edition.

CONTENTS

PART 1

INTRODUCTION TO OFFICE AUTOMATION

CHAPTER 1

Concepts of Office Automation

OBJECTIVES

After studying this chapter, you should understand the following:

1. The definition of office automation
2. The socioeconomic trends that have affected the office
3. The changing office environment
4. The significance of computer, office, and communication technologies in office automation
5. The role of office automation in white-collar productivity
6. The advantages of office automation
7. The disadvantages of office automation

Office automation emerged as a popular buzzword during the early 1980s. Tremendous enthusiasm and interest was displayed for office automation by corporate America. During the eighties office automation moved from obscurity into the commonplace. For example, *The Wall Street Journal* in 1985 ran an article expressing the belief that as much as 90 percent of corporate America did not know what office automation was.[1] Yet only

---

1. John Marcum, Jr., "Computer Firms Fight to Win Market Share in Office Automation," *The Wall Street Journal* (April 8, 1985): 1.

a few years later Walter A. Kleinschrod wrote in the AMS (Administrative Management Society)-sponsored study, *Update 1987–1988: Approaching the Automated Office*, that now "everyone 'understands'" office automation because of the impact of the personal computer.[2]

Although some experts believe that the influence of office automation has waned, a more likely belief is that its tremendous potential has yet to be unleashed. While the current direction of office automation is not as clearly focused as in the past, its future seems solidly assured. This text is designed to help you understand the many forces, technologies, and management strategies that have shaped office automation and continue to affect its future. This is the story of office automation.

DEFINITION OF OFFICE AUTOMATION

Because of the many facets of office automation, people often mistake one or a few of its many areas for the real thing. Why should such misunderstanding exist when office automation has become so widespread? The reason is that the concept of office automation is broad and complex. What passes for office automation in one organization may be quite different in another organization or even within the same organization. Yet all of these different offices might properly be labeled automated.

Even the term "office automation" is challenged by some industry professionals as too mechanistic or not very expressive of the real meaning of office automation.[3] Other names in common usage are advanced office systems, advanced information systems, advanced information technology, and end-user computing. While all of these terms are acceptable, none has yet to achieve the status at the popular recognition level of the term "office automation." Considering the difficulty encountered in deciding upon just a name for the concept of office automation, imagine the complications in trying to define office automation.

Some experts say there are as many definitions of office automation as there are users. Actually, office automation can be defined from many different perspectives. For example, office automation can be approached from a technological viewpoint, focusing on equipment. Another approach might involve office automation as an improved method of communication. Still

---

2. Walter A. Kleinschrod, *Update 1987–1988: Approaching the Automated Office* (Willow Grove, Pa.: Administrative Management Society Foundation, 1987): 11.

3. *Ibid.*, 5.

another approach might be to study the design, implementation, and management of automated office systems. All of these approaches contain valid aspects of office automation. To understand the full scope of office automation, however, a broader view is required. A **sociotechnical approach** appears to be useful in this respect. Such an approach considers the behavioral aspects as well as the technical aspects of office automation. While these aspects can be studied independently, their interrelatedness is what gives office automation its distinctive character.

Using a sociotechnical approach, **office automation** can be defined as the concept involving the interaction of people in offices using technology to meet their organization's goals. Such a definition allows all of the elements of office automation — people, environment, equipment, and procedures — to be examined. The social aspect focuses on the people and their environment. The people include every classification of personnel — managers, professionals, technicians, secretaries, and clerks. The environment, while typically an office in an organization, can be anywhere today because of technology — from an airplane cabin to a hotel room to one's own home. The technical aspect focuses on the use of equipment and its related procedures. Office technology involves equipment such as computers, word processors, printers, copiers, dictation systems, and telecommunication systems. With this equipment, office activities such as data processing, word processing, electronic mail, electronic filing, graphics, desktop publishing, and personal computing are supported. With the use of these automated systems, office personnel are in a better position to contribute to the goals of their organization. Office automation has become commonplace in corporate America because of both internal and external forces of change.

INTERNAL AND EXTERNAL FORCES OF CHANGE

Historically the office had been neglected as a focus of concern by management. A large pool of well-trained clerical workers always had been available at relatively low wages. If the office work load increased, the solution had been for management to hire more clerical workers. By the late 1960s, however, the effects of a changing society gradually would force management to give more attention to the office.

IMPACT OF THE INFORMATION AGE

The postindustrial era has been labeled the **"information age."** This era generally is regarded as beginning during the mid-1950s. Two major events occurred then that changed the course of history. The first event was the shift in the work force from predominantly blue-collar occupations to white-collar occupations. The second event was the launching of Sputnik by the Russians, marking the beginning of the feasibility of satellite communications. These events were important to office automation because they signaled the beginning of the information age.

The most important resource in the information age is information. The products of the agricultural and industrial eras were goods, but the product of the information age is knowledge. In fact, the workers of the information age have been dubbed **"knowledge workers."** Their jobs involve the creation, processing, and distribution of information. Increasing numbers of the work force will be engaged in producing knowledge as technology reduces the need for people to grow food or manufacture goods.

SOCIOECONOMIC TRENDS

During the decades of the 1960s and the 1970s, many changes of a political, social, and economic nature occurred in society. The civil rights movement spawned other social movements where individuals felt that past practices were unfair or unreasonable. The women's liberation movement was one of these movements. Women were encouraged to select careers based on personal choice and not tradition. Responding to the movement, women opted for careers in nontraditional occupations. Thus some women became lawyers or managers instead of entering traditional occupations such as teaching and office work. What resulted was a national shortage of qualified office workers, presenting a problem for office management.

Another problem for office managers resulted from the extensive amount of paperwork generated in modern offices. Knowledge workers require information to make decisions. Most of this information arrives in printed or handwritten form on paper. Since 1960 the amount of paperwork generated in American businesses has increased almost 90 percent. Attempting to keep up with this overwhelming amount of paperwork often is referred to as the problem of **information overload**.

Other problems arose during the 1970s and continued into the early 1980s. A period of high inflation and high interest rates beset the American economy. For example, the prime interest rate (the rate charged by a bank to its best customers for short-term loans) at some banks was a modest 4¾ percent in 1972; but by late 1980 the prime interest rate had skyrocketed to 21½ percent, the highest level ever in U.S. history. Inflation also had a particularly strong impact on office costs. Workers demanded higher wages to keep up with a rapidly increasing cost of living. For example, in January, 1980, the consumer price index spurted

1.4 percent or at an annual rate of about 17 percent. This spurt represented the sharpest one-month increase since August, 1973. The effect of these price increases was significant for office operations. Since office work is labor intensive, approximately 75 percent of office costs are related to labor. Other office overhead, including rent, supplies, and utilities, also increased so that office costs represented a significant 40 to 50 percent of the total cost of doing business in most organizations.

Along with the problems of the clerical labor shortage, information overload, high interest rates, and inflation, there was a problem relating to national productivity. **Productivity** refers to the relationship of output to a unit of effort, usually measured in hours, by labor. The productivity levels in the business sector of the U.S. economy rose at an average annual rate of 3 percent from 1948 to 1973, but from 1973 until 1981 the rate of increase was only 0.8 percent. This decline in the national productivity level is associated with accelerating costs of production and price inflation.

Even by the end of 1988 the state of the national economy had failed to improve in many respects. The economist Herbert Stein noted that the inflation rate was still twice as high as the average of the years 1947 to 1967, that in only two years between 1947 and 1973 were unemployment rates as high as in 1987 (6.1 percent), and that between 1980 and 1987 the rate of growth of productivity was half as great as between 1947 and 1973.[4] Faced with difficult national economic problems, organizations struggled to maintain their competitiveness against aggressive business organizations abroad. In addition, the late eighties found numerous organizations coping with mergers, takeovers, deregulation, and aggressive international competition. Organizations were not the only ones dazzled and frazzled by the many political, social, economic, and technological forces of change besetting society. Individuals also experienced the impact of change.

THE CHANGING OFFICE

Revolutionary changes have occurred in the office because of the introduction of recent technology. Because of the continued advancements in technological development, these changes will continue to occur. The results of these changes have focused unprecedented attention and interest in the office. What is so remarkable about office automation, however, is the relative

4. Leonard Silk, "Economic Scene," *The New York Times* (September 2, 1988): D2.

Figure 1-1 Today's technology has
advanced far beyond the machines
displayed in this typical 1955-era
office.
The Bettmann Archive

swiftness with which these changes have occurred. To appreciate
how change has affected office work, consider the case of Jane,
the reentry office worker.

Jane Collins graduated from a business program in high
school in 1955 and went to work in the typing pool of an office at
the National Life Insurance Company. Jane had studied typing,
shorthand, business machines, filing, and bookkeeping in school
and was well prepared to assume her office duties. She used an
electric typewriter, made carbon copies of her typed work, and
stored the copies in a filing cabinet. She calculated totals on a
10-key adding machine and used the telephone to place and receive calls. After a year she was promoted from the typing pool
to private secretary for Ron Blake, one of the company's young
executives. In this position Jane moved to a desk located outside
of Ron Blake's private office. She took dictation in shorthand,
transcribed her notes on the typewriter, did the filing, and was
responsible for answering the telephone. After working for five
years, Jane left her job to get married.

In 1980 Jane decided to reenter the work force, since her children were grown. She applied for an office job once again at the

Figure 1-2 Jane interacts with co-workers in a contemporary office setting.
Piedmont Airlines

National Life Insurance Company. Because of Jane's previously fine work record at the company and the fact that she had maintained her typing skills, she was rehired. As Jane was shown to her workstation, she quickly realized that the office had undergone many changes over the last thirty years.

Jane was impressed with the new look of the office. Despite the many pieces of operating equipment, the office was quiet and also very attractive, with colorful panels separating the work space of individual workers. Jane's new position was as a trainee in the Word Processing Center. She reported to a word processing supervisor, whom she recognized as one of her former friends from the typing pool. At first Jane was afraid that she would not be able to deal with her new job, but with help from her supervisor Jane soon became a proficient word processing operator. Her duties included keyboarding machine dictation into a word processor. When the documents called for figures to be totaled or copies to be made, the equipment performed these functions easily.

About a year after Jane returned to work, she noticed on the company bulletin board a job announcement for a position as an administrative assistant to a team of managers in the Information Systems Department. This department was headed by Ron Blake, Jane's former boss. Jane applied for the position and was promoted; however, Ron Blake was not to be her boss. Instead she reported to an administrative support supervisor. In her new position Jane performed all nontyping secretarial functions, such as scheduling department meetings on the computer. Jane felt challenged as she mastered new equipment and procedures.

She was able to make a smooth transition to her new position because the National Life Insurance Company had a training department that provided help to employees like Jane.

The story of Jane, the reentry office worker, illustrates some of the major changes that have occurred in the office. These changes involve much more than the physical changes evident in office layout and equipment. Other changes involve office relationships, specialization of tasks, career mobility, and supervision.

In the traditional office, relationships generally were structured according to a one-on-one boss-secretary relationship or a typing/steno pool structure. Secretaries typically received promotions from the "pool" to become secretaries to individual bosses. In these positions secretaries functioned as generalists, performing all duties requested by their bosses. Secretarial duties ranged from the traditional ones, such as typing correspondence, to the performance of personal favors, such as shopping for gifts. Typically, career mobility of secretaries was tied to the career progression of their bosses. If their bosses advanced in the company, the secretaries generally moved right along with them. The work load of secretaries was determined by the work load of their bosses. Consequently, work loads in the traditional office frequently were uneven. Secretaries could spend much of their time waiting for work from their bosses or experiencing periods of idleness when their bosses were out of the office. The job performance of secretaries was supervised and evaluated by their bosses. Often these bosses were not aware of the skills and talents required for office work. Such a lack of knowledge by their bosses could result in a less than accurate job appraisal of the work of their secretaries.

The appearance of the automated office gradually is altering many of these traditional boss-secretary relationships. Organizations today with increasing frequency are recognizing the importance of teamwork. For the automated office, teamwork can mean that the work of several managers is supported by one or more secretaries and clerks. Advancement for the support staff is based on individual merit rather than on automatic career movement with a boss. The job duties of office workers may be specialized and technically oriented. Work assignments are distributed by an office-supervisor specialist who can provide more assurance of even work loads and fair evaluations.

The story of Jane, the reentry office worker, is only an example. Her experiences, however, would not be so different from the hundreds of thousands of office workers who have found themselves swept up in change. Let's take a few moments to examine how office automation has evolved into the highly regarded position it holds in corporate America today.

A CHRONOLOGY OF OFFICE AUTOMATION

Automation as a term first appeared in print about 1948 and usually is associated with the computer. However, **automation** can refer to any augmentation of the physical and mental capabilities of individuals by technology. Therefore, automation has earlier origins than the development of the computer.

Office automation evolved from three distinct areas involving data processing, word processing, and communication technologies. The evolution in office work can be traced by observing the development of these technologies. As computer technology became more pervasive, it caused a blending of these three areas so that clear-cut distinctions were more difficult to identify. Figure 1-3 illustrates the evolutionary progression of the technologies contributing to the development of office automation.

Figure 1-3 Technological Contributions to Office Automation

600 B.C.	Abacus (Chinese counting device)
1642	Mechanical adding machine (Blaise Pascal)
1822	Difference Engine (Charles Babbage)
1832	Telegraph (Thomas Edison)
1847	Boolean Algebra (George Boole)
1868	Typewriter (Christopher Latham Sholes)
1876	Telephone (Alexander Graham Bell)
1881	Dictation equipment
1885	Calculator (William S. Burroughs)
1890	Punch card and tabulating equipment (Herman Hollerith)
1915	Teletypewriter
1930	Analog computer—processes physical data (Vannevar Bush)
1932	Automated paper-tape typewriter
1933	Electric typewriter (IBM)
1935	Facsimile
1939	Electronic calculating machine (John V. Atanasoff and Clifford Berry)
1942	Mark I—forerunner of modern computer (Howard Aiken)
1945	ENIAC computer—processes digital data (J. Presper Eckert Jr. and John W. Mauchly)
1949	EDVAC (John Von Neumann's stored program concept)
1951	UNIVAC I (U.S. Census Bureau delivery)
1954	UNIVAC (first commercial use)
1961	Selectric typewriter (IBM)
1963	Minicomputer (Digital Equipment Corporation, DEC)
1964	MT/ST (IBM)
1969	MC/ST (IBM)
1971	Microprocessor (Intel)
1972	Video display system for word processing

Figure 1-3 **Technological Contributions to Office Automation** *(continued)*

1973	Diskette system for word processing
1977	Microcomputer (Apple)
1978	Electronic typewriter (EXXON)
1981	IBM personal computer
1980s	Networks

Note: Historians differ in reporting years for technology development. Some cite the year the design was conceived and others the year the design was completed. For that reason some of the above dates might vary from other sources.

COMPUTER TECHNOLOGY

Early computers of the 1940s had been used primarily for academic research and defense purposes. However, computer development during the 1950s had advanced sufficiently so that business could make practical use of their powers. The Remington Rand Corporation in 1954 made its first commercial installation of the UNIVAC at the General Electric Appliance Park in Louisville, Kentucky. The first impact of computer technology on business

Figure 1-4 In the 1950s, the UNIVAC was used primarily for data processing.
Photo courtesy of Sperry Corporation

was limited to data processing. This area of processing is concerned with operations dealing mainly with numbers for such activities as accounting and payroll. The computer was ideally suited to handle such large volume operations requiring rapid, repetitive calculations. Using the computer for data processing in business proved to be a more efficient way to process many time-consuming, routine business tasks. Later the computer's tasks would expand to include other types of office operations, including word processing and communications.

OFFICE TECHNOLOGY

Prior to the late nineteenth century, office work was accomplished by manual methods. Documents were prepared by clerks using pen and ink. The movement to the mechanical stage of office work began in the late nineteenth century with the invention of the typewriter. This event reduced the tedious task of handwriting documents, lowered the chance of error caused by illegible handwriting, and increased the quality and speed of document processing. The advent of typewriters also resulted in women entering office employment for the first time. Prior to 1880 almost all office workers were men. The inventor who perfected the design of the typewriter for commercial production, Christopher Latham Sholes, was proud of the social impact of his invention, which served to open the door for women to enter the business world.

In later years, another typewriter was to contribute to the development of office technology. While this typewriter did not have the vast social ramifications that the original typewriter did, it did have a significant impact on office technology. This

Figure 1-5   Before the typewriter was invented, clerks prepared handwritten office work.
The Bettmann Archive

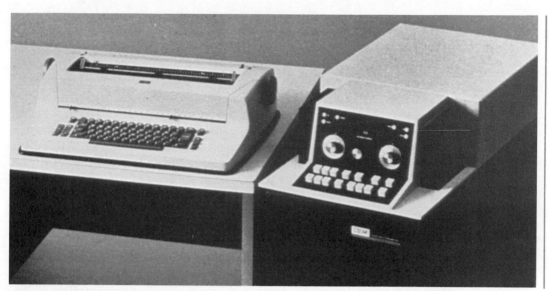

Figure 1-6   IBM's MT/ST
typewriter was a prototype of the
modern-day word processor,
developed in 1964.
*Courtesy of International Business
Machines Corporation*

typewriter was called the **automatic typewriter**. Its development
was the result of the efforts of the manufacturers of player pianos
to extend their market. The piano market had begun to fall off in
the 1930s as the radio became a more popular form of home
entertainment. Just as the player piano had, the automatic typewriter used a cylinder covered with paper tape with punched
holes. As the cylinder spun, it activated the keys for the typing of
repetitive documents. However, these typewriters were not particularly successful because of the difficulty of plugging up the
holes in the paper tape if revision of a document was necessary.

A later development of far more importance occurred in 1964
with the introduction of the **MT/ST** (Magnetic Tape/Selectric
Typewriter). With the new medium of magnetic tape, documents
could be edited easily, stored, and new material could be recorded
over the older document. This piece of equipment was the brain-
child of Ulrich Steinhilper of the IBM Office Products Division
in West Germany. He called this process "textverarbeitung,"
meaning "text editing." An improvement in 1969 by IBM in this
technology led to the introduction of the **MC/ST** (Magnetic Card/
Selectric Typewriter), which allowed the recording, storing, and
editing of text onto magnetic cards. The impact of these new

typewriters was of equal significance to the impact of the original typewriter. This equipment heralded the entry into the office of computer power for the production of documents. This new focus of technology would become known as word processing. The computer was now manipulating text as well as numbers.

During the early 1970s advancements came rapidly as word processing equipment became more sophisticated using **video display screens** (TV-like screens) and **diskette systems** (magnetic storage devices with a phonograph-like appearance). Although the idea of word processing met with relatively quick acceptance as a more efficient system with which to produce documents, the cost of the early word processing equipment ($10,000–$13,000) did restrict its widespread use. However, the cost factor was modified with the introduction of microcomputers in the late 1970s. These desktop size computers could be used to do word processing and were in a price range (under $10,000) that even small offices could afford. By the late 1970s the piece of equipment most synonymous with office work—the typewriter—was predicted to become obsolete by the end of the following decade.

Figure 1-7 By the 1970s, the word processor had evolved into video display terminals linked to diskette systems.
Photo courtesy of Wang Laboratories, Inc.

COMMUNICATION TECHNOLOGY

In addition to the computer and office technologies, the third area from which office automation derived its roots is that of communication technology. The process of **communication** involves the transmission of information. Offices have been transmitting information for some time. In the nineteenth century the communication process was aided by the inventions of the telegraph, the telephone, and dictation equipment. In the twentieth century these office staples were supplemented by the teletypewriter and facsimile equipment. The teletypewriter enabled the transmission of printed messages over the telephone lines. **Facsimile** refers to the process of transmission and exact reproduction of printed messages, photographs, and drawings over telephone lines. Further developments of communication technology in the 1970s, however, were destined to become vital to office automation.

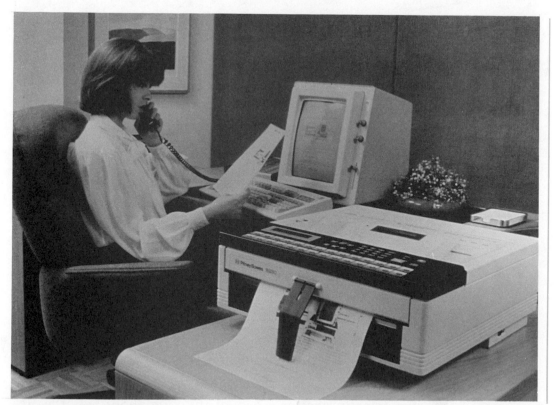

Figure 1-8 The FAX machine reproduces images over great distances almost instantaneously.
Pitney Bowes

Figure 1-9 The teletypewriter
transmits printed messages over
telephone lines.
Western Union Corporation

Previously, information had been transmitted primarily over
telephone lines, but now other methods included coaxial cable,
microwave transmission, satellites, and fiber-optic cable. Instan-
taneous communication could occur from workstation to workstation within the same office, same building, relatively close
geographical location, or even to remote sites around the world.
This improvement in communication technology was an important development for office automation because it enabled the
development of a systems approach to office work.

A **systems approach** is a way of thinking about how the elements of the office (people, environment, equipment, and procedures) can work together systematically to achieve organizational
goals and objectives. In the past, office functions tended to be

departmentalized and isolated. With a systems approach the interdependencies of office functions are emphasized. Such a development has been achieved with the use of new communication technology. Such technology has enabled the concept of networking to be applied to the office environment. **Networking** involves the linkage of office equipment electronically to enhance the communication process. Such linkage acts to generate greater efficiencies than previously possible with independent functions. Using traditional communication channels, such as interoffice mail, messages might take a day or even longer to reach their receivers. Networking allows messages to be transmitted electronically in just a few seconds even to remote destinations. For more than two decades now, advanced computer, office, and communication technologies have been impacting the office. Just how have these technologies affected the production of office work?

NEED FOR INCREASED OFFICE PRODUCTIVITY

Despite the application of advanced technologies to office work, **white-collar (office) productivity** remains low. Meanwhile, costs, especially salaries, continue to spiral. According to a Stanford Research Institute study, between 1960 and 1970 office productivity in the U.S. increased only 4 percent while industrial productivity rose 83 percent.[5] The President's Council of Economic Advisers reported declines in productivity between 1973 and 1986 in the industries most intensively involved in office work— finance, real-estate, and insurance. Yet, during the same period, factory productivity rose overall.[6] Another dramatic example of the low productivity problem is illustrated by **Olson's Theory.** This theory is based upon Olson's investigation regarding the productivity of the white-collar work force. According to Olson's Theory, white-collar workers produce on the average only four hours of effective work out of each eight-hour work day.[7] This imbalance between productivity and costs has fostered aggressive efforts on the part of organizations to increase productivity and decrease costs.

5. Alan Purchase and Carol F. Glover, *Office of the Future,* Stanford Research Institute Business Intelligence Program Guidelines (1001) (Menlo Park, Calif.: SRI International, April, 1976).

6. David Wessel, "Service Industries Find Computers Don't Always Raise Productivity," *The Wall Street Journal* (April 19, 1988): 37.

7. Val Olson, *White Collar Waste, Gain the Productivity Edge* (Englewood Cliffs, NJ: Prentice-Hall, Inc., 1983): 4.

Reports of low productivity rates should not be interpreted to mean that office workers are lazier or work more slowly than factory workers. Sometimes this unfavorable comparison is attributed to the fact that industrial workers until quite recently were supported by a higher capital investment than office workers. Olson and other consultants believe that office workers do not manage their time well. Whatever the reason, measuring office productivity is more complex than measuring industrial productivity. Substituting automated equipment in the office for human activity may simplify or speed up tasks, but it will not always guarantee increases in output.

p25 # 10

The low rates for white-collar productivity have become an issue of national concern. The farm and factory have been successfully automated with increased productivity as a result. The white-collar sector must also become more productive if our nation is to stay competitive in the global economy. The reason for the significance of office productivity to the U.S. economy is because more than half of the U.S. work force is employed in the white-collar labor sector as illustated in Figure 1-10. The **white-collar labor sector** refers to work groups titled clerical, professional/technical, managerial/administrative, and sales. The blue-collar sector refers to industrial workers. The service sector refers to occupations such as beauticians and waiters/waitresses. The sales sector includes store clerks as well as high-level marketing representatives. The farm sector includes agriculturally related occupations. The dominance of office-related work groups in the white-collar labor sector is illustrated in Figure 1-11.

Efforts to improve office productivity have, thus far, concentrated on the clerical office population because clerical work is easier to measure than managerial/professional work. The latter work group, however, has the most potential to improve office productivity levels because managers/professionals receive higher salaries than clerical workers do. Essentially the white-collar productivity problem is that workers earn more each year

Figure 1-10   Composition of U.S. Labor Force (Projected for 1990)

Type	Number in Millions	Percent
White collar	60.7	51
Blue collar	37.7	32
Service	18.9	16
Farm	2.2	2

Source: U.S. Department of Labor

Figure 1-11 **Composition of the White-Collar Work Force (Projected for 1990)**

Type	Number in Millions	Total Labor Force, %	White Collar, %
Clerical	22.2	19	34
Professional/technical	20.1	17	32
Managerial/administrative	10.4	9	18
Sales	8.0	7	15

Source: U.S. Department of Labor

while producing less. Since office automation has been touted as a means to increase productivity, but productivity levels have remained low, how then should top management view office automation?

THE STATUS OF OFFICE AUTOMATION

The reports from corporate America provide mixed reviews regarding the status of office automation. In a survey conducted by the United Research Company, a Morristown, NJ, consulting firm, 53 percent of insurance company chief executives said computers significantly reduced overhead costs. Yet in this same survey a sizable 37 percent of the executives claimed office automation did not lower overhead while 10 percent were undecided. Such statistics are not due to a lack of commitment to investment in office automation by the insurance industry. As much as 20 percent of their budgets are devoted to computers and the people who operate them. Expenditures by U.S. insurance companies on hardware alone amount to about $7 billion a year.[8]

In *Update 1987–88: Approaching the Automated Office,* the AMS study referred to previously, 83 percent of the executives who had been involved with office automation for a number of years resoundingly concluded that office automation does pay. In addition, four out of five of the executives said that they have plans to enlarge or upgrade their current office automation systems. Although overall white-collar productivity gains in the insurance industry and other industries are not very encouraging, evidence exists to suggest that office automation at the individual corporate level has proven beneficial.

8. David Wessel, *loc. cit.*

Perhaps some managers have discovered that their expectations of office automation were unrealistic. Office automation should not be relied upon as the only management strategy to cure the many problems facing organizations today. The more likely solution will require several management strategies.

The use of a variety of approaches to solve the problem of low office productivity is illustrated in a study conducted by the American Productivity Center. Organizations generally reported using one of three distinct approaches to improving office productivity. Some organizations employed human resource development programs and claimed productivity increases of up to 16.7 percent. Other organizations emphasized environmental design and cited gains of up to 11.6 percent. Organizations that focused on the use of automated systems reported increases ranging from 2 to 21.5 percent. Figure 1-12 illustrates the actual benefits realized from the use of automated systems to increase office productivity. Although the increases in productivity from the use of automated systems appear impressive, a conclusion of the study was that even greater productivity gains could have been achieved by organizations if a mix of methods involving human resources, environmental design, and automated systems were used.

Figure 1-12   Outcomes of Office Productivity Using Automated Office Systems

Outcomes	Percent of Users Who Recorded Improvement	Average Percent of Improvement
Staffing Requirements Reduced	66.7	10.4
Task Difficulty Reduced	81.5	15.4
Errors Reduced	85.2	8.5
Distractions Reduced	20.4	7.5
Response Time Reduced	70.4	21.5
Absenteeism Reduced	9.3	2.0
Turnover of Staff Reduced	11.1	6.0
Staff Grievances Reduced	22.2	6.0
Travel Time Reduced	18.5	5.0
Office Space More Efficiently Used	31.5	10.7
Necessary Communication Made Easier	61.1	11.4
Work Output Increased	87.0	16.3
Quality of Product or Service Increased	72.2	12.5
Timeliness of Delivery Increased	68.5	10.6
Needs of Client Better Met	61.1	9.4
Image/Credibility of Office Increased	55.6	10.9

Source: The American Productivity Center, *White-Collar Productivity: The National Challenge* (Grand Rapids, Mich.: Steelcase, Inc., 1982), pp. 28–29.

ADVANTAGES OF OFFICE AUTOMATION

Managers in great numbers generally have been willing to implement office automation because the concept arrived at the right time and at the right place to fill a real need. Some of the following benefits could be challenged by critics of office automation as relatively undocumented, but their statement here could be considered as ideals toward which organizations strive. Consequently, managers are seeking to attain the following advantages for their organizations:

1. *Support of organizational goals and objectives.* Automation contributes to the efforts of people in offices who desire to achieve the goals and objectives of their organization.
2. *Increases in productivity.* Worker output increases relative to hours worked.
3. *Increases in profitability.* If productivity climbs, expenses are decreased, thus increasing an organization's profits.
4. *Optimization of office staff.* Automation enhances human capabilities and compensates for labor shortages.
5. *Improvement in the speed of office output.* The time for creating, processing, storing, and distributing information is reduced.
6. *Improvement in the quality of office output.* Appearance, accuracy, and timeliness of information is enhanced.
7. *Improvement in managerial decision making.* Managers receive relevant information faster and can become aware of more alternatives for problem solving.
8. *Improvement in control over office work.* Managers can have more detailed knowledge of office worker output, often calculated automatically on computerized equipment.
9. *The linkage of office systems.* Users of automated equipment can be connected with other users for more efficient communication.
10. *Improvement in the quality of office work life.* Work can be more interesting, satisfying, and challenging as automation eliminates routine, repetitious tasks.
11. *Provision of new services.* Organizations can offer customers new services such as exclusive communication links for speedy order entry or access to company databases for tracking the status of their orders.
12. *Achievement of a competitive edge.* Because of the rapid pace of business, often conducted on a global basis, automated systems have become vital for accomplishing business transactions more efficiently.

DISADVANTAGES OF OFFICE AUTOMATION

Although organizations can receive many advantages from office automation, its use also can create some problems. These difficulties need to be addressed. In some cases the implementation of office automation has been delayed because of the following organizational concerns:

1. *Nature of office automation.* Without knowledge of the value of office automation, managers can exhibit inertia or resistance to change.
2. *Cost justification.* Many benefits of office automation are intangible—for example, improvements in the appearance of documents—and thus difficult to cost justify to top management. Also, office work traditionally has not been subject to work measurement, so data are unavailable for justifying the benefits of office automation.
3. *Organizational structure.* Often power struggles occur regarding the administration of office automation. Data processing, word processing, or other departments may clash.
4. *Organizational procedures.* New technological systems often are superimposed on older, outmoded procedures.
5. *People.* Issues relating to health and safety, privacy, morale, job displacement, training, unionization, and other matters can surface when office automation is implemented.
6. *Vendors.* Conflicting performance claims, incompatibility of equipment, rapid obsolescence of models, and business failures of vendors make selecting equipment hazardous duty.
7. *Software.* Off-the-shelf packages are often inappropriate, difficult to learn, or require extensive customizing by programmers.
8. *Security.* As more office staff members acquire access to computers, questions can arise regarding the extent of that access to organizational files.
9. *Legal.* The growth of computer usage presents increased opportunities for computer-based crime, such as illegal electronic transfer of funds or theft of computerized data.

A GROWTH INDUSTRY

The office automation industry is one of the prime areas of growth in the information age. The level of capital investment in technology for end user support was projected for 1990 to represent as much as 10 percent of the U.S. GNP (Gross National Product represents the total cost of all goods and services produced). A similar investment trend appears to exist on a global scale.[9] Knowledge workers total an estimated 100 million in the world, with more than half of these workers in the United States. A 1986–1987 study conducted by Arthur D. Little, Inc., and reported in the AMS study referred to previously, reached the conclusion that the penetration of office automation is actually much less than the literature would lead one to believe. Thus much opportunity for continued growth of office automation still remains.

The future of the office automation industry appears almost unlimited and subject to further advancements as computer-related technologies continue to emerge. The direction of office automation is not as clear-cut as in previous decades, but its multiple dimensions are permitting organizations to design individual solutions to fit their diverse needs. The changes that office automation has thus far brought about in the office workplace in a relatively short span of time have been nothing short of revolutionary. Few other developments have produced such major changes in the way people work and relate to one another.

WOHL'S BUSINESS PERSPECTIVE

What is Office Automation and How Does that Concept Continue to Change?

The idea underlying the concept of office automation is really quite simple. In any time period, it means applying available technology to support the work of the office.

In the past, technology could be applied, but it couldn't really provide automation. Individual tasks could be mechanized (e.g., a typist could type a letter instead of a secretary writing it), but the human element still outweighed the technological one. Most of what happened needed continuing input from human decisions.

Inherent in the idea of automating something is that we can string a whole group of useful tasks together—rather like a string of pearls—and describe the task to the technological support system (in this case, of course, a computer) in some way that permits the computer to make a significant number of decisions on its own. Of course, these decisions are based on human knowledge and input, but in a well understood process, quite a bit is possible.

The possibility of this kind of office automation has raised expectations (and fears!) in the business community. Frankly, very little of the office automation that has occurred so far would meet so rigorous a test. Much office automation today remains within the popular concept of simply applying available technology as it comes along.

9. Paul A. Strassman, *Information Payoff* (New York: The Free Press, 1985): 236–237.

This means that the automation of the office is often bumpy and sometimes illogical. Few companies are yet ready to build their own office systems and the expense of custom software development and maintenance may always make this impractical. We take what we can get and we apply it as best we can.

New, larger and more powerful hardware platforms and operating systems may soon change all this. We may be able to choose to build our own sets of office tools, combining them to suit the needs of individual organizations and to optimize the possible results. This would mean secretaries and professionals could share documents, but use different tools to operate upon them. Engineering firms could have a different set of tools than advertising agencies. And novice users could be supported differently than experienced ones.

Actually, like many technology-related concepts, office automation depends not upon revolution, but upon a steadily expanding evolution. Computers become faster, so they can process more and more difficult work. Tools become more sophisticated, more refined, and more integrated with one another. Users become more computer literate—and so do the organizations they work for.

Office automation depends upon our skills in blending available technology with available and changing people skills to support the work of this office. This means that as we process more and more information our tools must do more and more of the work. Otherwise, the value of the information we can create cannot be realized in the finite time we humans have to read, select, analyze, and use the overwhelming amount of data that continues to grow each year.

Successful organizations recognize that rapid and insightful processing of data leads to informed decisions. The tools for that are here. Now it is up to us to learn how to use them.

SUMMARY

Office automation can best be understood from a sociotechnical perspective. Such an approach considers both the behavioral and technical aspects of office automation. The elements of office automation involve people, environment, equipment, and procedures.

Socioeconomic conditions have affected the office. Advent of the information age, the women's liberation movement, demands for increased information, rising labor costs, and low productivity rates all contributed to the motivation for organizations to implement office automation.

The evolution of office automation can be traced from developments in computer, office, and communication technologies. Events of major significance include the first application of the computer for business data processing in the mid-1950s and the introduction in the mid-1960s of the MT/ST which evolved into word processing. During the mid-1970s the move to link separate office technologies into interdependent office systems became the focus of office automation. Advancements in technology will continue to infuse change into the office environment.

Although office automation has impacted the office for more than two decades, overall white-collar productivity rates remain low. Despite these statistics, top management continues to demonstrate faith in the promise of office automation to solve organizational problems.

Trends indicate that extensive opportunity still exists for the continued growth of the office automation industry. Office automation has been responsible in a relatively short period of time for nothing short of revolutionary changes in the way people work.

KEY TERMS

sociotechnical approach	video display screens
office automation	diskette systems
information age	communication
knowledge workers	facsimile
information overload	systems approach
productivity	networking
automation	white-collar productivity
automatic typewriter	Olson's Theory
MT/ST	white-collar labor sector
MC/ST	

REVIEW QUESTIONS

1. Why is the concept of office automation so often misunderstood?

2. What is a sociotechnical approach? How can a sociotechnical approach be used to understand the concept of office automation?

3. What is the relationship between the information age and office automation?

4. What socioeconomic trends influenced management to accept office automation?

5. How did the computer contribute to the development of office automation?

6. Using a sociotechnical approach, explain the role of the typewriter in the history of office automation.

pg 15 7. What is the role of communication technology in office automation?

pg 17 8. What is the value of a systems approach to office functions?

pg 17 9. After more than two decades of corporate involvement with office automation, what has been its impact upon productivity?

pg 18 10. Why is improvement of office productivity an issue of national concern?

11. Identify the benefits of office automation and the problems associated with implementing office automation.

pg 22 12. What are the prospects for growth in the office automation industry?

CASE STUDY: THE CASE OF THE CONFUSED VICE PRESIDENT

Monica Rivera, age 29, is the manager of fifteen office employees in the Administrative Services Department of the Pershing Corporation. Harold Smith, age 45, is the manager of five employees in the Data Processing Department at the Pershing Corporation. Both managers were sent recently by the vice president of Pershing to attend a conference on office automation sponsored by a computer vendor. Upon their return to work, the managers discussed with the vice president the feasibility of implementing office automation in their organization.

Monica Rivera told the vice president that office automation would be a perfect solution to the problems in her department. Her department has been unable to recruit qualified office workers to keep up with the mounting backlog of paperwork. Thus many office employees had to work overtime, increasing costs and hurting morale. However, Harold Smith told the vice president, "Office automation is just a fad and nothing more than a bunch of fancy typewriters." The vice president became so confused about office automation that he decided to employ the services of a consultant at Advanced Office Systems, Inc.

QUESTIONS/ACTIVITIES

If you were employed as this office automation consultant, how would you ease the confusion of the vice president?

SUGGESTED READINGS

Augarten, Stan. *Bit by Bit: An Illustrated History of Computers.* New York: Ticknor & Fields, 1984.

Bostrom, R.P., and J.S. Heinen. "MIS Problems and Failures: A Socio-Technical Perspective, Part 1: The Causes." *MIS Quarterly*, Vol. 1, No. 3 (1977): 17–32.

Harris, C.L., et. al. "Office Automation: Making it Pay Off." *Business Week* (October 12, 1987): 142.

Kleinschrod, Walter A. *Update 1987–1988: Approaching the Automated Office.* Willow Grove, Pa.: Administrative Management Society Foundation, 1987.

Marcum, John, Jr. "Computer Firms Fight to Win Market Share in Office Automation." *The Wall Street Journal* (April 8, 1985): 1, 7.

Meyer, N.D., and M.E. Boone. *The Information Edge.* New York: McGraw-Hill Book Co., 1987.

Naisbitt, John. *Megatrends: Ten New Directions Transforming Our Lives.* New York: Warner Books, Inc., 1982.

Shurkin, Joel N. *The Engines of the Mind: A History of the Computer.* New York: W. W. Norton & Co., Inc., 1984.

Strassman, P.A. *Information Payoff.* New York: The Free Press, 1985.

Tapscott, Don. *Office Automation: A User-Driven Method.* New York: Plenum Press, 1982.

Toffler, Alvin. *The Third Wave.* New York: William Morrow & Co., Inc., 1980.

CHAPTER 2

Organizational and Systems Concepts

OBJECTIVES

After studying this chapter, you should understand the following:

1. Organizational concepts
2. Organizational development, goals, climate, structure, and systems
3. Behavioral concepts
4. Office concepts
5. Office taxonomies
6. Office systems
7. The information center
8. Information center services and benefits
9. The integrated office systems concept
10. Strategies for implementing integrated office systems
11. Obstacles blocking the implementation of integrated office systems
12. Solutions to obstacles blocking the implementation of integrated office systems

   The study of office automation should not be viewed as an end in itself. Equally important is the total environment in which office automation exists. That environment generally consists of an organization involving numerous systems. Therefore, a knowledge of organizational and systems concepts complements the study of office automation.

ORGANIZATIONAL CONCEPTS

Office automation has met with rapid acceptance in the organizational environment. Therefore, individuals interested in office automation should develop an awareness of the dynamics of organizations. Knowledge of organizational concepts involves many different characteristics of the organization, including its development, goals, climate, structure, and systems.

ORGANIZATIONAL DEVELOPMENT

The modern organization emerged in the nineteenth century during the early days of the industrial era. Organizations in the United States began to mass manufacture goods and operate large enterprises, such as the railroads. Prior to the mid-nineteenth century, small, family-owned businesses were the common form of business organization. However, by the turn of the century (1890–1910), which coincided with the expansion of American enterprise and the development of machine technology, large organizations dominated the business world. Associated with organizational development was the emergence of the white-collar work force. Large organizations needed professional managers to plan and make decisions and clerks to keep records and process the paperwork.

ORGANIZATIONAL GOALS

The chief purpose of an organization is to accomplish its mission. This mission can be expressed as its overall goal toward which the organization's activities are directed. For example, a publishing company would have as the prime reason for its existence the servicing of its targeted market with the publication of appropriate books. Besides this goal other goals would contribute to further the purpose of the organization, such as efforts to diversify the nature of the organization to ensure its future economic growth and stability.

Within the publishing company other units would adopt complementary, specific objectives to help achieve the goals of the organization. Objectives indicate what performances are necessary to achieve the goals of the organization. One such objective might be that the acquisitions editor of the publishing company might scout prospective authors at conferences. The mission of office automation is to assist the organization in accomplishing its goals and objectives. Examples of applying office automation directly to organizational functions include applications such as providing immediate responses via facsimile to customer requests for price quotations and providing sales representatives with portable computers to strengthen on-site presentations.

ORGANIZATIONAL CLIMATE

One of the major methods used to portray the characteristics of an organization is with the concept of climate. **Organizational climate** refers to the perceived characteristics present in the work environment. The concept is important because it can affect such things as personnel recruitment, employee morale, productivity, management style, and philosophy. Ultimately, organizational climate affects the manner in which the goals of the organization are accomplished.

Organizational climate can be thought of as environmental personality. Because of the complexities inherent in an organization's personality, it is best described multidimensionally. Three such major dimensions of the work environment each with its own set of characteristics, include the following:

1. *Relationship dimensions.* This area involves the relationships among employees and between managers and employees.
2. *Personal development dimensions.* This area involves the extent to which employees are encouraged to be self-sufficient by making their own decisions and the extent to which the climate emphasizes good planning, efficiency, and getting the job done.
3. *System maintenance and system change dimensions.* This area involves such characteristics as work pressure, the functioning of the work group, the extent of change and innovation, and the degree of pleasantness of the physical surroundings.

Figure 2-1 lists in more detail the characteristics associated with each dimension of the organizational environment.

Figure 2-1 **Work Environment Characteristics**

RELATIONSHIP DIMENSIONS

Involvement.   The extent to which workers are concerned and committed to their jobs, including their enthusiasm and constructive activity.

Figure 2-1 **Work Environment Characteristics** *(continued)*

Peer Cohesion. The extent to which workers are friendly and supportive of each other.

Staff Support. The extent to which management is supportive of workers and encourages workers to be supportive of each other.

PERSONAL DEVELOPMENT DIMENSIONS

Autonomy. The extent to which workers are encouraged to be self-sufficient and to make their own decisions.

Task Orientation. The extent to which the climate emphasizes good planning and efficiency, and encourages workers to get the job done.

SYSTEM MAINTENANCE AND SYSTEM CHANGE DIMENSIONS

Work Pressure. The extent to which the press of work dominates the job milieu.

Clarity. The extent to which workers know what to expect in their daily routines and how explicitly roles and policies are communicated.

Control. The extent to which management uses rules and pressures to keep workers under control.

Innovation. The extent to which variety, change, and new approaches are emphasized in the work environment.

Physical Comfort. The extent to which the physical surroundings contribute to a pleasant work environment.

Source: Adapted and reproduced by special permission of the Publisher, Consulting Psychologists Press, Inc., Palo Alto CA 94306, from *Combined Preliminary Manual Family, Work and Group Environment Scales* by Rudolf H. Moos, Paul M. Insel, and Barrie Humphrey © 1974. Further reproduction is prohibited without the publisher's consent.

ORGANIZATIONAL STRUCTURE

Structure is common to all organizations, although its particular form within individual organizations may vary. The chief basis for determining organizational structure is function. Work of the organization usually is classified by functional specialization, such as production, marketing, and administration. Structure is a means of classifying organizations and may be formal or informal. An organization's **formal structure** is depicted on an organizational chart. An organizational chart is a tool indicating who is responsible for what and who reports to whom. An organization's informal structure is not represented graphically on an organizational chart.

The concept of the **informal structure** refers to self-groupings that humans naturally form. The informal structure can be as important as the formal structure in accomplishing the goals of the organization. Generally, the formal structure would be more important in situations where decision making is governed by well-defined organizational policies. The informal structure might be more important in situations where the less precisely defined circumstances of organizational politics occur. For example, a staff position of assistant-to-the-president may exist on the organizational chart, but the most influential person with the president might be a spouse or secretary. An understanding of organizational politics is generally necessary for the achievement of business success, including the successful implementation of office automation. However, the concept of organizational politics will be discussed in more detail in the human factors chapter.

Line and Staff.   One of the most typical structures shown on an organizational chart is called line and staff. Line and staff designations refer to positions of individuals located on the organizational chart. Whether a position is classified as line or staff depends on the nature of the organization. Persons occupying **line positions** are responsible for those activities pertaining to the achievement of goals directly related to the purpose or purposes of the organization. For example, line positions in a manufacturing organization would include the vice presidents for production and marketing. The production department deals with the manufacturing of goods, and the marketing department deals with the distribution of those goods. Both of these departments function to carry out the primary purposes for which a manufacturing organization exists.

Persons occupying **staff positions** are usually specialists such as lawyers, accountants, and engineers. These individuals assist those in line positions in the organization. Staff specialists have line responsibility in their own departments, but the organizational chart would reflect only their advisory responsibilities. Staff positions within a manufacturing organization would be located in departments such as accounting, finance, purchasing,

personnel, and administrative support. In the accounting department, business and financial transactions are classified, recorded,
and analyzed. In the finance department, management deals with
its capital resources such as credit and investments. The purchasing department involves the procurement of materials and
supplies to be used by the organization in its operation. The personnel department is concerned with employee selection, placement, training, and services. The administrative-support function
provides the office services necessary for conducting the business
affairs of the organization. Figure 2-2 illustrates an organizational chart with a line and staff structure.

Figure 2-2   Partial Organizational Chart for Line and Staff Structure in a Manufacturing Organization

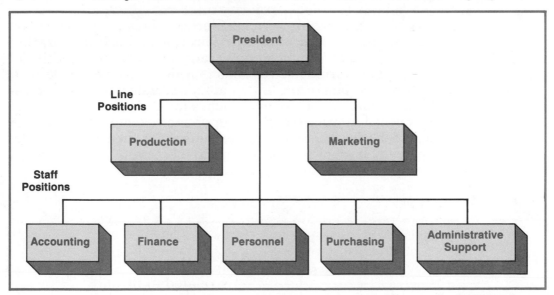

Power. Another characteristic of organizations closely related
to line and staff structure deals with power or the flow of authority. Power can be centralized, decentralized, or in a matrix design.
With a **centralized design**, authority is concentrated at the top
management level and flows down to the ranks. Planning and
decision making are not viewed as responsibilities to be shared
with employees. With the **decentralized design**, policy making,
planning, and decision making are dispersed throughout the
ranks. The guiding philosophy of decentralization is that decisions should be made at the lowest possible level. With the **matrix
design**, authority is based on the concept of project management.
Here the work of the organization is carried out by a group or

groups of people who are responsible for the completion of a particular job. Individuals from the traditional functional structure are assigned to a project based upon their expertise. These individuals have a dual-reporting relationship to the functional department head and to the project manager. Project managers usually report to a project coordinator. Figure 2-3 illustrates the flow of authority in an organization with a matrix design.

Some of the benefits of the centralized approach include a uniformity of management operations, a reduction in duplication of effort, and a reduction in the risk of inadequate decision making by subordinates. With the decentralized plan, the motivation of employees can be enhanced because of their participation in management operations. Also, decision making can be speedier and adapted to local conditions. Top management thus has more time available for higher priority matters.

The matrix design is not considered to be a replacement for the traditional structures of centralization and decentralization but is added to an organization's traditional structure. This design has a useful role in situations that involve a clearly defined project with a temporary life. In actual practice, most organizations use a combination of approaches for their power structure. The choice of approach depends upon many factors, such as the nature of the organization, its size, complexity, management style, competency level of personnel, and the extent of automation.

Figure 2-3   Matrix Design

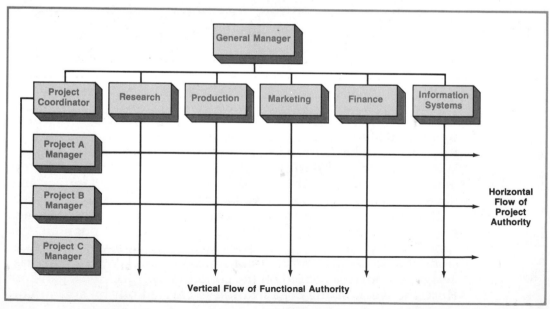

ORGANIZATIONAL SYSTEMS

The systems concept can be applied to the study of organizations. A **system** is defined as a set of related elements that interact with each other to achieve a purpose. Examples of systems include the solar system and the digestive system. The entire organization represents the total system, and its various subdivisions compose its subsystems. These subsystems can be organized in a variety of ways, such as by geographical location or type of customers served, but typically organizations use a functional structure and organize by department. Those departments directly related to the purpose(s) for which the organization exists are referred to as primary systems, such as the production department in a manufacturing organization. Those departments that exist to assist the primary systems in helping them achieve their purpose(s) are referred to as **support systems**, such as the personnel department.

Other systems broadly identified as social and technical also can be used to describe internal forces affecting organizations. The social system involves the behavior of the members of the organization. Influencing this behavior are a number of social forces, including employee needs, values, motivations, attitudes, and expectations. The technical system of an organization includes its physical facilities, technologies, structure, and procedures needed to accomplish its goals. In addition, a variety of systems external to the organization influence its operations. These include physical, political, legal, ethical, economic, social, and technological systems. Brief descriptions and examples of these external systems are given in Figure 2-4.

A systems model appears in Figure 2-5. This model depicts how external systems enter the organization and become integrated with its internal systems. According to the systems model, forces enter the organization as input. The processing stage transforms the input in some way. The end result of this transformation is the output. Following this stage, however, the cycle may continue because of feedback. The term feedback refers to information received about the transformation process and can be the basis for its future modification.

An organization that operates without consideration of its external environment is a **closed system**. An organization that considers the external environment in its operation is an **open system**. Managers who fail to follow an open-system approach place their organizations in jeopardy. If, for example, management ignores technological advancements and continues to operate without such advantages, the organization may become unable to compete effectively. In some cases management can choose which systems will influence their organizations. In other cases external systems encroach upon organizational territory without invitation. Therefore, managers need to be alert to trends in society's systems and attempt to prepare for their effects. For example, when the clerical labor shortage affected the recruitment of qualified office personnel, some organizations reacted by establishing their own office training departments.

Figure 2-4 External Systems

Physical. Environment of the land, sea, and air. *Example:* Organizations monitor their emissions and waste products to safeguard land, water, and air quality.

Political. Governmental units (national, state, local). *Example:* Organizations lobby with legislative bodies in efforts to obtain favorable laws regarding taxation, trade, zoning, etc.

Legal. Laws. *Example:* Organizations comply with all laws affecting operations, such as safety, employment practices, and taxation.

Ethical. Morals and values. *Example:* Organizations generally follow prevailing standards of morality and conduct to maintain a good public image. Refusal to sponsor controversial television programs or accept advertising conflicting with such standards is not uncommon.

Economic. Activities involving the production, distribution, and consumption of goods and services. *Example:* When slumps occur in the economy, organizations may lay off employees, suspend operations, or file bankruptcy.

Social. Interrelationships between individuals, groups, and institutions. *Example:* Organizations include individuals on their governing board from outside the organization, recognize ethnic groups in advertising, and engage in philanthropy.

Technological. Applications of scientific knowledge to practical purposes. *Example:* Organizations use computers for information processing needs.

Managers faced with the complexities of society as well as the complexities present in their own organizations can benefit from use of the systems approach. With a systems approach managers can analyze and integrate the numerous internal and

Figure 2-5 **A Systems Model**

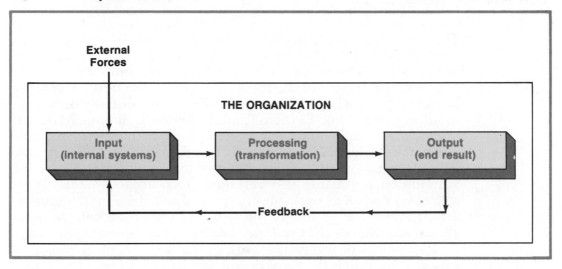

external forces affecting their organization. Such an approach can be vital to organizational survival. Managers need to understand how a change in one system affects other systems. A systems approach provides management with an orderly, unifying vision necessary for comprehending numerous, diverse systems.

BEHAVIORAL CONCEPTS

The social system of an organization involves the behavior of humans both internal and external to the organization. Human behavior can also be analyzed using the systems approach. The input into an organization, the processing affecting all of its activities, and its output are significantly affected by individuals and groups of individuals. For example, as employees, individuals contribute their skills, knowledge, attitudes, motives, needs, and values; whereas groups supply their cohesiveness, norms (standards of behavior to which conformity is expected), ideas, and conduct.

The social system internal to an organization is inherent to its success. Without this human element an organization could not achieve its goals and objectives. The student of office automation needs to be aware of how human factors affect the organization. The topic of human behavior as it impacts the organization will be discussed in more detail in the human factors chapter. In addition, behavioral concepts will be stressed in the chapters dealing with the work environment and personnel management.

OFFICE CONCEPTS

The office can be defined as a support system in which people process information using technology to serve the needs of an organization. The office developed as a significant support system with the growth of the modern organization in the late nineteenth century. The presence of an office is practically universal to all organizations. Large or small, domestic or international, organizations depend upon an office to meet their external and internal administrative needs. Although the term office is still widely used to refer to a specific physical location, the effect of automation is causing this reference to become archaic. With technology, such as portable computers and voice mail (computerized telephone systems), the work of the office can be done almost anywhere—for example, while at home or when traveling.

Regardless of where the work of the office is performed, its primary mission is the provision of services to support the organization. The nature, volume, and frequency of these services are usually determined by factors outside of the office. For example, office workers initiate processing in response to orders received, shipments to be made, or letters to be answered. Because of the reactive nature of office work, it is considered less structured than some other functional areas in organizations.

People who work in the office are called white-collar workers. They are composed of two basic groups. In the first group are the **knowledge workers**, consisting of those who use information to make decisions. Included in this group are people who are managers, such as the vice presidents of various departments; professionals, such as lawyers or architects; and technicians, such as systems analysts or engineers. The major work responsibilities of knowledge workers include the traditional management functions of planning, organizing, directing, staffing, and controlling. The second category of workers is called the **support staff**. These workers manipulate or provide information for knowledge workers and may have some responsibility for routine administrative decision making. Classification of support staff workers includes executive secretaries, administrative assistants, word processing specialists, data-entry operators, bookkeepers, and clerks.

OFFICE TAXONOMIES

Taxonomies (classifications) can be helpful in understanding offices and office work. Traditional descriptions of office activities probably would include typing, filing, and answering the telephone. Perhaps mention might be given to the taking of shorthand dictation, the keeping of books, or doing paperwork. While these activities might have been adequate to describe the offices of the past, are they appropriate in describing the automated office? The diverse nature of office work often is obscured by generalizations. In reality, not all office environments are uniform or standardized. Understanding the differences and complexities present in offices is important to the implementation of office automation. Offices support various information needs and therefore require different information systems and strategies. The use of office taxonomies will help those responsible for office automation in an organization to recognize and distinguish among office types and their information processing requirements.

Office Types. A useful, broad taxonomy describes offices as type I or type II. The distinction between the types is based upon the nature of the office work performed. In **type I offices**, information processing is of a fairly routine nature and includes activities related to the handling of ordinary correspondence, business forms, regularly scheduled reports and documents, and clerical procedures such as filing. In **type II offices**, knowledge work predominates and includes nonroutine or customized activities involving problem solving and decision making at a nonclerical level. In actual practice, offices in each classification might engage in a mix of some routine and nonroutine information processing activities, and no office may fit a type I or type II category exactly. However, with this taxonomy a greater degree of clarity can be attained regarding office types. Figure 2-6 provides more details regarding this taxonomy of office types.

Figure 2-6   A Taxonomy of Office Types

	Type I Office	**Type II Office**
Activities:	Routine information processing such as payroll, accounting, billing, check writing, reservation systems	Nonroutine information processing such as work of line managers, staff managers, legal or engineering departments
Procedures:	Extensive	Loose
Staff:	Primarily clerical	Primarily managers and professionals and their secretaries
Evaluation:	Efficiency measures (production/cost with certain quality considerations)	Effectiveness measures (right operations with some consideration to efficiency)

Office Work.   A more complex taxonomy of office types can delineate the nature of office work with even more accuracy. The type I category can be divided into subcategories of flow, batch, and custom offices, and the type II category can be divided into the subcategories of executive, line, and professional offices. Figure 2-7 provides descriptions for these subcategories of office work.

OFFICE SYSTEMS

Office functions are part of the support system of an organization. If office functions are organized as separate divisions, then the office function is composed of subsystems. Most frequently

Figure 2-7   Anatomy of Office Work

TYPE I

Flow.   One main procedure executed repeatedly; relatively rare in business; examples include reservation or credit department

Batch.   Switches back and forth between kinds of jobs; highly routinized and automated but with some diversity; most work governed by strict guidelines

Custom.   Each event handled specially because of complexity; example: contract administration department; extensive guidelines and procedures with repetitiveness of events

TYPE II

Executive.   Offices of corporate executives; broad jobs involving mostly telephone use and face-to-face meetings; complex, loose procedures; heavy secretarial/staff support.

Line.   Offices of lower and middle line managers; 20–30 percent of their time spent at desk work; fairly complex jobs.

Professional.   Offices of nonline managers or executives such as lawyers, architects, or planners; about 40 percent of their time spent at desk work; secretarial support usually limited.

these subsystems are referred to simply as office systems. The office systems are introduced briefly in Figure 2-8 and will be discussed in much greater detail later in this textbook.

Office systems might function as independent departments or might be activities incorporated into a general-purpose office. The goal of office automation is to integrate all of the office systems.

Figure 2-8 **Office Systems**

Administrative Support. A system involving a variety of office activities generally performed for knowledge workers by support staff often with the use of the computer to do tasks such as scheduling, calendaring, and list processing (accessing items on a list to use in a variety of ways, such as sorting a mailing list by geographic territories for a salesperson).

Decision Support. A system involving a variety of activities usually performed by knowledge workers with the computer for accessing organizational files, planning and tracking projects, calculating, analyzing, projecting, modeling financial information, and using graphics.

Data Processing. A system usually associated with large-volume operations whereby raw data (detailed facts and numbers) are converted into useful information.

Word Processing. A system involving the use of specialized personnel, the environment, procedures, and automated equipment for document production.

Reprographics. A system for obtaining copies of written or graphic information with a variety of techniques including duplicating and printing as well as computerized and filming (micrographic) processes.

Phototypesetting. A system by which information is converted into type using a photographic process.

Records Management. A system involving activities related to the storage, retrieval, maintenance, and disposition of information as well as its supervision.

Telecommunications. A system involving the movement of information from one location to another location by a variety of transmission methods.

THE INFORMATION CENTER

A relatively new support system within the organizational structure is the **information center**. In some organizations the information center is a permanent physical location, but in other organizations the approach is more conceptual. The information center concept was first promoted in 1976 by IBM of Canada to increase job productivity and decrease data processing backlog. The information center became firmly established in most large organizations during the early to mid 1980s when microcomputers and their many end users began to increase significantly. The end user clients of the information center represent all levels of organizational personnel—professionals, managers, supervisors, and clerical staff—who use computer power at their workstations. The information center provides end users with training and support services for computer skills so that they can use information resources to improve decision making and increase job productivity.

INFORMATION CENTER SERVICES

The types of services provided by information centers are changing in response to the increasing computer sophistication of end users. The findings of the annual CRWTH[1] information center survey of large organizations housing information centers illustrates this transformation. Originally, training was the most common service associated with information centers. (The role of information centers in training end users will be discussed in more detail in a later chapter.) Now, according to the survey, the most frequently reported service of information centers was analysis of end user requirements. Another trend reported in the survey was the take over by the information center of the function of selecting end user hardware and software from the data processing area. The survey also reported a leap in popularity in user demands for mainframe-micro connectivity and application development. Figure 2-9 illustrates typical services provided by information centers and the percentage of centers reportedly offering those services.

---

1. CRWTH (pronounced "crooth") refers to an obsolete Celtic musical instrument somewhat like a violin. The name is symbolic of melodic harmony, which can be likened to the harmony possible among organizational functions with integrated office systems.

Figure 2-9   **Information Center Services**

Type of Service	Percentage Offering Service
Analyze end user requirements	92
Train end users	86
Select end user hardware & software	86
Provide mainframe-micro link	84
Provide hotline support	81
Provide access to corporate data	80
Provide computer graphics facility	68
Provide application programming	33

Source: Third Annual CRWTH Information Center Survey. *CRWTH News for Better Training* (Information Center Survey Special Report, 1987), pp. 1–7.

INFORMATION CENTER BENEFITS

Information centers have been successful because of the many benefits they provide organizations. The CRWTH information center survey, however, indicates that the nature of these benefits is changing as the information center matures within organizations. In the early eighties, the chief benefit organizations received from information centers was the development of computer literacy among end users. Although information centers still provide that benefit, the chief benefit received by organizations today is the increased job productivity afforded end users. End users also benefit from assistance in the use of information technology for faster and better decision making. Additional benefits include improved relations between end users and the data processing personnel, improved quality of end user applications, and reduction of the data processing backlog. The benefits derived from the information center are moving end users beyond the processing of routine information. The information center is becoming instrumental in helping end users sharpen the competitive edge of their organizations. The introduction of the information center into organizations is making dramatic changes in the way work gets done. Another dramatic change affecting organizations is the integration of office systems.

THE INTEGRATED OFFICE SYSTEMS CONCEPT

The linkage of separate information systems into one system accessible to a number of users is referred to as **integrated office**

systems. Although a popular buzzword of the 1980s, the concept was conceived in the 1970s in conjunction with discussions of the office of the future. In most organizations, however, the implementation of integrated office systems remains a goal instead of a reality.

INTEGRATED OFFICE SYSTEMS

The central idea behind the integration of office systems is that each system, such as data processing, word processing, and records management, becomes connected with each other system. In this way each system becomes more valuable because when systems are linked, access to information and speed of communication increases considerably for users. In the traditional office, each system within the organization addressed only a specific task or set of tasks and remained isolated. With integrated office systems, information processing becomes more efficient and convenient. The goal of integrated office systems is for all office personnel—managers, professionals, technicians, and clerical workers—to have computer power for a variety of information processing functions at their own workstations or in a nearby location.

The information processing functions performed by users of integrated office systems can include the gathering, storing, modifying, reviewing, analyzing, and moving of information from one physical location to another. The most basic form of an integrated office system generally includes word processing, data processing, records management (electronic filing), and telecommunications for electronic mail/message distribution. More advanced integrated office systems might include administrative support, decision support, and voice mail systems. Other integrated office systems may allow teleconferencing (meetings conducted electronically with participants at remote sites), access to phototypesetting, and security and time-attendance monitoring.

Integrated office systems represent a true information system—many individual technologies functioning in concert to serve the information needs of those who carry out an organization's goals. The greatest single influence on the blending of technologies to form integrated office systems was the introduction and acceptance of the personal computer. This phenomenon created an atmosphere in which millions of nontechnical office personnel began to expect and demand more and more computing capabilities to perform their work. With an integrated office system these users have a more powerful system than with independent technologies.

The benefits of an integrated office system to an organization are many. Primarily, the productivity level of the office should be affected positively because of reliance on the same or even fewer resources. The impact of integrated office systems can result in cost reductions in labor and materials with time savings in formatting, keyboarding (entering data or text on a typewriterlike device), filing, searching, and delivering. Also, teamwork generally increases among organizational members, often resulting in improvement in customer service. Ultimately such improvements can result in increases in an organization's profits. All of these benefits, of course, are not likely to occur without a well-designed plan for integrated office systems.

STRATEGIES FOR IMPLEMENTING INTEGRATED OFFICE SYSTEMS

Planning is necessary to develop an integrated office system. Because of the complexity of office systems and the rapidity with which changes occur in this area, a strategic plan is recommended. **Strategic planning** involves a long-range, holistic approach. An organization can tailor an integrated office-system plan according to its own needs and desired future direction. This sense of strategic vision is very important for the organization so that all planning, purchasing, and implementation can be directed toward achieving its goals. Consideration of such a plan for integrated office systems often necessitates restructuring the entire organization.

Restructuring might be necessary because an integrated office system impacts on every aspect of an organization. Not only will the way that work is initiated and processed be affected but also the way that the organization delivers its products or services. For example, stockbrokers who use computers can inform their clients immediately about the status of their accounts. With computers, communication also can be established instantaneously with the marketplace to carry out clients' transactions. The use of the computer has changed the way that stockbrokers deliver their services, just as with countless thousands of other occupations. Organizations, however, do not restructure their work environment overnight but generally follow a more evolutionary progression.

Offices usually pass through certain phases of growth in approaching the ideal of an integrated office system. In the first phase, a company might acquire electromechanical equipment such as a copier (a device that reproduces an exact image on paper) or micrographic equipment (devices that reduce a document in size and reproduce it on film for storage and retrieval). These machines are purchased for the office with the idea of reducing the volume of paperwork and clerical costs. In the second phase, word processing equipment and personal computers might be added to the office in a further effort to reduce paperwork and clerical costs. In the third phase, attention becomes focused on integrating data processing and word processing by some means of communication technology, such as a local area network. Future phases might include the addition of other equipment for voice mail or teleconferencing.

Obstacles to Implementation of Integrated Office Systems. Relatively few offices have been able to realize a fully developed integrated office system. Several obstacles exist which serve to block the implementation of such systems. These obstacles primarily concern cost, management, and the compatibility of equipment. Although the high cost of integrated office systems can act as an effective barrier to their implementation for many organizations, the managerial and compatibility obstacles appear to be the more serious impediments.

The management-related obstacles involve several facets. Some managers lack awareness of the benefits of integrated office systems; other managers lack the expertise to assemble and coordinate an integrated office system. Also, in some organizations, managers of independent information systems try to impede integration for fear of losing managerial turf. The compatibility obstacle frequently surfaces when organizations acquire office automation equipment without a strategic plan. Thus, offices tend to become multivendor environments. Care needs to be exercised from the earliest phase of office automation to deal with vendors whose equipment has interfacing capabilities.

Linking various equipment together can be either impossible or extremely difficult and costly. Until recently, most vendors concentrated on making their equipment incompatible with other brands. This approach was favored so that customer reliance and loyalty would be directed toward only one manufacturer. Vendors finally have realized that this plan has been a roadblock to the projected growth of the office automation market, and some cooperation is evident now among vendors. This cooperative effort is being assisted by the work of several groups devoted to the development of standards such as the International Standards Organization (ISO), the American National Standards Institute, and the Electronic Industries Association (EIA).

Solutions to Obstacles Blocking Implementation of Integrated Office Systems.   Several solutions exist to overcome the obstacles in implementing an integrated office system. The first solution involves the acquisition of equipment from a single vendor. With this approach, compatibility generally would be assured.

In some cases, however, compatibility does not exist even between models of the same brand. So caution is still needed by persons responsible for implementing an integrated office system. In addition, this solution would not be practical for organizations that have already purchased equipment from different vendors.

The second solution involves the acquisition of interface devices (black boxes) and the use of translation and interface programs to accommodate diverse systems. This approach can be expensive and time consuming. Often high-level technicians must spend much time interfacing the devices or eliminating program errors (debugging) in order to get the separate systems to "talk" to each other.

The third solution involves the use of a **network**. Networks can link diverse equipment together over long distances or within a limited geographical location. The latter are called local area networks (LANs) and connect equipment either within the same building or to other buildings generally within a ten-mile radius by telephone wires, cables, or other transmission methods. Examples of commercially available networks are Ethernet™ and Novell™. Networks will be discussed in more detail in a later chapter.

The fourth solution involves the acquisition of a totally integrated office system. Several such systems are now on the market, for example, the ALL-IN-1™ from Digital Equipment Corporation. With such systems, office personnel can perform multiple information-processing functions from their workstations using a single software package (instructional program).

The most common approach to an integrated office system is the use of an existing data processing system with added-on office system capabilities. The architecture (system structure) of such an integrated office system includes software and hardware, including workstations and letter-quality printers linked with a separate, large "host" computer. The workstations may be personal computers or computer terminals. These units might function independently for most office automation functions with need to access the host system only for extensive data processing. In other cases the personal computers or terminals might be totally dependent upon the resources of the host computer. Figure 2-10 depicts a model of an integrated office system.

An integrated office system is made possible through the use of **user interfaces**. This term refers to system capabilities allowing individuals to perform various information processing functions from a single software package. These interfaces are composed of standard commands, menu structures, system prompts, and file procedures. Standard commands enable a user to deal

Figure 2-10 A Model of an Integrated Office System

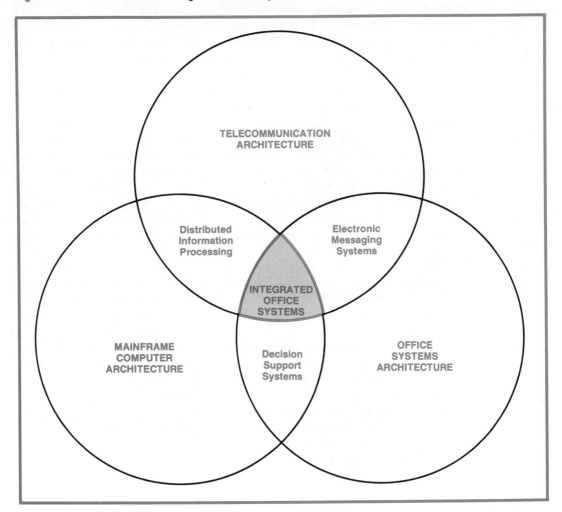

with uniform language in performing similar computer operations such as creating a file, saving a file, or transferring a file.
(A file is a collection of related information treated as a unit and
may be stored on cards, tapes, disks, or in the internal memory
of a computer system.) A menu is a "help" feature and refers to a
list of options available to the user, such as word processing and
electronic mail, and allows easy movement from function to
function. **System prompts** refer to another help feature that provides cues to users for computer operations, such as entering
the name of a file in response to a question presented on the
screen of the computer. File procedures involve electronic record

management for the organization, allocation, and control of files, such as erasing a file, viewing a file, and accepting data processing input into a word processing file.

Several problems are associated with the selection and use of an integrated office system. One of these problems concerns vendor selection. Some vendors may be too narrow in the scope of their equipment offerings or lack the financial and/or technical resources to remain abreast with the rapidly changing technologies of office systems. Another problem is that not all functions are available. For example, data and text applications might exist but not voice or graphics. Systems need to be evaluated carefully to be sure that their functions meet the requirements of their users. In addition, the office-system functions might be available but not truly integrated. This situation causes users to learn several different commands for similar functions. Therefore, retrieving a file in the word processing function would require a different command from retrieving a file in data processing. Another difficulty might be that certain operations initiated on one part of the system cannot be transferred to another part of the system. For example, figures developed in a financial-analysis function may not be compatible with a file created in the word processing function.

All of these obstacles are holding back the implementation of integrated office systems in organizations; however, with time they are expected to diminish. The transition from independent office systems to integrated office systems will depend upon technological advancements, which will reduce their cost, increase equipment compatibility, and allow easier use. In addition, users must accept such systems as a viable means to accomplish their work. In the years to come, the use of integrated office systems is expected to become a significant force in the daily operations of medium-to-large organizations.

WOHL'S BUSINESS PERSPECTIVE

How Does Office Automation Fit Into an Office?

There are as many ways to implement office automation as there are offices. Each office, each organization has its own culture and a successful office automation strategy always understands that culture and plans office automation to complement and support it.

Most large organizations have been supporting various kinds of computing for a long time now, dating back into the 1950s and 1960s. The computer organizations have themselves gone through many changes, reflecting changing technology costs, changing opportunities to utilize computers, and changes in management philosophy and style.

Most large organizations have been moving for some time away from the notion of controlling all computing centrally, and toward the idea of more local involvement and control. Office automation, which is intended for widespread local use, falls right into the middle of this ongoing debate.

There is a kind of natural conflict between the needs of individual members of the organization to control their own computing environments and the need for the organization to maintain enough control to permit intra-organizational communication and to facilitate the problem of integrating data and applications. In today's office, this conflict is often observed in the demands of personal computer users for more control and the organizational desire to converge decision making—offering fewer (but better supported) choices to permit integration.

The answer to this seeming conflict is education and participation. Users must be educated about organizational goals, as well as how group (rather than individual) decisions support such goals. Many large organizations now prefer a kind of participatory model, a sort of representational democracy. Users' needs and preferences are carefully solicited. Time is taken to educate the user sufficiently so he or she can participate meaningfully in the system design process.

Where users help to design the automation of their offices, they have been enlisted in advance to help implement these solutions and drive them to success. When solutions are imposed without user participation, users have little reason to move from their personal preferences and systems go unused or underused. The system may be perfectly all right technically, but the organizational culture hasn't given it permission to exist!

The organization needs a focus for this activity. Office automation, which started off as part of the administrative system, is now clearly an information services activity. Most large organizations support the office and its automation efforts through an Information Center. Even firms which didn't use an Information Center in the old days (when IC's parceled up excess mainframe memory and offered it— stingily—to users), have created Information Centers to provide office automation leadership and end user computing (usually personal computing) support.

Organizations automate not to have office automation but because office automation supports their business goals. Effective CEOs do not spend the millions a full-blown, large scale automation project requires unless they are certain it is not only necessary, but also critical to the continuing success of the organization. Office automation works when it solves problems and permits new opportunities to be addressed. It is up to the office strategists to identify these problems and prove the worth of office automation in providing solutions.

SUMMARY

The study of office automation needs to be examined in its typical environment—the organization with its many systems. The use of a systems approach helps management acquire a unifying vision necessary for dealing with these numerous, diverse systems. One of the most important systems impacting the organization is the social system, involving the behavior of individuals and groups internal and external to it.

The office is a support system in which people process information using technology to serve the needs of an organization. Differences in types of offices and office work can be understood more easily with the use of an office taxonomy describing offices as type I (fairly routine) or type II (nonroutine). Office functions can be categorized as office systems involving administrative support, decision support, data processing, word processing, reprographics, phototypesetting, records management, and telecommunications. Through the use of office systems, organizations can be greatly assisted in accomplishing their goals and objectives.

Another support system relatively new to organizations is the information center. Its mission is to provide training and support services to end users in computer skills so that they can use information resources more effectively to improve decision making and increase job productivity.

The concept of integrated office systems refers to the linkage of separate information systems into one system accessible to a number of users. Benefits of integrated office systems to an organization include increased productivity, cost and time reduction, improved customer service, and possibly increased profits. Relatively few organizations have fully developed integrated office systems because of obstacles related to cost, management, and equipment incompatibility. Solutions to obstacles blocking the implementation of integrated office systems involve avoidance of multivendor office automation environments, use of interface devices and programs, networks, and acquisition of totally integrated office systems.

KEY TERMS

organizational climate
formal structure
informal structure
line positions

staff positions
centralized design
decentralized design
matrix design

system   word processing
support systems   reprographics
closed system   phototypesetting
open system   records management
knowledge workers   telecommunications
support staff   information center
taxonomies   integrated office systems
type I offices   strategic planning
type II offices   network
administrative support   user interfaces
decision support   system prompts
data processing

REVIEW QUESTIONS

1. Why is a knowledge of organizational and systems concepts important to the study of office automation?

2. How does organizational climate affect organizations and their employees?

3. Contrast an organization's formal structure with its informal structure. Do you think these structures always would be of equal importance? If not, when might one structure be more important than the other?

4. How might an open-system organization differ from a closed-system organization? Give several examples.

5. In what major way has automation changed the traditional concept of the office?

6. How do knowledge workers differ from support workers? Give examples of each.

7. How can a knowledge of office taxonomies be useful to someone implementing office automation in an organization?

8. What factor is responsible for the change in the type of services provided by information centers? Contrast the earlier type of service rendered with more current types of service.

9. Why is strategic planning recommended before the implementation of an integrated office system?

10. What kinds of solutions are available to organizations to overcome the obstacles preventing the implementation of integrated office systems?

11. What is the most common approach to an integrated office system?

CASE STUDY: THE CASE OF THE BROKEN PROMISES

The Golden Brand Corporation over the years had acquired automated equipment from many different vendors. This equipment included a large "host" computer system, computer terminals, word processors, an assortment of printers, a dictation system, electronic typewriters, phototypesetters, copiers, facsimile devices, and micrographic equipment. Despite all of this automated equipment, the Golden Brand Corporation never seemed to be able to reach the increased rates of productivity that the vendors had promised.

The large computer system of the Golden Brand Corporation was located in the Data Processing Department. Much of the word processing equipment was located in the Word Processing Center, but other equipment was distributed throughout the organization. Lately there had been a trend at the Golden Brand Corporation for department managers to acquire their own personal computers. The data processing manager complained to top management about this practice. The data processing manager felt that he should be the one to control all computing activities.

Top management called a meeting of all of the Golden Brand Corporation managers to address the concern of the data processing manager. At the meeting the department managers claimed that the response time from the Data Processing Department for requested information was not fast enough for efficient decision making. Also, each manager contended that he or she should be allowed to select the personal computer that could best meet the needs of each department. The word processing manager expressed the belief that the staff could be more productive with more cooperation from the Data Processing Department. Frequently the operators needed information from large organizational files to incorporate into word processing documents, and lengthy time lags were common between requests for information and its delivery. The top manager decided to impose a moratorium on the purchase of any additional personal computers. The manager also instructed the data processing and word processing managers to study the situation and file a written report.

QUESTIONS/ACTIVITIES

1. Why do you think the Golden Brand Corporation has had difficulty achieving the promised increases in productivity?

2. What recommendations do you think the study team should present to top management?

SUGGESTED READINGS

Deal, Terrence and Allan Kennedy. *Corporate Cultures—Rites and Rituals.* Reading, Mass.: Addison-Wesley Publishing Company, 1984.

Kanter, Rosabeth Moss. *Men and Women of the Corporation.* New York: Basic Books, Inc., 1979.

McQuade, H. A. "Dealing with Office Rituals." *Administrative Management* (July, 1986): 17–19.

Plant, Roger and Mark Ryan. "Managing Your Corporate Culture." *Training and Development Journal*, Vol. 42, No. 9 (September, 1988): 61–65.

Raudsepp, E. "Establishing Creative Climate." *Training and Development Journal*, Vol. 41, No. 4 (April, 1987): 50–53.

CHAPTER 3

Careers in Office Systems

OBJECTIVES

After studying this chapter, you should understand the following:

1. The industries in which office systems careers appear most promising
2. The job opportunities and projections for office systems careers
3. Descriptions of current and emerging jobs in office systems
4. Career planning activities
5. The job search process
6. The career development process within organizations
7. Career tracks and career stages for technical personnel
8. Career mobility options for office systems personnel
9. The manager's role in the employee career development process
10. Professional growth and development activities available to office systems personnel

Automation has had a profound effect upon career opportunities. Familiarity with computer technology has become integral in almost every job. Many workers in office, managerial, and technical positions are involved in the use of office systems technology. Most of the positions are located within organizations, but some of the positions offer possibilities for self-employment. Because of the diversity of jobs available in office systems, individuals with widely different educational backgrounds, skills, interests, and values can find rewarding careers in this field.

In this chapter, a **job** is defined as a set of tasks related to a particular position. A **career** is used to refer to the sequence of jobs held during the course of a person's work life. Career implications related to the various office systems are discussed in this text in their respective chapters. This chapter provides an introduction to office systems career opportunities and offers suggestions for the planning and development of an office systems career.

OFFICE SYSTEMS CAREER OPPORTUNITIES

Despite the many types of jobs discussed in this chapter, the list should not be considered final. As technology continues to affect the labor market, jobs are eliminated, created, and changed. Robotics, for example, is currently a technology with few office applications. In the future, however, robots could become as commonplace in the office as computers. According to the U.S. Department of Labor, the fastest growing jobs through the year 2000 will be in executive, managerial, professional, and technical fields requiring the highest levels of education and skill. By contrast, occupations requiring little formal education are expected to stagnate or dwindle in number.

THE INFORMATION INDUSTRIES

Industries that are involved with the processing and distribution of information rather than the production of goods are part of the service sector of the economy and are known as **information industries**. These industries are among the fastest growing in the U.S. economy. By the year 2000 nearly four out of five jobs will be in industries that provide services in such areas as finance, insurance, data processing management, and consulting. Job growth in business services, such as word processing and computer support is expected to be especially rapid. The U.S. Department of Labor has made the following projections regarding the following information industries:[1]

1. U.S. Department of Labor, Bureau of Labor Statistics, *Occupational Outlook Handbook* (Washington, D.C.: U.S. Government Printing Office, 1988–1989 edition).

Finance, Insurance, and Real Estate.   The industry of finance, insurance, and real estate is of major importance as a source of jobs in office systems. More professional, managerial, sales, and clerical workers in the U.S. are employed in the finance, insurance, and real estate industry than any other industry. Figure 3-1 compares the construction industry and the finance, insurance, and real estate industry according to professional, managerial, sales, and clerical employment. Job growth in this industry will result if the demand for financial products and services continues unabated as expected during the nineties. However, technological advancement in such areas as automated banking is expected to put a damper on some job categories.

Figure 3-1   Industry Comparison for Employment Type

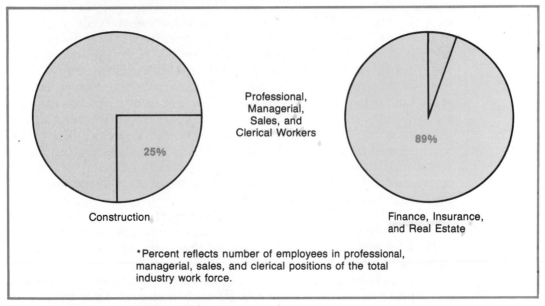

Source: Bureau of Labor Statistics, 1982.

Communication.   Communication is another key industry providing job opportunities in office systems. Employment growth in the communication industry, however, is expected to slow, despite the demand for telecommunication services, because of the increases in productivity prompted by the competitive industry climate.

Service.   Service is the fastest growing industry. This classification includes business services, such as data processing and computer repairs. However, other types of jobs, such as those in health care, are also included in this category, distorting employ-ment projections for those interested in office systems careers.

Most of the job opportunities in office systems will be avail-able not only in the information industries but in other industries as well, such as construction and transportation. Most individ-uals employed in careers related to office systems work in office, managerial, and systems-related positions, which will be dis-cussed in this chapter. However, job opportunities also exist in many other capacities such as sales representative, librarian, writer-researcher, instructor, and trainer. Additional informa-tion on training as a career will be presented in a later chapter.

OFFICE POSITIONS

The category of office work is classified as **administrative support** by the U.S. Department of Labor. This broad category is composed of a variety of office jobs, including secretaries, typists, clerks, bookkeepers, and word processing operators. Their job duties consist of processing, transmitting, and distributing information for internal and external use by others. Many of these positions involve the use of word processors, information storage equip-ment, and other automated equipment. Job requirements include a minimum of a high school education, although training at the postsecondary level may be required. Skills generally needed include oral and written communication, typing, shorthand (for some positions), spelling, punctuation, and grammar. Personal traits desired are discretion, good judgment, tact, organizational ability, initiative, and adaptability.

The category of administrative support is considered by the U.S. Department of Labor to be one of the slowest growing occu-pational areas. However, because of the large size of this employ-ment area and its substantial replacement needs, job opportu-nities are still considered to be abundant for qualified job seekers during the nineties. The area's slow rate of growth is generally attributed to changes brought about by technological advance-ments. Typists' positions, for example, are expected to decline because the increased use of word processing equipment has affected the productivity of typists.

Job opportunities for self-employment also exist in the career category of administrative support. Business ownership of such services as temporary office workers, data entry, word process-ing, media conversion, reprographics, micrographics, office training, and consulting are possible.

MANAGEMENT POSITIONS

People in managerial occupations direct the activities of others in organizations of every kind. The skills needed vary with the industry, managerial level, and nature of the particular function managed. Educational requirements usually include a college degree and specialized training. According to the U.S. Department of Labor, familiarity with computers is a "must" for managers in a growing number of firms due to the widespread use of computerized management information systems. Managers generally should possess abilities in organizing, decision making, and communicating; and they should demonstrate initiative and good judgment.

Employment opportunities in management are expected to increase about as fast as the average for all occupations through the year 2000. An example of an office systems managerial position would be that of records manager. Responsibilities of this position generally include coordinating an organization's records—paper, film, and electronic—and forms control. Employment of general managers and top executives in the computer and data processing services industries is expected to more than double as computer use expands. Employment of marketing managers in charge of sales and support for a wide variety of computer-related equipment, products, and services, including telemarketing, is expected to experience growth faster than average for all occupations through the year 2000.

The administrative position of **chief information officer (CIO)** is being created in many organizations. The CIO can be responsible for office automation, computer resources, records management, telecommunications, and all other information needs of an organization. Qualifications for the position include in-depth technical knowledge, a broad understanding of the business functions of the organization and its overall industry, and the ability to work with nontechnical senior executives to determine their information needs.[2] The CIO position is still relatively uncommon in most organizations but is expected to acquire much of the status associated with the position of chief executive officer (CEO). Such increased status will occur as organizations realize the key role that information systems can play in overall strategic planning.

SYSTEMS AND PROCESSING POSITIONS

Many jobs are classified in the systems and processing category. A wide range of skills is required from entry level to advanced levels. Positions related to office systems include computer,

2. Peter J. Nofel, "The Information Center," *Modern Office Technology* (February, 1984): 74–75.

peripheral equipment, and data-entry operator, programmer, analyst, user liaison, and systems consultant.

The jobs of **computer, peripheral equipment,** and **data-entry operator** all primarily involve the use of computer and computer-related equipment. In large organizations such operative-level work may be performed by specialist operators, but in smaller organizations such work may be performed by the same individual. Educational requirements include a high school education with special training often provided on the job. Personal traits needed include the ability to reason logically, to work quickly and accurately, to feel comfortable with machines while doing repetitive tasks, and to work as part of a team. Employment opportunities for computer and peripheral equipment operators are expected to rise much faster than the average for all occupations through the year 2000. Positions for data-entry operators, however, are expected to decline during this same period because of the increasing use of direct data entry by all categories of employees as well as the use of optical scanners and other data-entry devices.[3] Figure 3-2 illustrates these employment projections.

Figure 3-2 Employment Demand for Computer Operators

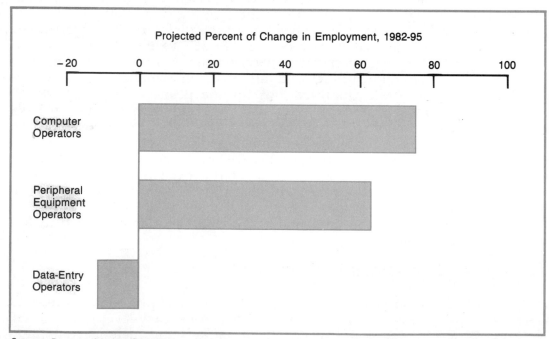

Source: Bureau of Labor Statistics.

3. Dorothy Sandburg, "Career Opportunities in Office Automation," *Office Automation and Administration* (April, 1985): 79.

The job of **computer programmer** involves the writing of detailed instructions called programs that list in logical order the steps the computer must follow to perform a task. Employment of computer programmers is expected to grow much faster than average for all occupations through the year 2000. However, employment in programming is not growing as rapidly as in the past because of the increased availability of packaged software and advancements in programming techniques that simplify or eliminate the need for some programming tasks. Educational requirements generally include postsecondary education in programming languages, logical thinking, and ability to work with details.

An **analyst** plans, develops, evaluates, and implements systems for an organization's information needs. Educational requirements for analyst positions usually include a college degree in information systems. Characteristics desirable for those in analyst positions are the ability to think logically, communicate effectively with technical and nontechnical personnel, address a number of tasks simultaneously, and work both independently and in teams. Analyst positions are projected to grow much faster than average for all occupations through the year 2000. A trend is developing toward the specialization of analyst positions. An **office-systems analyst**, for example, specifically works with the office automation needs of an organization and develops plans for their implementation.

The position of **user liaison** is relatively new to organizations. An individual employed as a user liaison may be housed in an information systems department or an information center. This person would act as an in-house consultant, providing computer support to organizational members for their system hardware, software, and applications.

The position of **systems consultant** is available in-house or with organizations that offer computer-related consulting services. Job duties include conducting feasibility studies, making recommendations to management, and implementing systems. Consultants also work as advisers to office designers, software developers, and manufacturers of office equipment and furniture. Consulting opportunities exist for work on a part-time, free-lance, or entrepreneurial basis.

CAREER PLANNING

Before individuals make a career choice, planning should occur. **Career planning** involves a variety of activities including self-assessment, job exploration, and goal setting. A satisfying, pro-

Figure 3-3 Career counselors help
job applicants assess their interests
and aptitudes.

ductive career usually depends upon how well individuals can
use their personal skills and traits. Because a job consumes a
major share of an individual's time, energies, and talents, career
planning helps to ensure a more satisfying personal as well as
work life.

SELF-ASSESSMENT

The first step in career planning is self-assessment. A **self-assessment** includes an analysis of an individual's aptitudes, interests,
values, and skills. Individuals who desire help in assessing these
characteristics can seek career counseling. Career counselors
can administer various inventories and tests and provide guidance in career decision making. Educational institutions and
private and public agencies generally offer career counseling
services.

Self-assessments enable individuals to determine their fitness
for various careers. Useful categories to help individuals assess

their career interests are people, data, and things. **People people** prefer jobs that require a high degree of social interaction. Examples of people jobs in office systems include those of manager and trainer. **Data people** prefer jobs that emphasize details and the planning, organizing, and analyzing of information. An example is that of an office systems analyst. **Things people** prefer jobs that involve the manipulation of machines. An example is the position of a word processing operator.

Individuals also need to assess their skills acquired both on and off the job. Office workers in particular often fail to recognize that many of their job tasks are transferable to other job categories. For example, some of the job skills of an administrative support specialist could be classified as managerial. When individuals realize the full nature of the job skills they possess, a broader range of career opportunities can be considered.

Another vital part of a self-assessment concerns values. Values are important because they concern the priorities of individuals. Values relating to status, power, money, security, and family bear a strong relationship to an individual's determination of career success. Career counselors generally recommend that individuals determine their own definition of career success. Harmony among the aptitudes, interests, skills, and values of individuals and their definition of career success can promote job satisfaction as well as satisfaction in their personal lives. Once individuals arrive at a level of self-understanding, they need to investigate job opportunities.

JOB EXPLORATION

Individuals interested in office systems careers should investigate in great detail the jobs described earlier in this chapter. Methods of job exploration include reading career literature and talking with job holders in office systems careers (**information interviews**). Gaining experience in a job is an excellent method of trying out a possible career. Such experience might be paid or unpaid and may be acquired from part-time work, summer jobs, internships, or volunteer work. Once individuals determine what type of job they desire, they can decide where they want to go in their careers.

GOAL SETTING

The setting of goals is the next step in career planning. Both short- and long-term goals need to be determined, as well as appropriate strategies for reaching them. Career goals might specify what education, skills, and experiences need to be acquired for career entrance. Then individuals might set a time frame for attaining different levels within the career tracks. For example, an individual could begin a career as a word processing operator and aim to become a word processing supervisor within three years. This individual might set a goal to become a manager within six to eight years.

. Career targets need to be reexamined periodically to determine if progress is being made toward them. If barriers to goal attainment arise, individuals must decide on a course of action. Strategies might include a plan to overcome the obstacles or to reset the career goals. For example, job relocation might be a necessary prerequisite for career advancement in a particular organization. If an individual has a spouse who resists relocation, serious conflict could arise. Compromise on the desired career goal or risk of a major change in a personal relationship are difficult choices, but attainment of high-level career positions demands enormous personal sacrifice and commitment. After specific career goals have been established by individuals, the next step in career planning is to begin the job search.

THE JOB SEARCH

The job search is a process that is likely to occur several times during a person's work life. One popular estimate is that the average person will experience five different careers. Whether the job search is the first or the fifth, though, the preparation of certain documents is recommended to help individuals find a job.

Document Preparation.   A resume and a letter of application are documents used by many job seekers to gain interviews. A **resume** is a written summary of a job seeker's previous education and employment. In addition, other information such as job-related skills, membership in professional and civic associations, and personal information indicating distinction, such as awards and honors, should be included. References may be cited or information given on how to obtain them. If the job seeker is in doubt as to how to prepare a resume, write a letter of application, or take a job interview, help is available from several sources. Such sources include books on job-hunting skills, placement offices of educational institutions, and career workshops.

Extra effort should be put into the development of the resume and letter of application because they totally represent the job seeker, who is in competition with all other job seekers. These documents should help the job seeker stand out and yet not be overly flashy. Career counselors recommend that the documents be businesslike in tone, attractively formatted, and error free. Tailoring the documents for particular organizations is preferable to the mass mailing of resumes. Special effort should be put into having the documents show how the job applicant's employment history can be of benefit to the organization. If such effort is not made, job interviews may not be granted. In order to tailor the documents for a particular organization, the job applicant needs to gather appropriate information about it.

Organizational Research. Data gathering about organizations can be done informally. However, if the job search is to be conducted over a wide geographic area or the job seeker is unfamiliar with organizations where desired job opportunities exist, a visit to a library is recommended. Figure 3-4 lists sources available in most libraries that would be helpful to individuals conducting organizational research.

Conducting organizational research can be helpful to job seekers in gaining a competitive edge. The following information about an organization can be learned from such efforts: size, nature of business, number of administrative and office employees, competitive boundaries, geographical reach, economic status, executives' names and addresses, and organizational culture. Every organization shares a common culture of values, traditions, and behaviors. Achieving career success in a particular culture requires acceptance by its group members. Recognition of the appropriateness of **organizational fit** by the newcomer needs to occur at the peer, subordinate, and superior levels. The probability of a successful career diminishes greatly when organizational fit does not occur. Organizational research, therefore, can be a useful tool for the job seeker; but it is not the most recommended procedure to use for locating actual jobs.

JOB SOURCES

Many methods are available for locating sources of employment. These methods include personal contact, placement offices, job fairs, personnel offices, employment agencies, and classified advertisements.

The most recommended method for locating a job is by personal contact. Seeking the assistance of family, friends, co-workers, current employers (if feasible), teachers, and career counselors frequently leads to employment. These individuals might know of job openings or contacts within organizations. Often organizations encourage their employees to recommend new personnel because of the probability that they will be like-minded individuals. Organizations believe that the organizational fit of new employees will be better when current employees recommend their organization to job seekers. Also, employees generally would

Figure 3-4 **Selected Sources for Organizational Research**

Annual Reports. Some libraries collect annual reports of major corporations.

Million Dollar Directory. Annual. Alphabetical, geographical, and standard industry classification (SIC) listings provided for 120,000 U.S. companies with a net worth of over $500,000. Includes address, annual sales, number of employees, officers, etc.

Moody's Manuals. Annual with semiweekly supplements. Company history and financial information provided in separate manuals — Industrial, OTC (Over the Counter), Bank and Finance, Municipal and Government, Public Utility, and Transportation.

Standard and Poor's Corporation Records. Looseleaf with bi-monthly supplements. Descriptions provided of public corporations listed on AMEX (American Stock Exchange), NYSE (New York Stock Exchange), and larger unlisted and regional exchanges.

Standard and Poor's Industry Survey. Looseleaf. Current and basic industrial analyses published quarterly and annually, respectively. Arranged alphabetically by industry, with subject and company indexes.

Standard and Poor's Register of Corporations, Directors, and Executives. Annual. Access provided to information on approximately 37,000 U.S. and Canadian corporations, arranged by company name and by individuals' names in the first two volumes, respectively. The third volume provides SIC and geographic indexes, parent company, obituary and new individual and company addition sections.

Standard Directory of Advertisers. Annual. Officers, products, sales personnel, etc., provided for companies that advertise nationally. Arranged by industry with company index.

Thomas Register of Manufacturers. Annual. Information provided on over 100,000 U.S. manufacturers arranged by product and service with brand name index, company listings, and catalogs in separate volumes.

not recommend someone who would reflect poorly upon their own judgment.

If the job seeker is enrolled in an educational institution, a placement office is a convenient place to search for a job. Services usually are free and include listings of job openings, access to campus recruiters, and distribution of the job applicant's credentials.

A **job fair** is an event frequently sponsored by educational institutions or civic groups. Numerous organizations set up booths for prospective job seekers. Each employer provides information about the organization and its career opportunities. Attendance at a job fair enables job seekers to learn a great deal in a short time about different organizations and current employment opportunities. Job seekers who appear to be of potential interest to an organization can be invited for formal interviews.

Personnel offices in organizations usually accept job applications made in person and sometimes conduct preliminary interviews. Many organizations like to maintain a current file of job applicants who have been screened initially for employment. Pounding the pavements to find a job, however, can be tiring and discouraging. The reason for this is that job seekers often do not know whether positions are available for employees with their qualifications.

Employment agencies screen job applicants and select individuals for job interviews. Positions are listed with the agencies by organizations seeking qualified employees. Both public and private agencies exist. Public agencies are operated by every state and offer free job services such as job counseling, testing, and referrals for job interviews. Private agencies offer similar services, but some differences do exist. For example, private agencies may specialize in certain career areas such as data processing, office services, or management. In addition, a fee is charged for these services which has to be paid by the organization, the job seeker, or both. A variety of agencies offer employment assistance to special categories of job seekers such as the handicapped, minorities, women, older workers, veterans, and ex-offenders.

Searching the classified advertisements in newspapers and professional and trade publications, while probably the most popular method, is also the least likely to produce results. Help-wanted advertisements can produce a flood of responses, making it more difficult for a job seeker's resume and letter of application to stand out. Another problem with classified advertisements is that many jobs, sometimes said to be as high as 70 percent, are not advertised. Classified advertisements, therefore, should not be relied upon as the sole method of finding a job. Job seekers, however, can get a feel for the types and locations of jobs and their requirements, salaries, and fringe benefits offered in a particular area. Therefore, subscriptions or library copies of out-of-town newspapers are recommended particularly to job seekers who desire relocation.

THE JOB INTERVIEW

When job search efforts finally result in a job interview, great care should be exercised in preparing for the event. Anxiety over an interview can be relieved somewhat by the feeling of self-confidence derived from careful preparation. A professional appearance and promptness are prerequisites in contributing to a good first impression. Recommended procedures are to carry two copies of the resume. One can be used as a guide if a job application needs to be completed, and the second one can be given to the job interviewer if necessary.

The first few seconds of an interview are critical. When greeted by the interviewer, job applicants should smile and respond with a firm handshake. A composed, self-confident image should be projected and genuine interest in the position should be demonstrated. Job applicants should be prepared to answer typical interview questions such as why this particular organization is of interest and how their education and experience qualify them for the position. In addition, job applicants should be ready to discuss their personal strengths and weaknesses and their immediate and future career goals.

Generally, interviewers will ask professionally related questions, but some questions considered illegal by the EEOC (Equal Employment Opportunity Commission) might arise. For example, a question concerning marital status or child care could be asked. Tactful evasion might be possible, but outright refusal to answer the question could result in loss of the job offer. Some individuals, however, could decide that illegal interview questions might indicate the presence of other undesirable employment practices. Thus, these individuals would seek employment elsewhere.

Another area where the EEOC can affect the interview process is in testing. Job applicants for positions in office systems, especially in operations and administrative support, might be asked to take an employment test. Typical employment tests include typewriting, word processing, clerical aptitude, and stenography. According to the EEOC, no test should be administered unless the test corresponds to the knowledge and skills actually required on the job. For managerial positions, a different type of testing might be encountered.

Some organizations operate **assessment centers**. In such centers, job applicants perform a variety of activities designed to simulate a job. Assessment can extend over several days and include in-basket tasks, case studies, and teamwork exercises. Trained administrators evaluate the job applicants' performances and make reports to management regarding their employment suitability.

Figure 3-5 Care in preparing for the interview helps create a positive impression.

Following the job interview experience, job seekers should send follow-up letters to their interviewers. Such letters should include mention of appreciation for the interview opportunity and reinforce the job applicant's interest in the position.

CAREER DEVELOPMENT

Development of a career in office systems depends on several factors. Individuals seeking a career in office systems should be aware of personal as well as organizational factors. The personal factor includes both work content skills (what one knows) and self-management skills (how one uses what one knows). The organizational factor is important to the career development process because to have successful careers, most people must become experienced in organizations. Figure 3-6 illustrates a model of the career development process for employees within an organizational setting. The model defines the roles and responsibilities of its three components—the employee, the manager, and the company. Employees are the focal point in the model because employees need to assume primary responsibility for their own career development. However, the career development process also is dependent upon employees' interaction with the managerial and organizational components. If employees understand themselves and their career needs and goals, the manager can serve as a career catalyst, providing employees with information about organizational opportunities. Also, managers can provide feedback to employees regarding the realism of their career aspirations (a form of reality testing). Organizations that encourage employee career development benefit from heightened employee morale, which can result in increased productivity. An

Figure 3-6 Employee Development Process

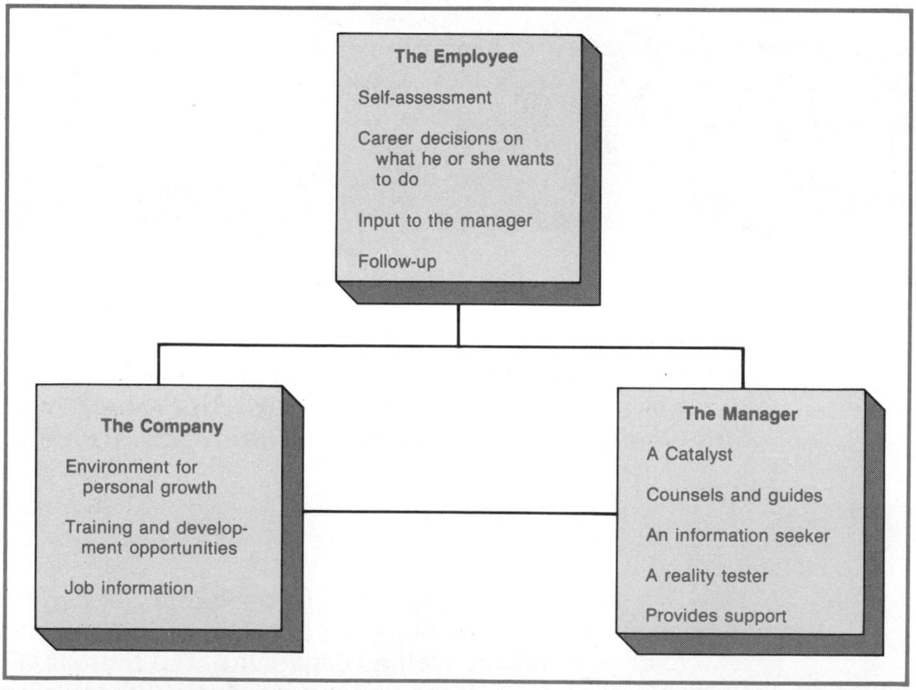

Source: Carolyn A. Bardsley, "Hooking Management on Career Development: A Workshop," *Training and Development Journal* (December, 1984), p. 77. Copyright 1986, *Training and Development Journal,* American Society for Training and Development. Reprinted with permission. All rights reserved.

explanation of how each component in the employee development process functions in relation to office systems careers follows.

THE ORGANIZATION

The organization is critical in a number of ways to the development of an office systems career. Factors include the extent and level of office automation and the nature of the management culture. The attitude of management toward office systems is especially important because it will affect the internal growth of office systems and, accordingly, opportunities for promotions and the creation of new positions.

Career Tracks.   Most organizations maintain **career tracks** or paths leading to advancement. For example, a word processing operator may progress to the level of word processing supervisor. Before the arrival of office automation, advancement in office occupations often was limited, and the label "dead end" was associated with such work. Advancement, of course, was possible for some office workers; but well-defined career tracks leading to managerial positions were uncommon in the traditional office. One of the benefits attributed to office automation has been the establishment of career paths for office workers.

Even today, office systems personnel experience difficulty in career advancement if top management has a negative perception of their work. Office systems should be viewed as a viable organizational function from which promotable talent can emerge. Personnel in computer operations and administrative support, however, are not the only office workers who may experience frustration from lack of career advancement. This problem also affects knowledge workers in technical positions.

Often, distinctly separate career tracks for general management and technical personnel are maintained by organizations. Figure 3-7 illustrates one company's dual-track system. Both career tracks generally do not provide equal access to advancement, and crossover between career tracks is often difficult. A problem for those in the technical track arises when advancement into a general management "fast track" is desired but appears contrary to organizational practice. As with traditional office worker positions, top management may not perceive technical personnel as capable of being promoted into general managerial ranks. One reason for this perception is that technical personnel are often isolated in their departments, resulting in limited contact with nontechnical managers. Also, extensive display of technical expertise can be misinterpreted by top management as a lack of interest in or knowledge of general management concerns.

Figure 3-7   Dual Career Track Models and Career Stages

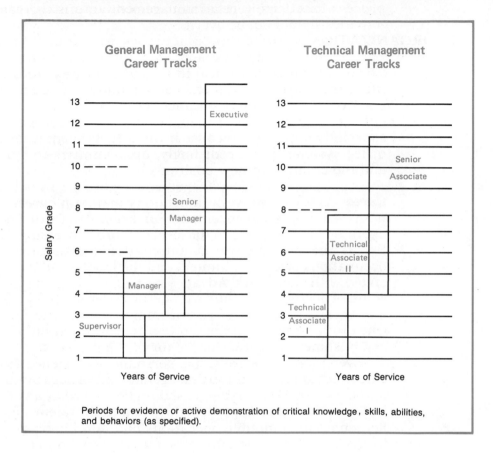

To counteract any managerial misperceptions about their career aspirations, technical personnel need to demonstrate their concern for the total organization. Highly recommended would be the development of knowledge of the industry and an understanding of the organization's needs. If technical personnel can use the information resources of their organizations creatively to enhance profitability, top management generally will take notice.

Another recommendation for technical personnel would be to heighten their organizational visibility. Formal activities such as volunteering for an organizational task force, presenting a report at an executive meeting, and doing extra work on key projects could prove beneficial to the technical employee who desires a move into general management. Informal organizational activities should not be overlooked either by technical personnel. Attending socially oriented activities with executives present, such as lunches, parties, and recreational activities, increases contact with management. Thus, through participation in formal and informal activities, technical personnel may be able to move into different phases of their careers.

Career Stages. Various phases of career development, or **career stages**, can exist in the technical-professional career. These phases represent four stages: (1) apprenticeship, (2) self-dependence, (3) mentor, and (4) senior management. Figure 3-8 illustrates these career stages. Inherent in the idea of career stages is the belief that certain knowledge, skills, and critical activities need to be mastered before passage to the next stage. Typically, the technical professional becomes well grounded first in technical competency

Figure 3-8 **Career Stages of the Developing Technical-Professional Career**

Stage	Name	Characteristics	Critical Activities
I	Apprenticeship	Close supervision Work assignments parts of larger projects Acceptance of direction Exercise of initiative/creativity within well-defined area Learning by observation	Adjustment to dependence Self-discipline for detail Show initiative potential Develop good relationship with mentor
II	Self-dependence	Assume responsibility for definable portion of project Relative independence Results identified with person Develop credibility, reputation Responsibility for management of one's own time and outcomes Technical depth in assignments	Demonstrate capacity for professional work and increase visibility Avoid overspecialization Develop peer relations Rely less on mentor, supervisor Achieve competency: technical first, then administrative
III	Mentor	Affect others' careers and development Broaden technical skills Deal more with external environment Roles may include: informal mentor; idea person/small group leader; supervisor/manager	Achieve self-confidence Achieve ability to feel secure with success Accept responsibility for others Develop ability to cope with change and conflict Demonstrate ability to produce over a long period Administrative duties may equal or exceed technical duties

Figure 3-8 Career Stages of the Developing Technical-Professional Career *(continued)*

Stage	Name	Characteristics	Critical Activities
IV	Senior Management	Assume significant organizational responsibility and direction Achieve orientation to external and internal environment Sponsor and develop promising employees Roles may include: idea innovator; internal entrepreneur; upper-level manager	Outside contacts Delegate to subordinates Proactive rather than reactive Cope with change Ability to use power

Source: Elmer H. Burack, ''The Sphinx's Riddle: Life and Career Cycles,'' *Training and Development Journal* (April, 1984), p. 58. Copyright 1986, *Training and Development Journal*, American Society for Training and Development. Reprinted with permission. All rights reserved.

before advancing to administrative levels. With career progression, administrative duties gradually equal and then exceed technical concerns. For some individuals, however, movement to advanced career stages will not occur or may not be desired.

Career Mobility.   The interests, values, and life-styles of individuals greatly affect their career mobility. Typically, **career mobility** is viewed as advancement upward or vertical mobility but may actually involve movement in other directions. Some individuals may not be qualified or desire the increase in responsibility that accompanies upward movement. In such situations, horizontal mobility offers another option. Here the employee permanently changes from one career path to another but remains at the same level—for example, from word processing operator to administrative support secretary.

In some organizations a form of career mobility is practiced routinely. In such cases bilateral mobility or job rotation occurs. Here the employee moves between two job categories but does so on a temporary basis. For example, a word processing operator may spend several months working in a word processing center and then several months working with an administrative support team. Such a practice can inject variety and enrichment into an individual's career. In addition, a trained pool of workers becomes available to the organization to fill its employment needs.

The concept of career mobility can be extended to include demotion, or downward movement. Reasons for such movement can be many. Employees experiencing health problems or job stress may feel that a different position would provide them with relief. Poor job performance or job displacement caused by office automation could be other reasons for demotion. In some cases employees may prefer demotion to termination (permanent dismissal). For some individuals, however, termination might result in career advancement if the individual moves to another organization and acquires a higher position. Such outward movement may be necessary if the organization does not appear likely to offer career advancement to an individual. Typically, organizations do desire that their employees develop professionally, and they attempt to provide assistance in this area.

Career Aids.   One demonstration of an organization's support of its human resources is the sponsorship of a career development program. A career development program is a formal system for assisting employees in planning their careers. Such programs are not typical, however.

In a study of 142 companies in the Greater Philadelphia area, 35.9 percent reported no career development programs. Only 15 percent reported separate, identifiable career development activities, with the majority of the companies (48.6 percent) reporting that their career development activities are linked to their personnel system.[4]

Even when career development programs exist within organizations, their purpose often is directed toward the development of mid-level managers. Thus, certain categories of office personnel might find themselves shut out from any assistance provided by these programs. Government regulations and pressures regarding employment opportunities for women and minorities, however, have improved this situation.

Various forms of career assistance frequently can be found in the personnel office of an employee's organization. These personnel offices often post listings describing job vacancies. Here employees can become aware of higher level position requirements, helping them to prepare for career advancement. Personnel offices also might provide information about tuition-reimbursement plans, training programs, job transfers, promotion policies, job counseling, and referrals for other career aid. Another source of career assistance in an organization might be the employee's manager.

---

4. Marcia P. Kleiman, "Turning Career Development Lip Service into Action," *Training and Development Journal* (April, 1984): 78.

THE MANAGER

The role of manager is another critical component in the development of an office systems career. One study reported that in 76 percent of the organizations surveyed supervisors were involved in career development.[5] Because of daily contact with employees and personal contact with other managers, the manager can assist office systems employees in their career development in many ways. Managers can delegate to their subordinates assignments that promote growth. In addition, managers can provide realistic assessments of their subordinates' career potential. Such feedback can take the form of coaching employees to strengthen any personal or professional weaknesses.

Some managers might become mentors to their subordinates, thus improving their chances for career success. A **mentor** usually is a superior or experienced peer within the employee's organization. The mentor assumes a professional interest in another's career and acts in an advisory capacity to that individual. Generally a mentor arranges for the employee to meet the "right people" and to make the "right moves," thus helping the employee to acquire recognition of and acceptance by the managerial network. However, even when managers show an interest in their subordinates' careers, problems can occur.

Some managers might lack sufficient power within their organizations to be successful mentors or might be reluctant to assume a mentor role. For example, a male manager might be reluctant to become a mentor for an aspiring female employee because of the possibility of office gossip. Other managers might resist the mentor role because managers may not be rewarded by their organizations for engaging in career development activities for their subordinates.

Other dilemmas for both manager and subordinate could arise when the career development process is linked to the manager's task of performance appraisal. The career development process is not as effective when it is tied to employee assessment for job promotions and salary increases. Most employees would be reluctant to risk revealing any career inadequacies or doubts to their evaluators. Therefore, employees should take charge of their own career development.

THE EMPLOYEE

Taking charge of career development can begin with employees informing their managers of their interest in career advancement.

5. *Ibid.*

With this awareness, managers can do a better job in helping to develop their subordinates. However, even without managerial assistance, many professional growth opportunities are available for office systems personnel.

Educational Activities. An abundance of educational opportunities exists for office systems personnel to develop their career potential. For example, employees can enroll in college degree programs. Courses in office systems are offered at community colleges, universities, business schools, and trade schools. Other educational opportunities include in-house or off-site seminars, conferences, and trade shows. In addition, regular reading of technical and general business magazines and newspapers can add to the knowledge of office systems personnel. Figure 3-9 lists suggested reading materials.

Figure 3-9 **Suggested Reading for Office Systems Personnel**

General Business Periodicals	Office Systems Periodicals
Barron's	ARMA Records Management Quarterly
Business Week	Computerworld
Forbes	Datamation
Fortune	Datapro Reports
	Desktop Publishing Journal
Management Review	Information Center
	Information Executive
Management World	Infosystems
The Wall Street Journal	Infoworld
	MIS Week
	Modern Office Technology
	The Office
	Office Systems Research Journal
	The Seybold Report on Office Systems
	Today's Office
	The Wohl Report on End-User Computing
	Words

Professional Groups. Another excellent means of career development is through membership in professional groups. These associations include professional societies and user groups. Figure 3-10 lists some societies of interest to office systems personnel. The user groups may be organized locally or nationally and are composed of members with similar interests. These interests can include the use of the same vendor's equipment or similar office technologies. Examples of these two categories of user groups include the International Society of Wang Users and the International Electronic Facsimile Users Association, respectively. By active participation in group meetings, committee work, or in leadership roles, members can increase their professionalism. Additionally, members can engage in networking. **Networking** is the process of forming connections with others who might prove helpful to one's career.

Figure 3-10 **Professional Societies for Office Systems Personnel**

Association for Information Management (AIM)
7380 Parkway Drive
La Mesa, CA 92041

Administrative Management Society (AMS)
2360 Maryland Road
Willow Grove, PA 19090

Association for Systems Management (ASM)
24587 Bagley Road
Cleveland, OH 44138

Association for Computing Machinery (ACM)
11 West 42nd Street, 3rd Floor
New York, NY 10036

Association of Information Systems Professionals (AISP)
104 Wilmot Road, Suite 201
Deerfield, IL 60015–5195

Association of Record Managers and Administrators (ARMA)
4200 Somerset Drive, Suite 215
Prairie Village, KS 66208

Association for Women in Computing (AWC)
P.O. Box 21146
St. Paul, MN 55123

Computer Society of the Institute of Electrical and Electronics Engineers (IEEE-CS)
1730 Massachusetts Avenue NW
Washington, DC 20036–1903

The Computer Software and Services Industry Association (ADAPSO)
1300 North Seventeenth Street, Suite 300
Arlington, VA 22209–3899

Data Entry Management Association (DEMA)
P.O. Box 16711
Stamford, CT 06905

Data Processing Management Association (DPMA)
505 Busse Highway
Park Ridge, IL 60068–3191

Independent Computer Consultants Association (ICCA)
P.O. Box 27412
St. Louis, MO 63141

Figure 3-10 **Professional Societies for Office Systems Personnel** (continued)

The Institute for the Certification of Computer Professionals (ICCP)
2200 East Devon Avenue, Suite 268
Des Plaines, IL 60018

National Micrographics Association (NMA)
8719 Colesville Road
Silver Spring, MD 20910

Office Automation Society International (OASI)
6348 Munhall Court
P.O. Box 374
McLean, VA 22101

Office Systems Research Association (OSRA)
501 Grise Hall
Western Kentucky University
Bowling Green, KY 42101

Professional Secretaries International (PSI)
301 East Armour Boulevard
Kansas City, MO 64111

Certification. Many professional associations promote programs leading to professional certification for their members. **Certification** is a formal designation representing distinctive achievement in a particular career. Typical requirements include passing a rigorous, multipart examination, completing periods of professional work experience, and subscribing to high standards of personal and professional conduct. A number of such voluntary certification programs is offered by the Institute for the Certification of Computer Professionals (ICCP). Figure 3-11 lists examples of certification of interest to office systems personnel.

Figure 3-11 **Certifications of Interest to Office Systems Personnel**

Certified Administrative Manager (CAM)
    Sponsor: AMS

Certificate in Computer Programming (CCP)

Certificate in Data Processing (CDP)

Certified Systems Professional (CSP)
    Sponsor: ICCP

Certified Office Automation Professional (COAP)
    Sponsor: OASI

Certified Professional Secretary (CPS)
    Sponsor: PSI

Certified Records Manager (CRM)
    Sponsor: ARMA

Note: For more information regarding certification, write to the sponsoring association. Addresses are listed in Figure 3-10.

WOHL'S BUSINESS PERSPECTIVE

How are Office Jobs Changing?

The office of the fifties, filled with electric typewriters and mechanical calculators, barely exists today. The office of the seventies, with its dedicated word processors and electronic calculators, is nearly gone too.

Each office technology alters the way we perceive office work and changes the opportunities for future employment.

In our business lifetimes, we can expect technology to continue to evolve, sometimes slowly, sometimes so rapidly that the educational system, and the employers who depend upon it, can scarcely run fast enough to keep up.

Business is often at odds with the educational community as to how to best prepare new entrants for the job market. Educators try hard to provide fully trained individuals, but the technology is changing so fast that such training is often obsolete before it can be used. Who remembers the word processors of yesteryear, with their clumsy coding sequences? Or typesetting before the WYSIWYG screen and the desktop publisher?

While business needs trained employees, what it really needs to exploit ever evolving technology is employees who are educated to learn new things.

Students who focus their learning on how a particular computer works are only prepared to use that computer. Students who understand computing are prepared to sit down in front of *any* reasonable computer and figure out what needs to be done.

Moreover, we need students for our management rank who are trained beyond *using* technology. We need employees who understand how to manage technology. This means knowing:

- How to choose among available technology investments to maximize the organization's investments.

- How to identify problems which technology might be able to solve—and how to separate out management problems which can be obscured, but not solved, by technological investments.

- How to decide when to ask for compromises to permit integration, and when decentralization and local control is best.

- How to spot emerging technologies and when to incorporate them into their organizational planning horizons.

We also desperately need students who are trained in specific business areas, from accounting to marketing, from manufacturing to quality control, but who also have strong backgrounds in the business uses of technology. These special people will have the dual skills required to have insights into how new technologies can be used to solve specific line-of-business problems.

Today, we have such employees in place only by accident or by luck. We waste precious time trying to train systems analysts to understand the business or business professionals to understand the technology. Tomorrow, we hope to have employees who know both, who refresh their knowledge of both on an ongoing basis, and who can lead our organizations into the thoughtful implementation of just the right technology, at just the right moment in time.

SUMMARY

Numerous and diverse career opportunities in office systems exist now with growth rates projected for most through the year 2000. The industries of finance, insurance, real estate, communication, and various service industries appear most likely to produce jobs in office systems. Job opportunities in office systems primarily include positions in office, management, marketing, and systems categories. Although most careers in office systems occur within organizations, opportunities do exist for self-employment.

Career planning is recommended for the office systems job seeker. A career plan involves a self-assessment, job exploration, and goal setting. Organizational research might be necessary to tailor the resume and letter of application to particular organizations. Locating job sources can involve personal contact, placement offices, job fairs, personnel offices, employment agencies, and classified advertisements. Job interviews require that the applicant be prompt, project a professional appearance, answer typical interview questions, and take necessary employment tests. Follow-up letters should be sent after the interview by the job applicant.

The career development process in an organization is an interactive process dependent upon the individual, the individual's manager, and the organization. Career advancement in organizations often proceeds on dual-career tracks for technical and general management positions. A technical-professional career can involve successive career stages of apprenticeship, self-dependence, mentor, and senior management. Not all office systems personnel will engage in vertical career mobility but may experience movement horizontally, bilaterally, downward, or outward.

Formal career development programs typically are not offered to employees by organizations, but career development assistance might be obtained from the employee's manager. Career development may be enhanced if the employee develops a relationship with a mentor. Individuals in office systems careers can avail themselves of a wide variety of professional growth activities, including education, professional groups, and certification.

KEY TERMS

job	data people
career	things people
information industries	information interviews
administrative support	resume
chief information officer (CIO)	organizational fit
computer operator	job fair
programmer	assessment centers
analyst	career tracks
office systems analyst	career stages
user liaison	career mobility
systems consultant	mentor
career planning	networking
self-assessment	certification
people people	

REVIEW QUESTIONS

1. Should the type of industry in which a position is located be a factor in considering a particular job offer? It yes, why? If no, why not?

2. How might each holder of the following job pairs differ in educational background, interests, skills, and values?
   a. computer operator and office systems analyst
   b. chief information officer and computer programmer

3. How do an individual's interests, values, and personal characteristics affect career choice and success?

4. Do you think the setting of career goals is necessary for career advancement? Why or why not?

5. How can employees determine whether "organizational fit" is occurring?

6. If upon college graduation you desired to work in a major city over a thousand miles away, what methods could you use to find employment before relocating?

7. If you were asked a question concerning your practice of religion by a job interviewer, what factors would influence your reaction?

8. If an office systems analyst wishes to attain a senior-level, general management position, what organizational factors probably would have to be present for such career mobility to occur?

9. Whom do you think would make the best mentor for an office systems employee—the employee's manager or an experienced peer? Defend your answer.

10. What professional growth opportunities are available for office systems personnel desiring career advancement?

CASE STUDY: A CASE OF OFFICE SYSTEMS CAREER FRUSTRATION

Cindy Feinberg is employed at Global Enterprises, a large, international telecommunication firm. Cindy joined Global six years ago after graduating from a community college with an associate (two-year) degree in word processing. Cindy has earned an excellent reputation as a capable word processing operator and was promoted rapidly through the word processing ranks to lead operator.

When she was hired, Cindy thought she would just work a few years, marry, and eventually leave her job to raise a family. Since these plans did not materialize, Cindy has become more interested in her career. She now desires to move up in the company but is not quite sure how to go about doing so.

Cindy visited the company's personnel office and learned that Global has a management trainee program. Cindy asked her supervisor for a recommendation for entrance into the program. Her supervisor told Cindy that top management does not view individuals from the Word Processing Department as potential candidates for this program. She also told Cindy that she had been with the company for fifteen years, eight of them as supervisor, and has never been considered for a higher management position. In addition, Cindy's supervisor stated that all Global managers have bachelor's degrees. That evening Cindy pondered her career situation.

QUESTIONS/ACTIVITIES

1. What career options does Cindy have?

2. What do you think would be her best course of action?

SUGGESTED READINGS

Bolles, Richard N. *The Three Boxes of Life, and How to Get Out of Them.* Berkeley, Calif.: Ten Speed Press, 1978.
——, *What Color Is Your Parachute?* Berkeley, Calif.: Ten Speed Press, 1978.

Cornish, Edward, Editor. *Careers Tomorrow: The Outlook for Work in a Changing World.* Bethesda, MD: World Future Society, 1988.

Leach, J. and B. J. Chakiris. "The Future of Jobs, Work, and Careers." *Training and Development Journal* (April, 1988): 48–54.

Mirabile, R. "New Directions for Career Development." *Training and Development Journal* (December, 1987): 30–33.

Moses, B. "Giving Employees a Future." *Training and Development Journal* (December, 1987): 25–28.

Slavenski, L. "Career Development: A Systems Approach." *Training and Development Journal* (February, 1987): 56–60.

U.S. Department of Labor, Bureau of Labor Statistics. *Occupational Outlook Handbook.* Washington, D.C.: U.S. Government Printing Office, latest edition.

U.S. Department of Labor, Bureau of Labor Statistics. *Occupational Projections and Training Data.* Washington, D.C.: U.S. Government Printing Office, latest edition.

PART 2

OFFICE SYSTEMS AND TECHNOLOGIES

CHAPTER 4

Computer Information Systems

OBJECTIVES

After studying this chapter, you should understand the following:

1. The common components of computer systems and the role that each plays in information systems

2. Characteristics of computers used in comparing their performance and capabilities

3. The basic hardware elements of a computer system and the information processing functions performed by each

4. Computer software types, uses, and alternative sources

5. The differences among various computer system configurations

6. The basic distinguishing characteristics of computer systems

7. The application of various combinations of computers and terminals to create distributed data processing environments within an organization

8. The difference between computer installations for the management information systems environment and computer installations for the office automation or end user computing environment

9. The use of computers to create information systems for small organizations

The generic term **information systems** encompasses all administrative information handling: creation, communication, storage, and retrieval. Office systems function within the organization's total framework of information systems. In recent years, significant and rapid changes have occurred in office systems, and most of these changes have hinged on the computer. This chapter presents the fundamental characteristics of computer information systems, a review of the management information systems (MIS) environment, and the concepts of office automation and end user computing.

THE COMPUTER — AN OVERVIEW

The computer has been defined, described, and dissected in texts, popular magazines, and professional journals. Most students of office systems, whether college students or practicing managers, have probably been sufficiently exposed to computers to know their makeup. They understand the power of computers, their speeds, their limitations, and their sensitivities. This overview is offered for the benefit of readers with limited or no exposure to computers.

Computer hardware of some type forms the basis for all office automation systems. The size, cost, capacity, and capability of computers varies among systems.

COMPUTER SYSTEM COMPONENTS

Computers come in many different sizes, capabilities, and capacities. Even with these vast differences, the computers used for business applications share common characteristics. Knowledge of these characteristics will enhance your understanding of office technologies for which computers supply the basic power.

The word *computer* almost defies definition. Identified according to common characteristics, however, a **computer** is a system of interconnected components that electronically processes (calculates, correlates, selects, and compiles) information according to a set of instructions and has a capacity for storage of information. A computer is referred to as a system because all computers consist of separate but interlocking components that are coordinated by a central processing unit to accomplish information processing tasks. Computer components to accomplish these tasks are

1. *Input units* receive information (for example, optical scanners, keyboards, data-communication or voice-recognition devices).

2. *Processing units,* called **central processing unit (CPU),** manipulate information according to programs. A **program** is a set of instructions that tells the computer how to manipulate the information that has been provided.
3. *Memory units* hold programs and data within the computer during processing.
4. *Storage units* permit processed data to be held externally (recorded) for later use.
5. *Output units* such as disks and/or tapes display, print, or transmit information. Screen displays, printers, and modems are examples of these units.

COMPUTER SYSTEM CHARACTERISTICS

The capacity for receiving information (input), manipulating (processing) data (numbers, symbols, or letters) to serve a need, and producing usable information (output) are the common characteristics of all computer systems. Technical jargon, classifications, and measurements have provided common descriptive characteristics used to identify system capabilities.

Figure 4-1 All computers consist of separate but interlocking components coordinated by a central processing unit, called a mainframe.
Courtesy of Unysis Corporation

As computers of varying sizes, capacities, and physical structures developed, technical jargon to label the various computer types evolved. Even though such jargon often has a specific meaning for a very short period of time, the terms *mainframe*, *minicomputer*, and *microcomputer* have developed somewhat standard meanings.

A **minicomputer** is one that is usually smaller in capacity, processing speed, and physical size than a **mainframe computer**. This description was accurate until the development of personal computers or **microcomputers**. Minicomputers are physically small (occupying no more than three or four square feet of floor space), but they are complete computer systems. They may support multiple users who compute from a desktop terminal. The introduction of large, powerful microcomputers further complicated the description of small computer systems. The definitions in 4-2 offer some clarification. However, the capacities, capabilities, operating speeds, and costs of computers may overlap from one type to another.

The traditional characteristics for differentiating between minis and micros were physical size, memory, operating speed, portability, multiuser capabilities, multitask capability, and even price. Minicomputers were smaller than mainframes, larger than micros, and sold for many times the price of a micro and a fraction of the cost of a mainframe. Micros were physically small, stand-alone systems that sat on a desktop and operated with very limited speeds and memory capacities, compared to the others. However, these characteristics no longer apply.

Figure 4-2 **Computer Systems Definitions**

MAINFRAME COMPUTER: (1) The central processing component of a physically large, complex computer system, the component that houses the processing apparatus, software, and operations controls; (2) any large, general-purpose computer capable of processing information for an entire organization.

MINICOMPUTER: A physically small computer (compared to a mainframe) with the same capabilities of a mainframe but with lower capacities and operating speeds; typical features include proprietary (manufacturer supplied) operating systems using stored programs and operating speeds of 1.5–2 million instructions per second.

MICROCOMPUTER: A very small, complete computer system available in desktop or laptop (briefcase-sized) configurations;

Figure 4-2 Computer Systems Definitions *(continued)*

features usually include 640K—one megabyte of **RAM**, hard or flexible disk storage; capable of multiuser applications or as stand-alone systems in small organizations and by individuals in large organizations; may be used as a remote workstation connected to centralized minicomputers, mainframe computers, or local area networks; operating speeds of five **MIPS** are possible.

Speed.   A common criterion for comparing computers is their speed in processing data. Characters per second, millions of instructions per second (**MIPS**), and billions of characters per second are measures of capability. Speed becomes important when computers must process large quantities of data or the work of multiple users.

Figure 4-3 Minicomputers sometimes serve multiple users who store and retrieve data through terminals.
Courtesy of Wang Laboratories, Inc.

Data Structures. Systems of today get their speed through their memory data structures. To understand data structures, you must understand bit (one binary digit or one item of information recorded as an "on" or an "off" condition) and byte (a group of bits). A byte represents a character—a number, letter, or symbol—that is recognized by the computer. Computer memories and processors, through their electronic circuitry, treat information as groups called words. A word is a unit of one or more bytes organized for computer handling and processing. These computer units vary in length—8-bit, 16-bit, and 32-bit are popular word lengths. Figure 4-4 clarifies the use of data structure terminology.

Figure 4-4 Computer Data Structures

BIT. One binary digit

BYTE. A group of bits usually representing one character

WORD. A group of characters at one storage location treated by the computer as a unit

Data structures provide a basis for comparison because word length (8-bit, 16-bit, 64-bit, etc.) influences processing speed. The greater the word length, the more characters processed in a given quantity of time.

Capacities. The capacities of computer memories and some of their storage devices can be measured by applying data structures. Capacities identify maximum numbers of characters of data and are measured in thousands (Ks) of bytes or characters. Actually one K of data is 2^{10} or 1,024 characters. Because some computer capacities are so great, the **megabyte (MB)** is used as a measure. A megabyte is 1,024 K or 1,048,576 characters; it is frequently rounded to and expressed as one million. **Gigabyte** (one billion bytes) may be used to measure the capacity of storage media.

Applications. A final criterion for comparing computers is their use. **General-purpose computers** can be programmed to perform a wide variety of processing tasks. A **dedicated computer** is employed for a single type of activity; it may be permanently and internally programmed. Early stand-alone word processors were dedicated computers; they performed no tasks other than text editing. Their programs were "installed" (permanently recorded in memory) or "booted" (transferred from a magnetic disk) each time the program was used.

HARDWARE COMPONENTS

Computer hardware consists of the physical components of a computer system. The basic hardware piece is the CPU. Peripherals are accessory hardware pieces connected (usually by cable) to the CPU. The following discussion of hardware components is grouped according to an **information-processing cycle:** input, processing, storage, output, and communication of information.

Input.   Keyboards and various scanning devices, such as **optical character recognition (OCR)** equipment, that "read" printed, typewritten, coded, or hand-lettered characters are the two most popular input peripherals for today's computer systems. OCR units convert information into electronic impulses that can be accepted and used by CPUs at a rate of more than 300 pages of typewritten copy per hour. Specially printed characters such as those produced by credit-card imprinters as well as ordinary typewritten copy can be read by such devices. Other scanners read bar codes, document images, and numerical data for input into the system. The **mouse** can input data when the operator uses it to select commands or items from a screen menu. Display screens may permit input when the user touches a touch-sensitive screen in a designated spot. Voice-recognition input devices exist, but applications are not widespread. These devices convert the human voice into digital electronic impulses for processing by computers.

Alphabetic, numeric, and alphanumeric keyboards remain popular as input devices, especially with small computer systems. Standard keyboards (also called **QWERTY keyboards** to indicate the top row of letters) are used almost exclusively for the English language. However, the **Dvorak keyboard** (named for its inventor August Dvorak and introduced in the early 1930s) is more efficient than the standard keyboard because of the placement of its characters. Educators and business trainers, however, did not adopt the Dvorak keyboard out of fear that Dvorak-trained typists would not be able to use existing equipment. However, a single keyboard can now function as either a QWERTY or Dvorak keyboard. The keys have two characters each—one representing each arrangement. This feature may bring new life to the Dvorak keyboard if, in fact, keyboards remain necessary as input devices. Perfection of voice input may eventually lessen the need for keyboarding as an input method. Figure 4-5 illustrates the location of characters on the Dvorak keyboard.

Figure 4-5 The Dvorak Keyboard

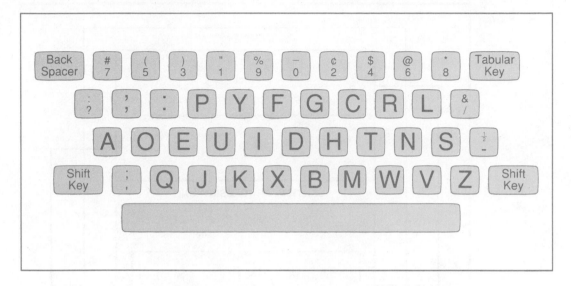

Processing.   References have already been made to the CPU or central processing unit. The CPU is that portion of the system, regardless of size, that executes the data manipulation directed by a program. It contains the computer's control unit, which enables the computer to run through a list of instructions, and an arithmetic/logic unit (ALU) for performing comparisions and calculations. Programs and data processed by the CPU are stored temporarily in internal memory—also called main memory or primary storage. Processing does not take place in memory; this contains the programs and data that support CPU functions.

Central processing units are sometimes called microprocessors, microprocessor units, or **microcomputer processor units (MPU).** In small computers, small chips, which are less than one-fourth inch wide, contain the integrated circuitry of the CPU. In older systems, 50,000 or more transistors or other components would have been required to perform the functions of these chips. Popular microcomputer CPU chips are the Intel 8086, 8088, 80286, and 80386 chips. The model in Figure 4-6 illustrates the relationships among the components of a computer system.

Figure 4-6   **Memory and Central Processing Units**

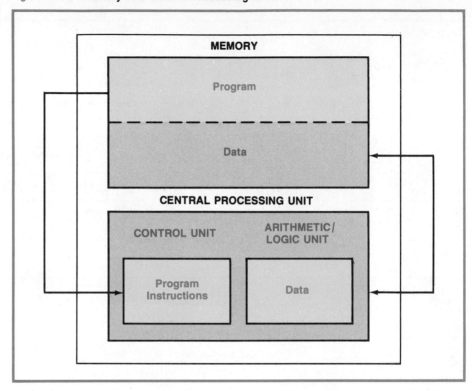

A CPU is referred to as the system's brain because of its key role. CPUs select, compare, calculate, and display information. Microprocessors, which are built into office equipment to aid in its manipulation, are said to give the equipment intelligence—thus the terms intelligent typewriter, intelligent printer, intelligent terminal. Actually, there are some miniature computers in this equipment that serve specialized functions.

Storage.   One of the great values of computers as the basic tool of office automation is their capacity to store information. Some information is stored internally (in the computer); other information is stored externally (on some medium outside the computer). A **storage medium** is a device on which information is recorded electronically. Examples are magnetic tape, magnetic disks, and optical disks.

From another viewpoint, storage may be considered data that is either accessible to the CPU or data that must be loaded into the system before it can be accessed. **On-line** is the descriptor for information stored in such a manner that it is accessible.

Information stored on a hard disk is accessible (on-line); data stored on a floppy disk or a tape and removed from the system must be reloaded before it is accessible.

Internal information storage devices are **random access memory (RAM)** and **read only memory (ROM)** devices. Actually, both memories use random access; the computer can go directly to a set of data without "reading" through all the data that is stored ahead of it. Some memory devices allow the computer to write new data to the device (record new information). These are RAM memories. ROM memories can be read, but no new information can be added to them. ROMs are "installed" memories. The manufacturer installs them permanently in the computer's CPU.

Internal memories may store instructions that help the computer operate or store information that is being accumulated for processing. RAM capacity affects the speed at which computers operate. Memory resides on chips as small as one-fourth inch square. Most RAMs are volatile; they require a constant flow of electricity and are erased when the equipment is turned off or when electricity is interrupted. Figure 4-7 summarizes popular internal storage devices.

Figure 4-7   **Internal Computer Data Storage Devices**

RAM. Random access memory; a volatile memory, erased when power to the CPU is turned off

ROM. Read only memory; manufacturer installed; contains permanent programs. ROM programs translate programs and provide the mechanism for creating programs and managing the operation of the computer. May be called "firmware" (not soft); access to ROM is also random.

PROM. Programmable read only memory: may be "custom designed" for a particular user

EPROM. Erasable-programmable read only memory: can be changed under certain conditions

Off line storage is accessible, but it usually requires operator intervention (use of an external storage device). External or secondary storage media include magnetic recording media in various shapes and configurations and various optical (laser) storage media. They expand the information storage capacities of computers to unlimited quantities by transferring RAM information to a medium that can be removed from the computer. Various peripherals record information to these media and read information from them for reuse and manipulation as instructed by programs and user commands.

Computer technology has passed through many phases of information storage. Early systems relied on punched paper cards and tape, magnetic tape, magnetic drums, and magnetic cores. More recent developments have used magnetic disks, optical disks, and **cryoelectronic storage** devices (a highly sensitive storage medium kept at zero degrees to improve storage). Currently, the most-used medium is the magnetic disk. The peripherals that read information to and write information from magnetic disks are **disk drives**. They use either hard (rigid) disks or floppy (flexible) disks.

Hard disks are rigid disks coated with a magnetic recording material similar to ordinary audio recording tape and are used to store information in digitized code (electronic impulses representing alphabetic characters and numeric quantities). Figure 4-8 illustrates a hard disk drive and Figure 4-9 illustrates a removable hard disk.

Floppy disks (diskettes) are manufactured from flexible magnetic recording material that is either 8, 5¼, or 3½ inches in diameter. The disks are housed in plastic folders. Figure 4-11 illustrates a 5¼-inch floppy (flexible) disk, and Figure 4-12 illustrates a 3½-inch floppy disk. The housing of the 3½-inch disk is rigid; and, therefore, the disk is less susceptible to damage.

Figure 4-8   Schematic Diagram of a Multi-Disk Hard Disk Drive

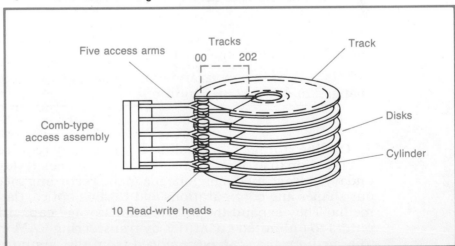

Figure 4-9 The removable hard disk stores information much like an audio recording tape. *Control Data Corporation*

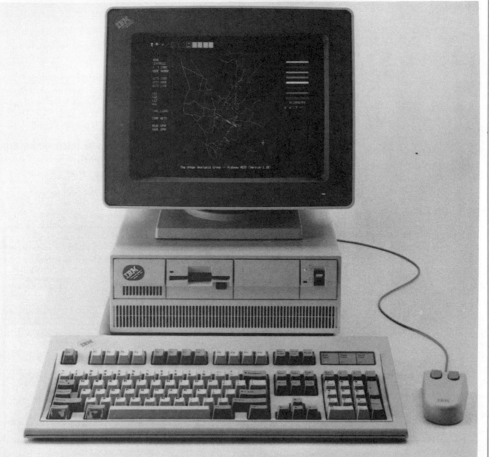

Figure 4-10a This microcomputer contains a hard disk drive. *Hewlett Packard Corporation*

Figure 4-10b **Some hard disks are permanently installed.**
Wang Laboratories, Inc.

Figure 4-11 **Anatomy of a Floppy (Flexible) Disk**

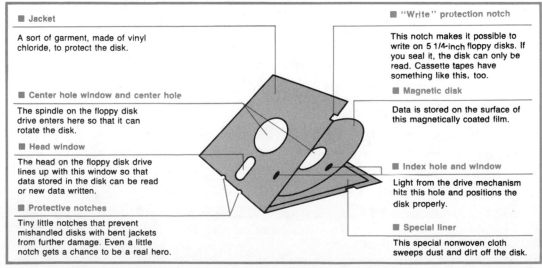

■ **Jacket**

A sort of garment, made of vinyl chloride, to protect the disk.

■ **Center hole window and center hole**

The spindle on the floppy disk drive enters here so that it can rotate the disk.

■ **Head window**

The head on the floppy disk drive lines up with this window so that data stored in the disk can be read or new data written.

■ **Protective notches**

Tiny little notches that prevent mishandled disks with bent jackets from further damage. Even a little notch gets a chance to be a real hero.

■ **"Write" protection notch**

This notch makes it possible to write on 5 1/4-inch floppy disks. If you seal it, the disk can only be read. Cassette tapes have something like this, too.

■ **Magnetic disk**

Data is stored on the surface of this magnetically coated film.

■ **Index hole and window**

Light from the drive mechanism hits this hole and positions the disk properly.

■ **Special liner**

This special nonwoven cloth sweeps dust and dirt off the disk.

Source: Fuji Photo Film Company, *The Floppy Disk Story*, (1984), pp. 9–10.

Figure 4-12 This entire book can be stored on a single, high-density floppy disk.

The capacity of hard disks far exceeds the capacity of flexible disks. A hard disk drive for a microcomputer may have a capacity of 70 or 80 megabytes. Floppy disk capacities have been greatly improved in recent years. High density versions of the 3½-inch disks will hold up to 1.44 megabytes of information—a capacity that would make it possible to store the contents of this entire book on one floppy disk.

Hard disks may be removable disk packs or permanently installed disks in a disk drive. Hard disks may also be built into expansion cards for microcomputers. Figure 4-13 illustrates a "hard card" information storage device.

Optical disks represent the storage medium with the greatest capacity for information. They are available in 5½-, 12-, and 14-inch diameters and can store more than a gigabyte (one billion bytes) of information per side. Chapter 6 discusses the technology used for storing information on these media.

Microcomputer popularity introduced millions of people to the 5¼-inch flexible magnetic diskette as an information storage medium. Disk drive capabilities and data structures influence the information storage capacity of a disk. The packing density

Figure 4-13 Hard disk drives are
only visible when the CPU is
uncovered.
Plus Development Corporation

Figure 4-14 Optical disks, which
come in various sizes, store more
than magnetic media.
Amdek Corporation

of data tracks varies. Some drives use both sides of the disk;
others use only one side.

Office automation literature sometimes refers to any external
storage medium as mass storage. The term also may refer to
peripherals that combine hard disk and magnetic tape storage.
Data can be transferred at high speeds from these devices to a
computer's internal memory for processing, updating, and eras-

ing. Some mainframe computers still use magnetic tape as a standard information storage medium. In microcomputer and minicomputer systems, the magnetic tape storage medium is likely to be used as a backup storage medium to protect information from power failures and other hardware failures that might destroy information.

Output.   The product of the computer is information in some usable form. That may be a printed form, document, or report. It may be a display screen image of data, text, graphics, or document images. It may be a magnetic medium created for possible future use. Computers can now produce microfilm images and human voice responses from stored human voice responses or computer-created audible output.

Communication.   Information must be communicated (moved) from one component to another for processing, retrieval, and application. The internal mechanism that controls communication is a **bus**, a cable or wire network that connects the microprocessor, memory units, and peripherals.

The path between one component and another over which data travels is called a **channel**. Over telephone lines, external peripherals (called **modems**) communicate information from one system to another or from a central system to remote terminals — devices at another location that communicate directly with a computer. In addition to modems, networks and satellite systems are used to communicate information. These and other technologies used to communicate information are discussed in Chapter 8.

SOFTWARE

Contemporary office technology requires **software** (programs containing directions to computers for carrying out complicated information processing activities). References to software usually indicate such a set of computer readable instructions.

Sources.   Software is now available from a variety of sources: hardware manufacturers and vendors, **software houses** (firms that develop and market software), and staff programmers (user-developed software). Office supply houses, computer shops, and even bookstores also market packaged software for the microcomputer market.

Early computer users thought in terms of developing their own software or using software developed by computer manufacturers to perform the information processing activities desired from the computer system. Users of medium-to-large-scale computer systems still rely heavily on programs developed, tested, and perfected by their own programmers. Large-to-medium-scale computer manufacturers or vendors have traditionally included software with the system package, sometimes providing alterations necessary to customize the programs to user needs. These packages have represented significant portions of the purchase or lease price of systems.

The microcomputer revolution in the early 1980s brought with it the concept of the commercial software publisher (software house). Companies were formed to engage in writing and marketing software for all types and sizes of computers, but those producing software for microcomputers were especially numerous. Major hardware manufacturers began to market software produced by these software specialists with their systems. The quality of the programs and the training materials that accompanied them were frequently poor. Because of the ease with which users could duplicate software, prices remained high. Yet, those high prices were frequently preferable to the cost of programs developed in-house. Experience and competition have increased the quality of both programs and instructional materials, which has led to a decrease in the price and an increase in the value of software.

Software Types.   Three major categories of software important to computer users are (1) systems software or **operating systems** programs, (2) applications programs, and (3) operating environment software. Operating systems are programs that control the computer and direct the processing of information. Operating system (OS) refers to any computer operating system software; **disk operating system (DOS)** usually refers to microcomputer operating systems stored on disks.

An operating system is actually a collection of programs, including directions for passing information between the computer and its peripherals, communication with the operator regarding status of program execution, managing languages for writing programs, and actually making calculations required by the applications programs. Additional components of the operating system, called **utilities**, permit users to carry out housekeeping chores, such as copying files and preparing blank storage media for receiving information.

Applications software programs instruct the computer to carry out specific information processing tasks, such as performing accounting or word processing. Figure 4-15 identifies several categories of applications software. Software for an office automation environment may perform a single function, such as word processing, or it may perform a combination of functions, such as spreadsheets, graphics, word processing, telecommunication, and databases. Software that performs a combination of functions is called **integrated software**.

Figure 4-15 **Computer Applications Software Categories**

Category	Function
Accounting/Finance	General record keeping, payroll, accounts receivable and customer billing, accounts payable and check writing, producing financial reports, financial modeling, financial forecasting, investment analysis
Inventory	Records additions to and deductions from inventory; produces status of individual items
Engineering and Scientific	Computer assisted design, graphics design
Decision Support	Uses mathematical and statistical models to support decision making, particularly in operations research and major management decisions; allows managers to predict the effects of alternative decisions
Database Management Systems	Creates collections of records that have common elements; permits updating and manipulating records to organize and compile reports from information contained in records
Communications	Allows computers to send and receive information through communication links
Electronic Mail	Transmits messages, such as documents produced by word processing software, from one computer or terminal to another
Word Processing	Text creation and editing, merging stored text components to produce documents, mail list management, spelling and grammar checks, merging text, data, and graphics elements to produce documents
Graphics	Produces graphic representations of statistical information, enables computer to record responses to user input devices such as the light pen and the ''mouse''
Administrative Support	Managerial support such as schedule management, tickler files, calendar reminders, list management
Tutorial	Computer-aided instruction, training
Electronic/Desktop Publishing	Designing page layouts, selecting type style, type size, and other features to produce professional quality documents
Statistics	Regression calculations, application of statistical formulas to available information
Vertical	Applications software developed for the information processing needs of highly specialized industries or businesses (real estate, attorneys' offices, medical facilities, insurance agencies, churches)

Large computer systems software may be very complex, including more than a dozen types of programs. Computer manufacturers provide the operating systems for large computers. The system may be permanently installed in the computer, and users may not be aware of the existence of the software. Some microcomputer manufacturers also design their equipment for operation with their own operating systems software. Small systems may require that the operating system be transferred from a magnetic disk to the memory of the computer each time the system is turned on. Others store the operating system on a hard disk from which it can be retrieved each time it is needed. Applications software disks may also contain the operating systems software.

Operating environment software functions between operating systems and applications software to instruct the computer's handling of information storage and retrieval. The basic purpose of the software is to simplify computer use for people in an office environment. The user may be able to move the cursor (a location indicator) to a symbol on the screen instead of keying a two- or three-step command. Early examples of this type of software were IBM's TopView®, Microsoft Corporation's Windows®, and the MacIntosh® series from Apple Computer.

An important characteristic of software is the **user interface**. Whether supplied by operating environment software or built into applications software, the user interface represents what the computer user sees on the display screen, the ease with which he or she can interpret the software's capabilities and enter commands (directions) to get the software to respond quickly and easily. For example, some users who feel awkward using a keyboard can be relieved of some of that discomfort if information can be entered by touching a spot on the display screen or moving a cursor with a pointing device, such as a mouse. A **mouse** is an apparatus that is moved about a spot on a desktop; simultaneous movement of the cursor takes place on the screen. Clicking the controls on the mouse substitutes for commands that would require keying without the use of the mouse.

Programming Languages.   Language is a set of symbols that carry somewhat uniform meanings. Human language includes verbal symbols that carry meaning. Machine language is made up of symbols that computers recognize. A set of symbols or instructions (words, phrases, codes) to which computers will react is called a **programming language**. Hundreds of programming languages exist, and they are written at different levels for different uses.

Machine, assembly, and compiler languages are low-level languages. Computers react to machine language. Because high-

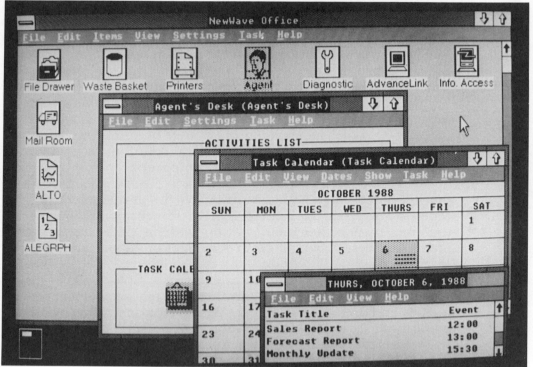

Figure 4-16 A friendly user interface provides screen prompts and
other devices that make manipulation
of software easy.
*Courtesy of Hewlett Packard
Company*

level languages are difficult and cumbersome, compilers and
assemblers convert high-level languages to machine languages.
High-level languages use English-like words as symbols in writing
program instructions. Popular business languages are **COBOL**
(Common Business-Oriented Language), **RPG** (Report Programming Generator), and **BASIC** (Beginners' All-purpose Symbolic
Instruction Code). BASIC is the most popular high-level language
for microcomputers. Higher level or artificial intelligence languages are now common. These **natural languages** are installed
in systems that convert human language to machine language.

THE MIS ENVIRONMENT

Computers were originally developed to serve either scientific
applications (analog computers) or business data processing

applications (digital computers). Over the years, this distinction became less pronounced, but the professional discipline for business computer applications assumed the title "data processing." The department that housed and administered computer operations for processing business and administrative information was called the data processing department of the organization. College courses, majors, and instructional departments also used the term data processing. Corporate data processing departments functioned rather independently of other organizational departments and emphasized highly technical solutions to routine information processing needs using computers.

As these departments began to branch out from routine information processing and concentrate on the development of systems to solve management problems for entire organizations, the title "management information systems (MIS) department" identified these departments in organizations and in educational institutions.

As data processing technology evolved, various facets of office work were realigned to take advantage of mass processing capabilities and greater processing speeds. Routine clerical and accounting tasks or any information processing that could easily be processed in batches were prime candidates for data processing/MIS divisions of organizations. Later, more complex data-handling and decision-support applications also moved into these divisions.

Routine tasks that could be automated (performed with the aid of a computer) were removed from the traditional departments where they had been handled and labeled DP functions. Nonautomated clerical functions, such as manual bookkeeping tasks, correspondence, and records management, remained in functional offices or were centralized, particularly where the volume of such tasks remained low. These remaining clerical functions were labeled office functions. Those who managed computer functions had the title *data processing manager*, and managers of nonautomated information processing activity were called *office managers*. In many organizations, the nonautomated functions were widely distributed among functional specialties and were not supervised by professional managers.

Beginning in the 1960s, advances in computer technology enabled organizations to automate additional clerical, secretarial, and communication functions in offices. Three distinct categories of information technology developed: data processing/MIS, word processing, and telecommunications. These technical systems were managed and operated independently with very little interaction.

Most organizations operate within a somewhat common structure. This structure is molded differently from one organization to another, but common functions and activities create similarities. This was true as data processing/MIS departments evolved. The common elements, from one organization to another, were job content, job titles, procedures, professional vocabulary, and the tasks for which computers were used. Relatively few manufacturers produced hardware, and training was provided by manufacturers. IBM dominated hardware manufacturing and training. These circumstances created a professional environment which influenced the goals, philosophies, and roles of data processing professionals.

PRODUCT/OUTPUT

Historically, the product of data processing departments has been quantitative data. The tangible products were reports of quantitative data—accounting reports, financial reports, production reports, research and quality-control data, and customer reports (invoices, statements, summary data, etc.). Files of quantitative data (for reference purposes) were accumulated.

PERSONNEL

Any professional discipline develops around the people in that profession and the work they do. Roles, orientation, contributions, and professional development of those employed by one organization are influenced by the profession as a whole. The data processing profession influenced new professionals joining the field; and the education, skills, and career expectations of new professionals tended to reflect those held by older members of the profession. The profession influenced the role of data processing, the job structures, departmental orientations, and the education of professional employees—both formal education prior to employment and professional development after employment.

ROLE IN ORGANIZATION

Data processing departments operated for many years as independent administrative services within organizations. They were attached organizationally to finance or accounting functions or functioned independently with the departmental manager reporting to a vice president or some other relatively important official. Some organizations include a vice president for information systems or a chief information officer who coordinates all information systems. Data processing departments are still very much a part of successful organizations. However, they have become less centralized, physically. Very often data processing hardware sits in the end user department.

ORIENTATION

Because of the technology involved and the lack of understanding by professional managers in other disciplines, data processing managers were able to get the departments they served to alter procedures to fit DP designs. While service to others was their reason for existing, DP professionals called the shots about the nature of that service. The designs called for highly structured, quantitatively oriented tasks processed in batches. Relatively long lead times were required for designing systems and producing results. The raw material was numeric data; the output was quantitative reports and statistical data.

As a group, data processing professionals were rather independent, and the computer's "desires" and requirements were blamed when a manager or executive requested changes in processing procedures or system output. "The computer won't accept . . ." and "the computer can't . . ." were phrases to which managers became accustomed. This orientation has been labeled a "technology-driven approach."

The 1970s brought many changes in this orientation. Managers from all disciplines became computer literate and better understood the capabilities of systems. Data processing professionals became more aware of the importance of the human element in their systems planning. Systems analysts considered the total effect of their systems and tried to develop them according to user needs. Information managers began to strive for a "user-driven approach" to technology and its applications. In this orientation, the individual or department requesting technical assistance is the prime consideration; they participate in the planning and design of systems to serve their needs. In most organizations, this condition has not been achieved.

HARDWARE USED

The traditional computer system throughout the 1960s and 1970s was a central system that handled all automated data processing for the entire organization. Some of these systems communicated with remote terminals and other peripherals, and some organizations had several large computer installations. Organizations sometimes shared a single installation; however, the bulk of data processing activity took place in a single, centralized location in most organizations. During much of this period, mainframe computers (large, centralized, high-capacity, expensive systems) were the only computers, so the term *mainframe* was not necessary to distinguish it from other systems. Mainframes were characterized by their capacity and speed.

DISTRIBUTED DATA PROCESSING

As computer hardware became less expensive and managers became more comfortable with computer use, the demand for **distributed data processing** increased. This term has been used to describe two concepts. First, it may refer to remote, independently-operating computer systems in the functional departments of organizations. These systems are more accurately referred to as **stand-alone systems** because they do not communicate with mainframe computers or other distributed systems. They distribute the work load, but they may not improve information communication (see Figure 4-17). In fact, they may duplicate the efforts of the mainframe computer. The installation of microcomputers in the offices of managers, professional staff, secretaries, and other support employees was the first wave of a concept that would later be labeled "office automation" and, still later, "end user computing."

The second concept of distributed data processing describes the installation of communication links between central computing facilities and end users (Chapter 8 describes communication links). This concept involves distributing processing power to the departments. Ideally, each department would have its own system with individual users connected to that system. Each user is capable of executing applications programs and storing data. Departmental systems are connected to each other and to the central computer. Central processing systems connect individual users to the central computer without a department computer in between. Personal computers in departmental offices or the offices of individual employees may be linked to central systems, providing information processing powers and access to mainframe-stored information in remote locations. Some organizations may use a combination of these approaches. Either arrangement may enable users to engage in a variety of office automation functions such as electronic mail or downloading data into a computer.

In organizations that follow the first concept, the user departments are likely to purchase and control their own systems. In organizations following the second concept, data processing or MIS departments are likely to coordinate and control the systems, including hardware and software purchases. In some organizations, an office automation or an office-systems unit may coordinate and control the use of computers by individuals throughout an organization. Multiple mainframe computers may form the distributed information processing environment, but it may also include minicomputers and microcomputers.

Figure 4-17 **Examples of Computer Worked on By Users**

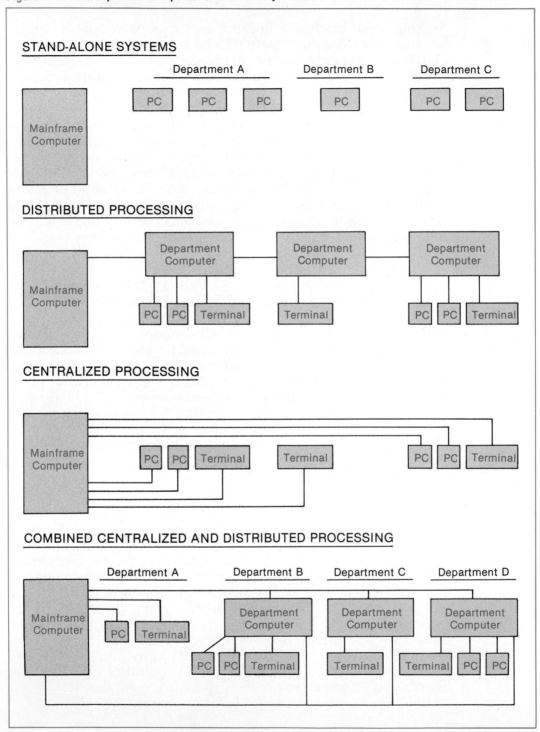

Figure 4-18 Remote terminals
allow users to access data and use
software stored by a computer in
another location.
Unysis Corporation

OFFICE AUTOMATION ENVIRONMENT

End user computing is the term frequently used to describe the use of computers to enhance the productivity of individual managers, executives, staff personnel, and support employees. Computing power in individual offices allows these persons to perform small-scale information processing involving the functions and tasks of a single department or an individual. Among the more popular applications are financial analysis, accounting, administrative support, word processing, and other communication activities. The technical nature of these applications is discussed in Chapter 5 and other chapters of this text.

The popularity of end user computing can be demonstrated by the fact that by 1987, after only about seven years of active personal computer sales, the sales (dollar volume) of microcomputers had equalled the dollar volume of mainframe computer sales.

Distributed processing through electronic workstations will provide office support employees with major information processing responsibilities, including programming. However, implementation of distributed processing must be carefully coordinated with DP/MIS departments so that individual departments' efforts coincide with organization-wide information processing. For greatest effectiveness, hardware and software in and among individual departments must be compatible with mainframe computers networks and other communication devices that connect them.

MANAGING END USER COMPUTING IN LARGE ORGANIZATIONS

Responsibility for end user computing in large organizations takes many forms. In some organizations, there is no central responsibility. In others, managers of end user computing coordinate computer use from a position in a MIS department. In a few organizations, office systems managers or end user computing managers operate independently of the MIS department. A unit called the **information center** may coordinate these activities. Information centers are training and support centers for end users. They assist in the selection of hardware and software and provide training and software support for users. Some organizations have begun to employ **office systems analysts** to assist with strategic planning and implementation of end user computing.

COMPUTER INFORMATION SYSTEMS FOR THE SMALL ORGANIZATION

The discussion in this chapter has concentrated upon computer information processing technology and the application of that technology to the large organization. Much of the discussion explored small-scale, end user computer applications for managers, professional staff, and administrative support workers in large organizations. Another vast potential for productivity improvement through information processing exists within small organizations. Through the computer, office automation is available for the smallest organizations, even one- and two-person firms.

Microcomputers with quality peripherals can support the complete spectrum of information processing for the small organization. Packaged software is plentiful and relatively inexpensive. It can support accounting and other record keeping systems, databases, word processing, and special applications for most organizations.

Many small business managers are skilled in programming and can create their own custom software. Vendors are available to supply and support hardware and software even in small cities. Multi-user systems and communication of data among multiple locations are also possible. Networks, modems, and communications software can be used to communicate information among small organizations or among multiple workstations of a single organization.

The rebirth of the small business and entrepreneurial spirit has been enhanced by these office automation opportunities that have enabled small businesses to process their own information at relatively low costs.

CAREER IMPLICATIONS FOR COMPUTER INFORMATION SYSTEMS

Careers involving computer information systems can be found in many working environments, including the data processing/management information systems function of large organizations, the office automation/office systems function of large organizations, the telecommunication function of large organizations, or a wide variety of functions in organizations too small to support separate functional units for information systems.

The following career information is typical of jobs offered in the MIS environment. Similar information in Chapters 5–8 includes information about careers in office systems, reprographics and desktop publishing, information/records management, and telecommunications.

Job titles and definitions in this list are adapted from the 1988 *Datamation*[1] salary survey. In some cases, the title indicates a level of employment rather than an actual job title. Many organizations would not employ separate job titles for each level.

---

1. "What Are You Worth In '88?," *Datamation* (October 1, 1988): 53.

SPECIMEN JOB TITLES IN THE MANAGEMENT INFORMATION SYSTEMS ENVIRONMENT

Data Entry Positions
Operator
Supervisor

Production and Input/Output Control
Clerk
Scheduler
Lead Controller
Supervisor

Computer Operations
Magnetic Media Librarian
Operator
Lead Operator
Shift Supervisor
Manager

Operating Systems Programming
Junior Systems Programmer
Intermediate Systems Programmer
Senior Systems Programmer
Manager

Systems Analysis/Programming
Junior Systems Analyst/Programmer
Intermediate Systems Analyst/Programmer
Systems Analyst/Programmer
Senior Systems Analyst/Programmer
Lead Systems Analyst/Programmer
Manager

Applications Programming
Junior Applications Programmer
Intermediate Applications Programmer
Applications Programmer
Senior Applications Programmer
Lead Applications Programmer
Manager

Systems Analysis
Junior Systems Analyst
Systems Analyst
Senior Systems Analyst
Lead Systems Analyst
Manager

Staff Level
Technical Services Manager
Director of DP/MIS
Vice President DP/MIS
Vice President, Chief Information Officer

The following definitions from the *Datamation* survey indicate the nature of education and experience requirements for many of the positions identified above.

Junior — two to four years of college and six months' experience; directly supervised.

Intermediate — bachelor's degree or equivalent and minimum of two years' experience; requires some direction.

Senior — bachelor's degree or equivalent and minimum of three years' experience, including some experience in a supervisory capacity.

Lead — bachelor's degree or equivalent, and minimum of four years' experience (two in a supervisory capacity); performs supervision as a project leader.

Manager — master's degree or doctorate and minimum of five years' experience (or equivalent combinations); strong management skills; performs personnel evaluations, budgeting, progress reporting, project management.

WOHL'S BUSINESS PERSPECTIVE

Choosing an Information System

The information systems market today represents an embarrassment of riches. Dozens of companies offer hundreds of systems. Each system could be configured in a nearly infinite number of ways. Just figuring out what to buy — and worrying about whether you've made the right choice — is an enormous burden, particularly for non-technical managers.

Vendors offer to help you choose, but they can only do so on behalf of their own product offerings. Thousands of consultants offer to help — but how do you know you've picked the right consultant?

The miracle of computing as we enter the nineties is in its diversity — something for nearly anyone — and in its value. Today we can buy the performance equivalent of a large mainframe computer of a few years ago, write a check for $10,000 or less, and fit the entire system onto a single desktop. Expect that miracle to continue; computer systems will offer more and more performance for diminishing prices.

Business means making decisions, and decisions about computing will be an important part of everybody's organizational strategy. Businesses will require that *every* manager know enough about computer systems — their uses, their cost, and their value—to participate in such decisions. But all managers will depend upon the special skills of a systems staff to offer guidance and expertise, especially in the selection of large, complex systems.

But something important has changed in the design, selection, implementation and management of systems. Once data processing management made such decisions on behalf of the user organization. Users, they felt, could not make decisions about computers, because they lacked the appropriate technical expertise.

Many systems were designed, bought, and built but rarely used because they failed to correctly identify and serve the needs of a user community.

Today, systems are designed with user input at every stage. A new design process, called iterative design, is widely employed. This permits the user to see how the system will look before enormous (cost and time) investments are made in actually creating the software programs. At each iteration (sample system), the users for whom the system is intended can fine tune the design. Only when all are in agreement does the coding proceed. The design document acts as an accurate specification, greatly speeding up the final programming process.

A wise industry analyst has stated, "Remember that end users are workers who choose *not* to be data processing analysts." This means that systems designed for end users must employ every bit of knowledge we have to make the system not only user friendly, but user seductive, catching the potential user's attention and inviting him/her to try the system.

Given the enormous costs of training and retraining users and the cost of their ongoing support, systems must also be intuitive, permitting the user to get started with a minimum training investment.

The systems of the future will be built out of processors and workstations, storage and communications, hardware and software—just like the systems before them. But the emphasis for future systems will clearly be on user participation and ease of use, and that will make them happily different.

SUMMARY

Knowledge of computer information systems is essential to understanding the potential for office automation. Computers provide the basic technology. Hardware ranges from tiny microprocessor chips to giant mainframe computer systems. Business computers share common elements such as input, processing, storage, and output components. A variety of hardware types can be used for each of these elements. The speed, capacity, and capability of computers are characteristics that can be used for comparison.

Software is the key to computer applications in office automation. Software consists of operating systems, programs which manipulate the computer, and applications programs, which perform actual information-processing tasks. Internally developed software or purchased software may be used.

Traditional data processing/MIS applications involved quantitative information processing, specialized and technical personnel, and large mainframe computers. Contemporary information systems may include smaller systems and distributed data processing employing minicomputers and microcomputers that communicate with mainframe computers. The application of computers to the work of individuals throughout an organization is sometimes referred to as office automation or end user computing.

Even the smallest organizations now install and benefit from computer systems.

KEY TERMS

information system
minicomputer
microcomputer
mainframe computer
computer
central processing unit (CPU)
program
computer
megabyte
gigabyte
general-purpose computer
dedicated computer
information processing cycle
optical character recognition
  (OCR)
mouse
QWERTY keyboard
Dvorak keyboard
microcomputer processor
  unit (MPU)
storage medium
on-line
random access memory
  (RAM)
read only memory (ROM)
off-line
cryoelectronic storage
disk drive

hard disk
floppy disk
optical disk
bus
channel
modem
software
software house
operating system
disk operating system (DOS)
utility
applications program
integrated software
operating environment
  software
cursor
user interface
programming language
COBOL
RPG
BASIC
natural language
distributed data processing
information center
office systems analyst
stand-alone system
end user computing

REVIEW QUESTIONS

1. Contrast the term *information system* with the following terms:
   a. computer information system
   b. office automation
   c. data processing
   d. management information system

2. Identify five categories of computer hardware elements, citing specific elements in each category, and discuss the basic function of each element.

3. How do you measure computer speed? Is it important to measure speed?

4. What is computer software? Contrast the two major categories of software.

5. Contrast the general meaning of the terms microcomputer, minicomputer, and mainframe computer. Why is this comparison now more difficult than it was 10 years ago?

6. What have been the distinguishing characteristics of traditional electronic data processing?

7. What is distributed data processing? When this concept is applied, what has been distributed? Contrast stand-alone processing, centralized processing, distributed processing, and combination arrangements.

8. How does the use of computers for end user computing or office automation differ from the use of computers for central management information systems?

CASE STUDY: THE WARREN COMPANY—PREPARATION FOR REORGANIZATION—PART I

This is a two-part case involving an insurance company. As a preliminary activity, examine an insurance firm's annual report or read about the insurance industry in a library. (Standard & Poor's *Industry Surveys* would be a good source.)

The questions that follow the case will require application of concepts from Chapters 2, 3, and 4. Depending upon the extent of your background studies in business administration, your instructor may wish to assign additional readings or conduct a class discussion of the following concepts:

   1. *typical organizational structures for corporate service firms*
   2. *organization charts: techniques and guidelines*
   3. *the difference between functional units and support or service units in large organizations*
   4. *a comparison of private organizations and government organizations*

At the end of Chapter 5 additional information and additional questions are presented. The basic description of the firm follows.

THE ORGANIZATION

Warren Corporation is an insurance company that writes policies in the fields of casualty (automobile, home, business property) and term life insurance. Some independent insurance agencies represent the company for sales, but most of the selling is done directly by telephone and by mail. Several large professional groups endorse Warren Corporation's group policies for term life insurance and automobile insurance.

The firm employs 283 people at its headquarters, including top management, departmental managers, and various administrative service and professional service units. Several units in the firm have some degree of responsibility for information processing activities.

The MIS Department is managed by a director who reports to the corporate controller. The staff of this department handles typical data processing tasks for management, for policyholder accounting, and for routine projects for most departments. The MIS Department generates standard monthly and annual financial reports for the accounting department. Occasionally, it gets involved in projects related to market analysis, forecasting, and actuarial statistics. The activities of the MIS Department are scheduled far in advance. New systems analysis and design activities for the next two years are already scheduled because most of the staff's time is devoted to keeping existing systems running smoothly. Any new design work must be lifted into the schedule.

The Word Processing Center is managed by a WP manager who reports to the manager of administration, a person to whom several administrative service units report. (The manager of administration reports to the vice president of operations.) This center produces transcripts of phoned-in dictation and big jobs: mass mailings to policyholders, routine special reports (including copy for the annual report), and particularly large reports that require several revisions.

A Central Records Department is managed by a records manager who also reports to the vice president of operations. This center is responsible for central files, records storage, a large copy center, and a small print shop. Among other things, this department maintains a folder for every policyholder.

The other service areas that report to the manager of administration include the mail room (one supervisor and several employees), the building receptionists, who also serve as the telephone operators (no supervisor), and the director of security (building and parking lot). The manager of administration is personally responsible for the firm's telephone switching system.

Gradually, information management technologies have crept into Warren Corporation. The computer center is adequate for the immediate future; among their scheduled activities are plans to computerize several procedures that are now done manually. Stand-alone word processors in several departmental offices and the large system in the WP center are recent updates from major manufacturers. Some departments don't use their WP systems more than three or four days each month. Telephone service is adequate. Very little state-of-the-art equipment is being used in the mail room or central records area, but they appear to be functioning adequately.

There are no major complaints except for occasional comments from workers and supervisors who object to changing procedures to accommodate demands of new computer programs.

For reasons that have nothing to do with office systems directly, a corporate management team is examining reorganization potential for the firm. The team members' ideas about most areas have been developed over a period of years, and they know what they want to do. However, the management team knows very little about office automation. They have heard enough to know that greater productivity may be possible from their office staff. Some comparisons with industry data regarding percent of revenue dollar spent for administrative costs suggest that they spend significantly higher amounts than the industry as a whole.

Top management believes that if any improvements are forthcoming in the office and in administrative costs, they should begin changes now during the general reorganization. Examination of salary and benefit structures indicates that the firm is about average for the industry. One member of the team has pointed out that the firm has modern equipment in most areas and that "we are up to our ears in information technology around here, but we don't appear to have the integrated information systems that we hear so much about."

QUESTIONS/ACTIVITIES

Assume that you are a member of the team that is investigating possible future directions for information processing at Warren Corporation.

1. Construct an organization chart of the portion of the Warren Corporation described in this case, filling in the chief executive officer and any other top management positions that you would expect to be above the vice presidential level positions indicated in the case description.

2. How would communication among the MIS Department and the other departments be affected by the organizational structure as you perceive it?

3. Compile a list of computer hardware that you would expect the MIS Department of this firm to be currently using.

4. For each of the following groups, identify information output that you would expect the MIS Department's information systems to produce: corporate top management, policyholders, and the federal government.

5. To what extent has Warren Corporation achieved "integrated office systems"?

6. Would you characterize Warren Corporation's information systems as user driven or technology driven? Why?

SUGGESTED READINGS

"The Future Is Always Beginning." *Datamation* (September 15, 1987): 44.

Betts, Kellyn S. "Magnetic Media: The Memory Lingers On." *Modern Office Technology* (July, 1985): 78–86.

CHAPTER 5

Word/Information Processing Systems

OBJECTIVES

After studying this chapter, you should understand the following:

1. Basic information formats

2. Ingredients of systems for written communication systems—the people, procedures, and technologies for information capture, initial processing, communication, storage, and retrieval

3. The significance of the business document to business information systems and the technologies involved in document production

4. The evolution and current status of word processing technology and its role in business document production

5. Printer technology for office systems and factors influencing the choice of technology

Office automation technologies originated with the application of computer technology to the tasks of secretaries, clerical workers, and other administrative support employees. Later developments expanded applications to the tasks of managers and professional staff persons. The concept of office systems can be applied narrowly to systems for the use of one individual or department or in a broader sense to the components of systems that serve an entire organization.

This chapter introduces a series of chapters that detail the technical and conceptual aspects of the office systems introduced in Chapter 2. All of the chapters involve the computer technologies discussed in Chapter 4. This chapter introduces concepts associated with office information systems and explores word processing as the basic technology for written document production—information capture, initial processing, and distribution or communication. In addition to word processing, the chapter explores printer technology, a very important supporting technology. Chapters 6, 7, and 8 deal with three additional supporting technologies: electronic publishing, information resources management, and telecommunications.

OFFICE INFORMATION SYSTEMS

Office systems help to satisfy the information processing needs of organizations. They are associated with information processing for units (departments and divisions) within organizations and for individual employees. Understanding these systems requires knowledge of system components. Information itself is the major component, so the discussion begins with descriptions of *information formats*. Other components include the methods for *capturing information* in usable form for *initial processing*, the *communication* (movement) of information from one place to another, the *storage and retrieval* of information, and the *people* who perform the tasks associated with these activities.

The following descriptions of information processing concepts serve as a framework within which entire office systems or individual subsystems can be examined. Each system or subsystem must deal with one or more of the information formats and include a scheme for capturing, processing, communicating, storing, and retrieving that information. The discussions in the remainder of this chapter and the following three chapters will deal with these information categories and system elements.

INFORMATION FORMATS

Knowledge workers generate, receive, and use information in a variety of types and formats. Office systems may be designed to handle information in only one format or they may handle multiple information types. Several distinct information categories have been defined and are useful in designing office systems and describing their capabilities. These categories include voice, text, data, graphics, and image.

Voice.   Since a large percentage of the communication within organizations is oral communication, **voice communication** represents an important information format. Systems for recording and transmitting voice communication have functioned since the invention of the phonograph and the telephone. More recent developments have concentrated on the storage and retrieval of voice communication. Even though very high-quality voice recordings were possible through analog technology, single systems for efficiently transmitting, storing, and retrieving information in the voice format became possible only when these technologies were combined with computer technology and digital formats. Chapter 8 includes the technologies associated with voice communication systems.

Text.   Written information in the form of words, sentences, and paragraphs is referred to as **text**. Office systems must provide procedures and mechanisms for creating, transmitting, storing, and retrieving text. Although text is usually associated with paper documents, it may appear in any medium. Computer video screen images and microfilmed images are two popular nonpaper text media. The primary function of text is the communication of information, but it also assumes evidentiary value when it serves as proof that communication has been accomplished. Word processing and reprographics technologies are used for generating, manipulating, and reproducing text. Text is document oriented. Systems that manage text must be capable of maintaining document format.

Data.   The highly quantitative category of business information referred to as **data** involves statistical, financial, and accounting information. Even though the quantitative values receive major attention in this category, data also include alphabetic information such as words to name accounts and identify collections of quantitative information. Because of computers and electronic data processing, data are sometimes assumed to represent only electronically processed information. Any quantitative information might be labeled as data. Basic dictionary definitions of *datum* (data is the plural form) include such things as "a fact known" and "information from which conclusions are drawn." When the advent of office systems for processing text and document-sensitive information required clarification, the data/text designation became more necessary. Figure 5-1 offers a comparison between text and data.

Graphics.   Charts, graphs, and illustrations that depict quantitative values comprise the information category called **graphics**.

Figure 5-1   A Comparison of Text and Data

TEXT:

July 8, 19--

TO: Stanford Walsh, Engineering

FROM: Brenda Cook, Office Systems

SUBJECT: Training for Electronic Workstations

You may schedule training sessions for your staff's introduction to the new electronic workstations during the first three weeks of August. We can accommodate six employees at a time. The training lasts two full days, but the two days need not be consecutive.

Work out a tentative schedule for your staff and call Maija Avots, who will be your trainer. She will confirm the schedule and arrange a meeting with your entire staff. That meeting should take place several days before the training begins, so call her within the next few days if possible.

lwr

DATA:

```
****************************************************************************
                    F E B R U A R Y    S A L E S
                         (by district)
****************************************************************************
                                  Unit Sales
                    ****************************************************
District/Product Code     #7892     #7893     #7896     #7897     #7899
--------------------------------------------------------------------------

Auburn                   35638     34692      2789       378       233
Rockfield                 6836      3786       278       322       192
Richardsville            57389      3865      1873       233      1267
Marrowbone                 387      3899      2981      1547       876
Bee Springs               9992     10330       227       709       987
```

Because graphic presentation of quantitative information communicates more readily than raw numerical data or textual descriptions of quantitative values, written and oral communication is frequently supplemented with graphic presentations. Before the perfection of computer software and hardware elements to create graphic information, these communication supplements were created manually and required substantial time. With sophisticated software, computers can now create elaborate, full-color graphic representations of most quantitative information. This technology is further explored in the section of this chapter devoted to integrated office systems.

Image.   This fifth information format category is added to prevent confusion. As Chapter 4 described, business information is frequently stored in digital format and retrieved when necessary in a variety of formats (screen image, paper printout, or even a voice response). Most data processing systems are capable of processing, storing, and retrieving quantitative information (data); however, there may be no specified format to the retrieved information. Format may not be a critical element when retrieving data; but for other information types, the **image** may be quite critical. Image technology makes possible the creation or replication of document images, photographs, line drawings, and art work. An image of a business document may contain logos, signatures, or line drawings that would be lost if only text and data were stored.

Information systems must be capable of replicating and transmitting the exact image of a stored document, photograph, map, or line drawing. Both computer technology and microfilm technology are important in processing images. A text processing system can reproduce the words and format of a document, but it cannot reproduce signatures and handwritten notations affixed to those documents. An image processing system can electronically store an image of a document, including text, drawings, signatures, and other handwritten information which might appear on the document. For some applications, image processing is very critical. The sections of Chapter 7 that are devoted to micrographics and optical-disk technologies further explore this concept.

A subcategory of the image format is **video**. This category represents photographic information stored electronically and retrieved through video players and television screens. The medium may record both video (picture) and audio (sound) and is retrieved as either **full motion video** images or still images. The still images are called **frozen video** and are used in teleconferences. Other aspects of this information category are discussed in Chapter 8.

PROCEDURES AND TECHNOLOGIES
FOR INFORMATION CAPTURE

Information must be captured before it can be processed. In an electronic information processing system, capture is associated with the input function, but it may also be associated with other activities. A stenographer captures information through recording dictated messages. An executive who records dictation is both creating and capturing information. A data-entry clerk who keyboards information into a system is capturing information in a form that is usable by the system. The goal of any office automation system is to accurately capture information—at the time it is being created if possible.

MTST – IBM COMPUTER First word processor

Figure 5-2 Optical character recognition (OCR) is one example of information capture technology that doesn't involve the keyboard. *Computer Indentics Corporation*

The keyboard is still the most-used mechanism for information capture in office systems. Administrative support and clerical employees use alphanumeric keyboards and 10-key number pads to capture information. Managers and professional staff persons frequently keyboard their own information. This alleviates some of their dependence upon administrative support employees to assist in this process. Employees at all levels work with systems that permit electronic information capture. Examples include airline employees who key in passenger flight data, nurses who key patient charges into nurses' station terminals, and bank employees who key in customer transactions.

Figure 5-3 **The mouse is another example of information capture technology separate from the keyboard.**
Xerox Corporation

Other technologies for information capture are gaining popularity. Optical character recognition (OCR) and other electronic scanning devices may read typewritten or printed information, capturing it for electronic processing. Through responses to screen menus and the use of a mouse, computer-based office information system users can capture information. Light pens and touch-sensitive video displays are other methods of capturing information. Future office information systems will make greater use of voice input as an information-capture technology.

PROCEDURES AND TECHNIQUES
FOR INITIAL PROCESSING

Processing the information of office systems is similar to the processing performed by data processing systems. Captured information must be manipulated. Examples of processing include text editing, combining text with data (or text with graphics) to produce a document, or generating multiple copies of a basic message each of which is addressed to a different recipient and may contain varying quantitative data (an account balance, for example). Software and hardware evaluations permit comparisons between the organization's needs and office automation capabilities.

Software and systems with increasingly sophisticated capabilities are improving the capability of processing administrative information and business communication. Many of the technologies discussed in this unit involve initial information processing. Computer technology that plays a role in this phase includes word processing, electronic publishing, graphics, spreadsheet, and database software and their supporting hardware elements.

COMMUNICATION, STORAGE, AND RETRIEVAL

The important elements of communication, storage, and retrieval of information are critical to efficient office systems. Chapters 7 and 8 describe these elements in detail. Communication (the movement of captured information from one component of a system to another and among various physical locations) is the very essence of office automation. Without this capability, the automated office cannot reach its full potential. As technologies develop, however, paper distribution of information remains an important communication medium. Word-processing, electronic publishing, and reprographics technologies support the communication of information.

Communication capabilities make possible both the initial transmission of information and the retrieval of information after it has been stored. The storage devices described in Chapter 4 are used to store information created in office systems. Development of office automation was hampered during the 1950s and 1960s because storing text required an enormous amount of storage capacity. The introduction of removable magnetic tape reels and magnetic cards for word processors introduced the concept of external storage to the office environment. This development made the electronic storage of text practical. Technologies such as the hard disk and optical disk are enhancing the development of truly automated office systems.

PERSONNEL

Office personnel is the subject of a separate chapter in this text (Chapter 15); however, human factors must also be considered when evaluating systems. People throughout organizations and even people outside the organization are affected by office systems. As each technology or subsystem is examined, the people who are affected by that technology must be considered.

Employees create, capture, and retrieve information, and this information enhances the work of managers and professionals. Even though some technical understanding of a system is necessary, the human reaction to the system ultimately determines its success. Since office automation tools are used by employees at every level and among every specialty, the magnitude of the human factors in office systems is great. Chapters 10 and 17 are especially devoted to human factors concerns, but their importance must be associated with every technology.

Figure 5-4 Word processing altered the traditional administrative-support systems that provided secretarial and clerical services. Many professionals now use electronic administrative support.

WORD PROCESSING AND THE BUSINESS DOCUMENT

Businesses, governments, institutions, and private citizens rely upon documents. They are an integral part of every business transaction, every accounting or financial procedure, and every effort to record human history. Many of these documents contain text. The production of documents containing text—reports, memos, letters, advertising copy, speeches, training materials, manuals of policy and procedure, and any other written communication—is the concern of word processing technology.

The history of computer development in Chapter 1 reviewed the introduction of electronic text editing and text storage. Although introduced as modernized versions of automatic typewriters, word processors eventually developed into systems for generating and managing written communication. Word processing has always been computer based, and much of the hardware and software has been produced by the same manufacturers who produced computers. However, word processing was born and grew as a discipline apart from other information processing technologies.

DOCUMENTS—THE PRODUCTS OF WORD PROCESSING SYSTEMS

Text (words) for business documents has been and remains the major product of word processing systems. Text is the word processing counterpart of quantitative data in traditional data processing systems. Although document production now depends upon many supporting technologies, word processing is the foundation technology for the production of written communication. As office systems have developed and matured, word processing has been blended with many other technologies. Examples of this blending include the ability to perform math functions when quantitative data is used in a document, the ability to select from almost unlimited type styles and sizes for the output of word processing, and the ability to import the products of other office systems technologies—spreadsheets, database information, graphics, and so on.

A review of the development of word processing as a document production technology will provide a clear prospective of the current status and probable future of this technology.

Early word processing installations were concentrated in applications where originally typed (not printed or copied) messages were required in large numbers. The technology was viewed as yet another substitute for highly repetitive typing. Its techniques were similar to the punched paper-tape automatic typewriters that had been used for years to produce "original" documents. Magnetic recording of information and microprocessors for manipulating hardware provided vast improvements.

Form letters with automatic inserts for inside addresses, salutations, and unique variable data items within the paragraphs were early products of word processing. Another popular application was *boilerplating*, the selection of prewritten and stored paragraphs to fit particular situations requiring reports or correspondence. These were particularly popular in legal document typing where long, complicated (but standard) components of documents were required. Unique data items were manually typed. These products have been joined by many other applications, which will be discussed later in this chapter.

TRADITIONAL WORD PROCESSING ORIENTATION

The traditional orientation of word processing as an office technology has been an extension of the secretarial function. That is, the systems (hardware, software, people) concentrated on automating the tasks traditionally performed by secretaries as support tasks for executives, managers, and professionals. Early installations emphasized correspondence tasks. The hardware was a dedicated word processor with installed software. The value of word processing as a communication tool used by management and as a medium for writing text was all but nonexistent during most of word processing's first twenty years.

Although the phrase "user friendly" (meaning that the system has built-in aids and tutorials for users) was coined much later, word processors became user friendly before general purpose computers. Early systems that created messages on paper (not on screen) as the document was generated were cumbersome, but rapid developments involved special-function keys, which simplified commands to the system.

Personnel. The advent of word processing affected the traditional administrative support systems that were designed to provide secretarial and clerical services to executives, managers, and professionals in all types of organizations. Especially affected was the role of the secretary. Many of the routine typewriting tasks of secretaries were transferred to word processing installations. In many organizations this meant that someone in another physical location would be doing work previously done in the department where the document was being originated.

Job titles were never universally applied, but many organizations adopted the recommended job titles and structures offered by the International Information/Word Processing Association (IWP) (now Association for Information Systems Professionals)

(AISP). Three word processing operator-level jobs (correspondence secretary, senior correspondence secretary, and executive correspondence secretary) and a supervisory-level position were created. Jobs for central support groups who performed non-automated tasks were administrative secretary, senior administrative secretary, and executive administrative secretary.

The typical arrangement included a supervisor for each section and a manager of word processing/administrative support who was responsible for the whole operation. Some clerical employees remained in departments, and most high-level executives continued to employ executive secretaries. The title administrative assistant became prevalent for this position in some organizations.

Role in Organization. In organizations where full-blown word processing systems (as opposed to stand-alone, distributed hardware) were implemented from the mid-1960s to the late-1970s, the system was usually centralized. The central installations and their employees served departments throughout the organization. They created large-volume mailings to specified mailing lists, transcribed recorded dictation, and filed magnetic media versions of documents (magnetic tape cartridges and magnetic cards) for rapid recall and revision. They operated on a principle of "type it once." The objective was to increase productivity among administrative support employees.

These early word processing centers and the work they did made some things possible that had not been possible before. Professional supervision of clerical employees was more affordable from a centralized service; highly repetitive typing was reduced or eliminated; and original documents were possible for applications where duplicated documents had been used previously.

Problems also developed. Operators' work was frequently more boring than it had been in traditional secretarial roles; some of the equipment was extremely noisy; and the employees' association with the principals they served was eliminated by the centralized service concept. This "exciting new technology" turned text creation into an assembly-line activity in many organizations. Operators rebelled and principals rebelled, sometimes refusing to use the service.

Word processing managers have reported to various middle- or top-management personnel, depending upon the importance attached to the work and the position. In some organizations, the person to whom this manager reported was a vice president for administrative systems or held a similar position title.

CONTEMPORARY WORD PROCESSING ORIENTATION

Word processing of the past has been discussed because it represents the traditional approach—the practices in effect when the field was being formed in the 1960s and 1970s. Contemporary word processing is less standard. Some word processing centers and dedicated word processors remain, but many other configurations for accomplishing word processing tasks exist: managers who create their own documents using a personal computer, satellite and departmental word processing systems, and integrated workstations with word processing capabilities are some examples. Cottage industry word processing operators and "offshore" word processing service bureaus are also possible arrangements. In small organizations, word processing is likely to be one of many office functions performed by any employee—not just highly skilled persons.

SOFTWARE

Word processing software enables computers to create and manipulate text. The software is an application program that works in conjunction with the computer's operating system. These programs are produced by software development firms or hardware manufacturers and marketed either with hardware or through retail outlets. Some word processing software may be installed permanently in the hardware.

Word processing software may be written for any computer system; some of it will run on any hardware type with minor variations. Although the hardware may affect the ease or sophistication of the text generation and editing process, most reputable word processing software carries standard basic features.

Word processing software is document oriented—designed to create written communication equal to or surpassing the quality of typewritten documents in the traditional office environment. It can be used to create computer programs and other nondocument files, however. The typical documents created by using word processing software are either printed on paper or transmitted electronically to another location.

Selection of word processing software is determined by its special features and its adaptability to existing hardware and operating systems. Software features should control the document characteristics that typists controlled in traditional environments. Those features fall into five categories: text/document creation, text/document editing, printer controls, file management, and related applications. Because many professionals and managers create their own written documents with computing facilities and integrated office hardware, software features should be easy to control. The intended application may affect the features sought. Figure 5-5 and the following discussion cover major software features. Software developers are continuously adding new capabilities and upgrading existing software, so a particular package may contain features not included here.

Text Document Creation. Word processing software assists the operator in creating text or documents by simplifying or automating certain procedures. The operator can control page layout (margins, spacing, pagination) and move the screen cursor about the document freely if the software contains basic features. Time-consuming tasks such as centering words and lines, correcting keyboarding errors, and creating tables or columns are simplified with most software.

Figure 5-5 **Word Processing Software Features**

TEXT/DOCUMENT CREATION

Formatting and Page Layout

Set top, bottom, left, and right margins; right margin justification
Set and clear tabs; multiple tabs
Set page length
Set character width
Set type font
Set vertical line spacing
Automatic paragraph indention
Margin release
Temporary margin changes
Column formatting
Manual/automatic page breaks
Center lines

Cursor Movement and Scrolling

Move the cursor up or down by line, screen, or page; to beginning or end of document
Move cursor left or right by character or word or to beginning or end of line
Move cursor to specified page
Return cursor to location prior to save
Scroll continuously up or down, by line or screen

Figure 5-5 **Word Processing Software Features** (continued)

TEXT/DOCUMENT CREATION

Automatic Features

Wordwrap
Right margin justification
Blank line between single-spaced paragraphs
Case commands
Pagination
Pagination in headers, footers
File backup
Reformatting after edits
Footnotes

Screen Layout and Appearance

Full horizontal page
Full vertical page
Controllable printer commands
View document on screen as it will print
Status lines, file directories, and help cues
Windows for calling up alternate files or systems

TEXT/DOCUMENT EDITING

Insertions/Deletions

Insert character, word, or line
Insert current date, time
Delete character, word, line, paragraph, or block
Delete from cursor to end of line, paragraph, page, or document
Insert "return" (end of paragraph)
Change from insert mode to type-over mode

Reformatting

Reformat paragraphs or entire documents to new margins
Sort a list of words

Block Operations

Mark beginning and end of block
Move block to another location within the document or to another file
Copy block to new file or to another storage medium
Delete block
Find beginning or end of block

Figure 5-5 **Word Processing Software Features** *(continued)*

TEXT/DOCUMENT EDITING

Delete block markers
Hide, display block (toggle)

Search Operations

Search forward or backward for string of characters
Replace string with or without verification
Global replace with or without query
Ignore specified string when searching, replacing
Search and delete
Repeat last command
Find beginning or end of block
Find format instruction

Hyphenation

Soft or hard hyphens
Hyphen help in reformatting

Printer Output Controls

Control pitch
Pagination on or off; book-style pagination (odd numbers at right margin; even numbers at left margin)
Overprint (or emphasized print)
Boldface
Doublestrike (shadow)
Superscripts, subscripts
Underscore, double underscore
Headers, footers
Move orphan lines
Proportional spacing
Alternate pitch, alternate font within document
Line, form feed
Pause printing for paper change
What you see is what you get (print quality same as screen image)

Printer Manipulation Controls

Continuous printing multiple documents
Print specified page
Begin or end printing at specified page
Begin print at cursor
Print multiple copies

Figure 5-5 **Word Processing Software Features** (continued)

TEXT/DOCUMENT EDITING

Interrupt printing
Pitch-independent line lengths
Display and/or change print format
Print spooling (multiple documents continuously)
Convert to all uppercase or to upper/lower case
Choice of type fonts
Proportional spacing
Pause printing

FILE MANAGEMENT

Save, rename, or copy a file
Save document and resume creation or edit
Save document and exit to application program
Save document and exit to operating system
Copy files
Rename files
Copy whole file into text
Copy whole file to separate file

RELATED APPLICATIONS

Miscellaneous
Dictionaries: spelling, law, medical (check, correct)
Automatic spell check with audible warnings
Personal or temporary dictionary creation
Word count
Thesaurus
Grammar and syntax checks
Readability level calculation
Electronic-mail compatibility
Mail lists
Merge features
Table of contents and indexing features
Security controls (access to document files)
Math capability within documents
Facsimile transmission system compatibility
Import graphics, spreadsheets, database files
Collaborative writing/editing features (maintain edits for approval)

PROGRAMMING CAPABILITIES

Nondocument (programmer) mode
Integer, string, dollar, system variables
Input to variables (from disk and from operator)

Figure 5-5 **Word Processing Software Features** (continued)

PROGRAMMING CAPABILITIES
Prompt operator from input
Output variables to disk
Conditional branching

Text/Document Editing. Editing text and documents is simplified if the software provides procedures for insertions, deletions, reformatting text, and moving blocks of copy within the document. The equivalent of a cut-and-paste approach to editing typewritten documents can be accomplished in a few seconds with word processing software.

Other editing features on sophisticated word processing software include the ability to search for a word, phrase, or block of text; to automatically replace one word with another at every occurrence in a document; to check the spelling as a document is being created; and to display lists of synonyms for a particular word.

Printer Controls. Software sends various messages to printers that control the quality and physical appearance of documents. The software may provide for such characteristics as multiple fonts (the shape or style of the characters), varying type sizes, boldface and underlined text, and a variety of print qualities. Printer controls may be capable of handling some of these features, but they are accomplished more quickly if the printer is driven by the software.

Recent versions of the popular word processing packages are able to send many printer controls that were previously possible only with desktop publishing or photocomposition systems. Type sizes ranging from headline-sized type to "fine print" character widths in a variety of type fonts and the ability to mix type size within documents makes possible the creation of professional-looking reports, forms, and other text.

Word processing software must be "installed" for a particular printer in order for the system to function properly. The more sophisticated word processing packages offer numerous files of installation data that make installation for a particular printer relatively simple. However, major difficulties may be encountered for users whose software does not contain data for their particular printers or who are not able to alter the software to accomplish printer compatibility.

File Management. Documents generated by word processing systems are usually stored electronically for possible future use

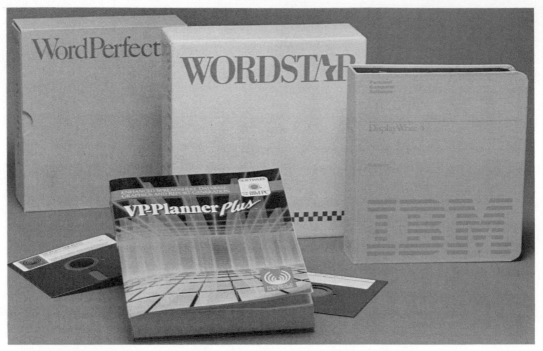

Figure 5-6 Sophisticated word
processing software packages provide similar capabilities for text
generation and editing.

or as evidence of the content of documents. The software controls
the nature of these files and the ease with which documents can
be added to and retrieved from the files. Files are usually stored
on a medium such as a hard disk or a flexible disk. Software can
assist with a classification system for naming these files and
producing backup files, which can be used if a document is inadvertently destroyed.

Other Features.   Numerous programs have been developed that
assist in the creation of text. Dictionary software packages, which
check the spelling of words in a variety of languages, and programs that analyze text for syntax errors and excessive word
repetition and sex-biased phraseology are examples of these features. The software should contain a provision for operator verification of changes controlled by these features. For example,
the operator should be able to authorize a change in spelling to
the dictionary version and should be able to add industry—or
organization—specific words to the dictionary.

HARDWARE

Word processing software packages enable computers to manipulate text. These packages are used on a variety of hardware types, which are reviewed in the following discussion.

Electronic Typewriters. Microprocessor chips as components of electronic typewriters distinguish them from ordinary electric typewriters and give them limited word processing capabilities. They can store text for recall in repetitive typing situations, and limited document formatting commands (margins or tab stops, for example) can be stored for later recall. Limited display screens on electronic typewriters display text as it is being generated. Some displays show only a few characters; others display one or more full lines; and some of them display up to 24 lines of text. Some electronic typewriters can be changed from one type pitch to another and can be switched from one type font to another.

Early models of these typewriters were called memory typewriters. They had no displays, but they were capable of storing and recalling many pages of text. Current models offer less storage space but more editing and formatting features.

Several features of electronic typewriters speed up document typing: alignment of columns around a decimal; automatic features, such as centering, underlining, error correction (through backspacing), and indentions; and easy recall of standard phrases.

With special interfaces, electronic typewriters can be used as computer printers. The printing speeds are somewhat slow (15–50 characters per second), but they may be adequate for low-volume work and short documents.

Dedicated Word Processing Systems. A dedicated word processor is a computer dedicated to one task—word processing. Most manufacturers have ceased production of dedicated word processors, because general purpose computers are able to run word processing applications as well as multiple other applications; and their cost is lower than dedicated word processors. However, many dedicated systems manufactured by IBM, Lanier, Wang, Xerox, and CPT are still in use.

Dedicated systems are among the most sophisticated word processing hardware. Their special features include numerous special-function keys, high-resolution display screens, full-page displays, and rapid processing speeds. Spelling checkers and other editing software are easily invoked by the operator.

Stand-alone Systems. A standalone system is a single system of hardware and software with its own CPU. The very first word

Figure 5-7   Electronic typewriters
have taken on many of the characteristics of computers and word
processors.
*Courtesy of International Business
Machines Corporation*

processors were in this category (IBM MT/ST and Mag Card
models). Stand-alone systems in use now more nearly resemble
microcomputer systems. They use disk software, display screens,
and detached printers. Most of them are capable of communicating with other word processors or other peripherals, but that configuration would put them in the clustered or shared categories.

Clustered Systems. Some dedicated word processors support
multiple input stations or otherwise share resources. Multiple
terminals may share a printer, a CPU, or a hard-disk storage unit.
Workstations in the cluster (those sharing some component) may
be able to communicate text from one station to another.

General-Purpose Computers.   A general-purpose computer is
capable of performing a variety of information processing applications, and one of these is word processing. Some organizations
that use a computer primarily for general data processing want
to use it for word processing also. Small, general-purpose com-

puters with word processing software and a good printer offer an inexpensive means for quality document production.

General-purpose computers of any size can provide the central processing power and the operating system to run word processing software. The greatest number of such systems in existence now are in the microcomputer category. Since 1984, personal computer sales have totaled four to six million units annually. The most popular software package purchased for or included with personal computers is word processing. Many of these systems are used in homes and by executives for general computing applications; however, many of them form fully functioning word processing systems in small organizations and departmental operations of large organizations.

Minicomputers and mainframe computers with remote terminals for input may be used to form word processing systems. These computers are either **shared logic** or **concurrent logic** systems. In either case, terminals for word processing applications share a central processing unit. If that unit is used for word processing only, it is a shared logic system; if it is used concurrently for word processing and other computing tasks, it is a concurrent logic system. Shared systems are not as prevalent as dedicated, clustered, and microcomputer systems; but the technology and some applications have been in existence for several years.

SYSTEM COMPARISONS

Obviously, many factors influence the choice of a particular word processing system. Organizations wishing to integrate and coordinate information processing for the entire organization will not consider their word processing system independently. Instead, they will consider this need along with the total information needs of the organization.

The choice of a word processing system will be greatly influenced by the user and by other computing facilities already in place. Users who desire general applications capability must use general-purpose computing equipment. An organization that already has office automation software installed on a mainframe computer or one that operates with a local area network will probably use these facilities to accomplish word processing needs also.

Hardware elements include keyboards, display units, central processors, disk drives (or other recording devices), and printers— the same as for any other computer system. These may exist as five or more separate components, or any number of them may be combined into a single hardware element.

Software features and the possibility of running a variety of software on the system would greatly influence the choice of a system. (Chapter 13 deals with implementation of office automation technologies and includes detailed analyses of hardware and software capabilities for word processing.)

WORD PROCESSING IN INTEGRATED OFFICE-SYSTEMS ENVIRONMENTS

As the concept of integrated office systems (See Chapter 2) develops, word processing technology will become available to more and more employees through their individual workstations. They will be able to perform a variety of text-editing functions and to combine the results of other technologies with text—such as spreadsheets and reports from the organization's databases—to produce reports and other documents.

Word processing components of integrated office software must be easy to use because users do not have time to devote to long learning processes. Operating environment software, of the type introduced in Chapter 3, and access to a variety of peripherals will help to provide assistance. Since integrated office systems will bring electronic mail capabilities to greater numbers of people, many documents will be transmitted electronically to their recipients. The creation and transmission of documents by individuals will probably cause the quality of written communication to decline, because its quality will not be monitored by administrative support employees or staff. This will necessitate greater dependence upon related software for such things as spelling, grammar, and syntax checks. Current software for these purposes is user friendly and easy to operate. Nevertheless, administrative support employees still need to assist with the preparation of important documents.

SELECTING PRINT TECHNOLOGY FOR OFFICE SYSTEMS OUTPUT

The "office of the future" arrived on time, but it failed to produce the promised paperless office. Users still want paper output from information systems. The printer provides this output. Printer technology has become an integral part of office systems technology. In a survey of personal computer users,[1] 98 percent of users indicated that they had printers hooked up to their personal

---

1.   John Dickinson, "The Fifth Annual All-Printer Review," *PC Magazine,* Vol. 7, no. 18 (October 31, 1988): 94.

computers. Seventy-three percent of those printers were dot-matrix printers, five percent were print wheel printers, and twenty-two percent were using laser printers or some other non-impact printer. A basic knowledge of printer technology and selection criteria is necessary to select the printers that will produce high quality documents as the output of word processing and other office systems applications.

PRINTER TECHNOLOGY

Two major categories of printers are used in office systems: impact printers and non-impact printers. **Impact printers** involve a mechanism that makes physical contact with paper by forcing a ribbon against the paper to create characters and, in some cases, graphics. Non-impact printers "plant" character images and graphic images on the page without a physical impact.

Impact Printers. Among the many possibilities for impact printers, the most popular in office systems installations is the dot-matrix printer. Print wheel or "daisy wheel" printers, once popular and still used in some offices, have almost disappeared

Figure 5-8 A Dot-Matrix Print Head Mechanism

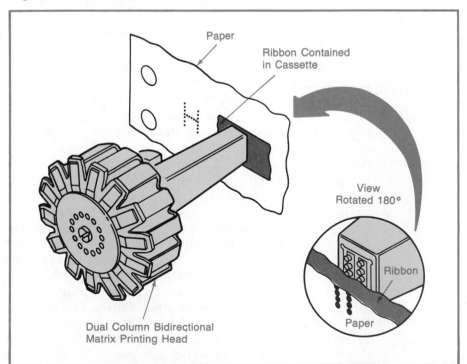

from the market. Their popularity has been reduced because of their limited speeds and the fact that excellent quality is now available from non-impact printers. **Dot-matrix printers** receive signals from computer systems, which trigger steel pins to strike the ribbon, creating images on the paper. A print head forms characters with nine, eighteen, or twenty-four pins. Literally, they form characters from a matrix of dots. A high-density matrix (meaning that many lines of dots make up the matrix) creates high-quality, legible characters. If the dots are close together, they form almost solid characters. The term that describes the output of these high-density printers is **near letter quality**. Low-density matrices can create fewer rows of dots, and the dots that form the characters have small spaces between them. These characters are more difficult to read, and the text and graphics that they create are less attractive. Most dot-matrix printers are capable of printing at high speeds in a low-density or **draft mode** and also at higher-density, near letter quality modes.

Print wheel printers create text from rotating character sets with molded alphabetic and numerical characters on individual "petals" of the wheel. These printers have been labeled **letter-quality printer** because they produce text that is equal to type-writer quality in density and sharpness. A hammer forces the character mold against the ribbon, which creates the image on paper.

Nonimpact Printers.   Among the printer processes that create characters on paper without physical impact or ribbon are laser, liquid crystal shutter (LCS), light emitting diode (LED), ink-jet, and ion-deposition printers. These printers may also be called **page printers**, because they create a page of images then transfer those images to a sheet of paper before proceeding to the next page. Non-impact printers that support personal computers in offices are likely to be laser, LCS, or LED models. Printers in the non-impact category are usually faster and considerably more expensive than impact printers. However, low-end costs of non-impact printers have fallen below the high-end prices for impact printers.

To simplify the discussion of printer technology, the term *laser printer* will include all of those using a light source to create characters (laser, LCS, and LED machines). **Laser printers** (some-times referred to as electrostatic or xerographic also) use a light source to reflect character and graphic images through a series of mirrors onto a photosensitive drum. The drum attracts par-ticles of a substance called **toner** to the charged images on the drum and transfers the images to paper. A heat process then fixes the toner to the paper. The process is similar to electrostatic

Figure 5-9 Laser printers produce high-quality documents with letter quality print type at six to ten pages per minute.
Courtesy of Hewlett Packard Company

copy-machine processes. These printers are capable of very high speeds and quality of output that justifies "letter quality" status. In addition, the machines are practically noiseless.

LED array printers and **LCS printers** create characters and graphics by focusing light from a light-emitting diode or from a fluorescent or halogen light source to form characters on the photosensitive drum.

Many additional technical differences distinguish these three popular non-impact printer technologies, but the printer selection criteria discussed below become the observable and identifiable factors to consider in a choice among them.

Ink-jet printers spray fast-drying ink character images onto paper in a dot-matrix configuration to form printed images. If the matrix is dense, the output from these printers rivals the quality of laser printers and printwheel impact printers. **Ion-deposition** printers create images using a drum, as do electrostatic printers. However, this process requires no light or heat. The ions (electrically charged particles) are deposited directly to a dielectric drum (capable of holding an electrostatic field without conducting current) to form character and graphic images. The drum transfers the images to paper as print.

PRINTER SELECTION CRITERIA

Printer selection is influenced by many factors: printer cost, speed of output, quality of print, compatibility with central processors and software, special features, paper sizes and qualities accepted, anticipated maintenance, sound level, and flexibility required for the range of word processing and other applications for which the printer will produce output.

The purchase price of a printer can be a poor measure of its real cost. Cost comparisons should take into consideration the total cost of a package (printer plus necessary or desirable options) and the cost of operating the printer at the volume required in a particular office over some specified period of time, such as a year. Supplies to operate a printer can cost more than the printer itself within the lifetime of a machine. In addition, all the other selection criteria discussed here should be considered. Laser printers are considered to be extremely expensive; however, competition has reduced the price significantly since their introduction. In addition, when considering all factors and the environment for which output is being generated, the expense of a laser printer may be the most desirable choice.

Printer speed is measured in characters per second, lines per minute, or pages per minute. Non-impact printers are extremely fast, reaching more than 200 pages a minute for some systems. However, typical page printers for office applications produce five to eleven pages per minute. Dot-matrix printer speeds are measured in characters per second (CPS) and may reach 300–400 CPS, but for office printers 175 CPS for a nine-pin printer and 225 CPS for a 24-pin printer are considered high speeds. Speeds are significantly reduced when the printer is switched to near letter quality or proportional spacing modes.

Special features that influence printer selection include the paper size that the printer will accommodate, its capability for feeding cut sheets as well as continuous paper sheets, and the size and variety of type sizes and styles that the printer will produce. Popular capabilities include the ability to produce justified margins, proportional spacing (space consumed by characters varies), and type of a variety of sizes (double high, double wide, compressed) and fonts (style of character shapes). Some printer literature discusses type size in typewriter terms relative to the number of characters per horizontal inch (pitch size). Ten-pitch type is the equivalent of 10 characters per inch or typewriter *pica*. Twelve-pitch type is the equivalent of 12 characters per inch or typewriter *elite*. On the other hand, points or picas—terms popular in the printing industry and associated with desktop publishing software—refer to 1/72 of a vertical inch or 1/6 of a horizontal inch. The character size variability of printers may be extremely limited. Even if the printer is capable of multiple sizes, the word processing software may not be capable of selecting those sizes.

Printer noise may be extremely important. It is measured in decibels of sound produced in various modes. Impact printers produce significantly more noise than laser printers that should be considered noiseless for the sake of comparison. Dot-matrix printers may produce noise at a level of 80 decibels or more. Chapter 10 discusses the ergonomic effect of printer noise and other environmental factors in the office.

The type of output may be critical to printer selection. Requirements that a printer be able to print labels, envelopes, cut sheets, business letters with the first page on a letterhead and the second page on plain paper, and documents of various sizes may be a critical test for printer selection for some offices.

A final criterion that may be the deciding factor in printer selection is the support of page-description languages used by desktop publishing software to define pages and improve the quality of graphics within documents. Two popular page description languages are Adobe Systems' **PostScript Language** and Hewlett Packard's **Printer Control Language**. The Apple Laser-Writer was the first printer to support the PostScript language. Now several other manufacturers also support the language. If the output of desktop publishing software will be required of a printer, support of one or both of these languages may be important considerations.

WORD PROCESSING VERSUS DESKTOP PUBLISHING FOR DOCUMENT PRODUCTION

The distinction between word processing and **desktop publishing** is sometimes confusing. Chapter 6 will point out that desktop publishing refers to a collection of software and printer technology for producing near-professional quality documents on desktop computers. Page design, type font selection, incorporating text, graphics, and other illustrative materials into documents, and high-quality output are characteristics of these systems. Word processing, on the other hand, has, in the past, concentrated upon text generation and editing. Word processing software is used to create and edit text for document pages designed by desktop publishing software. The development of both applications to the point where word processing software carries "desktop publishing features" (type-size manipulation, type style selection, and so on) and desktop publishing software that has built in text editing features contributes to the confusion. The differences lie in the purposes for which the software is used and the range of tasks to be performed by the software. Your study of Chapter 6 should clarify some of these features.

CAREER IMPLICATIONS FOR WORD/INFORMATION PROCESSING

Chapter 3 discussed careers for office systems in general. However, there are employment opportunities that are specific to word processing and general information processing positions. Trainees for many of these positions may be selected from graduates of associate degree programs. In some cases baccalaureate degree candidates will be sought for supervisory, managerial, and specialist positions.

Highly specialized jobs that require word processing skills only are becoming less prevalent. Positions for persons with broader training in information processing or office systems are becoming more prevalent. The following job titles are typical of positions available for persons with preparation in word processing and information processing.

Word/Information Processing Operations
- Data Entry Operator
- Word Processing Operator
- Supervisor of Data Entry
- Supervisor of Word Processing

Word/Information Processing Specialists
- Correspondence Specialist
- Transcriptionist
- OCR Operator
- Electronic Publishing Specialist
- Proofreader
- Word Processing Trainer
- Text Editor
- Manufacturer's Representative (sales)

Office Automation Specialists
- Microcomputer User Support Specialist
- Information Center Trainer
- Office Systems Analyst
- Local Area Network Administrator

Staff Level Positions
Manager of Information Processing
Manager of Word Processing Operations
Manager of Administrative Support Services
Office Manager
Manager of End User Computing

WOHL'S BUSINESS PERSPECTIVE

What will the next generation of word processors look like?

Word processors are no longer systems, bundled offerings of hardware and software. Today's word processors are software products, often running on multiple hardware platforms. (One very popular product, WordPerfect® runs on nearly ten!)

The original word processors were designed to trick the recipient of a letter or memo into thinking he held an originally typed, unique document. Letters not only needed to *look* typed, they had to be created on a type of printer which would emboss the page, just like an electric typewriter!

Today's word processors are clearly children of the personal computer era. They replicate all of the functions of traditional, dedicated word processing systems, but they also offer features suited to the *authors* of documents as well as to typists and secretaries. Built-in outliners help authors plan their documents; reference tools help them pick just the right words; review tools let multiple authors collaborate.

Just as we thought word processing software was a mature marketplace, with little additional function to offer, all the rules are about to change.

The next word processors (a few are already in the marketplace) go way beyond our desire to put words on paper and make them appear perfectly typed. Today, we want documents that include graphics as well as text, plus the ability to embed data from a variety of personal and organizational sources. Moreover, moving beyond the printed page, we want to be able to create electronically-based documents, capable of being automatically linked to their data sources, and automatically updated as changes to their underlying data occur.

The next generation of word processors will look different:

- Modern interface metaphor—consistent menus and a point-and-pick selection

- Editable WYSIWYG screen, with full typographic fonts and layout

- Not just word processing, but wp plus draw graphics and desktop publishing, at a minimum

And users in large organizations are already enthusiastic about the possibility of getting all of this functionality in a single product. Such integration points to both lessened software costs and decreased training costs as well.

When a universally used category of software (everyone needs to process words sometimes) goes through a basic change, the fallout can be formidable. Existing vendors will scramble to preserve their current market shares, while new vendors will enter the market, eager to feast at this enormous, emerging opportunity.

As we enter a change point, users need to handle change decisions with care. Change too soon and you may need to change again—after the winning product emerges. Wait too long and your competitors may gain market share at your expense, as their more elegant, more graphical, and ultimately more communicative documents reach the customers.

Word processing has always been a market where learning to live' with change was important. That capability will be much more important as we enter the nineties.

SUMMARY

A systems approach to office automation begins by recognizing the categories of information format that may be processed by office automation technologies. Each system may involve one or more of the information types—voice, text, data, graphics, and image—and include techniques for capturing, processing, communicating, storing, or retrieving that information.

Procedures for processing text include information capture, initial processing, communication, storage, and retrieval. Since technologies for information processing tasks evolved and were applied to isolated categories of tasks, word processing technology developed independent of other information technologies. Now word processing may be performed in any office environment. Word processing involves any system for producing and managing text with the aid of computers which assist the editing and manipulation of this text. Although the first word processing systems were used in centralized facilities with highly trained operators, any employee or manager at any level may now engage in word processing activities. The word processing centers still exist, but much word processing is now done in individual departments.

Text for business documents is the major product of word processing. The software that controls word processing hardware includes features for document creation and editing, file management, and printer control. Although some word processing output is now transmitted electronically, most of it is produced as paper output. A variety of printers produce word processing text. Some of them operate at high speeds and produce letter-quality documents. Printer technology includes impact and non-impact printers in a variety of models. Features examined when selecting printer technology include hardware cost and a variety of features that control the quality of printer output. Recent improvements in printer technology have included both the popular dot-matrix printers and the laser printer.

KEY TERMS

voice communication	dot-matrix printer
text	non-impact printer
data	print wheel printer
graphics	letter quality printer
image	page printer
video	laser printer
full motion video	toner
frozen video	LED display printer
mouse	LCS printer
dedicated word processor	ink-jet printer
shared logic system	ion-deposition printer
concurrent logic system	CPS
impact printer	pitch
near letter quality	PostScript language
draft mode	desktop publishing

REVIEW QUESTIONS

1. What are the components of an office information system?

2. Name and describe five information formats used in the business office environment.

3. Profile and contrast traditional and contemporary word processing applications in the office.

4. What is the difference between the product of a word processing system and the product of a data processing system?

5. Identify the major features of word processing software that are associated with each of the following categories:
   a. text/document creation
   b. text/document editing
   c. file management
   d. related applications software

6. Among the three major hardware types used to run word processing software, which is currently the most prevalent? What is the status of the other two?

7. What are the differences between WP in a stand-alone environment and WP in an integrated office environment?

8. What is the relationship between word processing and desktop publishing?

CASE STUDY: THE WARREN COMPANY—PREPARATION FOR REORGANIZATION—PART 2

Review the information about word processing and the Central Records Department at the Warren Company presented in Chapter 4. Using the information presented in the case and the content of Chapter 5, answer the following questions.

QUESTIONS/ACTIVITIES

1. What problems might be caused by the location of the word processing function in the firm's organizational structure?

2. Study current reviews of word processing software and computer hardware in information processing publications and, if possible, interview vendors of hardware. Then recommend hardware and software systems you would expect Warren Company to have in order to satisfy its present word processing needs.

3. In light of the team's current task, what would be the implications for word processing at Warren Company if the firm does, indeed, move toward integrated office systems?

4. Even though you have not yet been exposed to detailed analyses of all the office technologies, revise the organization chart for the firm to better provide for management of word/information processing in the firm's offices.

SUGGESTED READINGS

Allen, Robert J. "Office Technology: Putting the Pieces Together." *Management Technology* (January, 1984): 40–45.

Bergerud, Marly, and Jean Gonzalez. *Word Processing: Concepts and Careers,* 4th Edition. New York: John Wiley & Sons, 1988.

Casady, Mona, and Dorothy Sandburg. *Word/Information Processing: A System Approach.* Cincinnati: South-Western Publishing Co., 1985.

CHAPTER 6

Desktop Publishing and Reprographics Systems

OBJECTIVES

After studying this chapter, you should understand the following:

1. The technology and possible output or products of desktop publishing systems

2. The differences and similarities among desktop publishing systems, other office technologies, and traditional printing systems

3. The technology and product of reprographics systems

4. The potential benefits of incorporating desktop publishing systems into office systems

5. The major hardware and software components of desktop publishing systems

6. The differences among low-level, mid-range, and high-level desktop publishing systems

7. The basic user skill requirements involved in operating desktop publishing systems

8. The decisions necessary for an organization to effectively implement desktop publishing into its strategic planning for office systems

9. The concepts and technologies associated with reprographics

The word *publishing* as used in *desktop publishing* is actually a misnomer. Traditionally, the term has described "the business or profession of the commercial production and issuance of literature, information, musical scores or sometimes recordings, or art."[1] In reality, desktop "publishing" is an effort to avoid the cost and time consumed by traditional, commercial printing services. Before desktop publishing, organizations either established internal print shops, purchased the services of commercial printers, or opted to produce typewritten and computer-printer generated documents and replicate them for distribution with photocopy systems. Many organizations used all of these methods.

For many organizations, outside commercial printers remain a viable option for high-quality printing needs and form manufacturing; but desktop publishing offers a fast and relatively inexpensive alternative for many.

WHAT IS DESKTOP PUBLISHING

Businesses and other organizations still depend upon written documents to communicate and to record their events and transactions. Methods and techniques of creating and reproducing the written word have evolved throughout history. This evolution has included the replacement of manual methods with such mechanical methods as the printing press, the typewriter, and various document duplicating systems.

Desktop publishing is the most recent development in this evolutionary process. Prior to the development of this technology, organizations produced a variety of documents in-house by using copying machines, duplicating systems, and sophisticated printing processes. Only very large organizations could justify the cost of in-house printing facilities. Good quality document production services were purchased from outside agencies such as print shops. **Desktop publishing** is a system employing computers, printers, specially designed software, and, in some cases, other hardware components to produce high-quality documents in-house. In most cases, the total system will fit on a single desktop.

The quality of documents produced with desktop publishing systems rivals those produced on more sophisticated printing systems. Desktop publishing systems permit the combination of text, graphics, line drawings, and photographs on a page. It provides a control over document appearance that was not possible with typewriters and word processors. These controls include the

---

1. *Webster's Ninth New Collegiate Dictionary,* (Springfield, Massachusetts: Merriam-Webster, Inc., 1983), 952.

ability to specify page design, type style, and type size. Additional features will be described in the remainder of this chapter.

This chapter explores desktop publishing and reprographics, an older technology, and their use in producing in-house documents or preparing copy for reproduction by outside agencies. It is an introduction to the hardware and software of desktop publishing, the variety of systems available, and the decisions that face organizations that contemplate the addition of desktop publishing to their office systems.

PRODUCTS

Although the output of desktop publishing systems varies with the sophistication of the system, even the relatively simple systems are able to produce a variety of documents with an appearance that is professional and superior to "nonprinted" documents produced in-house. Examples include business forms, letterheads, business cards, newsletters, system documentation, employee manuals, job descriptions, advertising copy, announcements, reports, graphics for presentations, brochures, proposals—even books and magazines. Practically any written document is a candidate for production by this method; however, simple correspondence and many internal reports are probably more efficiently produced by traditional methods.

Figure 6-1 A variety of publications are produced with a desktop publishing system.
Apple Computer, Inc.

Figure 6-2   A desktop publishing
system produces high quality
reports.
Xerox Corporation

In addition to the wide variety of document types, a variety of document sizes and appearances is also possible. The output of a desktop publishing system may be a "master" copy of a document for reproduction using in-house copying or printing processes, or it may be an "original" copy from which an outside service agency will reproduce or print multiple copies. Either is likely to result in cost reductions for the organization, compared to the cost of conventional printing services. Traditional methods of page design and layout creation for such documents, whether done by in-house specialists or printing firm specialists, have been an expensive process.

SOFTWARE

Although many popular microcomputer applications software packages are labeled "desktop publishing," desktop publishing software actually requires several software capabilities. These capabilities may be delivered by several software packages working together. The basic requirement is **page composition software** which permits the user to bring to a document page the text, graphics, illustrations, drawings, and physical features necessary to create that page with the desired appearance. This may include text arranged in columns, supported by a statistical table and a line drawing. Standard headers on every page of the document and the ability to surround illustrations with text may be desirable elements. Headlines in a variety of type sizes and text with high quality bold and italicized words may be the desirable elements. Page composition software makes these things possible.

Additional software that may be necessary includes a word processor for creating and editing text and software for the creation of a variety of graphic elements that may be needed for documents. Figure 6-3 shows a screen image of a popular page composition software package with a partially completed page design.

Figure 6-3 **With page-composition software, the user is able to see the page design on the computer screen.**
Xerox Corporation

HARDWARE

Desktop publishing requires powerful computers and additional hardware components. Although the process is possible on floppy disk microcomputer systems, any of the systems above the very minimum in quality require memory capacities and processing speeds that can only be supplied by computers with powerful central processing units and hard disk storage systems. The more sophisticated the software capabilities, the greater the memory capacity and speed of the computer system required for effective use of the software.

The printer is a key element in the desktop publishing system. Dot-matrix printers with graphics capabilities are capable of printing the pages produced by desktop publishing software, but a laser printer is required for serious applications. In addition, various other hardware pieces, such as image scanners and graphics cards for computers without built-in graphics capabilities, may be necessary.

RELATIONSHIP TO OTHER OFFICE SYSTEMS TECHNOLOGIES

Desktop publishing is highly dependent upon other office systems technologies. Although some page composition software has built-in text editors, they do not have the capability of creating and editing complex text. For this part of the task the process depends upon word processing software. As word processing software has developed, it has taken on more characteristics of desktop publishing—the ability to select type style and size and to perform draw functions, for example. Future generations of word processing software will be capable of performing most of the functions now found in low-to-midrange desktop publishing software.

RELATIONSHIP TO PRINTING

Many page composition software features represent characteristics of a technology first applied in the printing industry through **electronic publishing** techniques. Electronic typesetting—computer-driven hardware that controls the production of print-quality text—was being used long before desktop publishing. This equipment was able to produce text in infinite sizes and type styles; however, the cost of the equipment and the technical expertise required for its operation were significant. Now much of the same capability can be achieved through desktop publishing. Although the term *electronic publishing* is sometimes used synonymously with the term *desktop publishing*, electronic publishing represents a much higher level of sophistication in equipment and operator skill in its operation.

Even though the final product of desktop publishing systems does not match the quality of electronic publishing, the input from desktop publishing can drive the output of expensive, high-quality printers and produce commercial printing quality output.

Recent word processing software packages and the combination of word processing and desktop publishing software makes possible the production of high-quality documents at relatively low costs. The quality of these documents rivals the quality of electronic publishing to the casual observer. However, commercial quality output and documents with the aesthetic qualities that we have come to expect from commercial printing still require complex systems, expensive systems, and high-level skills of the employees who produce them. Figure 6-4 illustrates the relationships among these factors and how they affect the quality of output.

Figure 6-4   Hierarchy of Printing Processes

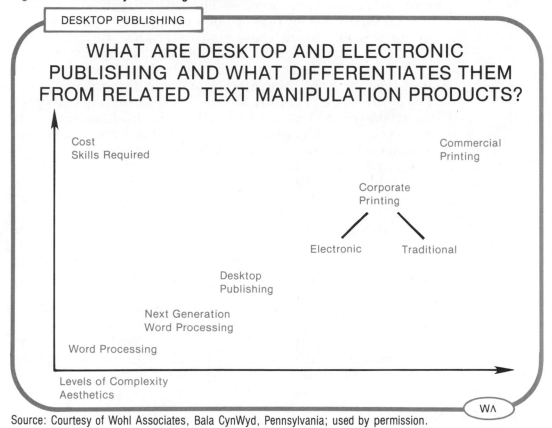

Source: Courtesy of Wohl Associates, Bala CynWyd, Pennsylvania; used by permission.

BENEFITS

What are the benefits of desktop publishing? Has the multi-billion-dollar investment in this technology been a hoax? Emerging as the most frequently mentioned reasons for using this technology are time and cost factors. With the cost per original page of published material ranging from $300 to $2,500 in direct costs, in-house desktop or electronic publishing systems can frequently reduce these amounts substantially.[2] Some firms are able to jus-

2.   Jonathan Seybold, ''The Revolution: Companies Discover the Benefits of Corporate Publishing,'' *National Association of Desktop Publishers Journal,* vol. 2, no. 2 (spring, 1988): 2.

tify the cost with very short payback periods (the time required for savings to accumulate to the point that they equal the cost of the system).

In addition to the cost of having documents printed by outside firms, there are frequent time delays. Printed documents require a more time-consuming process. The resulting delays are frequently expensive for the organization purchasing these services. Other less tangible benefits may also materialize. Because of the time and cost, many organizations may opt to produce inferior in-house documents rather than employ the services of an outside printer. Desktop publishing offers another alternative.

The preparation of copy from existing information resources (files, databases, and so on) and getting the information ready for professional publication may be more time consuming and expensive than in-house desktop publishing. Existing data (text, graphics, databases) can be imported to documents through a desktop publishing system. In the same time that it takes to assemble data for an outside publisher, the document can be completed in-house.

The competitive edge provided by fast turnaround—or the loss of a competitive edge if all or most of your competition is taking advantage of this technology—is another benefit. Add to these the information security enhancement of having documents produced in-house.

Even though there are clear benefits to using this technology, there can also be drawbacks. Employees without knowledge and experience in document design, failure to properly edit content, and failure to establish internal control over the technology can cause negative results.

SYSTEM COMPONENTS

Desktop publishing represents a system of technology and people; the technology includes both hardware and software components. The human factor can be any employee with sufficient computer skills and desktop publishing training. Computers and related peripherals represent the major hardware components. Several independent software packages or integrated software packages represent the software components.

HARDWARE

Computers. Desktop publishing software was originally designed for the Apple Macintosh® computer. The easy-to-use screen images and the graphics capability of this computer enhanced its ability to handle page composition software and to incorporate multiple type sizes, graphics, and line art into documents.

Adapting desktop publishing to the MS-DOS world required new versions of software, graphics cards, and sometimes different display screens. This environment adjusted quickly. Now most MS-DOS machines have built-in graphics capabilities. Either a dedicated system or a general-purpose computer can be used for desktop publishing. Many vendors provide turnkey systems— all the computer hardware, peripherals, and software necessary to begin a desktop publishing operation in one package.

Displays. Monochrome or color screen displays may be used for desktop publishing. If the computer system does not have graphics capabilities built in, a graphics expansion card must be used to achieve screen images that are described as **WYSIWYG** (pronounced *whiz*-i-wig)—what you see is what you get. The image on the screen has the appearance in proportion and style of the image that will print out. High resolution displays may be quite expensive; they sometimes cost as much as the computer.

Typical computer screens display a maximum of 24 lines of text. With desktop publishing applications, this may be inadequate. The ability to see a complete page of a document or even two complete pages—in a size that approximates the size of the finished document—may be desirable. Large, expensive screen displays can provide this benefit.

Scanners. To simplify one of the great benefits of desktop publishing—the ability to incorporate graphics and art into documents—the scanner is used to scan line drawings, graphs, charts, or photographs to digitize their contents and store them for manipulation by the desktop publishing software. Graphics software and other software packages that permit the creation of artwork on the display can be used to import graphics and art to the page design, but scanners offer a faster and simpler solution.

The scanner is a device that looks at an existing image and converts that image—text, art, graphic, hand-written note—to either characters or a series of dots that can be stored in the computer. A **text scanner** looks at text characters and converts them to code that the computer will recognize as text characters— just as striking a keyboard key records a character in a word processing document. Text scanners are either OCR units or **intelligent character recognition (ICR)** units. Both can read typed information, but the latter is much more flexible. It is capable of reading virtually any type size and shape and storing the text electronically.

Optical **image scanners** scan an entire page and record the image as a series of dots. The greater the density of the dots, the better the reproduction of the image. An important difference between text and optical image scanners is that text scanned by an image scanner cannot be edited; text scanned by a text scanner can be edited.

Scanners may cost as little as a few hundred dollars or $50,000 or more. Of course, the quality of the input—and ultimately, the document—are affected by the level of the equipment. Scanners range from small, hand-held devices to desktop models resembling copy machines or microfilm cameras.

An important consideration when selecting a scanner is the resolution or density of the product. This is measured in **dots per inch (DPI)**; the higher the number, the better the output. For scanners the range is from 100 DPI to 1,000 DPI or more. Scanner selection can be influenced by very technical considerations (See Figure 6-5) that are beyond the scope of this discussion. For ex-

Figure 6-5 **Variances in Quality of Resolution**

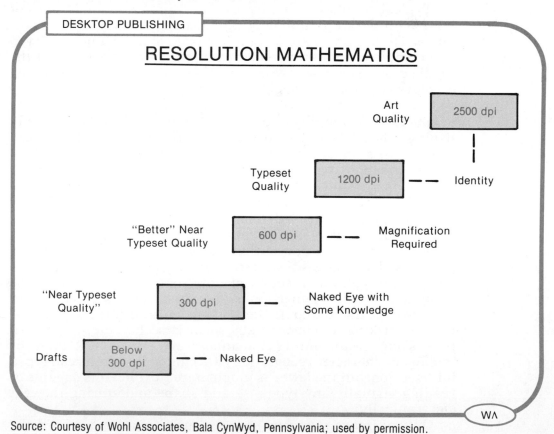

Source: Courtesy of Wohl Associates, Bala CynWyd, Pennsylvania; used by permission.

ample, the memory requirement of the computer may be greater than that offered on many personal computers. Special features include the ability to scan material in a variety of shades of gray **(gray scale)**; a less-expensive alternative to gray scale called **dithering**; and the ability to scan color images and record them in color.

Printers.   Although dot-matrix or ink-jet printers with graphics capabilities can be used to produce desktop publishing output, a laser printer is necessary to achieve the high quality for which desktop publishing systems are designed and a reasonable output speed. Laser printers are manufactured in the same variety of qualities and prices as most other desktop publishing hardware. The selection of a printer is based upon the volume and quality of output.

Printers for desktop publishing must be considered simultaneously with a software decision—**page description languages (PDL)**, a computer language that tells the printer how to print the copy that has been created by the combination of desktop publishing software packages. This software may reside within the page composition software or within the printer. The latter is the most popular method. Regardless of the location of the software, the printer and the page composition software must both support the same page description language.

Several page description languages have been developed, but in the office automation environment (mid-ranged desktop publishing systems) the choice has narrowed to two popular languages: Hewlett-Packard's Printer Control Language (PCL) and Adobe Systems' PostScript®. Other popular languages are Xerox's Interpress® and Imagen's Document Description Language® (DDL). PostScript is generally regarded as the most sophisticated and powerful. Combined with a high resolution laser printer, this language is capable of producing very high-quality output, particularly when that output combines text and graphics. This software is relatively transparent to users (the user may not be aware that the software is there), but they will be able to observe the results in desktop publishing output.

Printer control languages define a page as a unit, rather than considering each element (text, graphic, etc.) as a unit. PostScript type characters are stored as outlines that can be expanded or shrunk without affecting the quality of the image. Other languages create characters by a bit mapping process that may result in "ragged" lines in graphics, line drawings, and large type. PostScript can create type in about any size and style; other languages may restrict output to a list of font sizes and styles stored in the printer or downloaded from the computer software.

PostScript is less document oriented and more graphics oriented. PostScript works well with documents that are to be printed in color—a recent capability that has been added to the desktop publishing output spectrum. Operations that print mostly text or long documents with relatively few graphics may do just as well with one of the non-PostScript languages. Printers that support the PostScript language are about twice as expensive as those that support PCL. Because of the popularity of the Hewlett-Packard laser printers, which until recently supported only the PCL language, PCL printers are much more popular than their more expensive PostScript counterparts. A few printers support both languages.

Since most popular page composition software packages support a variety of PDLs, the selection of a printer is more affected by page description language than the selection of page composition software.

Figure 6-6 A complete desktop publishing system includes a PC, laser printer, and scanner.
Xerox Corporation

Printer Selection Criteria. Of course, *cost* is a major factor in printer selection, but the printer investment should match the total investment in a desktop publishing system. Failure to select a printer that will produce the output needed to justify the system is self defeating. Other considerations are *memory* (sufficient to handle type fonts and images), *output quality* (resolution, appearance), *type fonts supported* (total number and variety, number per page or per document), *graphics quality, paper handling capabilities* (continuous forms or cut sheets), and *speed of operation* (measured in pages per minute).

SOFTWARE

As introduced earlier, desktop publishing operations require a variety of software types, in addition to the page description language discussed above. As text editing software (word processing) and page composition software features continue to overlap, descriptions of the individual software ingredients become more difficult. However, considering the software in at least four separate categories—page composition, text editors, graphics, and font libraries—offers a convenient classification for discussion.

Page Composition. Page composition software is the central software tool in a desktop publishing operation. This is the software tool that builds the document. Page composition software enables the user to import text, graphics, photographs, and special features into a page layout or document design that will create output in the desired format, design, and aesthetic quality. This software ingredient is the one that manipulates type style, type size, and features such as bold type, italics, reverse type, columns, headers, footers, rulings (lines), bars, and underlines. With this software, users rearrange document layout to experiment with appearance; crop and scale (expand, contract) illustrations and photographs to match page and document dimensions.

Since the introduction of desktop publishing, two page composition packages have dominated the market: PageMaker® by Aldus Corporation and Ventura Publisher by Xerox. Because of computer/printer/page description language combinations, PageMaker was originally considered more effective in the Macintosh environment and Ventura more effective in the IBM/MS-DOS environment. PageMaker now runs in both environments. Original versions of the two leaders were quite different with PageMaker considered to be better for short, graphics-intensive documents and Ventura, for long, text-oriented documents such as employee manuals and long reports. Revisions have brought the two closer together. Dozens of page composition software packages have been produced. Recent entries such as NBI's Legend® represent a new breed of similarly priced integrated software (combining page composition, text editing, graphics, and font control features into a single package) that may challenge the leaders.

Features that may be important in the selection of a page composition package include the ability to "snake" text from one column to the next, the quality of documentation, the time required for employees to learn the system, the availability of style sheets (sample document layouts), treatment of hyphenation, and typographic concerns. A later section of this chapter deals with typographic skills.

Text Editors.   Some page composition software packages have built in text editors, but they may have limited capabilities. Any word processor can create text for desktop publishing documents. As in any other application, the word processing package is used for creating and editing text. Formatting text can be left to the page composition software.

Graphics.   Graphics files may be imported from software that creates statistical graphics—pie charts, line graphs, and bar graphs, for example. Two other types of software may be used to create graphics for documents: draw and paint programs. Limited versions of these may be built into the page composition software or included with mouse software. Collections of graphic design files called **clipart** may also be used as sources from which to import graphics to documents.

SYSTEM CONFIGURATIONS

Much of the discussion in this chapter has emphasized the variety of options available for every component type. This variety creates the possibility of building desktop publishing systems with a variety of capabilities. These can be divided into three or four categories that are influenced by the quality of the output.

LOW-LEVEL SYSTEMS

At the low end of the spectrum, many of the desktop publishing features can be accomplished without page composition software or sophisticated hardware. A Macintosh or IBM computer with a hard disk and at least 640K RAM, graphics monitor, a mouse, and an inexpensive laser printer—combined with word processing software capable of selecting a variety of type fonts and sizes—will build a modest system that can improve the quality of forms, reports, and simple brochures. An inexpensive page layout software system could be used.

MID-RANGE SYSTEMS

For serious desktop publishing, the computer system needs to be in the power range of the PC-AT (80286 based central processor) and include a color display, a scanner, and at least a 40 megabyte hard disk. Software would include a sophisticated page composition package, a compatible word processing package, graphics software, and a utility for hard disk management.

HIGH-LEVEL SYSTEMS

High-level systems for complex documents and processes would include an 80386 or equivalent computer with extended memory and 60–80 megabyte hard disk, a tape backup system, a full-page display, a high-speed/high-quality laser printer supporting Post-Script, and probably more than one page composition software package, and additional font software. The system would probably be networked for file retrieval and printer sharing.

PROFESSIONAL-LEVEL SYSTEMS

Professional-level systems would include up to two megabytes of expanded memory, the capability of producing very long documents, extensive hard disk storage and tape backup, large high-resolution video display with true WYSIWYG, automated document management (complex pagination and layout), and the capability to interface with sophisticated electronic typesetters.

BASIC USER SKILLS

Users who expect to create documents with desktop publishing systems must develop basic typographic and document design skills. These elements from the traditional printing environments are unfamiliar to most users. The ability to manipulate the software to produce text and graphics on a page with multiple type sizes and type fonts is not sufficient. They must also develop an appreciation for the aesthetics of effective page design and a sufficient knowledge of the technical side of type design to create effective document pages.

TYPOGRAPHIC SKILLS

Typography refers to the shape, style, or appearance of printed alphabetic and numeric characters. **Typeface** refers to a specific category of type design. Hundreds of typefaces exist; and each has a name, such as Helvetica®, Bookman®, and Glypha®. Within a typeface, styles and sizes may vary. Creating type in bold characters changes its style, but not its typeface. The technical meaning for **font** is a complete alphabet and related numeric and character sets of one typeface in one size and one style. However, the term is frequently used interchangeable with *typeface*.

Points, picas, and characters per inch are all popularly used measures of type size. Points and picas are common in the printing and electronic typesetting fields; traditionally typewriter type and computer printer type has been measured in characters per inch. **A point** is $\frac{1}{72}$ of one inch; a **pica** is $\frac{1}{6}$ of an inch or 12 points. Printers have built-in type fonts (character sets) in a variety of sizes. Additional type fonts may be selected from desktop publishing software or purchased font libraries (software).

Figure 6-7 illustrates elementary typography features: uppercase/lowercase, ascenders/descenders, serif (the opposite is sans serif—without serif), the baseline, type height, and point size. Three other terms are important typographical considerations. **Leading** refers to the space between baselines of lines of type. **Kerning** refers to the overlap of some characters (See Figure 6-7).

Figure 6-7   Elementary Typeface Elements

Proportional spacing refers to the space left between characters on a line of type. Point size refers to the vertical height of a character—not necessarily the width of the character. Within a particular typeface, some characters, such as W and M are much wider than other characters, e.g., i and l. A printer without proportional spacing capabilities assigns the same horizontal space to every character; printers with proportional spacing capabilities assign only the required space to each character.

Figure 6-8 **Comparison between Kerned and Unkerned Type**

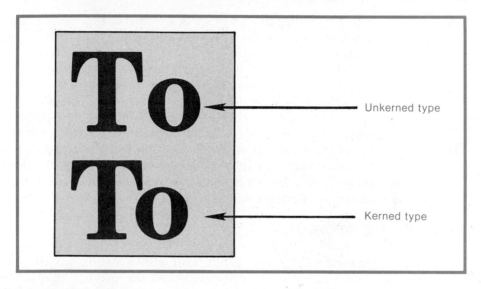

Unkerned type

Kerned type

DOCUMENT DESIGN SKILLS

The second set of skills needed to create documents with a professional appearance is document design skills. Page layout is the design of a document page; it is the plan that indicates the number of columns for text, the location of graphic elements, the number and size of headlines and subheadings, the number and location of rulings, the typeface, and various type style characteristics. The limitless combinations of these factors can be bewildering to a novice user. Experimentation plus advice from a professional typographer enable users to develop an appreciation for appropriate design.

IMPLEMENTATION DECISIONS

Decisions regarding whether or not desktop publishing fits into the overall office systems scheme for a particular organization can be difficult. Once a decision to use this office system technology is made, subordinate decisions involving the extent of system sophistication, specific hardware and vendor selection, and the startup activities, such as user training, must be made. Cost is a vital consideration underlying all of these. Cost-benefit analyses of desktop publishing systems, however, must be preceded by some basic decisions about system sophistication, hardware, vendors, and training sources.

SYSTEM SOPHISTICATION LEVEL

The preceding discussions of system components has pointed out a wide range of complexity and sophistication in every system component. The quality, complexity, and volume of document production to satisfy the needs of a particular organization or organization division determines how sophisticated the desktop publishing system or systems must be. If the objective is to produce in-house all the documents, forms, and publications now requiring the services of an outside printer, the system requirements will be far more sophisticated than the one required to produce only an informative newsletter for employees. So the first decision is to determine the applications for which the system will be used.

HARDWARE DECISIONS

Armed with a decision about applications, hardware capable of producing those applications in the quality desired must be selected. Factors such as software complexity and the computer capacity required for selected software must be determined. Compatibility among software, computer, and printer affect these decisions. Several decisions about whether to perform tasks internally or purchase services externally affect this decision. For example, modest operations may include plans for purchasing scanning services and actual printing services. Very large volumes and fast turnaround times may suggest purchasing the necessary hardware to do these internally.

VENDOR SELECTION

As is the case with any other office system component, support is the major consideration in vendor selection once the desired system components have been selected. The vendor may offer assistance in making decisions about components and levels of sophistication, but support after installation, whether this support is included with the purchase price or purchased separately, may be critical. The availability of support from equipment manufacturers and software developers will also influence vendor selection.

USER TRAINING SOURCES

Training is essential for any serious desktop publishing user. Any of the systems will require considerable time and effort to learn. The thorough understanding of hardware and software required for reaping maximum benefits from their capability requires a formal training effort with a live trainer. Interactive video or self-study courses may be adequate, but there is no substitute for live trainers for those organizations that can afford the cost of the trainer and provide blocks of time for the learner. The weekend-with-the-users' manual approach will be inadequate for most users.

To some extent, decisions about the system to install suggest the level of training needed. Hardware, software, page design, and typography training may all be necessary for many users, particularly with sophisticated systems.

REPROGRAPHICS

Reprographics, another previously independent office information technology, is now becoming a component of office automation and is closely related to desktop publishing. **Reprographics,** as a technology, represents all reproduction of document images. The objective of reprographics is dissemination of written communication through reproduction of documents, drawings, or designs. Reproduction processes include various copying, duplicating, printing, and film-duplication processes. The technology of reprographics includes fundamental reproduction processes and related technologies such as photocomposition or electronic printing, telecommunication systems to transmit images among component hardware, and paper handling (document assembly and binding) processes.

From the viewpoint of office automation, the interest in reprographics must involve both its technology and its management (control). Efforts to integrate office technologies will involve distribution of information. Decisions must be made relative to distribution medium and process. Paper, electronic transmission of images, and film are the choices.

Reprographics influences both the effectiveness and the efficiency of office systems through its influence on communication and public relations. Communication quality is affected by the legibility and availability of information. Organizational image is affected by the quality of tangible things produced by that organization, including its documents. Document quality may play an important role in the image that people hold for a particular organization.

Organizational efficiency is affected by the cost of information-distribution systems. Reprographics decisions—alternative systems and alternative approaches—will greatly influence information-distribution efficiency. For example, a decision whether to copy a short memo or to record an oral message on a voice-mail system will have significant impact in an organization that must send the message to a thousand employees in remote locations.

REPROGRAPHICS TECHNOLOGY

A short historical perspective is essential for understanding the current status of reprographics. Before the introduction of copy machine technology, reprographic processes offered a choice of professional printing (from movable or molded type), duplicating (from some reproducible "master" of the image to be reproduced, or carbon paper. Among the duplicating processes were stencil (ink), spirit (alcohol), and offset (ink) processes. Offset printing evolved into a variety of processes producing varied quality of output. Photocopy machines offered another alternative. All of these processes still exist and are in use in various forms. Only two of the categories significantly affect today's reprographics scene: photocopy processes and offset printing processes. Photocopy equipment has been improved to the point where some systems are referred to as copy/duplicators because they produce large numbers of copies very rapidly, and offset systems have improved to the point where they are considered the ultimate in printing quality. High volume and good quality are possible from either system. Professional appearance (impeccable quality) still requires an offset printing process.

PHOTOCOPY PROCESSES

Most copiers produce document copies by a combination of electrostatic (attracts ink to image on paper) and heat processes. They are called photocopiers because they reproduce an exact image of most documents. The quality of the image varies with the sophistication of the equipment and the quality of the original document. Hardware prices range from less than $1,000 to more than $125,000. Speeds range from a few copies a minute to more than 120 copies a minute. Developments that have enhanced the quality of copiers include color copying, copying on both sides of a sheet, reduction of and enlargement of image size, collating and binding capabilities, the production of copy from digitized (not paper) input, communication capabilities for remote copying, and self-diagnostic maintenance. This means that machines that need service analyze themselves and cue the operator about the machine component that needs service or replacement.

PRINTING PROCESSES

Offset is a duplication or printing process involving the preparation of a master image from which copies are reproduced. Low-end systems may involve paper masters that are produced on hardware similar to a copy machine. They are more likely to be called "offset duplicators." The master attracts ink to the image and "offsets" it to a series of rollers and finally to paper.

Extremely high-quality reproduction is possible from the offset process. These high-quality processes are in the offset printing category and reproduce copies from a metal plate that has images of documents, possibly including photographs and line drawings, etched into the plates. These plates may be produced from the output of a desktop publishing system. Electronic typesetting and complicated photographic processes may be involved in producing the plates, so this increases the expense for such reprographic processes.

Other printing processes include **letterpress**, a process that creates images directly from inked, raised characters such as molded type, and **offset lithography**, a process usually reserved for high-quality artwork and color reproduction of images from several plates.

Improvements in technology and overlapping capabilities have complicated the discussion of reprographics. Copy machines have taken on characteristics of duplicators and have achieved quality near that of offset printing. Their basic function is to replicate images of paper documents or produce another image like the one they see. This is called direct copying or photocopying. However, some intelligent copiers can produce an image from electronic digitized input. This capability puts them into the family of computer printers. Machines that have both direct copy and printing capabilities are called intelligent or electronic printers or copiers.

PHOTOCOMPOSITION

Equally important to reprographics technology is the preparation of copy (document images or text matter) to be reproduced. Microprocessor technology has revolutionized the methods for producing text matter. Photocomposition involves original production of high-quality text, graphics, and documents that will serve as the "master" for producing multiple copies.

Photocomposition is a method of creating text by a process that exposes light-sensitive paper to the text characters one at a

time. The paper is developed to create a photograph-like repro-
duction-quality master. The type for this book was generated in
a similar manner with photocomposition equipment reading the
output of a word processing system from a magnetic disk. Recent
innovations in low-cost photocomposition enable systems to
produce publisher-quality copy on plain paper. Laser beams are
used (in a manner similar to that used by laser printers) to produce images in a variety of fonts. Other systems may create masters electronically by printing the images on special paper with
a high-quality laser printer. Extremely high resolutions (more
than 2,000 DPI) in photocomposition and electronic typesetting
systems are now possible. They also offer a choice among thousands of typeface designs.

Microprocessors make photocomposition possible. Software-
manipulated processes enable the typesetter to select from an
infinite number of fonts. Proportional spacing, right justification,
and automatic hyphenation are adjusted to the particular type
choice automatically.

Physically and operationally, photocomposition hardware
resembles word processing equipment or any other small-to-
medium-sized computer. Because it is designed for producing
high-quality "printed" text, however, the product is more specialized and the process more complex. Some photocomposition
hardware will run popular word processing software such as
WordStar®, WordPerfect®, and Microsoft Word®. With high-
quality printers that are able to read the output of desktop publishing systems, including typeface selections and type size commands, the distinction between word processing and photocomposition is disappearing.

Without page composition software, electronic printing still
requires pasteups (cutting portions of text produced by photocomposition equipment and hand-produced graphics to build a
page). This may produce a quality that is superior to that of many
desktop publishing systems.

The differences between word processing and photocomposition still exist, but they are not as pronounced as they once were.
Word processing software, combined with desktop publishing
and laser printers, is able to produce high-quality output. Most
sophisticated word processing software now permits typeface
and type size selection that eliminates the need for electronic
typesetting of many documents.

REPROGRAPHICS AND COMMUNICATION

Communicating documents and text from one office system component to another represents still-fertile potential for improving
communication in organizations. The ability to reproduce hard

documents in remote locations may result in substantial savings in distribution costs and turnaround time. Telecommunication systems are quite capable of transmitting documents created in one location for reproduction in another location. Chapter 8 describes the technology that is required for such transmission.

Until systems that eliminate the need for paper documents are functional, reprographics will remain a vital office information technology which should be carefully coordinated with other technologies.

CAREER IMPLICATIONS FOR DESKTOP PUBLISHING AND REPROGRAPHICS

Knowledge or skill in the areas of desktop publishing and reprographics are more likely to supplement one's career preparation than to offer direct career opportunities. Many jobs are affected by desktop publishing; few have been created specifically for this purpose. Aside from the specialized graphic arts careers that are associated with traditional publishing structures, reprographics is not an area for career specialization. Likewise, desktop publishing offers great opportunities as a job component but few opportunities for specialized careers.

Large organizations with specialized centers for the production of documents may employ **desktop publishing specialists** or **electronic publishing specialists**. More likely, however, is the probability that employees in a variety of positions will incorporate this knowledge and skill as job components. The range of people who use desktop publishing for creating documents includes such diverse positions as writer, word processing specialist, administrative assistant, secretary, graphic artist, personnel assistant, marketing employee, engineer, artist, and design consultant.

Careers for those who become desktop publishing specialists require thorough computer skills and a knowledge of desktop publishing hardware and software. Perhaps the most critical is design skill. Page layout, typographical decisions, and document design require visual and design skills. Many office employees lack skill in these areas, and therefore, special training is necessary.

WOHL'S BUSINESS PERSPECTIVE

How Will Desktop Publishing Change the Office?
Starting with the Aldus PageMaker™ product for the Macintosh™ in 1985, Desktop Publishing has truly changed the office.

Standards for office documents have changed. No longer is a typed letter or report considered appropriate. For many applications—even for documents which are entirely distributed internally—type fonts, multiple type sizes, and elaborate graphics are the order of the day.

This is entirely appropriate. Before 1985, office document producers had two choices: typewritten or typeset. Typeset meant enormous differences in cost and time. It had to be reserved for formal documents, mainly for documents intended for customers rather than employees. Most internal communications and training materials were typewritten, making them harder to read and understand, but much cheaper and quicker to produce and revise.

After 1985, we had three choices:

1. Typewritten (mainly computer-based word processing);
2. Desktop published (with laser printer output); or
3. Typeset (but often inexpensively created with a desktop publishing front end).

Even more important, we could choose to move from one output option to another, using word processed text as an input to desktop published documents, or even moving to typesetting when higher quality output was required.

Desktop publishing has caused a revolution (not always a tranquil one) in where documents are produced. Printing empires (internal or external) can crumble quickly when their economics are undermined.

It is important to remember that desktop publishing, while an important technology, is not the answer to every office output question. Already, office users have noted such irritations as "ransom notes" (documents published in too many type faces) and documents whose layouts are so confused that no one can read them.

Electronic publishing tools can be found to suit every need, but office managers need to direct the right project to the right environment. A few simple rules seem in order:

Wohl's Rules of Office Publishing

1. Desktop publishing tools do not make the user an artist or a typographer. Unless you're a publishing professional, be sure to keep it simple. Use professionally designed templates, styles, and guidelines.
2. Direct work to the simplest platform that will get the job done. Sometimes this will be a word processor with enhanced layout features, sometimes a next generation word processor (which can be almost a desktop publisher), sometimes a desktop publishing package and sometimes only a more elaborate intermediate or production publishing system will do.
3. Big, complex jobs don't belong on little systems with little tools. Learning how to divide things up (and when to do them yourself as opposed to when to get professional help) is important. Some jobs (lots of photos, high quality, high volume, color) just aren't ready for the desktop yet.

SUMMARY

The combination of desktop publishing and reprographics technologies can be used to produce high-quality business documents, including reports, brochures, manuals, newsletters, and other printed documents. These products of the system may include graphics, photographs, and other qualities formerly available only through expensive printing processes.

Desktop publishing systems involve a variety of components. The basic hardware piece is usually a microcomputer with a graphics-capable display, supported by a laser printer and, sometimes, a scanner. Software includes a combination of applications packages—text editing, graphics, and page composition. Page composition software allows the user to design document pages on screen before printing. A variety of systems configurations is available, and they involve great variances in hardware and software sophistication.

Although designed to replace traditional printing processes for many tasks, desktop publishing incorporates many printing features. Users must understand the mechanics of typeface design and know something about the physical dimensions of type.

The decision to install desktop publishing systems requires careful analysis of document production needs and a comparison of these needs to available hardware and software. This will be influenced by the types of documents produced, the audience for which they are produced, and their volume.

Reprographics, the older technology, is a companion system for contemporary desktop publishing systems. Reprographics systems replicate the output of desktop publishing for distribution to recipients. Photocopy processes and several alternative printing processes comprise the choices for document reproduction.

KEY TERMS

desktop publishing
page composition software
electronic publishing
reprographics
WYSIWYG
text scanner
optical scanner
intelligent character
  recognition (ICR)
dots per inch (DPI)
gray scale

dithering
page description
  language (PDL)
clipart
typography
typeface
font
point
pica
leading
kerning

proportional spacing   letterpress
offset   offset lithography

REVIEW QUESTIONS

1. What is the motivation for organizations to install desktop publishing systems?

2. Describe the output of a desktop publishing system and identify several document types that this output might be used to produce.

3. What hardware components, other than a computer, may comprise a desktop publishing system?

4. Identify several software components that are common to all desktop publishing software and others that are available only on the more sophisticated packages.

5. Identify several supporting software packages and indicate how these relate to page composition software in a desktop publishing system.

6. Compare low-level desktop publishing systems, medium-range systems, and professional-level systems by indicating features and capabilities of systems at each level.

7. What skills and knowledge will a user of desktop publishing need to acquire in addition to text editing software familiarity?

8. What factors influence an organization's selection of a particular system for desktop publishing—beyond the desire to reduce costs and to produce high quality documents?

9. What is the relationship between desktop publishing and reprographics technologies?

CASE STUDY: INNOVATIONS AT KYLE CORPORATION

The word processing center at Kyle Corporation serves about five hundred executives, managers, technical staff, and administrative support employees in the firm's headquarters. Recent innovations at the center include new laser printers and desktop publishing systems. The center now produces about fifty thousand pages of copy a month, including correspondence, standard reports, special reports, speeches, and publications of various kinds. Most of these documents are distributed as produced by personal computer word processing software and one of four laser printers that serve the word processing systems. The laser printers replaced daisy wheel impact printers. The output rate of the laser printers is more than 40 pages a minute—about one twentieth the time required for daisy wheel printers.

Frequently the word processing output is reproduced by high-speed copiers for distribution within the firm or to outsiders. However, many projects require text, art work, and photographs within one document, which are designed by desktop publishing specialists. Many are documents for which high-quality appearance is desired (reports and publications for customer or employee publications and documents with some permanence). Three desktop publishing systems that share a high-quality, high-speed laser printer produce these documents. Some of them are reproduced by copy machines, but most of them serve as the original from which the company's print shop prints documents.

Prior to the innovations at the center, the annual external typesetting cost was about $40,000 and the annual printing costs were more than $700,000.

The print shop, which printed medium-quality documents in a traditional mode previously, is able to reproduce high-volume documents using the output of the word processing and desktop publishing systems.

In the center, software decisions control the type font choices, output is offset quality, and text can be communicated to or from remote locations. The size of type (ranging from half to four times the size of elite typewriter type) and the shape of type (several hundred font possibilities) are selected by software decisions selected from menu choices.

Critical documents, such as the corporate annual report and advertisement copy, are still reproduced by outside photocomposition services and printing firms.

QUESTIONS/ACTIVITIES

1. Using the information presented in the case, in this chapter, and in the previous chapters in this text, compile lists of hardware and software that you would expect the word processing center at Kyle Corporation to be using.

2. Compile a list of benefits that you would expect the company to have realized after the installation of laser printers for word processing and the installation of desktop publishing.

3. Which of the benefits identified in No. 2 would be quantifiable?

4. Discuss any sacrifice in quality that you would expect the firm to have experienced. Compare these sacrifices to the benefits that you described in No. 2. Do the potential sacrifices outweigh the potential benefits?

SUGGESTED READINGS

Blum, Greg. "The Changing Face of Laser Printers." *PC Publishing* (June, 1988): 20–29.

Brown, Alex. "Desktop Publishing: A Guide for Skeptics." *National Association of Desktop Publishers Journal*, vol. 2, no. 3 (summer, 1988): 11–23.

Buche, Don. *Desktop Publishing Using PageMaker® on the IBM-PC*. Englewood Cliffs, New Jersey: Prentice-Hall, 1989.

Feldman, Len. "The New Wave in Scanners," *PC Publishing*. (November, 1987): 8–20.

Lesser, Hartley. "Scanners." *PC Publishing* (August, 1987): 11–22.

Mullins, Carolyn J. "The Layout of Desktop Publishing." *Information Center* (June, 1987): 19–27.

Seybold, Jonathan. "The Revolution: Companies Discover the Benefits of Corporate Publishing." *National Association of Desktop Publishers Journal*, vol. 2, no. 2 (spring, 1988): 2.

Sorensen, Karen. "Corporate Desktop Publishing: Who's in Charge?" *Publish* (June, 1987): 56–61.

CHAPTER 7

Information Resources Management

OBJECTIVES

After studying this chapter, you should understand the following:

1. The concept of information value

2. Three categories of information media

3. Five categories of information value

4. The nature of management control of information resources

5. The rationale for labeling information resources as a corporate asset

6. Paper records as information resources

7. The elements of the records life cycle and the nature of management need for each element

8. Microfilmed records as information resources

9. The technology for micrographic information resources

10. Databases and electronic files as information resources

11. The role of computer output microfilm in managing information resources

12. The combination of technologies used to create computer-assisted retrieval of information resources

More than eighty percent of the information generated and used by organizations in the United States is distributed through a paper medium. Much of this paper is generated as output from computers; however, a rapidly increasing quantity of information is being communicated and retrieved without ever being committed to paper. Regardless of the medium through which information is recorded and used, it must be effectively managed in order for it to have value or usefulness. The office is the nerve center that brings life to the organization's information resources. This chapter explores the management of information resources in organizations and the enhancements that technology, combined with sound management practices, can bring to that information.

THE CONCEPT OF RECORD/INFORMATION

The very essence of organizations is information. When recorded, information becomes a very real and tangible element in the operation and management of organizations—private or public, profit or nonprofit, large or small. Information has no usefulness, however, unless it can be retrieved, manipulated (sorted out or combined), and placed at the disposal of those who need it. Information is created within organizations; it may be transmitted within the organization, to another organization, or to individuals (customers, clients, consumers, or the general public). Computerization of the processes of creating, transmitting, storing, and retrieving information brought a new awareness of the value of information. In some organizations, the use of information in management decision making has reduced the number of mid-level managers as administrative assistants become more proficient in the use of information systems. Since the inception of organized business activity and professional management, the need to use and store information has been recognized. Rapidly changing information technology has increased the challenges in managing the total information needs of organizations.

In this chapter, the terms record and information are used interchangeably. **Record/information** refers to "that which informs or has the potential to inform"[1] and is recorded on any medium. The medium may be a computer's memory, a magnetic medium such as tape or disks, a film medium, a paper medium, or one of the newer media such as optical/compact disks. "**Information resources** (plural) are the information holdings and information-handling tools within or available to an organization."[2]

---

1.   Cornelius F. Burke, Jr., ''Working Definitions of Terms Related to IRM Concepts,'' *Information Management* (May, 1985): 8–9.

  2.   *Ibid.*

Information resources management (IRM) addresses the need for a systematic approach to managing an organization's records throughout their life cycle from creation to final disposition.

RECORD/INFORMATION VALUES

Decisions about what we do with information are affected by the values we attach to that information. Some of the values represent internal needs (within the organization). Internal information is needed for the everyday functions of the organization. It is used to satisfy the needs of the organization's employees and management as they perform their activities.

Other values represent external requirements or needs. For example, the Internal Revenue Service may require that corporations maintain certain kinds of information. That information takes on value (usefulness) because it enables the organization to satisfy a government requirement—even though there is no other perceived reason for creating or maintaining the information.

The value of recorded information will be categorized as administrative, operational, documentary, legal, or archival. Information has **administrative value** when it enables management to make effective decisions. The size and complexity of organizations and the influence of outside elements lessen the effectiveness of judgment alone as a basis for decisions. Managers must consider multiple decision elements such as economic conditions, competition, financial factors, human factors, legal implications, and timing factors. Up-to-date information about the status and effects of various decision elements can be very valuable.

Information has **operational value** when it supports or documents the routine activities of the organization. Production records, sales records, and accounting and financial data are examples of operational records.

If recorded information provides necessary proof of past events or conditions, that record has **documentary value**. This type of value cannot always be predetermined. Some organizations routinely document communication, activities, events, and conditions because of the potential documentary value of those records.

Legal values are added to information collections by the legal systems under which we live and operate. Statutory laws specifically require certain types of record keeping, information communication, and records preservation. Organizations are affected differently by these requirements, depending upon their nature. A public utility, an agency of government, or a bank, for example, must follow strict regulations which require that certain types of information be generated. These regulations determine when and how the organizations must communicate the information and how long it must be maintained (some information must be maintained permanently). Records that enable compliance with these requirements have legal value. Records that are not required but that would prevent legal entanglements also have legal value.

A sometimes neglected value of information is its **archival value**. This is the potential value of information for future scholarly research or historically valuable documentation. For the most part, recognition of this value and subsequent steps to protect information are voluntary actions. However, many organizations are recognizing that such values exist and are taking steps to identify and preserve records for their archival value.

INFORMATION AS A CORPORATE ASSET

For years accountants have defined assets as anything of value in an organization. They have categorized assets as tangible and intangible. The organization's plant, office buildings, and equipment are its tangible assets. Monetary values also represent intangible assets, such as customers' goodwill or an organization's reputation with the public, which must be paid for when businesses change hands. More recent thinking has also begun to consider an organization's human resources (the value of talented, well-trained personnel) and the information resources they command to be of equal worth to an organization's tangible assets.

Information resources management (IRM) at its best manages information like other corporate assets (such as personnel or equipment). It assures that information is accurate and available throughout an organization. Information resources management focuses on the development of organization-wide systems for identifying and managing information resources. This discipline views information as a corporate resource with systems (usually electronic) that enhance communications and the availability of information for the organization as a whole. While hardware and software are part of this discipline, they are viewed as tools or means. IRM recognizes that organizations spend billions to bring information to the organization in order to accomplish the mission of the organization as effectively as possible.

INFORMATION LIFE CYCLE

Records management specialists recognize the following stages of the **information life cycle**: creation, storage/retrieval, manipulation, distribution, and disposition. With slight variations, this cycle can be applied to the management and control of information in any form. Each of the stages is a discipline, complete with systems, procedures, terminology, hardware, and issues.

CREATION

Creation, also called input, is the first step in origination of information. This information is usually known as a document or record. The person creating the document starts with an idea or information about a transaction or event and builds it into some form of business record or communication such as a letter, memorandum or report. However, all input is not original. Previously created documents may be entered into a system to allow further editing and distribution. These issues will be developed later.

There are several methods available for use in creating a document. The method of creation is directly related to an individual's knowledge and the availability of technology. Some methods of creating a document are longhand, shorthand, optical character recognition (OCR), composing at the system, machine dictation, and voice recognition.

Traditionally, the most common method of creating documents in an office is by writing it in longhand using paper and pen. This method is relatively slow, as an individual can only write at an approximate rate of 20–25 words per minute. If this document requires further editing or processing by another individual, that person may have difficulty in reading the creator's handwriting, which may cause delay in producing the final document.

Another method that is quickly being replaced by automation is shorthand. Originally, shorthand was the writing of symbols or abbreviations for a document dictated by the author to a secretary. However, shorthand systems include both manual (with pen and tablet) and machine using various technologies. The manual method is rapidly being replaced by machines, which have the capability to record an excess of 200 words per minute. The most common form of machine shorthand is operated by the court reporters who enter into the machine a set of letters that represent the spoken word. Some shorthand machines have the ability to work directly with a computer. This process is called computer-aided transcription (CAT). Whether manual or machine shorthand is used, this method is at least double the speed of longhand.

OCR technology allows for computers to read the printed word from paper directly into the word processing unit. The OCR system "reads" or recognizes data directly from paper and records it on a computer disk or into a mainframe computer. Most OCRs work in about the same way. A page is fed into the system, characters are digitized, then each character is compared to a table of known characters in the OCR's memory. An OCR can be ten to twenty times faster than a typist and many times more reliable. Some OCRs can read handprinting, typing, and certain graphics. Most OCRs in the office read only typing of specified type styles. The most common everyday use of OCR is found at the local grocery store. Many now use OCR scanners at the checkout counter.

Though this form of creation of information is indirect, it is a form of input that will then allow for further manipulation of that data. The integration of OCR equipment with other technologies such as facsimile and electronic mail will enhance its importance in the future.

Composing at the computer by the originator is becoming increasingly common as computers appear at each workstation. Creators key in their own documents, which may then be edited by support staff or the originator. Integration of word processing, graphics, and spreadsheets allow managers the option of producing their own reports more easily than explaining to support staff how they need it done. It should be noted that individuals can create documents at least three times faster by composing at the computer than by longhand methods. However, individuals must be willing to adjust to the changes in technology and retrain themselves when needed.

Machine dictation is the process of talking into a machine that records the words on a magnetic medium. Machine dictation provides increased productivity by both originator and support staff. Machine dictation is a fast method for inputting a document. We can generally dictate at a rate of 60 to 80 words per minute. This is four to five times faster than writing in longhand and usually faster than dictating to a secretary.

Some training is required for the originator to dictate the document and for the support staff to transcribe the document. However, the advantages outweigh the initial training time. Machine dictation can be combined with several other technologies and allow origination from many places. For example, a traveling salesperson, before normal business hours, could call in orders, reports, and office staff directives from the road and have work in progress while returning to the office.

Many types of dictation equipment exist. The range includes hand-held or portable units, desk-top units located in office settings, and centralized units that combine the use of telephones, transcribers, and word processing systems. The nature of business, location, size, and number of employees will determine the need for dictation equipment.

Voice or speech recognition represents another input/creation method. Voice-driven typewriters are now available which allow the creator to speak directly into the typewriter and have the recognized words printed by the typewriter. Further development is underway in this area, however the future combination of voice recognition and word processing will allow for an even greater volume of information creation.

The method of creation for some documents is clear. An accountant may use a worksheet as a means of input for a budget; or that same budget may be created on a computer using a spreadsheet program. Eventual use of the input may determine the best method for creation. Some documents may never be printed as we know them; for example, the creation of a document by voice mail or voice messaging. This system is computer based, and the message will follow the normal life cycle path of information creation, storage, and distribution but in a form utilizing a new technology. This system will be explained further in the chapter on telecommunications.

STORAGE/RETRIEVAL

The organization of paper files, computer disks, tapes, and microform records for storage and retrieval by a systematic method is a complex and time-consuming task. The maintenance of paper records typically requires a large number of filing cabinets and ever increasing amounts of floor space. Therefore, records managers have been deeply committed to the development of cost effective alternatives to paper records storage systems for many years. The recent development of computerized filing, micrographics, and the integration of micrographics and computers is changing the way we deal with information storage and retrieval.

Records maintenance concentrates on the useful, active life of documents. Classification systems for housing records in an organized fashion are utilized. Equipment is selected and procedures are developed which concentrate on easy retrieval of information for those who need it for administrative and operational purposes.

Active records (those that are used frequently) may be housed in centralized facilities or in the accessible physical location of the department or unit that uses the records most. A combination of centralized and decentralized housing of active records is the plan most frequently used. Even though maintenance procedures may allow decentralized control, there should be centralized coordination of systems, procedures, and equipment procurement.

In records management circles, **records storage** represents the phase of a record's life after it has passed active status. It may still have legal, archival, or even administrative value; but its chances for retrieval are very low. At this point the record is

Figure 7-1   Active records may be housed in the department that uses them the most.

physically removed from active status and stored somewhere so that it is still retrievable and protected. Stored records are housed in less expensive space and less expensive containers than active records.

Not to be confused with destruction, records disposition refers to decisions about the existence of records at the end of the storage stage. Some records are destroyed at this point. Many that are not destroyed should be. If records have no legal, archival, administrative, or operational value, there is little justification for consuming space and complicating the retrieval of other records by keeping them around. Their removal improves efficiency and, if they are recycled, produces revenue as well.

If archival value is recognized, disposition involves a plan to protect and preserve documents. Paper records are especially vulnerable to the environment and special attention is required to preserve them even for relatively short periods of time. Some unprotected records will literally disintegrate.

Vital records are those that would be essential for an organization's survival and continuance following a disaster. Examples of natural disasters that may occur include floods, tornadoes, earthquakes, and hurricanes. Disasters of human origin — such as fires, vandalism, deliberate destruction of information, and employee error — may be just as devastating. Information management must include identification of records that should receive special protection.

Figure 7-2 Inactive records are stored in less expensive space and containers.

Accounts receivable information, client and customer data, and records of organizations whose primary "product" is on paper (such as an architectural firm) are examples of vital information. Off-site storage of information, duplicate copies, and backup magnetic records are examples of efforts to provide information protection. Many firms exist now to provide this service. By means of data links, disaster recovery companies maintain duplicate data for their clients.

RECORDS RETENTION SCHEDULES

A **records retention schedule** is a comprehensive list of all records in the organization (papers, disks, tapes, microforms) for which retention periods have been assigned. The retention period might be one month, two years, seven years, or indefinite. Each organization must develop a retention schedule that suits its operational needs.

Listings on a records retention schedule are usually "records series" titles rather than individual document titles. To use a paper record example, a "customer folder" would be the records series. However, one organization might have two thousand customer folders and each one might contain numerous items or documents: invoices, purchase orders, copies of correspondence, and other documents.

Effective schedule development requires extensive investigation of administrative and operational needs for records, legal requirements that might affect their retention, and potential archival value of the records. Every person in an organization who might have some future need for a record should have a chance to examine the proposed retention time before it becomes a policy. Frequently, legal counsel, trade association advisers, and representatives of other firms in an industry are consulted in making the decisions. Government agencies are affected by commissions and legal restrictions in the retention of their records.

Because paper records are often physically moved at the end of each retention period, their schedules get more attention than less bulky or intangible records. There may be a greater need for a retention schedule for electronic records, however. When electronic records, retained on a disk or in valuable computer memory, are beyond their usefulness, they create unnecessary burdens upon equipment. On the other hand, precautions are necessary to prevent their premature and inadvertent destruction. Figure 7-3 presents a portion of a records retention schedule. Notice that a variety of records media are represented.

INFORMATION MANIPULATION

Manipulation or processing is another step in the information life cycle. Though some consider this to be the step prior to stor-

Figure 7-3   Records Retention Schedule

Record Name	Type	Years Active	Years in Storage	Disposition
COM = Computer Output Microfilm I = Indefinite P = Permanent				
Accounts Payable Ledger	Printout	1	3	Destroy
Subsidiary Tax Returns	Paper	3	3	P Archives
Personnel Record, Individual	Paper	I	15	I
Branch Weekly Reports	Fiche	1	2	Destroy
Master Vendor List	COM/Tape	3	COM: 1	Destroy
			Tape:	Reuse after update
Report of Sales	Fiche	1	2	
Annual Report	Printed	(three copies to archives)		

age/retrieval, a document is usually first stored and retrieved by computer before it is manipulated. In this step, the information is changed in some way so that it will be in a useful form.

In the past, processing numbers (data processing) and processing words (word processing) were considered separate, distinct fields. Data processing was associated with computers, while word processing was accomplished on equipment referred to as word processors. Of course, these "word processors" are also computers. The widespread use of the microcomputer and the availability of popular word processing software has brought word processing into the hands of many data processing workers, managers, and home users. Thus, the distinct areas of word processing and data processing are disappearing as the technology improves and both are handled on the same equipment. Therefore, the term information processing perhaps will more accurately describe the work handled in the office.

An additional example would be a letter retrieved on the word processor so that corrections or additions to the text may be accomplished. Possibly a table or graph is inserted into the text, or spacing of the final document is changed to single spacing in order to save paper during printing. Nonetheless, manipulation is the changing of a document so that it will be in a more useful form.

INFORMATION DISTRIBUTION

Distribution and permanent storage are the last steps in the information processing cycle. Distribution is the transfer of information from one place to another. Distribution assures that the input that was entered into and processed by the system is distributed to the people who need it. Once, distribution was a slow and sometimes inefficient process. Now, modern systems of distribution deliver information more quickly, sometimes using new forms of electronic distribution and transmission.

In the past, the process of making copies also was slow and the copies were sometimes unreadable because they were produced on old, inadequate copy machines. Reprographics has changed the method and speed of making copies. Refer to Chapter 6 in order to review the various methods.

This distribution takes place both inside and outside an organization. The distribution may utilize automated systems. These systems include data communication between computers, electronic mail, including facsimile and fiber optics transmission, and both local and remote networking.

After information has been inputted (creation), processed (manipulation), and distributed, a copy of the document will be stored in some way. (As stated previously, document storage/ retrieval may take place before output and distribution of the information.)

MEDIA SELECTION

In managing information resources, the medium may be the key to an effective system. Even more important is recognition of the fact that numerous information resources are available for carrying out the work of an organization. The medium is a vehicle, a tool, or a container for holding information; the information itself is the thing of value.

Three popular categories of information media are paper, film, and electronic storage devices. The media choice must not be viewed as a choice among these three, however; it must be viewed as an opportunity to select from a multitude of media possibilities in combinations that build effective systems. In many instances the person responsible for information-resource management is not the person who determines the medium in which information will be created. In such a case, the manager of a firm's information resources faces a challenge in making a significant contribution to the organization's objectives.

For effective management of information resources, media conversion may be necessary. This may include keying or scanning paper documents to convert them to electronic media. Other processes convert electronic media from one format to another. For example, disk files created on one system may not be compatible with another system. Various hardware and software combinations can be used to convert files to formats that equipment will accept. For information generated within organizations, this necessity of making systems compatible may be eliminated by cooperative planning. However, very little control can be exercised over the media used to generate information that comes to your organization from the outside.

The medium for information may be selected to satisfy a need that exists when information is created and communicated. For example, a paper record may be created because of its portability and because no special equipment is necessary for later references to that information; electronic transmission may be selected because it is the fastest means of communicating information. A firm may use electronic mail because a network already exists for on-line computer communication. The additional application may cost less than postage to mail paper memos.

PAPER SYSTEMS

Paper has been the traditional medium for information since it was invented. Established procedures are difficult to change. However, most managers agree that the creation, storage/retrieval, distribution, and use of paper is more time consuming and less efficient than some of the alternatives. This agreement has not lessened our dependence on it, however.

Widespread discussion of the "paperless office" and existing technology that makes that goal achievable has not been matched by performance. Some specimen or "model" offices, such as the one called The Paperless Office in Washington, D.C., have been created to demonstrate that offices can operate without paper. Many offices now concentrate on reducing paper to a minimum. These organizations transfer information from the paper medium in which it is received to some other medium as quickly as possible. However, the same technology that makes it possible for us to communicate and house information without committing it to paper also makes it possible for us to produce unlimited tons of paper records.

The manager of a progressive industrial organization boasted that his firm generates no paper records. "Everything's on microfilm or in the computer," he said. Yet a tour of his facility reveals nonstop, high-speed printers, multiple high-speed copiers, and a room containing 76,000 paper documents. "Those aren't records; they're engineers' specifications," the manager explained. Our knowledge of technology's capabilities and our embarrassment when we are unable or unwilling to use those capabilities prevent a realistic view.

Rather than pretend that paper does not exist, managers who are thoroughly familiar with their information resources will develop effective systems for controlling and managing paper information systems. Such a system requires consideration of the life cycle of paper records within that organization and planning for each phase of that cycle.

Documentation of the frequency of records use is difficult and time consuming. Attempts at such documentation and reasonable estimates by employees who work with paper records reveal that many records are never referred to again after they are housed and that most paper records are not used after they have been in existence for more than 12 months. The data in Figure 7-4 is typical of such attempts to quantify references.

The best way to manage paper records is to prevent them from becoming a problem. Formal programs to control the creation

Figure 7-4 **References to Paper Documents**

Percent of Records	Reference History
35%	Never accessed
60%	Accessed only during the first 12 months
5%	Accessed after 12 months

Source: Reprinted with permission from *Office Automation: A Survey of Tools and Techniques*, by David Barcomb. (Bedford, Mass: Digital Press, 1981), 104. Copyright © 1981 by Digital Press/Digital Equipment Corporation.

of records achieve this goal by limiting the number of copies of documents produced, requiring approval for the development of paper forms, and analyzing information handling procedures that rely upon paper documents. Such analyses can frequently eliminate documents or reduce the number of copies produced.

MICROGRAPHIC SYSTEMS

Micrographics refers to the whole field of filmed records: the equipment, the technology, and management decisions regarding the nature of systems that will be used and how those systems will be integrated with other information systems. Microfilm technology was developed as a photographic medium more than a hundred years ago. Except for the filming of canceled checks by banks, however, very little use was made of the medium until it was dramatized by developments for the communication of intelligence data during World War II.

Following World War II, records management applications of microfilm technology were developed by governments and private business firms. The Social Security Administration has been a leader in the use of filmed records systems. Initial installations sought an alternative to storing inactive paper records. Later applications involved the filming of library materials and newspapers. More recent developments have used film for active information management.

MEDIA AND TECHNOLOGY

Microfilm is a complex technology no longer limited to a photographic process. In early applications, micrographic images involved some type of photograph of a paper document — either transparent film photographs or printed miniature paper photographs called micro-opaques. Micrographic images that have never been on paper are now possible. Laser technology and photography involving computer images can commit information to film directly from a computer's memory or a magnetic medium. Applications of these systems are discussed under the section of this chapter devoted to electronic systems.

Film. Films used in microfilm applications vary in price, processing time, processing method, and in the quality of the processed image. Equipment and film selection will be affected by the nature of the use of the film and the length of time for its active use. Some film types are more durable than others. The physical width of film is critical because it is directly tied to all of the equipment manufactured for its use, and they come in a variety of colors from black and white to shades of blue and gray. Full-color microfilm is available and used for special applications.

Microforms. Microfilm is developed, sliced, and rolled or mounted into formats that are labeled roll film, microfiche, aperture cards, jackets, or micro-opaques. These microforms

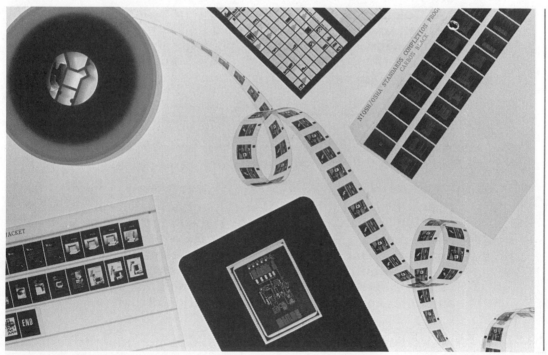

Figure 7-5 Microfilm is developed, sliced, and rolled or mounted into roll film, microfiche, jackets, or aperture cards.

are sometimes used as they emerge from the processing phase, or they may require special containers or mounting.

Several containers for **roll film** are available. Open reels require hand loading and rewinding; cartridges are merely dropped into place on the reader. Cartridges contain reels of film that readers and other equipment will automatically load. Cassette containers involve a continuous loop of film. **Microfiche** is the name given to unitized collections of images on a single piece of film (about 4" by 6") cut from a 105mm roll of processed film. These film sheets contain from 96 to several thousand images, depending upon the size of the document images. They are referred to as unitized records because they can be retrieved manually and placed on a reader to locate the desired image quickly without rolling past hundreds of feet of film to find the desired image. Related documents are filmed together on one microfiche (a unit).

Aperture cards are filmed images mounted on paper cards with an opening (aperture) or window the size of the film image. A card may contain only one image or a strip of film with two or three images. They are especially useful for mounting filmed images of very large documents such as blueprints (engineer's drawings).

A **micro-opaque** is not film; that is, it is not transparent film through which light passes for reading as in other microforms. Micro-opaques are miniature photographs printed on paper. They are viewed through magnifying readers in much the same way that transparent microforms are read.

Microfilm jackets are similar to microfiche in size, but the filmed images are on strips of film or chips (single images), which are inserted into clear plastic pockets on a microfiche-sized sheet of clear plastic acetate. These jackets are sometimes duplicated to produce a microfiche-type copy.

Equipment. Microfilm information systems can function with relatively little equipment. Outside service agencies will process and film records and deliver the filmed images ready to use. All that is required for records use is a reader to magnify the images. Some organizations choose in-house systems, however. In-house systems require cameras, film processors, film inspection devices, readers, reader-printers, and sometimes film duplicators and other equipment for the preparation of film.

SYSTEM EVALUATION

The most dramatic and obvious reason for installing a microfilm system is to save space, and that is probably the most common reason for using filmed information. Compared to paper systems, the space savings is phenomenal. Records requiring a room full of file cabinets can be housed in one desk drawer when they are committed to microfilm. Filmed resources consume only about 5 percent of the space consumed by their paper counterparts.

Space saving is not the only reason for using microfilm, nor is the usefulness of microfilm confined to stored, inactive records. Active records may be filmed because film can be retrieved, duplicated, and used more quickly than paper records. Multiple sets of records can be produced easily and inexpensively. A microfiche containing thousands of images can be reproduced at a cost that rivals the cost of a copy machine reproduction of one paper document. Organizations with branch facilities that need access to records sets find microfilm especially useful.

Updatable microfilm systems now have opened microfilming to applications requiring that collections of data be updated. Images are filmed and ready for inspection in six to ten seconds. The fiche may be returned to the camera any number of times for adding additional images. Images may be removed from the film, and limited notations to existing images can be made. This

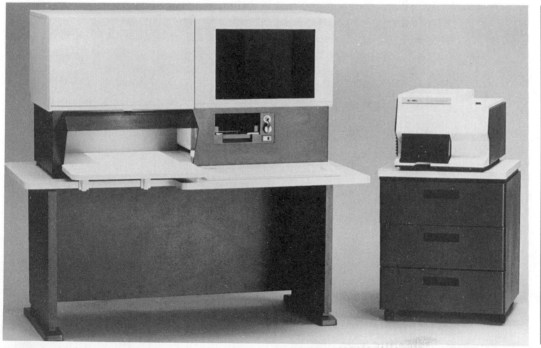

Figure 7-6 With an updatable microfilm system, the fiche can be returned to the camera for additional images.
MICROX Bell & Howell Co.

can now be done without destroying existing images. A microfiche containing images of previously existing documents can have images of new documents in the same collection added to the same microfiche.

Information or **file integrity** is improved with filmed records. File integrity involves the degree to which a collection of records remains intact or the extent to which a group of related documents can be brought together and kept together for reference purposes. The integrity of paper records can be destroyed when portions of the record are removed and lost or misfiled when they are returned. Filmed records remain in the sequence in which they are filmed.

Limitations and disadvantages of film systems should be considered when selecting information systems. The initial investment in equipment for an in-house operation can be significant. If the volume of records to be filmed is small, other approaches to information management may be less expensive. While updatable microfilm systems permit the addition of new images to a film, only limited notations to existing film data are possible. Documents that are continually changing because new information is being added are not good candidates for film. Where large numbers of employees need to access information frequently, the number of readers required may be prohibitive. The fact that records sequence cannot be rearranged may be considered a drawback, but unitized microfiche and computerized indexes that determine document location have all but eliminated this disadvantage.

RELATIONSHIP TO OTHER INFORMATION SYSTEMS

Micrographic systems can be used in conjunction with other information systems. They can supplement paper records systems by reducing the bulk of selected records types. Microfilm images can now be digitized, stored electronically, and transmitted via telephone lines or satellite for reproduction in remote locations. Computerized indexes to microfilmed images can greatly reduce the expense of information storage compared to the cost of on-line computer storage. These and other relationships to office automation technologies are discussed in greater detail in the following section.

The **micrographic disk** is a blend of electronics, optics, laser, and electron-beam technologies. A 12-inch disk carries reduced images of documents and graphics, digital bar-coded recordings of text, and an index to the disk's contents. Up to 6,000 pages of 8½-by-11-inch documents and four megabytes of digital information can be stored. The production process is somewhat complex, but duplicate disks are easily made in a manner similar to that used to stamp out phonograph records.

ELECTRONIC SYSTEMS

Computers and related technologies have brought new approaches to information storage and retrieval. Some confusion still exists, but software, media, and hardware developments are improving and enhancing the concept of electronic files. New developments in electronic document storage through technologies such as the compact/optical disk offer exciting new possibilities.

Numerous applications of technology to the storage of information have been labeled electronic files. Some of these systems refer to software/hardware combinations that make possible the filing of either a document image or the data contained in a document. Other uses of the term refer to databases of selected information—usually information that has never existed in document format. These information collections may be updated, rearranged, and printed in the form of reports. This chapter will highlight databases, various other forms of electronic files, and computer-assisted retrieval.

DATABASES

A **database** is a collection of related information (as opposed to a collection of documents). Although any collection of categorized or classified information is a database, the term usually refers to an electronic file of information. The most common example of a printed or hard copy of a database is the telephone book, which is now computerized for use by operators. Databases may be either (1) internal or based within the organization's own computer system and containing records created, arranged, updated, and manipulated within the organization; or they may be (2) external or based in computer systems of outside firms, which charge a fee for access to the data. Early external databases, such as those of Mead Data Control and System Development Corporation, were specialized and intended for business use. Public databases are now accessible for relatively small fees with the aid of a microcomputer and a communications device with a telephone hookup. Companies that now supply database information to users include Dialog Information Service Inc., Dow Jones News/Retrieval Service, and Compuserve Information Service Co.

A **database management system (DBMS)** is the software that makes possible the use of the database. The software directs the creation of records, addition of data to the records, calculations, sorting and combining data from the database, and production of reports containing data from the database. Mainframe computer database management systems may involve complex programs, limited access to portions of the records, and expensive hardware. However, relatively inexpensive and highly capable database management systems software is available for mini- and micro-computer systems. With DBMS, users (perhaps departments or individuals within a firm) can create, manipulate, and access the database to fit their own needs.

Hierarchical databases and **relational databases** are categories of DBMS that indicate how data are handled by the system. To retrieve information from a hierarchical system, the computer must search through successive layers of information, each more detailed than the previous one. The relational system allows the user to go directly to a set of specific data without searching through successive files. For example, the system would find the names of all employees who have scheduled vacations for a particular month if that information is stored in each employee's record. Relational database management systems are considered more user friendly than hierarchical systems.

HYPERTEXT

Recent developments in a rather old technology have created the possibility for vast information resources. **Hypertext** is a concept conceived in the 1940s, improved upon in the 1960s, and made available for microcomputer applications in the 1980s. This concept involves a database of stored information in multiple forms containing segments of information that can be linked together to form collections of information, the components of which have some common theme.

Unlike the databases described above, which follow a file/record/field pattern, hypertext files are collections of information called **nodes**. A node is usually no more than a display screen full of information. However, that information may be text, document images, graphics, video images, or audio signals. Collections of nodes are sometimes associated with index cards of information on a particular subject. Built-in links to related information enable the user to retrieve vast amounts of interrelated information.

Software for hypertext systems is actually a collection of software—a text editor, a database management system, a graphics package, and various tools that make it possible to browse through collections of information on a selected topic. High density graphics displays, a windows-type user interface (pull-down screens containing information or menu-type commands to which the user responds to get more information), and a mouse are standard features in hypertext situations. Moving a cursor to an icon or a menu choice (preferably with the aid of a mouse) moves from one node to other related nodes. Related nodes are retrieved very quickly—in no more than a second.

Hypertext applications may involve retrieving existing information on a selected topic, locating statistical data for use in problem solving, or identifying bibliographic data about existing works related to topics being researched. The more sophisticated systems use mainframe computers and intelligent workstation terminals for information retrieval, but systems such as Guide, HyperCard, Knowledge Pro, and KRS (Knowledge Retrieval System) are available for IBM, IBM-compatible, and Apple Mac microcomputers.

ELECTRONIC FILES

Electronic files can be any collection of information that is recorded in digitized code (a code that can be read and stored by a computer), and stored on some medium from which it can be retrieved, viewed, and used. Hard disks, reels of magnetic tape, optical disks, and floppy disks might all serve as the medium for electronic files. The recall of information is accomplished by a computer. The memory or disk storage of a computer or a word processor may serve as the storehouse of electronic files.

Because the literature of information management uses the term electronic file to refer to a variety of data storage arrangements, some differentiation of those arrangements is desirable. Separating electronic files into two broad categories provides some clarity. These categories are databases and electronic document files.

As you just learned, a database is a collection of computer-stored and retrievable data. Databases are most valuable for organizing standard data related to a variety of entities. An example would be the names, mailing addresses, telephone numbers, and products used by a thousand customers. The electronic database is even more important if multiple users need to be able to retrieve information about those customers. The information in databases can be manipulated and viewed or printed out in endless configurations.

Electronic document files, on the other hand, contain electronic versions of documents that have been generated in the communication of information. These "documents" are either text- or image-based files. Text-based files contain electronically stored text with stored instructions for formatting that text when it is printed. These files are generated by word processing systems. Image-based files contain electronically stored codes representing images of documents that were originally paper documents. These files are created by a scanning process or by means of graphic programs such as computer-aided design or presentation art programs. The computer can reproduce an image of the document—exactly as it appeared when it was a paper document.

Until recently, electronic document files could contain only text. They did not contain graphics or other nontext elements, such as signatures, for example. Most of the documents were computer generated by word processors or word processing software on general-purpose computers. The technology available now makes true electronic document filing possible. Various facets of this technology are explained in other chapters.

OPTICAL DIGITAL
DATA DISK TECHNOLOGY

In addition to magnetic media and computer memories, which contain databases, text files, and document files, two developments have opened the doors for the first practical electronic document files. These developments are digital image processing

Figure 7-7 Optical disks come in a
variety of sizes.
3M Optical Recording

and optical-disk technologies. Digital image processing involves hardware that scans a document with a laser beam converting the document image to digitized code. The **optical digital data disk** (sometimes referred to as OD3) is the medium on which this code is recorded in a density far greater than magnetic media. (Density refers to the quantity of information recorded on a given amount of space.) An optical disk drive is used for recording digitized codes representing images on the disk. Small versions of these disks are called **CDROMs (compact disk read only memory)**; however, erasable optical disks now permit the optical disk drive to write new data over existing data as is the case with magnetic media.

These developments are significant because they make possible the preservation of graphic elements in documents, the maintenance of documents as evidence, and the reproduction of legally acceptable images of original documents. Many information systems do not provide for electronic document storage, because the code representing a document consumes huge quantities of storage capacity in traditional computer information processing systems. The optical disk permits extensive electronic document storage.

Understanding the significance of electronic files requires an understanding of the concept of a document. The following definition clarifies that concept:

> A **document** is a recording of graphic and/or textual information which, because of its evidentiary or reference value, is maintained in its original recording medium or is converted to another medium from which a legally acceptable reproduction of the original can be obtained.[3]

Digital image processing (also referred to as electronic image processing and picture processing) makes possible computer storage of images—graphic or textual data—by converting the images to code and storing and retrieving them without manually keying the information into the system. Laser and other scanning devices are used to scan the document and transmit digital information representing the image to optical disk drives.

The optical digital data disk (frequently shortened to optical disk) is a glass or plastic disk ranging from 5¼ to 14 inches in diameter. Information is recorded in the form of microscopic pits or holes burned into the surface of the disk by a laser beam. The pits or holes are one-sixtieth the diameter of a human hair. These recordings are permanent. They can be duplicated, but

---

3. Edward N. Johnson, "The Document as an Information Source," *Information Management* (May, 1983): 22.

the information cannot be removed. One 12-inch disk will hold up to 1.2 gigabytes (1,200,000,000 bytes) of information per side, representing up to 20,000 8½-by-11-inch documents. If both sides of the disk are used, this capacity is doubled. The information, recorded in digital code, can represent data, text, graphics, or scanned document images or photographs.

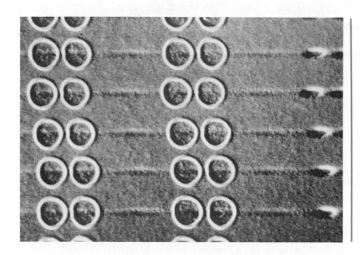

Figure 7-8   Information is stored on optical disks in digital code (here magnified by 10,000). *Optical Storage International*

Laser-pitted optical disk data storage systems were marketed as early as 1982, but early versions of the equipment experienced problems. Since erasing data was not possible, correcting errors required rerecording portions of the disk; this consumed disk capacity or required creating a new disk. Those problems have

Figure 7-9a   Optical disks are available in cartridges. *3M*

Figure 7-9b **The disk drive allows access to stored information.** *Amdek Corp.*

now been solved by systems that detect and immediately rewrite incorrectly recorded information.

Erasable disks are now available. They too are plastic disks, but they contain a layer of magnetic material. Data are recorded in code in a manner very similar to the write-once disks described above. The laser beam heats a tiny spot on the disk and changes the polarity of the magnetic field. A laser-powered beam reads the data. Data are erased when new material is overwritten.

Documents stored on optical disks are located, retrieved, and displayed on a screen in five seconds. Optical-disk equipment consumes about the same amount of space as or less than an ordinary office desk.

An optical-disk system involves four categories of hardware: a document entry station, an image management system, an integrated workstation, and a printing station. The document entry station contains the scanner and laser recorder (digital image processor), which are controlled by a small computer that is labeled a "server" in the model. Optical disks are housed in a device called a **jukebox** or **disk library**, which selects and plays the disk by inserting the disk in the disk drive for information access. An integrated office systems workstation or any video display terminal can retrieve images from the disks or direct the printing station to print a copy. (See Figure 7-10).

COMPUTER OUTPUT MICROFILM (COM)

As an information medium, filmed records may be more efficient than paper records—particularly the paper records generated by computers. Technology that permitted the information output from computers to be recorded in the form of microfilm instead

Figure 7-10   Model of an Optical-Disk Document-Management System

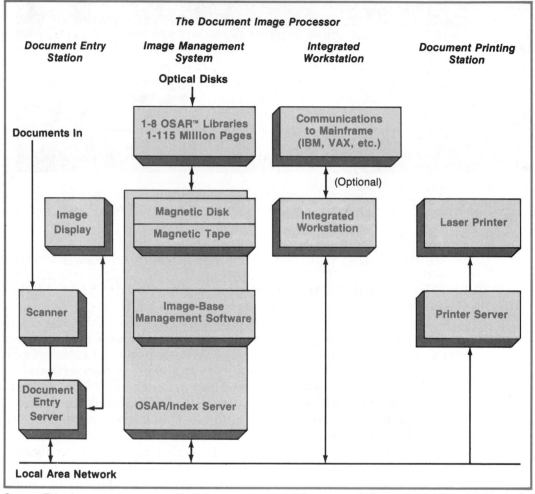

Source: This document image processor diagram was provided courtesy of FileNet Corporation. (FileNet and OSRA are trademarks of FileNet Corporation.)

of paper printout was developed in the early 1950s and labeled COM **(computer output microfilm)**. Early applications concentrated on graphic data output, particularly scientific and engineering documents.

In the 1960s, capabilities of this process were refined, and organizations began to consider the medium as a substitute for paper and magnetic output. The technology has been gradually improved and now is an integral part of many office automation and "paperless" systems. A variety of technical arrangements are available to produce COM, but the important thing for office automation is the fact that technology exists that is capable of producing filmed images that look like photographs of documents and computer printout. The continued use of this technology will depend upon its ability to compete with some of the new media for recording information, such as the optical disk.

COM offers distinct advantages over paper computer printout. When large volumes of paper printouts are produced and remain in the organization (not sent to customers or clients), COM offers a viable alternative. The space consumed by the film is about 5 percent of that consumed by paper. Retrieval of information from film can be faster and easier; computer-assisted retrieval can be employed; and inexpensive duplicates of microfiche (four to eight cents each) can be made available for employees to use at their workstations.

COM systems are available that will integrate graphically filmed images and computer-generated alphanumeric data. Both are recorded on the same image. The process is called **integrated source graphics (ISG)**. Data being input to a COM recorder for film production can be transmitted via telephone lines and special communications hardware. COM images are usually recorded on 105mm film rolls and sliced into microfiche-sized sheets.

COMPUTER-ASSISTED RETRIEVAL (CAR)

Computer-assisted retrieval (CAR) is a system for retrieving records—usually filmed records. The term computer-aided retrieval means the same thing. Used in a combination with COM and document filming systems, the organization's records can be housed on film outside expensive computer memory and without expensive, space-consuming systems for housing paper records.

By entering a code or index number, usually provided by the computer, the user may direct the computer to either locate and display the desired image or to identify its location. Less sophisticated systems require user handling of the film or the film container (cartridge or reel) at some point in the process. A single disk library may contain 200 or more disks capable of storing up to 65 million page images. Any image can be retrieved in about 15 seconds.

CAREER IMPLICATIONS FOR INFORMATION RESOURCES MANAGEMENT

MANAGEMENT CONTROLS

If information resources are to be used effectively and efficiently, someone must manage them. Unfortunately, management of information resources receives fragmented and sometimes conflicting attention.

Again, differences in interpretation of role and jurisdiction complicate the picture. Some organizations develop records management programs; others have no program at all. Some organizations have centralized systems for controlling the flow and maintenance of information; others leave the management of information to the unit that receives the information from an outside source or the unit that generates the information. Some organizations have formal programs for management of computerized information and separate formal programs for the management of paper or manually generated documents.

A formal assignment of responsibility for the organization's total information resources management is the most desirable arrangement. This responsibility may require the full-time attention of one individual or a whole staff. It may be a part-time responsibility for one person. The breadth of the responsibility is affected by the size and nature of the organization. Regardless, someone must give attention to the nature of information, its origin, its characteristics, and the procedures, systems, and equipment for its creation, maintenance, use, and disposition. Planning and control, two fundamental management functions, are necessary for effective information management. Otherwise, waste and ineffective systems prevail.

EMPLOYMENT OPPORTUNITIES

Records/Information management is an increasingly important area in the world of expanding information. For businesses, the expansion of information has resulted in increasing numbers of paper documents, magnetic media (tapes, disks), and microforms to be stored. The task of systematically storing all types of information is handled by the records management personnel. However, studies show that filing and records management rank in the top 10 percent of all office activities and that over 90 percent of all office workers do some filing.

The Association of Records Managers and Administrators, Inc. (ARMA) has published guidelines for a career path in the records and information management profession. Job descriptions range from records and information clerk to records and information manager. The typical career path in records management, from entry-level to more advanced positions include records clerk, records technician, records center supervisor, and records manager.

The various duties of each position include the following: A records clerk indexes, sorts, files, and retrieves records. A records clerk also locates and investigates information in files and classifies records. A records technician organizes, maintains, and transfers records in accordance with the standards and procedures established by management. A records center supervisor operates and maintains a records center; selects and supervises records center staff; and is responsible for the protection, storage, and disposition of vital records. Finally, the records manager develops and implements records management policies and practices. The manager is responsible for the design of the information center and the work flow of the center. The manager also selects personnel, designs and oversees training programs, and develops procedures manuals. In addition, the manager communicates and works with other company managers and directors.

Depending on the size of the organization other specialized positions are available in the area of records management. For example, in micrographics, jobs exist for clerks, technicians, and supervisors as well as for computer output microfilm operators. In forms management, jobs are available for clerks, analysts, and supervisors. Special positions may also be created in some organizations to handle the archiving and destruction of records.

WOHL'S BUSINESS PERSPECTIVE

Who should manage Information?

Most companies (and their employees, for that matter) agree that corporate information is a valuable corporate asset. Disagreement occurs quickly, however, when the organization then decides that valuable assets are best kept in the company safe!

The era of personal computing has allowed millions of business users the opportunity to be in charge of their own data—in effect, to be their own data processing manager. While they often fail at some of the job requirements (users are notorious for not backing up data, for instance), they nevertheless see the computer on their desk as a personal device and are loath to give up control of the data inside it.

Moreover, early experiments at storing data files in shared repositories (usually file servers on local area networks) have pointed to some woeful inadequacies in current systems implementations.

1. Users have to decide who is to have access to each file. Often they take the lazy man's way out and make all files public (with potentially devastating security consequences) or private (in which case they might as well not exist). Default values that make most files public might help here.
2. User-written labels (especially in the cramped IBM PC-DOS and OS/2 naming conventions) are hard to write and harder to remember. Another user would no doubt find labels on the shared file meaningless.

3. A business user often wants all the files on a particular subject, rather than all the files with a particular label. File retrieval software is becoming much more common, but it's still hard to use and rarely integrated with the rest of office functionality.

In the long run, new storage technologies and artificially intelligent storage and retrieval software will solve most of our information resources management problems. The problem of storing compound documents, with embedded graphics, for instance, goes away with such high density storage as optical disk. Getting users to willingly put up with security diminishes when we use built-in physical security such as reading fingerprints or retinal patterns rather than requiring the memorization and frequent changing of complex passwords and codes.

But some problems will, tantalizingly, remain much longer:

- As we get more and more information in the information resources, seeing only those things which are valuable becomes more and more important. We will need filters at both the individual and the organizational level to choose between the important and the trivial, the things which are actually for me and those I would choose to delegate, had I but time to read them.

- We need the ability to find things not by what we call files or the words we store in them, but rather what the words describe. This will require much more interesting software than the string retrieval software beginning to be used today. And it will require very clever indexing algorithms (computer rules) to be able to store complex indices without significantly and unacceptably increasing the storage overhead for indexed documents.

Eventually, we will get to the goal: I can get anything I need from wherever I am, without learning anything new about computer systems other than my own!

SUMMARY

Information resources (records/documents) of organizations exist in the form of paper, film, and electronic media. They are held for various time periods according to their value. Managerial decisions and controls affect the effectiveness and usefulness of information resources. These include the assignment of responsibility for managing resources, selection of media, and the design of systems for housing and retrieving records.

Paper resources remain important because more than 80 percent of business information exists on paper media. Even though many paper records are never accessed and few records are accessed after they are twelve months old, systems must provide for easy retrieval of those records which are needed. These systems include storage equipment, retention schedules, and the identification and protection of vital records.

Micrographic resources consume only a fraction of the space of paper records and offer opportunities for improving retrieval procedures. Micrographics technology is complex and involves either photographic or computer-imaging systems. Film images are produced in a variety of microforms: roll film, microfiche, aperture cards, jackets, and micro-opaques. Hardware includes cameras, film processors, readers, reader-printers, and film retrieval equipment. Recent developments include updatable microfiche, which permits adding or deleting film images without disturbing other images.

Technology now permits organizations to maintain electronic files. These resources are stored in computer memories or on electronic storage media: magnetic tapes, flexible disks, compact/hard disks, or optical disks. Some electronic files such as databases contain collections of categorized data; others contain digitized representations of document images, which can be reproduced by printers. Optical disk and CAR technologies have created new opportunities for document-based management systems.

KEY TERMS

record/information
information resources
information resource
   management (IRM)
administrative value
operational value
documentary value
legal value
archival value
medium
media conversion
information life cycle
records creation
information manipulation
records maintenance
records storage
vital records
records retention schedule
micrographics
roll film
microfiche
aperture card
micro-opaques

microfilm jacket
updatable microfilm
file integrity
micrographic disk
database
database management
   system (DBMS)
hierarchical database
relational database
hypertext
node
digital image processing
CDROM
optical digital data disk
document
jukebox
disk library
computer output microfilm
   (COM)
integrated source graphics
   (ISG)
computer-assisted retrieval
   (CAR)

REVIEW QUESTIONS

1. Consider the descriptions of information/records values in this chapter and identify one or two specific examples of records that would illustrate each of the values: administrative, operational, documentary, legal, and archival.

2. Describe the concept of a records medium, identify the three categories of media, and give examples for each category.

3. Referring to the chapter discussion of the manager who believed that his firm had no records, discuss his concept of "record." Contrast that concept with the concept of record discussed in this chapter.

4. Define and contrast the terms maintenance, storage, and disposition as they apply to paper-records systems.

5. Identify five microforms of records and briefly describe each of them.

6. What are the potential advantages of paper, film, and electronic records systems?

7. How can computer and micrographic technologies be combined in the design of information resource management systems?

CASE STUDY: THE CASE OF THE BULGING FILES

Brown Corporation owns a chain of more than one thousand retail stores that are located in twenty-six midwest and southeastern states. Merchandise is distributed to the company-owned outlets from three district warehouses, one of them in the town where the headquarters offices are located. Except for a few supervisory and clerical employees at the branch warehouses, all administrative activities are conducted in the headquarters office—purchasing, marketing, personnel, legal, real estate, accounting, finance, data processing, employee training, shipping and receiving, and transportation.

Most of the records generated by the firm can be attributed to two departments: data processing and accounting. The computer center, operated by the Data Processing Department, maintains very few on-line records. Most of the center's work is batch processed, generating magnetic tape and magnetic disk data that produce paper printout when necessary. Tapes and disk files are updated periodically.

Because of the nature of Brown Corporation's outlets (they are small and operated by a manager and two or three assistants), very few records are maintained on the store premises. Records are forwarded to headquarters daily or weekly. There are frequent communications between headquarters and outlet managers. Headquarters maintains a file in the accounting department for each retail outlet. These files contain all records for that outlet for the current fiscal year. As the firm grows, this collection of records grows. The collection contains a wide assortment of documents. Some are generated by DP; some come from vendors of merchandise; many of them involve outlet requisitions for merchandise, shipments of merchandise, and even cash register tapes. They provide the source of answers to questions asked by outlet managers who call checking on the status of shipments, credits, requisitions, and so on. Clerical staff members check the files while an outlet manager is on the phone. Many of the records circulate to many places within the firm before they find their way to these files. Information is sometimes added to documents in the outlet files.

The problem is volume. The four-drawer file cabinets are overflowing. Management must do something; more office space must be built or the records system must be changed.

QUESTIONS/ACTIVITIES

1. What alternatives are available to management? What additional information would you need to develop a solution to this problem?

2. How might office automation technologies relate to this firm's information-management needs? What special problems might each alternative that you have identified pose for the firm?

SUGGESTED READINGS

Bellamn, Pat and Beth Freedman. "Database Firms at Forefront of OS-2 Applications Development." *PC Week* (January 5, 1988): 1.

Canning, Bonnie. "Regulatory Requirements for Records." *Administrative Management* (February, 1988): 10.

Dykeman, John. "Optical Disk—A Technology on the Move." *Modern Office Technology* (June, 1988): 82–88.

Fiderio, Janet. "Hypertext: A Grand Vision." *Byte* (October, 1988): 237–244.

Fisher, Marsha J. "IBM, Customers Continue Work on Document Image Processor." *Datamation* (October 1, 1988): 23–24.

Folts, Harold C. "OSI's Coming of Age: From Concept to Products." *Computerworld* (May 4, 1988): 47–50.

Francis, Robert. "The Age of Friendly DBMSs Draws Closer for Micro Users." *Datamation* (January 15, 1988): 85–90.

Frisse, Mark. "From Text to Hypertext." *Byte* (October, 1988): 247–253.

Kalthoff, Robert J. "Document-Based Optical Mass Memories?" *Information Management* (September, 1985): 1.

Neubarth, Michael. "Erasable Optical Drives: An Infant Ready to Soar." *MIS Week* (October 10, 1988): 9.

Zehr, Leonard. "The Paper Palace: Technology Changes, But Paper Is Forever" in "Technology in the Workplace, A Special Report." *The Wall Street Journal* (September 16, 1985): 40.

CHAPTER 8

Telecommunications

Communications — means understanding

for understanding

analog transmission — continuous transmission
telephones use analog
computers use digital
fibre optic cables p223

OBJECTIVES

After studying this chapter, you should understand the following:

1. The difference between communication effectiveness and communication efficiency

2. The five telecommunications media categories

3. Alternative technical configurations for passing information electronically from one component of an information processing system to another

4. The description, basic technology, and alternative transmission media used for local area networks

5. Utilization of voice technology, including switching equipment, voice input/output, and voice mail

6. The field of electronic mail and its potential for voice, text, and image communication

7. Teleconferencing as a communication system

8. Data communication terminology and its function in the information processing system

9. The technology involved with fiber optics, cellular phone systems, the various telephone technologies, and speech synthesis

Communication is the most pressing concern of any organization. Research projects analyzing the needs of organizations and identifying their problems continue to discover that communication is a challenge for all types of organizations—small entrepreneurs, corporations, governments, and institutions. This challenge involves the organization's internal communication among its own units and employees and its external communication with customers, clients, suppliers, and the like.

Managers and planners share concern for two elements of communication: efficiency and effectiveness. Efficiency relates to the cost of communication; effectiveness relates to the quality of communication. Technology plays a monumental role in the delivery of both of these elements. Since neither efficiency nor effectiveness is an independent goal, communication strategists strive to help organizations best communicate (effectively) at the lowest reasonable cost (efficiently).

This chapter reviews the process of communication, introduces basic information about telecommunications technologies, describes several applications that are used to automate the office, and discusses the technology of fiber optics, cellular phones, and the trends in telecommunications.

THE COMMUNICATION PROCESS

The Latin root for the word communication is *communicare*. The common element in communication is understanding. Communication quality depends upon common understanding of what is communicated. When people communicate, they assign common meaning to a message. Technology that assists in the quality of understanding or the speed of transmission of a message improves communication.

COMMUNICATION EFFECTIVENESS

The quality of communication is a managerial concern. **Communication effectiveness** is a measure of quality, and anything that improves quality is a potential benefit for the organization. Technology may enhance effectiveness or it may impede effectiveness. If technology permits immediate feedback and the opportunity for communicators to question each other and probe for exact meaning, effectiveness is improved. If technology requires that people act upon incomplete information or messages that could easily be misinterpreted, effectiveness is destroyed.

As you encounter the various technologies discussed in this chapter, analyze them for their ability to contribute to communication effectiveness. Look for applications that would destroy effectiveness.

COMMUNICATION EFFICIENCY

All organizations must be aware of the economic implications of their activities. **Communication efficiency** deals with the cost of communication. This cost should be considered broadly as the expenditure of resources to accomplish communication. Since the people who work for organizations spend more time communicating than in any other activity, the efficiency of this activity is critical. Too frequently, managers think narrowly about the cost of communication. They consider the cost of a written message to be the cost of materials and postage, the cost of a telephone call to be the long-distance charge, and the cost of a technological enhancement to be the hardware and service costs. The most important cost ingredient in all of these examples is the cost of employee time.

Communication efficiency is measured by the expenditure of resources. Direct communication costs include employee time, equipment, and supplies. Indirect costs include items such as rent and electricity and can also be calculated in terms of the number of people reached by a message. For example, a duplicated memo to 1,000 employees is more efficient than a series of 50 small-group meetings of 20 employees each to communicate the same information—even if the meetings last only 15 minutes each. If the average wage of the employees is $10 an hour, the cost of lost productivity is $2,500 for all of these employees.

MANAGEMENT CONCERNS

All managers are concerned about the proper blend between effectiveness and efficiency, particularly in decisions involving technology. How much can a firm afford to spend for a system that will improve communication effectiveness? Is it possible that spending the smallest amount will result in diminished effectiveness? What blend of technologies (computers, telephone systems, connections to remote databases, and devices for transmitting text and television pictures) will best enable an organization to compete in the marketplace?

TELECOMMUNICATIONS TECHNOLOGY

The word **telecommunications** has had various meanings among communication and information processing professionals and in professional literature. Literally, the word means "far communication." Nineteenth-century efforts developed wire telegraph and telephone systems; and, until the 1960s, the term was applied mostly to telephone transmission of voice communication. The use of telephone lines and related paraphernalia to transmit computer-generated electronic information was termed data communication. Later this process was labeled telecommunication. Eventually, five separate and distinct categories of information transmission technologies emerged, each considered a part of the telecommunications family. These categories are voice, image, data, video, and text.

Because the telephone industry has been considered a public utility and controlled as such, early development of component technologies was very slow. There is less incentive for research and development in a controlled environment. However, several legal actions have significantly deregulated the industry and created numerous changes. Figure 8-1 briefly summarizes these changes.

Figure 8-1   **Legal Acts Affecting Telecommunication**

Date	Event	Impact
1954	890 Decision	Organizations could install their own facilities for telephone communication
1968	Carterfone Case	Allowed two-way radio use on telephone networks and (after several years of appeals) the use of telephone equipment manufactured by firms other than AT&T
1969	MCI Case	Microwave Communication, Inc., was permitted to enter the long-distance telephone market using a microwave transmission system, and eventually other firms were permitted to enter the long-distance telephone market
1982	AT&T Antitrust Case	AT&T agreed to sell its operating companies, much of the industry was deregulated, and hundreds of firms entered the various facets of the telecommunication industry

INFORMATION CATEGORIES

The following discussion describes the five categories of telecommunications technology along the lines of traditional distinctions.

Voice. Voice communication transmission evolved around analog (continuous) transmission technology because voice is by nature analogy, and at the time telephone and radio were invented the technology did not exist that enabled an analog signal to be broken into enough discrete pieces to be digitized. Voice technology has concentrated not only on the transmission of voice communication but also on automated switching equipment (direct distance dialing), internal control of telephone traffic (switchboard systems), and equipment enhancements (Touch Tone). Much of today's communication is digital.

Data. Data communication involves the movement of data from one component of information processing equipment to another. For short distances, this is accomplished by direct connections through cables or networks; telephone transmission has been the traditional medium for greater distances. Data communication has concentrated on the transmission of quantitative data.

Data communication is more efficient when digital transmission (on-off) is used. Because digital transmission is sent in spurts, several transmissions can use lines simultaneously. In order to use telephone lines for data transmission in the most efficient manner, signals are converted from digital to analog transmission and back to digital for applications at the receiving end.

Image. Various forms of image communication have been in use since facsimile services were introduced in 1935. Facsimile (FAX) facilitates the electronic transmission and reproduction of images. Image transmission involves the communication of text, drawings, charts, photographs, or any graphic paper element. A scanning device at the sending station transmits the image a line at a time. When the image is reproduced in a like manner at the receiving end, a duplicate of the original image is produced. Most facsimile transmission systems have used analog transmission in the past, but some systems now use digital transmission, which is faster and can scan an entire document rather than reading it line by line.

Text. The output of word processing systems is transmitted in much the same manner as data processing output. However, because the technologies were developed and managed separately, transmission among component parts of word processors (CPU to terminals, for example) and from one location to another was also handled separately in past systems. Applications involve communication from central processors to remote printers or screen displays.

Video. Video transmission has been a combination of video (television) and audio signals. This technology can now be combined with others to provide complex teleconferencing systems. It can also substitute for facsimile in image transmission of graphic data.

Figure 8-2 This office environment
is shaped by a variety of communication processes with corresponding
equipment.
NCR Corporation

DATA COMMUNICATION SYSTEMS

Although the technical differences between data communication
and voice communication are narrowing, the systems for moving
quantitative, digital information from one location to another
are still a distinct technology for most organizations. Data communication refers to the transmission of electronically encoded
information over distance using some type of telecommunication
link. Any information processing system may generate digital information in order to transmit it to another system's components.

The concept of distributed information processing has gradually replaced the idea that all electronically processed information must be processed in a single physical location. Minicomputers, to some extent, began the transition. Microcomputers
accomplished it. However, distributed standalone, mini- and

micro-computers have many disadvantages if they cannot communicate with other hardware within an organization. The same is true of any information processing component. Files generated on one system may not be accepted by another system. Software must be purchased for each individual system—an expensive procedure. Peripheral equipment must be duplicated at each hardware installation. However, telecommunications technologies along with uniform standards will eventually eliminate most of these problems.

In the future, data communication will become as critically important to most organizations as voice communication has been in the past. External communication with suppliers, customers, clients, and governments now depends upon data communication links for communication effectiveness and efficiency. Data communication creates the opportunity for significant changes in the way work is accomplished. Firms need not be hampered by physical distance among their branch facilities. The necessity for separate organizational units for physically separated facilities may be lessened. The concept of the "electronic cottage" (using computers and telephone lines for employees to work at computer terminals at home) may increase in popularity. This practice was brought to public attention by the books *The Third Wave* and *Megatrends*. Work-at-home ("telecommuting") staggered work schedules, and flextime are made possible by telecommunication developments. The human and social issues raised by these developments are discussed, along with the technologies with which they are associated, in later chapters.

DATA TRANSMISSION TERMINOLOGY

Data communication technology involves numerous complex devices that enable information processing systems to communicate information among various components. The following discussion and Figure 8-3 present some of the basic terminology. Understanding these terms is basic to developing an understanding of most telecommunication applications. The terms that are defined in Figure 8-3 apply not only to data communication but also to all telecommunication technology.

Figure 8-3 **Data Transmission Terminology**

Interface: A system of devices, protocols, and (in some cases) software that accomplishes the communication of electronic information among hardware components. This may involve distances ranging from a few

Figure 8-3 **Data Transmission Terminology** (continued)

feet to thousands of miles and have connections that can be categorized by the connecting device or the protocol.

Interface Device: A physical link over which electronic signals representing information travel or any hardware component necessary to convert signals to make them compatible with the communication link and/or the hardware to which information is communicated.

Communication Link: The pathway or route over which signals travel from one hardware system or component to another; may be a hard (physical) link, an air-wave link, an optical (light-beam) link, or any combination of these.

Twisted Pair Wire: A physical, two-wire communication link used for ordinary voice telephone systems and other telecommunication links.

Coaxial Cable: A physical link made from shielded cable with a center wire and a surrounding braided wire sleeve.

Fiber-Optic Cable: A physical link made from tiny strands of glass over which laser beams carry information signals. There are usually multiple strands in one cable.

Microwave Transmission: An air-wave communication link that transmits signals over relatively short distances in a straight line.

Radio-Wave Transmission: An air-wave communication link that uses radio frequencies identified by the Federal Communication Commission over which business information may be transmitted.

Infrared-Beam Transmission: An optical communication link involving transmission of signals on infrared light beams.

Laser-Beam Transmission: An optical communication link that transmits signals on laser beams for short distances.

Dedicated Line: Telephone lines or other communication links permanently assigned to a specific communication task. They are either owned by the user or leased from long-distance telephone companies.

Broadband: A communication link that can be divided into channels for transmitting simultaneous multiple signals (as in cable television).

Figure 8-3 **Data Transmission Terminology** *(continued)*

Baseband: A communication link that uses the whole link for one transmission at a time (as opposed to broadband, which transmits multiple signals simultaneously); may transmit multiple signals alternately.

Protocol: Sets of conventions (customs or guidelines) governing the format of electronic data, the nature of transmission paths, and the speed of data transmission.

Transmission Mode: The nature of the signals representing characters and the indicators that tell receiving equipment where the signals for each character begin and end.

Asynchronous Mode: Transmission mode that communicates each character, one at a time, and separated by a start signal and a stop signal (start signal-character code-stop signal).

Synchronous Mode: Transmission mode that communicates groups of characters a block at a time with control characters before and after each group; requires clock-synchronized sending and receiving equipment.

Transmission Paths: The direction of the flow and the possibility of simultaneous flow in two directions on the communication link.

Simplex: Transmission path carrying information in one direction only.

Duplex: Transmission path that carries two-way information flow.

Full Duplex: Transmission path that permits simultaneous two-way flow (both directions at the same time).

Half Duplex: Transmission path that permits two-way flow but in only one direction at a time.

Baud Rate: Measure of data transmission speed; bits of information per second.

High-Speed Transmission: A category of transmission speeds 4800 baud or faster (4800 or 9600 baud; 9600 baud = about 960 characters a second).

Low-Speed Transmission: A category of transmission speeds 1200 baud or less (1200 or 300 baud).

In order for electronic information to be transmitted accurately, the various devices that carry or transmit information must be compatible or the system must employ devices that make them compatible. **Interfaces** are (1) the physical devices that connect components and transmit information and (2) the protocols under which these devices operate. Figure 8-4 outlines the relationships among various telecommunications devices and protocols. The devices represent the actual media (communication links) over which information travels and the numerous components that may be used to convert or translate signals during transmission. Protocols are sets of conventions (standardized guidelines) governing the format, electrical conditions, and transmission speeds of electronic information. Some protocols come into existence when a popular manufacturer adopts a set of standards for its own systems, but many protocols are defined by the International Standards Organization (ISO). The ISO's X.25 protocol has become an international standard. It describes electrical, procedural, and equipment characteristics necessary for direct communication. If component equipment does not operate on the same protocol, a translator device, a modem, (sometimes called a black box) is necessary.

DIRECT COMMUNICATION

The earliest method for connecting computers to remote facilities (input devices, output devices, and other computers) was some type of permanent, direct connection. Cables serve this purpose for short distances, and switched or leased telephone lines connect computing facilities at greater distances. The most popular

Figure 8-4a   **Data Communication Interfaces**

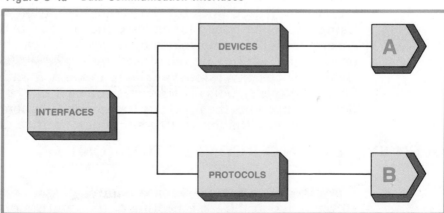

Figure 8-4b **Data Communication Interfaces** *(continued)*

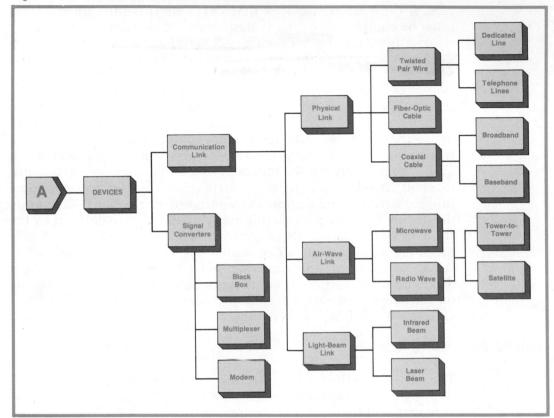

applications in early data communications were the connections between mainframe computers and remote terminals or printers. Although terminals are relatively inexpensive, both cable installations and leased lines for data communication are expensive. Using telephone lines may involve the conversion of computer-generated digital pulses to analog waves which can be transmitted over copper wire cable telephone lines. The device that is still used for such conversions is called a **modem**. A **multiplexer** combines multiple signals for transmission over one communication link. This prevents the necessity for paying telephone line charges for each device that needs to communicate with a distant device.

OPEN SYSTEMS INTERCONNECTION (OSI)

When **Open Systems Interconnection (OSI)** was created just over 10 years ago at the first meeting of the International Standards Organization (ISO) Subcommittee for OSI, a new direction in

Figure 8-4c **Data Communication Interfaces** (continued)

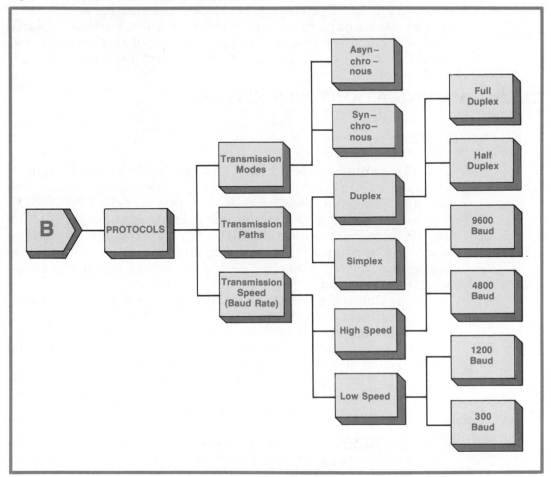

establishing standards for information technology applications was developed. The goal of OSI was to allow the free interchange of information among networked computer resources that could be assembled from a multivendor marketplace. The ISO coordinated its efforts in establishing OSI with the International Telephone and Telegraph Consultative Committee to ensure that telecommunications interests were appropriately considered. IBM Corporation and Digital Equipment Corporation have been actively involved in the development of OSI.

The purpose of OSI is to provide protocols for different vendors'/manufacturers' products to connect with each other, thus allowing an open system interconnection of user applications. The work has proceeded, and several layers of the model have now been defined. The seven layers of the OSI model include physical, data link, network, transport, session, presentation, and application. Each layer's services are defined concisely with specifications of its functions to the peer layer. Further explanation of the OSI layers are beyond the scope of this text but may be obtained in other advanced texts on data communications.

TELECOMMUNICATIONS APPLICATIONS

ELECTRONIC MAIL

The office automation industry has accepted electronic mail as the generic term for a whole class of electronic text transmission systems. **Electronic mail (EMail)** is a system for electronically forwarding written messages and displaying them on a video display screen or storing them in the receiver's "mailbox." Messages may be printed at the receiving end, usually at the discretion of the receiver. They may be stored for future recall or deleted after they are read.

Subsystems of electronic mail include the communication of teletypewriter communication, word processor output, computer-based message system output, and computer conferencing messages. Communication distances range from intraorganizational transmission of messages via direct cable or local area networks to long-distance communication through telephone systems, satellite transmissions, and leased telephone lines (the user pays a fee for full-time use of a long-distance telephone line).

Teletypewriters.   The oldest forms of electronic mail are the teletypewriter networks such as TWX™ and Telex™ which feature typewriter-like terminals. Messages are typed on a sending unit, transmitted over telephone lines, and printed by the receiving station's terminal. Responses can be transmitted immediately. A vast network and thousands of terminals are in operation. The major disadvantage of this system is the slow transmission speed.

Communicating Word Processors.   Most dedicated word processors that are still in existence offer electronic mail options that work for limited applications. As long as communication takes place within the organization and software and hardware are compatible, communication is usually possible. Transmitting documents between processors made by different vendors can be difficult. Software and network technology improvements have eased this problem somewhat by offering devices that will convert the coded data produced by one system into formats and codes that are compatible with other hardware. Careful planning and network design can create internal and external links for electronic mail generated by word processors.

Computer-Based Message Systems.   Practically any computer terminal can be a vehicle for electronic mail if the right software is accessible to that terminal. Terminals that have access to networks can be used for sending electronic mail to any facility on the network. Some of the available software simply provides the possibility for one user to put a message on the screen of another user. Others allow storage of messages in electronic mailboxes.

The software-hardware-network combination, which creates sophisticated electronic mail systems (for example, message storage, signals to senders that messages were received, and signals to receivers that messages are waiting), is called a **computer-based message system (CBMS)** or simply **electronic message system (EMS)**. Terminals, intelligent workstations, and personal computers are the vehicles for sending messages. EMS offers more than a simple screen-to-screen message system. Users call up electronic mailboxes through their terminals, workstations, or personal computers. Incoming messages are scanned and filed, erased, or printed. Responses require a simple word processing operation that creates and sends a message. System arrangements determine whether documents arrive as hard copy or electronic (screen) messages.

Internal direct cabling systems, local area networks, private networks, and public access networks can all be used for electronic mail. Even home computers can become electronic mailboxes with the aid of a modem and a connection to a public network through phone lines. These devices can communicate with any other system that has similar devices.

Computer Conferencing.   Computer Conferencing makes use of a central computer (mainframe, mini, or powerful micro) to allow multiple users to interact with each other. This new application is very much like electronic mail except that it simultaneously displays comments from all participants in the conference. Like electronic mail, this new kind of communicating is not like normal written communication because it is interactive. Unlike oral communication, it allows more time for formulating reactions. Computer conferences can continue over several months, which gives all participants time for reflective thinking and allows for a thorough analysis of the issues.

This new application is not widely used and may take some time to catch on. Computer conferencing is a relatively impersonal form of communication and therefore is useful in contexts that do not require the subtleties of voice cues (rate, pitch, volume, and tensity) and nonverbal cues to enhance the meaning in face-to-face or voice interactions.

IMAGE AND DATA COMMUNICATION SYSTEMS

Facsimile. A system for image transmission, facsimile systems communicate drawings, longhand, illustrations, and copies of any printed page. Equipment transmits images of pages by scanning the page and encoding the image. Equipment on the receiving end converts the encoded image to a copy of the original document that looks much like one from a copy machine. Early analog transmission speeds range from less than a half minute to three minutes per page; however, the transfer to digital transmission is improving this rate allowing transmission speeds of a few seconds.

Until recently, **FAX** transmissions used analog systems and public dial-up telephone networks for the transmission. Digital transmitters, now referred to as electronic facsimile, and better communication links have speeded the transmission and lowered the cost for many systems. Facsimile is the fastest and least expensive method of communicating exact duplicates of paper

Figure 8-5 FAX machines can be programmed to transmit documents at specific times.
AT&T

images at low volumes. Other technologies can communicate documents more rapidly than facsimile, but they involve expensive installations requiring high volume for cost justification.

Facsimile equipment offers a number of features that facilitate its use. The store-and-forward feature allows the user to send documents over telephone lines at times when rates are cheaper than usual. The operator reads a stack of documents into the machine's memory and tells the machine when the documents should be sent and to what destinations. The equipment automatically transmits the documents according to the schedule without any further operator intervention. New developments in FAX involve the use of boards inserted into a pc, or even a network to receive and transmit.

VIDEOTEX

Videotex systems combine text, low-resolution graphics, and data applications in a hybrid system that enables users to interact with each other and various databases through minicomputer-based systems. For example the Buick Motor Division of General Motors has a videotex system called the Electronic Production Information Center (EPIC), which allows salespersons to directly access information about the optional equipment for a given model, the monthly payments for a given loan amount, and check the status of a car that has been ordered. When the system is not being used interactively, it displays a series of advertisements for the company's products. Videotex is actually a system for remote access to databases containing information that is textual and, sometimes, graphic.

ELECTRONIC BANKING

Electronic Banking is the general idea of carrying on bank transactions without direct interaction with tellers. The automated teller machines are the most common form of the new electronic banking data service. CitiCorp introduced in 1988 an automated teller machine that utilizes "touch screen" technology. Customers make selections by touching the desired function on the screen rather than pushing various buttons.

A new electronic banking service currently being offered by several large banks allows customers with personal computers and modems to perform most of their banking functions from home. The goal of the banks offering these services is to automate most of the traditional bank teller functions that are labor intensive. This service also provides customers with more convenience by allowing them to do their banking at home.

TELECOMMUNICATIONS NETWORKS

The integrated office information systems concept requires that hardware components in all phases of information processing technology be able to communicate with other hardware components. Data communication technology is the key to integrated systems. Without communication capability, systems are not integrated; the components are independent. A technology that has struggled through rapid growth along with the entire information management field is the data communication network. The **network** is a device for connecting physically separated information handling devices (see Figure 8-6) by some data transmission link similar to the way telephone lines have connected telephone systems for years. The communication link among information processing facilities within a building or a building complex (technically, confined to the premises of the owner) comprise a **local area network**. Geographically dispersed facilities may be connected by similar networks called wide area networks, remote networks, or long-distance networks. Networks that combine the transmission of text, voice, video, and images are now possible.

LOCAL AREA NETWORKS

Local area networks are internal communication tools. The users electronically exchange messages and files of information and share some hardware such as printers and other devices. They may provide gateways to external public or private communications networks; and they can contribute to communication efficiency because they may offer a less expensive route to information communication than alternative routes.

Local area networks (LANs) are highly technical systems that offer numerous alternative solutions and technical decisions that complicate the choice of a system. This discussion will be confined to the potential benefits of LANs and a brief introduction to the technology that would influence decisions about hardware and software. Popular LANs include several versions of Ethernet: EtherLink™ (3COM), AST-Ethernet™ (AST Research), and DECnet™ (Digital Equipment Corporation); Netware™ (Novell Corporation); ARC (Datapoint); Starlan™ (AT&T), PC Network™ (IBM); Token Ring (IBM); Office Works™ (NBI); Net/One™ (Ungermann-Bass), and 3+ (Novell Corporation). The large number of systems available and the technical variations among them complicate decisions.

Benefits.   Although the benefits of networks might be associated with any communication network, they are most frequently asso-

Figure 8-6   Information-Processing and Communicating Devices Which May Be Linked to Data Networks

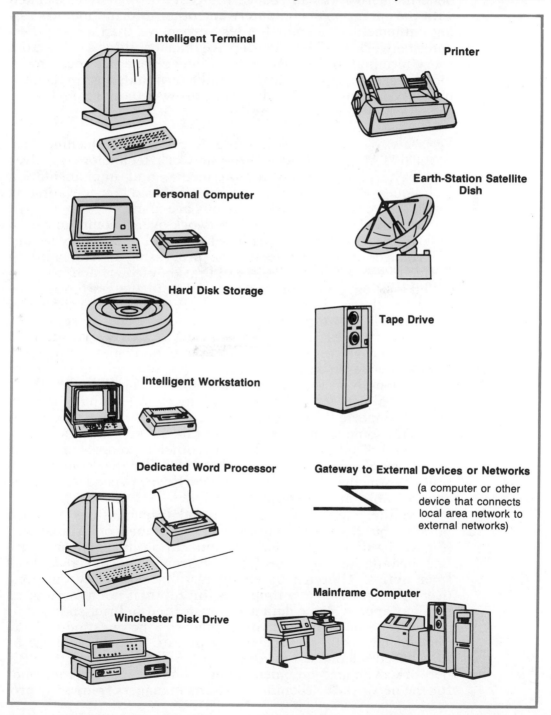

ciated with local area networks. Aside from their communication benefits, networks can reduce the costs ordinarily associated with the operation of computers and other information processing equipment. A terminal is less expensive than a computer, and a network may be less expensive than installing a cable from every terminal to the host device. Some companies spend more money rearranging terminals than the terminals cost in the first place. With a network, facilities can grow without removing old systems and starting over again.

Technology.   Without getting too deeply into the technical aspects of LANs, basic local area network technology involves topology, physical transmission media, and implementation techniques. Other technical aspects also need consideration by firms before final network decisions are made.

Information travels along a network over a communication link. Intersections along this link are called nodes; they permit the connection of an information processing or transmitting device to the network. The configuration of lines and nodes is called **topology.** As in other applications of the word, topology describes the geography of the network and the area served by the network. **Star** topologies require that all nodes be connected to all other nodes (it looks likes a star) and communicate with each other via a central controller; **ring** topologies arrange the links and nodes in an unbroken circle; and **bus** topologies feature a single length of cable, along which nodes are installed, without any central controller. The ends of the cable in a bus topology are not connected. Figure 8-7 summarizes these three topologies, identifies some of their vendors, and lists their features, advantages, and disadvantages. There are other topologies and other variations of each of these. The three most popular communication links (media) for local area networks are twisted wire pairs, coaxial cable, and fiber-optic cable.

Satellite, microwave, and infrared transmissions are also possible; but these are not used by great numbers of installations. (Figure 8-4 defines possible communication links.) Most future LAN installations are expected to be broadband coaxial cable or fiber optics. Although baseband installations allow only one user's transmission at a time, this limitation is not as serious as it might appear, since data are transmitted in brief spurts.

An issue involving networks concerns the question of independent networks versus existing private branch exchange or PBX-based telephone networks. With a star topology, the PBX network switching equipment is sometimes used as the controller for the network. Telecommunications managers frequently pro-

Figure 8-7 Local Area Network Topologies

Configuration	STAR	RING	BUS
Vendors	AT&T Northern Telecom Rolm InteCom	A. B. Dick Prime Computer Ztel	3 COM Corvus DEC Xerox
Features	Uses central control unit All data passes control unit Popular with private branch exchange (PBX) and WP networks	Uses "token" signal for access Continuous ring cable	Collision detection No control unit
Advantages	Handles greatest number of nodes Works well with MultiLANS	One-way flow of data Can use fiber-optics Repeaters permit data flow of greater distances	Inexpensive Reliable record Problem at one node does not affect others
Disadvantages	Expense of controller Controller failure stops network	Break in channel stops flow Installation of modes requires shutdown	Limited distance (3,000 ft.) Does not use fiber optics

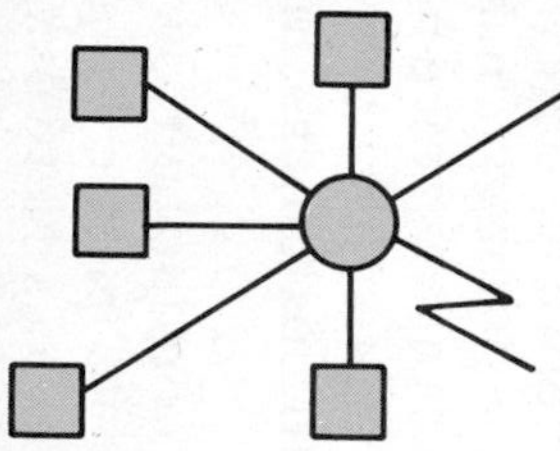

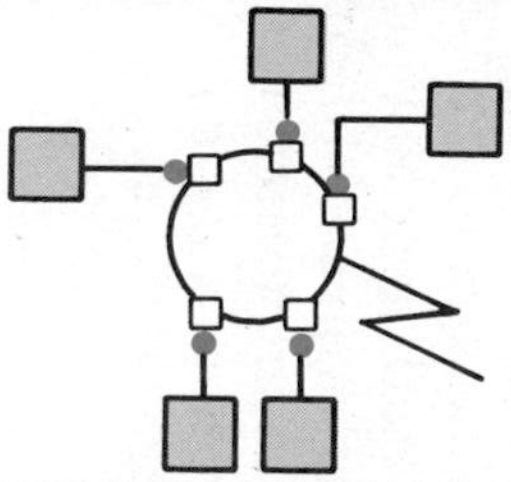

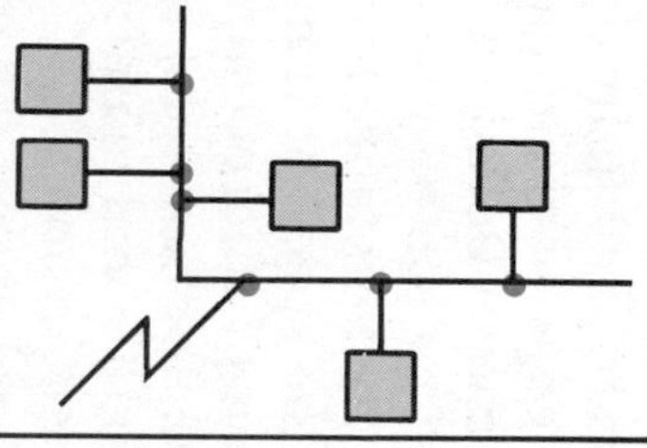

□ —Repeater (a device to "push" the data along the network)

▨ —Information-processing device

○ —Network controller

⨅ —Gateway to external network or device

• —Node

pose the **PBX** as the hub of office automation and technology integration; an opposing view still sees the organization's mainframe computer as the potential hub of all activity, including data communication.

Choices of communication methods for any individual organization must be made with full knowledge of the organization's needs and knowledge of the alternatives. Decisions about an individual installation will be affected by the number of anticipated devices to be connected, the required distance for the transmission medium (wire or cable), and the speed of transmission. Developments such as the introduction of microcomputers, advancements in operating systems (OS/2, for example), and acceptance of the LAN as a substitute for traditional mainframe communication will continue to affect the decision.

The major impact of network technology on the integration of office information systems has probably not been seen yet. Even though ". . . only 11.6 percent of all PCs in use were networked in 1987, 58 percent will be connected to LANs by 1992, according to the market's current growth rate."[1] With proper planning and careful spending, LANs offer great potential. Even though they are expensive, they should contribute to an environment that will eventually reduce administrative costs through greater efficiencies.

LONG-DISTANCE NETWORKS

Networks are available for external (even global) data communication through public networks and several varieties of private networks. Wide area networks (also called long-haul networks) were developed long before local area networks, but their numbers have remained relatively low because of the expense involved in their development. The most popular long-distance network is the private SNA (Systems Network Architecture) network sold and installed by IBM for connection to customers' mainframe computer installations.

Organizations that cannot afford to build their own private long-distance networks may subscribe to public long-distance carriers such as AT&T Information Services Network, Telenet, Tymnet, Uninet, Cylix, MarkNet, or IBM Information Network. These offer time-sharing plans for using value added networks (VANs). The "added" services include high-speed transmission,

1.   Christine Strehlo. "The Promised Lan," *Personal Computing* (January, 1989): 94.

access to public databases, electronic mail, links to syndicated databases, and linking firms' geographically scattered branches. Airlines use them to connect thousands of travel agencies to their reservation services.

The voice/data integrated **PBX** may be used to connect to a long-distance network. Whether public or private, the long-distance network offers the same capabilities as the local network. The geographical area of coverage and the possibility of communication with other firms and organizations, in addition to one's own geographically dispersed facilities, are the major differences.

NETWORK APPLICATIONS

Office automation technologies that are available to one user on a standalone system can be available to many users if their computing or other information processing systems are connected by a network. Electronically stored information can be accessible to any user on the network. On the other hand, most networks have controlled access to prevent unauthorized access to confidential information. Software stored in one central-processing unit of the network can be made available to any user on the network.

Popular applications for networks have been database access, mainframe computer access, and electronic mail. Networks can also be used for word processing because they provide access to the software and they communicate messages or documents from a personal computer, standalone word processor, or terminal to printers or to other users along the network. Other applications include electronic messaging and administrative support (calendaring, schedule management, and other supports discussed in Chapter 9). More recently, LANs have provided access to external networks. Communicating from individual workstations to public databases, external organizations, and facilities along wide area networks is now possible. Before microcomputers were introduced, the only firms using networks were those that had large numbers of users (airlines, for example) that were sufficient to justify the cost of using computer equipment that controls the networks. Microcomputers and standardized software to control the communication function (enabling the linking of various manufacturers' equipment) have lowered the cost of networks and made them more practical for small organizations. These factors have especially influenced the installation of local area networks.

INTEGRATED SERVICES DIGITAL NETWORK (ISDN)

The **integrated services digital network (ISDN)** is an emerging set of data communications standards that integrates nearly all forms of electronic communications, including voice, data, video, graphics, and facsimile, by enabling them to travel over the same lines. One of ISDN's major goals is to replace analog components with digital ones and to convert voice into digital signals at the customer's telephone, rather than at switching centers.

The ISDN consists of a series of recommended standards, published by The Comite Consultaif Internationale de Telegraphique et Telephonique (CCITT), that defines an end-to-end digital network, offering a wide range of user services with a limited set of user-network interfaces. CCITT is a standards body under the International Telecommunications Union, an agency of the United Nations. The CCITT is the primary organization for developing standards on telephone and data communications systems among participating governments. It is an influential body responsible for the development of standards. United States membership on CCITT comes from the State Department.

One might reasonably ask, "Why should I have one network for everything?" The answer is simple: to reduce duplication, complexities of interfaces, and (eventually) costs. Many organizations use six to ten separate networks to handle their data communications requirements (telephone switched, telephone nonswitched, telex, teletex, telegraph, public packet systems, private packet systems, etc.) The intent of ISDN is to use one technology to service all these heretofore disparate systems. Further discussion of ISDN's structure and functions will be left to high-level texts or in-depth study of data communications.

VOICE COMMUNICATION SYSTEMS

Much has already been said about voice communication in the discussion of data communication systems. Although telephone systems are considered to be an established technology, recent developments in this field offer potentially far-reaching changes. The divestiture of the Bell System brought both opportunity and confusion for those who must manage voice communication systems for their organizations. The eventual outcome will probably be positive, however, because greater competition for telecommunication business will speed development of technology.

TELEPHONY

Telecommunication decisions, even for the smallest firm, now involve the selection of hardware vendors and the selection of a long-distance telephone carrier. For larger firms, this responsibility requires the selection of private branch exchange (**PBX**) switching equipment (apparatus to connect telephones to dialed numbers and route incoming calls) and the already-discussed decisions regarding data communication.

Dozens of companies now manufacture telephones that offer a variety of features. The trend toward purchasing telephone equipment (as opposed to leasing), which began with the deregulation that made such purchases possible, increased after the divestiture of the Bell System. Some firms still prefer to lease equipment because they can easily exchange it for upgraded versions when they become available.

AT&T, MCI, GTE Sprint, Western Union, ITT, SBS Skyline, Alinet, and numerous small firms now offer long-distance network services. Some of them own their own networks; others lease the networks from larger firms and resell the service to

Figure 8-8 PBX switching equipment is used by larger firms to connect telephones to dialed numbers.
AT&T

customers. Selection of a carrier may depend upon the type of service desired—direct dial, leased lines, WATS (wide area telecommunication service) lines, credit-card calling, and sufficient lines to support multiple simultaneous telephone calls into the business—all are possible services. The cost of these services will be affected by the number of calls, the distance involved, the time of day, and the number of people needing to make calls at one time.

Five or six vendors, in addition to AT&T, are now in the private branch exchange business. For large organizations, a **PBX**, or some variation of that configuration, is more economical than the alternative—a line for each telephone to the telephone company's central exchange. Figure 8-9 further describes typical levels of switching systems.

If telephone switching systems become the "hub of the office information system" as communication managers predict, the telephone system will take on new significance and will require greater coordination with other communication systems.

VOICE INPUT/OUTPUT TECHNOLOGY

Many office automation specialists now consider voice input/output technologies to be crucial to future productivity gains. Existing technologies permit voice commands to equipment,

Figure 8-9   Levels of Switching Systems

Private Branch Exchange (PBX): An automatic switching system accepting and transmitting analog signals. For data communication applications, analog signals are converted to digital signals. Originally, the term referred to a switchboard through which an operator manually connected callers to various lines.

Computerized Branch Exchange (CBX): Signals are converted to digital for switching and back to analog for transmission. Computerized switching completes calls faster.

Digital Branch Exchange (DBX): Sometimes labeled "Digital PBX," a CODEC (COder/DECoder) chip is installed in the telephone. The chip converts voice signals to digital signals, which are switched and routed by a computer and reversed to analog signals by another CODEC chip before being transmitted to receivers. These conversions are, for all practical purposes, simultaneous. There is no detectable lapse in transmission time. The technology is used in voice mail applications, which are discussed later.

voice responses to information queries, storage and management of oral messages and other information, and security clearance using equipment that can recognize voice patterns. Although automatic transcription machines that transcribe ordinary voice dictation have been granted patents by the U.S. Patent Office, this technology is yet to be perfected. However, it is available in rudimentary forms today.

A few basic definitions of voice technology are necessary for understanding the status of the technology and probable future developments. Figure 8-10 defines some of the terms that identify voice input and output developments.

Current voice technology systems do not depend upon recorded sounds on audio recording tape. Instead, the human voice is converted to digital signals resembling the signals that store alphabetic characters and numbers keyed into a computer or other

Figure 8-10 Voice Technology Vocabulary

Speaker-dependent Recognition (SDR): Voice input system that allows identified users to record a vocabulary of words that the system will later recognize and respond to. Words must be prerecorded and stored in the system. Input must be pronounced clearly and slowly.

Continuous Speaker-dependent Recognition (CSDR): Voice input system that allows the speaker to use a continuous stream of words in a normal conversational pattern with no special or awkward pronunciations or pauses. System will respond to prerecorded vocabulary, which appears in the "stream."

Speaker-independent Recognition (SIR): Voice input system using equipment that recognizes words within limited vocabulary without the necessity for equipment "training" (prerecording vocabulary).

Speaker Verification: Voice input system that matches speakers' unique voice patterns to stored patterns for security purposes; no-match prevents entry to system.

Voice Response: Audible voice output from a system which, in a digitized format, has accepted and stored the human voice. Output carries inflection and intonation of the original voice input (recreation sounds like the person who recorded it).

Voice Store and Forward: Input/Output "voice-mail" systems that digitize and store oral messages, dial receiver(s), deliver messages, record and store responses, or "flag" failed attempts to deliver.

Figure 8-10   **Voice Technology Vocabulary** *(continued)*

Voice Key Software: Software to sequence computer command key-strokes and associate them with spoken vocabulary. With the aid of this software, user gives oral commands instead of keyboard commands.

Voice Processing Unit: The computer that controls voice input, storage, and output through controls provided by voice management software.

Digital Speech Compression: When voice input is stored as digitized signals, extraneous components (pause, ahs, uhhs) are eliminated; compression requires less storage capacity.

information processing device. The digitized signals are stored electronically in whatever manner the organization's other information is stored (such as hard disks). The equipment configurations necessary for accepting voice data and converting it for storage constitute the voice input component of the system.

A voice processing unit controls the storage and manipulation of the information. Voice output components convert the information to audible signals and play them when output is needed.

Status.   Voice technology has moved from a state that required an extremely limited vocabulary and slow, deliberate enunciation of words (speaker-dependent recognition or SDR) to systems that will recognize words (still within limited vocabularies) uttered in normal conversational speeds and tones. This technology is referred to as continuous speaker-dependent recognition (CSDR). Speaker dependent means that only those individuals whose spoken words are recorded into the system (using the system's limited vocabulary) are recognized by and able to interact with the system. This process is called training the system. It requires that each person who will use the system pronounce each word in the vocabulary twice.

Speaker-independent recognition (SIR) technology is in place but still under development. These systems recognize words from anyone speaking the English language or other identifiable language without their having trained the system. Further refinement of this technology by broadening the vocabularies of the equipment and the variety of recognizable speech patterns will lead to automatic transcription systems. Spoken words will appear on a screen for verification and editing; then they will be printed or stored as documents from a word processing system.

"Busy hands/busy eyes" make up another category of applications. This category includes oral commands to computers or word processors via voice key software. Long sequences of command keystrokes necessary for computer commands can be reduced to an oral statement that the computer's microphone will pick up and respond to as if the command keys had been struck in proper sequence. This process saves time and improves productivity because the user can concentrate on screen content (busy eyes) and data entry (busy hands) rather than keying in cumbersome commands.

Various equipment control commands and voice data-entry systems are under development. Some of these have more potential for manufacturing applications than for office systems. Figure 8-11 gives possible applications of voice technology in offices and four specific industry categories.

The Human Factor. As voice technologies are improved and implemented, their success will depend upon the reactions of personnel and, to some extent, the general public. The goal is improved productivity, and the technology offers potential for improving the productivity of managers, professionals, and support personnel. However, developers and users must anticipate personnel-related problems and potential employee frustrations that could result from this technology. For example, employees will probably rebel if digital speech compression, the technology that removes extraneous sounds from digitized oral recordings, distorts the sounds of their voices or the fluency of their speech. Communication effectiveness will be hampered—not enhanced—if recorded messages are incoherent, mechanically incorrect, or confusing. There is no less need for accuracy in oral memos than in paper or screen memos.

VOICE MAIL

The most advanced applications of voice technology are in the voice mail category (sometimes referred to as voice store and forward or electronic mail). **Voice mail** systems manage oral telephone communications by storing and forwarding messages to other people, receiving and storing incoming calls, and performing other related procedures. Although these systems are sometimes referred to as electronic mail, this term usually refers to electronically transmitted written communication. Voice mail systems are discussed in the following section.

Figure 8-11 **Voice Technology Applications by Industry Categories**

Generic Application	Specific Applications by Industry				
	FINANCE/BANKING	MANUFACTURING	MEDICAL	DISTRIBUTION/ MERCHANDISING	OFFICE OF ANY INDUSTRY
DATA ENTRY	Account records	Factory floor Data collection Quality control and instruction	Medical records Lab analysis	Point of sale Inventory	Order entry
INFORMATION RETRIEVAL	Account inquiry Stock quotations	Inventory status	Patient records Organ transplant	Product availability Exchange inventory	Executive workstation Database
VOICE STORE AND FORWARD	Voice mail Customer service Customer orders	Voice mail	Voice mail Diagnosis dictation Patient record updates	Orders Voice memos to branches Outlet reports	Voice mail dictation
REMOTE TRANS- ACTION PROCESSING	Funds transfer Market transactions	Maintenance Work orders	Ambulance service Appointments	Catalog sales	Customer service scheduling
EQUIPMENT CONTROL	Check logging	*CAD/CAM Process control Robot control	Instrument control Equipment analysis	Warehouse control and organization	Voice key commands
SECURITY	Credit card verification Customer ID	Facility access Time cards	Records control	Customer ID Credit authorization	Facility access File access

*CAD/CAM stands for computer-aided design/computer-aided maufacturing.
Source: Ann E. Conrad, "Voice Systems are a 'Sound' Investment," *Data Management*, Vol. 21, No. 11 (November, 1983), pp. 20–23.

Voice mail systems should not be confused with telephone answering systems using magnetic audio recording tape, although there are similarities. Voice mail is far more sophisticated and, consequently, more expensive. Systems prices range from around $50,000 to more than $500,000. They store messages from callers, permit callers to edit messages, store messages for delivery to identified callers, store standard messages for delivery to "mailing lists" of telephone numbers, and record status messages regarding disposition of assignments. For example, if a mailing-list number is busy, that fact will be recorded and the system will keep trying until the called party answers or signals the fact that delivery was not possible. These signals are called "message certification." Figure 8-12 and Figure 8-13 present capsules of voice mail procedures.

Figure 8-12 Voice Mail Procedures

HOW VOICE MAIL WORKS

Using voice mail is like having a combined mailbox and telephone. Instead of picking up letters, memos, and phone messages, you pick up your phone, dial up your personal mailbox number, and listen to your messages as they are played back to you. You can reroute or reply to the mail you receive this way or send messages of your own by dialing someone else's mailbox and speaking your thoughts. This can be done from anywhere in the world, at any time, and from virtually any touchtone telephone.

Voice store and forward lets you talk right into a telephone and have the message or memo recorded, even when your intended recipient is out of the office, in a meeting, or on another telephone line speaking to someone else. Computerized "voice prompts" guide you whether you are sending or receiving messages. Your voice messages are digitized, stored on a hard disk or on tape, and then forwarded at the appropriate time to one recipient or several. Other features follow:

- You generally receive your messages in the order in which they were left.

- You can save, replay, or erase messages at your convenience.

- Each mailbox will hold either a prescribed number of messages or a maximum total time volume, depending on the manufacturer.

The ultimate point, of course, is to have information and thoughts worth communicating—that depends more on people than technology.

Source: "How Voice Mail Works," *Management Technology* (April, 1985): 14.

Figure 8-13   **Sequence of Events In a Voice Mall System**

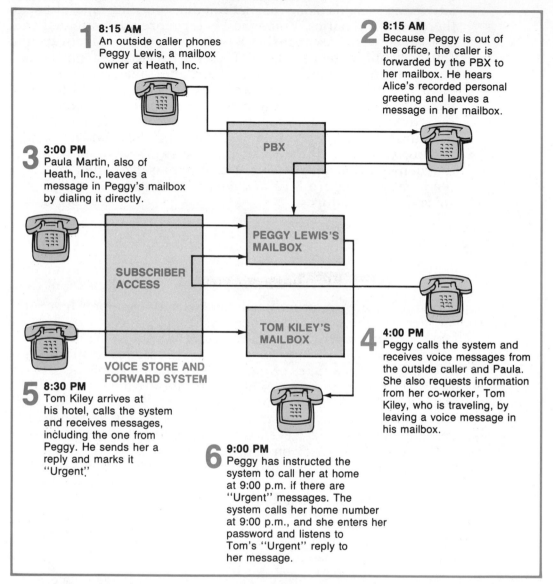

1   8:15 AM
An outside caller phones
Peggy Lewis, a mailbox
owner at Heath, Inc.

2   8:15 AM
Because Peggy is out of
the office, the caller is
forwarded by the PBX to
her mailbox. He hears
Alice's recorded personal
greeting and leaves a
message in her mailbox.

PBX

3   3:00 PM
Paula Martin, also of
Heath, Inc., leaves a
message in Peggy's mailbox
by dialing it directly.

SUBSCRIBER
ACCESS

PEGGY LEWIS'S
MAILBOX

TOM KILEY'S
MAILBOX

VOICE STORE AND
FORWARD SYSTEM

4   4:00 PM
Peggy calls the system and
receives voice messages from
the outside caller and Paula.
She also requests information
from her co-worker, Tom
Kiley, who is traveling, by
leaving a voice message in
his mailbox.

5   8:30 PM
Tom Kiley arrives at
his hotel, calls the system
and receives messages,
including the one from
Peggy. He sends her a
reply and marks it
"Urgent."

6   9:00 PM
Peggy has instructed the
system to call her at home
at 9:00 p.m. if there are
"Urgent" messages. The
system calls her home number
at 9:00 p.m., and she enters her
password and listens to
Tom's "Urgent" reply to
her message.

SPEECH SYNTHESIS

Another factor in the voice technology area is **speech synthesis,**
a computer-driven system that "builds" audio responses representing stored quantitative or textual information. Although the
information is stored on magnetic media as data or text, the system converts it to word sounds. The system includes a dictionary

of words pronounced differently from standard pronunciation guidelines. Voice synthesis is not the same as voice mail, which converts human voice signals to digital code and back to voice signals. This system creates audible "voice" responses that have never been uttered by a human.

Voice synthesis applications have concentrated on voice output (responses to telephone inquiries such as requests by bank tellers for account balances). Georgia State University, Atlanta, Georgia, uses the system to dispense information to students about closed classes during registration.

VOICE INPUT FOR WORD PROCESSING

Voice or speech recognition by computers allows data entry without the use of hands. The IBM Personal Computer Voice Communications option can recognize voice commands for input to applications programs, including word processing, convert text to speech for playback over a speaker or transmission over a telephone line, and detect and act upon instructions input from touch-tone telephones. The voice recognition feature can be trained to recognize several different voices or vocabularies. Other voice recognition devices with the IBM PC utilize a microprocessor to transmit the spoken command through the keyboard cable just as if the command had been typed.

Most current microcomputer speech systems can handle a vocabulary of about 200 words. The basic obstacle in this form of technology seems to be the amount of storage space on disk that a single speech sound requires. Another is that voices and styles of speech vary widely among individuals; in fact, one person's voice changes pitch and timbre from hour to hour to day to day. In addition, the computer is also confronted by the vast vocabulary spoken by people. Research in this entire area is moving rapidly because the potential rewards are so great. The Kurzweil system is just one system that is commercially available today.

CELLULAR TELEPHONE SYSTEMS

Cellular telephone technology was developed by Bell Laboratories to meet the huge demand for efficient, high-quality mobile communications. The technology in mobile telephone communication is equal in quality to telephone calls placed in the home or office.

Car phones have been available for years, but the old transmission severely limited the number of subscribers. Cellular radio uses computers to make better use of radio frequencies, thus opening up thousands of new mobile links. Through highly efficient use and reuse of the radio spectrum, cellular telephones permit thousands of simultaneous conversations to take place in a given geographic area, where earlier only hundreds could be handled.

In terms of operation, an area to be served by the new system is divided into many small geographical grid units. They are called "cells," each with a radius of about 8 miles. Within each cell a low-powered radio transmitter-receiver unit carries the calls over an antenna system for as many as seventy-two radio channels. A sophisticated computer-controlled call-switching system that is centrally located in the area controls the transmitter-receiver in each cell. It performs the switching task.

As the customer drives from one cell to another, sophisticated electronic equipment transfers or "hands off" the call to another cell site. This permits highly efficient use and reuse of the same radio spectrum.

AIRFONES

Making telephone calls while flying the skies is also possible. **Airfone** was the first air-to-ground telephone system designed for the commercial airline passenger. The same cellular technology utilized in car phones is used by the airline industry. Initial use of the airfones was mainly within the continental United States. However, transcontinental airlines are now offering this service by means of satellite technology. Thus, passengers will no longer be "out of touch" while traveling cross country or across the world.

TELECONFERENCING

Teleconferencing combines video, voice, and facsimile transmission to permit persons in various geographical locations to conduct a conference. The term may be used to describe conference-type telephone (voice only) communication, but the more prevalent meaning applies to the combined transmissions. Participants can see and hear each other and can exchange documents with each other as the conference proceeds. Some prefer the term video teleconferencing to describe this integrated concept.

Objectives.   Although the technology is quite expensive, one of the primary motivations for using teleconferencing is the reduction of travel costs, particularly for top-management meetings in firms whose facilities are widely dispersed and for employee training at all levels. A firm that must employ legal counsel to sit in on numerous meetings around the country, for example, must either pay travel expenses for a legal staff or employ attorneys in each location. Through teleconferencing, one staff person can handle this assignment from the home base. Equipment costs have declined from the level of the first systems.

A second reason for using teleconferencing is that meetings requiring more than a telephone conference can be conducted without taking employees away from the office for long periods. Some firms use teleconferencing as an alternative to cross-town travel for meetings in large metropolitan areas.

Finally, the technique has become a medium for marketing products. Clients and potential customers can be gathered at teleconferencing centers around the country for one presentation. Complete interaction through cameras, microphones, and facsimile transmission devices is possible.

Technology. Teleconferencing involves either rented facilities or, more likely, privately owned facilities. Firms with their own facilities build a teleconferencing room at each location. Some hotels now install such rooms for the use of their guests and conference clients. Cities are building teleports to link facilities with major communication satellites, hoping to attract businesses requiring such facilities.

A typical arrangement for teleconferencing involves transmission of signals through an earth-station satellite dish. Signals are bounced off satellites to receiving stations at other locations. Conference rooms are equipped with multiple television cameras for pictures of conference participants, screens for viewing remote participants, a television graphics production facility, microphones, viewing screens that show images from each participating location, and facsimile or graphics transmission devices. Smaller scale installments may involve transmissions from ordinary offices, fewer amenities, and lower costs.

HUMAN CONCERNS

How are people affected by teleconferencing? Communication specialists quickly condemned teleconferencing after its introduction in the 1970s. They cited the harshness of the equipment, the coldness of the environment, the absence of the "feel" of closeness, and the lack of non-verbal elements (for example, eye contact and body language that would be observable if everyone were in the same room). Others criticize teleconferences because microphones and television pictures magnify poor speech patterns, one's monopoly of the conversation, rambling conversation, absence of graphic data to support oral data, and lack of creativity in presentations. These factors can be avoided through careful planning.

Figure 8-14   Remote participants in a teleconference are viewed on a large screen next to graphics transmissions.
Hotel Inter-Continental (New York)

Is the quality of interaction comparable to face-to-face meetings? With experience, managers have come to realize that teleconferences cannot be exact duplicates of face-to-face conferences. They require a different approach. When a teleconference is costing thousands of dollars per hour, planning is crucial. Careful planners will consider the people who will be participating in the conference, anticipate their needs relative to the subject matter, and provide preliminary information (agendas and written reports) and supplementary communication aids (graphic data, video tapes, and overlays, which guide the discussion) to overcome the potential strain of the electronic environment. The teleconference need not be a cold, empty experience for participants, but it can be just that if attention to these details is not provided.

TRENDS IN TELECOMMUNICATIONS

Historically, telecommunications has passed through many stages and technological phases. Chronologically, these phases represented the telegraph, telephone, teletype, facsimile, microwave, fiber optics, and satellite transmission technologies.

Distinct trends are evident in telecommunication technology (some of these have already been identified). These trends involve (1) product development and enhancement, (2) integration of telecommunications with other technologies, and (3) rapid developments in systems for transmitting all five categories of information.

PRODUCT DEVELOPMENT

Development of telecommunications technology was greatly influenced by the Bell System until the breakup of the system in 1984. Influenced by the changes in the Bell System, by the development of digital technology for voice transmission, and by the fading distinctions between the five separate technologies, rapid and far-reaching developments began. Manufacturers formerly associated only with communication devices began to explore possibilities in the office and data processing areas; those formerly associated with either office or data processing hardware began to develop telecommunications hardware and software.

Recent developments such as teleconferencing and the electronic blackboard involve multiple technologies. The whole field of telecommunications is merging with data processing and office systems technologies to form integrated information systems.

TRANSMISSION ENHANCEMENTS

New developments involving digital transmission, voice-data integration, and voice recognition devices comprise the third trend. Because private branch exchanges are now offered with digital technology instead of the traditional analog technology, they are less expensive, more reliable, and more compatible with text- and data-transmission equipment. From another viewpoint, the capability of converting voice to digital form for transmission makes possible the use of internal networks for all forms of information communication, including voice. Voice recognition technologies that are still being perfected, combined with digitized voice transmission, will make possible the communication of voice messages and their conversion to text messages when necessary.

Fiber Optics. Perhaps the most exciting recent telecommunications advancement is fiber optics. Fiber optics is transmission over glass or plastic strands of cable the diameter of a human hair, which allows a quantum leap over copper wire or coaxial cables in terms of the number of transmissions that can be sent on a single cable. In addition to the significant increase in transmission capacity, fiber optic cables are immune to traditional forms of electronic noise caused by heat, moisture, cold, or other environmental factors. This significantly improves the signal-to-noise ratio of the transmission when fiber optic cables are used.

Fiber optic cables are currently much more expensive to produce than copper cables because of the complex manufacturing process used to create the fiber optic cables. At present, the cost of the equipment (special lasers) used to produce the fiber optic signal is high compared to the traditional equipment needed to produce a signal for copper cable. As the costs for fiber optic transmission continues to come down, the use of this medium will grow rapidly because of the large number of transmission channels that can be carried on fiber optic cable compared to other communication links.

EXPECTED FUTURE ENHANCEMENTS

In addition to these trends, enhancements in several categories are expected. Data communication will be improved by local area networks, electronic mail, and personal-computer-to-mainframe-computer interfaces. Voice communication upgrades will improve voice mail, provide better long-distance telephone services and add more capabilities to in-house telephone equipment.

By 1998, the analog-to-digital transformation will be complete, most computers will operate in a networked environment, and telecommunications management will be functionally integrated with data processing management. In 1998, it seems likely that:

1. Integrated services digital network services will be past the experimental stages.
2. Fiber-optic cable will be the most common communication link.
3. Local area networks, with gateways to other networks and to wide area networks, will be commonplace.
4. Mobile communications systems will be as common as local area networks.
5. No single network design or architecture will dominate.

CAREER IMPLICATIONS FOR TELECOMMUNICATIONS

Although career opportunities in telecommunication fields are numerous, they are somewhat difficult to pinpoint at the entry level. Many positions are highly technical and require persons with technical degrees in electrical engineering or similar fields.

Even with such degrees, entry-level personnel are likely to spend long periods of time in training programs. Eventually, they fill positions such as telecommunication specialist, network technology specialist, or data communication technician.

Jobs in traditional voice communication firms tend to be either very technical or no different from jobs in any other firm.

Careers for persons with extensive study in office systems, computer information systems, or management information systems might include the following:

LAN Administrator
Electronic Mail Administrator
Voice Mail Administrator
Teleconferencing Specialist
Manager of Teleconferencing
Manager of Data Communication
Telecommunication Consultant

With experience and, perhaps, graduate study at a school offering advanced study in telecommunications management, these individuals would be qualified for positions such as telecommunications systems analyst or telecommunications manager.

WOHL'S BUSINESS PERSPECTIVE

Voice Technology and Practical Office Applications

There is always a lag between the promise of technology and its practical implementation in broadly used (and broadly useful) business applications. Various kinds of voice processing technology have been wandering about the office for a number of years now, looking for appropriate homes.

Voice mail is finally a success. After more than ten years in which voice mail was initially used only by a few businesses, especially those with the need to manage a large, geographically dispersed employee force, many business users now employ at least some voice mail.

Perhaps this is because of the underlying consumer acceptance of telephone answering machines. Voice mail is, after all, like a very sophisticated, super-powerful answering machine. More likely, it is due to the integration of voice mail into new telephone switches, so that as companies move to new premises or upgrade to larger and more powerful telephone systems, voice mail comes with their new telephones.

Many users are still reluctant to use the technology; as with any new technology, education needs to precede training, and help the new user understand why a time investment in learning the new technology makes sense.

Other voice technologies also lag behind other telecommunications technologies such as data communications and telephony.

Voice annotation (the ability to tie a voice message to a piece of text or other data) is finally coming into its own. More powerful computers and more storage make it possible to offer voice annotation as an additional interface for nearly any computer application—and executive users and secretaries both find it handy, permitting a broader channel of communication than keyboarded information alone.

Voice recognition is also coming along. Too bad that our movie experiences lead us to expect some kind of human-like computer, with highly developed abilities to understand us (and to talk back). Today, computers can only understand speakers they have been trained to expect, and then only if they speak words individually, distinctly, and within somewhat limited (but growing) vocabularies.

Natural language processing (which would permit the computer to analyze your idiomatic emissions and understand the *meaning* as opposed to recognizing the *words*) is coming along just fine, but it still takes a mighty big computer and more than real time processing before your messages can be understood. This is probably the real barrier to man-machine interfaces as we'd like them.

We are in the process of building a telecommunications infrastructure for the 21st century. When it is completed, we will be able to send data of any type—from voice messages to text to graphics to data—anywhere where humans and computers try to manage information, as cheaply, as reliably, and as quickly, as we pick up the telephone today.

SUMMARY

Communication is a basic concern of any organization. Because most information systems are really communication system components, office automation is deeply involved in communication. Information managers and supervisors of knowledge workers need to understand the communication process and to consider the consequences for communication effectiveness and efficiency when making systems decisions.

The field of telecommunication is a broad one. The term is used in this chapter to describe the technologies that enable information to move from one place to another. That information might be quantitative data, text, voice messages, video images, graphics, or document images. Telecommunications involve the interconnection of information-processing components. Any stem becomes more powerful, more functional, and more effective if it can interchange information with a variety of other systems. This is accomplished through direct cable connections, telephone lines, or various configurations of networks.

Traditional telephone voice-communication systems have been upgraded and modified to fit into the total information management picture for many organizations. Recent changes in level and nature of regulation have opened new markets for voice communication enhancements. Voice recognition and manipulation technologies are developing rapidly. Current applications feature limited vocabularies for commands to equipment, but a goal is complete sentence recognition, which would allow for machine creation of text from the spoken word. Voice mail is a sophisticated component of the telephony system that permits storing, forwarding, and retrieving voice messages — using the telephone.

Electronic mail is a family of technologies used to communicate and manage text transmissions. Recent developments in this field have provided systems that store and forward text and rapidly transmit complicated drawings and photographs.

Teleconferencing/video teleconferencing combines the technologies of video, voice, and text transmission to permit conferences among people in widely dispersed (even world-wide) locations.

Although great strides at integrating the various telecommunications technologies have already been made, further integration of these technologies with all information management technologies appears likely.

KEY TERMS

communication effectiveness
communication efficiency
telecommunications
interface
interface device
communication link
twisted pair wire
coaxial cable
fiber-optic cable
microwave transmission
radio-wave transmission
infrared-beam transmission
laser-beam transmission
dedicated line
broadband
baseband
protocol
transmission mode
asynchronous mode
synchronous mode

transmission paths
simplex
duplex
full duplex
half duplex
baud rate
high-speed transmission
low-speed transmission
modem
multiplexer
Open Systems Interconnect
  (OSI)
electronic mail
computer-based message
  system (CBMS)
network
local area network (LAN)
star topology
ring topology
bus topology

Integrated Services Digital
  Network (ISDN)
private branch exchange
  (PBX)
computerized branch
  exchange (CBX)
digital branch exchange
  (DBX)
speaker-dependent
  recognition (SDR)
continuous speaker-
  dependent recognition
  (CSDR)

speaker-independent
  recognition (SIR)
speaker verification
voice response
voice store and forward
voice key software
central voice processing unit
digital speech compression
voice mail
speech synthesis
cellular telephone
airfone
teleconferencing

REVIEW QUESTIONS

1. If you were in charge of telecommunication planning for a large organization, how would your organization's goal of "maintaining communication efficiency while achieving communication effectiveness" be affected by the installation of a system such as electronic mail?

2. Identify and discuss the impact of legal decisions affecting telecommunication. To what extent should telecommunications firms be considered public utilities?

3. Contrast the nature of messages transmitted by the five telecommunications categories.

4. Describe how (a) a local area network and (b) a **PBX** might be considered the integrating force for office technologies.

5. If you want to communicate a document created by word processing software from a personal computer to an electronic file managed by a database management system, what are some of the alternatives for getting that document to the file?

6. Identify eight or ten information processing devices that might be linked by a network.

7. Contrast local area networks and wide area networks.

8. What is the difference between electronic mail systems designed to communicate voice mail and those designed to communicate textual mail?

9. In your role of manager of office automation, what applications could you identify as possible uses of voice input or voice output systems (a) using available technology and (b) using technology expected to be operational during your career.

10. What is the difference between a telephone answering service, which records messages on magnetic tape, and a voice mail system?

CASE STUDY: YAR CORPORATION

The Finance Department at Yar Corporation maintains data about the firm's credit customers, handles stock records, and keeps tabs on the status of the organization's debt—among other things. Fifteen people work in the department. They have installed the following information processing equipment within the department: five IBM PCs (8088 chips and two floppy drives each); four IBM PS/2s, Model 50 (with 30MB hard disk drives); one Compaq 386; one IBM PC-AT; six dot-matrix printers; one HP LaserJet IID printer; a 40Mb external hard disk (connected to the AT), and a terminal to the firm's IBM mainframe computer. In addition to the mainframe terminal, several modems are used for sending data to the mainframe from the micros.

Some of the old PCs are shared by two or more people. Files are stored on floppy disks or in one of the hard-disk systems. For the old PCs, software is in disk form; software for the newer models is installed on the hard disks. The laser printer is installed at one of the PS/2 computers because this is the one most used for word processing applications to produce reports and correspondence. Each PC and the terminal has a dot-matrix printer.

Some work in the department requires access to mainframe terminal databases; other work deals with small databases stored on the hard disks (KeepIt® database and pfs:File® are used); pfs:Write® and WordStar® are used for word processing. Important word processing files are stored on hard disks and backed up on floppy disks; other WP files are stored on floppy disks at the workstations of the persons who created the documents. Each workstation has software for at least one DBMS and one word processing software package. Other software that is passed around the department includes Lotus 1-2-3™, Super-Calc™, pfs:Report®, and ChartMaster™. One of the PS/2 machines has Byline™ installed (the one with the laser printer) for desktop publishing applications.

Except for occasional waits for the mainframe terminal, or trips to borrow a 286 or 386 machine in a neighboring department to run a program that requires more memory than their old machines have, there appears to be no major system problems. The staff members who use the old PCs use them very little and consider them adequate for now. The department manager sometimes wonders, however, whether things should be more efficient than they are, considering all the money the company has invested in hardware and software.

QUESTIONS/ACTIVITIES

1. What communication technologies might have potential application in this department?

2. Describe some of the changes that could be made using the technologies that you have identified. What steps would you take to implement the changes necessary to incorporate your suggestions?

SUGGESTED READINGS

Barcomb, David. *Office Automation,* 2nd ed. Bedford, Mass.: Digital Press, 1988 (see sections on telecommunications).

Bowen, Terry. "Wiring the Open Office for Fiber." *Telecommunications* (April, 1988): 70–75.

Braue, Joseph. "1987: The Year When Networking Became Part of the Bottom Line." *Data Communications* (January, 1988): 165.

Bylinsky, Gene. "Technology in the Year 2000." *Fortune* (July 18, 1988): 92.

Gantz, John. "The Network of 1988." *Telecommunication Products & Technology* (January, 1988): 20–36.

Miller, Shelley. "Your Phone System: Advanced or Antiquated?" *Management World* (July–August, 1986): 13.

Olson, Bob M. "How Telecom Managers Integrate Voice and Data Today." *Telecommunications* (September, 1988): 37–40, 52.

Strehlo, Christine. "The Promised Lan." *Personal Computing,* (January, 1989): 92.

Tannenbaum, Jeffrey A. "Speed, Cost, and Cachet Aid Growth of Electronic Mail." *The Wall Street Journal* (July 27, 1988): 29.

Warr, Michael. "Fiber Gets Faster—Again." *Telephony* (November 16, 1987): 58.

Lan Magazine, monthly publication devoted to local area networks.

The Blackbox Catalog of telecommunication devices and supplies. The descriptions of the various components are an excellent "text" on telecommunication.

CHAPTER 9

Administrative Support

OBJECTIVES

After studying this chapter, you should understand the following:

1. The nature and evolution of the administrative support concept

2. The redefining of office roles and relationships

3. The benefits of administrative support for secretaries and principals

4. How administrative support can be organized

5. The procedures that accompany administrative support

6. How the electronic workstation meets administrative support needs

7. How software helps meet administrative support needs

8. The career path and job outlook for administrative support

Just what is administrative support? This chapter explores the concept's evolution, benefits, organization, procedures, and career implications. Special attention is devoted to the effect of automation on this vital office function.

THE CONCEPT OF ADMINISTRATIVE SUPPORT

The concept of **administrative support** in its broadest sense refers to the secretarial services provided to an organization's principals (generally members of the supervisory, managerial, and professional staff). Administrative support emerged as a more distinctive office function with the introduction of word processing. This advent of office automation brought work concepts typically associated with industrial or factory work into the office. For example, based upon the **division of labor** principle, word processing advocates recommended that the secretarial role be restructured into two distinct functions—typing and nontyping. These same advocates, applying the principle of **work specialization**, recommended that these functions be performed by specialists. Thus, word processing operators performed the typing tasks, whereas administrative secretaries performed the nontyping tasks.

Figure 9-1 An administrative secretary is shown proofreading with a member of her support staff.

These recommendations for restructuring the secretarial function were made because of the need to justify to management the high cost of early word processing equipment. Without the constant interruptions that generally accompany secretarial work or the performance of nontyping duties, secretaries dedicated to the production of documents could be more productive. Thus, maximum use of the organization's equipment investment could occur. Greater secretarial efficiency was also expected as the word processing and administrative support secretaries concentrated on performing their designated functions.

Today, however, the validity of this cost-justification argument has diminished substantially because of the reduced cost of automated office equipment as well as a change in management thinking regarding office functions. Organizations have generally reunited the previously split secretarial role. Typically, administrative secretaries do some typing and/or word processing even in organizations with word processing centers. Nevertheless, for those interested in the automated office, a knowledge of the administrative support concept remains desirable because this once primarily manual office function has become increasingly affected by office technology. In addition, many of the initial developments associated with administrative support have had a permanent impact upon office roles and relationships.

CHANGES IN OFFICE ROLES AND RELATIONSHIPS

The role of the administrative support secretary resembles closely the role of a traditional secretary with the exception of the performance of major typing tasks. Although the administrative support role has experienced changes, these have not been as dramatic as those associated with word processing. With the word processing secretary, the changes were more obvious. Typically, the word processing secretary was relocated to a newly designed word processing center, given a distinctive new title, trained on new equipment complete with new procedures, and received direction and guidance from a word processing supervisor. This situation was often in stark contrast to the situation for the administrative secretary. In many organizations the administrative support role was unplanned, unrecognized, and was not professionally supervised. When stripped of the most visible symbol of the secretarial role—the typewriter—the administrative secretary and others in the office could easily become confused regarding the nature and status of the administrative secretarial role.

Another important and possibly even traumatic change for the administrative secretary was the loss of the boss (principal)-secretary relationship. This relationship, popularly referred to as the **office marriage**, was dissolved with the introduction of the word processing and administrative support concepts. This dissolution occurred because administrative secretaries typically serve a group of principals instead of just one principal. The ramifications of this separation were felt acutely, not only by the secretary but also by the principal. Principals experienced the loss of one of their perquisites (status symbol "perk" of the private secretary), and secretaries experienced the loss of their intimate working relationship and convenient access to their principals. This change in office relationships can be viewed more positively for the secretary when considered from a career perspective. Freed from the one-on-one relationship, the secretary could now be perceived not as an "assistant to" but as a professional performing a designated function of the organization.

LEVELS AND REPORTING RELATIONSHIPS

The number of levels and the reporting structure for the administrative support function depend significantly upon the organization in which they are located. For example, in one organization an individual may be designated as a manager for all of the administrative support functions. In another organization two positions might exist—administrative support supervisor as well as administrative support manager. In addition, the administrative support function might involve management by managers of various functional areas, such as personnel or marketing.

Reporting relationships also can be quite varied depending upon the organization. Supervisors might report to principals in functional areas, an administrative support manager, an office manager, or a manager of information systems or secretarial support. Administrative support managers might report to higher level managers of functional areas, an information systems manager, or even the chief executive officer. Figure 9-2 illustrates a functional staffing structure.

BENEFITS OF ADMINISTRATIVE SUPPORT

The concept of administrative support endured in organizations because of the many benefits realized by organizations with its implementation. The most apparent benefit is the constant availability of secretarial support afforded by the clustering of admin-

Figure 9-2 Functional Staffing Structure

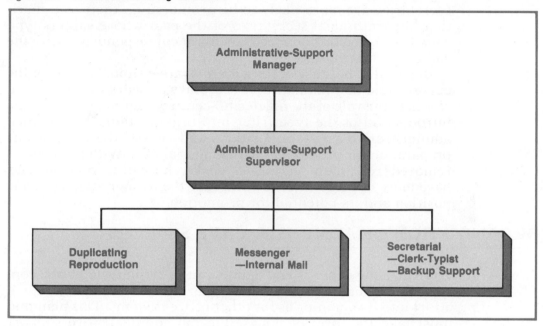

Source: Arthur L. Thursland, ''Restructuring a Support Staff,'' *Words* (February-March, 1984): 16.

istrative secretaries. This approach to administrative support work provides a constant source of secretarial services for principals who are not dependent upon the personal presence of an individual secretary. A further benefit of an administrative support work group can be a boost in the productivity level of the principals. Tasks can be delegated to administrative secretaries of a paraprofessional nature, thereby providing principals with more time to deal with higher priority matters. (The term **paraprofessional** refers to work similar to that of the principal but performed at a lower level, usually by an individual without the full credentials of the principal—for example, in the way a paralegal assists an attorney.)

Secretaries, too, may derive benefits from implementation of the administrative support concept. Opportunities for increased job satisfaction and new career paths are possible. Individual secretaries' work interests can be brought more in line with their own personalities and aptitudes. While some secretaries might enjoy producing a heavy volume of typed work, others might not. Thus, the administrative support concept allows individuals who enjoy the helping role to achieve personal satisfaction while contributing to the goals and objectives of their organizations. With the existence of two distinct career paths—word processing and administrative support—secretarial work could be more appealing to some individuals than in its traditional form. In addition, secretaries are more likely to be promoted on their own merit than the traditional secretaries of the past whose careers typically flourished or floundered in direct correspondence with the careers of their bosses.

Ironically, because of the administrative support concept the current role of administrative secretary appears to be modeled closer to the role of the nineteenth-century secretary. Before the introduction of the typewriter into organizations, males filled administrative assistant positions and viewed the positions as preparation for promotions to managerial jobs. With typewriters removed from many secretaries' desks, those in secretarial roles have more opportunities to recapture the former status of their position and its potential for promotion.

ORGANIZATION OF ADMINISTRATIVE SUPPORT

To realize the benefits and opportunities possible from the concept of administrative support, organizations should put as much effort into its planning as for other office systems. This planning must take the form of integrating the administrative support concept into the total organization. Goals and objectives for this function need to be developed and its structure established within the organizational hierarchy. Just how this planning is accomplished for the administrative support function depends upon the requirements of the organization.

Some important factors that need to be considered in designing an administrative support system include the following:

1. The size of the organization
2. The number of principals
3. The managerial level of the principals
4. The nature of the work
5. The volume of the work
6. The location of the offices of the principals
7. The location of equipment

Once these factors are analyzed, the administrative support system can be designed according to several configurations. The organization of administrative support can be fashioned in a centralized, decentralized, matrix, or mixed process configuration.

CENTRALIZED PLAN

With a **centralized plan** all of the support needs of the organization are performed at one physical location. Such a location could be referred to as an administrative support center similar in design to a word processing center. The size of the centralized administrative support group depends on the needs of the organization. In a centralized plan, a work group or **team approach** generally is used. The team may be a team of two (principal and secretary); but more likely the team will be composed of one or more secretaries and several principals. For example, two secretaries may serve the administrative support needs of eight principals. Figure 9-3 illustrates an administrative support system configured according to a centralized plan.

Figure 9-3 **Centralized Design for Administrative Support in a Manufacturing Organization**

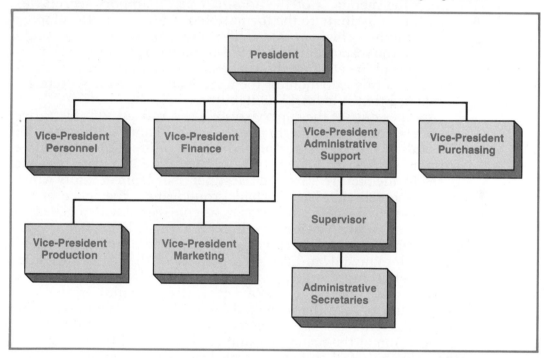

Secretaries in the administrative support team usually are assigned to serve the needs of a group of principals on a **priority basis**. Thus, the work load of certain principals would constitute a secretary's primary responsibilities, and the work load of other principals would be performed on a secondary basis. If the work load becomes unbalanced within the team, the members are expected to provide backup assistance for each other. Although some members of the group may be specialists in particular tasks, all of the members of the group generally are knowledgeable about all of the services because of **cross-training**. With this arrangement, principals are assured of a constant and steady level of secretarial assistance.

With the team approach, support will be provided even with absences of a temporary or long-term duration by individual members of the group. Under the traditional boss-secretary relationship, all work of a principal could come to an abrupt halt because of a secretary's illness or vacation. Even minor interruptions in service, which occur when secretaries are away from their desks, can be eliminated with the inclusion of a position of messenger or page to perform errands and other tasks that require off-site attention.

The close working relationships and cooperation fostered among the members of the administrative support secretaries generally contribute to the formation of team spirit. Developing and maintaining high morale in the secretarial work group would be one of the responsibilities of the administrative support supervisor. One of the chief methods used by the supervisor for ensuring high morale is to monitor the work load among the secretaries to be sure that it is fairly distributed.

Another duty of the supervisor of a centralized administrative support group would be to conduct performance appraisals of the staff. Evaluations performed by a qualified administrative support supervisor generally would be more accurate because of the inside picture afforded the supervisor from actually working in the center. Also, the background and experience of the administrative support supervisor, as contrasted with a principal who does the supervision, would tend to provide a much deeper insight into the work performances required of the secretaries. Although many advantages are apparent with a centralized administrative support center, disadvantages also exist.

One of the disadvantages of a centralized administrative support center is that the principals might find it inconvenient to access the center's services. Distance must not be so great between the location of the principals and the location of the center that the principals fail to avail themselves of the center's services. Such inconvenience leads to principals doing the work themselves, which reduces productivity. Another limitation might be a lack of close communication between the secretaries in the center and the principals. This communication gap could result in services not being performed to the satisfaction of the users and could cause possible frustrations among the secretaries regarding a lack of clarity in work specifications. The administrative support supervisor would have to be alert to the possibilities of these dangers of the centralized plan. The supervisor's work would include preventing or improving such conditions or, if necessary, even instituting a different type of plan, such as one that is decentralized.

DECENTRALIZED PLAN

In a typical **decentralized plan,** the administrative support secretaries are placed in physical proximity to the principals they support. Figure 9-4 illustrates such a plan. Close communication and rapport among the principals and the administrative support secretaries would be expected with this arrangement. An administrative support supervisor might be used to direct the activities of the secretaries and/or the secretaries might be supervised by the administrators of the particular departments or areas served by the support group. Specialization of functions by the secretaries may or may not exist in these decentralized work groups, which would be distributed throughout the organization.

Figure 9-4   **Decentralized Plan of Administrative Support for a Personnel Department**

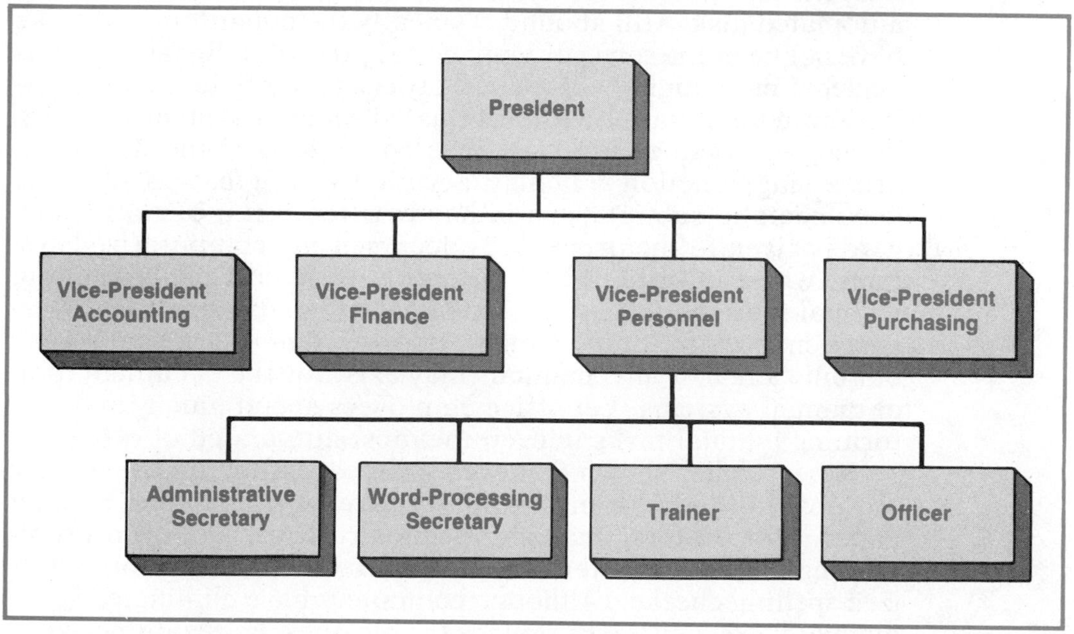

OTHER PLANS

In some organizations the matrix plan may be used. In the **matrix plan** some areas of the organization may have decentralized administrative support groups even though there is a centralized administrative support center to serve the entire organization. A further variation in administrative support organization is to merge the administrative support and word processing functions into the job descriptions of secretaries. This **mixed process** approach has been labeled administrative support in some organizations. At first glance the mixed process plan may seem contradictory to the original principle, which divided word processing and administrative support into two distinct functions. However, the trends prevalent in automated offices reveal that the roles of the typing and the nontyping secretaries have become blurred. The integration of word processing and administrative support functions is occurring because of the increased availability of technology and greater expectations among management regarding secretarial responsibilities. To understand this development, an in-depth examination of administrative support procedures is necessary.

ADMINISTRATIVE SUPPORT PROCEDURES

Despite the introduction of automation in offices, many nonautomated tasks still abound. Typically the nonautomated tasks have not been the focus of managerial attention. Because of this neglect, many highly automated offices run efficient computerized systems parallel with antiquated manual systems. For example, an organization may have computerized the document processing function but may permit the originators of those documents to submit them in handwritten form. Usually much care is given to the procedures documenting computerized systems, whereas little, if any, attention is given to documenting manual systems. Therefore, extensive manuals and other references may exist for documentation of computerized systems, but only a few, if any, manuals may exist for the documentation of manual systems. Yet office employees spend much time performing manual tasks in even the most automated of offices.

Research has shown that even the most computerized activity requires four or five manual procedures; for example, loading paper into printers, changing printer ribbons, and even proofreading documents after they have been checked by a computerized spelling checker. Although computers have eliminated some manual tasks, new tasks replace the old ones. For example, without a voice mail system office personnel will be frequently interrupted by the telephone and have to respond immediately to "live" inquiries. With a voice mail system users must discipline themselves to listen to their messages and then respond electronically in a timely fashion.

Managers must come to recognize that tasks, both manual and automated, affect the performance of office activities and that the manual procedures are just as important to office operations as the automated processes. A systematic study or audit of the manual procedures, many of which are administrative support tasks, could enhance the productivity of the office as impressively as automation has. Such an opportunity is being lost by not bridging what amounts to a costly gap in office operations because of this oversight in managerial perspective.[1]

Administrative support procedures actually involve both administrative secretaries and principals. Therefore, a knowledge is necessary of both their work activities to understand fully the administrative support concept. Figure 9-5 illustrates how the time of principals is distributed. An examination of the work distribution of principals reveals that although much of their time is spent in meetings and on the telephone, relatively routine, nonadministrative tasks, such as proofreading and copying, also consume their time.

Figure 9-5 Composite Distribution of Executive Time by Work Activity

Activity	Upper Management	Middle Management	Both Together
Paper handling	8%	6%	6.2%
Writing	5	9	8.6
Searching information	6	12	11.4
Proofreading	2	3	2.9
Incoming mail	6	5	5.1
Reading	8	6	6.2
Filing	—	1	0.9
Dictation	6	3	3.3
Telephone	16	12	12.4
Typing equipment use	—	1	0.9
Calculating	2	6	5.6
Unscheduled meetings	9	6	6.3
Scheduled meetings	11	6	6.5
Copying	—	1	0.9
Travel	14	7	7.7
Other	7	16	15.6
TOTAL	100%	100%	100.5%*

*Because of rounding, this column does not equal 100%.

Source: "Executives Change with Office Automation Tide," *Data Management* (February, 1982), p. 39.

One of the advantages of the administrative support concept is its ability to free up more time for principals by using the skills of secretaries to perform administrative tasks. However, some

1.   Charles J. McDonough, "Meanwhile, Back at the Paperwork Ghetto," *The Wall Street Journal* (May 21, 1984): 24.

principals are reluctant to delegate duties of an administrative nature. Some principals are unaware of how to delegate. Other principals use the administrative secretaries but do not use them to their fullest potential, delegating only clerical tasks such as filing, copying, and telephoning. Principals generally need to be made aware of the capabilities and quality of services afforded by the use of administrative secretaries.

The types of administrative duties that could be delegated to administrative secretaries include answering routine correspondence, completing forms and questionnaires, data gathering, and project work. With the skillful delegation of such tasks by principals, more time would become available for other tasks. If the principals and secretaries coordinated their work efforts to be complementary, synergism could occur. **Synergy** refers to the concept that a group generally accomplishes more work and achieves better results than individuals working independently. This concept often is illustrated by the expression "one plus one equals three." An example of synergy could be that of a team formed specifically to conduct a procedures audit in an organization. The members of the team would include representative principals and secretaries who would work together on a peer basis. Once the study was completed, the team would be disbanded.

With a team approach, secretaries contribute input to the decision-making processes of principals. When secretaries and others are encouraged to participate in decisions that affect their work activities, a greater degree of job satisfaction generally occurs. Although the team approach can be important to the principals in expanding their sources of input for decision making, it is particularly important for secretaries. Their talents and creative abilities generally have been overlooked in the decision-making processes affecting office operations, frequently to the detriment of those operations.

Previously, the work of the secretary was to complete tasks assigned by principals. With the changes brought to the workplace by such trends as the team approach and automation, the role of the secretary is evolving. Under new procedures secretaries may be required to initiate work and follow it through to completion. Skills that formerly were required only of managers may be required of secretaries, as they will need to learn how to motivate other team members to complete their portion of a project. Skills once considered basic to the secretarial role, such as typing, shorthand, and filing, will drop to the bottom of secretarial job requisites as more office functions become impacted by new office trends. These trends will affect both the typing and the nontyping functions. Automation already has altered the typing function; and now the nontyping functions, of which administrative support is such a large element, is next. The catalyst for changing the way the administrative support function is handled is the electronic workstation.

ELECTRONIC WORKSTATIONS

At the beginning stages of automation in the 1950s, only data processing personnel used computers. In the 1960s and 1970s, other members of the office staff, particularly secretaries, began to work on computerized equipment such as word processors and computer terminals. In the 1980s and into the 1990s, the growth in the use of desktop personal computers transformed almost all members of the office staff into computer users. Having computing power at one's desk has been labeled the **electronic workstation**. The purpose of the electronic workstation is to improve the productivity and decision making of its users. The degree of computing power and range of capabilities of the electronic workstation depend upon its system configuration. For example, with distributed data processing or networked personal computers, on-line, independent processing as well as access to the host computer system can be achieved.

Figure 9-6 **The 1980s have ushered in the electronic work station by most staff members.** *Kimball International, Office Furniture Division*

Electronic workstations have dramatically contributed to the redefinition in progress of the roles of administrative secretaries and principals. Prior to the onset of desktop computing, office workers maintained use and control of office technologies such as electronic typewriters, copiers, and word processors. With electronic workstations, however, principals began sharing responsibility for the execution of many office tasks. For example, principals may key in rough draft from their own speeches or reports simply because it is easier than dictating or writing them out by hand. A secretary may then finish the document as a final draft. Some tasks, such as the keying of a short memo and its distribution via electronic mail, might even be performed solely by the principal.

WORKSTATION APPLICATIONS

Workstation applications used by office employees were surveyed by COMP-U-FAX™, a computer trends reporting service. Figure 9-7 illustrates the top ten PC-based office applications and their percentage of use. The survey also ranked the top ten applications in the following order of importance: word processing, spreadsheets, database, electronic mail, telecommunications, data processing, data entry, graphics, desktop publishing, and calendars. The comparison between use and importance led to the conclusion that electronic mail and telecommunications are more important than their use would indicate.[2] The lower levels of use for electronic mail and telecommunications are reflective of their dependence upon networking, which is not yet at the popularity level of independent electronic workstations. However, PC networking is expected to reach this mass level in the decade of the 90s.

SOFTWARE

Appropriate software, however, must be available for the users in order for any of these workstation applications to be realized. Some software can be purchased from vendors off the shelf and be ready to run immediately. Frequently, however, such software needs to be customized by programmers to suit the requirements of a particular business. Sometimes programmers create entirely new software to meet the needs of an organization. If the user is working on an intelligent terminal or networked personal computer, software can be stored within a host computer system

2. COMP-U-FAX™, "Survey Reports on PC-based Administrative Support Tasks," *Data Management* (May, 1987): 25.

Figure 9-7 **Workstation Applications**

Top 10 PC-based Office Applications	Percentage of Use
Word Processing	100.0
Spreadsheets	90.4
Database	69.0
Data Entry	54.7
Data Processing	52.3
Graphics	42.8
Telecommunications	40.4
Calendars	26.1
Desktop Publishing	23.9
Electronic Mail	19.0

Source: COM-U-FAX™, ''Survey Reports on PC-based Administrative Support Tasks,'' *Data Management* (May, 1987): 25.

and **downloaded** (directly transferred) to the workstation. If the user is working on a personal computer with independent disk drive(s), the software can be in diskette form, stored on hard card or hard disk, or stored within the microchip of the personal computer itself. Literally thousands of software programs exist that are manufactured by thousands of vendors. According to a study conducted by Newton-Evans Research Company, software expenditures are expected to reach $7.6 billion in 1992.[3]

New software packages, offering a vast array of applications, enter the market regularly. These include Lotus's Agenda, a personal information manager that helps users organize information, and Xerox's Colab (for collaboration), which generates "living minutes" during computer-assisted meetings. The latter is a product from an entirely new category of software called groupware. **Groupware** refers to diverse software products designed to support "workgroup computing," as opposed to independent "personal computing." With **workgroup computing**, teams can have the same computing power to manage information, communicate, and coordinate work that individuals now have. Several specialized applications can exist within groupware that are layered on top of electronic mail in a workgroup network, such as scheduling and appointment calendar maintenance, project management, and messaging systems. Products available for workgroup computing include Broderbund Software's ForComment, Action Technologies' The Coordinator, and Lotus Notes.

3. ''PC Software Spending Exceeds $25 Billion by 1992,'' *Inside DPMA* (February, 1989): 16.

Capabilities of electronic workstations usually center on the categories of communications, financial analysis (spreadsheet), information management (database), personal support, decision support systems, and integrated software. Each of these software categories is described below.

Communication (word processing/graphics/electronic mail). Users can create, format, edit, file, retrieve, and transmit documents. The spelling and accuracy of keyboarding can be verified through the use of a dictionary package. Form letters can be created as well as mailing labels and envelopes. Bar and pie charts and other graphic representations can be included with reports for greater clarity and impact. Examples of such software include WordPerfect®, Harvard Graphics©, and Crosstalk.

Financial (spreadsheet) analysis. Users can work with electronic spreadsheets, which allow the manipulation of figures and formulas. A common application includes the entry of a set of figures to calculate a "what if" condition: e.g., if the price of an item increases to a certain level, what will be its effect on profit? Examples of such software include Lotus 1-2-3™ and SuperCalc™.

Information (database) management. This software allows the creation, editing, addition, deletion, and manipulation of internal organizational files. Examples of this software include dBase IV and RBase. In addition, external databases can be accessed via subscription services such as H & R Block's CompuServe®, Reader's Digest's The Source℠, and Dow Jones & Co.'s Dow Jones News/Retrieval®. These services provide a wealth of information, such as current news, sports, weather, stock market quotations, airline schedules, theater listings, bulletin boards, and electronic mail.

Personal support. This type of software offers a way for users to organize their time and work through the use of an on-line calendar. This calendar can be used for keeping track of appointments, deadlines, and special occasions such as birthdays and anniversaries. Such software can also be used as a tracking system, a "to do" list, a scheduling tool, and for the creation and maintenance of list processing. Examples of software packages with a calendaring function are PROFS and Office Works.

Decision support systems (DSS). Such software can be classified into two categories: decision aid and decision modeling. Decision-aid packages are used for strategic planning. The user typically assigns weighted values or sets up a range of limits for the variables of a business problem. The package generates options based on this input regarding the best paths to follow. An example of a decision-aid package is Decision Aide. After strategic plans are decided, a decision-modeling package can be used for building models required for the technical and tactical decisions that follow. A lower-level decision-modeling package is the electronic spreadsheet, which allows manipulation of numbers and formulas; however, more sophisticated decision-modeling packages offer features such as simultaneous equation solving. Examples of decision-modeling packages include IFPS/Personal and Encore® for handling such tasks as budget allocations, personnel assignments, market and production planning, projections of revenues, and calculation of profit margins.

Although some similarities exist between **management information systems (MIS)** and decision support systems (DSS), the two systems are distinct from each other. MIS tends to concentrate on transaction processing and the production of reports based upon past business activities for the information of managers. DSS tends to concentrate on present and future activities in an interactive fashion; hence it is often referred to as a **query system.** Its users typically are principals who may not be managers and who desire assistance in making decisions. MIS usually involves the production of standardized reports produced on a regular basis. DSS frequently involves ad hoc analysis of data files instituted at the discretion of the user.

Integrated software. This software combines applications enabling the user to do multiple tasks without switching disks or quitting one program and loading another if on a network or hard card or hard disk. Features of such software usually include word processing, graphics, communications, financial analysis, and database management. Examples include Symphony™ and Framework III™.

ISSUES RELATED TO WORKSTATIONS

The growing use of electronic workstations in the office has raised several important issues. These issues include the effect of workstations on support personnel, workstation use by principals, data security, and the technical problems associated with the networking of personal computers.

Effect on Office Support Personnel. With principals using the capabilities of their electronic workstations to perform many of the administrative support tasks, a reduction in the office support force might be a logical consequence of such activity. One study reported that data were most frequently processed by the secretary with only a "slight margin" over the manager.[4] However, initial interest by managers and professionals doing their own administrative tasks might be short lived. Personal computers can "glamorize" clerical work, and principals should eventually recognize that such tasks may not be the best use of their time. This realization might already be reflected, as the previously cited COMP-U-FAX™ survey reported that administrative support employees spend more time on a personal computer than any other category of office employee.[5] Figure 9-8 illustrates the categories of office employees surveyed and what percent of an average day is spent on a personal computer.

Not only administrative secretaries but also other support personnel, such as data analysts whose jobs have been to gather and analyze data to present to management in report form, are being affected by easy access to computers. If top managers become inclined to analyze their company's data with their desktop PC rather than allowing midlevel managers to perform this function, some midlevel managers may lose their positions. This tactic would result in greater centralization of the decision-making process within an organization. Even some personnel in data processing may have cause for concern regarding the trend toward electronic workstations. While data processing personnel are losing their former status as the sole gatekeepers of corporate information, however, they are gaining a new status as in-house consultants for the new breed of computer users.

Figure 9-8 **Office Employees' Time Spent on PC-based Tasks**

Category of Employee	Percent of Average Day
Administrative Support	36.73
Professionals	24.57
Executives	10.08

Source: COMP-U-FAX™, ''Survey Reports on PC-based Administrative Support Tasks,'' *Data Management* (May, 1987): 25.

Usage by Principals.   Some principals enthusiastically gravitate toward use of the computer, while others resist its appeal. Reasons for resistance are frequently attitudinal or emotionally based. Some principals resist because they feel uncomfortable

4.   Rhonda Rhodes and Joyce Kupsh, ''Do Top-Level Executives Use Computers to Make Their Decisions?'' *Office Systems Research Journal,* Vol. 6, No. 2 (spring, 1988): 12.
    5.   COMP-U-FAX™, *Ibid.*

or are unskilled at a keyboard. Others might not want to risk ridicule or embarrassment in front of other office staff members. Those principals who have not had the opportunity for computer-based education or exposure might feel intimidated by the technology. Some developments in technology, however, have improved the "user friendliness" of electronic workstations. For example, instead of complex command codes to initiate functions, **icons** or pictures of functions can appear on screen. A picture of a wastebasket can be pointed to by the user to tell the computer to discard a file. Another example would be the use of windows. **Windowing** allows a user to view several files on a screen simultaneously and transfer information from file to file.

Most of these problems involving the resistance of principals to computers are expected to fade away because of several factors. Keyboarding has been predicted to become outmoded and to be replaced by voice technology in the 1990s. Thus, lack of keyboarding skills or negative attitudes toward keyboarding are expected to become a moot issue. Many companies that want their principals to use computers are enticing them with free take-home computers so that they can experiment in the privacy of their own homes. Also, companies are offering training in computer usage to principals. In addition, future managers and executives are becoming computer literate in elementary, secondary, and postsecondary schools.

Figure 9-9 Voice technology will most likely take the place of keyboarding in the 1990s.
IBM Corporation

Data Security. As more individuals acquire electronic workstations with the capability to access corporate databases, a security problem can arise. Determination of the legitimacy of certain corporate users to access the data can be a difficult issue. Advancements in technology are helping to control the problem. For example, with voice "fingerprinting" the computer would be programmed to allow only certain recognizable voices to access the information. More details on this issue regarding the protection of databases will be discusssd in Chapter 14.

Linkage. The issue of linking or networking the electronic workstations with a local area network (LAN), a mainframe, or other communication systems can be a difficult, technical problem for organizations. Generally technical expertise is required to oversee installation, maintenance, and upgrading. Developments in networking have encouraged many more individuals to desire and use electronic workstations; however, organizations frequently face a shortage of telecommunication specialists to meet end user demands. This issue is expected to be resolved gradually as networking technology advances and as more individuals become knowledgeable about computer networking.

CAREER IMPLICATIONS FOR ADMINISTRATIVE SUPPORT

The job category of administrative support with its over three million workers constitutes one of the largest occupational groups in the United States. Organizations often use different job titles for individuals who perform the administrative support functions; however, the titles administrative secretary, administrative assistant, and executive secretary are quite common. Also, just as with the word processing function, a career path exists for administrative support personnel which extends to supervisory and managerial level positions.

Figure 9-10 lists job titles and descriptions for administrative support positions and related positions according to the classification system of the AISP (Association of Information Systems Professionals).

WOHL'S BUSINESS PERSPECTIVE

Once, while the fad to sharply divide word processing from administrative support was at its peak (circa 1976), I visited IBM's Office Products Division headquarters.

Believing in practicing what it preached, IBM had taken all typing implements away from administrative support. Keyboarding was to be done in the word processing center, using state-of-the-art word processors.

"We can't get anything done," a friend of mine confessed. "If you need to send a letter out after lunch, you have to hand write the envelope or wait until tomorrow!"

Time passes. Today, *both* word processing and administrative support in most organizations are likely to be highly decentralized, with support functions located near the professionals and managers to be supported. In fact, many no longer remember the experiments in office work engineering of the 1970's.

Electronic workstations are now very cost effective. We don't need to move all the word processing onto a few word processors, because they cost so much. In 1964, word processors cost about $10,000 per workstation. This is about $40,000 in 1989 dollars. Secretaries cost about $5,000 per year and spent about 20% of their time in typing. Obviously, rearrangement was needed to cost justify these relatively expensive systems. Today, a word processor is likely to be a personal computer—about $2,500 of hardware and a few hundred dollars for software. At that price, anyone can play.

In fact, it's important for administrative support that support staff and professionals be on well-matched systems. Too often, we give the professional a brand new, high-end personal computer with lots of processor speed, memory, and storage. The secretary may have anything from an electronic typewriter to an old, dedicated word processor, to a PC. Usually that PC is a small memory, small storage, hand-me-down, incapable of running the best new user interfaces and software.

But professionals and their support staff are a team. The electronic office is intended to help them work better together, not drive them further apart.

To deliver on this promise, we need to insure that

- The services that we provided professionals in the past are still provided. Of course, they can be provided differently, using the capabilities of electronic workstations and interconnected networks, but the end result should always be more service, not less.

- Workstations for team members need to enable the same software. This permits work to be moved around as needed. Pity the poor secretary with an electronic typewriter, working for a professional with a personal computer and laser printer—his correspondence might look better, completely undermining her pride in their joint work and significantly lessening her ability to help.

- We need to take full advantage of the electronic environment. I don't want all of my electronic mail, any more than I opened paper junk mail and things that need to be passed to others. I want my automated office to support the filtering and delegation that my secretary and I enjoyed in the past, but supported at the higher levels that technology can now provide.

SUMMARY

Administrative support is a broad concept that refers to a wide range of secretarial services provided to an organization's principals. In the early development of office automation, many organizations divided the secretarial role into two distinct functions—typing (word processing) and nontyping (administrative support); however, in organizations today the functions may not be so precisely defined. The introduction of the administrative support concept to organizations frequently resulted in the loss of private secretaries for principals and the loss of an intimate working relationship between principals and secretaries. However, the implementation of the administrative support concept generally has provided secretaries with an opportunity for a greater degree of job satisfaction and a career path. For the principals, benefits include a readily available source of secretarial support and the opportunity to become more productive through the delegation of tasks to the administrative secretaries.

The administrative support function in an organization can be organized according to a centralized, decentralized, matrix, or mixed process plan. Although the automated tasks in the office have received the greatest amount of attention, management should devote just as much attention to the planning of the administrative support functions.

Automation is affecting the administrative support functions of the office with the use of the electronic workstation. These workstations are used by secretaries and principals for purposes of communciation, financial analysis, information management, personal support, and decision support. A necessary adjunct to the electronic workstation is appropriate software. Some important issues that have arisen regarding the use of the electronic workstation involve their effect on support personnel, their use by principals, data security, and their linkage.

Administrative support is one of the largest occupational groups in the United States; however, job titles for the administrative support function vary considerably within organizations. The specific job skills and activities of the administrative secretary closely resemble those of the traditional secretary but may include more complex tasks involving decision making. The outlook for administrative support jobs through the year 2000 is generally positive.

KEY TERMS

administrative support   work specialization
division of labor   office marriage

paraprofessional
centralized plan
team approach
priority basis
cross training
decentralized plan
matrix plan
mixed process
synergy
electronic workstation
downloaded
groupware
workgroup computing

financial analysis
   (spreadsheet)
information management
   (database)
personal support
decision support systems
   (DSS)
management information
   system (MIS)
query system
integrated software
icons
windowing

Figure 9-10   **Job Titles and Descriptions for Administrative Support Personnel**

Administrative Secretary: Someone who works for a group of principals as part of a team under the direction of an administrative support supervisor or manager. Responsibilities include such support functions as filing, photocopying, maintaining calendars, records, and lists, and providing special secretarial services.

Senior Administrative Secretary: Has a record of exceptional performance. At times may act as assistant to the supervisor of an administrative team and is qualified to compose and edit documents for principals, provide research support, and perform other paraprofessional duties. The senior administrative secretary handles special projects and is fully aware of company standards and practices.

Administrative Support Supervisor: May have the responsibilities of the senior administrative secretary position in addition to scheduling and administering work flow to a team of administrative secretaries. Responsible for liaison with and training of individuals who benefit from administrative support. Evaluates staffing requirements, prepares management reports, recommends new methods of handling administrative secretaries. Reports to the administrative support manager.

Administrative Support Manager: Exempt (salaried). Has full responsibility for developing, maintaining, and evaluating all services under administrative support within an organization, such as filing, telephone, mail, and paraprofessional support. Monitors the success of the administrative support group and is familiar with the company's goals and objectives. Works closely with the word processing manager to ensure cooperation of the two functions. May manage other major administrative duties such as records and retention schedules, microfilm, print shop, purchasing, and so on. Reports to the information manager (in large organizations).

Staff Analyst: Exempt (salaried). Responsible for consulting and assisting word processing and administrative support supervisors and managers. Conducts studies, reviews operations, and determines and recommends appropriate staffing, procedures, and equipment. Reports to information manager, word processing manager, or administrative support manager.

Director of Secretarial Support Systems: Exempt (salaried). May be vice president or assistant to vice president in some organizations. Has total responsibility for all aspects of an organization's office system, including word processing, administrative support, and other information processing functions. Ensures the collaboration (integration) of all support functions. May report to vice president or chief executive officer in some organizations.

Source: ''Job Titles and Descriptions,'' Eleventh Salary Survey Results 1984 (Willow Grove, Pa.: Association of Information Systems Professionals, 1985).

REQUIREMENTS

The requirements desired by organizations for administrative support positions generally include at least a high school diploma or its equivalent and experience in secretarial work. Many individuals who hold administrative support positions have additional education acquired from business schools or at the collegiate level. Typical prerequisites for administrative support positions may include knowledge and skills in typing, shorthand, transcription, grammar, spelling, human relations, organization, communication, business and office principles, procedures, and practices. In addition, employers also seek people who are team players with professional business attitudes and work values. The actual requirements, however, for attaining an administrative support position would be determined in accordance with the needs of the particular organization. Also, the levels and areas of expertise required of holders of administrative support positions vary considerably based upon the needs of the principals served. Figure 9-11 gives a detailed description of the major skills and corresponding job activities for administrative support secretaries, supervisors, and managers.

Figure 9-11   Skills and Activities for Administrative Secretarial Functions

Skills	Activities
	ADMINISTRATIVE SECRETARIAL FUNCTIONS
Administrative	Confers with principals regarding needs and requirements
Planning	Makes arrangements for travel, meetings, luncheons, and conferences
Organizing	Prepares agendas, programs, and itineraries
Priority setting	Scans and monitors literature related to principal's work
Problem solving	Maintains and orders supplies and business forms
Decision making	Contacts vendors for repairs and maintenance of equipment
Communication	Screens telephone calls and callers; takes messages; places calls to obtain
Listening	information
Oral	Greets visitors; answers inquiries; makes referrals
Written	Interprets company policies and procedures
Nonverbal	Opens, scans, annotates, routes, and distributes mail
Interpersonal	Composes responses to routine correspondence
	Dictates correspondence to word processing center or other secretary
	Proofreads and edits documents for principal(s)
	Fosters harmonious working relationships among staff
Records Management	Maintains logs, information lists, budgets, personnel records, and schedules
	Adds, deletes, retrieves, and purges files
	Routes material to central files
	Designs new filing systems
Research	Locates and collects data; develops and compiles reports, speeches, briefings, and so on
Equipment Usage	Types short items: labels, cards, forms, and envelopes; calculates figures and statistics; uses micrographic equipment for filming, viewing, and splicing; uses reprographic equipment for copying, collating, and binding; uses audiovisual equipment for slides, transparencies, tapes, and so on
Courier	Makes rush or confidential deliveries and pickups of materials; runs errands
Personal	Attends professional meetings; continues self-development; displays willingness to learn
Miscellaneous	Carries out tasks as delegated by principal(s)
	SUPERVISORY AND MANAGERIAL FUNCTIONS
All of the above skills with the addition of the following:	One or more of the above activities may be required by the organization with the addition of the following:
Coordination	Coordinates and monitors the administrative support work flow
Implementation Interfacing	Coordinates work flow with word processing area
	Distributes work load
	Serves as a backup

Figure 9-11   Skills and Activities for Administrative Secretarial Functions (continued)

Skills	Activities
	SUPERVISORY AND MANAGERIAL FUNCTIONS
	Helps review and update the policies and procedures affecting administrative support
	Documents the policies and procedures affecting administrative support
	Helps to establish performance standards
	Prepares productivity reports and other reports
	Recommends change; implements changes
	Evaluates administrative support employees
	Builds team spirit
	Maintains effective working relationships in administrative support groups
	Orients new employees (principals and secretaries) to the administrative support functions
	Trains office employees and temporaries in the administrative support functions

JOB OUTLOOK

The outlook for jobs in administrative support remains generally positive despite predictions that office automation would bring about the "death of the secretary." The U.S. Bureau of Labor does forecast that employment of secretaries is expected to grow more slowly than average for all occupations through the year 2000 primarily due to productivity gains made possible by office automation. This decline in jobs, however, is offset by the especially large number of job openings that arise yearly because of replacement needs.[6] Also, a national shortage of qualified secretarial workers is said to exist with over 80,000 secretarial jobs remaining unfilled each year.[7] The market demand for secretaries is expected to continue in every industry and on every corner of the earth.

REVIEW QUESTIONS

1. Discuss how office automation affected the administrative support function (a) during the early days of office automation, and (b) currently.

2. How has office automation affected office relationships between principals and secretaries?

6. U.S. Department of Labor, Bureau of Labor Statistics, *Occupational Outlook Handbook,* 1988–1989 Edition, 12.

7. Neil Chesanow, "The Manager's Manager: The New Breed of Secretaries," *New Woman* (March, 1989): 91.

3. What benefits are derived from implementation of the administrative support concept (a) for principals? (b) for secretaries?

4. (a) Describe the configurations available for administrative support. (b) How can an organization decide which configuration for administrative support would be best suited for it?

5. Why is a knowledge of the work activities of principals necessary for an understanding of the administrative support concept?

6. How can the concept of synergy be applied to principals and secretaries?

7. How have electronic workstations contributed to the redefinition of the roles of administrative secretary and principals?

8. (a) What are the top three PC-based office applications? (b) Why are electronic mail and telecommunications not more highly ranked?

9. (a) How does "workgroup computing" differ from "personal computing?" (b) Describe some of the specialized applications that can exist within groupware. (c) Give examples of this new product.

10. Why should MIS and DSS not be considered interchangeable systems in an office?

11. What organizational effects might be realized from the use of electronic workstations by principals?

12. Should resistance to computers by office principals be considered a short-term or long-term issue? Defend your position.

13. How has office automation affected the job outlook for the employment of secretaries?

CASE STUDY: THE CASE OF THE WORRIED ADMINISTRATIVE SUPPORT MANAGER

Carmen Ramirez is the administrative support manager for the Sun West Corporation, a large, growing manufacturing organization. Carmen reports directly to Mrs. Gilmore, the chief executive officer of the firm. Several years ago the Sun West Corporation reorganized its office into two divisions—word processing and administrative support. Sun West has a decentralized plan for word processing, which is operating very successfully. Currently its administrative support division also is organized according to a decentralized plan. The administrative support secretaries are supervised by the various functional department managers with Carmen Ramirez managing the overall function.

Lately Carmen has begun to worry about the administrative support function at the Sun West Corporation. For the past several months some of the department managers have been complaining about the ability of the administrative secretaries to keep up with their work loads. In addition, some secretaries do not complete their tasks correctly; and when the experienced secretaries are absent, the more complex tasks go undone. A few principals have confided in Carmen that the turnaround time for the support services is becoming so poor that they are doing some of their own clerical work at their newly acquired electronic workstations.

The situation appears to be getting worse. Carmen has recently heard that some of her best administrative secretaries are thinking of quitting. Apparently some of the principals in the various departments favor the more experienced secretaries by leaving them overworked while other secretaries are underworked. This condition is resulting in poor morale in the secretarial work groups.

The problem reached the critical stage when Carmen's superior, Mrs. Gilmore, called Carmen into her office and told her that she wanted the administrative support situation cleared up immediately.

QUESTIONS/ACTIVITIES

1. What appears to be the real problem at Sun West?

2. Has the company done anything correctly regarding the administrative support function?

3. Develop a plan of action for Carmen.

SUGGESTED READINGS

Blake, Robert R., Jane S. Mouton, and Artie Stockton. *The Secretary Grid.* New York: AMACOM, 1984.

Chesanow, Neil. "The Manager's Manager: The New Breed of Secretaries." *New Woman* (March, 1989): 88–92.

DeJean, David. "The Electronic Workgroup." *PC/Computing* (October, 1988): 72–84.

Kirby, Margaret S. and J. Dale Oliver. "Information Processing Specialist: A Redefinition of the Administrative Support Function." *The Delta Pi Epsilon Journal,* Vol. XXX, No. 1 (winter, 1988): 14–24.

LaRue, Adella C. "Is the Secretary a Professional? Says Who?" *The Balance Sheet* (November/December, 1988): 13–15.

Rhodes, Rhonda and Joyce Kupsh. "Do Top-Level Executives Use Computers to Make Their Decisions?" *Office Systems Research Journal,* Vol. 6, No. 2 (spring, 1988): 7–13.

Thursland, Arthur L. *Administrative Support: Economic Justification for Automation.* Willow Grove, PA: Association of Information Systems Professionals, 1984.

U.S. Congress, Office of Technology Assessment. *Automation of America's Offices,* 1985–2000. Washington, DC: U.S. Government Printing Office, OTA-CIT-297, December, 1985.

PART 3

MANAGEMENT STRATEGIES FOR OFFICE AUTOMATION

CHAPTER 10

Ergonomics in the Automated Office

OBJECTIVES

After studying this chapter, you should understand the following:

1. The concept of ergonomics in relation to the office environment

2. How and why office designs have evolved

3. The factors involved in planning for office design

4. The importance of power, atmosphere, sound, and lighting systems in office building design

5. Effects of the physical environment on people, equipment, and procedures in the office

6. The systems approach to workstation design

7. Effects of workstation design on office workers

8. Issues of safety and health in the automated office

9. Methods of stress reduction

Environment is recognized by behavioral scientists as having a strong influence on human behavior. Such influence can affect the body, the mind, and the way humans interact with others. For example, prolonged exposure to an excessively noisy environment can impair hearing; even short-term exposure can interfere with concentration and communication. The physical condition, attitudes, and behavior of employees can also be related to the effects of the work environment.

With the growth of office automation, much concern has been generated regarding its effects on the office environment. Concerns range from fears of dehumanization of the office to reported declines in the physical and mental health of workers. Planners of office environments have responded to these concerns by using **human factors engineering.** Such an approach enables planners of office facilities, equipment, and furniture to incorporate into their designs the physical and psychosocial needs of users.

DEFINITION OF ERGONOMICS

The study of the interaction between people's performance and their work environment is called **ergonomics**. Early studies that explored the relationship between workers and their environment were conducted during the years 1924–1932 by Elton Mayo, a social scientist. In a long series of experiments at the Hawthorne plant of the Western Electric Company in Chicago, Mayo assessed the effects of working conditions such as lighting and rest periods upon factory workers' productivity. A major conclusion of the studies was that psychosocial factors can exert even more influence upon productivity than physical working conditions.[1]

More recent studies of the work environment continue to acknowledge its importance to employees. Landmark studies of the office work environment have been conducted by Steelcase, Inc. (1978[2] and 1980[3]) and the Buffalo Organization for Social and Technological Innovation, Inc. (BOSTI, 1984[4]). These studies will be referred to throughout this chapter. A significant finding of the BOSTI study was that a well-designed office environment can affect job performance and satisfaction and increase productivity to equal up to 15 percent of a worker's annual salary. The 1984 BOSTI study supported the finding of the 1978 Steelcase study in which 92 percent of the surveyed office workers reported that their job performance was related to their personal satisfaction with their office surroundings. In the 1980 Steelcase study, office workers had ranked the environmental conditions

1.   Elton Mayo, *The Human Problems of an Industrial Civilization* (New York: Macmillan Publishing Co., Inc., 1934).

2.   *The Steelcase National Study of Office Environments: Do They Work?* (Grand Rapids, Mich.: Steelcase, Inc., and Harris & Associates, 1978).

3.   *The Steelcase National Study of Office Environments, No. II:Comfort and Productivity in the Office of the 80s* (Grand Rapids, Mich.: Steelcase, Inc., and Harris & Associates, 1980).

4.   Michael Brill, *Using Office Design to Increase Productivity* (Grand Rapids, Mich.: Westinghouse Furniture Systems, 1984).

of comfort and quiet second and third (after more pay) as changes that would contribute most to improving productivity. Figure 10-1 lists the rankings of all of these environmental changes.

Figure 10-1 Important Changes for Improving Productivity

Changes	Percent of Office Workers
Knowing that if you produce more in a day, you'll be paid better	48
More comfortable heat, air conditioning, and ventilation	45
More quiet when you need to concentrate on your job	40
More experience with your job	37
More encouragement from managers and supervisors	37
More desks and files that store papers where you can easily find them	29
Better or more office equipment such as more photocopiers, computer terminals, or typewriting machines	28
A more comfortable chair with good back support	26
More stability in the office—less moving around of people	26
Better lighting	22

Source: *The Steelcase National Study of Office Environments, No. 8: Comfort and Productivity in the Office of the 80s* (Grand Rapids, Mich.: Steelcase, Inc., and Harris & Associates, 1980), 8.

Ergonomic studies also have indicated that most organizations do not have ergonomic guidelines in their corporate policies and do not have a systematic approach toward making improvements in the office environment. Fragmented efforts by diverse groups such as architects, engineers, industrial psychologists, facilities planners, interior designers, vendors, and systems analysts are common. With a systems approach, managers can attain the integrated perspective needed to unify all of the environmental factors present in the office. Without coordination, the impact of management's efforts to increase productivity by introducing changes into the work environment will be reduced significantly. Managers need to consider several major issues in coordinating ergonomically designed offices. These issues are office design, building systems, workstation design, worker safety and health, and training. This chapter will examine these issues with the exception of training, which will be addressed in depth in Chapter 16.

TYPES OF OFFICE DESIGN

Office design involves the physical arrangements within an organization to meet its needs. The design needs of an organization can be concerned with planning for the construction or remodeling of an entire building or just the rearrangement of a work area or individual workstation. Historically, organizations have put great care into the exterior of their buildings, since this exterior presents their corporate image to the world. Now organizations are using the same degree of care to design office interiors. These interiors reflect many corporate considerations besides style, function, and cost effectiveness. The organization's concern for employees' health, safety, comfort, and general well-being also can be demonstrated by office interiors. The introduction of automation to offices is a frequent reason for instituting new office designs, but the original motive for changing the design of offices preceded office automation.

THE OPEN PLAN

For over a century offices appeared much the same, but during the late 1950s a new concept in office design developed. A group of designers known as the Quickborner team (named for the German town where the members practiced) introduced to their clients a design that became known as the **open plan**. This plan was designed to foster the free flow of information and egalitarianism (belief that all individuals should have equal rights). The open plan is characterized by the lack of interior walls and the free-standing placement of desks, partitions, and other office furnishings.

When the open plan (also translated as office landscaping from the German *Bürolandschaft*) originally was introduced, it presented an ideal solution for the office needs of the time. The terms open plan and office landscaping came to be considered synonymous. However, the term **office landscaping** actually refers to the planning process of matching design to needs.

With the open-plan design, functional areas are designated by workstations typically surrounded by movable panels. The open-plan design can be used in several different physical arrangements, providing various degrees of enclosure. These arrangements can include any of the following:

1. standalone panels with suspended work surfaces and storage areas serving as workstations.
2. workstations composed of standalone modular storage and work surfaces acting as work dividers.
3. conventional office furniture separated by standalone panels.

Figure 10-2a The open plan office
is designed with free-standing
desks and partitions.
Steelcase Inc.

4. offices laid out in circles with wedge-shaped workstations radiating from a small core. (Such design accommodates one third more people and one third more storage than a space occupied by conventional rectangular or square office design.)

The open plan became popular because of some of its advantages over conventional office design. These advantages include better accommodation for office technology, flexibility in the physical arrangements for furniture and work functions, facilitation of the communication flow, and cost effectiveness. The disadvantages of the open plan generally concern loss of privacy and status, high noise levels, and lack of security for information processing. Although one survey of designers and facilities managers indicates that the open plan is expected to continue to dominate office design throughout the decade of the nineties,[5] other evidence indicates that the open plan has reached its peak of popularity as the ideal solution for office design.

5. "Odds and Ends," *The Wall Street Journal* (June 24, 1988): 17.

Figure 10-2b The hybrid design evolved to accommodate the highly automated office.
Haworth, Inc.

The open plan flourished during the period from the early sixties into the eighties. Approximately 80 percent of new U.S. office construction was in the open-plan design. The open plan appeared ideal for office layouts of the time because it eased the flow of communication, which was then mostly face-to-face and paper-based. Transmission of such types of communication made proximity of workstations an important consideration. However, as automation's impact on the office increased, the need for a different approach to office design became apparent.[6]

THE HYBRID APPROACH

Office landscaping for the highly automated office requires a hybrid approach to office design. A **hybrid approach** encompasses both open and closed spaces with easy and economical convertibility. A survey in the late eighties sponsored by the Admini-

6. Walter A. Kleinschrod, *Update 1987–88: Approaching the Automated Office* (Willow Grove, Pa.: Administrative Management Society Foundation, 1987), 102.

strative Management Society (AMS) illustrates the reasons for this change from the open plan to the hybrid approach for office design. When office automation planners were asked to indicate their toughest environmental problems, the cost and difficultv of making layout changes, open plan or not, were cit' most severe.[7] (See Figure 10-3 for the ranking of the environmental problems of office automation planners.)

Figure 10-3   Office Automators' Toughest Environmental Problems

Environmental Problem	Percent of Respondents Rating Problem as Severe
Expense of layout changes	51
Difficulty of making layout changes	31
Poor workstation design	26
Noisy equipment	21
Inadequate security	20
Lighting/glare on CRT screens	20

Source: Reprinted from *Update 1987–88: Approaching the Automated Office,* © (Willow Grove, Pa.: Administrative Management Society Foundation, Trevose, PA.

The requirements and costs of the automated office have resulted in offices becoming less flexible with the need for more closed, rather than open, space. Office communication is now more electronic than paper-based and thus is routinely transmitted to remote sites as frequently as to the next desk. In addition, computerized work often entails intense concentration giving rise to users' needs for private space. Because of the extensive and expensive cabling, equipment, and furniture installations in the automated office, facilities managers are increasingly reluctant to reconfigure office layouts. Some facilities managers simply leave existing wires and lay new cables over them, sometimes resulting in an overgrown jungle of wires beneath floors, under carpeting, or in overhead ceilings.[8]

Figure 10-4 illustrates several office designs. These plans include the conventional office with fixed walls, a "pool" arrangement usually associated with groups of workers performing typing tasks, and versions of the open plan. Whatever design is

7. *Ibid.,* 98–102.
8. *Ibid.,* 102–105.

Figure 10-4 **Office Designs**

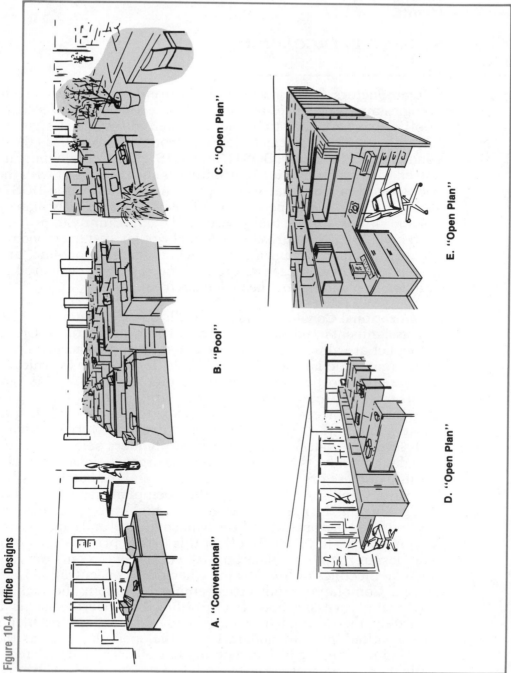

A. "Conventional"

B. "Pool"

C. "Open Plan"

D. "Open Plan"

E. "Open Plan"

Source: *The Steelcase National Study of Office Environments: Do They Work?* (Grand Rapids, Mich.: Steelcase, Inc., and Harris & Associates, 1978), p. 28.

chosen, its selection requires careful consideration of ergonomic factors.

FACTORS INVOLVED IN ERGONOMIC PLANNING

Human Factors.   The needs and requirements for office technologies and procedures as well as the desires and preferences of office workers need to be incorporated into office design. Information of this type can be learned from studies such as those conducted by Steelcase, BOSTI, and AMS. However, planners involved with specific office environments should consult with the people who inhabit that work space. According to the BOSTI study, though, only 25 percent of office workers (usually managers and supervisors) actually receive the opportunity to provide such input. Other concerns that should be of interest to ergonomic planners include organizational, technological, economic, and aesthetic factors. These factors also need to be considered in ergonomic planning for the office environment.

Organizational Considerations.   Tradition often determines office assignments and the type of decor in organizations. Office personnel are allocated work space and amenities according to their organizational status. For example, top executives typically receive large corner offices with big picture windows. Assignments of such preferred surroundings are justified on the basis of managerial needs for a private space to handle confidential matters and a quiet space in which to perform work requiring high levels of concentration. If office planners select an open-plan design, conflicts can arise within the organizational hierarchy because of these organizational traditions and the human desires for privacy and status. Although the open plan was designed to be egalitarian, in many organizations high-ranking managers have retained their private offices while mid-level and supervisory-level managers have not. To offset this loss of privacy, the open-plan design frequently incorporates conference rooms for confidential meetings or for working when deep concentration is required. Complaints from office employees about the lack of privacy and excessive noise have produced a moderate backlash regarding the open plan. Attempts to reduce these problems have resulted in some moderation to the open plan such as the use of almost ceiling-high **demountable walls.** These upholstered walls serve to increase privacy and decrease noise levels, yet retain flexibility for any needed regrouping of furniture or functions.

Space.   Another organizational consideration includes the amount of space required or available for office functions. A recent trend has been to use the computer in planning office floor space. Computers can provide projections of space usage for up to five years and enable designers to simulate models of floor space arrangements. Increasingly, these models include buffer zones. A **buffer zone** is an open space available for future expansion within an organization.

Technology. Ergonomic planning for office design also includes attention by planners to organizational needs for the equipment necessary for office functions. Information regarding the amount, size, electrical requirements, and location of equipment must be obtained. In addition, planners need to look for equipment that is flexible, functional, sturdy, attractive, and within an organization's budget.

Economic Factors. The economic factor is critical in office design and has been a significant advantage of the open plan. Its building, remodeling, and energy costs can account for considerable savings. The initial costs of installation for open-plan design may be as much as 10 to 25 percent less than the traditional office. Changing the layout in open-plan offices costs about 75 cents per square foot compared with approximately $17.50 when changing traditional office layout. Usable floor space of the open plan may be increased by as much as 15 to 20 percent. Energy consumption may be reduced for heating, cooling, ventilation, and lighting as the absence of walls promotes efficiency in these systems.[9] Cost factors such as these, plus increases in office rents, have resulted in a trend toward reductions in office size. By 1993 clerical and secretarial work spaces are expected to decrease about 5 percent.[10] The open-plan design uses as much as 20 to 30 percent less work space than conventional office design. Some of this space savings comes from the use of previously wasted vertical space. For example, the space over the workstation can be used to house storage or shelving units.

Aesthetics. Aesthetics is another important factor in ergonomic planning. Beauty and sensory appeal can be created in the office environment through the use of attractive furnishings, interesting textures, and color. The latter especially has implications for office design as color affects the moods of individuals and their perceptions. For example, light colors make a room ap-

---

9. Zane K. Quible, *Administrative Office Management* (Englewood Cliffs, N.J.: Prentice Hall, Inc., 1989), 99.

10. Arthur R. Williamson, "OA Ergonomics . . . Changing the Workplace to Fit the Worker," *Words* (February–March, 1985): 21.

pear larger, and dark colors make a room appear smaller. Figure 10-5 illustrates how different colors can affect environmental perceptions and cause certain emotions to be stimulated.

Figure 10-5   Color Effects on Environmental Perception

Color	Suggested Effects
Red	Heat, action, excitement
Orange, brown, yellow	Warmth
Blue, green, beige	Coolness, relaxation
Purple	Dignity

Source: Betty L. Schroeder and Diane Routhier Graf, *Office Technology* (New York: John Wiley and Sons, 1984), 9.

Organizations can choose color schemes for their decor according to the psychological effects desired. For example, color can be used to enhance the corporate image and to establish the office atmosphere. If an organization wishes to convey a modernistic, high-tech image, the office decor might feature a color scheme of black and white with accent pieces in acrylic and chrome. On the other hand, if an organization wishes to convey a conservative, formal image, then office decor might feature shades of burgundy and cream with accent pieces in natural wood and dark leather. Another application of color psychology would be in the choice of color for certain functional areas in an organization. For example, a reception room should not be painted apple red since such a color might cause visitors to become impatient. A better choice might be a color conveying warmth or relaxation, such as yellow.

Plants are commonly used in all styles of offices and not only contribute to the aesthetics of the work environment but also can serve functional purposes as work dividers and sound absorbers. The services of professional interior designers should be consulted when planning office decor. Consultants would be able to coordinate all of the elements involved in an aesthetically appealing office design, ensuring an integrated effect throughout the organization.

BUILDING SYSTEMS

Vitally important to contemporary office design are building facilities which are hidden beneath floors, inside walls, in ceilings, and in work dividers. These facilities increasingly are computerized; hence, one of the latest buzzwords in office building construction is **intelligent building.** This term involves the use of a computer, typically a mainframe augmented by microprocessors in strategic areas, to regulate building services and utilities. This idea has been applied to building functions before in such areas as climate control and elevator service, but what is new is the effort to integrate all building systems. Intelligent building construction can offer reduced costs for building maintenance, labor, and operation. For example, sensors can automatically shut off lighting when no motion is present in a room, thus saving on energy costs. Currently, such construction has been confined to urban, prestige buildings. Notable examples include the City Palace in Hartford, Connecticut; Tower Forty-Nine in New York City; the LTV Center in Dallas; and the Citicorp Center in San Francisco.

Intelligent buildings can offer to tenants on a monthly leased basis a continuum of capabilities, ranging from independent to

Figure 10-6 A computer-controlled
building system regulates utilities
and other building services.
Johnson Controls, Inc.

integrated. This sharing enables the tenants of intelligent buildings to access services such as teleconferencing that otherwise might be too costly on an individual basis. Intelligent buildings require a structural interface, meaning some kind of linkage so that the system components can interact together. These systems may include the following:

1. *Automation*—to monitor and control temperature, pressure, humidity, lighting, fire and security protection, and maintenance.
2. *Telecommunications*—to provide telephone systems for internal and external data and voice communication, possibly involving sophisticated microwave and satellite facilities.
3. *Information systems*—to provide data processing and word processing capabilities, often integrated.
4. *Video communications*—to provide teleconferencing and viewing of remote sites in the building such as the parking structure.

Despite the advantages associated with intelligent buildings, the sharing of computer systems can lead to problems for tenants regarding security. Such a trade-off has resulted in an uncertain future for the concept. Several intelligent buildings reportedly are having trouble making a profit. The 1401 New York Avenue building in Washington got only 50 percent of its tenants to use shared services. The Tower 49 project in Manhattan originally designed to provide shared services changed course because of tenants' disinterest.[11]

POWER DISTRIBUTION SYSTEMS

In offices of the past, usually only the computer room had distinctive power needs. However, as automation spread in offices, especially in those with the open plan, even general office areas required special electrical planning. Because of increased power demands from automated equipment, the heating, cooling, and air-conditioning systems are impacted heavily. The automated office results in a 15 to 20 percent average load increase in power demand compared to the traditional office.[12] Planners can determine the increased need for power by reading the specification sheets for equipment or by checking with appropriate vendors.

Special methods for distributing power have been developed for the automated office. One such power system, that of access

---

11.   Walter A. Kleinschrod, *op. cit.,* 112.
12.   Randle Pollack, ''Where Automation is Taking Office Design,'' *Office Automation and Administration* (January, 1983): 83.

floors, is favored for its convenience and ease of maintenance. **An access floor** is a floor raised above the slab base and typically covered by squares of metal tile. These tiles lift up easily to allow access to the cables and conduits of the power system below. Located at intervals beneath the access floor are fixed junction boxes which carry power to predetermined locations. At these locations flush-to-floor outlets provide a source of power for electronic workstations and other electrical needs.

Another means of distributing power to office workstations is through the use of raceways. **Raceways** are channels that are fitted in the bottom or middle of panel dividers and are usually accessible from both sides. With the use of access floors and raceways as power distribution systems, greater flexibility is available for the arrangement of workstations and equipment. Consequently, office equipment can be positioned wherever planning indicates is the best location instead of determining arrangement by proximity to power sources.

ATMOSPHERIC CONTROLS

More comfortable heating, ventilation, and air conditioning (HVAC) was ranked by office workers as the second most important change in the work environment that could improve productivity (see Figure 10-1). HVAC systems typically are part of the heating-cooling system in buildings and affect not only temperature but also circulation of air and air quality. Designers need to be knowledgeable about factors affecting HVAC. These factors include atmospheric conditions, HVAC's interface with office technology, federal energy regulations, and comfort standards. Figure 10-7 lists standards developed by the American

Figure 10-7   Comfort Standards

Quality	Standard
Temperature	73°–79° Fahrenheit (summer)
	68°–74.5° Fahrenheit (winter)
Relative Humidity	30–60 percent (year-round)
Air Velocity (indoor)	.15–.25 m/second
Satisfies 80 percent of an average population	

Source: Ansi *ASHRAE Standard 55–1981* (Atlanta, Ga.: American Society of Heating, Refrigerating and Air-Conditioning Engineers, Inc.). Reprinted by permission.

Society of Heating, Refrigerating and Air-Conditioning Engineers (ASHRAE), which satisfy the comfort levels of 80 percent of the average population.

Four factors constitute the atmospheric conditions within the office environment — temperature, humidity, air conditioning, and air quality:

Temperature.   Arriving at the "right" temperature to suit all office workers might be an impossible task. The degree of warmth or coolness in the office was reported as "not right" by over half (55 percent) of the office workers surveyed in the 1980 Steelcase study. Preferences varied by sex and age, with women tending to prefer warmer temperatures than men, and younger employees preferring cooler temperatures than older employees. In the BOSTI study, temperature fluctuation rather than specific temperatures was cited by office workers as most bothersome.

Help may soon be on the way to solve this common office dilemma caused by conflicting personal preferences in heating and cooling. **Advanced comfort systems,** the very latest idea in office design, enable workers to have personal control over their environmental elements. Such systems are catching on in Europe but are still rare in the U.S. With advanced comfort systems each worker can control temperature, velocity and direction of air, and lighting surrounding a workstation.[13]

Temperature is so significant that it not only affects employee comfort but also job satisfaction and job performance. Excessive coolness can distract from concentration, and excessive heat can cause drowsiness. Both factors can result in diminished worker productivity. In addition, temperature extremes can damage office equipment. The temperature limits for computerized equipment are commonly between 60 and 100 degrees Fahrenheit. If the temperature falls or rises outside of these limits, such as during an extended period of power failure, equipment problems can occur. Excessive heat also can affect automated office supplies, such as printer ribbons and floppy disks. Such office supplies should be stored in a cool, dry place to avoid any problems. Current designs that contribute to the control of temperature problems in the office are zoning and heating recovery systems.

Zoning allows temperature variations in certain functional areas without interfering with the comfort of employees located in other areas. Examples of areas with a need for extra cooling would include a computer room or an area with a heavy density

13. "When Some Like It Hot and Some Don't," *The Wall Street Journal* (May 2, 1988): 27.

of workers. Where extra heat is generated by office equipment such as computers or systems such as lighting, **heating recovery systems** are being used to capture otherwise wasted heat and recirculate it to other areas. Organizations have become interested in energy conservation measures such as zoning and heating because of rising energy costs. In addition, organizations need to comply with federal government energy regulations.

Prompted by the "energy crisis," the Carter Administration in 1979 initiated an energy conservation law, which set temperature limits for public buildings. The temperature limit for winter is no higher than 65 degrees Fahrenheit and for summer no lower than 78 degrees Fahrenheit. Although offices have been impacted by energy regulations, office workers often counteract the effects of the energy regulations by using supplementary heating and cooling devices.

Humidity.   Humidity is the amount of moisture in the air. This moisture affects the comfort level of office employees and may also affect equipment and supplies. A relative humidity range of 30 to 60 percent is comfortable for most workers. The normally accepted range for humidity for automated equipment is between 20 and 80 percent. If humidity drops below the lower level, static electricity will build up causing equipment problems. If the humidity level increases above the higher limit, moisture could condense inside equipment causing a short circuit. Also, paper can curl and become heavier because of increased moisture content, which can cause problems with jamming in paper feeders. In addition, magnetic media can react negatively to humidity levels outside of their normal tolerance range. Both temperature and humidity can be controlled, however, with the use of air conditioning.

Air Conditioning.   In offices of the past, workers opened windows to permit fresh air and breezes to enter the office environment. In the BOSTI study, office workers indicated a preference to be located near a window; however, this preference did not affect their job performance and was only slightly related to their job satisfaction. In the 1980 Steelcase study, two thirds of the office workers reported that they could not open the windows in their offices because buildings increasingly are designed for energy conservation. Consequently, many offices are without fresh air because of lack of windows or windows which do not open. This situation has given rise to the condition known as **tight building syndrome.**

Consequently, workers are relying on air-conditioning systems for air circulation. Such systems, however, while improving air circulation, can bring discomfort to some workers because of drafts. Nevertheless, good air circulation is important because stagnant air can lead to problems such as headaches, nausea, and fatigue, as well as unpleasant odors. Even more serious problems of respiratory illness and cancer can occur due to indoor pollution caused by the presence of asbestos and radon. (Asbestos is a fiber commonly used in the past to insulate buildings, and radon is a radioactive gas that can accumulate in tightly constructed buildings built upon certain types of rock foundations.)

Air Quality.   Cleanliness of air in offices is important for the health of workers since poor air quality can harm the eyes, nasal passages, and lungs. Common pollutants in office air include dust, tobacco smoke, and pollens. Such pollutants can become trapped in office environments, adhering to drapes, carpeting, and upholstered furniture. These pollutants can lead not only to human discomfort but also to equipment problems. For example, disk drives particularly are prone to problems caused by dust and dirt in the air. Dust particles can attract static, resulting in faulty operation by disk drives. Damage from dirt and dust also can be done to disk drives themselves, resulting in expensive repairs. For this reason, smoking by employees in the vicinity of computerized equipment should not be permitted.

Offices have become battlegrounds in the war between smokers and nonsmokers. Although fewer than ten states have laws restricting smoking in the workplace, employees under tort law (wrongful acts not involving breach of contract for which civil action can be brought) can sue employers who compel them to work in a toxic atmosphere. Companies are responding in a variety of ways to their employees' concerns regarding passive smoking (the inhalation of the smoke of others). According to a survey by the American Society for Personnel Administration, 38 percent of companies have a smoking policy; 21 percent are thinking about one; while 41 percent had no plans to create one. Some companies have established segregated areas for smokers and installed ventilation systems that keep smoke away from nonsmokers.[14]

SOUND TREATMENT

Another system to be considered by office designers is sound. A unit measurement of the intensity of sound is the **decibel.** The

14.   Robert Barr, Associated Press, "Workplaces Becoming a Front in War Over Smoking," *The Daily News,* (Bowling Green, Ky.; May 17, 1987): 17-B.

average office sound level is 50 decibels, but the sound level in a highly automated environment such as a data processing center can reach 80 to 90 decibels. Maintaining control over the sound level in offices is important for several reasons. Prolonged exposure to excessive noise can impair hearing as well as affect job performance. In the BOSTI study the noise levels from people talking and phones ringing were cited by office workers as most annoying. Also, the study reported a relationship between increased noise levels and decreased job satisfaction among office workers. Recall that a quiet environment was ranked third by office workers in the 1980 Steelcase study as one of the most important factors likely to increase productivity. Noise can reduce workers' ability to concentrate and lead to irritability and decreased efficiency.

Noise was previously cited as a possible disadvantage of the open-plan design. Such a problem can be minimized with proper sound treatment incorporated into the office design. Sound-proofing methods are used widely in automated offices because of the high noise level associated with some types of equipment. Reducing the noise level can be accomplished in a variety of ways. One common way is the installation of **acoustical hoods** on printers. These coverings, which fit over the tops of printers, serve to deaden the noise. The loud noise associated with impact printers is fast becoming history as offices replace them with soundless, nonimpact printers, such as the laser. However, the newly found office quiet may be only short-lived as voice technology impacts the office and workers begin to talk to their computers and their computers talk back. Figure 10-8 illustrates the decibel level of some common noises, including printers.

Other sound-control treatments include the use of sound-absorbing materials such as cork, fabric, and fiberglass incorporated into ceiling tiles, wall coverings, and panel dividers. Draperies, carpeting, upholstered furniture, and plants also help to absorb noise. The objective of sound control, however, is not to eliminate all sounds in the office. Psychological studies have shown that the complete absence of sound is a form of sensory deprivation and can produce negative effects on people.

Sound systems that can mask noise while providing a background sound have been introduced into the office environment. These sound systems are known as **white sound** or **white noise** and may include such sounds as blowing wind, crashing waves, rustling leaves, and music. The use of music, however, can be controversial in an office environment because of individual preferences for different types of music. Interpersonal conflicts can arise among office workers because of disagreements regarding types of music. In addition, the music preferences of the of-

Figure 10-8   Sound Levels

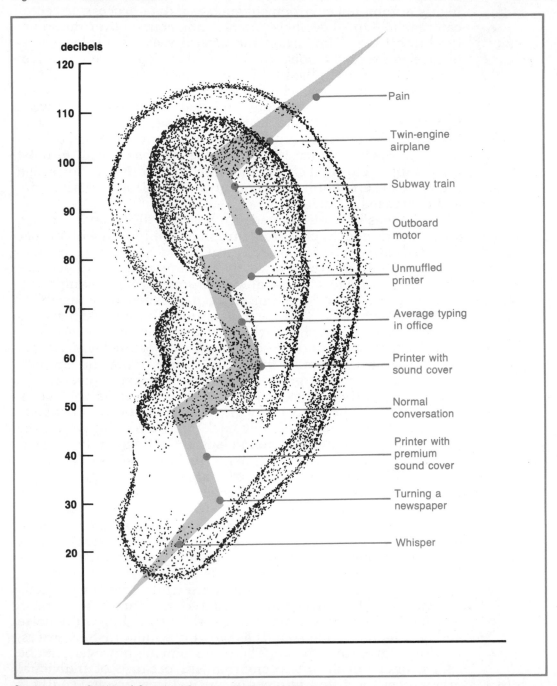

Source: Inmac Catalog of Computer Supplies (August, 1985), p. 31.

fice workers might not be compatible with the organizational image desired by management. Therefore, music played by a radio station and broadcast into the office environment is not recommended.

However, musical programs especially designed as background music can be purchased. Such music is unobtrusive, often intermittent, and involves a variety of rhythms. Used effectively, musical programming can be perceived by employees as contributing to a more pleasing work environment and can result in improved office productivity. For example, as the afternoon progresses and workers experience fatigue, the tempo of the music could increase, providing workers with a morale boost.

LIGHTING SYSTEMS

Another important system in buildings is lighting. **Footcandles** and **lumens** are the units used to measure the quantity of light and the flow of light, respectively. The necessity of providing proper lighting for office workers appears to be a high priority for management. The 1980 Steelcase study noted that 88 percent of the office workers felt comfortable with their office lighting. In the BOSTI study, however, clerical workers who were involved in the most demanding visual tasks reported the least satisfaction with office lighting. This study also reported that the level and distribution of lighting affected the job satisfaction of office workers. Special attention, therefore, needs to be given by management in providing lighting for the office environment.

In the automated office, fluorescent lighting (light produced by a glass tube coated with a light-producing substance) is preferred to incandescent lighting (light produced by a coiled tungsten wire filament contained in a heated vacuum bulb). Reasons for this preference are that fluorescent lighting is more economical and produces less heat and glare. Another lighting recommendation for the automated office is the use of both overhead and workstation lighting. Overhead lighting, often referred to as **ambient lighting,** can be suspended from the ceiling, recessed in the ceiling, or located in troughs along the top of the wall. Ambient lighting usually is used in combination with **task lighting,** which is installed as part of the actual workstation. Thus, office workers are afforded both indirect and direct lighting sources.

In conventional and open-plan office designs, artificial lighting may be the only source of illumination. An additional source, however, can be natural lighting in the form of skylights or windows. Windows can complement the use of artificial lighting as well as provide the psychological benefit of temporary relief

Figure 10-9   Fluorescent lighting is
ideal for automated offices.
G.E. Lighting

from the internal environment. In the automated office, the size
and location of windows can be critical. Different light ex-
posures, such as north or south, can have a decided effect upon
atmospheric conditions in the office and affect the HVAC systems. Thus, some buildings are designed without any form of
natural lighting. Other problems that can occur as a result of
natural lighting are shadowing and glare. In addition, glare can
be increased by reflections from shiny surfaces, such as glossy
paint, glass-topped furniture, or highly polished surfaces. Such
problems can be detrimental to office employees working with
video display terminals.

   A new trend in office lighting is the use of solar energy. Solar
technology can become practical for some buildings in the near
future partly because as much as 40 percent of air conditioning
costs goes to disperse heat from electric lights. **Solar lighting** for
offices is accomplished through the use of empty tubes of clear
acrylic plastic scored on the inside with grooves used as prisms.
These prisms reflect light along the interior of the tubes while
releasing enough light to make the tube glow like a conventional
lighting fixture.[15]

   15.   "What's New," *The Wall Street Journal* (July 7, 1986): 33.

WORKSTATION DESIGN

Electronic workstations are part of the burgeoning multibillion-dollar office furniture industry. Dramatic changes have occurred in this industry because of the influences of the open-plan design, automation, and ergonomics. Basic components of a workstation involve a chair, a work surface, and storage facilities. In designing workstations, manufacturers consider the requirements of the tasks to be performed and the needs of the workers who will perform them.

SYSTEMS FURNITURE

In order to accommodate the needs of the automated office, a systems approach has been used by office furniture manufacturers. Consequently, the term **systems furniture** frequently is used to describe contemporary office furniture designs. A systems approach means that modular, interchangeable components such as work surfaces, desk pedestals, auxiliary tops, end supports, storage units, dividers, and other equipment are combined into whole units so that the total effect created is greater than any part could contribute independently. These components, when combined, create custom-designed workstations for each type of work performed in the office. Just as the job tasks of the executive, administrative assistant, and VDT operator differ, so should their workstations.

Furniture manufacturers adopted a systems approach to design because traditional office furniture generally was unsuitable for the automated office. For example, a personal computer placed on a standard office desk is too high for proper typing height, resulting in an uncomfortable position for operator efficiency. Another special need for the automated office is storage for magnetic media such as cassettes and disks. Figure 10-10 illustrates an ergonomically designed workstation integrating various system components.

HUMAN FACTORS

Systems furniture can cost about twice as much as traditional office furniture. However, the gains in productivity to the organization because of its design can range up to 30 percent. In addition, the BOSTI study reported that furniture design was a factor affecting environmental and job satisfaction as well as ease of communication. These gains have been achieved not only because of task and equipment requirements but because human factors have been incorporated into furniture design.

Figure 10-10 **Ergonomic Workstation Layout**

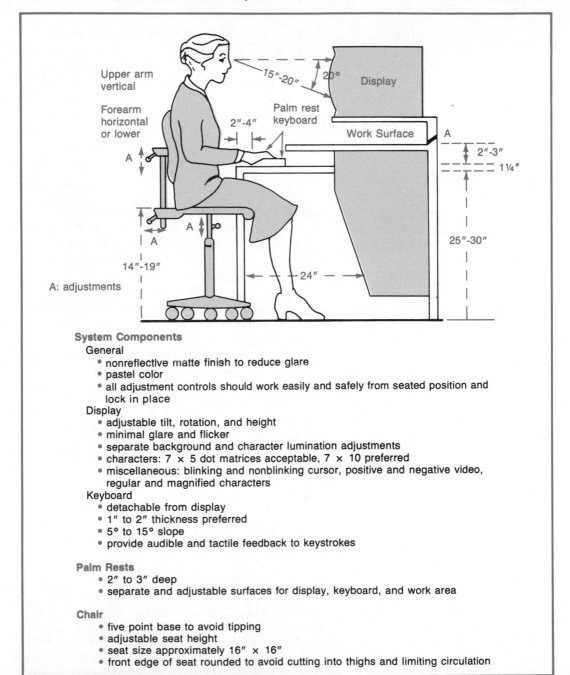

System Components

General
- nonreflective matte finish to reduce glare
- pastel color
- all adjustment controls should work easily and safely from seated position and lock in place

Display
- adjustable tilt, rotation, and height
- minimal glare and flicker
- separate background and character lumination adjustments
- characters: 7 × 5 dot matrices acceptable, 7 × 10 preferred
- miscellaneous: blinking and nonblinking cursor, positive and negative video, regular and magnified characters

Keyboard
- detachable from display
- 1″ to 2″ thickness preferred
- 5° to 15° slope
- provide audible and tactile feedback to keystrokes

Palm Rests
- 2″ to 3″ deep
- separate and adjustable surfaces for display, keyboard, and work area

Chair
- five point base to avoid tipping
- adjustable seat height
- seat size approximately 16″ × 16″
- front edge of seat rounded to avoid cutting into thighs and limiting circulation

Source: Sandy Thompson, ''Is the VDT A Terminal Disease?'' The Secretary (February, 1984), p. 9.

Psychosocial Needs.   Behavioral scientists tell us that individuals possess a desire to establish a space to call one's own, referred to as **territoriality.** In addition, people also desire social contact with others. These two needs can be satisfied by the effective use of work dividers. The dividers or panels are manufactured in floor-to-ceiling height or standard sitting height and used to separate workstations. When seated, employees are afforded a private work space free from distractions and protected from excessive noise. Yet, when standing or when moving about the office area, visual contact and occasions for socializing with others are available. In addition, employees have the opportunity to define their work space by personalizing their workstations. With the use of photographs and other personal items, employees can develop a greater degree of ownership of their work space.

Anatomical and Physiological Needs.   Much effort has been made by designers to create a more comfortable workstation. Originally, efforts centered on anatomical factors involving human body structure, body dimensions, and bodily movements. Through such study, designers incorporated into equipment, furniture, and furnishings accommodation for a variety of human shapes and sizes. Typically this accommodation was done by introducing adjustability into the design of the product. In order for adjustable features to be beneficial to office workers, however, they must be aware of the features and understand how to operate them. Office supervisors need to communicate the benefits and explain the operation of adjustable furniture. Evidence exists that such efforts frequently are not made and that adjustable furniture once installed is seldom adjusted by office workers. Office workers also should be aware of proper posture and correct body movements to derive the most benefit from ergonomically designed furniture.

Even with ergonomically designed workstations and perfect posture, however, office workers may still experience problems. Office work is sedentary; remaining seated for long periods of time at a workstation, especially if using a VDT, can be uncomfortable. This condition is known as **muscle loading** and is caused by the effect of gravity on the body and being seated with the legs in a fixed position for long periods which creates muscular strain and fatigue. This problem can be alleviated somewhat by allowing employees a choice between standing or sitting for the performance of some tasks.

When employees are seated at their workstations, the design of their chairs is of critical importance. Chairs designed especially for use at an electronic workstation are referred to as **task seating.** These chairs are recommended because sitting for long periods of time in a static position builds pressures on the spine, thighs, and neck. The importance of a comfortable chair to office workers was acknowledged in the 1980 Steelcase study. Desirable characteristics for office chairs include adjustable seat and back height for desk and work; sufficient thickness of padding; a breathable chair covering that resists absorbing extreme heat or cold; lower back support; casters, a swivel base, arm rests, and chair tilt; and overall comfort.

In addition to chairs, the physical arrangement of the workstation can affect worker comfort. An improperly designed or arranged workstation can lead to unnecessary worker stretching, bending, and moving about the office, resulting in fatigue and possible strains. Consequently, the physical arrangement of the work surface should allow the most frequently performed activities to be reached by hand movement. Less frequently performed activities could be reached by extension of the arm or require some leaning and bending. Figure 10-11 illustrates the optimum working areas for different activities.

Workstations in the office can be arranged in groups or clusters to facilitate communication and efficient office operation. A cluster arrangement might be in the form of a Y, an X, a line, or a circle (see Figure 10-12). Whatever physical arrangement is used, work flow should be promoted and unnecessary traffic patterns

Figure 10-11 Workstation Arrangement

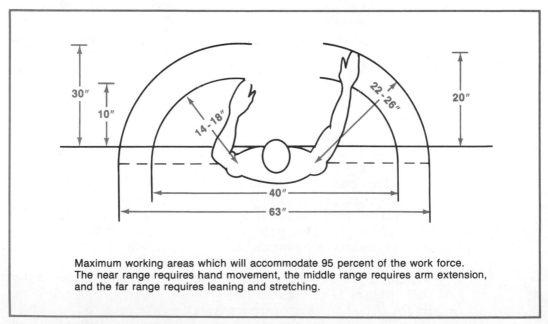

Maximum working areas which will accommodate 95 percent of the work force. The near range requires hand movement, the middle range requires arm extension, and the far range requires leaning and stretching.

Source: Illustration Courtesy of National Office Products Association (NOPA).

Figure 10-12   X, Y, Line, and Circle Clusters

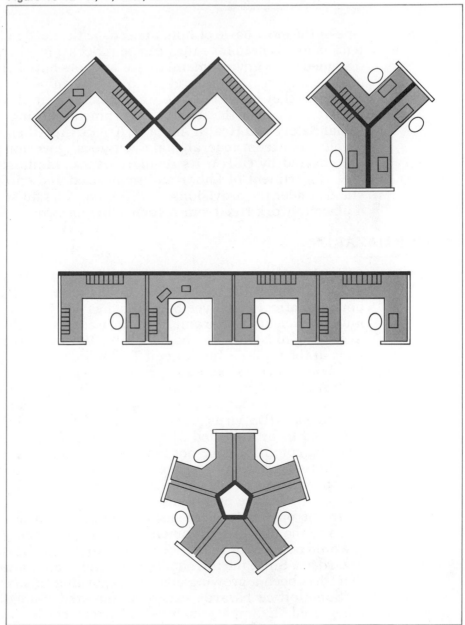

eliminated. While improvements in office and workstation design are important considerations in an ergonomically designed environment, the issue of employee safety and health cannot be ignored.

OFFICE SAFETY AND HEALTH

One of the most basic of human needs is the need to feel safe. Attention to this need for safety can be reflected in an ergonomically designed work environment. Office workers have benefited from a general increase in interest by diverse groups in working conditions as they affect the safety and health of employees. This interest resulted in the federal government passing the Occupational Safety and Health Act of 1970 (OSHA). All employees and employers except federal, state, and local government workers are covered by OSHA. Its regulations are administered by the U.S. Department of Labor and monitored and enforced by the states. Under the provisions of OSHA, workers must be provided a place to work free from recognizable hazards.

OFFICE HAZARDS

Office hazards generally are not perceived as potentially threatening or shortening to one's life. If such fears do exist, they are bound to affect employee behavior. Fear of AIDS (Acquired Immune Deficiency Syndrome, a fatal disease) is such an example. According to a study by the Center for Work Performance Problems at the Georgia Institute of Technology, 37 to 66 percent of the 2,000 workers polled expressed various fears of mingling with AIDS victims in the workplace.[16] Despite the fact that no evidence exists that participating in normal work activities can spread the AIDS virus, such fears can be potentially disabling and need to be dispelled by management. If safe and healthful working conditions are not maintained, unnecessary employee discomfort can occur. The result can be extensive cost to organizations in terms of lost work days, poor morale, and increases in medical insurance premiums.

In the days before the automated office, little thought was given to the office environment as being potentially dangerous. It would be rare for the office worker to think of an office job as hazardous. Since the introduction of office automation, however, there has been a growing concern regarding this issue.

Some office hazards can be eliminated immediately, once recognized. Examples include electrical cords and cables in walking paths of employees, frayed cords, improperly grounded equipment, and electrical outlets protruding above floor level. Other hazards associated with the automated office, however,

16. "Georgia Tech Poll Finds AIDS Fears in Workplace," *The Wall Street Journal* (February 2, 1988): 14.

are not so obvious or easily remedied. The source of many of these other hazards has been attributed to the use of the video display terminal.

PROBLEMS WITH VIDEO DISPLAY TERMINALS

Video display terminals (VDTs) were introduced into the work environment in the late 1960s, but problems did not surface until the mid-1970s. Health and safety hazards associated with VDT use involve problems of a musculoskeletal nature as well as those of vision, radiation, and stress.

Musculoskeletal Complaints. Complaints from VDT users about aches and pains in the neck, shoulder, lower back, and wrists are common. Many of these musculoskeletal problems occur because of **repetitive straining injuries (RSI)** caused by the many repeated, forceful motions essential to computer operation. Ergonomic features in workstation design can help reduce such complaints. For example, one form of RSI, carpal tunnel syndrome, a disabling wrist ailment, can be alleviated through the use of a wrist rest. Other ergonomic features include adjustable controls for chairs and workstation height, conveniently reached storage facilities, detachable keyboards, tiltable and/or adjustable monitors, and the use of a document holder. The latter device can be helpful in reducing neck strain caused by repeatedly turning from the source document to the screen. Also, less refocusing by the eyes is required to accommodate different eye levels and color differences between copy and screen.

Vision. Complaints regarding vision by VDT users include eyestrain, fatigue, tearing, burning, blurring, twitching, deteriorating vision, and cataracts. While no evidence exists to justify the cataract complaint, explanations can be provided for the other vision problems. According to vision experts, eye problems are likely to occur to VDT operators because of their prolonged periods at the screen requiring a continuous focusing and refocusing of the eyes. Such focusing is contrary to the natural inclination of the eye to view things at more of a distance. Because of these extra focusing and shifting tasks for the eyes, vision experts believe aggravation can occur to the eyes. Vision problems can become pronounced if preexisting, uncorrected defects are present. Vision experts believe that as many as 20 to 30 percent of the population have these defects.

Many recommendations have been made by vision experts to diminish eye-related problems associated with VDT use. One suggestion has been that people over forty years of age should not be permitted to work on VDTs. The reason for this recommendation is that the eye begins to change significantly at this age. Other recommendations are not as radical, however. Regular eye examinations would be a wise procedure for VDT users to follow, because eyes are changing constantly. VDT users who wear prescription lenses should take care to ensure that they are proper for VDT work. For example, people who wear bifocals may need an entirely different lens prescription when working on a VDT. While VDT users are on the job, regular breaks (ten minutes every hour or twenty minutes every two hours) are recommended to reduce eyestrain.

Other recommendations to protect the eyes include the use of a screen filter to reduce glare and the use of different colors to improve screen contrast. The recommended character colors for display are amber (orange) or green on a dark background or black characters on a white background. Wearing white or light-colored clothing also might have to be avoided if screen glare results from such apparel.

Another problem associated with VDTs is flicker. **Flicker** involves the movement of displayed characters on the screen. Images projected on VDTs generally are made up of a series of light pulses. If conditions are not right, the images will not be steady. Flickering can result in operator eyestrain and irritation, although individual perceptions of flicker vary.

Radiation.   Radiation from VDTs is a controversial issue. Originally, groups such as the National Research Council, the National Institute for Occupational Safety and Health (NIOSH), and the Federal Drug Administration maintained that the level of radiation emitted from VDTs was not likely to be hazardous. However, a study conducted at the Kaiser Permanente Medical Care Program in Oakland, California, found that female clerical workers who use VDTs more than 20 hours a week had more than twice as many miscarriages as women who didn't work with VDTs. In addition to miscarriages, other instances of pregnancy-related problems have been reported by VDT users including premature births, birth defects, and newborn deaths. The implications of such problems are obvious considering this sobering fact: of the 10 million or so Americans who use a VDT much of the day, about half of these are women of child-bearing age.[17] No definitive conclusions can be made as yet on the effects of VDT radiation upon the female reproductive system until long-term studies are conducted.

17. Bill Paul, "Latest Study on VDTs Adds to Safety Fears," *The Wall Street Journal* (October 20, 1988): B1, B4.

The Kaiser study and other evidence point to the need for further research on the effects of radiation from VDTs and make caution necessary. Feminist groups and unions have taken note of these alleged effects of VDT radiation and have responded with demands for immediate action. These demands include protection devices such as lead aprons for female VDT users, metal shielding for VDTs, the right of transfer to a position not requiring VDT use, or an unpaid leave of absence from the VDT position.[18]

Stress.   Use of a VDT by clerical operators has been linked with stress according to studies conducted by the National Institute for Occupational Safety and Health (NIOSH) and other researchers. **Stress** involves a pattern of physiological, psychological, and behavioral responses to environmental demands that exceed an individual's capacity to cope. Symptoms of stress may include anxiety, boredom, chronic fatigue, nervousness, headaches, and depression. When such stress symptoms occur in workers in an automated environment, they are said to be experiencing technostress. Effects of stress vary widely among individuals, depending upon their stress-tolerance levels. Not all stress is undesirable, however. A certain degree of stress can be beneficial in priming workers for peak job performance when required. When stress levels are unhealthy, they can interfere with an individual's physical and mental well-being as well as job performance.

Stress from the work environment, including the office environment, is not anything new. The use of VDTs on the job, however, is relatively new, and such use appears to produce stress unlike that associated with traditional office work. Clerical VDT operators, for example, have reported higher levels of job stress than other clerical workers.[19] When individuals experience high levels of job stress, their organizations are likely to feel its effects. These effects of job stress among workers can be indicated by high levels of absenteeism and turnover as well as low morale and low levels of productivity.

Some causes of VDT operator stress appear to originate from the nature of the job activity rather than the VDT itself. For example, viewing the VDT for long periods of time without a break or change in task activity may produce stress symptoms in some individuals. Other VDT-related job stress is associated more

---

18.   Joann S. Labin, ''Fearing Radiation, Pregnant Women Win Transfers From Work on Video Terminals,'' *The Wall Street Journal* (April 6, 1984): 25.

19.   Michael J. Smith et al., ''An Investigation of Health Complaints and Job Stress in Video Display Operations,'' in *Human Factors,* Vols. 23–24 (Cincinnati: National Institute for Occupational Safety and Health, August, 1981), 387–400.

with the general nature of the automated office environment. Tasks might become so simplified and routine that workers are not challenged or stimulated when performing them.

In addition, workers might suffer from technophobia, which is a fear of technology. Such fears arise because office workers might worry that the new technology will be difficult to learn, leading to loss of self-esteem before their supervisors and peers. Other workers might worry that automation will replace them on the job. Some office workers might hold "antitechnology" attitudes, even resorting to attempted sabotage of the new office systems. Frustrations among office workers can develop when they are forced to learn new technology on the job while trying to keep up with their regular work load. Also, employers may expect increased productivity because of the new technology, leading to increased demands upon workers. Fortunately, help exists to assist office workers in combating the effects of stress.

METHODS OF STRESS RELIEF

Reducing stress in the work environment has become big business. The multimillion-dollar stress-reducing industry offers a multitude of products and services, including soothing sound machines, relaxation chairs with vibrating cushions and stereo, stress management seminars, and high-tech devices. An example of the latter includes the use of a technique called **electromyographic (emg) bio-feedback** as shown in Figure 10-13. The VDT operator wears a lightweight headset connected to a portable monitor and is alerted to the presence of muscle tension by an audible signal. With this device the VDT operator can be trained to avoid improper posture and muscle stress.[20]

Another sophisticated approach to reducing stress is the use of computer programs. Such programs range from the harmless to the potentially harmful. One example of the former is Chuckle Pops, software allowing users to call up a series of jokes on screen when boredom strikes.[21] Another program, The Messenger, displays calming images of mountains and streams along with subliminal messages such as "My world is calm." Subliminal messages are presented so rapidly on the computer screen that they cannot be consciously detected. The potential for harm arises

20.   Clifford M. Gross and Elissa-Beth Chapnik, "Ergonomic Training for Tomorrow's Office," *Training and Development Journal* (November, 1987): 60.
21.   Jan Sheehan, "High Tech Toys for Treating Tension," *Sky* (November, 1988): 111.

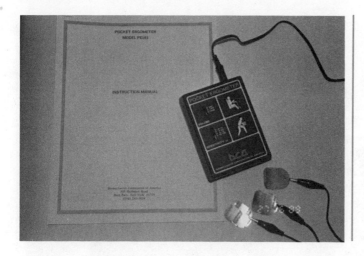

Figure 10-13 **A pocket ergometer pinpoints the location of muscle tension.**
Biomechanics Corporation of America

with such software because management can insert messages (like "work faster") into the program without the knowledge of the VDT operator.[22]

Figure 10-14 **Stress-Reducing Exercises at the VDT Workstation**

Head Rolls: Roll your head slowly clockwise and then counterclockwise, three times each way, allowing it to drop heavily.

Neck Stretches: Slowly allow your head to drop forward, then to each side, then to the back. In each direction, stretch as far as possible. Repeat ten times.

Shoulder Stretches: Shrug both shoulders together, and then each alternately. Raise them as high as you can and allow them to drop heavily.

Backstretch at Desk: Slowly raise your arms behind the back of your chair, clasping your hands together. Squeeze your shoulder blades together. Then gradually lean backward, arching your upper back.

Source: Jan Sheehan, "High-Tech Toys for Treating Tension," *SKY*, (November, 1988): 111. This article has been reprinted/republished through the courtesy of Halsey Publishing Co., publishers of Delta Air Lines *SKY* magazine.

22. Gary T. Marx and Sanford Sherizen, "What Bugs Workers?" *Best of Business Quarterly* (summer, 1987): 44–45.

Figure 10-14a **The Executive Stretch**

Figure 10-14b **The Short Shrug**

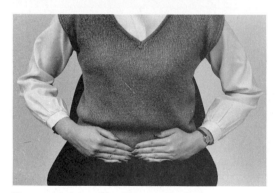

Figure 10-14c **The Tummy Tucker**

Figure 10-14d **The Agile Ankler**

Supervisors of office workers impacted by automation can do many things to help them avoid or reduce job stress. Examples include the following:

1. Instituting initial and follow-up training for the new technology.
2. Instructing VDT operators in stress-reducing exercises (see Figure 10-14) and providing other forms of ergonomic training.
3. Establishing VDT-user support groups.
4. Providing information regarding the effects of automation on office jobs.
5. Ensuring that VDT operators receive regular breaks.
6. Assigning operators a variety of tasks.

7. Allowing operators to complete a total job.
8. Permitting operators to maintain a degree of control over their work.

Implementation of these supervisory activities coupled with an ergonomically designed work environment can do much to contribute to the physical and mental well-being of office employees.

WOHL'S BUSINESS PERSPECTIVE

When office automation was in its first flower (early eighties), the ergonomics of the office was on everyone's hot list. Now that office automation is much more common, it has become more of a background issue, not ignored but much less emphasized.

But a properly designed office is not a fad, a bit of business chic, here today and gone tomorrow. A carefully designed office makes the difference between less work done and more work, less employee comfort and health and a pleasant, safe workplace.

Employers are often penny wise and pound foolish. Concerned about the large investment required to automate each desk, they may choose to postpone much smaller investments in preparing the office to permit automation to be installed in an optimal environment.

For instance, computers are often placed on ordinary office desks. For most average-sized humans, this means the computer keyboard is a few inches too high. Trivial? Not at all. Those few inches can be shoulder, neck and back pain at the end of each day, decreasing employee effectiveness and productivity—and leading to increases in absenteeism.

Elaborate desks with multiple work levels are not required to solve this problem. In fact, such work stations are not only overly costly, but may be inconvenient for users to work on. (The paperless office is still filled with paper and most of us work on our computers while referring to mounds of paper all around us!)

Simple, inexpensive techniques can solve many ergonomic woes. Desks can be lowered—some are adjustable, others can be fixed by the office handyman. Or inexpensive metal shelves can be purchased that can offer a lower work surface for the keyboard. At worst, occasional typists can simply open their desk drawers and put the keyboard on that ad hoc lower level.

Other problems can have simple, informal solutions. Wall surfaces can be softened (to control noise) and enhanced aesthetically or color-corrected by mounting inexpensive decorative fabrics over wood lathing and hanging the result, rather like an over-sized painting. The area behind the fabric becomes a sound baffle. The fabric itself can offer a fresh point of view—what about a mountain scene, serene clouds, or your favorite color?

Lighting needs to change, but users can gain the most individual control with some easy-to-implement choices: Turn *down* the ambient (over-all) lighting by placing light diffusers over existing fixtures or removing some of the fluorescent bulbs. Make up for this kind-to-the-computer change by *adding* light with inexpensive clamp-on lamps. Pick sturdy ones with lots of user adjustments, so they can be pointed on the paper surfaces where extra light might be needed. Turned upside down (pointing at the ceiling), they can be indirect lighting, too. We've bought lots of these at discount stores for less than $20 each.

This brings up an ergonomics-related issue: automated offices need lots of electric outlets. There's simply more equipment to plug in. Be sure you handle this problem ergonomically (and safely). Don't use octopus plugs. Buy power strips with surge protection, if needed, and be certain that you're not asking for more power than your electrical system is prepared to provide.

SUMMARY

Ergonomics is the study of the interaction between people and their work environment. According to studies of office workers, improvements in the comfort and quiet in the office environment lead to increases in job productivity and job satisfaction. An ergonomically designed office can be planned most effectively with a systems approach.

By combining the elements involved in office design, building systems, and workstation design, a totally unified effort can be made to improve the comfort, safety, and health of office workers. Initially, the open plan was a popular design for use in automated offices; however, a mix of open and closed spaces enabling economical, easy convertibility has become the more ideal solution for the design requirements of the automated office.

With ergonomic planning, human needs and requirements become a major consideration in the design of office facilities, furniture, and furnishings. Planners need to consider the human aspect underlying organizational, technological, economic, and aesthetic factors. Offices increasingly are serviced by computerized building systems that control power, heating, ventilation, and air conditioning. An emerging trend in office construction is the intelligent building concept, offering integrated, computerized services and utilities. Office designers need to be knowledgeable about atmospheric conditions, office technology requirements, federal energy regulations, and comfort standards to deal effectively with the many elements involved in building systems. Sound treatment by a variety of means is typically a part of a well-designed automated office environment. Lighting systems involving ambient, task, and natural lighting are used currently in the automated office; and, in the future, solar lighting may become feasible.

Because office furniture manufacturers are combining modular components into flexible workstations, these units are called systems furniture. Such workstations feature ergonomic designs based upon task requirements and human factors.

The issue of safety and health in the automated office is a controversial one because of the video display terminal. Some problems associated with VDT use involve workers' muscles, eyes, mental health, and radiation; however, no definite conclusions can be reached yet on possible radiation effects because of the lack of long-term studies.

KEY TERMS

human factors engineering	buffer zone
ergonomics	intelligent building
open plan	access floor
office landscaping	raceways
hybrid approach	advanced comfort systems
demountable walls	zoning
heating recovery systems	systems furniture
tight building syndrome	territoriality
decibel	muscle loading
acoustical hoods	task seating
white sound	repetitive straining injuries
footcandles	(RSI)
lumens	flicker
ambient lighting	stress
task lighting	electromyographic (emg)
solar lighting	bio-feedback

REVIEW QUESTIONS

1. How is the study of ergonomics related to office productivity?

2. Why would an understanding of a systems approach be helpful in planning office environments?

3. Why has a hybrid approach come to be recognized as the ideal solution for the design needs of the automated office?

4. Why is an understanding of atmospheric conditions (temperature, humidity, and air) important to a planner of an automated office?

5. As an office automation manager, how would you handle the smoking issue (a) in regard to equipment, (b) in regard to employees?

6. Describe the five types of lighting recommended for the automated office.

7. How have office furniture manufacturers applied a systems approach to office furniture design?

8. How has the study of psychology, anatomy, and physiology affected workstation design?

9. What conditions or problems associated with the automated office might affect the safety and health of office employees?

10. How can supervisors of automated offices help office workers avoid or reduce job stress?

CASE STUDY: THE CASE OF THE "INDUSTRIAL LOOK"

Mrs. Toshi Asano is the newly hired WP supervisor at the Eastern Industrial Corporation, a manufacturer of heavy construction equipment. When Mrs. Asano was interviewed, she was told that despite the company's heavy investment in automated equipment and systems furniture, the WP Center's productivity was low and absenteeism was high. On Mrs. Asano's first tour of the WP Center, she made several observations. The Center was located in a windowless basement room. Its bare cement block walls were painted a dark gray. Exposed pipes and incandescent light bulbs hung from the ceiling. The workstations lacked panel dividers and were devoid of any personal touches. Several printers without acoustical hoods operated simultaneously while a radio blared in the background.

On the first day that Mrs. Asano reported to her new job, she called a staff meeting. In her discussion with the operators, she learned that the last supervisor took great pride in operating the WP Center on a very low budget, resulting in its no-nonsense "industrial look." Mrs. Asano listened to more operators' comments concerning their work environment. Then she told the staff that she would put a high priority on the development of a plan for the improvement of their office environment.

QUESTIONS/ACTIVITIES

1. Develop a plan that you feel will help Mrs. Asano improve the office environment. Who should be consulted? What features, if any, of the current environment should be retained? Which features should be changed?

2. What strategy should Mrs. Asano use when presenting her plan to top management?

SUGGESTED READINGS

Brill, Michael. *Using Office Design to Increase Productivity.* Grand Rapids, Mich.: Westinghouse Furniture Systems, 1984.

Brod, Craig. *Technostress: The Human Cost of the Computer Revolution.* Reading, Mass.: Addison-Wesley Publishing Co., 1984.

Chusmir, Leonard H. and Victoria Franks. "Stress and the Woman Manager." *Training and Development Journal* (October, 1988): 66–70.

Cohen, B.G.F. *Human Aspects in Office Automation.* Amsterdam: Elsevier Science Publishers B.V., 1984.

Dainoff, Marvin J., Alan Happ, and Peter Crane. "Visual Fatigue and Occupational Stress in VDT Operators." *Human Factors,* Vols. 23–24 (August, 1981): 421–437.

Galitz, Wilbert O. *The Office Environment.* Willow Grove, Pa.: American Management Society, 1984.

Goldhaber, Marilyn K., Michael R. Polen, and Robert A. Hiatt. "The Risk of Miscarriage and Birth Defects Among Women Who Use Visual Display Terminals During Pregnancy." *American Journal of Industrial Medicine,* Vol. 13 (June, 1988): 695–706.

Gross, Clifford M. and Elissa-Beth Chapnik. "Ergonomic Training for Tomorrow's Office." *Training and Development Journal* (November, 1987): 56–61.

Kleinschrod, Walter A. "The Office Environment: Adjusting to OA," in *Update 1987–88: Approaching the Automated Office.* Willow Grove, Pa.: Administrative Management Society Foundation, 1987, 97–114.

Louis, Candace M. "Secretarial Stress: Causes and Solutions." *The Balance Sheet* (September/October, 1987): 21–22.

Majchrzak, Ann. *The Human Side of Factory Automation: Managerial and Human Resource Strategies for Making Automation Succeed.* San Francisco: Jossey-Bass Publishers, 1988.

Neubauer, Richard E. "The 'Intelligent' Building—Easier Access to Office Automation." Office Administration and Automation (November, 1984): 31–34.

CHAPTER 11

Strategic Planning for Office Systems

OBJECTIVES

After studying this chapter, you should understand the following:

1. Strategic planning for officc automation as a first step in the planning and implementation process

2. Conditions that are necessary for effective strategic planning

3. The relationship between organizational strategic planning and strategic planning for office automation

4. Stages in the planning process and basic procedures, instruments, and documents involved at each stage

5. Procedures and instruments used to conduct an office-systems study

6. Potential targets for an office-systems study

7. The role of budgeting in planning and control

Office automation, also referred to as office systems, provides the technology for improving the productivity of managers, professional staff, and office employees. If the technology is carefully planned, it can enhance the effectiveness and efficiency of office systems and improve the quality of work life for people who work in office environments. This chapter and the next two chapters deal with the planning and implementation of office systems technologies. Chapter 11 also examines the climate for effective planning, the assessment of existing conditions, and the tools and techniques for analysis. It reviews the probable contents of a strategic plan and reviews some of the issues associated with planning for office systems.

A MODEL FOR OFFICE SYSTEMS PLANNING AND IMPLEMENTATION

THE PLANNING PHASE

Strategic planning for office systems includes the following:

1. Assessing the organization and its existing office systems.
2. Identifying problems, inefficiencies, and ineffective procedures among existing office systems.
3. Collecting research data about identified system elements, and selecting elements that offer the greatest potential for improvement through changes in technology or procedures.
4. Planning a strategy for installing recommended changes.

The strategic planning element of this definition is extremely critical. Strategic planning is more than schedule making or forecasting. It is *visionary*. Dictionary definitions of *vision* use phrases such as perception of things not visible, mental acuteness, and keen foresight. John Naisbitt described the vision of strategic planning in the following statement:

> Strategic planning is worthless—unless there is first a strategic vision. A strategic vision is a clear image of what you want to achieve, which then organizes and instructs every step toward that goal.[1]

Another visionary planner captured the spirit of strategic planning for office systems when she admonished senior management to

> . . . visualize a system that will make exchanging information—data, text, or graphic material—almost as easy as using a telephone.[2]

Strategy involves careful plans and methods for reaching complex goals. Strategic planning for office information systems involves planning for an entire organization, because office systems affect every facet of the organization. Office technologies will achieve the greatest impact in organizations that analyze the entire organization, produce a general plan for improving office

1. John Naisbitt, *Megatrends* (New York: Warner Books, 1982), 94.
2. Anne Mayfield, "Memo to Senior Managers," *Management Technology* (February, 1984): 70.

systems, and develop a long-range strategy that is specific enough to guide implementation but flexible enough to permit changes when circumstances suggest them. The breadth of this vision is critical because office systems are supportive systems. They must support the organization's basic goals and objectives. Unfortunately, few organizations have followed this pattern. Failure to approach office automation with a broad perspective results in isolated installations that may duplicate efforts or inhibit interaction among departments.

THE ANALYSIS AND DESIGN PHASE

The analysis and design phase examines initial data gathered during the planning phase, profitability issues, cost justification, and the competitive position of the organization. During this phase the organization may conduct pilot studies and feasibility analyses to determine the impact of technologies being considered. Analysis and design involves deciding which technologies are going to be used and the level of sophistication to be employed. This topic is discussed in Chapter 12.

THE IMPLEMENTATION PHASE

With the basic information generated by the planning, analysis, and design processes, the organization is ready to implement these plans. The term **implementation** actually carries two different meanings when used in association with information systems. In its narrower context, the term is used to identify the range of activities associated with selecting and installing systems technologies recommended in a systems analysis and design process. That is essentially the interpretation used in this text. Chapter 13 explores implementation activities: hardware/software evaluation, vendor selection, installation of technologies, and follow-up evaluations.

In its broader interpretation, implementation may refer to the whole range of analytical activities beginning with planning, continuing with systems analysis and design, and culminating with hardware/software installation and followed by the evaluation of systems components. When used in this context, implementation refers to the total activities depicted in Figure 11-1.

Figure 11-1 presents a model for office systems planning and implementation. The highlighted portion of the model represents the strategic planning phase—the phase covered by this chapter. The whole model is given here to indicate the relationship between strategic planning and systems analysis, design, and implementation. The remaining concepts will be discussed in Chapters 12 and 13.

Figure 11-1 **Office Systems Planning and Implementation**

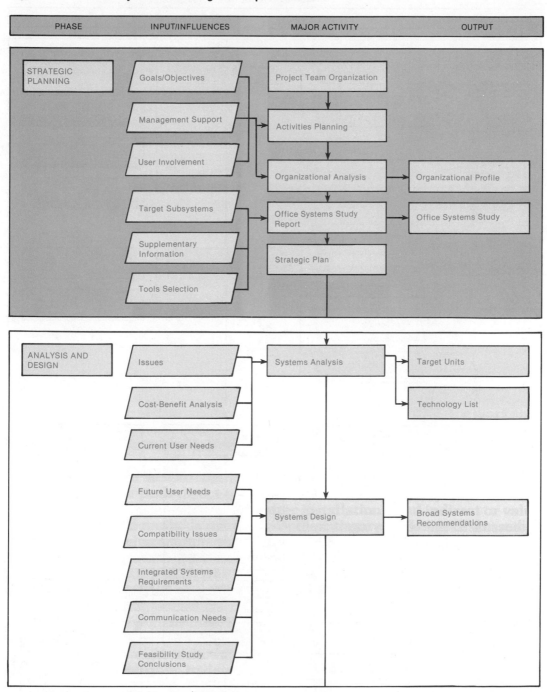

Figure 11-1 **Office Systems Planning and Implementation** *(continued)*

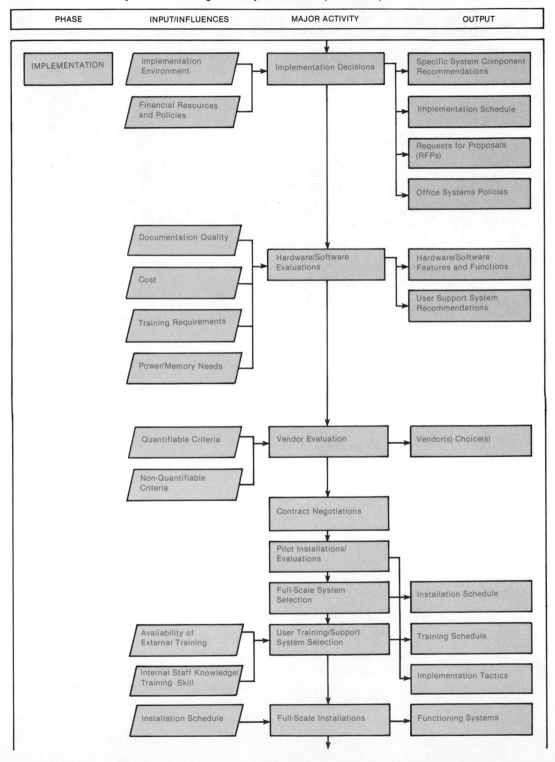

Figure 11-1 Office Systems Planning and Implementation *(continued)*

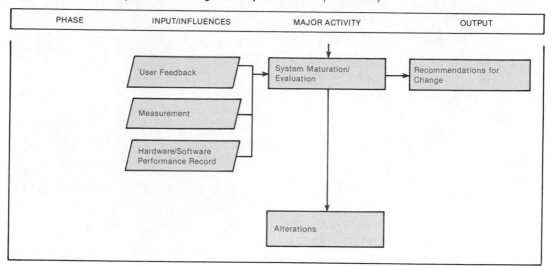

PHASE	INPUT/INFLUENCES	MAJOR ACTIVITY	OUTPUT

THE STRATEGIC PLANNING ENVIRONMENT

The complexity of office systems planning is related to the size and complexity of the organization and its mission. The experiences of organizations that have installed office technologies suggest that certain environmental conditions are desirable and that issues regarding these factors be addressed before extensive installation of technologies begins.

LEADERSHIP

Some individual or group of individuals should be formally assigned the responsibility for office systems planning and implementation. The establishment of this responsibility is itself an issue. Should these activities be a function of the existing MIS/DP department, an office support group, the telecommunications group, the word processing group, or the records management group? Whether an organization has all or none of these units in the existing structure, a person whose preparation is highly specialized and whose experience is narrow (one technology or discipline) is a poor choice for the leadership role in office systems planning and implementation.

The variations in philosophies of data processing, word processing, administrative support, telecommunications, and records management specialists are great. Their appreciation for and knowledge of technology and its potential applications to other disciplines is limited. A separate office systems or office auto-

Figure 11-2   An office systems
team composed of representatives
from various office or information-
management units will offer the
broadest perspective for the
strategic planning process.

mation project team is a better choice than adding this responsibility to any of the existing groups mentioned here. An **office
systems team** composed of representatives from MIS/DP, WP,
administrative support, telecommunications, and any other office
or information management units will offer the broadest perspective for the strategic planning process. A permanent office
automation or office systems unit within the organization may
become part of the strategic plan if the organization is large
enough to require ongoing coordination of implementation. An
office systems or office automation team composed of representatives from various office or information management units will
offer the broadest perspective for the strategic planning process.

The person who directs a permanent office systems unit will
preferably have had broad educational preparation, which includes a foundation in business administration as well as specialized courses in office systems. This education should have been
supplemented by experience in more than one discipline.

Assistance for office systems analysis and design and general guidance may come from outside the organization, but insiders are more capable of planning and directing implementation. Their understanding of the organization and its goals and objectives is far keener than that of an outsider. An insider's understanding, combined with the objectivity of an outside consultant, provides a workable implementation team.

IDENTIFICATION OF OFFICE FUNCTIONS

The office systems team must define existing office functions throughout the organization and select those that will become the targets of analysis and design. Those functions usually involve

1. the creation and production of written communication.
2. administrative support for managers, professionals, and staff (whether centralized or distributed among departments).
3. manual information processing activities.
4. paper, micrographic, and electronic records storage and retrieval.
5. telephone and other communication services, various office services (such as reprographics and forms design and control), and the mail room.

Data-entry functions in the MIS area and clerical functions in the accounting area may also be included in the office functions list. The important thing is to identify all office work without regard for the physical place where it is performed or the status of the people who perform it. Much office work will not lend itself to automation, but all of it should be considered.

A final area for consideration is the "office work" performed by managerial level employees and professional staff. These activities include database access, electronic files retrieval, electronic mail, voice mail, teleconferencing, and the types of administrative support functions suggested in Chapter 9. This area may offer greater potential productivity improvements than further automation of the clerical functions. Targeting only typewriting, data entry, and records storage is too narrow.

MANAGEMENT INVOLVEMENT

Because office work pervades the entire organization, involvement of management from throughout the organization is essential. Top-management support is especially important. Top-level managers should be involved in the selection of the office systems team and should be kept informed and involved at every phase of implementation. Of course, they must also approve any extensive systems analysis, organizational change, or technology acquisition. The more detailed the planning and the more extensive the investigation, the better the evidence to support the changes that may be recommended.

USER INVOLVEMENT

The most severe problem that has plagued the implementation of office systems technology has been the failure to involve the ultimate users of the technology in implementation. Two now-familiar phrases, "technology driven" and "user driven," describe the alternatives. Many organizations have installed technologies and have then altered their organizational structures and procedures to comply with the demands of the new technology. This approach is considered to be technology driven because users must conform to technical requirements. On the other hand, the user-driven approach involves analysis of user needs and the selection of technology that will assist in satisfying those needs. User involvement from the beginning benefits implementation in many ways. The technology is more likely to satisfy user needs if users participate in its selection. The systems study is likely to yield better information and maintain employee morale if users are gathering their own data. User involvement lessens employee resistance and lessens the belief that systems changes will be forced upon them.

As the data in Figure 11-3 indicate, in the early days of office automation implementation, organizations did not have a good track record for collecting information from users. Past and projected users were considered sources of information in very few cases in this study by The American Productivity Center.

EMPLOYEE ORIENTATION

The analysis and design of office systems must be objective. In other words, there must be no preconceived notions that additional office technologies will be installed or that every unit in the organization will be forced to install and use those technologies that are selected. Through the orientation of employees, preferably by their own supervisors, this point will be made clear and will reduce misunderstandings and rumors. This orientation should include an assurance that current employees will not lose their jobs because of installation of office technologies or major alterations in existing technologies. Explanation of planning and implementation procedures, identification of possible benefits, and an invitation for employees to participate by making suggestions and providing information should be included.

Figure 11-3 **Sources of Office Automation Planning Information**

Major Source of Information	Word Processing	(Percent of Firms/Technologies) Electronic Mail	Teleconference	Records Management
Persons in organization who had used same or similar technique (technology)	7	13	7	16
Person in organization considered "expert"	59	67	52	39
Persons in offices likely to be affected by change	9	4	7	26
Outside agencies or persons	25	17	31	8

Source: The American Productivity Center, *White-Collar Productivity: The National Challenge* (Grand Rapids: Steelcase, Inc., 1982), 22–23.

DOCUMENTING THE PLAN

As suggested by the introduction to this chapter, organizations whose leaders have a vision about future directions will react positively to changing conditions and the need for changing their approaches to information management. The **strategic plan** is a document that outlines implementation. The precondition to a systems study is that the organization recognizes the need for a strategic plan. The plan can be completed after an organizational profile has been developed.

THE ORGANIZATIONAL PROFILE

Some organizations already have strategic plans to guide them. These plans are likely to have been based on thorough analyses of strengths, objectives, and direction. They may concentrate on production, sales, market development or share of market, growth of the product line, or the nature of services to be provided.

Any existing plan can provide a starting point for office systems planning. These plans probably outline the organization's structure and identify its overall objectives. If there is no such description, the office systems team must identify this framework through interviews and discussions with top management.

Beginning strategic planning with an assessment of the organization and top-management involvement follows a generally accepted philosophy of top-down assessment. This philosophy suggests that organizational assessment should begin by defining the organization from the broadest perspective and proceeding to organizational units and their individual functions.

An **organizational profile** will identify objectives and goals or missions of the entire organization—its recognized strengths, weaknesses, limitations, and projected directions—including directions for information systems. The office systems team will be able to answer the questions "What is our present status?" and "What do we expect to be doing in the future?" The **office systems study** will answer these questions from the viewpoint of targeted units or departments; and the strategic plan for office systems will add answers to the question "How do we get there from here?"

The organizational profile should include identification of existing office systems at a depth that is sufficient for identifying

Figure 11-4   Thorough orientation of employees will reduce misunderstanding and rumors.

targeted areas for improvement. Through interviews or question-naires, the investigators attempt to identify and quantify activity associated with written communication, telecommunication, information processing in an office environment, records man-agement, and administrative support provided for each unit of the organization. The analysis should also attempt to identify problem areas, personnel shortages such as the need for addi-tional administrative support, and employee perceptions of unit objectives and organizational objectives.

Some information for the organizational profile can be gath-ered from existing documents (manuals, brochures, organization charts, management directives, and policy statements); but infor-mation not available from these sources must be gathered through interviews or a data-gathering instrument. Interviews with top management should confirm that existing statements of objec-tives and direction are still accurate. Figure 11-5 outlines types of data that may be sought in the attempt to develop the organi-zational profile.

Every element of the organization should be represented in the development of the organizational profile. There is no need to gather exhaustive data at this point. However, representatives from every functional area (production, marketing, finance, and accounting), every staff group (information systems, personnel, and administrative-support groups), and every employee classi-fication (managers at all levels, secretaries, clerical workers, the union, and any group that processes or communicates informa-tion) should be interviewed or asked to supply information. Many of these sources of information are ignored in such analyses, and this condition complicates employee acceptance of new technologies.

THE OFFICE SYSTEMS STUDY

A detailed study of units for which full scale installations are possible will best provide for OA in those areas. Although the study may be directed by a systems analyst from the office sys-tems team or an outside analyst, the best approach is for one of these specialists to work with departmental managers and super-visors to teach them to gather needed data. This provides user involvement and, eventually, understanding and support for recommended changes. It is at this point that user involvement becomes possible and critical.

The systems study examines targeted units, describing pres-ent systems, procedures, personnel, hardware, and software; identifying alternative systems for accomplishing the work; and

Figure 11-5   **Data for Organizational Profile**

From Top Management

1. Opinions of economic environment and industry condition.
2. Expected major influences on the future of the organization.
3. Assessment of the organization's strengths and weaknesses.
4. Identification of existing strategies (product line, markets, service line, diversification).
5. A description of the organization's major objectives.
6. Priority opinions regarding OA (routine information processing, communication, records/information retrieval, management support, decision support).
7. Opinions regarding OA team composition and responsibility for OA. (Is this to be, for example, top management, finance, existing DP or MIS group, or a separate OA team?)
8. Other organizational information.

From Representative Individuals

1. Individual function and unit function.
2. Unit personnel (number and functions).
3. Perception of organization's objectives.
4. Individual and unit contributions to organization's objectives.
5. Assessment of quality of work life, job satisfaction, physical environment.
6. Individual and unit involvement with communication.
   a. Media used (oral or written; letters, reports, or memos; conversations, meetings, or oral presentations).
   b. Tools used (telephone, dictation equipment, word processors, electronic mail, teleconferencing).
   c. Flow of communication (internal or external).
   d. Estimates of time spent with various media.
   e. Problems associated with communication.
7. Individual and unit involvement with records/information management.
   a. Information generated, captured, processed, or housed by individual or unit.
   b. Physical nature of tangible information media (paper, film, or magnetic).
   c. Volume of space consumed by records.
   d. Access to electronic information (databases or electronic files).
   e. Quality of information (accurate, retrievable, correct format).
8. Administrative support provided for individual and unit.
   a. Clerical assistance.
   b. Copying, calculating, filing, and communication activities performed by administrative-support employees.
9. Other information about individual responsibilities.

recommending available technologies that could improve productivity and lessen problems identified in the analysis. What are the office functions? Who is responsible for each function? What are the standard operating practices and procedures which involve office work? This study ferrets out problems with existing functions and the need for new applications of existing functions. It is similar to the popular "feasibility studies," which concentrated on one technology.

The most important trait of the analyst is inquisitiveness. What is done? Who does it? Why? The sections that follow are full of questions. They are only the beginning. For a specific organization, additional questions would be added.

TARGETING SUBSYSTEM ACTIVITIES

Subsystems frequently included in the office systems category include communication hardware, procedures, and systems; data processing hardware, procedures, and systems; records management personnel, procedures, equipment, and systems; and administrative support for managers and professional staff in the department. A questionnaire or interview guide will be needed to collect this information. The instrument for a particular firm would be influenced by the manner in which office work is accomplished in that particular firm. The following sections provide questions that would prompt the development of an instrument that would be appropriate.

Communication. For each department or other organizational unit, information about communication practices should be sought. If the firm has recently conducted a communication audit, such information might be available in the audit report. Otherwise, questions such as those that follow could be used to develop an instrument:

1. What media are used? (Written media include memos, letters, and reports; oral media include meetings and the telephone.)
2. What support systems are used? (Systems include word processing, electronic mail, voice mail, teleconferencing, conference phone, networks, secretarial support, and dictation systems.)
3. Are support systems centralized or distributed?
4. What tools are used in the unit? (Tools include telephones assigned to individuals, telephones not assigned to individuals, multi-line units, number of trunk lines to unit, number of WATS line trunks to unit, and use of FAX, TWX, TELEX, leased lines, networks, and so on.)
5. What is the annual cost of communication services (local and long distance)?

6. What is the path and purpose of communication? (Is it internal, external, informative, analytical, or customer information?) What messages originate in the department for communication to others outside the department? What messages come to the department from external sources?
7. What proportion of total communication is devoted to each medium? What proportion is internal or external, written or oral?
8. What standard operating procedures carried out by this department require the use of telecommunication technologies?

Data Processing. Of particular interest to the office systems study are manual data processing, preparation of information for entry to an electronic data processing system, and data input to a central computer system. The study should reveal existing application of technology to the processing of information within the unit. That portion of the study instrument devoted to data processing should provide answers to the following questions:

1. What is the source, medium, volume, and format of information that comes to the department requiring further processing?
2. What operations are performed with this information?
3. What documents are originated in the department? (Specify volume, destination, and number of copies.)
4. What files (manual or electronic) are accessed by employees in the department to perform their duties?
5. What data processing hardware and software are used by personnel in this unit? How many employees use a mainframe computer terminal, a minicomputer terminal, or a microcomputer? What software packages are used by each employee?
6. What information storage technologies are employed within the department (such as hard disk, floppy disk, mainframe memory, optical disk, magnetic tape, or computer-output microfilm)?
7. What information storage technologies that reside elsewhere are accessed via a communication link?
8. What information-output devices are used? (Are the printers dot matrix, letter quality, ink jet, or laser? Is computer-output microfilm used? What kind of terminals?)
9. What standard operating procedures involving data processing are carried out by this unit?

Records Management. The records management analysis identifies tangible records media housed by the unit or accessed from other sources. Electronic records accessed by the unit would also be identified. Answers to the following questions can help to build a profile of records management activities. Existing records inventory reports or records retention schedules may provide some of this information.

1. What tangible records (film, paper, tape, photographs, drawings, disks) are housed in the department? Which are housed for the department by a central facility? What is the volume in linear inches or cubic feet?
2. What is the source (point of origin) of each tangible record type?
3. What intangible records (databases or electronic files) are used by the department's employees?
4. What technologies are used to store and retrieve records?
5. What is the frequency of reference to each record type?
6. What is the disposition of each tangible record type? (When is it transferred to storage? When is it destroyed?)
7. Is there a records retention schedule?
8. Is there a plan for protecting vital records?
9. Is there an archive for the organization?
10. What is the reference history for each record type used?
11. What are the standard operating procedures carried out by this department that involve records creation, storage, or retrieval?

Administrative Support. Collection of data about administrative support activities should include secretarial and clerical activities not associated with telecommunication, information processing, or records management.

1. How many employees perform administrative support functions? (How many secretaries and clerical employees perform these functions?)
2. For how many principals does each support employee work?
3. What is the nature of the tasks performed and the percentage of time devoted to each? (Tasks involve dictation, filing, mail, telephone, copying, collating, receptionist duties, errands, and so on.)
4. What support services are available outside the department (from central files or a word processing center)?
5. What internal tools are used for word processing (dedicated word processors, microcomputers, minicomputers, terminal to mainframe computer, terminal to shared logic system)?
6. How is text originated (dictation equipment, longhand, dictation to support employee for transcription, self-input to word processing devices by managers and staff)? What is the volume of written communication produced by the unit (in terms of total pages or lines)?
7. How many typewriters are used? By whom?

8. What reprographic services are available to the unit (copy machines, printing services, desktop publishing)? Are these services available within the unit or from a central service? If both, what is the proportion of use?

9. What are the standard operating procedures for providing these services to principals in the unit?

10. What support services are provided by this unit for other units?

GATHERING SUPPLEMENTARY INFORMATION

The previous section concentrated on information about specific activities within the individual units or departments of an organization. There is also a need to gather supplementary general information regarding responsibilities for office functions, problems identified with these functions, and the nature of standardized procedures associated with each area.

Responsibility for Subsystems. The systems study should place responsibility for each of the functional areas. Who supervises employees performing these functions? To whom do supervisors report? Which employees are supervised by a professional supervisor with expertise and prior experience in the work being performed by the employees? Which are supervised only by a principal (manager or professional staff member) whose expertise and experience do not include the work of the employees being supervised?

Problems. Some effort should be made to identify problems recognized by departmental managers and supervisors with the quality of the office function. Are there problems with procedures (dependency on information that does not arrive, confusion, errors, bottlenecks)? Is the available administrative support adequate? Are there problems with work distribution (some employees with too much to do, others with not enough to do)? Does the department receive all the administrative support that it needs? What is the general assessment of the quality of work life for departmental employees (as indicated by comments, turnover, grievances, requests for transfers)?

Existing Standard Operating Procedures. Departments targeted for special attention because they are being considered for pilot installations will need detailed procedures analysis involving probing questions about the nature of standard operating procedures in those areas. Detailed scrutiny of other units may be postponed, particularly if implementation is expected to cover a long period of time.

SELECTING TOOLS AND TECHNIQUES FOR DATA GATHERING

An initial survey for the purpose of developing a strategic plan may be conducted by a specialist or team of specialists from the office systems team aided by personnel in the various departments of the organization. As departments are targeted for further systems study, however, the user departments should conduct as much of their own analyses as possible. User involvement in analysis will aid the adjustment to new technologies and to changes that may occur in office procedures as a result. A variety of tools and technologies may be employed to establish the nature of the information being used by the targeted department and the procedures used in carrying out information processing activities. Interview guides, questionnaires, work logs, and duplicate copies of documents generated by the information handling process can be used to document the nature of existing systems and procedures.

Figure 11-6 **To collect information about the nature of office systems, the analyst should interview departmental supervisors.**

Interviews. Interviews of departmental supervisors may be adequate to collect information about the nature of office systems. The analyst should probably avoid confronting the individual employees. The supervisor will be in a better position to collect information necessary to document the nature and volume of information processing activities at the worker level. Interviewees must be coaxed to be completely frank and open, especially when they are identifying problem areas.

An interview guide (see Figure 11-7) would attempt to identify the information processing activities carried out by executive- and professional-level employees in a particular department. The interview guide serves two purposes: It standardizes the questions asked of all interviewees, and it serves as an instrument for recording the answers.

Documentation. If interviews do not reveal a complete picture of the procedures in a department, some form of documentation

Figure 11-7   Interview Guide

OFFICE SYSTEMS STUDY
Interview Guide

Unit

Interviewee		Title	

1. Describe the structure of this unit. If it is divided into subgroups, identify each and indicate the number of supervisors, operatives, and professional staff, indicating the major function of each group.

Group	No. Supervisors	No. Operatives	Staff	Function

COMMUNICATION

2. Rank the written communication generated by this unit according to volume (1 is the most-used medium, etc.).

letters:	memos:	reports:	other:

3. Rank the oral communication generated by this unit according to volume (1 is the most-used medium, etc.).

internal conversation:	external conversation:	telephone:	other:

over a period of time may be desirable. Employee logs of daily activities and duplicates of documents and completed forms help to document the nature of the work being done and the time devoted to each task.

Analysts may attempt to quantify the volume of information processed. This measurement may involve the number of forms processed, pages of text keyboarded, number of customers served, number of telephone calls made, number of documents generated, and so on. This type of quantification resembles work measurement, which is discussed in another chapter of this text. **Work measurement** quantifies productivity for the purpose of establishing work standards or productivity expectations. Work measurement is a control technique; system studies merely attempt to quantify the volume of activity so that new systems can be designed to handle the work volume.

DOCUMENTING THE PLAN FOR IMPLEMENTATION

Documentation of the results of strategic planning may take several forms. Reports that communicate the projected role of office automation in an organization's overall information management scheme may be labeled "Office Automation Report," "Office Automation Feasibility Report," or "Strategic Plan for Office Automation." A single report or a series of reports may be used. Two possibilities are discussed in the remainder of this chapter—an office systems study report and a strategic plan. In this case, the office systems study report would be a rather specific description of the current status of office systems with sufficient detail to guide further analysis and implementation. The strategic plan, a separate document, would be broader in its scope, outlining in general terms the organization's short- and long-range strategies for implementation.

The strategic plan may call for further analyses of the office systems study data; additional data gathering activity, such as cost-benefit analyses; or pilot installations before final recommendations are made.

THE OFFICE SYSTEMS STUDY REPORT

Based upon the organizational profile and the office systems study, the office systems study report is prepared. If pilot installations were under way before the systems study, data from these experiments would also be included. The report might be called an office automation feasibility report; however, that term is more likely to be used when investigating the feasibility of a single technology such as word processing or electronic mail.

Assuming that analysts conclude that change is desirable (the investigators foresee improvements from office automation), the report will present recommendations, review cost-benefit analyses, and suggest a timetable that is consistent with the overall strategic plan. If the recommendations do not fit the organization's strategic plan, justification for altering that plan would be included.

The greater the degree of integration in the recommended plan, the more careful the planning must be. If several procedures that have been functioning independently (such as stand-alone word processing) are shifted to an integrated system (integrated office systems hardware and a network, for example), coordination of installations is more difficult. Almost all units within an organization react intensively with other units and with external organizations. Changes in procedures and technologies require changes in these relationships. Careful planning for implementation will result in minimum frustration during the change. The report would outline a timetable for these changes and for training employees. Depending upon the nature of the investigation and the breadth of coverage, the report would cover the following topics:

1. Executive summary (condensation of entire report).
2. Identification of potential technology installations.
3. Systems recommendations.
   a. Technological changes (system changes, automation of formerly manual systems).
   b. Human factors (job restructuring, effect of procedural changes, training).
   c. Environmental factors (changes in physical layout, workstation design).
4. Preliminary recommendations for:
   a. Hardware.
   b. Software.
   c. Changes in procedure.
   d. Communication systems.
5. Recommendations for additional analyses:
   a. Cost-benefit analyses.
   b. Cost justification.
   c. Pilot studies.
   d. End user policy development.

THE STRATEGIC PLAN

The strategic plan documents the plan for implementation of office automation in the organization in terms that are specific yet flexible. The strategic plan attempts to merge office automation recommendations for targeted areas with existing organizational goals and plans. Assuming a thorough organizational analysis, the implementation team will be able to describe the organization, present broad strategies for further investigation, and outline a procedure for installation, testing, and evaluation. The plan may project costs and expected benefits.

THE ORGANIZATION

This section of the plan should summarize the organizational profile and include statements about direction, position in the industry, financial stature, and overall objectives. Industry or organizational constraints affecting planning should be identified.

Brief descriptions of the organization's units and their functions should be included. Although this section may appear to restate the obvious, information about each unit's communication flow, information processing activities, administrative support personnel, and currently used technologies will assure that planners are attacking problems from the right perspective. Without such information, members of the implementation team may lack the necessary information to appreciate identified needs for each unit.

OFFICE SYSTEMS STRATEGY

This section of the plan recommends functions, units, or departments where the greatest potential for improvement of information activities exists. Systems, hardware, software, and vendor identifications may be reviewed. Assignment of permanent responsibility for coordination of office systems would be included. If a separate office systems or office automation unit exists or is recommended, its placement, authority, and staffing would need explanation.

The strategy should recommend timing and general procedures for installation decisions, and it should describe needed changes in job structures, training requirements, and personnel assignments. Anticipated benefits to users, including improvements in the quality of work life, would be reviewed.

A cost-benefit analysis may be a part of this plan. If it is truly strategic in nature, the plan will recommend budgeting procedures and include financial effects, such as anticipated payback periods and productivity improvements. These data are sometimes difficult and expensive to produce. Little research data are available to substantiate the benefits of integrated OA systems, but many firms report relatively short break-even points for individual technology installations. Cost-benefit analyses, budgeting, and issues regarding whether savings can be measured or whether they should be attempted are covered in Chapter 12.

IMPLEMENTATION SCHEDULE

Even though the implementation schedule will remain flexible enough to allow users to take advantage of technological developments, there is no merit in waiting for "new" developments before beginning to use technology. Several implementation approaches may be taken. Some organizations prefer to test applications on a relatively small scale, evaluate the results, and proceed accordingly. Others might prefer full-scale installation in a single department, withholding decisions about other departments until after evaluation of success in the experimental unit. Another plan would involve installing technologies in a cross section of the organization from top to bottom. The strategic plan should outline both the short- and long-run implementation strategies.

Short-Range Strategy. Typical short-range strategies involve **prototype** and **pilot** systems. Both involve experimental trials for systems and technologies. Prototypes are very small-scale installations. Sometimes vendors of hardware systems will lend a piece of equipment for a prototype analysis. Pilot installations are larger in scale (one whole department or one work group) but still small enough to allow the organization to abandon the system before extensive resources have been devoted to it. The strategic plan would identify the units (departments, divisions, and so on) within the organization that have been selected for prototype and pilot installations and the nature of the analysis that will be conducted.

Gantt charts are used to communicate short-range strategy. Figure 11-8 illustrates such a chart. (Because of the possibility that plans will be altered, these timetables are limited to relatively short periods; consequently, time periods for the last four items in Figure 11-8 are not projected.)

Long-Range Strategy. Even though implementation experiences in the short run may alter long-range plans, the strategic plan should outline anticipated long-range strategy. Several plans

Figure 11-8 Gantt Chart Implementation Schedule

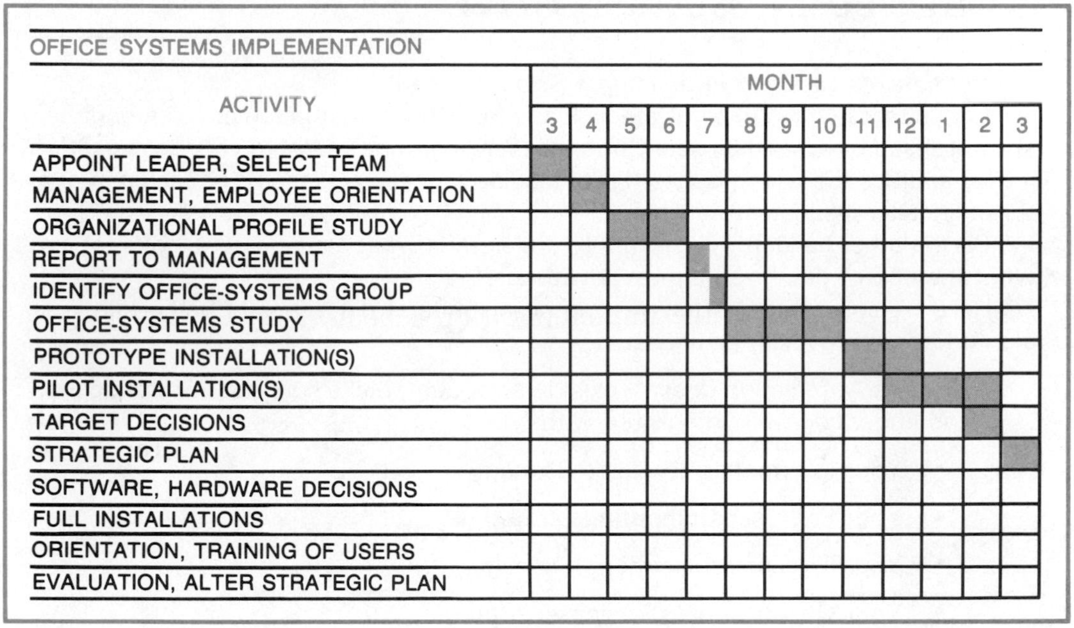
OFFICE SYSTEMS IMPLEMENTATION
ACTIVITY
MONTH
3 4 5 6 7 8 9 10 11 12 1 2 3
APPOINT LEADER, SELECT TEAM
MANAGEMENT, EMPLOYEE ORIENTATION
ORGANIZATIONAL PROFILE STUDY
REPORT TO MANAGEMENT
IDENTIFY OFFICE-SYSTEMS GROUP
OFFICE-SYSTEMS STUDY
PROTOTYPE INSTALLATION(S)
PILOT INSTALLATION(S)
TARGET DECISIONS
STRATEGIC PLAN
SOFTWARE, HARDWARE DECISIONS
FULL INSTALLATIONS
ORIENTATION, TRAINING OF USERS
EVALUATION, ALTER STRATEGIC PLAN

may be used. The one selected will be influenced by the choice between installation of independent technologies within various units of the organization and the use of some integrated approach such as a network or an integrated office system with multiple workstations. One strategy involves the installation of one technology at a time until that technology is available to all units that are scheduled to receive the technology. Another approach would install a variety of technologies until a single unit is fully automated. Other units would receive similar treatment until full installation is completed in all the units. A third variation would involve installing technologies according to a priority determined by needs without necessarily attempting to completely install a single technology throughout or a variety of technologies in a particular unit.

The strategic plan might call for pilot studies with a particular technology, application of that technology on a wide scale, then repetition of the process with another technology. Integrated office information systems may best be used when several technologies are tested in one or two departments with full-scale installation for other departments scheduled over time and based upon anticipated need.

WOHL'S BUSINESS PERSPECTIVE

Some Mistakes to Avoid in Building a Strategic Plan

Consultants who review Strategic Plans for Office Automation are often puzzled and surprised by what they see. Strategic Plans can't be useful to your organization if they address the wrong issues, fail to include the relevant issues, or seek approval for politically unsatisfactory goals.

On the other hand, it's important to understand what management looks for and what they can't grant you approval without.

Here are some of the often missing or misunderstood issues to be certain your plan addresses, avoids, or finesses:

1. Office Automation doesn't exist in a vacuum. Make sure your Strategic Plan is knowledgeably integrated with:

   - Your Information Systems Strategy

   - Your End-User Computing Strategy

   - Your Telecommunications Strategy

   - Your Organization's Business Strategy

2. Office Automation doesn't start with a clean slate. Everything you're using right now has to be used or eliminated. Make sure your plan includes an inventory of what's on hand and a reasonable plan to use it up, use it as part of the new system, or dispose of it.

3. Office Automation can only grow if the Strategy is consistent with your organizational culture. Dictatorial schemes where the Emperor of Office Automation decides nearly everything only work in existing dictatorships. Too much freedom in an organization with lots of structure would also be difficult to adequately support.

4. If you don't ask the users what they want and need, don't expect them to help you gain approval for the Strategic Plan—and don't expect their help and cooperation at implementation time.

5. In the real world, timing is important. Note the economic conditions in your company, your industry, your country, and internationally. No one invests large sums in office automation when catastrophe seems at hand. On the other hand, even if economics are in your favor now, the Plan should address how you'll handle a downturn.

6. Remember loyalties. What people use now (unless they hate their current products and/or vendors) is probably what they'd prefer to keep. If possible, have at least some familiar things incorporated into the plan.

7. Technology moves fast. Don't put the fine details of your fifth year into a Five Year Plan. You'll look silly when you get there. Go with details for the first year or two and get vaguer as to actual products after that.

8. Every Plan needs to include a mechanism for changing the Plan. Otherwise

it becomes useless when some important change point is reached. This could be as unlikely as the sale of your company to another or as likely as the need to incorporate new vendors and new technologies.

9. Don't forget this is a business decision. Management will demand to see the practical analysis, including the numbers.

SUMMARY

Implementation is the process of integrating new or redesigned systems within existing structures of an organization. Strategic planning includes all of the planning and evaluation activities that precede this process. Conditions that contribute to effective planning include informed and concerned leadership, top-management support, a knowledge of the office function throughout the organization, user involvement, and employee orientation. Strategic planning is a visionary exercise for the whole organization.

An organizational profile (objectives, nature of office systems, and existing technologies) is developed by the office systems team in the process of strategic planning. This is necessary because office systems serve an entire organization and are most effective if planned from this perspective. The strategic plan is a document that communicates the organizational profile, strategies for installing new systems, and the anticipated cost-benefit impact.

An office systems study of units targeted for office systems installations gathers detailed information about personnel, procedures, and problems within the unit. Communication, information processing, records management, and administrative support activities are emphasized in the study.

The strategic planning process results in documents that will aid implementation. The office systems study report targets functional areas for potential technology installations and may recommend further analysis. The strategic plan is a broader document setting forth goals and objectives for office automation and dividing strategies into long- and short-term time frames.

KEY TERMS

implementation
strategic planning
office systems team
work measurement
prototype system

strategic plan
organizational profile
office systems study
pilot system

REVIEW QUESTIONS

1. Discuss the three types of activity associated with strategic planning for office automation:
   a. assessing the organization
   b. the office systems study
   c. documenting the strategic planning process
   Indicate the nature and scope of each activity and point out the similarities and differences among them.

2. Present the rationale for declaring that each of the following environmental factors should exist in order to strategically plan for office automation implementation: specified leadership, identification of office functions, management involvement, user involvement, employee orientation, and a written strategic plan.

3. Why is an organizational profile necessary for office automation implementation? Is it realistic to expect top-management involvement in providing such a profile if the organization is large?

4. Contrast the scope of activities associated with the following: prototype installation, pilot installation, and full-scale installation. If electronic mail were the technology, describe the possible application of electronic mail at each of these levels.

5. Identify four categories (subsystems) of activity that are possible targets for an office systems study—activities about which you would gather data if you went to a department to conduct an office-systems study.

6. Review the supplementary information categories for which this chapter suggests gathering data (responsibility for office systems, problems, standard office procedures), and discuss the possible effects of gathering these data. (How would having this information affect the recommendation of the analyst?)

7. Contrast the concepts of strategic planning and implementation, using OA as the basis for comparison.

CASE STUDY: IMPLEMENTATION AT HOSPITAL CARE, INC.— PART I

(Parts II and III of this case will be presented in Chapters 12 and 13.)

Hospital Care, Inc., is a private firm that owns and operates sixteen hospitals in three states. This case involves planning and implementation for office systems at two levels: (1) at the corporate headquarters level and (2) in the administrative offices of one of the hospitals.

Exhibit A is an organization chart of the corporate headquarters. Exhibit B is an organization chart of one of the sixteen hospitals, a medium-sized

Exhibit A · An Organization Chart of Corporate Headquarters

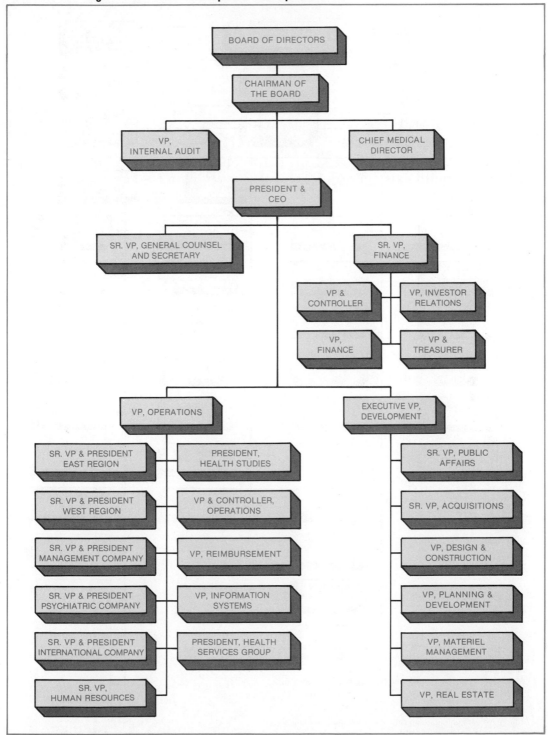

Exhibit B   Hospital Organization Chart

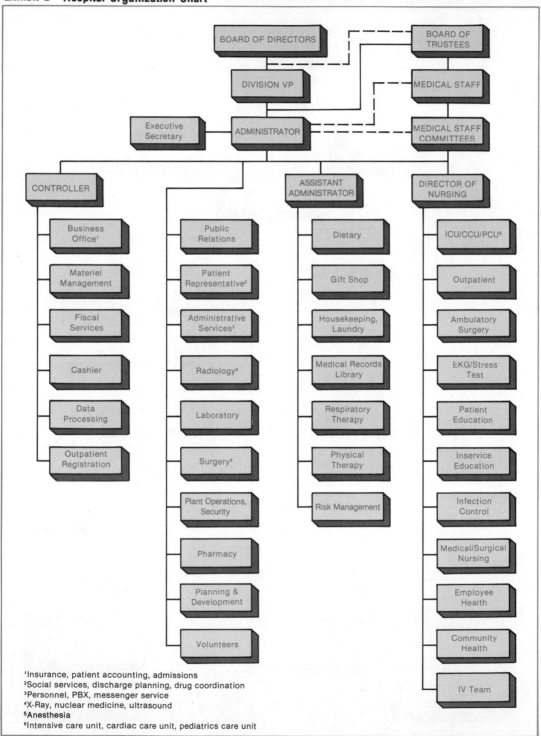

[1]Insurance, patient accounting, admissions
[2]Social services, discharge planning, drug coordination
[3]Personnel, PBX, messenger service
[4]X-Ray, nuclear medicine, ultrasound
[5]Anesthesia
[6]Intensive care unit, cardiac care unit, pediatrics care unit

hospital that has essentially the same organization as the other fifteen units. Exhibit C indicates existing office technology in the administrative offices and at each of the hospitals.

Study the charts and formulate probable answers to the following questions involving implementation.

Exhibit C Existing Technologies

CORPORATE HEADQUARTERS

- Mainframe computer (used for corporate financial accounting, cost accounting, financial planning)

- Electronic Document Center (serving word processing and desktop publishing needs of entire organization for large volume/high quality documents); supervisor reports to VP & Controller, Operations)

- PBX for telephone service

- Stand-alone word processing system operated by administrative support staff serving three VP offices and one microcomputer for staff of the VP, Public Affairs Office

- Microcomputer in VP Real Estate office

- Microfilm operation in Records Center (manager of center reports to VP & Controller, Operations)

- VP offices all have terminals to mainframe computer

HOSPITAL LEVEL

Data Processing

- Minicomputer for patient billing system and other activities such as room-use analysis, operating-room use analysis, etc.

- Facilities for batch processing and transmitting to corporate headquarters periodic data about local operations

Office Systems

- Clustered stand-alone word processing system (four workstations and one laser printer) and remote (phone-in) dictation systems in the medical records departments. These systems are used for transcribing physicians' dictated diagnoses and operation reports for patient records.

- A somewhat sophisticated telephone system. Although operator control of external calls is required, the system includes provision for conference calls, paging, and call forwarding and call waiting features.

QUESTIONS/ACTIVITIES

Corporate Level:
1. Each of the following questions asks that you identify a person (by title) or a group of persons from the corporate organization chart (Exhibit A). For each, supply the specific answer requested and briefly discuss your reasons for that selection.
    a. Which corporate official would you expect to initiate a corporate headquarters office automation study?
    b. To whom would the person identified in a. present his or her report?
    c. Discuss in a general way the probable contents of the office automation study report you would expect the person identified in a. to present.
    d. Whom would you appoint to the planning and implementation team? Since you don't have much information about these people, make any qualifying statements that would describe the circumstances that would influence your choices.

2. Outline each of the following strategic planning phases by (1) listing the steps you would recommend for carrying out each phase, or (2) briefly describing how you would handle that phase. (Refer to units or positions from the organization chart by title of the unit or the title of the position.)
    a. Establishing an organizational profile.
    b. Assuring the support of management for the study.
    c. Involving potential users in the study.
    d. Identifying targeted activity.

SUGGESTED READINGS

Carlyle, Ralph Emmett. "Advanced Technology Groups." *Datamation.* (November, 1988): 18–24.

Hawryszkiewycz, I. T. "Strategic Planning," in *Introduction to Systems Analysis and Design.* (Sydney: Prentice Hall of Australia, 1988.)

Kleinschrod, Walter. *Strategies for Office Automation: Planning for Success in the Office of 1990.* (Willow Grove, Pa.: Administrative Management Society, 1985).

Krebs, Valdis E. "Planning for Information Effectiveness." *Personnel Administrator.* (September, 1988): 34–42.

Strassman, Paul A. "Technology, Structure, and Strategy," in *Information Payoff.* (New York: The Free Press, 1985).

Tapscott, Don. *Office Automation: A User Driven Method.* (New York: Plenum Press, 1982). (See especially Chapters 6–9)

CHAPTER 12

Office Systems Analysis and Design

OBJECTIVES

After studying this chapter, you should understand the following:

1. Issues that affect the office systems analysis phase of the planning and implementation process

2. The process of office systems analysis, including the tools and techniques used to carry out the process

3. The concept of cost-benefit analysis and the distinction among efficiency benefits, effectiveness benefits, and value-added benefits

4. The distinction between hard-dollar benefits and soft-dollar benefits

5. Popular methods of measuring office productivity and the difficulties encountered when attempting to measure knowledge worker productivity

6. The concept of office systems design and the basic components included in the design of systems that improve the productivity of knowledge workers and their support employees

7. The evaluation of alternative designs

Strategic planning for office systems is followed by analysis of data gathered to determine the needs of the organization and the design or redesign of systems to satisfy those needs. The highlighted portion of Figure 12-1 represents the portion of planning and implementation devoted to systems analysis and design.

Figure 12-1   Office Systems Planning and Implementation

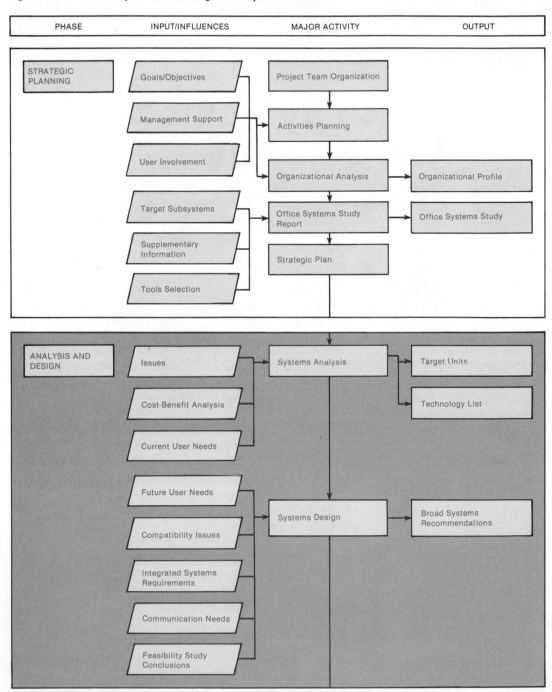

Figure 12-1 **Office Systems Planning and Implementation** *(continued)*

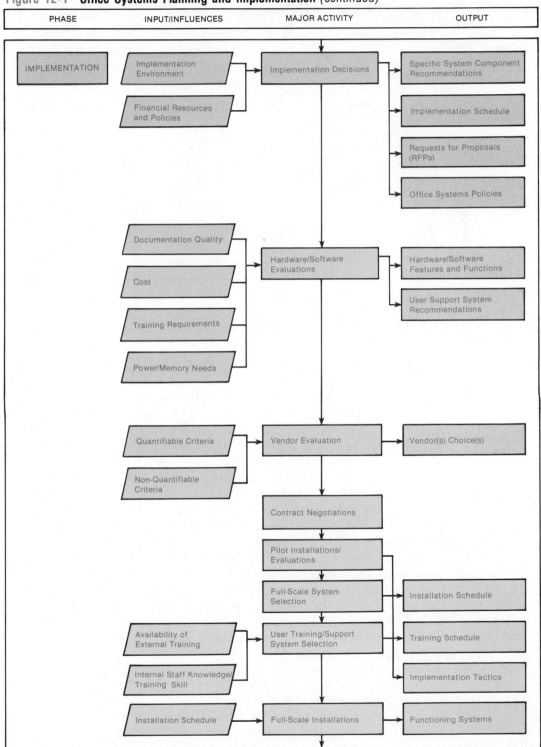

| PHASE | INPUT/INFLUENCES | MAJOR ACTIVITY | OUTPUT |

Figure 12-1   Office Systems Planning and Implementation *(continued)*

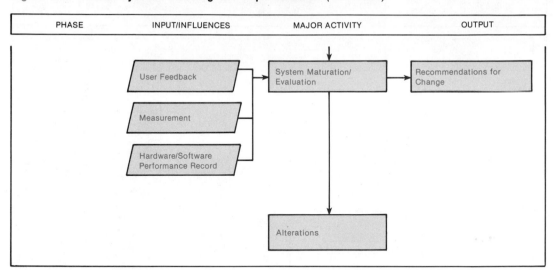

ISSUES AFFECTING ANALYSIS AND DESIGN

To justify office automation, organizations must conclude that the application of technology to the work of support employees, managers, and professional staff will in some way create a positive impact. This impact may come from reduced costs, avoided future costs, improvement of the quality of the work performed by one or more of the three identified groups, or may contribute to the organization's competitive position. Even if all of these phenomena develop, the impact is indirect. Administrative effort does not, in a direct manner, bring in revenues. Indirectly, however, it may influence the production of revenue because the quality of work performed is better or because the organization is in some way able to compete more effectively.

Numerous issues dealing with office automation influence those who make decisions about office automation technology. To some extent, effective analysis and design can minimize fears that expensive technology installations will not be profitable. On the other hand, the issues that consume time and energy remain. Several issues that survive deal with intangibles. Because of the probability that these issues will surface during analysis and design activity, several of them are discussed here. They involve continuing controversies about the profitability of technology, the measurement of knowledge worker productivity, the identification and measurement of benefits, and the ownership of information. No attempt is made to resolve the issues.

PROFITABILITY AND COST JUSTIFICATION

One issue facing information systems decision makers is whether or not the organization can justify the cost of office systems technologies—either before or after installations—by quantifying their effect on profit in private organizations or their effect on cost containment in public organizations. This chapter will introduce basic methodologies that organizations have used to attempt such quantification. To proponents of cost justification, their methods appear reasonable and necessary. Others suggest that the effort is an unnecessary expense. They would attempt to measure the costs of alternative solutions, perhaps, but not the profitability contribution of the solution selected.

PRODUCTIVITY MEASUREMENT

Even more controversial is the issue regarding the possibility of measuring office productivity, particularly the productivity of knowledge workers. If it can be measured, then before/after comparisons would certainly provide data to evaluate efforts to automate. As the material presented in this chapter will suggest, many organizations and individuals support the theory that any productive effort can be measured and that scientific methods of inquiry and evaluation can be applied to the work of managers and executives. Others contend that because of the unpredictable and nonstandard types of productivity in the office, the work that goes on in this environment cannot be measured—as the work in an assembly line or a sales environment can be.

Among those who accept the premise that office productivity can be measured, there is another issue—the method of measurement. Both direct measurements, such as attempts to measure productivity before and after installations, and indirect or value added methods are used. Both of these efforts are discussed in this chapter.

BENEFITS IDENTIFICATION AND MEASUREMENT

Management theorists have for many years labeled control as a function of management. Control is considered to be an evaluation mechanism—a set of checks and balances—that enables the organization to determine whether or not it is reaching its goals. Controls can be effectively applied to revenue-producing effort— the production of goods and services. Measuring the benefits of change in the office environment is another matter. Related issues involve the justification of cost by predicting the benefits that will result from having incurred the cost. If a benefit results, can it be measured in increased revenue/profit (as the result of decreased cost)? Are non-measurable benefits really worth anything? Various opinions about the answers to these questions are offered in the discussions of office systems analysis, office systems design, and evaluation later in this chapter.

INFORMATION/SYSTEM OWNERSHIP

Finally, the analysis of information systems, particularly analyses that may lead to integrated office systems, may create controversies over the ownership of information. Does information generated by, processed by, or held by a department or other organizational unit "belong" to that department. Who should have access to that information? Who controls access to that information? This issue hasn't been settled either. In a particular organization, the design of a system may need to reflect that organization's philosophy about access to information, however.

All of these issues remain in the background as office systems professionals attempt to analyze data gathered in preparation for office systems implementation.

OFFICE SYSTEMS ANALYSIS

After the systems study has gathered information about procedures and the volume of activity, analysis of this information is necessary. **Systems analysis** is the process of examining the data gathered in the systems study to determine what is being done within the units being analyzed and whether office technologies offer any potential for improving the units' ability to serve the organization. The analyst and the user must clearly understand existing systems before they can intelligently visualize alternative systems. Not only must they understand what goes on within each unit, they must also understand interdepartmental relationships and various external contacts.

Tangible descriptions of existing systems and procedures may simplify the analysis. Simple tallies of data gathered in the systems study, flowcharts that trace the flow of information, and various analysis tools can be used to depict the status of existing systems and to identify categories of activity that could be improved by using technologies. The written report of an office-systems study may be used as an analysis tool.

TOOLS AND TACTICS

Some compilation of data gathered in the office-systems study is necessary. This may take the form of narrative descriptions, logs of activity in various areas of the office, statistical tables quantifying the level of activity in the logs, or a combination of these. A paper drawing of the physical layout of an office complex with the various departments identified and the flow of information depicted is another example. Data that identify the number of personnel in each unit—both principals and support employees—would be helpful. Organizing data by subsystem, office, employee, or department are all possible choices.

Symbol flowcharts, block-diagram flowcharts, bubble flowcharts, and flow-process charts are valuable tools for analyzing or visualizing the nature of existing procedures. The symbol flowchart (Figure 12-2) is the most formal. It is especially helpful for analysts and users who are familiar enough with standard information processing symbols to understand the nature of what the symbols represent with a minimum of text accompanying the symbols. The tasks or methods of a particular individual within a particular department are frequently segregated to various sections of the chart.

Figure 12-2 Symbol Flowchart

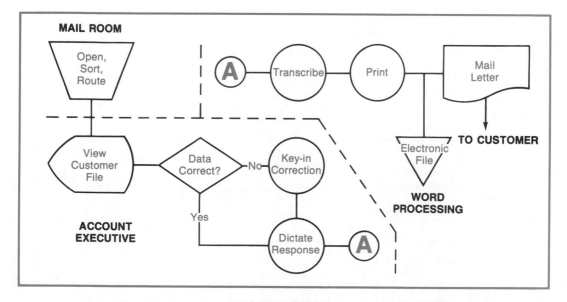

Block diagrams may be sufficient to document procedures if the number of people involved is small and the detail of the systems is not too minute. Figure 12-3 illustrates such a chart.

The least formal flowchart is the bubble chart; it identifies the flow of information and the nature of processing. It may not give enough detail to explain exactly what happens in a procedure, but it does give a picture sufficient to explain information needs, document preparation, and general procedure. Figure 12-4 illustrates a bubble flowchart.

With a vision of the current status and knowledge of existing technology, the analyst is able to draw conclusions and make recommendations. The conclusion is an informed judgment of existing conditions. For example, conditions may be adequate to serve the organization into the foreseeable future. On the other hand, the conclusion might be that change would improve productivity and effectiveness. If the need for change is the conclusion, recommendations outline the targets, the technologies, the timetable, and the procedures.

At this point there is some value in an attempt to upgrade productivity without reorganizing work groups. That strategy will meet less resistance from employees. If restructuring is necessary, the recommendation should involve cautious and careful planning. The results of the analysis are presented to the appropriate management group in a written report supported by an oral presentation by the implementation team.

Figure 12-3 Block Diagram Flowchart

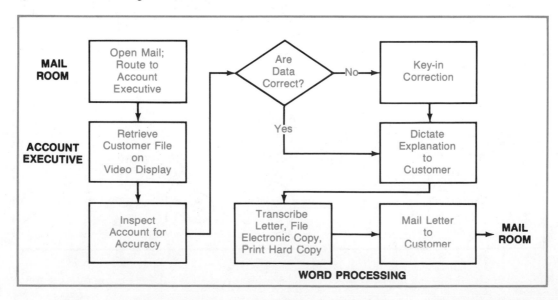

Figure 12-4 Bubble Flowchart

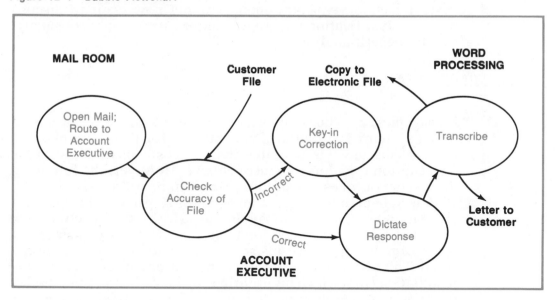

IDENTIFYING ALTERNATIVE SOLUTIONS

With the benefit of the information gathered about existing systems, procedures, and information needs, someone must begin to identify alternative courses of action that will provide end users with the technology and environments they need to be productive and to communicate effectively. These decisions must deal not only with the technologies at the disposal of the organization but also with the scope of automation efforts. Who gets new technology? What procedures do we automate? If we install a network, who will be connected to the network? If we upgrade workstations, who needs the more powerful workstations? Should we install technologies on an organization-wide basis or piecemeal? Do we provide users with PC workstations or terminals to shared systems? Do we purchase multiple applications software packages or networked software? Should users be able to create their own file media or operate with diskless workstations and departmental or centralized files?

This phase of the analysis process must produce alternative plans, alternative technologies, and recommendations for their implementation. When specific choices are made, management will want information about expected costs and benefits. Cost projections must deal with the cost of technology (hardware, software, needed services, supplies, and maintenance) and the cost of support staff, user training, and administrative support management. Although the typical approach concentrates on the cost of technology, many managements now want to discuss benefits. Justification may require equal attention to cost analysis and benefit analysis.

COST-BENEFIT ANALYSIS

Management may insist upon a cost-benefit analysis for proposed office systems installations, particularly for first-time installations. As discussed later in this chapter, cost-benefit analyses for office automation may be inconclusive. However, the following discussion outlines a procedure that can be followed.

A **cost-benefit analysis** is an attempt to project the cost of a system or a single technology and to identify the benefits to be expected from that system or technology. The management of some organizations will insist that expected benefits be quantified. This analysis is easier if it comes after a pilot or prototype installation from which information can be gathered. Since dollar benefits of office systems are usually indirect (office systems do not produce revenues directly), their justification on a purely quantitative basis must take the form of reduced or avoided costs rather than increased revenues. Office productivity is difficult to quantify. Projecting future productivity is even more difficult. Procedures vary greatly among organizations, and measurement attempts do not exist in many organizations. These complications suggest that office-systems analysts provide decision makers— those whose approval is required for systems installations—with all the quantitative information possible and supplement this with qualitative information.

COSTS

Cost projections should include the cost of systems installations and the ongoing operational expenses for those systems. They are influenced by the procurement method. Outright purchase of hardware, leasing or rental plans, and lease/buy options represent alternatives available for procuring office automation systems. Initial capital outlay, cash-flow data, and maintenance cost estimates are some of the factors which should be projected. Costs should be tied to some time span, such as a monthly or annual cost. Initial cost plus annual operating cost for five years, for example, would give effective cost comparisons among procurement plans and among potential vendors.

If pilot installations have been used, data generated during these trial periods provide valuable cost insights, particularly for the unexpected costs. Without such information, careful estimates must be made. The volume of work identified in the office-systems study or other attempts at identifying and quantifying the work that goes on within the organization can provide a basis for making estimates. Among the costs that should be projected are:

1. Hardware (purchase, lease, or rental).
2. Purchased software (including vendor charges to customize it or the cost of internal programming to alter software).
3. Internally developed software.
4. Training (including outright cost of training, lost employee time during training, and initial "lost productivity" until employees know systems well enough to be fully productive).
5. Hardware maintenance.
6. Communication costs (line charges, and so on).
7. Additional labor (supervision, support staff, and so on).
8. Supplies costs.
9. Cost of space consumed (if greater than current system).

Some of these costs may actually represent reductions from current expenditures to provide the same service or process the same information, but projected costs are necessary for comparisons.

BENEFITS

Unless office automation projects are inspired by an organization's competitors having gained an edge by such installations, projected benefits from installations must surpass projected costs. However, analysts must be careful to recognize both quantitative and qualitative benefits.

As the focus of office automation has moved from the operative level (routine clerical tasks and secretarial activities) to the supervisory, managerial, and professional staff levels, quantification of benefits has become more difficult. The expected benefit has now become increased productivity and enhanced productivity of those served, rather than in a reduction of clerical costs. The variety of functions and tasks performed by knowledge workers and their support employees, combined with a mind-set by the people who work at this level (the assumption that their work is so diverse and unstructured that it cannot be quantified) creates quantification problems. The impact of office automation for administrative support (see Chapter 9) is observable and identifiable, however. The impact of office automation upon the work of managers and professional staff may eventually be more significant than the impact of word processing and other technologies at the clerical and secretarial levels.

MEASURING BENEFITS

With the renewed interest in productivity has come a new concern: measuring the quality of output in offices. Quality control has been a manufacturing production control activity for many years, and it has been a concern to those who provide services to other firms or to consumers. Managers of the office environment have been concerned about accuracy, timely information, and the quality of office products. Few organizations, however, have concerned themselves with quality measurement in office environments. Because measurement has been associated with raw quantitative counts, office work has eluded control efforts. Now that managers realize that the activities of office workers (even managers and professional staff) can be quantified, there is also a renewal of interest in quality. At least when something comes along that improves the quality of office work effort, this improvement can be recognized.

There appears to be a consensus that the quality of output is more important to managers of office systems than the quantity of output. A survey of managers by the American Management Association revealed the following reactions regarding managers' concept of white-collar productivity:[1]

1. Quality of output as well as quantity of output must be considered—95 percent.
2. Overall efficiency and effectiveness of an operation are significant—88 percent.
3. Customer and/or client satisfaction must be included—64 percent.
4. Measures of productivity should also consider employee loyalty, morale, and job satisfaction—55 percent.

Quantification of the product of office operations has valuable and useful applications. However, the combination of efficiency, which concentrates on quantity of output and investment of resources, and effectiveness, which concentrates on the quality of output, is the real measure of the value of productivity. Cost-benefit analyses attempt to consider both of these factors.

Because the expenditures for a manager's time are greater than the expenditures for an operative employees' time, managerial productivity offers great potential for improving the quality of productivity. The reality of the benefit depends upon the effective use of time saved. For example, improving the productivity of operatives or managers produces a benefit only when the im-

---

1.   Michael J. Major, "The Quality Measure of White-Collar Productivity," *Modern Office Technology* (October, 1984): 166.

provement results in fewer dollars spent or an increase in the quality of their output. No benefit is realized if OA reduces report writing time for a manager who then wastes the time in trivial conversation. OA may then, in fact, be counterproductive.

Productivity benefits can be divided into four types—two that represent efficiency benefits and two that represent effectiveness benefits. Figure 12-5 outlines these benefits and summarizes their descriptions. Identifying all benefits and quantifying those benefits that lend themselves to quantification lifts technology decisions above the "guesstimate" level and provides better information to influence the decision.

EFFICIENCY AND EFFECTIVENESS BENEFITS

Benefits take the form of enhancements to efficiency or effectiveness. (Review the discussion of these concepts in Chapter 8.) **Efficiency benefits** are those that can be quantified by identifying reduced expenditures for capital, labor, and operating expenses. Their identification is achieved by measuring output and costs— before and after technologies are installed. These efficiencies are economic and can be measured in terms of dollars.

Figure 12-5 Identifiable Office Automation Benefits

Outcome Category	Benefit Type	Characteristics
Efficiency	Hard Dollar	Direct savings, measurable in dollars
Efficiency	Soft Dollar	Indirect savings, measurable in dollars but not resulting in immediate real-dollar savings
Effectiveness	Qualitative	Improves the quality of performance of employees, systems, or the product of the unit employing technology—observable, but not immediately measurable
Effectiveness	Quality of Work Life (QWL)	Improves work climate, job structure, employee morale—measurable, but not in dollars

Effectiveness benefits involve quality and are difficult, if not impossible, to measure. Identifying qualitative benefits and confirming that they exist, however, is not difficult. The problem is pinpointing the degree of such benefits. Analysts must identify effectiveness benefits because without them cost-conscious decision makers may overlook the potential that OA offers for improvement of managerial productivity.

The systems approach to productivity improvement does not eliminate quantification. Quantification may be essential to system selection, planning staff needs, and making before-and-after cost-benefit comparisons. Standards of performance at the individual employee level may even be valuable for training, employee counseling, and group productivity appraisal; but they should not be used to browbeat employees into higher productivity levels. If managers know what to expect, they can evaluate productivity. If productivity is less than what should be expected, that is an indication something is wrong with the system—a signal to examine the system.

Identifying potential benefits of office automation or any other change must first focus upon the impact of the proposed change for the organization as a whole. Office automation holds many potential benefits for the organization through the units targeted for office-systems technology and the impact of these units upon the whole organization.

Most units that are targeted for office technologies provide organization-wide services, so an improvement in their efficiency or effectiveness impacts upon the entire organization. The measurable benefits in a profit-oriented organization will be reflected in increased profit through decreased administrative costs (cost avoidance) or improvement of competitive position. **Qualitative benefits** affect customer relations and image. In nonprofit organizations, measurable benefits result in stretched budget dollars. These benefits may also be reflected in improved relationships with clients or the public.

Rather than attempt to measure benefits in terms of dollars, an attempt to contrast the level of service with and without the investment in technology may be more effective. What is the value of being able to answer a customer's question immediately instead of waiting until the records are searched and a telephone call is made or a letter dictated or a form completed?

Hard-dollar benefits, sometimes referred to as direct-dollar benefits, are measurable in dollars and represent actual before and after reduction in costs or avoided costs because of the introduction of improved systems. If OA is the ingredient that has been introduced, reduction in costs can usually be attributed to the OA system change. However, history has taught us valuable lessons about the fallacy of assuming that improvement can always be attributed to the change, as happened, for example, in Western Electric's Hawthorne studies.[2] Although productivity improved

---

2.   The 1927–1933 studies in the Hawthorne Plant of the Western Electric Company in Chicago were conducted by Harvard University researcher Elton Mayo and others. See Stuart Chase, *Men at Work* (New York: Harcourt, Brace, & World, 1941): 21–22.

after changes to physical factors, these studies concluded that social and psychological factors were more influential than the physical changes. If systems installations were accompanied by reorganization and other changes, identifying the variable that produces decreases or increases in productivity may be difficult. However, if work loads can be accomplished with fewer overtime hours after a system change, improvement can usually be attributed to the change. The same would hold for a system change that allows for level expenditures for administration during a period when the organization's overall volume of activity is increasing. These savings will usually be accepted as hard-dollar benefits.

Without prototype or pilot installations to produce comparative data, hard-dollar benefits must be estimated. Carefully quantified productivity records and cost data for existing systems can be used for such estimates.

Soft-dollar benefits are measurable in dollars, but they result in no immediate change in the profit picture (reduction in expenditures). Electronic files may eliminate the need for overtime work by file clerks or the employment of temporary service employees during peak periods (hard-dollar benefits). At the same time, this conversion may free 800 square feet of office space. Unless that space can be leased or rented to generate revenue or released to the landlord to reduce rent expense, there is no reduction in expenditures or identifiable improvement in profit. This soft-dollar benefit may have an indirect effect on efficiency, however. If the extra space enables employees to perform effectively, the result will be an eventual improvement in productivity. Improvements that save employee time are soft-dollar improvements if they do not result in a lower payroll; but at the point when they prevent the necessity for an increased staff, they become hard-dollar benefits.

Quality-of-work-life (QWL) benefits, the second effectiveness benefit type, are not measurable in dollars; but they improve the environment for employees. They enhance the working climate and improve employee morale. In organizations that regularly measure job satisfaction or climate, measurable differences may appear as a result of OA and related changes such as ergonomic improvements. These benefits can be expected, but they are difficult to predict. The potential for such benefits should be identified in a cost-benefit analysis.

Some effectiveness benefits improve the quality of employee performance, the quality of office systems, or the quality of the office product. These are labeled qualitative benefits. They are not directly measurable in dollars, although the long-term effect of such benefits may be improved revenues for profit-oriented organizations. Better communication, executive time freed for more important functions, and easy-to-interpret customer documents represent benefits in this category of effectiveness benefits.

VALUE-ADDED BENEFITS

Proponents of one approach to benefits measurement, such as Strassman, use a technique that they call value-added measurement of productivity.[3] Value-added calculations attempt to measure the effect of administrative effort, systems changes, innovation, and office technology by observing the effect of such changes on the profitability of the organization as a whole. Changes in these areas, it is assumed, are effective if the organization becomes more profitable as a result.

The combined long-range effect of efficiency and effectiveness benefits may be called **value-added benefits.** Ultimately, these benefits represent increased profitability for a private enterprise and more efficient use of revenues for public organizations. For office systems, this increase is represented by improvement of organizational performance because the systems exist and function well.

EXAMPLES OF OFFICE AUTOMATION BENEFITS

Office automation experiments reported by Strassman reveal a variety of improvements.[4] Figure 12-6 contains the results of these experiments in a variety of organization types. In addition to the measurable differences in productivity, numerous quality benefits are reported. These include quality of substantive conversations during meetings, secretaries' improved job satisfaction because they had time to assume more people-oriented tasks, and enhanced professional status of principals. In a semiconductor design firm, workers using intelligent workstations with embedded graphics software were able to custom design high-quality semiconductors at a cost that was the same as those previously mass produced. The quality of the mass-produced product was inferior to the custom designs.

The data were gathered from experiments involving control groups that continued to perform within well-designed manual systems and experimental groups performing the same functions in the same organizations within systems employing various office-systems technologies.

---

3.   Paul A. Strassman, *Information Payoff* (New York: The Free Press, 1985), Chapter 8.
4.   *Ibid.*

Figure 12-6   Office Productivity Improvements in Three Organizations

Example 1—A Patent Attorney Firm

Subjects: Three secretaries and four attorneys in each of two groups—the control group and in the experimental group.

Technology or experimental group: electronic workstations for all seven persons with individual computing power; communication network capabilities among all stations, including one office 200 miles away from the others; centralized electronic files and a high-quality laser printer

Summary of results:

	Control Group	Experimental Group
Document turnaround time (all documents)	21 hrs.	less than 1 hr.
Document turnaround time (complex documents)	20 days	7 days
Predictability of delivery (range of time prediction exceeded)	8–46 hours	0–2.5 hrs.
Telephone calls (control group = 100%):		
Incoming calls	55%	—
Outgoing calls	—	72%
Per-attorney reduction (time per day)	27 min.	—
Revision time for complex patent report	133 min. average	61 min. average
Unproductive document revision and retyping	22% of typing time	15% of typing time
Secretaries' handling of attorneys' telephone inquiries	1% of total time	12% of total time
Per-employee text production (average of control group = 100%)	—	200–250%

Example 2—A Training Department

The data below represent time required for preparing and revising training materials, graphic exhibits, and visual aids for technical skills training by a control group and a pilot group. The pilot group had access to graphics technology, a network, and electronic storage and retrieval of text and graphics. The control group continued to use traditional methods for preparing and retrieving materials. The experiment involved 25 professional trainers and six to eight support personnel.

	Production Time	
Item	Control Group	Pilot Group
Progress report	186 min.	75 min.
Trip report	156 min.	60 min.
Memorandum	144 min.	60 min.
Transparency	8 hrs.	2 hrs.
Graphic chart	10 hrs.	4 hrs.
Forms design	80 hrs.	16 hrs.
Sales notebook	10 days	5 days
Annual report	5 days	3 days
Executive program summary	4 days	2 days
Teaching text, lesson plan	5 days	2 days
Instructional manual	40 days	23 days

Figure 12-6 **Office Productivity Improvements in Three Organizations** *(continued)*

Example 3—A Public Agency

This example involves the time required to complete a routine expense report requiring a budget amendment in a public agency. This was a before/after experiment that involved keeping detailed records of time consumed before and after installation of office automation.

Process Step	Hours Before	Hours After	Percent of Time Gain (+) or Loss (−)
Organize process	1.1	2.6	− 135%
Analyze and write	12.6	9.3	+ 36%
Draft	1.4	3.8	− 168%
Edit	5.6	1.1	+ 81%
Meet	1.1	1.0	+ 10%
Complete	9.3	2.6	+ 72%
Type	.7	1.5	− 99%
Distribute	.9	.1	+ 88%
TOTALS	32.7	21.9	+ 33%

Source: Paul A. Strassman, *Information Payoff* (New York: The Free Press), 32–33 and 254–255. Reproduced by permission.

FEASIBILITY ANALYSES

While the term *feasibility study* sometimes has been used to identify the study that we have labeled *office systems study* in this text, a feasibility study or feasibility analysis is actually one that attempts to determine whether an action is possible or whether the results of an action are likely to be positive or profitable. Actually, several types of feasibility considerations may be given the attention of the systems analyst: technical, cost, legal, and operational. Detailed analysis of a proposed technology or system should provide these data.

If the technology exists to accomplish what the study indicates as needs of the organization, the project is technically feasible. If the cost is within reason and if the projected benefits suggest a payback or an improvement in quality that seems to justify the move, the project is feasible from a cost standpoint. Technologies that affect information may have legal ramifications. A project is legally feasible if it does not violate the law or the regulations of government agencies. Finally, a project is operationally feasible if the proposed system or technology can fit within existing organizational and technical frameworks. If the people who must work with the system are willing and able to perform the tasks associated with the technology, it is technically feasible.

OFFICE SYSTEMS DESIGN

Following the information gathering and the analysis comes the design of systems that will meet user needs. Organizations have a fair track record of analyzing technology before they purchase it, but they have a poor record of actually considering user needs in the design process. This is complicated by the fact that technologies have been designed by people who did not understand users. Office automation **systems design** involves the creation of systems that employ technology to enhance knowledge worker productivity and communication, without sacrificing the human factors or the quality of work life for users. This creative process may be applied to the establishment of new systems or the redesign of existing systems.

The design process may be somewhat informal—a subjective matching of user needs (determined in the analysis phase) and the availability of technologies to satisfy those needs. A more formal approach involves complex analyses of user tasks, applying sophisticated formulae to alternative designs.

PRELIMINARY SYSTEM RECOMMENDATIONS

The design process involves a specified plan for solving the problems or satisfying the needs identified in the analysis process. Preliminary recommendations involve hardware, software, communication systems, and user interfaces. For most organizations, this process involves selecting from existing hardware and software packages. In some cases it may involve altering or customizing hardware or software to fit the organization's needs. The more global design features are settled first. For example the choice of a network and an operating system and a decision about integrated voice/data communication systems would come before the selection of a workstation for each individual user.

Hardware Selection. The major ingredient of the office automation system design is the user workstation—usually a personal computer. Information gathered in the office systems study should provide information about current and anticipated user needs. Although users will not have identical needs, the hardware decisions should reflect compatibility issues for sharing information and communication purposes. Chapter 13 discusses this process in detail.

Other hardware decisions will involve network hardware (servers, cabling, workstation cards) file servers, and peripherals such as printers. Telecommunication decisions will affect these choices.

Software Selection.   Off-the-shelf software is usually selected for end user applications for such applications as word processing, spreadsheets, database management systems, graphics, personal productivity tools, and work group tools. In addition, decisions regarding operating systems, network software, and information security must be made.

Communication Systems.   Since standalone workstations do not constitute office automation, some system for linking users must be considered. This may involve shared intelligence, shared files, and various networking options. Communication links should permit communication among the users and between each user and the organization's central computing facilities, as well as gateways to external sources of information. Only with such communication capability does an organization have integrated office systems.

User Interface.   One of the most critical phases of the office systems design process is the **user interface.** This concept represents what the user sees when he or she sits at the workstation display. It is the system that has been created for user-machine interaction—a scheme that enables the user to tell the machine what to do and for the machine to guide the user through the necessary procedures.

Although some organizations may think in terms of using their management information systems designers to "build" or design a custom user interface, a more appropriate approach for many organizations is to *select* a user interface from those available from software design firms. User interfaces represent complex combinations of command languages, screen displays, and system feedback methods. However, the user need not know about all the complicated technology that resides behind the display. As office automation introduces more and more nontechnical users to computing, the user interface becomes more important. Nontechnical managers and professional staff persons will not tolerate the detailed interfaces that administrative support employees have been forced to learn through extensive training (and technical employees learned with very little difficulty). In the past, employees who used computers extensively for fairly routine but limited tasks could be taught to respond to complicated, non-helpful interfaces. This won't work for users who have dozens of applications at their disposal and must be able to use them easily in order to realize their benefits.

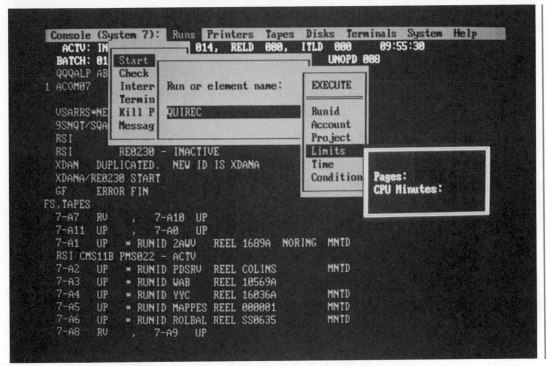

Figure 12-7 The ''friendly'' user
interface allows the user to direct
the computer, with guidance.
Unisys Corporation

The user environment introduced by the Apple Macintosh™
interface and continued by Microsoft Windows™ software combined with devices such as the mouse and the touch-sensitive
screen were early attempts to accomplish a graphical interface.
Now such interfaces are common.

DESIGN EVALUATIONS

The design process involves the evaluation of identified alternative solutions to end user information needs. For this process to
constitute more than an educated guess, a systematic approach
must be used. The designer must know about and understand
technology, as well as the people and the organization in which
technologies will be installed.

Modeling.   The more formal approaches to evaluating alternatives may involve some type of **modeling** process. A model is a
prediction of a future system. Modeling has been somewhat more

successful in financial and production systems than for office environments, because those areas are highly quantitative. For the office environment, the technology can be successfully predicted, but the human reactions to the technology are very difficult to predict.

Formal models may involve computer analyses of alternative courses of action or, in a simpler application, spreadsheet software. The spreadsheet can simplify the dozens of calculations that may be required as designers speculate about the effect of various alternatives.

Pilot and Prototype Trials.   If designers are able to learn enough about user needs to design one or more alternative systems to serve those needs, pilot or prototype installations may be used to make further analyses before organization-wide systems are adopted. Users who currently have access to office automation tools may be able to evaluate those tools and to recommend features for replacement tools. These recommendations could form the basis for prototypes or pilots. However, users who have not been exposed to office automation may have difficulty in visualizing new ways of performing old tasks.

Pilots and prototypes must not be solutions in search of problems; they must involve better means to reaching an organization's objectives than the current configuration. Even though they represent small-scale applications of technology, they must be thoroughly designed before implementation. Users must be thoroughly trained. This need is just as critical for an experimental system as for a permanent installation. Constant contact with users is essential. Their reactions and feedback form the basis for evaluating the trial system. The ultimate reaction will be modification, acceptance, or rejection of the system.

RELATING ANALYSIS AND DESIGN TO THE STRATEGIC PLAN

As in any systems approach to analysis and management, the systems approach to analyzing potential technologies considers all the ingredients in the system, including the overall organization and its relationship with the external world. Application of the strategic plan to office systems involves all of these ingredients: the organization's basic objectives; a structure that allows for effective communication among units; clearly defined systems for carrying out information processing and communication activities; procedures that function smoothly; and simple methods that employees understand. These ingredients are employed in an environment that is conducive to productivity—both the physical environment and the communication climate. Management, using honest, straightforward communication with employees, approaches productivity improvement by looking at an entire system first, then refining the components of the system. Piecemeal productivity improvement efforts may produce favorable results, but the impact and the permanence of the improvements are likely to be greater if organization-wide approaches are used.

WOHL'S BUSINESS PERSPECTIVE

There are many ways to measure office work and measurement tools to calculate with infinite precision how long it takes to get work done. But there is much less agreement on what kinds of work changes would significantly and positively affect worker productivity. And there is almost no agreement at all on how to calculate the organizational benefits of such changes.

Too often, in the office systems analysis and design process we spend our time measuring what can be measured and fail to find out anything useful at all. Much wasted effort could be averted—and much better results achieved, if some basic rules can be observed.

This is not a project for a deep thinker in an ivory tower. Successful office systems analysis requires the participation of a generous cross-section of office workers. This works better on two levels:

1. **You get much better information.** The people who do the work are much closer to the work and its problems. More important, they can tell you about the things they *can't* do now (and need to). Often, this helps you design an office systems solution with a much stronger and more interesting cost/ benefits justification.

2. **You build consensus.** Office systems can't be *imposed* on the organization. They need to be *accepted* by the workers whose environment will be changed. If employees participate in identifying office problems and formulating their solutions, they've simultaneously bought into accepting the implementation of those solutions. Even when such participation takes longer and ultimately costs more (especially in employee time), it's often cheaper than after-the-fact exercises designed to ''sell'' a management-, consultant-, or (worst case) vendor-imposed system, built with little or no user participation.

Employee participation greatly enhances the chance that you'll identify problems which are broadly agreed to be worth solving. Such solutions are much easier to cost justify.

- Management will pay much more attention to a solution which addresses a long-term problem. Just getting rid of it (or lessening it) is clearly worth something.

- Employees are close to the customers. Experts have identified better customer relationships as the single most important thing a supplier can use to insure his future success. Your employees can help direct you to problems in inventory control, shipment tracking, quality, and response to complaints that can better satisfy customers and directly bring profits to the bottom line. And management knows that *profits* are what fund changes in the office system.

Lastly, be sure your office systems analysis and design addresses organizational issues as well as technology ones. Organizational changes are often required for the successful use of technology. And don't forget a user feedback loop. Systems often fail because there's no mechanism for reporting problems (and quickly correcting them). Be sure someone's in charge of identifying problems — and be certain they're a user friendly sort who knows the correct response to a reported problem in a new system is, "Thank you. We'll never get all the bugs out without your help."

SUMMARY

Office systems analysis and design involve the evaluation of information gathered about the need for office automation by potential users. Issues about the value of analysis, the measurement of productivity in the office, and the method of justifying the cost of technology surround the analysis and design processes.

Office systems analysts attempt to document activity in present systems and to document the needs of users so that new or revised systems and technologies can be recommended for improving their productivity. This analysis is assisted by tools and techniques that range from simple flowcharts to complex mathematical models that simulate systems activity.

Analysis attempts to identify alternative solutions — both to solve identified problems and to project unanticipated benefits. Since many organizations expect rather specific data about expectations for technology installations, cost-benefit analysis may be a part of the analysis process. A variety of methods may be used to project costs and benefits, but the projection should include both the direct dollar benefits (efficiency benefits) and the intangible or indirect benefits (effectiveness benefits) that may not appear directly or result in immediate quantifiable savings.

Analysis paves the way for systems design, the creation of new or revised systems for using technology to enhance productivity in the office environment. These productivity concerns involve managers and professional staff as well as their support employees. System design must involve hardware, software, and communication considerations. Critical elements of the design are the user workstations and the user interface. Once alternative systems are designed, they may be tested with pilot or prototype installations prior to full-scale installation.

Systems analysis and design are two steps in the office systems planning and implementation scheme. They will be more effective if carried out within the context of the strategic plan for the organization, as well as for its office systems.

KEY TERMS

systems analysis
cost-benefit analysis
efficiency benefit
effectiveness benefit
qualitative benefit
hard-dollar benefit

soft-dollar benefit
QWL benefit
value-added benefit
systems design
user interface
modeling

REVIEW QUESTIONS

1. Discuss the following activities associated with office systems analysis and design:
   a. Systems analysis
   b. Systems design
   c. Design evaluation
   Indicate the nature and scope of each activity and point out the similarities and differences among them.

2. Why are cost justification and productivity measurements issues when they involve analysis and design of systems for using office automation?

3. What is the value of a flowchart when analyzing systems and procedures?

4. What is analyzed in a cost-benefit analysis for office technologies?

5. Contrast efficiency and effectiveness as they apply to expected benefits from a revised or newly developed office system.

6. What is the difference between a hard-dollar benefit and a soft-dollar benefit? What is the basis for saying that they are efficiency benefits? Is it possible for a soft-dollar benefit to be transformed into a hard-dollar benefit? (What is your opinion?)

7. What is the common ingredient of qualitative and QWL benefits?

8. List the major components of an office system design. For which of these ingredients might "component selection" be just as appropriate as "component design"?

9. Describe the office automation component called the user interface.

CASE STUDY: IMPLEMENTATION AT HOSPITAL CARE, INC. — PART II

Review the description of Hospital Care, Inc. and the accompanying exhibits at the end of Chapter 11; then formulate suggestions for each of the following items.

QUESTIONS/ACTIVITIES

1. At the corporate headquarters level, what office automation technologies would you expect the planning and implementation team to include on a list of potentially beneficial technologies for the executives shown in Exhibit A and the middle managers, professional staff, and administrative support workers that you would expect to report to these executives?

2. Keeping in mind the suggestions for strategic planning in Chapter 11 and those for systems analysis and design in Chapter 12, would you have gathered information from all 16 hospitals as well as the corporate headquarters if you had been conducting an office systems study? Discuss the reasons for your answer.

3. Assume that your office systems study reveals no systems that you would call integrated office systems in the corporate headquarters. Further, only a few examples of distributed processing exist; these are in departments reporting to the Senior Vice President — Finance and the Vice President & Controller — Operations. Many departments are using personal computers, and they are about evenly divided among managers and executives and administrative support employees (who use them as standalone word processing and data base machines). Using the knowledge of office automation that you have acquired to this point,
    a. Identify possible hard-dollar benefits that could be realized by a firm like this with a concerted effort to upgrade its use of office technologies at the corporate headquarters.
    b. For what type of employee would you expect hard-dollar benefits to be realized in the short term?
    c. What types of soft-dollar benefits would you expect them to realize?
    d. Are effectiveness benefits possible in a firm such as this? Discuss. If yes, identify the effectiveness benefits that you would expect in a medical firm's corporate headquarters.

4. Describe an office automation pilot study that you envision for Hospital Care, Inc. Indicate the potential value of a pilot study, compared to a full-scale installation of the technology that you recommend.

SUGGESTED READINGS

Bair, James H. and Laura Mancuso. *The Office Systems Cycle* (Palo Alto, California: Hewlett-Packard, 1985).

Meyer, N. Dean, and Mary E. Boone, *The Information Edge*, (New York: McGraw-Hill Book Company, 1987).

Newman, William M. *Designing Integrated Systems for the Office Environment* (New York: McGraw-Hill Book Company, 1987).

Sassone, Peter G. "Cost Benefit Analysis of Information Systems: A Survey of Methodologies." *Proceedings: Conference on Office Information Systems*, (New York: Association for Computing Machinery, 1988), 126–133.

Tillmann, George. "Prototyping for the Right Results." *Datamation* (April 1, 1989): 42–45.

CHAPTER 13

Office Systems Implementation

OBJECTIVES

After studying this chapter, you should understand the following:

1. Four categories of factors that affect the environment for office systems installations within organizations

2. Tactics that are likely to improve the preparation for change faced by employees during systems installations

3. The nature of decisions that must be made regarding design features prior to system installations

4. The office systems software functions and features that should be evaluated during final software selection

5. The office systems hardware functions and features that should be evaluated during final hardware selection

6. Quantifiable and nonquantifiable techniques for evaluating vendor products and services

7. Approaches to systems installation

8. The role of evaluation in office systems implementation

As discussed in Chapter 11, office systems implementation may be viewed as a broad, complex collection of activities associated with planning, analyzing, designing, and installing or putting into place any change in procedure or working environment. For major changes in information systems, implementation tends to be perceived narrowly as the final phases of this activity involving final decisions about basic system components—the selection of hardware and software; the purchase or lease of these components; their installation; other activities associated with "start-up" procedures; and the evaluation of the system.

The final component of our model (See Figure 13-1) represents these activities. This chapter amplifies the decision-making activities introduced in the discussion of the design phase and presents a framework for selecting hardware and software, choosing vendors, and installing user technologies.

THE IMPLEMENTATION ENVIRONMENT

The complexity of office-systems implementation is related to the size and complexity of the organization and its mission. The experiences of organizations that have installed office technologies suggest that certain environmental conditions are desirable and that issues regarding these factors (See Chapter 12) be addressed before extensive installation of technologies begins. Human factors, relationships among employees, the organization's structure and strategic plans, and the nature of existing systems all affect the implementation environment. These factors are discussed individually in the following paragraphs.

HUMAN/SOCIAL FACTORS

Even small-scale implementation involves change, and change affects the people who work for organizations. Therefore, careful consideration of the human factors, as well as making astute systems purchasing decisions, is advisable. Chapter 17 explores these human factors. This chapter concentrates on the procedure and the process of implementation.[1]

Many of the same factors that influence systems design also influence the implementation phase. Failure to address these factors will result in consequences that threaten the success of the systems. End users will either refuse to use the systems or will not use them to the extent that is possible. User rejection means that benefits will not match expectations.

Human factors to be considered include the level of computer knowledge and skills already possessed by users of office systems. These factors are critical to implementation. User education and training needs will affect the pace and sequence of installations.

---

1. See R. A. Hirschheim, *Office Automation: A Social and Organizational Perspective* (Chichester, England: John Wiley & Sons, 1985), for the social factors affecting office systems implementation. Chapter 7 and Appendix A review research and popular models of the change factors associated with implementation.

Figure 13-1   Office Systems Planning and Implementation

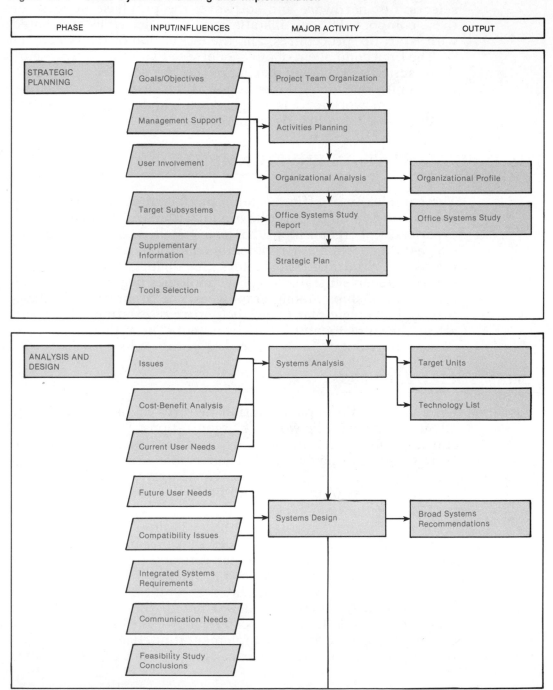

Figure 13-1 **Office Systems Planning and Implementation** *(continued)*

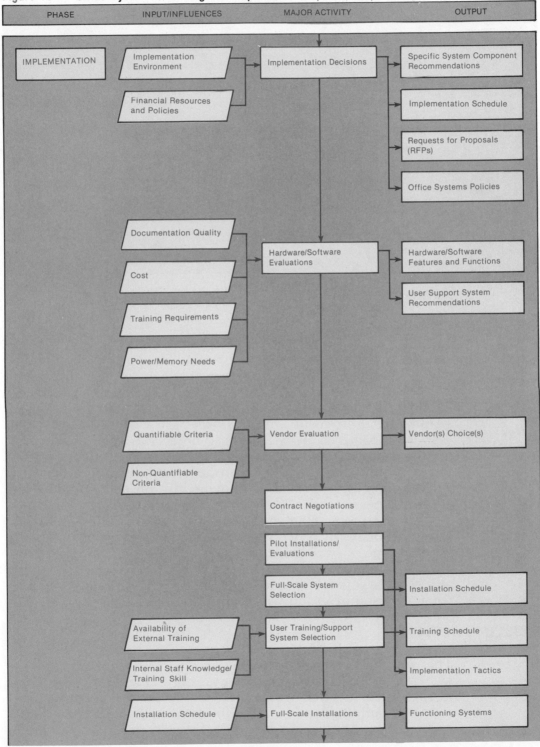

Figure 13-1 Office Systems Planning and Implementation *(continued)*

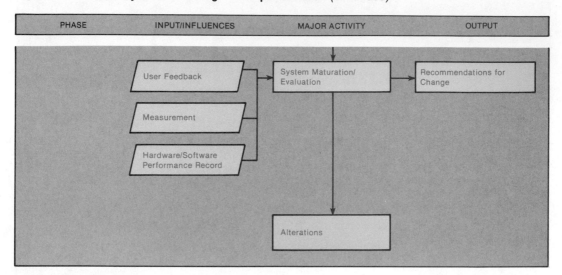

ORGANIZATIONAL FACTORS

The organization's strategic plan, including short- and long-range goals, and the provision for office systems and other information systems within those plans must be followed during implementation. The decisions made in the strategic planning process regarding the desired outcomes of office systems installations must also be considered. Whether these objectives take the form of specified improvements in specific activities or broader "improving the quality and quantity of productivity" objectives, they will set the tone for the pace of implementation and influence the choice of personnel assigned to implementation tasks.

If the strategic plan specified a person or group who would have authority for office systems, that person or group should be in charge of implementation. If such a provision was not included in the strategic plan, the team that has conducted analysis and design activity should be responsible for recommending such a person or group with permanent responsibility.

EXISTING SYSTEMS

The organization's existing physical facilities and information systems will influence implementation. Considerations include geographical location of end users, distances that separate users within a building, and existing information handling and document processing procedures. Weaknesses of existing systems identified in the analysis phase and addressed in the design phase may affect the approach to implementation. Implementation plans should provide for the correcting of these weaknesses. If they are numerous and extensive, the implementation schedule should provide adequate time for corrections.

FINANCIAL RESOURCES

The strategic plan should include a commitment to finance the plan. The level and timing of that commitment will influence hardware and software decisions and the installation schedule. This factor may force implementation decision makers to choose between "nice to have" features and "essentials."

IMPLEMENTATION TACTICS—PREPARATION FOR CHANGE

Many attempts at office automation have failed. Some failures are attributable to the absence of strategic planning. Inappropriate technologies are installed; the wrong systems are "improved"; the wrong employees or functional areas are targeted; or inadequate data are used to influence decisions. Major failures have also been attributed to lack of upper management support. Upper management approval must be accompanied by real commitment.

Even if all of these bases are covered, success may still evade the office-systems professional if tactical matters—the little things—are ignored. If users decide that the system will not work, it won't work.

Implementers must select work units where success of pilots is guaranteed; this will build confidence among other units. One of the major advantages of pilots and prototypes is that system-friendly individuals can help implementation teams locate bugs and develop alternatives without creating politically adverse conditions. The following tactics should smooth the implementation process:

1. Use a systems approach
2. Communicate clearly
3. Train the users
4. Prepare alternative plans

A SYSTEMS APPROACH

Implementers must encompass all the ingredients of the system—people first, then software, hardware, office procedures, and training—according to the strategic plan. Potential users have the best information about what goes on in their units, and they offer the best possible support. Success breeds success. When users are involved, they recognize that prototype installations improve productivity. They will help implementers sell the idea to the next user. After users and analysts have identified needs, the hardware, software, training, and procedures plans should be molded with input from every element that will be affected.

COMMUNICATION

At all stages of the process, the implementation team must explain systems to people in words they can understand. Communication is critical—from the initial organizational profile through prototypes, pilots, and systems studies to full installations. Define terms, explain changes, seek input, describe jobs, outline procedures, and help every user and every person who will be affected by a potential change to anticipate and prepare for that change and its ramifications.

TRAINING

Implementers, in cooperation with the existing training staff, must train those who will use and interact with each new system. Classroom training, hands-on training, and quality documentation are all necessary; but the technology itself provides the best training. Select systems software that is supplemented by guidance and support for users (on-screen menus, prompts, and other user-friendly features). The less technical the background of the user, the greater the need for training.

ALTERNATIVE PLANS

Expect the unexpected. Installation of technologies will bring predictable consequences, but the unpredictable ones always surface. Murphy's law ("That which can go wrong will go wrong") prevails. There are always people around who will oppose any technology and wait in the wings for signs of wavering or difficulty. "I knew this thing would never work" is their theme. Having alternative plans ready before something goes wrong will disarm those who may have been looking for something to criticize. The following list of dos and don'ts suggested by James H. Bair and Mary J. Culman[2] provide a basis for developing implementation tactics:

2.   James H. Bair and Mary J. Culman, "But Where Do You Start?" *Management Technology* (July, 1983): 40.

1. Maintain an adequate level of use. Daily use is necessary for support of interpersonal communications. The more services that are available through the system, the greater will be the attraction to the users. When adequate services are provided to encourage daily use of the technology, the levels of skill will improve quickly.
2. Install enough hardware and software to provide units for every potential user at all times.
3. Encourage all co-workers to use the system themselves, rather than depending on a few people to act for them.
4. Extend the system through a large enough part of the organization to create a "critical mass" of users with access to it. Otherwise, a user will have to fall back on traditional methods to communicate with nonusers.
5. Provide adequate support for the users. First, there should be clear encouragement from top management to make use of the system. Then there must be continuing help for the users in the form of training, documentation, and regular consultation on the most effective methods.

IMPLEMENTATION DECISIONS

Implementation decisions create the future environment for office systems use. These decisions fine tune the system components recommended in the broad design process; they include decisions about policies, interconnection, integration of systems, hardware, software, and evaluation. Decision making of the type discussed here will be necessary for any major technology change. The process will be more specific for the implementation of totally new systems than for the alteration of existing technologies.

OFFICE SYSTEMS POLICIES

The activities associated with implementation should produce policies that will guide implementation and future monitoring of the systems. Policies, which should have been initiated during the strategic planning process, should be refined before installation begins. These policies should deal with authority and responsibility for systems.

If not already complete, the organization's definition of "office systems" or "office automation" should be finalized. The organizational unit to which office systems will be attached is determined and assigned or reassigned. Decisions regarding the relationship between office systems and MIS/DP systems management and between office systems and telecommunication systems management must be made. The control of initial and future hardware and software purchases should be determined.

Attention to these policies during the implementation phase will avoid difficulty in the future.

INTERCONNECTION TACTICS

The nature of existing and planned systems will dictate interconnection tactics — the scheme for enabling users to communicate with each other, to access central files, to communicate with peripheral devices, and to communicate with external systems. A myriad of possibilities exists, but three categories of arrangements represent the majority of the choices and indicate the influence that these tactical decisions have for implementation decisions. These three categories are integrated office systems, multi-user departmental systems, and local area networks. The choices made during system design regarding these factors will affect remaining decisions such as applications software and workstation selection.

Integrated Office Systems.   **Integrated office systems** refers to systems for delivering applications software, communication tools, and files access to users throughout an organization. It is the combination of computing equipment, software, and telecommunications systems. Such systems are usually controlled by a mainframe computer or large minicomputers that are powerful enough to provide office automation and data processing capabilities to an entire organization or a large segment of an organization.

Now that networks are improved and more prevalent, integrated office systems have become more prevalent. The software that runs such systems is usually called **integrated office automation software** (or just OA software). While all software that performs office automation tasks might be so labeled, this term is used to refer to integrated office software, particularly when it is centralized and made part of a mainframe system. Through integrated office systems, users have access to functions that others perform on standalone or departmental computers: text processing, electronic mail, data communications, file sharing, electronic document retrieval, spreadsheets, graphics, and other administrative-support tools. Digital Equipment Corporation's ALL-IN-1, Data General's CEO (Comprehensive Electronic Office), and IBM's PROFS/DISOSS (Distributed Office Support System) are examples of integrated office automation software. IBM's Office Vision/2 is a new entry in this field. It runs under the OS/2 operating system.

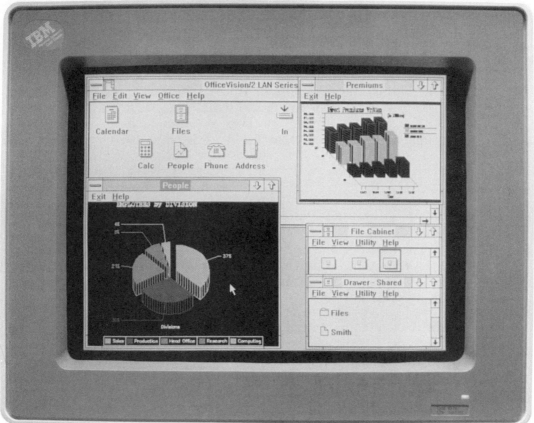

Figure 13-2 Integrated office automation software presents a common user interface throughout an organization.

Most of the software in this category is designed for mainframe and minicomputer applications. However, software firms that formerly concentrated on dedicated word processors now offer multifunction integrated systems software. Wang Laboratories (Wang VS Office) is one of the popular vendors in this category. Applications reside within the central system, but users have access to these applications through communication links with the mainframe. Figure 13-3 illustrates important considerations for selecting integrated systems. Advantages of these systems are (1) the ease with which the products of data processing and office automation systems can be accessed and used, (2) the common user interface that they provide, and (3) the lower costs for software. Even though software is very expensive, the

Figure 13-3   **Important Requirements of an Integrated Office System**

- Provides facilities for execution of WP, DP, user programming, electronic mail and desk management.

- Provides facilities for the integration of DP output with WP text in a single document.

- Provides access to these facilities by means of a logically unified user interface.

Source: Wohl Associates, Bala Cynwyd, Pennsylvania

cost of integrated systems software may be less than the cost of individual packages for huge numbers of users.

The number of available software packages for integrated office systems is somewhat limited. Figure 13-4 lists examples of these packages. These packages may be referred to as "mainframe OA software."

Multi-User Departmental Systems.   The approach to interconnectivity that involves departmental processors with multiple users is called a **multi-user system.** These systems may also be called **shared-logic systems** because the users share a central processor. Users may operate with workstations that are **intelligent terminals** (capable of some computing functions independent of the central processor), **dumb terminals** (capable of no computing functions without the central processor), or personal computers (capable of independent or shared processing). The departmental processor may also be connected to the organization's mainframe computing facilities or to other departmental computers.

Local Area Networks.   Local area networks connect users—usually those in a department or other small group. These networks can also be used to connect one network to another network. Through **bridges** (connections to other networks) and **gateways** (connections to mainframe computers and other devices), the users on a network may communicate with other networks and computing devices. Special network versions of applications software are required for networked users.

SOFTWARE DECISIONS

Software is the heart of technologies that are computer based. Office automation is no exception. Hardware is useless without software, so decisions about software become very important.

Figure 13-4   Integrated Office Systems Software

Manufacturer	Product
DEC	ALL-IN-1
Data General	Comprehensive Electronic Office (CEO)
Hewlett-Packard	Personal Productivity Center (PPC)
IBM	System 36 Office PROFS MVS/PS/370 Office Vision
Wang	VS Office

The availability of off-the-shelf software and inexpensive personal computers made office automation possible, because users learned this software could be valuable in their jobs.

In order for office automation to achieve the productivity improvement that it is capable of providing, technologies must be applied to management and professional tasks as well as to the secretarial and clerical tasks of administrative support employees. Packaged, user-friendly software has helped to create an atmosphere that will make these applications possible.

Software decisions involve the identification and evaluation of specific software packages and matching software to users' needs. Details of software selection are addressed in a later section of this chapter.

HARDWARE DECISIONS

The status of existing office systems installations within the organization will influence hardware selection. Planners must evaluate existing hardware in targeted areas to decide whether to keep or replace it. For most organizations that already have technologies installed, efforts to continue using existing hardware is the preferred general direction. Expansion of technology does not necessarily require scrapping existing installations.

Departments or offices that have no installed office automation technologies are in a favorable position when it comes to hardware selection. They can select hardware that will run the software needed to satisfy their needs. All-new installations may create difficulties with employee training and acceptance, however. Employees who are accustomed to technology can learn software and adjust to technology quite easily.

Although hardware and software decisions may be considered a "chicken and egg" dilemma, the applications should be selected first. Then hardware to manage those applications should be selected. For each application, planners must decide between independently functioning hardware (and software) or components that will share a central computing facility. After this decision, planners must decide whether to purchase or lease the hardware. Some of these decisions may be tightly controlled by the organization's financial planners, so systems planners will need to provide careful justification for their recommendations. More specific guidelines for hardware selection are given in a later section of this chapter.

EVALUATION TACTICS

Prototype and pilot installations, trial use of hardware and software (if vendors will permit), research of other organizations currently using systems, and expert advice from consulting services are among the tactics used to evaluate preliminary systems design components. The implementation schedule may call for pilot installations followed by further evaluation and an opportunity to change directions if problems with the pilot installation are discovered.

REQUESTS FOR PROPOSALS (RFPS)

The implementation process may yield documents called **requests for proposals (RFPs).** These documents describe systems, hardware components, and software components and invite vendors to submit bids for supplying the entire system or specified components. This bidding process is more prevalent in governmental and institutional organizations than in the private sector; but it may be used by any organization, especially those that are negotiating for the purchase of large volumes of equipment or software.

SOFTWARE EVALUATION—FUNCTIONS AND FEATURES

The three categories of software are operating systems, applications, and utilities software. All of these software types were introduced and defined in Chapter 4 and are discussed below.

OPERATING SYSTEMS

The choice of operating system software will be a part of the overall design, and this choice may affect the applications software selected. It will certainly affect the utilities available to individual users. For example, an organization's decision to use the OS/2 operating system will affect both software and hardware decisions.

Since operating systems serve as managers of the central processing unit of a computer system, this software determines whether or not the CPU can serve more than one user at a time (multi-user systems), whether or not individual users can be working on more than one application at a time (**multi-tasking**), and the extent to which a computer can access multiple sources (input devices, peripherals) at one time.

In most office environments PC-DOS or variations of this disk operating system were standard during the 1980s. Throughout the existence of the microcomputer, however, many users have selected the equipment that required proprietary operating systems (unique to the equipment of one manufacturer). The Apple Macintosh is an example of this category. Recently older operating systems such as UNIX and newcomers such as OS-2 have gained popularity. If multi-tasking applications is a goal of the system, one of these may be preferable. If extensive graphics capability is desired, OS-2 would probably be the choice.

UTILITIES

Utilities such as files management and disk management software are part of the operating system. Additional utilities of interest to individual users would include hard disk management tools, programming languages, and housekeeping tools that recover lost files, make backup copies of software, and present classification systems and naming conventions for electronic files.

APPLICATION TOOLS CLASSIFICATION

Applications software packages are made available to end users to assist them in the work that they do at their individual workstations. These tools fall into two categories: (1) **individual user application tools** and (2) **work group tools.** The first group refers to tools used by users to perform the tasks they would ordinarily do without the aid of technology. They use the tools at their workstations by themselves (although the products and files generated by such tools might be transmitted to others). The second group refers to tools that multiple users share as a group. These tools are also used at the workstation (or elsewhere), but their use is centered around group activity or projects. Most of the tools discussed here are software based, but their use may require special hardware components.

Some organizations use a system that allows users to share applications software. The software is installed on a network or provided in an integrated office automation software package. Other organizations choose to buy independent packages for each user. **Shared application tools** reside in some central or departmental system. Users have access to this software through their workstations. On the other hand, **independent application tools** reside at the workstation—either on floppy disks or the workstation's hard disk or some other storage medium. System design will have determined which method is appropriate for a particular organization.

Implementation decisions regarding application tools include not only the method of delivery but also decisions about which users will have access to which packages. The systems analysis will have examined user needs, and the design process will have identified tools with potential for serving those needs. Individuals should be supplied the tools that they are likely to use and that have potential for improving the effectiveness of their jobs. The final analysis should identify those users who have genuine need for tools. In some instances, the volume of need may result in quantity purchases that make it possible to purchase the tool for even marginal users at very low costs.

APPLICATIONS SOFTWARE FOR INDIVIDUAL USERS

Because most of the following tools have been introduced and discussed in previous portions of this text, the following discussion is restricted to comments affecting implementation decisions. Those that have not been introduced previously are discussed in greater detail. All of these tools are available for a variety of operating environments: independent software packages for individual workstations, components of integrated software packages for individual workstations, or components of centralized integrated office software managed by mainframes or minicomputers.

Word Processing/Desktop Publishing Tools.   Text editing software is the most-used software available. For some users these two packages are considered separately, but the functions and features of the two have overlapped so much that they will soon be considered as one tool. Some users will continue to need more sophisticated versions of the tool, however. Because almost everyone creates documents at one time or another, word processing software should be available for every user who requests it. In some cases, users who do not request it should be encouraged to learn this application.

Spreadsheets.   The second most popular applications tool is the spreadsheet. Spreadsheets were designed for financial analyses, but they can be used for numerous projects requiring large volumes of quantitative information. As is true for other tools, available spreadsheet software represents a wide range of capability. The price usually varies with the level of performance. Most users in an office environment will find productive applications for a spreadsheet tool.

Database Management Systems.   Users may have access to central databases, but they may also need to be able to create their own databases. Individual database management software enables them to do this. The value of database tools is the endless variety of reports that may be generated from the information contained in the records of a database and the ease with which information can be retrieved from the database. With the appropriate com-

Figure 13-5 **Software is the heart of office automation.**

munication software tools, users can also access external data-bases, such as those provided through CompuServe™ and the Dow Jones News Retrieval Service™.

Graphics Tools. Because graphic information is communicated more easily than statistical tables or text, graphics software is valuable for creating visuals to supplement written reports, statistical publications, and oral presentations. A category of graphics software called **presentation graphics** is a tool for producing supplements for oral presentations. This software is capable of producing color slides and projection transparencies and capturing video images.

Decision Support Tools. A special category of tools called **decision support systems (DSS)** is designed to assist managers who must make decisions that are affected by numerous variable conditions. Spreadsheet software is sometimes referred to as decision support software, because it can be a helpful tool to those who are making important decisions. Decision support software or financial modeling software is more complex than a spreadsheet, however. These systems, particularly those that incorporate artificial intelligence, query the user for input that simulates problem identification, alternatives identification, and other phases in scientific decision making processes. The queries are based upon "rules of good practice and judgment" stored in the system. Input is compared to databases of information and to stored "reasoning strategies" in the system. The combination of these activities simulate human judgment, logic, and reasoning. A major difference between DSS and "manual" decision making is the rapid speeds with which this information is processed.

Obviously, many users do not have a need for decision support tools at this level; for those who make complex decisions, however, these tools may be critical.

Communication Tools. Communications software manages the conversion of information into formats for transfer from one workstation to another and to remote peripherals. This software facilitates the transfer of information via modem over telephone lines and the access of information from remote locations. If users do not have access to communication software through integrated systems, separate communication software should be provided.

Administrative Support Tools. This family of software, which may also be referred to as "desktop management" or "personal productivity" tools, includes electronic counterparts of ordinary workstation tools: calendar, calculator, clock, to-do list, tickler file, and postanote reminders. In addition to these ordinary tools, administrative support software may also contain features to organize hard disk files, index and catalog other collections of electronic files, manage the user's personal calendar, coordinate the user's schedule with the schedule of work group members, and manage electronic address books.

Other Tools. Hundreds of additional user tools are available. Some of them fall into the novelty category; others have legitimate productivity benefits. Specialized tools such as accounting, inventory, or computer-assisted design (CAD) tools may benefit specific users. Users with specialized jobs are sure to find tools designed to assist them in those tasks.

SOFTWARE APPLICATIONS FOR WORK GROUPS

Work groups may be the users in a particular department or functional unit, the employees in a particular facility, the members of a project team, or all employees of the organization. The most prevalent applications software for the improvement of communication, information retrieval, and productivity improvement for these groups are electronic mail and various forms of files retrieval. Applications that are growing in popularity include voice mail and centralized administrative support software. For users who have a need, this category may include **collaborative writing software** (multiple writers contributing to the creation of reports and other documents with provision for editorial comments and revisions) and computer-based training from remote facilities. This category may also include facsimile transmission and complex files query systems.

SOFTWARE SELECTION CRITERIA

Important software selection criteria include cost, vendor support, and training. Mass marketing of software for standard applications has greatly reduced the cost, compared to the cost of software that is internally developed or manufacturer developed. Developer support after the purchase may be critical if alterations in software are necessary or when difficulties with the execution of software arise. Decisions about a software package should not be greatly influenced by its popularity in the marketplace. The most popular software packages may require more training than some of those that are less popular and less expensive. Likewise, the most popular packages may fail to serve user needs adequately.

Software reviews in professional journals are good sources of evaluations. Publishers and office systems consulting firms publish software evaluations on a regular basis through news-letters. Software capabilities are numerous and sometimes complex. As an example of the scrutiny which should be directed toward software, review the features presented in Figure 5-2. That figure illustrates some of the features that should be checked by potential purchasers of word processing software. Similar reviews of other applications software should be made. The services of a DP/MIS software expert or an office automation consultant for software evaluation may be advisable, particularly if the software must function in an integrated environment and be compatible with existing software.

SOFTWARE OWNERSHIP

Decisions must be made about purchasing software versus licensing with permission to copy. A license may be less expensive than large-volume purchases. Licensing has become a somewhat controversial subject because of agreements offered by developers of off-the-shelf software (ready-to-use software purchased in retail outlets). Statements called **shrinkwrap agreements** indicate contractual arrangements that begin when the software wrapper is broken: They declare the "purchaser" to be a licensee—not an owner. This permits circumvention of some of the provisions of the 1980 Software Amendments to the Copyright Law. These amendments to the Copyright Law permitted limited software copying for internal use. If the user is a licensee, not an owner, any copy of the software not authorized by the developer violates the agreement.

Most states (Louisiana was the first) have passed laws that uphold these license agreements protecting the software developer against would-be software pirates. Since state laws may conflict with federal laws, legal tests have generally allowed the state law (purchaser is a licensee) to prevail. Under either law, giving away and selling copies of copyrighted software are illegal acts. Prosecution is difficult, but many vendors have succeeded in prosecuting unlawful copying. Rampant illegitimate software increases the cost of software for legitimate users, but methods of prevention are not yet in place. Attempts to control it through software safeguards proved cumbersome for legitimate owners. Implementation should provide for an adequate number of legal software copies.

HARDWARE EVALUATION—FUNCTIONS AND FEATURES

Hardware selection for office automation installations will concentrate on the user workstation but will also include peripherals, such as printers and other hardware to support user communication and file retrieval. The following general guidelines and the specific recommendations for workstation selection detail the type of scrutiny that hardware evaluation should involve.

GENERAL HARDWARE—EVALUATION GUIDELINES

General systems design decisions and final implementation decisions about interconnectivity, files management, the level of user applications support, workstation configuration, and desired external communication capabilities will guide hardware selection in a general way. Research should document the organization's existing hardware capabilities and attempt to project future needs for at least five years. General guidelines for hardware decisions are as follows:

1. Identify criteria that management can accept and that are general enough to apply to any hardware selection decision involving office automation and end users. (For example, the hardware has the capacity to serve the organization's needs for the next five years.)
2. Match hardware components to planned applications. (Will this hardware component still work when the LAN is installed in eighteen months?)
3. Investigate compatibility with existing hardware and software applications, even for departments with which no immediate interface is planned.
4. Coordinate hardware selection with information security systems (see Chapter 14).
5. Select hardware that can be used in multi-user groups, even if that is not part of the current system design.
6. Consider training and programming implications. (Who will provide these elements—the organization, a vendor, or an outside agency?)
7. Identify a member of the office systems implementation team who will become the authority on hardware information (latest enhancements, prices, capabilities). Hardware exhibits, demonstrations, and business shows provide valuable information for this purpose.

8. Recommend a plan for system maintenance (both hardware and software). This element can be critical to the success of any installation.

SPECIFIC USER WORKSTATION SELECTION GUIDELINES

Selecting hardware to support a specific application requires detailed research. Equipment features, capabilities, costs, capacities, speeds and ergonomic implications must all be considered. The ergonomic factors that influence hardware selection are discussed in Chapter 10. Specific hardware evaluation guidelines should be developed for user workstations. As office automation moves toward integrated office systems and a "maturity" phase, major hardware decisions will include selection of workstations for those who need access to office automation.

The term *user workstation* may refer to the physical place where an employee works—the furniture, the work surface, the supporting equipment and the surroundings—or to the electronic computing device provided for each user. Chapters 10 (Ergonomics) and 17 (Human Factors) contain material related to the first interpretation, and Chapter 10 presents the concept of delivering electronic user support through workstations. The following discussion relates to the latter interpretation and includes implementation considerations likely to be raised when workstations are selected. We are rapidly approaching the "one computer per one office worker" ratio, so there is no question that this selec-

Figure 13-6 User workstations are becoming more powerful and capable of a greater variety of tasks.

tion process will take place. Implementation strategy can bring order to what has been chaos (the uncoordinated purchase of hardware) in the past.

The choice of user workstations is first a choice between a terminal to a departmental or organizational computer and a personal computer. Strategic decisions about the overall operating environment (mainframe orientation, departmental minicomputer orientation, or local area networks) will influence this decision. Regardless of the operating environment, many users will request and need personal computers as their workstations.

Workstations are becoming more powerful and capable of a greater variety of tasks. Figure 13-7 summarizes some of the factors that influence workstation selection, including printers. If office automation is to improve user productivity, workstations must be powerful enough to handle the users' tasks. Some consideration may be given to future requirements. However, predicting needs and workstation developments is difficult. Workstations that are the equivalent of the 386 machines (reference is to the Intel 80386 cpu chip) or better are rapidly becoming standard for many users.

Figure 13-7 User Workstation Selection Factors

Job Design
  Managerial/executive
  Specialized professional staff
  Administrative support

Nature of Operating Environment
  Multi-user departmental system
  Networked departmental
  Standalone

Complexity of Applications
  RAM consumed
  Required storage
  Operating speeds required for efficient use
  Need for multi-tasking

The workstation should fit the user's needs. An administrative support employee who specializes in document page layout will need a powerful computer and a full-page color display with high resolution graphics capability. The features outlined in Figure 13-8 should be analyzed during the selection process.

Figure 13-8　User Workstation Component Features

Component	Feature
Keyboards	Layout, location, and adequacy of special-function keys
	Detachable and movable keyboard
	Key touch, general comfort, and ''typewriter'' feel
	Number pad for numeric data entry
	Minimum interference for touch operators (no poorly situated special keys)
	Special-function keys, including some that can be customized to user need
	Cursor-movement keys
	Relationship of layout and features to user's major function
Displays	Column (character) width (may be a software or CPU feature)
	Screen color: Monochrome: positive or negative? 　　　　　　　　green, white, or amber? Color: color intensity, quality and number of colors to support applications
	Highlight visibility
	Absence of screen glare
	Graphics quality
	Data-entry capabilities (touch screen or voice commands)
	Screen resolution (horizontal and vertical pixels-picture elements and dot pitch)
	Adjustable to user preferences
Central Processor Units	RAM capacity (640K is standard and the limit of usable RAM with some operating systems)
	Operating speed
	Operating-systems supported
	Communication ports, software required
	Peripheral ports
	Compatibility with networks, peripherals
	Interfaces required
	Expansion slots available
	Support of additional storage devices

Figure 13-8 **User Workstation Component Features** *(continued)*

Component	Feature
	Support of input devices (mouse, wand, microphone for voice input)
Storage Devices	Type (hard disk, flexible disk, optical disk, magnetic tape)
	Physical size of device
	Size of medium (flexible disks are manufactured in a variety of sizes)
	Disks: density of storage, capacity per disk
Printers	Type (laser, dot matrix, ink jet)
	Speed in draft and letter quality modes
	Pitch capabilities (at least 10, 12, 15)
	Typeface capabilities
	Page description languages supported
	Typeface quality (true descenders—y's, p's, and g's in the lower-case extend below writing line)
	Underscore, bold print, emphasized print capabilities
	Single sheet and tractor feeding
	Graphics capabilities
Communication Devices	Protocols
	Interfaces
	Transmission speeds

VENDOR SELECTION

Office systems installations are almost sure to involve relationships with more than one vendor. If the hardware selected comes from a major manufacturer that produces most of the needed hardware or from a vendor that specializes in combining products from multiple manufacturers and software developers, the number of vendor relationships may be held to a minimum. Even though the systems are likely to cost more if this is the arrangement, service may be enhanced. Considering the possible sources and applying the criteria discussed here should enable organizations to establish effective vendor relationships.

HARDWARE SOURCES

If workstations and other equipment of a major computer manufacturer (one that is involved in the manufacture of all three CPU categories—mainframes, minicomputers, and microcomputers) are selected, most of the hardware could be obtained from the same source. Even though a firm may not manufacture all of the components, it would have established contractual agreements with manufacturers of the "missing links." Other sources include manufacturers that produce microcomputers only, personal computer retailers, and "vertical market" (highly specialized clients) assemblers of turnkey systems.

Some manufacturers distribute directly to customers; others distribute through their own retail outlets; and still others establish networks of dealerships.

SOFTWARE SOURCES

Software sources offer an even greater variety of possibilities. Software is either developed internally, contracted out to independent programmers, or purchased as an off-the-shelf package. The package might accompany hardware and be included in the system's purchase price.

A purchased software package consists of (1) a piece of recording medium (disk or tape) on which program listings are recorded, and (2) documentation (paper or disk-recorded text) which instructs the user in the installation and use of the software. Manufacturer-supplied or vendor-supplied software may require alterations to fit users' special applications needs.

Recent developments in software delivery have included **"software on a chip."** Software is permanently recorded on a microchip instead of a disk and is either permanently installed in a computer's central processing unit or encased in a matchbook-sized cartridge which plugs into a computer port in a fashion similar to the use of video-game cartridges.

Downloading involves the purchase of software that is transmitted electronically to the user over a communications link such as a telephone line. Instead of buying a disk on which the software is recorded, you pay a fee for the transmission of the software to your system. There is some concern about the ease of software piracy with such arrangements, but piracy is probably no more likely with this system than with software peddled on traditional recording media.

The high-tech supermarkets that are opening around the country and the many retail computer shops may allow potential buyers to try out versions of various software packages before making decisions. Users examine documentation, make a selection, and pay a fee to have the software written to their blank disk. Of course, the same copyright restrictions that apply to other purchased software would apply to this software.

QUANTITATIVE EVALUATION SCHEMES

The selection of vendors for either hardware or software may be improved if a quantitative evaluation scheme is selected. Such a system requires the following steps:

1. Identify criteria that are important. Criteria represent yardsticks against which products can be measured. Print quality and cost are examples of two criteria for selecting a printer vendor, for example. One of these (cost) is easy to quantify; the other requires subjective judgment.
2. Assign weights to the criteria. Even though you have four or five criteria, you may prefer that one criterion influence the decision to a greater extent than any other. To use the printer example again, you may be forced by budget restrictions to weight cost twice as heavily as print quality. Assigned weights should involve a specified scale, say a scale of five or ten. If cost is not a restraint, that factor would receive a low rating.
3. Identify alternative vendors of products.
4. Evaluate the product of each alternative vendor by assigning quantitative values that represent the extent to which that vendor's product satisfies each criterion, compared to each other vendor's satisfaction of the same criterion.
5. Complete the calculations in a chart such as the one that appears in Figure 13-9. By the way, a spreadsheet works effectively in making these calculations.

In the example in Figure 13-9 the evaluator would have enumerated the reasons for rating each alternative as it was. In some cases, the reason is obvious—the presence or absence of a particular feature. In other cases, such as output quality, the user would need to look at the output and exercise a judgment.

Quantifiable criteria are outlined in Figure 13-10. For some of these criteria, such as cost, the absence of a feature, or the presence of a feature, quantification is easy. If a text editor has no draw feature and that is an important criterion, for example, it gets no points. For other factors, such as documentation quality, quantification would require a value judgment and the selection of a value on some type of scale (superior = 5, excellent = 4, acceptable = 3, poor = 1).

Figure 13-9 Quantitative Scheme for Evaluating Vendors

Product: Laser Printer

Criteria and Weights:

Criterion	Weight*
(1) Purchase Price	5
(2) Output Quality	10
(3) Support of PostScript Page Description Language	5
(4) Availability of support for maintenance and repairs	8

*Represents a scale of 10, with 10 being the most important.
Notice that this is a weighting—not a ranking.

Alternative Vendors:

Vendor No. 1, a manufacturer with a sales representative who visits the firm regularly.

Vendor No. 2, a local retail distributor.

Vendor No. 3, a mail order retailer.

Calculation:

	Vendor No. 1	Total	Vendor No. 2	Total	Vendor No. 3	Total
Criterion	1 2 3 4		1 2 3 4		1 2 3 4	
Evaluation*	5 3 0 3		3 5 5 2		5 5 5 0	
Weight	5 10 5 8		5 10 5 8		5 10 5 8	
Rating	25 30 0 24	**79**	15 50 25 16	**106**	25 50 25 0	**100**

*On a scale of 5.
In this case, Vendor No. 2 receives the highest total rating.

NON-QUANTIFIABLE CRITERIA

The quantifiable criteria may not be sufficient for making a choice. Other factors may carry equal or greater weight—even though they are difficult to measure. Among these criteria are vendor reputation and product reputation. Customer testimonials and the results of independent test laboratories would fall into this category. The vendor location, particularly coupled with a high regard for local maintenance, could be the determining

Figure 13-10 **Quantifiable Product Evaluation Criteria**

COST

FEATURES/FUNCTIONS OF PRODUCT

SUPPORT PACKAGE OFFERED BY VENDOR

DOCUMENTATION QUALITY

TRAINING REQUIREMENTS AND/OR COST

criterion for a vendor who is not represented locally. If this is the case, the quantitative evaluations should be adjusted.

VENDOR SELECTION AND NEGOTIATION

Armed with all the evidence and information of the planning, analysis, design, and implementation processes, implementers can make informed decisions. The final task of the process is vendor negotiation. This process is easier if several vendors offer products that rank high and nearly equal on factors other than cost. Negotiations can then elicit the best price.

Through negotiations with vendors, implementers frequently can secure contract provisions that are better than the original bid. Vendors may be willing to substitute new features or hardware items for those that received low ratings in the review process. Vendors may agree to install and troubleshoot new systems until they are working properly.

Purchase contracts are negotiated—either for pilot installations with provisions for additional purchases if trials prove to be effective or for initial full-scale installations. In some cases organizations' representatives are sufficiently familiar with products that they are willing to commit to full-scale installations if they get equipment for a reasonable price.

INSTALLATION

The installation phase may require extensive preparation. In many cases, physical changes to offices and buildings must be made. Cable is installed; floors are ripped up; workstations are relocated. New workstation furniture may be installed. In any case, staffs must be prepared for the changes that result.

Figure 13-11a Cable installation is one example of physical changes to offices and buildings.

PILOT INSTALLATIONS

Pilot installations are usually considered to be trial runs. Their scale is small enough that the organization can back out without having made too great a financial commitment if the trial is not successful. The knowledge that an unsuccessful project can be aborted should not affect preparation for installation, however. If the pilot is to provide a realistic evaluation, it must receive serious attention. Otherwise, the trial has no chance of being successful.

Staffs must be oriented to the changes that will occur and trained for the new applications and hardware they will encounter. In some cases, new employees (especially for systems requiring skilled operators) will be recruited and trained. System documentation may need to be adapted to the organization's operating procedures.

FULL-SCALE INSTALLATIONS

If an entire organization or a major portion of it will be changing to a new system abruptly, even greater preparation is required. User and operator support systems must be planned and implemented prior to the arrival of hardware and the start-up for new procedures. Extensive training may be required. Organizations

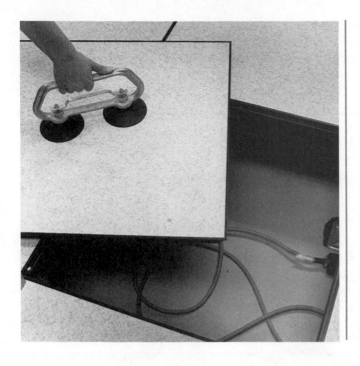

Figure 13-11b Floors may be ripped up during the installation phase.

with information centers that serve as a support mechanism will need to have these centers fully operational before major installations are made.

New personnel may need to be recruited, employed, and trained. A better solution for critical personnel positions would be to have newly required services performed by someone who has worked with the planning, analysis, and design process.

Vendors may be willing to maintain support personnel on the premises as new systems are being installed. Employed consultants and advisers may be retained to assist with the supervision of installations.

SYSTEM EVALUATION AND ALTERATION

Installation is not the final stage of implementation. Even while new systems are being installed, plans for evaluation and alteration should be in place. A systematic mechanism for obtaining user feedback should be planned. Departmental meetings, evaluation instruments, and interviews with users are possible ways to obtain such feedback.

The managements of some organizations will require measurements—at least during initial stages following installation. Even if an installation is full scale and irreversible, such information can form the basis for changing the design for future installations. Observations about the system's performance and evaluations of vendor support may be critical to future changes in the systems.

WOHL'S BUSINESS PERSPECTIVE

Often, the focus in picking an office system is on what will be delivered when the system is first installed. Users are concerned about the robustness of the hardware platform, its speed, power, and performance. If they think of software, it is as the "completer" for the system. Again, the focus is on what's available now and evaluation consists of picking the best choice.

But once the system is installed, users are locked into that decision for a significant length of time. Personal computers, for instance, may be technologically obsolete in three years, but they are often used for five years or more. Minicomputers and Local Area Networks are expected to last even longer.

This means that a successful system selection process should focus on more than today's products and today's needs. It should try to project how these needs will grow and change over some meaningful time frame (perhaps three to five years?) And it needs to guess how today's products will change and grow. Sometimes the best product in the short run turns out to be less than optimal when measured over some longer period of time.

Selecting anything, business or consumer product, always consists of a series of compromises. How much can I spend? What can I take delivery on right away? What tantalizing products aren't ready yet, but are worth waiting for? An office system selection is just like that.

Business consumers should be especially mindful of a few facts of computer life, circa the 1990's:

- Personal computer platforms change about every three years. That is, the old ones still work (and probably are still being sold), but newer products offer measurable advantages. Buy old equipment at the end of its cycle and you risk an early disappointment. Often that disappointment comes in the form of new software: optimized for the newest, most robust hardware platform, it simply won't run on older, less powerful machines.

   Older equipment is almost always *cheaper,* but it's rarely better. Users should consider buying less, but buying systems that will be durable.

   Don't take that to mean "buy the newest thing out." Some hardware announcements are noble experiments. If they fail to attract a critical mass of software, failure (or at least obscurity) is sure to follow. A good rule of thumb is to wait until at least a few of the most significant software developers commit to the new hardware platform. This is a good sign that the platform is slated for a long successful run.

• Try to size your requirements over time. Don't buy a system that is just big enough to do what you need to do right away. That system will be difficult and expensive.

If you can project your growth in users, in applications, and in volumes of data, you can pick a system which is small enough to be cost justified, but large enough to permit a few years' growth. Local Area Networks are particularly adept at this, permitting economical beginnings yet supporting substantial growth.

Be particularly wary of vendors whose product lines look continuous, but who require costly replacements rather than graceful, incremental upgrades. A good systems selection should remain a good selection for at least a few years!

SUMMARY

Office systems implementation may be interpreted broadly to encompass all planning, analysis, design, and installation activities. Another interpretation is somewhat narrower and includes the final design decisions and installation activities. This phase may also be interpreted very narrowly to mean installation and start-up activities only. The middle interpretation is used in this chapter.

The implementation environment for office systems is affected by a variety of human and organizational factors, as well as existing systems and the necessary changes to these systems. Decisions are influenced by the detail of systems analysis and design. Broad design parameters may leave decisions such as office systems policy and interconnection tactics to the implementation phase. Final software and hardware decisions will be made during the implementation phase. This may involve pilot installations and other systems evaluation techniques before final decisions are made.

The final software and hardware implementation decisions involve matching product features and functions to user needs and selecting products that fit into the organization's strategic plan for office systems.

Vendors are selected not only by the evaluation of their products, but also by the support, maintenance, and services that they offer. Since a single product may be available from multiple vendors, quantifiable criteria and nonquantifiable criteria such as vendor reputation and stability are important.

Installation and evaluation are the final phases of implementation.

KEY TERMS

integrated office system

integrated office automation
    software

multi-user system

shared-logic system

intelligent terminal

dumb terminal

bridge

gateway

request for proposal (RFP)

multi-tasking

individual user application
    tool

work group tool

shared application tool

independent application tool

presentation graphics

decision support system
    (DSS)

collaborative writing
    software

shrink wrap agreement

software on a chip

REVIEW QUESTIONS

1. What are the various interpretations of the term implementation when
    it is applied to office systems?

2. What are the human/social factors and the organizational factors that
    affect the environment for implementation?

3. Describe the concept related to the use of the word *system* in the sugges-
    tion that a "systems approach" be used for implementation? What is the
    key to "a systems approach" to implementation?

4. For implementation, how does each of the following affect the process?
    How do they contribute to smooth, effective implementation?
    a. existing systems
    b. office systems policy
    c. non-quantifiable vendor selection criteria

5. Contrast the following sets of terms that are related to implementation
    decisions:
    a. integrated office automation software and independent applications
        software
    b. integrated office automation software and independent integrated
        applications software
    c. multi-user departmental system and local area network systems
    d. multi-tasking and integrated software
    e. operating system software and applications software
    f. decision support software tools and administrative support software
        tools
    g. application tools for individuals and applications tools for work
        groups

6. What would you consider the major influences on the selection of a user workstation?

7. Divide the applications tools discussed in this chapter into the following categories and indicate briefly your reasons for categorizing them as you do:
   a. tools for all users
   b. tools for administrative support employees
   c. tools for managers and executives
   d. tools for those with special needs

8. Identify what you would consider to be the major hardware and software selection criteria for office systems.

9. Draft a software procurement policy statement that would guide decision makers in determining how many copies of applications software to purchase for the organization.

10. What are the four or five most important factors that would influence the decision about where to buy office systems hardware and software?

CASE STUDY: IMPLEMENTATION AT HOSPITAL CARE, INC. — PART III

Review the description of Hospital Care, Inc. and the accompanying exhibits at the end of Chapter 11. Using the information presented in the case and incorporating what you have learned about office systems to this point, formulate suggestions for each of the following items.

QUESTIONS/ACTIVITIES

1. Where would you locate a mainframe-powered integrated office automation software package within this firm? At corporate headquarters? At each hospital? Discuss.

2. If you were to install the software identified in No. 1, how would you connect (what communication link) individual workstations to the mainframe computer?

3. Discuss the probable number of offices from the organization chart that would be provided with the above office automation software.

4. Prepare a Gantt chart entitled "Office Systems Implementation at Hospital Care, Inc."

5. Draft a one-paragraph "Office Systems Policy" that would appear in the organization's policy manual and would prevent confusion about who is in charge of office systems decisions for the firm.

SUGGESTED READINGS

Bair, James H. and Mary J. Culman. "But Where Do You Start?" *Management Technology* (July, 1983): 40.

Bair, James H. and Laura Mancuso. *The Office Systems Cycle.* Palo Alto: Hewlett-Packard Company, 1985.

Bikson, T. K. and B. Gutek. *Implementation of Office Automation.* Santa Monica, California: Rand Corporation, 1984.

Hirschheim, R. A. *Office Automation: A Social and Organizational Perspective.* Chichester, England: John Wiley & Sons, 1985.

Long, Richard J. *New Office Information Technology: Human and Managerial Implications.* London: Croom Helm, 1987.

CHAPTER 14

Managing Office Systems

OBJECTIVES

After studying this chapter, you should understand the following:

1. The management functions of those responsible for managing the personnel and the technologies that comprise office systems

2. The nature and value of standard procedures for performing office tasks

3. Approaches to designing and communicating procedures

4. Issues associated with productivity analysis

5. Traditional and contemporary approaches to office productivity improvement

6. Work measurement as an approach to quantifying office productivity and the standards that are the result of work measurement

7. Security risks faced by organizations that automate office functions

8. Strategies for managing office information security risks

9. The special threat to information security created by computer viruses

10. The responsibilities associated with keeping hardware and software up to date

Office systems must be managed. Analysis of this task from the sociotechnical and systems viewpoints requires examination of the human factors, the behavioral aspects, and the organizational implications—along with the office automation or technical factors. This chapter and the two chapters that follow it explore management functions and tasks associated with managing administrative office systems. This chapter concentrates on the technical aspects; Chapter 15 examines the staffing function; and Chapter 16 deals with training office personnel.

The coordination of office systems is no more automatic than the technologies. Earlier portions of this text have considered the assignment of responsibility for managing office automation (OA) and the placement of that responsibility within the overall organizational scheme. This chapter deals with the nature of some of the responsibilities of those who manage office automation.

ADMINISTRATIVE SUPPORT MANAGEMENT

Because office automation and office systems exist for the benefit of professionals and the employees who support the efforts of professionals, the management of office technologies and office support employees may be referred to as administrative support management. Administrative support management involves the application of management functions (planning, organizing, leading, and controlling) to the components of office systems.

OFFICE SYSTEMS COMPONENTS

A concept presented early in this text is that "office automation" does not mean automatic offices. Office systems exist for the benefit of the organization and for the people who manage the organization. Effective systems depend upon effective procedures. Effective procedures get the job done well and protect the interests of the organization. *Office systems* components include people, technologies, and systems that add order to the interactions of people and technologies within formal structures called organizations. These components must be managed, and those who manage in this area must know something about the special systems, the special people who must be managed, and the behavioral principles involved in managing people.

THE ROLE OF MANAGEMENT

As organizations adjust their philosophies about managing people and as employees become more involved with the organization's success, the role of the manager changes. The number of infor-

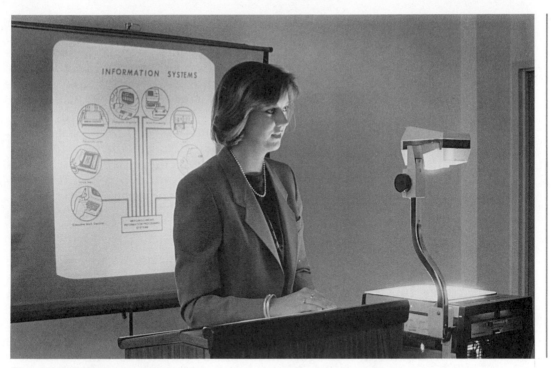

Figure 14-1 The new manager is more of a generalist who engenders a team spirit among employees.

mation workers has increased, and the educational level and skill levels of these employees have also risen. All of these factors have contributed to a role shift. Managers are not expected to rule their staffs. A team spirit among workers and managers is more likely to prevail.

Managers as Facilitators. The "new manager" who is evolving from the conditions described above is referred to as a facilitator: a coordinator or director of people, systems, and equipment. These managers are less likely to use their time as task assigners, production controllers, and disciplinarians. There will be less awe (and disdain) for managers from their subordinates. Both managers and workers will view the manager role as that of a team leader. Teamwork will prevail, but the teams may not be permanent. Groups are formed to accomplish tasks and projects and then they are disbanded. Employees at every level, including managerial levels, are less specialized in this new role. The breadth of professional managers' formal education in schools of business is evidence of this trend.

Education for business now concentrates upon the development of communication, critical thinking, and problem solving, in addition to specialized and technical education. Other evidences are the dependence on quality circles and other productivity improvement groups and the lateral moves by employees and managers into new fields.

The Staffing Function.   Someone must recruit employees, screen and interview applicants, and make hiring decisions. Much of this is done by human resource management departments, but at some point office systems managers get involved in the staffing of administrative support employees and technical specialists. This part of the management role is discussed thoroughly in Chapter 15.

Management-Employee Relationships.   Managers must cultivate a variety of relationships; and, to some extent, their roles vary as they function within these relationships. Many of them must deal with a group of subordinates for whom they are directly responsible, but they also report to a superior. They must maintain relationships with other managers. Within the office-systems environment, managers must direct employees who have their own formal and informal relationships with peers. For special projects, teams create temporary relationships. Managers must be capable of functioning in this variety of relationships.

The leadership functions—those associated with selecting, orienting, supervising, and motivating administrative support employees—will be discussed in Chapter 15. The functions presented in the remainder of this chapter are, for the most part, control functions. They deal with the tools and tactics necessary for the orderly functioning of systems and for the protection of the information with which office functions deal.

PROCEDURES, METHODS, AND DOCUMENTATION

A measure of a system's effectiveness is its effect upon productivity. Likewise, effectiveness is influenced by the efficiency of systems and their contributions to communication, decision making, and information protection.

Part of the process of managing office technologies is the development of work procedures and methods. Understanding systems at the procedure and method levels requires delineation of these terms. Throughout this text we have referred to systems as wholes; procedures and methods are subdivisions of those wholes. In this context, then, **system** is the broadest term, referring to a whole organization, an identifiable unit within an organization, or a family of related personnel, technologies, and plans for their accomplishment of objectives.

Procedures are subsystems and represent routines for carrying out the activities that make up a system. For example, every large organization has a purchasing system. This system is composed of numerous subsystems (procedures). One of those procedures would involve the submission and subsequent approval or rejection of a purchase requisition. Every person in the organization who requests permission to purchase goods or services would follow the same procedure regarding completion of forms, submitting them for approval, and so on.

Methods are the precise, specific tasks or activities that make up procedures. In our example, four tasks are associated with submitting a purchase requisition: (1) type or write a form, (2) secure approval, (3) submit the form, and (4) receive acknowledgement that the form has been received. Figure 14-2 illustrates this concept.

Some organizations develop procedures in a systematic, formal way; others allow procedures to evolve, never examining the reason for the format or sequence of the procedural steps in a process. Manual procedures seem to work for some organizations without extensive study or examination of their makeup and with no documented standard of performance, but office systems that are supported by technology require consistency in performance. This consistency comes from a decision to standardize the performance of tasks. These standardized patterns of behavior are labeled procedures.

The application of computer technology to routine clerical tasks, such as computing invoices and keeping accounting records, requires extreme standardization of procedures and is easily accomplished because the sequence of events for every occurrence is highly predictable. Because other office information-processing tasks are so unpredictable, however, many procedures cannot be reduced to rigidly standard patterns. Electronic systems that aid such procedures must provide for the required flexibility.

Analysis of the office-systems study (see Chapter 11) identifies the procedures that make up existing systems. Further study may be necessary to identify the detailed steps (the methods) in each procedure. Existing written procedures, frequently called **standard operating procedures** or office procedures, should supply such detail. Introduction of office automation will drastically change procedures; frequently they will be greatly simplified. However, there is still a need to standardize even simplified procedures; and to communicate these procedures consistently, they must be written. Before procedures are written (or rewritten, in the case of existing procedures), the incorporation of accepted systems and procedures-design techniques should be considered.

Figure 14-2 Systems, Procedures, and Methods

The System	The Component Procedures	The Methods of One Procedure*
RECEIVING SHIPMENTS	1) Receiving raw materials	Receive a telephone call that shipment has arrived
		Meet driver at gate
		Secure shipment documentation from driver
		Return to receiving office
		Retrieve document image of purchase order on PC
		Verify quantities by comparing shipment documentation and purchase order
		Key data for receiving report, including short or over data
		Print receiving report
		Initial receiving report
		Key shipment to daily receipts log
		Sort copies of receiving report
	2) Receiving product containers and packaging	
	3) Receiving merchandise	
	4) Receiving equipment	
	5) Receiving miscellaneous shipments	

*For the purpose of this illustration, only the methods of one of the five procedures is shown. These methods might differ from one organization to another. Similarly detailed procedures would exist for each of the other four procedures.

Some phases of office procedures design can be approached in a manner similar to traditional transaction data processing systems design. However, many office procedures do not lend themselves to the types of design that were intended as preparation for writing computer programs. Office procedures involve the actions of people as they carry out routine activity. Some of these activities involve administrative support employees who support the work of managers and professional staff, and some of them are performed by managers, staff, and professional specialists for themselves.

Many office procedures describe the tasks associated with financial transactions, but other activities also require procedures: communication among employees, communication with outside individuals and groups, retrieval of information, routine accumulation of information, and the support of decision-making activity. A procedure may commence because someone applies for a job, calls the organization for information, seeks reimbursement for travel expenses, or requests 500 copies of a form. These examples involve standard procedures, but their initiation is sporadic. Other procedures occur at regular intervals and under predictable circumstances: reports are written monthly and annually, files are purged, documents are filmed, and databases are updated. Regardless of the nature of the procedures, the organization will function more efficiently and effectively if procedures are followed consistently.

PROCEDURES AUDIT AND DESIGN

One by one, the procedures that combine to form a system must be audited and, if necessary, redesigned. Office procedures elements include input (information and conditions), processes (actions) involving personnel and technology, and output (product). Figure 14-3 presents an example of a portion of a written procedure.

People who perform procedures are assisted by whatever technology is available. The **procedures audit** involves examining all procedures and their tasks or methods for possible improvement. This scrutiny frequently reveals the need for technology. Highly repetitive tasks, frequent information retrievals, and minor alterations of existing documents to create new documents are signals that OA technologies may be helpful. Involvement of numerous employees in a single procedure, spreading the procedure over long time periods, and the identification of errors or communication malfunctions are evidences that procedures need to be improved. A few questions will help to design an effective procedure:

1. What is the primary function of the procedure—the one thing that it is designed to accomplish?
2. What is the product of this procedure (for example, information on a paper document, in a database, or in an electronic file)?
3. How does this procedure affect the organization as a whole?

Figure 14-3 A Portion of a Written Procedures Description

STANFORD & SONS, INC.
T-6
STANDARD OPERATING PROCEDURES

Procedure:	Employee Travel Expense Reimbursement
Purpose:	Approve, document, and reimburse employee expenses for extraordinary travel
Department(s):	All departments
Conditions:	1. Applies to extended travel (overnight) other than travel required to fulfill basic job requirements
	2. Examples: continuing education, attending professional association conferences

---

Person	Tasks
EMPLOYEE	1. Complete TRAVEL AUTHORIZATION (Form T-09). 2. Submit all three parts to immediate superior.
EMPLOYEE'S SUPERIOR	1. Examine and evaluate request. 2. Approve or reject request by signing appropriate line of form T-09. 3. If approved, enter budgetary and accounting codes. 4. Distribute Form T-09: Part 1—Accounting Part 2—Employee's Department Part 3—Employee
EMPLOYEE	1. Document out-of-pocket expenses and company credit-card charges according to "Travel Guidelines" (POLICIES AND PROCEDURES MANUAL, 16.42.3) 2. Complete and submit TRAVEL EXPENSE VOUCHER (Form T-10) within 30 days of completion of travel.

(For example, does it produce revenue, improve cash flow, facilitate production or sales, improve capital performance, enhance communication, or provide the foundation for decision-making?)

4. What action or condition initiates the procedure?
5. What information is necessary for the employees who perform the procedure?
6. What personnel are involved with the procedure?
7. What records are originated as the procedure progresses and what is their form (electronic, film, or paper)?
8. What decisions are made as the procedure develops? By whom?
9. What other procedures are dependent upon this procedure?

10. What are the critical elements of the procedure? What are the supplementary elements?
11. What hardware units are involved in the procedure?
12. What elements of the procedure are accomplished by software?
13. What elements currently accomplished by manual methods could be converted to automated methods?
14. What controls will assure that this procedure will function properly?
15. Given the ideal environment (ideal personnel, hardware, and software), how should this procedure be performed?

Answers to these questions will provide fuel for designing or redesigning a procedure. Many questions can be answered by examining existing written procedures documents; others must come from interviews with involved personnel. Whether an improvement to an existing procedure or the design of a new procedure, some type of flowchart will enable the designer to refine the detail of the procedure. The flowchart and a written description of the procedure can be used as training materials for instructing employees who will perform and interact with the procedure.

SYSTEMS DOCUMENTATION

Written procedures become the documentation for employees who work with procedures. Many organizations adapt standard formats for office procedures. They may be coded according to the system that they support and made available to any person who needs to know the details of the procedure. The traditional written procedure is a printed or typewritten document—frequently a procedures manual; however, office automation permits electronic storage and retrieval of written procedures. The care needed in writing procedures is not affected by the medium through which they are communicated, however.

Written procedures should detail the elements of the procedure in the sequence in which the elements are encountered. They identify input or conditions that necessitate the procedure, identify documents or records created or affected as the procedure is performed, and cross-reference other related procedures. The steps in the sequence are frequently enumerated, and they communicate more effectively if each item begins with a verb. Figure 14-4 illustrates a portion of a procedure description written in an "action" format. It details the action performed by any person performing the procedure. The procedure illustrated in Figure 14-3 was written in a "role" format—the employee and the role or methods performed by that employee were listed in proper sequence.

Figure 14-4 **Written Procedure for Electronic File Query**

LAURIE COUNTY BOARD OF REALTORS   OFFICE PROCEDURES

Page 1 of 4
Effective Date: 10-16-90
Previous Rev.: 10-16-87
          Code: MLS-7
  Distribution: All Participating Firms
          Title: **Market Search/Match Prospect With Active Listings**

PREPARE SYSTEM:
1. Turn on video data terminal (or personal computer), modem (if external), and printer.
2. Set modem transmission speed at "1200 BAUD" (some systems may use a setting of "High" or "Medium" for this speed).
3. Set telephone switch to "DIAL."
4. "Dial" 286-4277 and wait for a dial tone.
5. Set telephone switch to "COMPUTER" and hang up phone.

SECURE CLEARANCE TO HOST SYSTEM:
7. Depress <RETURN> or <ENTER> two times.
   Screen Image: >
8. Type "HELLO 9.1" <ENTER>
   Screen Image: > HELLO 9.1
                 PASSWORD:
9. Type "MLS" <ENTER>
   Screen Image: > HELLO 9.1
                 PASSWORD: MLS
10. Type "GO" <ENTER>
    Screen Image: HELLO 9.1
                 PASSWORD: MLS
                 > GO
                 SECURITY CLEARANCE:
11. Type "(Your Security Clearance Key)" <ENTER>

Note: Type your security clearance key carefully; the characters will not appear on the screen. If you make an error, the system will respond with "NO CLEARANCE FOR THIS KEY; TRY AGAIN." If you do not enter the correct key by the third attempt, the communication link will be locked. You must call the board office for instructions to unlock the link.

PRODUCTIVITY ANALYSIS

Productivity remains the number one concern among managers in the United States and Canada. Because our economic systems are rapidly shifting from industrially oriented systems to service and information-oriented systems, office productivity has gained significant attention among corporate, government, and institutional planners in recent years. Even though this concern has existed for several decades, serious action directed at improving white-collar productivity did not come to the forefront until the late 1970s. The productivity of those who produce or manage the production of tangible goods and quantifiable services is easier to measure than the productivity of those who work with information or manage others who work with information.

ISSUES

Even though there is general agreement that organizations should attempt to improve office productivity, there is little agreement about the target of such efforts, the approach to measuring productivity, the role of information in productivity, or even the definition of productivity. Understanding the basis of these issues is necessary to develop an understanding of the concern about office productivity improvement.

Definition of Productivity. The traditional definition of productivity has been the value of measurable output (essentially the monetary value of goods and services) compared to measurable input (an hour of a worker's time). This definition creates problems when information and knowledge workers are singled out. The products of their efforts are not sold. Organizations don't sell reports or databases or profitable decisions.

For a profit-making enterprise, productivity is the portion of revenue represented by profit. That portion of profit that is added because of the efficiency and effectiveness of office personnel and office systems represents office productivity. A popular concept refers to this as value added. This value may be attributed to administrative management and staff and the systems within which they work. Pinpointing this contribution is a very difficult task. Many organizations do not even attempt to measure it.[1] The discussion of cost-benefit analysis in Chapter 12 included descriptions of effectiveness, efficiency, and value-added benefits which may be derived from improved office systems.

Measurement. Because the output of some administrative support employees can be quantified (number of lines keyed, number of references to files, or length of time consumed answering telephone calls), these activities can be measured. The previously

---

1. See Paul A. Strassman, *Information Payoff* (New York: The Free Press, 1985), Chapter 8, for an excellent discussion of productivity measurement. Portions of that discussion are reproduced in Chapter 12 of this book.

mentioned issues surrounding productivity measurement apply here, however. Some managers question the value of any measurement effort. On the subject of managerial productivity, there is disagreement about the possibility of measurement, the potential value of measurement, and the method to use. The measurement method called the value-added approach associates the productivity of management with total revenue less the cost of capital, materials, labor, and technology. This method may give a measure of total value added by management, but it gives no measure of the productivity of an individual manager or the management of a single unit.

Targets.   The traditional targets of office productivity improvement have been secretarial and clerical tasks. Significant improvements have been made in these areas through technology. Firms that use no technology in the office can expect improvements when technology is carefully implemented. Knowledge-worker productivity offers more potential for improvement, however. The cost of knowledge workers' time is greater and the results of increasing their effectiveness may be far reaching. So both the administrative support level and the managerial levels, depending upon the circumstances, should be targets for productivity improvement.

A BRIEF HISTORY OF OFFICE PRODUCTIVITY IMPROVEMENT

Between 1950 and 1980 several techniques were used to improve productivity in the office. The use of digital computers, work measurement, records management, and office systems and procedures analysis were among the techniques. Each made limited improvements.

In the 1950s and 1960s digital computers for processing information related to financial transaction accounting, inventory control, and financial planning improved productivity in the specialized offices that managed these activities. However, these efforts covered limited functions; and the size and cost of systems confined their application to large organizations.

A second technique that produced productivity improvements in office-intensive organizations was the work measurement approach to job design, procedures design, and information flow. The basic concept of **work measurement** is the quantification of productivity in a working environment. Productivity (in the traditional approach) is measured output divided by measured time. Application of the resulting ratio to the productivity of workers is the basis for **time standards.** A standard is expressed in measurable units and given times (for example, 80 words per minute as a keyboarding skill or five letters per hour as a transcription skill). Standard productivity is that of the average, well-trained worker. These workers, called **benchmark positions,** are observed or measured to gather data from which standards are determined.

The work measurement approach involved the creation of standards and the use of those standards as guides to designing procedures, jobs, and work flow. The standards identified possible productivity for given time spans so that planning and controls could become more accurate. Work measurement consultants assisted hundreds of organizations in improving office productivity. Even though these efforts were usually able to demonstrate improvements, work measurement was not perceived as a solution to low office productivity in many organizations. In fact, many organizations expressed no concern about office productivity. The concept of work measurement, as explained later in this chapter, is now applied to other productivity analyses.

A third significant but quiet contribution to office productivity improvement came from efforts to improve records management systems. Analyses of records systems, procedures for dealing with these systems, and facilities for housing, protecting, and retrieving them brought significant improvements to office effectiveness (if not to productivity levels). These were limited to organizations with large volumes of paper records. Government agencies made significant but unheralded improvements in records management programs in the post-World War II era. Because of the assumption that computers would eliminate paper, however, many organizations' leaders overlooked this opportunity for improvement.

A fourth category of effort used some of the techniques of systems and procedures analysis to redesign information handling and communication systems. This effort was called **work simplification,** an effort to examine procedures and redesign them without waste. Because most office work was manual and routine, analysis concentrated on the steps in a procedure, identifying the creative elements, the delays, distances traveled, and the number of inspections. It resembled the work measurement approach, but it did not concentrate on time measurements or performance standards. The emphasis was eliminating wasted effort.

In the 1980s the shock of global competition, particularly from Japan, brought new efforts to improve productivity. Concurrently, the computer revolution convinced us that we were, in fact, becoming an information-oriented society with more knowledge workers and service employees than production employees. These conditions brought new attention to profit-and-loss statements and to government budgeting for administrative activity. Rising "sales and administrative costs," "operations and administrative expenses," and "cost of administration" figures—those nebulous, but high, totals that appear in financial statements and budgets—caused many organizations to examine administrative costs and to look for ways to improve efficiency in units financed by these expenditures. The term "white collar productivity" improvement began to include managers and professional staff.

Many factors reflect the renewed interest in productivity improvement. One example is the American Productivity Center in Houston, Texas, a research organization funded by more than 300 corporations and foundations for conducting productivity-related research. A growing number of firms have on their staffs a specialist whose responsibility is productivity improvement—both in the production and in the administrative sections of their firms. Quality circles and other productivity groups (see Chapter 15) have helped to improve office productivity.

Today's manager of office systems is likely to get involved in some effort to contain or, at least, document the costs involved in these systems. Rather than these traditional techniques, the method is likely to involve some form of work measurement technique.

Figure 14-5 Many firms employ a specialist in productivity management to keep administrative costs down.

WORK MEASUREMENT

Even though the attention to office automation is shifting from quantification at the administrative support employee level to quality measurement at the managerial and professional staff levels, a review of work measurement techniques provides insight into current efforts to improve office productivity. Two formal programs that involve work measurement are time-standards programs, and office technology feasibility studies. In fact, work measurement now may be used to describe any effort to quantify productivity.

When work is measured to develop time standards, the process is called **methods time measurement (MTM)** or **time studies.** Because the measurement techniques resemble those used in industrial settings, the process may be referred to as an engineering approach to work measurement. This approach originated with the industrial-era efficiency improvement programs such as those pioneered by Frederick W. Taylor and Frank and Lillian Gilbreth.

TIME STANDARDS

Time standards represent the productivity of a well-trained employee in a specified period of time. A variety of approaches have been used to measure office work to develop time standards. Some of them are quite informal, requiring employee-generated records of productivity; others are quite formal, involving statistical sampling techniques and observers who collect information. Elaborate quantification efforts are required for some approaches to developing standards. Organizations either develop their own standards or employ predetermined **standard office time data.**

Work measurement for time standards has concentrated on the task level (procedures and methods) and the work of employees at the operative level (clerks, secretaries, and equipment operators). The desirability and value of such quantification is highly controversial. Before the advent of computer-based office technologies, many organizations were able to report significant improvements in productivity levels and in managerial effectiveness following formal work measurement programs. Such efforts led consultants in the field to conclude that typical office employees were only about 50 percent as productive as they could be. These low productivity levels were attributed to inadequate employee training, poor procedures planning, inappropriate job design, inadequate equipment support, lack of professional supervision, and poor information flow. There is little evidence that low productivity is the result of low employee effort.

Productivity improvement through work measurement is more likely to show significant gains when the volume of manually performed procedures is great, the number of office employees is large, and the nature of office procedures is routine and repetitive. Since these conditions represent the areas where office automation has been most frequently applied, the presence of technology-based office systems tends to diminish the need for this type of measurement.

Establishing standards requires selecting procedures to be quantified, developing methods for gathering statistics, and selecting employees to be measured. Work measurement does not concentrate on quantifying the total production for an employee or unit. Instead the measurement is applied to identifiable elements of a method. For example, keying, document handling, and idle time might be the elements of a data-entry clerk's method for entering a customer's payment to an account. Repeated measurements (possibly by an observer using a stopwatch) are averaged, and the average times for all elements are totaled to arrive at a standard for the method. Examples are documents processed per hour, lines keyboarded per hour, documents filed per hour, or documents filmed per hour. Appendix C illustrates the calculation of standards for an office task.

Less formal standards may be calculated by noting the beginning and ending times, counting production for the time period, and dividing the time consumed for the whole process (a WP operator keyboarding double-spaced reports is able to keyboard 50 pages in 250 minutes — or one page every five minutes). Several observations would be averaged to arrive at the standard. Standards are valuable for managers who must predict staff needs and equipment needs and schedule services.

FEASIBILITY STUDIES

When a feasibility study of a new technology is being conducted, quantification of the output of the system may be requested. Such quantification offers several potential benefits. Quantification of existing systems allows a comparison with projected output of proposed systems. Together with information about the capacities of proposed systems, information about the quantity of output permits accurate selection of system size and capacity and hardware operating speeds. Operating cost comparisons are also possible. For example, the fact that a department files an average of 1,830 documents each day, combined with the knowledge that an updatable microfilm camera will film and process a document every 10 seconds, suggests that one camera should be sufficient to handle the volume.

The targets of work measurement during feasibility studies is likely to be routine procedures, document production, information processing, and communication activities. The result of the quantification is a list of activities, documents, or information types and the quantity of production over some identified time span (usually one or two weeks). There is usually no attempt to equate these data to the productivity of a single employee. Through log sheets, activity lists, document copies, questionnaires, or personal interviews, the types of activity and quantity of production are identified. Quantification of productivity for a prototype or pilot installation provides hard data that can be extrapolated to other units if data regarding current productivity in these units is available. Figure 14-6 represents a portion of a tally of

Figure 14-6 Tally of Activity Logs for Productivity Analysis

Activity	Section One		Section Two	
	Principals	Support	Principals	Support
NUMBER	12	7	7	
ORAL COMMUNICATION*				
Telephone	10080	2940	5880	126
Meetings and presentations	12640	840	6901	36
One-to-one conversation	30600	1960	17850	84
Dictation to secretary	1680	1680	980	98
Dictation to machine	3360	——	1960	—
WRITTEN COMMUNICATION**				
From dictation to secretary	——	3362	——	281
From machine dictation	——	10084	——	847
From principal's longhand	——	4369	——	214
From boilerplate	——	2422	——	73
DOCUMENT STORAGE/RETRIEVAL***				
Filed in principals' offices	——	128	——	74
Retrieved from principals' offices	——	26	——	15
Filed at support employees' workstations	——	504	——	294
Retrieved from support employees' workstations	——	101	——	59
Filed in section files	——	1214	——	806
Retrieved from section files	——	243	——	161
Retrieved from central files	——	123	——	89

*Minutes per activity   **Quantity in lines   ***Document count communication and document storage and retrieval activities for office employees. These data would be collected by asking employees to keep a log of their activities over a time period sufficient to give a representative sample of their activities.

Even if no formal productivity-improvement program exists, managers of office systems will find a method for quantifying output and activity to be a valuable planning tool. Volume counts, activity logs, and records of the number of employees assigned to various jobs and tasks help to equate office activity to other measurable factors, such as sales or production. These records assist managers in planning for staff needs, equipment capacities, and budgetary requirements. Productivity estimates for planning purposes may take the form of cost-benefit analyses.

INFORMATION SECURITY

Information security has received considerable attention recently because electronically accessible information has been brought into the office out of the relatively safe environment of computer centers. Personal computers, computer terminals, local area networks, and other communication links have made access to information so widely available that security of that information is severely threatened. Not only do greater numbers of outlets exist, but larger numbers of people are now computer literate and capable of using electronic access hardware. This increases the possibility that they may accidentally or purposefully retrieve or destroy information that they would not otherwise have access to except through electronic means.

For small businesses, many records that were previously protected in special containers or secured files areas are now housed in electronic form and reside on floppy disks, hard disks, or in databases. Unfortunately, many managers who would have insisted that file cabinets be locked allow employees to leave floppy disk data files carelessly unprotected.

Managing information security involves risk awareness, knowledge of approaches to managing that risk, and a formal program for information security. The program may include some of the technological systems described in the remainder of this chapter; it must include the common-sense safeguards that are described. There are financial, legal, and moral reasons for securing information. The possibility of financial loss is the most obvious, but information managers may also be legally bound to protect the security of information about individuals and clients. Finally, there is an ethical bond between organizations and their employees, customers, and clients. Less-than-reasonable efforts to secure information that could be damaging to those individuals or could invade their privacy is considered by many to be a breach of ethical standards. Identifying risks and managing them fulfills these obligations.

SECURITY RISKS

Organizations with long-standing vital records management programs are in a good position to identify office information security risks because these programs require an awareness of security risks. Electronic records are vulnerable to the usual disasters (fire, flood, and storm) and more. The major new concern is that information will in some way become available to unauthorized individuals who will use it in a manner that is detrimental to the organization. Another concern is that destruction of information may occur because of inadvertent employee error, system malfunction, computer crime by employees or outsiders, undesirable environmental conditions, or any combination of these.

Employee Error. The most damaging risk faced by managers of office systems is the risk of loss through inadvertent human error or system malfunction. This risk receives far less attention than other more dramatic risks, but it is responsible for greater dollar losses than any other. The potential losses of this variety include accidentally deleting electronic files, incorrectly updating databases, exposure of electronic information to hazards that destroy the information, and a variety of equipment failures that destroy information.

A 1989 study[2] of Data Processing Management Association members cited 57.1 percent of mainframe managers and 61.3 percent of microcomputer managers who reported that people constitute the greatest threat to their information systems. Among this group, the greatest expectations (71.1 percent of mainframe managers and 69.8 percent of microcomputer managers) are that people errors will come in the form of "human errors, accidents, and omissions."

Computer Crime. Computer crime has probably received the most attention of any risk. Overall losses have been small in this area, but very large computer crimes have been perpetrated against individual organizations. For example, a man who worked

---

2. Karen-Ann Kievit, "DPMA Members Target Information Security Threats," *Inside DPMA* (Data Processing Management Association: March, 1989): 1.

Figure 14-7 Stealing hardware from the office is one example of computer crime.

as a word processing operator in a New York law firm smuggled information about clients to stock traders who used information about pending mergers to make huge profits in stock transactions. In California, an outsider posing as an international bank examiner was able to get security codes and swindle a bank out of $10.2 million in 1978. He used the security codes to transfer funds to a Swiss bank account.

Computer crime includes unlawful access to information, manipulation of information in a manner that provides unwarranted gains to the perpetrator, vandalism of hardware and software, and deliberate sabotage of systems. Employees represent the greatest criminal risk to information security. Employees who take information with them to jobs with competitors, manipulate information to their own advantage, or sabotage information as revenge for some ill feeling toward the organization are examples of employee computer crime. Employees have been discovered selling stolen mailing lists, paying insurance claims to their friends (instead of the company's policyholders), paying salaries to terminated employees, and removing penalties from drivers' license records. Dismissed employees and those who are planning to quit because they anticipate dismissal are risks for

Figure 14-8 **Some hackers use their high-level computer skills to manipulate electronic information for their own benefit.**

vandalism and sabotage, though the actual incidence of these crimes is quite low. An auditor in a big-eight accounting firm estimates the average amount stolen by a computer criminal at $100,000, "far higher than the $23,000 take of the old-style embezzler."[3]

The dispersal of information access through personal computers and terminals has created information access points in high traffic areas within the organizations. Combined with easy access through telecommunication links, the risk of computer crime is likely to increase dramatically in the future.

Criminal Mischief. Another category of risks that is somewhat innocent but very dangerous is the pilferage of information by hackers and computer professionals who pride themselves on being able to infiltrate computer systems. **Hackers** are computer buffs who are highly skilled in data communications. Some of them apply their skills to gain illegal access to information through

---

3. Toni H. Lydecker, "Computer Crime," *Association Management* (November–December, 1984): 62.

communication links and to break codes that can enable them to manipulate an organization's electronic information. The hacker risk is the smallest of the computer crime risks.

Computer Viruses. The year 1988 was "the year of the virus." Numerous incidents of "program diseases" crept into the files of computer users all over the world. **A computer virus** is a program that may be attached to electronic files. When transmitted and triggered by some pre-planned event, such as the arrival of a particular date or the entry of a particular command, the program is unleashed to accomplish its creator's mission. This may be to multiply itself into infinity or until it fills the memory and storage capacity of the system. The mission may be the destruction of files or the display of annoying symbols on computer screens. Some viruses whose creators intended innocent intrusions such as the display of a holiday greeting have gone astray and caused extensive damage.

The virus threat came to national attention in November, 1988, when a Cornell University student transmitted a virus that locked up computers all over the United States. Even though it destroyed no information, the cost of removing the unwanted information from computer systems was estimated at $100 million. The Computer Virus Industry Association documented nearly 90,000 attacks on personal computers in 1988. "There may have been as many as 250,000 occurrences of computer viruses in 1988 . . ."[4] The problems caused by these attacks brought rapid attention. In 1988 Louisiana and New Hampshire signed anti-virus bills into law. In 1989 a Texas court convicted a man of planting a virus that destroyed close to $200,000 worth of sales commission records at a securities firm. This conviction came on a broad law that makes interfering with computer operation or destroying electronic files a crime.

Since many viruses have come from bulletin boards and public domain software, managers are advised to avoid any software that does not come directly from the distributor and that is not sealed in protective packages when it arrives. Backing up files on a daily basis, restricting write privileges of the organization's files, and installing systems that require file and program users to sign on and off are other recommended procedures.

Disasters. Natural disasters such as floods, storms, and lightning represent a risk that can be managed. Unmanaged, the risk poses a huge potential for loss. Some not-so-natural disasters

---

4. T. R. Ackmann, "Assault on Computer Crime," *Inside DPMA* (Data Processing Management Association: March, 1989): 12.

are also potentially damaging: fire, broken water pipes, power surges, lapses in the flow of electricity, and power failures.

When information technologies moved from the controlled atmosphere of the computer center into offices throughout organizations and even into homes and hotel rooms, the effects of the environment posed significant new risks. Temperature, humidity, static electricity, and cigarette smoke pose some of the most troublesome risks.

SECURITY RISK MANAGEMENT

Office automation has brought a mixed bag of benefits and security risks for office systems managers. Integrated office systems, which improve the office function, also create the potential for increased levels of accidental information destruction, information tampering, and computer crime. A combination of general safeguards and technical applications is necessary to effectively secure information. A formal program will identify vital and critical records and result in the installation of systems that will provide adequate security. Elements of the program must balance the positive element of maintaining information security and the negative element of damaging systems effectiveness. The user-friendly status that makes office automation possible should not be destroyed. Time-consuming and bothersome safeguards may discourage effective use of systems.

Responsibility for Information Security.   Specific responsibility for security by some individual is essential. If a data processing or MIS group manages information security, those plans should be extended to office automation. If there is no organization-wide security plan, someone in the office systems group should be assigned the responsibility. Unfortunately, ineffective security systems have no squeaking wheels, so they attract no attention. Someone needs to be responsible for maintaining their effectiveness.

The person responsible for information security would be charged with the responsibility for creating procedures and developing policy that deals with security issues, for combining the organization's electronic file classification with the security issue (assigning security status to each file classification), and for the development of a security-conscious employee population through training and awareness programs.

Vital Records Program.   As discussed in Chapter 7, identification of vital records is crucial. The need for records is not diminished by the conversion of records to electronic media instead of paper media; it may be greater. A vital record is one that would be essential for an organization's continued existence following a disaster that destroys working versions of records. The record could exist in any medium.

Examples of vital records are accounts receivable, payroll records, support for tax returns, contracts, and records required by law. For manufacturers, production specifications or contracts may be vital. For insurance companies, policies and policyholder information may be vital. For universities, student transcripts and budgetary support data are vital records.

Critical records are those that could be damaging to the organization or to individuals if they fell into the wrong hands. Sales information, contract negotiations, product and market research data, product development information, confidential information about employees and clients, contract bidding, payroll information, and software codes are critical. Correspondence, reports, or documentation involving any of these may also be critical. These records may exist in any medium—paper, film, or electronic. Electronic records are probably more vulnerable to security risks than other forms.

Tactics.   Basic safeguards represent common sense tactics for information security. They include physical access controls, security procedures, and environmental precautions, Figure 14-9 summarizes some of these tactics.

Both software and hardware components—and combinations of the two—may be used to create security systems. Software can provide for access control through password requirements. A person with high security clearance would become the keeper of the password directory, and each individual for whom clearance to various databases and files has been approved would be given a password that would be needed to retrieve or update information.

Precautions are necessary for password systems. Since passwords are stored in the system, they should be stored in such a manner to prevent unauthorized access. Easily obtainable information about individuals who have passwords (social security numbers, license plate numbers, names of close relatives, initials, and words appearing on keyboards or video terminals) should not be used as passwords. A frequent breach of security occurs when individuals, fearing they will forget their passwords, tape them to personal computers or terminals or inside their unlocked desk drawers. Passwords should be relatively long and involve nonsense words or numbers.

In addition to preventing unauthorized access, software can also record unauthorized attempts to access restricted information. It will also break the communication link after a specified

Figure 14-9 **Office Systems Security Tactics**

PHYSICAL ACCESS CONTROLS:

1. Controlled access to offices containing high concentrations of hardware (where possible and practical) and to media libraries by a librarian or other employee who controls access
2. Positioning of video terminals so that they are not visible to high-traffic areas
3. Off-hours security (human and mechanical)

PROCEDURAL CONTROLS:

1. Formal approval (dual signatures) for software changes, verification of changes, and personal computer acquisitions
2. Off-site storage of vital and critical information, with frequent updates
3. Backup copies of electronic file media (even if not stored off-site)
4. Routine security orientation and bonding of new employees
5. Routine investigation of applicants for employment
6. Emergency and disaster plans (by specific emergency or disaster)
7. Rotation of personnel work schedules and required vacations
8. Unannounced audits of files and magnetic media by separate staff not directly involved with the units that produce the files to determine that file names and media labels are accurate
9. Identification of critical and vulnerable employees
10. Telecommunication controls (particularly downloaded information from mainframes to personal computers)

ENVIRONMENTAL TACTICS:

1. Humidity- and temperature-measuring devices and controls
2. Dust-free environment (dust damages hardware and magnetic media)
3. Static electricity controls (carpet selection, static arresting pads under equipment, and so on)
4. No-smoking rule (smoke damages hardware and magnetic media)
5. Water drainage devices
6. Fire extinguishers (gas systems, not sprinklers) and smoke detectors; fireproof containers (vaults or files) for files, software, and documentation
7. Lightning arrestors, power-surge controls, and emergency power supplies
8. Emergency power distribution systems

TECHNICAL TACTICS:

1. Access controls (passwords, voice prints, retina recognition)
2. Encryption
3. Anti-virus filters
4. Disaster recovery facilities preparation

Figure 14-10 Data encryptors protect information transmitted over telephone lines.
Racal-Milgo

number of such attempts. This would permit a legitimate user the privilege of entering an incorrect password once or twice.

Disaster backup services are provided by firms that specialize in disaster recovery. They sometimes offer complete office facilities, computer systems, and staff that would enable an organization to move its office operations to their facilities immediately following a disaster. Assuming that necessary precautions to provide backup records had been taken, business might be able to continue with no more than a few hours' delay. These services, which may include the use of huge mainframe computers, telecommunications services, and ongoing disaster simulation tests, are quite expensive. The alternative may be more expensive, however.

Recent hardware and software advances have made possible the development of **fault-tolerant systems.** These systems offer security from lost business and down time because of equipment malfunctions. This concept involves mostly mainframe computers with multiple or "tandem" CPUs, input/output processors, and storage facilities. When there is a failure in one, the others take over. The system diagnoses its own problems and tells an operator what part to order. Such systems are backed up by emergency power sources and power distribution systems. The same principle is applied to OA technologies in the form of self-diagnostic maintenance. A screen message on a lighted message panel helps service representatives guide employees (over the telephone) to make necessary adjustments.

Numerous hardware devices are being developed to control access to information. Among them are voice print, fingerprint, signature, and even eye retina analyses. These systems appear to control access better than password access. Like passwords, however, the identifying data are stored in the computer and can be accessed by skilled criminals. Other devices include smart cards, which are credit-card size microprocessors containing unique identification information, and audible alarms embedded into magnetic media such as diskettes. The alarms are triggered if diskettes are removed from the owner's premises.

Available as either a software or a hardware option, **encryption** is a security system that garbles information during transmission and ungarbles it when it is retrieved by a person with the key (a code similar to a password that is created by the user who generated the information). The value of encryption is that the user creates the key and only those people to whom the user gives the key can unscramble the data. The keys are not stored in the system; they are created by the user at the time of transmission. The more sophisticated systems use intelligent modems as the encryption device, but some relatively inexpensive software packages for use with many systems, including personal computers, are available. With this approach, the software accomplishes the encryption, and the key is required to retrieve decrypted files. Complicated keys and codes can slow the communication process and affect user friendliness of systems.

Insurance. Once reasonable precautions to manage risk have been employed, the standard approach to risk management beyond the safeguards and devices is to purchase insurance to cover potential losses that will not be prevented by these measures. Insurance companies have been hesitant to insure against computer and information crimes out of concern that the losses may not be measurable. However, the cost of recreating lost data, actual money losses incurred by financial organizations, and amounts spent to create information are measurable, and insurance companies are beginning to cover such losses. Such insurance has been available since it was introduced by Lloyds of London in 1981.

Computer Auditing. Auditing involves special periodic checks on information, procedures, and conditions of any kind. Its most popular application is to the accounting procedures and records for an organization. Auditing techniques powered by the computer can be used to help control information security. Special auditing software programs, both for accounting information and other information, may be used to pull information from systems and to pose questions that should reveal security threats.

An important consideration for any auditing procedure is that the person responsible for the audit not report to the person responsible for the system being audited. Auditors usually report to very high-level officials and are totally independent of accounting departments, finance departments, and central computer departments. **Computer auditing,** whether the term is used to describe the auditing of computers and the systems that they operate or using the computer as a tool for auditing all organizational information resources, may be best handled in large organizations by a person who is designated the information security specialist. This person is responsible for programs, training, periodic audits, and general security awareness for the organization.

Available software packages, called **asset management systems,** can assist with the task of inventorying information systems. Both mainframe and PC packages are available that keep track of an organization's hardware and software. These packages inventory hardware from the time it is ordered, keep records of dollar value and software supported, track the location of hardware and software, record scheduled and emergency maintenance, and analyze the applications for which each machine is used.

WOHL'S BUSINESS PERSPECTIVE

A major issue for a successful office system is the security of its data. But too often systems management focuses on the data's security and forgets the purpose of offering data and tools to manipulate it with. That is to say, data is useful only if workers can use it!

Security is a scarey business today. In addition to the problems of amateur users who accidentally lose or erase things, we need to worry about:

- Pranksters, not out for gain, but rather for the fun of tricking the system or its owners. Such users don't intend to cause any permanent damage, but they can cause substantial disruption to the use of your system—and surface concerns about less benevolent security violations.

  Education is the answer. Users need to learn that computers are a serious business and that the fate of the company rests on using them wisely. If your employees understand just how important the computer and its data are to their ultimate fate, they are far less likely to exercise their computer literacy in an abusive way.

- Unhappy employees (or ex-employees) may choose to "get even" by destroying or confusing data. The danger is small, particularly if you include the computer in your orderly dismissal process (change passwords, get back physical access devices like keys and computer access cards), but it is present.

  Often, changing passwords or other access devices on a regular basis will limit your exposure. Certainly, making the most critical information available only on a "need to know" basis, with stronger control, is also important.

- Computer viruses are a newer problem. Whether they're intended as harmless pranks or malevolent statements of power, they can have financially disastrous consequences.

  Some new rules seem in order: No more amateur software seems to be one of them. You may want to restrict software from bulletin boards and other shareware devices to a small number of computers, unattached to your other system.

But let's not forget the point of office computing: data shared is more valuable than data hidden away. So it's important not to become so concerned with computer security and data integrity that impossible barriers are placed between computers and users.

Users whose passwords are a multiple lengthy sequence of meaningless numbers aren't more secure. Often, they write those numbers down and place them in a handy spot. That's no security at all! Or, they simply decide the system is too tough for mere mortals and become non-users. That wasn't the point of all this.

In some distant future, we'll solve the problem differently. The computer will note our voice, our fingerprints, or perhaps the speed and rhythm with which we keyboard. All of them are unique identifiers, and none requires a key to lose or a password to write down or forget!

SUMMARY

Office systems, comprised of people and technologies, provide administrative support to the organization's executives, managers, and professional staff. Those who manage this support effort must first be managers and, second, knowledgeable about systems technologies.

Management of office systems requires a knowledge of procedures as subdivisions of systems and methods as subdivisions of procedures. Regular audits, redesigns of procedures, and careful documentation of procedures enable managers to maintain smooth-functioning operations.

Productivity is a universal concern, but there are many issues about its definition and measurement. Targets of productivity improvement through office automation seem to be shifting from administrative support employees to managerial and professional staff employees.

Effective use of technologies requires carefully planned procedures that are communicated, usually in writing, to employees who perform them. They are valuable as training and reference materials, and they standardize procedures throughout organizations.

Work measurement represents a variety of approaches to quantifying productivity in offices. Productivity is quantified in order to select technologies with sufficient capacities to support office activity, to form the basis for calculating time standards, or to plan staff and equipment needs. Work measurement as a basis for productivity improvement and job simplification works best when applied to the methods level of office work. It needs to be supplemented by a concern for the quality of output and the quality of managerial and professional staff effort.

Office automation may increase security risk because information is available at many places inside and outside organizations using OA. However, these risks can be managed through routine safeguards and technical devices that protect information. Both software and hardware devices may be employed to lessen the threat of information destruction or computer crime. The more publicized computer crime risks from outsiders accessing information systems are not as great as the risk of employee error and employee crime, although the computer virus has recently been recognized as a potential major threat.

Hardware and software updates represent a major responsibility of those who manage office systems. Management education, professional reading, and systems management software are methods of keeping hardware and software up to date.

KEY TERMS

system
procedure
method
standard operating
  procedure
procedures audit
work measurement
time standards
benchmark positions
work simplification
methods time measurement
  (MTM)

time studies
standard office time data
computer crime
hacker
computer virus
disaster backup service
fault-tolerant system
encryption
computer auditing
asset management system

REVIEW QUESTIONS

1. What is included in the role of persons who fall into the administrative support management category when this term is applied to the management of office systems?

2. What is the relationship between the "office procedure" or "standard operating procedure" documents and the concepts of "system," "procedure," and "method"?

3. Identify alternative media for communicating office procedures to employees of an organization.

4. Identify and briefly review four categories of activity that addressed office productivity during the past three decades.

5. Contrast the traditional use of the term work measurement for the production of time standards and the work measurement that might take place in a contemporary environment to determine the feasibility of purchasing a new office system.

6. What are the risks to information security? Which risk is the most prevalent?

7. Identify the management tasks involved with managing the risk of information loss.

8. What is a computer virus? Can an organization protect itself against the threat of computer viruses? Explain.

9. What is the value of retaining the services of an external disaster contingency firm as a part of information security risk management?

CASE STUDY: GUTERMUTH, KEMP & ASSOCIATES

Gutermuth, Kemp & Associates is a law firm in a city in the northwestern United States. The firm is relatively small and employs a minimum of electronic office equipment—two memory typewriters, for creating some very standardized legal documents, and dictation equipment.

The firm is considering a variety of office automation hardware and software that they hope will improve the productivity of its attorneys and its administrative support staff. Managing partners want to use work measurement techniques to document the current productivity levels and a cost-benefit analysis to estimate costs and benefits before selecting a system. The senior partners are not excited about office automation, but they appear willing to accept benefits that are supported as justification for the investment.

This case requires specific calculation of one potential benefit and general speculation about other potential benefits. As a part of the data-gathering process that has taken place, Clay Offutt, the office manager, collected information about the secretarial, clerical, paraprofessional, and legal staff members' activities for a two-week period. The attorneys enthusiastically supported the project because most of them believe that much of the routine of their jobs could be reduced with office automation.

Mr. Offutt has measured the time spent by legal staff (attorneys) proofreading second drafts of typewritten documents that were not generated on one of the memory typewriters. Policy requires such proofreading because when a document must be typed a second time, there is always the possibility that another error will be made. Paraprofessional employees do some of this proofreading, but the attorneys still read much of their correspondence and certain legal documents before allowing documents to leave the firm. The study reveals that each of the 12 salaried attorneys who originate documents spends an average of 20 minutes a day proofreading such documents.

Mr. Offutt believes that if all the office employees who create documents for the 12 principals had access to word processing systems, this proofreading time could be reduced by at least 50 percent. Because only the portion of documents with errors would be rekeyed, only those portions would need checking after the revision by the attorneys who insist on proofreading their own documents. Mr. Offutt also believes that this is a conservative estimate, but he wants to be safe in his estimates. He has gathered the following additional information for use in his analysis:

1. The office is open an average of 21 working days each month.
2. The working day for the 12 principals is eight hours.
3. The average salary for the 12 principals is $42,245.
4. The benefit package for the principals equals 18 percent of salary.

Using this data, information in the past three chapters, and your own assumptions about the potential value of word processing and other office automation technologies, answer the following questions about Gutermuth, Kemp & Associates.

QUESTIONS/ACTIVITIES

1. What would be the savings (for one year and for five years) if the office manager's estimate (a 50 percent reduction in proofreading time) is correct?

2. What type of benefit would this savings represent?

3. Could you justify any installation of word processing technology on the basis of this one factor alone?

4. What additional potential benefits would you expect the office manager to include in his investigation? For each benefit, identify the type of data you would gather to support the benefit and the nature of the benefit that would result.

5. Would the productivity of the support staff or the legal staff (or both) be enhanced by the proposed system?

SUGGESTED READINGS

Dido, Laura. "A Menace to Society." *Network World* (February 6, 1989): 70.
Farhoomand, Ali F. and Michael Murphy. "Managing Computer Security." *Datamation* (January 1, 1989): 67.

Hobus, Jim. "Managing Micros for Success." *Information Center,* (May, 1989): 27.

Honan, Patrick. "Avoiding Virus Hysteria." *Personal Computing* (May, 1989): 85.

McAfee, John. "The Virus Cure." *Datamation* (February 15, 1989): 29.

Malina, Deborah. "The Renaissance Manager." *Information Center* (April, 1989): 12.

Mandell, Mel. "Do You Know What You Own?" *Information Center* (September, 1987): 54.

Pujals, Joseph M. "How Safe Is Your Data?" *Information Center* (April, 1988): 36.

CHAPTER 15

Selecting and Managing Office Personnel

OBJECTIVES

After studying this chapter, you should understand the following:

1. The characteristics of administrative support workers

2. The contributions of the managers of office systems and the managers of administrative support to the personnel/ human resources development activities involved in staffing offices

3. The prestaffing activities that facilitate the selection of employees: job analysis, job design, and job evaluation

4. The typical procedures for locating and hiring office workers

5. The content and value of orientation programs for new employees

6. Approaches and outcomes of employee performance appraisal and compensation systems

7. The role of managers and supervisors in the office and three popular theories of leadership style

8. The concept of supervision and some essential skills for effective supervision

9. The concept of employee motivation

10. The challenges of women in managerial positions

11. The changing perceptions of the roles of women and men in management

12. The status of union membership among office employees

Office automation may suggest that managing the office is managing technology. This is far from the truth. The office is still an environment occupied by people performing functions critical to the organization. Staffing and supervising the office are still major tasks because the technological environment affects skill requirements, the nature of jobs, the systems for carrying out work, and the social structures within which people work.

This chapter explores the characteristics of administrative support workers, the human resources management activities of those responsible for office workers, and the organizational climate for effective office employee motivation. Management activities include selecting, compensating, and evaluating employees, providing a climate conducive to employee motivation, and examining the roles of professionals responsible for managing office systems and office workers. Technology is influencing all of these activities, and those who manage office workers. The managers that serve knowledge workers must attempt to understand the nature of their responsibilities and the potential impact of technology.

Most organizations will have a **personnel management** or **human resources development (HRD)** staff. This staff will have fundamental responsibility for recruiting, hiring, training, compensating, developing, and, in general, looking after the welfare of employees. They serve the entire organization by assisting the various units in selecting employees and by coordinating employee benefit programs and training and development programs. Managers of the individual units also must participate in these activities. The manager of administrative support employees knows more about employee qualifications than a staff member in the personnel department. Managers of support employees should know about the training needs, the trends in compensation, the conditions necessary for employee safety and well-being, and the special problems encountered by office employees. Together the personnel management staff and the office systems or administrative support management staff will be able to select capable employees, orient and train them, and develop them in a manner that will encourage them to stay with the organization and to grow professionally.

Some managers of office automation or office systems are directly responsible for administrative support workers (as line managers); other office systems professionals are in advisory or coordinating positions and are not directly responsible for these employees. Regardless of the relationship, managers of office systems should know about the education and skills needed by workers in these systems and about the recruiting, training and development, and job conditions unique to these positions.

CHARACTERISTICS OF ADMINISTRATIVE SUPPORT WORKERS

As previous chapters have suggested, managers and professionals who work in offices have recently been labeled knowledge workers because they work with information and make decisions. Knowledge workers have emerged as a category of workers that includes professional managers of all disciplines and professional staff members, such as accountants, systems analysts, financial analysts, and legal counsel. Support employees such as clerical workers, secretaries, technical operations employees, and paraprofessional employees are sometimes considered to be knowledge workers also. In this chapter the management of the latter group is considered. They will be referred to as office workers or support employees. This discussion emphasizes the management of office workers and technical specialists who support executives, managers, and professional staff persons.

The portion of society in the knowledge-worker and office-worker categories has increased, and futurists predict that this segment will continue to grow. Large organizations are recognizing the need for concern about office workers. For example, the Cincinnati office of one multinational organization employs a Manager of Office Automation—Technical Factors and a Manager of Office Automation—Human Factors.

To further establish the group of employees we are considering, the qualifications of these employees and some demographic information about their numbers will be helpful.

QUALIFICATIONS

Administrative support employees, such as clerical, secretarial, data entry, operations, reprographics, records specialist, and electronic publishing employees, must have special qualifications. The work they do requires special skills and training. Prior work experience may not be required, but managers must be able to equate work experience with training and placement. The educational level of administrative support workers is steadily increasing. Many of them have completed associate and bachelor degree programs at the college level. Special requirements for support employees in contemporary office environments include knowledge about organizations and good oral and written communication skills.

Because of the nature of contemporary office systems, office workers must interact with large numbers of people. Therefore, their human relations skills are critical. Many of them make important decisions and coordinate critical activities for those whom they serve. Their education must have included more than technical skill development. For example, an employee with superior communication skills and only average technical skills might be selected for a secretarial position over one with superior keyboarding and computer skills but low human relations skills. Preferably, entry-level employees who will work with office systems will have been exposed to computer technology and basic office systems. Knowledge of and experience with hardware and software associated with a particular job or organization are less important. Today's office workers may be more career oriented than the traditional office employee. They are less likely to settle in a job for long periods of time. Employers who have developed career paths and employee development programs are more likely to attract superior employees.

DEMOGRAPHICS

The "white collar" work force consists of the "managerial and professional specialty" and the "technical, sales, and administrative support" elements as identified by the U.S. Bureau of Labor Statistics. Both terms are interpreted very generally by the Bureau, but these two groups made up 57 percent of the employed work force in 1989. The administrative support group accounts for 15.6 percent (18,087,000 employees) of the total.[1] This group includes most operative-level workers such as computer operations personnel, secretaries, stenographers, typists, data entry employees, financial records processing employees, mail and messenger service personnel, miscellaneous administrative support groups, and their supervisors. Among the administrative support category, 82 percent are women, and 44 percent are in the under-30 age group. The percentage of women is much higher in some positions such as typist (97 percent) and stenographer (89 percent).

Office automation managers also may be directly responsible for staff specialists such as office-systems analysts, forms designers, and records managers. An appreciation for the professional interests, job responsibilities, and special needs of these employees is also important.

---

1. *Employment and Earnings*, April, 1989 (U.S. Department of Labor, Bureau of Labor Statistics): 29.

STAFFING THE OFFICE

The effectiveness of office systems depends upon quality employees; therefore, the managers of these systems should be active in the staffing process. If a personnel department handles basic staffing responsibilities, careful communication of job requirements to that department and early participation in the screening of prospective employees will improve the possibility of hiring capable workers who will stay with the organization.

Effective staffing requires planning and aggressively seeking the most qualified employees. Those who staff their offices by selecting from routine applicants may experience higher training costs, lower productivity, and higher turnover ratios than organizations in which an office-systems specialist is active in staffing.

One goal of managing any group within an organization is a low **employee turnover ratio** (the portion of a work force replaced each year). This ratio is determined by dividing the number of employees leaving the organization by the number of employees when all units are fully staffed. High turnover can be very costly because of the expense of recruiting, selecting, orienting, and training new employees and because of lost productivity during initial employment. Low turnover keeps these costs low and also contributes to good morale and productivity.

A staffing program, whether carried out by the office-systems staff or by a joint effort of that staff and the personnel-management department, should involve prestaffing activities, identification of appropriate sources of employees, and planned staffing procedures. Following effective practices and giving attention to the legal implications of employment can improve the process.

PRESTAFFING ACTIVITIES

Prestaffing activities, although not directly part of staffing and the documentation that results, can improve the staffing process. Prestaffing activities include job analysis, job design, and job evaluation. The resulting documents are job descriptions and job specifications.

These prestaffing activities are standard procedure for many organizations. They help to create conditions for effective staffing. All managers should be familiar with the activities and participate in the preparation of documents that describe jobs and specifications for employees who work in their units.

Job Analysis. **Job analysis** is the process of collecting data about job content and analyzing the nature of the functions, duties, tasks, and responsibilities that comprise a specific job.

Figure 15-1 The search for qualified employees begins with prestaffing activities, which identify the requirements of particular positions.

Data regarding job content are gathered through carefully constructed questionnaires and through interviews with employees currently holding the positions. **Job descriptions** are written documents that detail the results of job analysis and do the following: (1) concentrate on the minimum or typical activity that comprises a job, (2) serve as valuable training and reference documents, and (3) document job content. Finally, job descriptions simplify communication with the personnel department regarding the nature of the job for which applicants are sought. Without job descriptions, employees may be confused about their responsibilities, and multiple employees occupying the same job may disagree about their responsibilities.

Job specifications specify minimum and desirable qualifications for the person who holds a particular job. They concentrate on education, skills, and work experience; but they may also include such attributes as physical stature, specific education, or a specific skill level if these are bona fide job requirements. Managers and supervisors develop specifications through their experiences and observations. Figure 15-2 illustrates a job description; Figure 15-3 illustrates a job specification sheet. The specific language is deliberate. Specificity can avoid disagreements over qualifications and prevent Equal Employment Opportunity Commission action. Qualifications should be low enough to attract applicants and correspond to the actual work requirements and the pay. The career ladder section is not often seen in job descriptions, but these items are likely to become more prevalent in descriptions for office jobs.

Figure 15-2   **Job Description**

POSITION TITLE: Records Center Clerk
DIVISION: Information Systems
SOURCES: J. Kemp
ANALYST: H. Adams
DATE ANALYZED: 10–26–90
D.O.T. CODE: NA
DEPARTMENT: Office Systems
WAGE CATEGORY: NonEx
VERIFIED BY: Z. Layne
DATE VERIFIED: 11–1–90

JOB SUMMARY:
The Records Center Clerk assists in the operation and maintenance of the Records Center. The Records Center Clerk assists in reference, use, and disposal activities of the Center, maintains current status of information for accurate retrieval, and assists in maintenance of the vital records program.

DUTIES AND RESPONSIBILITIES:
—accesses, compiles, gathers, and issues requested records and information
—maintains accurate charge-out system
—receives and stores material for inactive storage by established schedules
—assists in orientation, training, and cross-training of new employees, junior records staff, and other organizational personnel
—maintains files and is responsible for records security according to established procedures in the facility
—provides suggestions and recommendations in establishing and revising procedures
—performs other minor duties assigned by superior

CONTACTS:
—reports directly to the Records Center Supervisor

Figure 15-2 **Job Description** (continued)

—interacts daily with co-workers and other staff members to exchange information

—has regular contact with other departments using the Records Center for records storage

JOB REQUIREMENTS:

—good oral and written communication skills equivalent to that of a high school graduate

—ability to maintain pleasant working relations with all levels of personnel

—ability to operate office equipment (calculators, reader/printer, typewriter, terminals for data entry, CAR retrieval system) after reasonable training

—ability to lift in excess of 40 pounds

—ability to operate mechanical equipment such as a forklift after training

—ability to handle boxes of files on ladders at heights up to 15 feet

—good sense of balance and height perception

CAREER LADDER: Records Center Supervisor
                  Records and Information Technician

Job design is necessary when a new position is being created or when a job needs to be drastically changed. In the latter case, the process involves job redesign. Equipped with descriptions of existing jobs and data involving desirable job content, managers create positions that are compatible with requirements of a system and the organization's structure.

Technology has had a significant impact on job content. Jobs have been created to plan, install, and run technology-influenced systems. In some cases, jobs must be changed, combined with other jobs, or eliminated because technology condenses or eliminates certain tasks. The necessity for job redesign is greater at the operative level than at the managerial or professional staff levels. Technology can drastically change the nature of a job without changing the job content. If technology is merely a tool for carrying out a job, the results of using the tool may not change the duties, responsibilities, or relationships of an individual. The only difference is increased productivity and improved product quality.

For some people the switch to technology makes drastic changes in their work environments. An executive who uses electronic mail may keyboard his or her own messages and develop a rapport with the office systems analyst who helped select and

Figure 15-3   **Job Specification**

POSITION TITLE: Records Center Clerk
DIVISION: Information Systems
SOURCES: J. Kemp
JOB ANALYST: H. Adams
DATE ANALYZED: 11–09–90
D.O.T. CODE: NA
DEPARTMENT: Office Systems
WAGE CATEGORY: Nonexempt
VERIFIED BY: Z. Layne
DATE VERIFIED: 11–19–90

JOB SPECIFICATIONS:

Education:
High school diploma or G.E.D. certificate or demonstrated capability to perform the job
One semester of typewriting or equivalent keyboarding skills

Experience/Training:
Minimum of six months work experience in each of the positions of Records and Information Clerk and Inventory Control Clerk
OR
equivalent experience
OR
40 hours of classroom instruction and Computer-Assisted *Instruction (CAI) Units RM1 and RM2*

install the system. The same executive may retrieve information from an electronic file instead of asking a support employee to physically retrieve paper or filmed records from a file. Both the activities of the executive and the relationships with other employees have been changed.

Job Evaluation.   Another prestaffing activity that enhances the staffing task is **job evaluation.** This is the process of placing a monetary worth on a particular job. If job evaluation has been done for the entire organization, the data can become the basis for a compensation plan. Otherwise, a decision must be made for every opening that occurs.

Some organizations use very informal job evaluations. For example, they may establish standard starting pay based solely on market conditions. Other organizations use the pay for the person who previously held a position for comparison or use the pay of other employees in the same position as a guide, with adjustments for new employees, depending upon their qualifications. Neither of these plans is as good as a carefully considered job evaluation that uses the market conditions (supply of and demand for persons who qualify for the job), the required qualifications, the level of the position compared to others in the organization, the nature of the responsibilities, and the demands that will be placed on the person who holds the job. The result of job evaluation is a hierarchy of jobs that indicates the relative worth of each job.

The Comparable Worth Issue. A major issue facing organizations and the managers who administer job evaluation and compensation plans is the issue of **comparable worth**, which refers to the comparison of pay for jobs dominated by females and jobs dominated by males. Although federal legislation requires "equal pay for equal work," this has little effect in a job category dominated by one sex. The pay differential, referred to as the **wage gap**, has been significant. Various groups report the gap at different levels. The ratio of overall female-to-male salaries remained at 59 percent for several years, prompting a campaign by a national women's group. Meager improvements were realized by women in the 25-and-older age group between 1979 and 1982; the ratio improved from 61 percent to 64 percent. Figures for 1984 placed the ratio in the 65–67 percent category; and by 1989, it had improved to 72 percent.[2]

Women have won settlements in lawsuits that challenged job evaluation systems. They have argued that there is no justification for assigning a greater worth to a factor (such as responsibility for making decisions) in a male-dominated job than is assigned to the same factor in a female-dominated job. Such litigation has also challenged the worth of different factors (for example, the act of lifting for a maintenance employee being rated higher than that of dexterity for a data-entry clerk). Other arguments have contended that job-evaluation factor weights were matched to existing jobs long before large numbers of women were employed and that such assignments are still very subjective processes frequently performed by men.

Organizations that wish to use job evaluation systems that are free of sex bias and minority bias should use an approach such as the one recommended by Fulghum (see Figure 15-4). With thoroughly trained evaluators and effective instruments, the hierarchy of job worth that results will be relatively accurate.

2. George D. Webster, "Wage Discrimination: An Issue for the '80s," *Association Management* (August, 1988): 224.

Figure 15-4 **Mechanics of a Comparable Worth Study**

JOB EVALUATION:
— collect job data through questionnaires and interviews
— write formal job descriptions in a format that is conducive to evaluation of predetermined job content values
— evaluate all jobs and market pricing of jobs
— develop final job-worth hierarchy

COMPENSATION ADMINISTRATION:
— develop pay structures (select benchmark jobs and develop wage/salary ranges)
— develop cost estimates

IMPLEMENTATION:
— implement plan and adjust wage/salary structures accordingly

Source: Based on materials from Judy B. Fulghum, ''The Newest Balancing Act: A Comparable Worth Study,'' *Personnel Journal* (January, 1984): 32–38.

RECRUITING AND HIRING ACTIVITIES

A solid plan identifying sources of capable employees and an active recruiting program can result in more qualified applicants from which to select employees. Such a plan is desirable even though some organizations are able to fill vacancies for administrative support employees without actively recruiting.

Recruiting involves someone's time to match prospective employees with job requirements. Experience helps this person to evaluate applicants. Someone involved in active supervision of administrative support employees should either direct the recruitment or closely advise the staff person who carries out this responsibility. Sources and methods that should be considered are current employee referrals, public and private employment agencies, school employment placement centers, advertisements, and unsolicited application files. For specialized staff positions, the services of a private recruitment firm or recruiting at colleges and universities may be helpful.

Screening. Once a pool of qualified applicants has been identified, screening begins. Managers or personnel staff members examine written applications and personal data sheets, interview promising applicants, administer tests, and check references. Some personnel groups now discount the value of general letters of reference, but telephone calls or evaluation instruments from identified references may be valuable. This is particularly true for office employees whose technical skills, communication skills, and human relations abilities are all critical elements in job performance.

Testing. For some office positions, employment tests may be valuable in selecting employees. Positions requiring extensive word processing work require skills and abilities involving the use of computer equipment for this specialized application. If complex software is involved, employers will increase their efforts to find employees who already have this skill. The Association of Information Systems Professionals (AISP) commissioned the development of a test for screening word processing operators. Called the Fogel Word Processing Operator Test, this test was designed to identify people who will be able to perform as word processing operators. It has been validated and meets equal employment opportunity guidelines.

If a test is to be an effective tool in employee selection, it must have several characteristics and must be used cautiously. **Standardized tests** are the best. These are tests that have been proven to have **reliability** and **validity.** A reliable test produces consistent results on multiple applications. Tests are written in multiple versions, but a job applicant who takes two versions of the same test should achieve similar scores; or a repeat of the same version after a reasonable lapse of time should produce similar results. Tests are valid if they measure what they are supposed to measure. For employment purposes, the test must measure the skill, knowledge, or ability necessary for adequate performance on the job. Tests are not likely to have these characteristics unless they are objective. The characteristic of **objectivity** means that different scorers (people who grade the test) will grade the test in essentially the same manner. Avoiding answers that require the scorer to exercise judgment accomplishes this goal.

Statistical processes measure test validity and reliability. Tests are revised and retested until their validity can be established. Organizations that do not want to validate their own tests may purchase them from firms that specialize in test preparation and validation.

Office employee tests may involve pencil-and-paper test items or performance tests. Many of them involve a combination of these. Depending upon the job, the test may involve keyboarding, transcription, editing, language, mathematics, proofreading, or programming skills. Questions about systems, procedures, hardware, and software applications may be desirable.

Legal Implications. Interviewers and recruitment planners must be aware of the legal implications of their activities. Personnel management groups usually are quite knowledgeable about such matters and can advise functional managers who participate in staffing activities. Anyone involved in recruiting should be thoroughly informed about anti-discrimination legislation and the factors that determine whether or not a particular employer is affected. Equal employment opportunity legislation affecting staffing includes the following:

1. The Civil Rights Act
2. Age Discrimination in Employment Act
3. Executive Orders 11246 and 11375
4. Veterans Readjustment Act
5. Equal Pay Act
6. State and local equal employment legislation

Recruiters and managers may be successful at selecting quality employees, but they may violate legislation in the process. Working closely with a personnel manager will enable unit managers who participate in hiring to avoid asking illegal questions inadvertently. Application forms, employment tests, and interviews are the three areas where unit managers are most likely to violate laws inadvertently. Employment tests may be very valuable tools for filling some positions, but they must measure job-related skills or knowledge. Because of the possibility that tests discriminate unfairly or illegally, employers should use them cautiously and evaluate the instruments carefully.

ALTERNATIVE EMPLOYMENT SOURCES

Temporary employment agencies and employee leasing firms are evidence that organizations are concentrating more on efficiency and productivity and less on the stability of a loyal work force. In the past, management has known very little about the volume of administrative work to accompany given levels of activity being supported. Staff size has been determined by the number of workers needed for peak times, and management has been unwilling to face the frustration and confusion caused by temporary employees at very busy times. These frustrations are lessening, however.

Temporary Employment. **Temporary employment** is very popular and probably will increase. Rather than recruit their own temporaries, organizations depend upon temporary service agencies. Employees work for the agencies, and the agency bills the organization that purchases the employee's time—at a rate greater than the wage-benefit package cost of the employee.

Many organizations now plan and budget for temporary labor for peak seasons and vacation periods.

Temporary employment firms now provide employees who have highly specialized skills and knowledge of work in a particular industry or office. Overall, they are more productive (spend more time actively working) than full-time employees. Scheduling continuous productive activity for full-time employees may be next to impossible; however, such productivity is possible from temporaries since they are only employed for the time during which work exists.

The word temporary in the phrase temporary employment refers to an organization's use of the employees and not necessarily to the employee's work pattern. Some workers called **career temps** work full time, moving from one organization to another. The flexibility of the working hours and the exposure to a variety of working assignments appeals to some employees.

Employee Leasing. Using agency employees on a leased basis or a "permanent temporary" basis is an alternative for some firms. A leasing arrangement involves a firm that provides workers who perform full-time duties under an arrangement similar to a temporary employment agency relationship. The worker is the employee of the leasing firm but is on permanent assignment at a client firm. The client firm pays the leasing firm instead of the worker. Managers of small organizations who wish to be free from recruiting, training, payroll accounting, and government employment reports may find this arrangement attractive. In large organizations, the leasing fees for this arrangement may cost no more than employing workers directly, especially if the firm or a particular department in the firm experiences high turnover rates.

Managing Temporaries. Managing temporary employees is different from managing full-time workers. Temporaries need immediate orientation and acclimation to the job. Procedures for introducing them to the work environment and supervising their initial work must be established. Placement counselors in service agencies can provide recommendations for orientation, supervision, and evaluation. Good communication between the employer and the agency improves the chances for an effective match between parties.

POSTEMPLOYMENT ACTIVITIES

Once employees have been selected and report for work, a series of postemployment activities becomes critical to their introduction to the organization and their eventual success as employees.

Orientation and training specifically prepare employees for working in a particular organization. **Orientation** is the introduction to the organization and the working environment; **training** is specific preparation to carry out the tasks and functions of a particular job. **Personal development** enables employees to maintain effective performance and productivity levels and should continue throughout each employee's career. (Training and development activities are the subject of Chapter 16.) Performance appraisal and compensation administration are continuing activities that involve managers and supervisors.

Orientation. Too many organizations skip or slight the orientation process. New employees are uncomfortable at best; depositing them in a working environment without orientation creates an even rougher beginning. New employees should be assigned to orientation, which should provide information about the physical workplace, policies, procedures, expected performance and routine information including payroll arrangements, breaks, benefits, and working hours. A review of manuals and written procedural descriptions, an introduction to fellow employees, and a preview of the training program are usually included.

Employee Performance Appraisal. Employee **performance appraisal** is a combination of formal evaluations, day-to-day informal evaluations, and planning for future performance. The routine evaluations are the day-to-day supervisor-employee interactions regarding the quality of the employee's work. This is probably the most important evaluation of a worker's performance.

Periodic formal reviews are desirable. Numerous formal systems and appraisal instruments are used for these reviews. They range from complex multiple-page checklists to simple essay descriptions of the supervisor's thoughts about the subordinate's progress.

If the organization does not provide an instrument (an evaluation form) and a system for performance reviews, the office-systems manager should develop an appraisal system for office employees, including an instrument for periodic formal reviews of performance. Although there is a tendency for performance appraisals to concentrate on history (the past), planning for the future should also be included. Sometimes called **performance planning**, this element should involve goals that the supervisor and the employee work out together and periodic evaluation of progress toward these goals. The formal system usually ends with a performance appraisal interview. This approach resembles the **management by objectives (MBO)** approach for appraisal of managerial performance.

Figure 15-5 Orientation familiarizes the new employee with the people, policies, and procedures of an organization.

MBO is a goal-oriented appraisal system that emphasizes written goals upon which superior and subordinate agree. The goals are job-related, quantifiable behavioral objectives (for example, to complete the installation of the electronic mail system by the end of the second quarter) that fit into organizational and unit goals. Both the goals and the employee's written plans for reaching the goals are emphasized. The process involves establishing routines for carrying out the responsibilities identified in the job description and the subordinate's developmental activities.

Most management authorities agree that the employee appraisal should be a separate activity from recommendations for pay increments, that future performance should be emphasized, and that criteria and evaluations should be behaviorally oriented. This means that an office worker's productivity (specific behaviors, accomplishments, or measurable productivity) would be emphasized rather than his or her attitude or overall performance. They also agree that the system should avoid second and third review processes that encourage supervisors to attempt to impress their own superiors as they evaluate subordinates. Some review processes involve several levels of approval. For example, the supervisor may evaluate the worker, and the department head approves or disapproves the supervisor's evaluation and passes it to the vice president who has the final approval. If the supervisor and the department head know that their superiors will be impressed with a particular stance, this expectation may destroy their objectivity.

Compensation Administration.   Organizations that can separate the processes of employee appraisal and **compensation administration** have accomplished a major step forward in the creation of a positive working environment. Because salary or wage reviews are part of the comprehensive program, the two activities are related; but they should be handled separately. In the mind of the employee, the appraisal should involve the quality of performance and plans for development of that quality. Compensation administration is the program that administers employee pay and benefits. In large organizations, the program is coordinated by a formal unit of the organization, usually a part of the personnel staff. However, every manager is involved.

Guided by the organization's job evaluations, the compensation administration program generates a framework of wages, salaries, monetary and nonmonetary incentives, and other fringe benefits. The program includes definite policy regarding each of these ingredients and a system for informing employees about them. Pay structures are developed for each job. These include pay ranges that allow for the variety of qualifications that employees will have and for merit increments within each range. Pay structures are coordinated with career ladders so that promotions take into consideration both the previous salary and the level of experience. Administrators of compensation select plans (straight salary, hourly wages, incentive plans), provide indirect compensation through fringe-benefit programs, and assist with wage negotiations with organized labor.

Those who administer compensation programs must coordinate the organization's policies, government regulations, employee market conditions, the cost of living, and union contract negotiations. Individual managers must provide compensation administrators with information regarding pay structures in their particular disciplines. The Administrative Management Society, Association of Information Systems Professionals, and Data Processing Management Association salary surveys are excellent sources of competitive pay practices for administrative support and information processing employees.

Compensation patterns have changed in recent years. New influences (employee preferences) are entering the picture and old ones (government regulations) are showing less influence. Global competition and intensified productivity improvement efforts have affected pay scales as organizations attempt to develop long-term programs. Employees have become more willing to accept pay increments that are equated with performance, they welcome flexible benefit packages, and they accept pay differentiation among job types, industries, and geographical areas. For example, in 1985 General Motors announced that it was abandoning cost-of-living increments for all salaried employees in favor of a compensation program based on merit and job content.

The pressures to equate pay rates for men and women will continue. The focus will be on differences in female-dominated jobs (such as secretarial, administrative support, and word processing positions) compared to those of male-dominated positions with similar education and skill requirements.

MANAGING ADMINISTRATIVE SUPPORT EMPLOYEES

The general role of managers and the nature of supervision are fairly consistent from one organization to another. All managers search for a leadership style that will be effective and strive to understand their subordinates and to develop their supervisory skills. This section reviews some of those common factors that affect the management of administrative support employees. Some of them, such as leadership style, can be controlled by individual managers; others, such as employee personality and work style require adaptation. Appropriate attention to these factors can enable managers to create an emotional climate in which systems can function properly and employees can work with a minimum of stress and strain.

THE MANAGER'S LEADERSHIP STYLE

Management theorists, in attempts to explain the successes and failures of managers, have ferreted out common characteristics of management style that reflect basic reactions to and beliefs about people. These theories have been used to describe organizations as well as their managers. In addition to Douglas McGregor's classic **Theory X** and **Theory Y** of organizations and managers, recent years have seen a style that has been labeled **Theory Z.**[3]

---

3. Douglas McGregor, *The Human Side of Enterprise* (New York: McGraw-Hill Book Company, 1960).

Theory X is a style that reflects the manager's assumption that workers need to be controlled and directed because they do not want to work and do so only out of necessity. This style is rigid, authoritarian, and distrusting. Theory Y reflects a style of a manager who assumes that the worker wants to work, will accept responsibility, strives to produce good things, and can be trusted to participate in the job effort.

Theory Z is a combination of Japanese and American management styles recommended by William G. Ouchi.[4] His approach to management combines portions of the Japanese style that appear feasible in U.S. culture with the participative elements of McGregor's Theory Y. Ingredients of the Japanese system that may have merit for application in this country, according to Ouchi, are long-term employment, decision making by group consensus instead of by individuals, carefully considered and infrequent employee promotions, less specialized career paths, and holistic (complete) concern for people. Employee productivity improvement groups called **quality circles (QCs)** or productivity groups have grown out of this combination style. Japanese automobile manufacturers operating in the United States have developed styles similar to Theory Z as they have adapted their styles to the American culture.

EMPLOYEE PERSONALITIES AND WORK STYLES

Administrative support workers cannot be stereotyped. Their personalities, job expectations, and life-styles vary. Some office workers are comfortable with definite work routines and close supervision; others prefer jobs that offer freedom and challenge. Employees are willing to invest in the organization through their time and talents, but they expect to be rewarded for these efforts. These rewards are not necessarily money rewards; they may include nonmonetary rewards such as flexibility in assignments and working hours. Flexible schedules, shared jobs, and the opportunity for leave without pay have increased during recent years.

Contemporary office employees are willing to accept pay increments and other incentives that are based on their performance, and they may prefer a choice of incentives. For example, they may prefer a profit-sharing plan over life insurance as a benefit. These attitudes differ from the attitudes of workers in past decades when basic salary was the major criterion. Today, office employees are willing to participate in decision making

4.   William G. Ouchi, *Theory Z: How American Business Can Meet the Japanese Challenge* (Reading, Mass.: Addison-Wesley Publishing Company, 1981).

Figure 15-6 Human relations skills
are important to today's office
worker who must interact with a
variety of people.

and to cooperate in group projects for special assignments that
deviate from the traditional work groups. For example, they may
be dispatched to cities where new facilities are being opened to
assist with support and training in a new office.

SUPERVISORY SKILLS

The word *supervisor* has different meanings and different applications. Any manager in a working environment may be considered a supervisor to his or her subordinates. The most popular
application of the term is to the first level of supervision—the
person to whom workers report. The term **first-line supervisor**
describes this group. The role of the first-line supervisor is to
coordinate the work of a group of **operatives** (workers), the **nonexempt employees** in wage-and-hour legislation terminology. If
employees are not managerial, professional staff, or supervisors,
they are operatives. Nonexempt status for this group means that

they are protected by minimum-wage laws, overtime pay provisions, and other legal restrictions.

Some supervisors are working supervisors, carrying out basic routines as well as coordinating the work of a group of workers. The need for first-line supervision has grown as organizations have grown in size and complexity. Automation may reverse that trend because fewer workers will be engaged in the very routine jobs involving mostly manual tasks. These jobs require more supervision.

The first skill that supervisors must develop is the ability to juggle themselves between their superiors and their subordinates. Supervisors are managers, but they are sometimes caught in the middle between upper management and the workers they supervise. They may find difficulty with situations that seem to demand loyalty to both groups. However, their job is to represent the employee to higher management and to represent the organization to the employee. As suggested earlier, supervisors are becoming less like taskmasters and more team oriented. However, they still must assign and prioritize work to be done, control the quality of work, and assume responsibility for productivity. Much of their time is spent in activities not involved with direct worker supervision—for example, in planning, preparing reports, attending meetings, and conferring with their own superiors.

Through education and experience managers develop numerous supervisory skills. The level of management determines the need to apply these skills. First-line supervisors are in more direct and constant contact with their subordinates than with middle managers. Although the skills required of a first-line supervisor are similar to those of any other manager, communication and conflict resolution skills are especially important for supervisors. Supervisors must expect communication problems and conflict. In the office, managers must cope with new and different problems with employees who experience difficulty adjusting to technology.

Communication Skills. Supervisors and managers are largely responsible for the quality of communication within the units they supervise. Communication flow (which occurs horizontally among the unit's employees and vertically between the supervisor and subordinates and between the supervisor and his or her superior) is a major responsibility. The organization is responsible for the overall communication climate, but the individual manager sets the tone within the unit and in communication with other units. Office systems serve the entire organization, so this opens multiple communication channels. The quality of communication will affect the quality of the service that can be offered to other units. Oral and written communication skills and knowledge of nonverbal communication are essential.

Conflict Resolution.   Supervisors and managers must deal with conflict between themselves and their subordinates and among the subordinates. Conflict is a barrier to communication, whether it is caused by basic differences in opinion or by personality conflicts that prevent communication on any subject. **Conflict resolution** is the process of seeking solutions to conflict. Managers must be able to institute resolution attempts when interpersonal conflict causes problems between themselves and other professionals or subordinates. They must coordinate resolution of conflict among subordinates. In either case, identifying real causes for conflict, looking for information and possible solutions, and attempting to maintain objectivity is the general approach to resolution.

THE MANAGEMENT ENVIRONMENT

Three conditions affecting the office systems management environment affect the lives of those who are preparing for careers that will involve working in this environment. The first condition involves a new awareness and understanding of employee motivation. The second involves the increased presence of women in managerial roles and a steadily changing attitude about the roles of women and men as they manage. Employee unions, the third condition, represents a condition that was predicted to change but has not. Understanding the status of these factors is desirable for those who anticipate supervisory or managerial positions in an office systems environment.

EMPLOYEE MOTIVATION

Employee motivation is not a supervisory skill (although many popular speakers today would have us believe that it is), but supervisors and managers at any level can improve their effectiveness if they understand motivation. Brief definitions of such a complex concept are dangerous, but the following will serve our purposes: **motivation** is an internal force within individuals — those conditions or aspirations that influence human behavior. If we accept this definition, the things that managers can do to motivate employees is to provide a climate that will get favorable reaction and, at the same time, contribute to the organization's objectives.

Assuming that office workers are able to satisfy their basic physical needs with the monetary rewards of their jobs, basic needs will have been met if the organization provides some feeling of job security, a reasonable salary for the type of work being performed, and a comfortable and safe working environment. If these needs are basic, and if the assumption that most office jobs meet these needs is correct, further motivation must deal with higher level motives such as the needs for belonging, self-esteem, and self-actualization.[5]

People are neither standard nor robotic; they do not react identically to the same conditions. The assumption that all office employees are challenged by the same type of work is incorrect. Several categories of office workers perform tasks that are either very routine or very tedious or both (word processing operators, data-entry employees, and programmers). These jobs are the subject of extreme criticism by those who refer to the automated office as the automated sweatshop. In the nonautomated office, the same characteristics are found in routine clerical positions such as those of the accounting clerk and file clerk. Yet many employees enjoy this work and gain satisfaction from the fact that they perform the work well and accurately. Other employees prefer jobs that involve more people interaction, problem solving, and decision making. They want to coordinate people, processes, and communication to accomplish the goals of their jobs.

Both of these groups are motivated (moved from within) by conditions that represent higher level needs: pride in accomplishment, progress toward a goal, and self-esteem. These conditions can be enhanced by recognition, praise, opportunity for advancement, and open communication. Few employees in either group are motivated by fear, admonishment, or money.

There is much disagreement over the motivational powers of pay. Some organizations, such as L'eggs, the hosiery manufacturer, operate elaborate incentive wage systems for office employees. The systems appear to work effectively. Others consider incentive wages for office workers to be degrading and dehumanizing. Employee reaction to incentive pay systems and other systems which affect the working environment determines the motivational power of these systems. Many factors affect this employee reaction: the jobs, the nature of the employees, employees' understanding of the system, employee perceptions of reasons for the system, and employees' trust in the organization and in their superiors.

---

5.   For further discussion of this concept of need hierarchy, see Abraham H. Maslow, *Motivation and Personality,* 2nd Edition (New York: Harper & Row Publishers, Inc. 1970).

Climate for Motivation in the Office.   Any system that creates an environment that gives employees feedback that they are effective in their jobs creates a climate favorable for motivation. If employees believe that they are contributing to a successful organization and that opportunity for advancement exists at whatever level they deem desirable, this climate is enhanced. If the opposite conditions prevail (no feedback or only negative feedback about job performance, lack of respect for the effectiveness of the organization, and little perceived opportunity for advancement), motivation is nil.

The important thing for managers of administrative support employees˙(and probably any other group) is the knowledge that employee expectations vary. Some like routine; they get satisfaction from participating in smoothly operating systems; others take pride in taming tumult. Everyone needs feedback, but some need it more frequently than others. Everyone aspires to some sort of advancement, but some employees have more aggressive plans than others. Recognizing these factors is important: A horizontal job change might satisfy career plans for one employee, while others would accept that only if they perceive it as necessary to prepare for a vertical promotion later.

Many conditions already described in this chapter and elsewhere in this text are among those necessary for a positive climate: systems implementation, recruiting, hiring, communication systems, compensation plans, interpersonal relationships. In the office, such simple matters as clearly communicated job tasks, properly maintained equipment, adequate supplies, and an opportunity to participate in anticipated changes improve the climate and, subsequently, job satisfaction and morale. These are things that most people would consider standard procedure, but they are neglected in many organizations.

A final element in the motivational climate is a reinforcement system. Rewards reinforce behavior, but people react differently and in varying degrees to individual rewards. Although pay is assumed to be a factor in motivation, pay increments have very little effect on employee behavior. For most employees, a far greater impact is realized from rewards such as special recognition, compliments for special achievement, opportunities to demonstrate abilities in more complex assignments, and opportunities for advancement. Rewards may be nothing more than a compliment for a well-executed project or for continued extraordinary effort. Undeserved rewards, administered as carrots to move lackadaisical employees, have no motivational effect.

Technostress.   Technology has brought new respect for the office environment and for the value of office systems to organizations. Unfortunately, these advances have also created new pressures for office employees and those who manage them — pressures that can have a negative effect upon employee motivation.

Conversion to office automation systems from traditional office systems or major conversions from one automated system to another may create a condition called *technostress*. (See Chapter 10 for additional discussion of this phenomenon.) Although the term is applied to various employee situations, it involves "a condition resulting from the inability of an individual or organization to adapt to the introduction and operation of new technology."[6] Added to the cost of new systems, the effect of technostress creates significant declines in efficiency. Craig Brod's three year research project analyzing technostress in the office environment revealed several variables that affect the probability that this condition will appear. These include the user's age, prior experience with technology, job security, and perceptions of his or her control over new tasks. Management attitude toward implementation of technology is also a factor. The combined effect of these changes can have a ripple effect. For example, employees object to the new equipment, managers become frustrated with low productivity, employees make more errors, and management becomes more frustrated.

WOMEN IN MANAGEMENT

Women have made great strides in their efforts to move into management positions. Although no statistics exist for the office systems area, women in the executive, administrative, and managerial category in 1989 comprised 40 percent of the total.[7] Of the total work force, 45 percent are women. Women overcame many challenges to reach this status.

In addition to low pay, women have encountered numerous other challenges in their attempts to move into managerial positions. For each challenge, there are dozens of explanations about why the challenge exists. Most explanations conclude with the fact that many organizations have been managed by males for most of their existence. In the past, both males and females accepted the stereotyped interpretations of women's roles in the business working environment. Women were perceived as secretaries, clerical workers, receptionists, and perhaps as supervisors of these groups or as supervisors of technical specialists such as

---

6. Craig Brod, "How to Deal With Technostress," *Office Administration and Automation* (September, 1984): 30.

7. *Employment and Earnings,* April, 1989 (U.S. Department of Labor, Bureau of Labor Statistics): 29.

programmers, computer operators, or micrographics technicians.

Many women who did not accept these roles made attempts to change the situation. Some men have difficulty working with women as team members, and many women experience difficulty with being assertive in a mostly male team environment. These conditions are changing; but, unfortunately, they still exist. Research among 30,000 men and women in 1988 revealed that large numbers of men and women agree with discriminating stereotype statements about women in the workplace. (See Figure 15-7.)

Figure 15-7 Reactions to Sex Stereotype Statements

Sex Stereotype Statement	Respondents in Agreement Women	Men
Many women obtained their positions only because they are women.	31%	58%
The increasing employment of women has led to the breakdown of the American family.	29%	49%
Pluralism will force us to lower our hiring and promotion standards.	25%	46%
Many women use their gender as an alibi for difficulties they have on the job.	21%	39%
Many women are not really serious about professional careers.	19%	24%
Many women are too emotional to be competent employees in the company.	7%	15%

Source: John P. Fernandex, ''New Life for Old Stereotypes,'' *Across the Board* (July/August, 1988): 24.

Only 9 percent of the men and 27 percent of the women disagreed with all of the statements reviewed in Figure 15-7. Women who have achieved high level positions have met this challenge.

Women's records for promotion have been significantly better in the emerging high-tech firms and in government; they have achieved far less in the older, established firms. Women are expected to move into management positions at a faster pace in the future as the male bias diminishes and female self-confidence increases.

Male and Female Traits. Issues abound regarding managerial traits of men and women. At the basic level, there is no difference between the analytical skills, leadership skills, or tolerance to boredom or detail of men and women. These are learned behaviors. Reality does not match perception, however. Women in management positions are perceived to be more supportive of subordinates in difficult situations and more people-oriented in their approach to management. Men are perceived to be more able to solve problems, to draw solutions from past experiences, and to work as team members. Men are perceived to be unaware of people's feelings and to internalize frustrations instead of talking about them. If these traits exist, it is because the two groups have had more experience with the situations described.

The Androgynous Solution.   The field of **androgyny** involves the study of male and female characteristics in the behavior of people —men and women—and suggests that all people have representative characteristics of both sexes. Two popular writers, Kenneth H. Blanchard and Alice G. Sargent, presented the theory that the best managers in the future will be androgynous managers— those who possess the best of both sets of behaviors:

> The "whole" manager will need to be able to express and accept emotions, nurture and support colleagues and subordinates, and promote interaction between bosses and subordinates and between leaders and members of work teams. . . . Since many of these behaviors traditionally have been regarded as feminine and therefore not rewarded in the marketplace, both male and female managers have avoided them.[8]

This same theme is reflected in the work of Felice N. Schwartz:

> Today, in the developed world, the only role still uniquely gender related is childbearing. Yet men and women are still socialized to perform their traditional roles. . . . Indeed, the male and female roles have already begun to expand and merge. In the decades ahead, as the socialization of boys and girls and the experience and expectations of young men and women grow steadily androgynous, the differences in the workplace behavior will continue to fade. At the moment, however, we are still plagued by disparities in perception and behavior that make integration of men and women in the workplace unnecessarily difficult and expensive.[9]

EMPLOYEE UNIONS

Managers of office employees must be prepared for the possibility that employees will be attracted to unions. In spite of the fact that traditionally unions have not made significant gains in membership among office employees, their membership has risen in some geographical areas in recent years. Several factors about

8.   Kenneth H. Blanchard and Alice G. Sargent, "The One-Minute Manager is an Androgynous Manager," *Training and Development Journal* (May, 1984): 84.

9.   Felice N. Schwartz. "Management Women and the Facts of Life," *Harvard Business Review* (January-February, 1989): 65.

Figure 15-8 In the future, the most effective managers will combine the best of both male and female sets of behavior.

the current office environment could encourage renewed interest in union representation.

The Administrative Management Society gathers data about union activity in its annual surveys of general office and data-processing salaries, employee turnover, and employee benefits. For the past 15 years, this survey has shown that about 2 percent of the reporting firms have active unions. Another 3 to 4 percent have some employees who belong to a union, but 93 percent deal with no union members at all among office employees. The unions themselves report modest gains in office employee membership, but even their data show total membership at fewer than 10 percent of office employees. Because of declining membership in the heavy industry segment, unions have worked hard to attract office employees and other white-collar groups.

Office workers may be attracted to unions in organizations where conditions cause them to be unhappy. If employees perceive their wage levels, benefits, promotional opportunities, job security, or overall work climate to be inferior to those for other employees or for office employees in other organizations, they may seriously consider unions. If morale and job satisfaction are low, the promises of organizers may become attractive.

Office automation factors that worry office employees and provide fuel for union organization are numerous. The number of purely clerical positions may be reduced in automated environments, and some former secretaries may view their new jobs as mere data-entry positions. Reorganization, centralization of information systems in very large organizations, and telecommunication improvements may have a significant impact upon job structures. Employees who are unable or unwilling to relocate or retrain may be affected. On the other hand, the infusion of technology has opened up new and challenging positions for many employees.

WOHL'S BUSINESS PERSPECTIVE

It is difficult to imagine an office without word processors and computers. Yet it has been only a few years (at most 25) since modern office technology first placed a timid and tentative foot in the door.

Before offices were automated, office work was rigidly divided. Principals created ideas and wrote the documents which contained those ideas. Secretaries typed (and retyped) someone else's thoughts. Some senior secretaries might be asked to compose an unimportant letter—or to proofread for grammar and spelling as well as typos—but were only rarely permitted to compose final documents without supervision. Office administrative staff was hired and promoted for its typing and basic language skills. (And new employees were measured by dictation and typing tests.)

Originally, word processing introduced further inflexibility. Only specially trained secretaries—word processing operators—could handle routine office documents. Ordinary mortals—professionals or secretaries—required special intermediaries to get their own jobs done. Originally, all word processing operators were trained from within existing secretarial employees. Later, as a pool of trained word processors became available in the marketplace, it was often easier and cheaper to pirate (recruit) an already-trained employee by offering a higher salary, better benefits or working conditions, or better chances for advancement.

In the heyday of dedicated word processing systems (c. 1975–1984), word processing operators were hired for their ability to produce large volumes of text with few errors, and to make complex revisions. This skill was always tied to a particular word processing system and only rarely would employers consider giving top salaries to a perspective employee trained on a different system. The idea of *how* word processing worked was transferable, but the *knowledge* of how to use a particular system productively was much less leveragable.

Enter the personal computer. Word processing became a skill that secretaries (who typed only a few hours each day) and professionals (who might type occasionally, often, or not at all), could more easily learn and use.

Today, we prefer office employees to come with some initial degree of computer literacy. But the skill we are looking for has changed substantially over the past 25 years. We want employees who are experienced in using computers, particularly personal computers. We're happy if they have specific experience in the same personal productivity tools (especially word processors, spreadsheets, and databases) that we use right now. But it is far more important that a new employee has the ability to leverage his current computer skills into learning new applications.

We have learned our lesson. Knowing how to use a specific application or a specific system is useful only so long as we keep that system in use. Technology opportunities move fast and successful companies need to move with them, changing applications and platforms as better, more suitable products offer competitive advantages.

We need employees who are as flexible as our use of technology demands. We especially need employees who have learned how to learn new applications, employees who look on this continued new learning as a challenge rather than a trial. In the future, we will pick new employees and promote old ones based at least in part on their computer skills, but smart firms will increasingly look at the ability to learn as being far more important than what you already know.

SUMMARY

Managing administrative support employees involves understanding their characteristics, staffing offices with well-qualified employees, orienting and training employees, and helping them to develop professionally throughout their careers.

Even though offices are now filled with computer-based hardware and technology-based systems, they still require people in order to function effectively. Because of changing job structures and employee qualifications, staffing organizations is a critical management function. In most organizations the staffing function is carried out by a combined effort of personnel groups and the managers of office workers. Both the technical and the human relations skills of office workers are important in their selection.

Important prestaffing activities include analyzing jobs, determining job content, evaluating jobs, and preparing job descriptions and job specifications. The managers responsible for the staffing function must develop plans for recruiting capable and qualified employees. This plan will provide for documentation of job structure and employee qualifications; a monetary worth for each position; routines for identifying, screening, and interviewing applicants; and procedures for postemployment activities such as orientation, training, and administering an effective pay system. These conditions should enhance low employee turnover rates, the goal of the staffing function.

Managers of office employees are responsible for creating an environment that is conducive to satisfied and productive employees. This is influenced by the manager's leadership style and managers' understanding of employee personalities and work style preferences. Open communication and skill at resolving conflict are conducive to an effective work environment. The conditions of this environment influence employee motivation. Although compensation is a factor in motivation, it influences most employees less than general working conditions and their perception of the quality of their contributions and their personal progress.

Managers of office personnel face many conditions that are somewhat different from other managers. A special problem for managers of office automation environments is technostress. Constantly changing technologies can be frustrating for employees unless implementation is combined with proper preparation. Many managers in the office environment are women. Even though women in management positions have increased their numbers and their acceptance, stereotype ideas still persist. Managers of office employees are less likely to work with unionized workers than managers in an industrial environment. Relatively few organizations in the United States have unionized office workers. However, they are quite prevalent in some portions of the country. Managers of employees who belong to unions must deal with circumstances that are different from nonunionized employees. Contracted conditions, benefits, and job structures involve different procedures.

KEY TERMS

personnel management
human resources
  development (HRD)
employee turnover ratio
job analysis
job description
job specification
job evaluation
comparable worth
wage gap
standardized test
test reliability
test validity
test objectivity
temporary employment
career temp
orientation
training

personal development
performance appraisal
performance planning
management by
  objectives (MBO)
compensation
  administration
Theory X
Theory Y
Theory Z
quality circle (QC)
first-line supervisor
operative
nonexempt employee
conflict resolution
motivation
androgyny

REVIEW QUESTIONS

1. Even though office automation is the popular term used to identify the application of technology to office systems, there is a connotative (suggested) meaning for this term. Discuss the following statement: The term office automation suggests that office work is carried out automatically by machines.

2. Describe the concept of knowledge worker.

3. Describe the concept of administrative support worker.

4. What activities are associated with "prestaffing" and what is the contribution of these activities to the staffing process?

5. Contrast the following terms:
   a. job analysis and job description
   b. job specification and job evaluation

6. Which staffing activities would you expect to be performed by (1) a personnel management or HRD department and (2) the manager of administrative support employees?

7. Contrast the terms temporary employment and leased employment. What is the impact of these practices for managers of office systems employees?

8. What is the difference between training and orientation?

9. Identify the problems associated with compensation and job assignments for women in the office environment.

10. Contrast the three popular descriptions of leadership style presented in this chapter.

11. What is the basis for the statement "Motivation is not a supervisory skill."

12. What is technostress? How can managers of office employees recognize this condition? What steps can prevent or minimize technostress among office employees?

13. Describe the status of union membership among office employees. Compile a list of conditions that might lead to increased interest in organizing a union among office employees.

CASE STUDY: OAHU INSURANCE

Oahu Insurance is a life insurance company with home offices in Hawaii. Takeshi Moriwaki is director of office systems in charge of five groups within the Division of Administrative Systems. He reports to the vice president—

administration and works closely with the director of MIS who reports to the same superior. The units for which Mr. Moriwaki is responsible are administrative support (23 employees); word processing (31 employees); office systems (5 employees); telecommunication and reprographics (5 employees, including responsibility for two LANs within the home office building); and corporate records (7 employees in a center for housing tangible records and managing several electronic and micrographic files systems). Three full-time clerical positions are filled by six students from the local high school and vocational school cooperative education programs. Each student works a half day.

Mr. Moriwaki is concerned about the practices currently being used to select employees for the administrative systems, word-processing, and clerical groups. The Personnel Department posts vacancies on office bulletin boards and advertises them in the local newspaper. Unsolicited and walk-in applications are kept on file for six months. When a vacancy occurs, Moriwaki sends a memo to the Personnel Department identifying the job and the requirements for the position and encloses a copy of the job description. Personnel screens applications, interviews top candidates, and selects two or three for a second interview. Moriwaki and the unit supervisor interview these candidates and rank them. Personnel makes an offer to the highest ranked candidate.

Several times during the past two years all of the candidates for the second interview have declined offers, requiring Personnel to go back to some of the previous rejects.

Because of the nature of the work involved, individual supervisors conduct orientation and training for new employees. When multiple trainees are hired at the same time, a combination of group training and on-the-job training is used. When a single trainee is involved, the supervisor moves to on-the-job training after any necessary preliminary presentations.

Moriwaki is proud of the general office environment. The ergonomic factors are sound, the hardware is state of the art, and the various units use carefully written training and reference materials. However, he believes that turnover is too high in the three areas where employees with the lowest educational levels are employed—word processing, administrative support, and corporate records. Most of the employees in these areas are associate degree graduates of community colleges. A few have bachelor's degrees, and a few are high school or vocational school graduates who worked for the firm through cooperative education programs. Although the three units each have a solid core of long-time, dedicated employees, turnover has averaged fifteen vacancies a year over the past three calendar years. Some positions have been vacated more than once (these are included in the count) in a single year. During this time, three vacancies were created by employees who were fired.

QUESTIONS/ACTIVITIES

1. What is the turnover ratio among the three identified groups? Is this too high, as the director suggests? Discuss your reasons for your conclusion.

What additional information would be necessary to make a complete evaluation of the staffing needs for office employees in this firm?

2. Assuming that the vice president—administration and the vice president—HRD agree to attempt to reduce turnover among office employees under Moriwaki, recommend a staffing plan for Oahu's office employees. Make any additional assumptions that you consider necessary (and reasonable) and explain your assumptions.

SUGGESTED READINGS

Brod, Craig. *Technostress: The Human Cost of the Computer Revolution.* Reading, Mass.: Addison-Wesley Publishing Company, 1984.

Danziger, James N. and Kenneth L. Kraemer. "Clerks and Computers: The Problem/Benefit Mix." Chapter 8 of *People and Computers.* New York: Columbia University Press, 1986.

Long, Richard J. "Effects on Clerical and Secretarial Employees." Chapter 6 of *New Office Information Technology.* London: Croom Helm, 1987.

Ouchi, William G. *Theory Z: How American Business Can Meet the Japanese Challenge.* Reading, Mass.: Addison-Wesley Publishing Company, 1981.

Ray, Charles M., and Charles L. Eison. "Appraising Employee Performance." Chapter 13 of *Supervision.* Chicago: The Dryden Press, 1983.

Sargent, Alice G. *The Androgynous Manager.* New York: AMACOM, 1981.

Wolman, Rebekah. "How To Deal With The Problem Employee," *Information Center* (September, 1988): 32.

CHAPTER 16

Personnel Training

OBJECTIVES

After studying this chapter, you should understand the following:

1. The effect of office automation on the training function
2. The steps to follow for design of a training program
3. How to incorporate motivational strategies into training programs
4. How the organization, its personnel, and choice of delivery systems affect training programs
5. The chief sources of office automation training
6. The skills and knowledge desirable for trainers of office automation
7. Methods of needs assessment for office automation training
8. The training needs of personnel in the automated office
9. The variety of training strategies and media available for office automation training
10. Guidelines for the preparation of procedures manuals
11. Guidelines for the selection of training strategies and media

12. Methods of evaluation and cost justification for office automation training

13. The benefits of office automation training for office personnel and organizations

The driving forces for training and development are the present and future business needs of organizations. According to the World Future Society, by 1990 an estimated 67 percent of the work force in the United States will be engaged in information processing work. Consequently, employees increasingly will need sophisticated skills and knowledge to maintain productivity in our information-oriented society. Business spending for the training of employees is difficult to estimate because of so much informal training. ASTD (American Society for Training and Development), however, estimates total annual business training cost at $210 billion, not far below the $238 billion the U.S. spends annually on formal elementary, secondary, and collegiate education.[1] How much of this amount is spent on training for office personnel? The answer to that question varies, depending upon the level of office employee. Organizations traditionally have directed training toward management, not management support staff. With the introduction of office automation, however, organizations with increasing frequency are extending such training to all levels of office personnel.

OFFICE AUTOMATION TRAINING

Just why did office automation start a new trend in training office personnel? Such training began in the mid-1960s with the advent of word processing. Vendors routinely provided operator training free of charge to organizations purchasing automated equipment. This training was necessary because the typical office employee lacked knowledge and experience with computerized office equipment. Early vendor training was merely functional; today office training must go beyond that level.

The need for more expansive training in office systems became evident as the use of computerized equipment spread within organizations. Organizations generally found themselves unprepared to cope with the growing demand for training prompted by new end users. Failure of organizations to meet end-user training needs can present a serious threat to the successful implementa-

---

1. "Public Education's Failures Plague Employers," *The Wall Street Journal* (June 21, 1988): 31.

Figure 16-1 Teaching employees
how to use the prototype word
processor in the 1960s wasn't as
complex as training is today.
International Business Machines

tion of office automation. To avoid such a problem, training
needs to be an integral part of an organization's strategic plan
for office automation.

THE TRAINING FUNCTION

How does training fit into organizational plans? **Training** is
viewed as a function providing adults with opportunities for
learning concepts, skills, or attitudes. Generally, when organizations offer training, it is expected to contribute to an improvement in employee job performance. However, a recent trend in
training has been the development of **holistic training.** Such
training is wide in scope and affects the individual not only as an
employee but also as a whole person. For example, office employee

training might include computer skills as well as career planning and wellness (health and physical fitness). With holistic training, organizations expect that improvements in employees' personal lives also influence their working lives. Regardless of the type of training, however, all training programs need to be well designed.

A TRAINING MODEL

A **training model** is useful as a guide in the design of training programs. Figure 16-2 illustrates a training model.

Figure 16-2 A Training Model

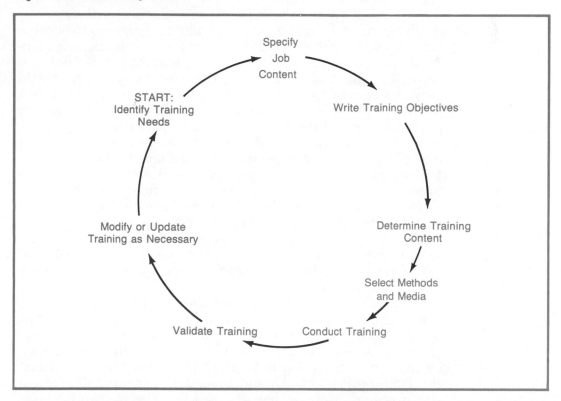

Source: ''A Systems Approach to Training'' from *Synergogy: A New Strategy for Education, Training, and Development,* by Jane Srygley Mouton and Robert R. Blake. San Francisco: Jossey-Bass, Inc., Publishers, Copyright © 1984, page 40. Reproduced by permission.

The training model illustrated in Figure 16-2 is cyclical and dynamic. Such characteristics are especially appropriate for office automation training where change is fast and frequent. The following steps of the model can be applied to the design of a training program for office automation: (1) identify training needs; (2) specify job content; (3) write training objectives; (4) determine training content; (5) select methods and media; (6) conduct training; (7) validate training; and (8) modify or update training. A brief explanation of each of these steps follows:

1. *Identify training needs.* An investigation should be made of the office automation training needs of all office personnel. Without identification of the areas where training is needed, the training offered could be irrelevant, unnecessary, and wasteful of resources. Further discussion of how an analysis of an organization's office automation training needs can be conducted will be presented in detail later in the chapter.

2. *Specify job content.* Job descriptions and job specifications, if available, are excellent means for training designers to become familiar with the required duties, responsibilities, and standards of job performance for office employees. If such job content is not readily available, the training designer should seek this information. Training programs can be designed then to fill the gaps between the desired levels of employees' job performance and their actual levels of performance.

3. *Write training objectives.* A **training objective** is a statement describing what task the employee must learn, what resources will be provided, what constraints will affect the learning process, and what standards of performance are expected. An example of a training objective is as follows: Given instructional materials and a practice exercise for use of a function key in a word processing software package, the employee will be able to associate the correct function key with a particular function and use it with 100 percent accuracy in the preparation of documents.

4. *Determine training content.* The content for an office automation training program should result from the identified training needs. Such needs, however, will not represent the actual training content. For example, if an organization's word processing center is having difficulty meeting turnaround times, the training designer should investigate specific causes for this problem. After the causes are identified, a training solution may or may not be appropriate. If training is needed, then specific programs can be designed to remedy the problem.

5. *Select methods and media.* The training designer must make decisions regarding the use of the most appropriate sources, methods, materials, and technology for a particular training program. For example, an in-house classroom training program could combine lecture, role playing, and a film for a managerial seminar on conflict resolution.

6. *Conduct training.* How, where, when, and by whom training programs are conducted will depend upon the sources, methods, and media selected by the training designer. For example, an office automation topic could be presented "live" or could be available on videotape.

7. *Validate training.* Validation involves evaluation of training programs. The evaluation process can yield useful information to management and training designers regarding the strengths and weaknesses of training programs. A variety of methods (discussed later in the chapter) can be used to justify to management the existence of training programs for office automation.

8. *Modify or update training.* If weaknesses in the office automation training program are revealed from the evaluation process, steps should be taken to correct the deficiencies. Existing training programs might need to be revised or terminated or redeveloped. For example, if the evaluation indicates that the directions in the training materials are confusing, such directions need to be clarified. In another instance, training manuals might need updating because of newly implemented procedures. Training programs need to be kept responsive to employee needs and organizational change.

MOTIVATIONAL STRATEGIES

Training designers need to prepare training programs that will advance organizational goals, yet human behavior is such that individuals work to achieve personal goals. These personal goals vary depending upon the individual. For example, goals can involve monetary reward, achievement, challenge, and the satisfaction of social needs. Thus, the key to successful training design is to incorporate motivational strategies that meet organizational goals and yet complement the personal goals of employees.

Motivation, a driving force that moves individuals to action, can be explained by many different theories of motivation. One such approach useful for applying to the training process was introduced in 1983 by J. M. Keller. This **ARCS (attention, relevance, confidence, and satisfaction) Model** allows training designers to infuse motivational strategies throughout the training process.[2] Each element of the model can be applied to training in the following ways:

2. Thomas W. Kopp, ''Making Trainees Want to Learn,'' *Training & Development Journal* (June, 1988): 43.

1. *Attention.* Training programs need to capture and hold the attention of their audience with a variety of instructional strategies. The training environment needs to be quiet, comfortable, pleasant, and stimulating. The person doing the training needs to demonstrate sensitivity in manner and voice to the needs of the individuals being trained. A wide range of methods and materials such as case studies and videos can enhance the attention-getting process.

2. *Relevance.* Training programs need to be based on the needs of the individuals experiencing the training. Also, understanding the why of the training and how its benefits apply to them as individuals will help maintain interest in the training. For example, in a training session involving the automating of a manual procedure, the tedious, time-consuming steps performed in the past could be mentioned and then followed with a focus on how much easier the task will be in the future when automated. Pointing out how the training will improve the quality of the individual's work life will encourage greater acceptance of the change.

3. *Confidence.* Training programs need to encourage a positive mindset in their participants. The individuals providing the training can assist in this effort by exhibiting a consistent, supportive attitude. One way to achieve this "can do" attitude involves moving from the simple to the complex in the course of the training. This progression will first produce instant success followed by a gradual buildup of confidence. Further confidence can be instilled among the individuals being trained if they understand that their organization is committed to their successful mastery of the training. For example, following their training, the individuals will be actively encouraged by their supervisors or managers to apply their new skills.

4. *Satisfaction.* Training programs should produce individuals who experience a sense of fulfillment from their training. Individuals derive self-satisfaction from rewards such as certificates of achievement, publication of their names in organizational newsletters, and notation of their accomplishments in personnel files. Knowledge that competence can generate external rewards, including the possibility of promotions and merit raises, can also generate internal feelings of self-esteem and a desire for further growth.

Undoubtedly more effective training can be delivered when training designers incorporate motivational strategies into training programs. Yet motivational strategies alone will not guarantee the success of training programs in organizations. Training designers also need knowledge of other factors affecting the training function.

TRAINING FACTORS

What makes office automation training strategically important in some organizations and unimportant or less important in others? Several organizational factors can substantially influence an organization's approach to training. Factors of considerable importance to training include the organization itself, its employee population, and its choice of delivery systems for training. The quality of the training function depends to a great extent on how an organization deals with each of these factors.

THE ORGANIZATION

The training function should be compatible with the overall goals and objectives of the organization that it serves. A healthy organizational climate for training would include management philosophy and policies supportive of the organization's most valuable resource—its employees. The philosophy of top management in an organization greatly determines the priority of the training function within that organization. A managerial priority for training would ensure adequate allocation of organizational resources for the training budget, staffing procedures, and facilities. The extent of these allocations for office automation training would need to be consistent with an organization's level of office automation. When management provides visible support to the training function, this communicates a commitment to employees' professional development.

THE TRAINING POPULATION

Who should receive training in office automation? All organizational personnel affected by office automation are potential trainees. Every employee in an office position from the highest level executive to the newest office employee will be affected by office automation. The focus of a particular office automation training program will depend greatly upon the category of the office training population being served. For example, entry-level office workers might need training to bridge the gap between their schooling and the job. Training might include new skills for the automated office or even training in basic skills, such as language arts and keyboarding. Because of the shortage of qualified office workers, some organizations have found it necessary to develop their own employees in order to fill vacant office positions. Reentry office workers as well as experienced office workers often find it necessary to update their skills as automation continues to affect all office positions.

A point of major importance is that office automation training should not be restricted to training for just new users of an office automation system. Because of the dynamic nature of office automation, systems frequently are upgraded, expanded, and converted. A group of employees will master the basics of a system only to be replaced by another group of novices. Meanwhile, other groups will have mastered an intermediate level of knowledge and will want to progress to an advanced level. Changes in systems—hardware, software, applications, procedures, personnel—all mean that training for office automation should be a continuous effort devoted to the professional growth and development of all levels of office personnel. However, in most cases, training in office automation has meant training only for those office employees performing computer applications, such as word processing.

This distribution of training can be explained easily. The effect of automated equipment upon certain forms of office work such as word processing was immediate and profound. Training became imperative if increased productivity and other benefits of office automation were to be realized. The work of principals, however, was not as directly affected by automation. Even now as the work of principals becomes increasingly affected by office automation, delivering training to principals can present problems to training designers. These problems are related to the fact that principals' jobs are not strictly standardized and vary considerably according to industry and management level.

Secretaries and administrative assistants (the administrative support group) constitute another group of office personnel who may be overlooked by their organizations for office automation training. Although companies are beginning to recognize the importance of providing training to administrative support staff, the type of employee who receives the least amount of formal training is the secretarial/clerical worker.[3] Administrative support personnel, however, need training for office automation too, as major changes are occurring in the way secretaries and principals work together. The role of the administrative assistant in the automated office has been characterized as that of an interface between the computer and principal. Only with an understanding of the concept and applications of the full range of office automation applications can administrative support staff members contribute effectively to the teamwork vital to the secretary-principal relationship. Figure 16-3 illustrates a promotion for a training seminar in office automation directed toward the administrative support staff.

---

3. "Training News," ASTD *Classe*, Vol. IV, No. 1 (Spring, 1988): 8.

Figure 16-3 The Secretary's Role in Office Automation

Description

This workshop brings secretaries up-to-date with the computer revolution. It shows them how word processors, personal computers, electronic mail, and other technologies are helping them work more efficiently. Their professionalism is enhanced through updated knowledge that gives them more confidence, improved communication skills, and an improved ability to resolve conflicts. Special emphasis is given on how to overcome stress unique to an automated environment.

Most importantly, this workshop motivates secretaries and enables them to better understand and appreciate their important role in office automation (OA).

You Learn How to

- Adapt to the secretary's new role in OA
- Understand OA concepts and terminology
- Adjust to and accept changes in responsibilities
- Relate to computer buzzwords
- Understand electronic mail
- Assist management in identifying OA applications and selecting equipment
- Resolve interpersonal conflicts and communicate more effectively
- Overcome physical and emotional stress in an automated environment
- Prepare your plan for success in an automated office
- Move up your career ladder

Who Should Attend

Any secretarial, administrative, or clerical employee who needs to understand the automated office.

Instructor

Kim Richardson
Principal, R. N. Patterson and Associates, Inc.

Course Outline

The Secretary's Role in OA — How To
- Get more work accomplished faster
- Recognize opportunities for new challenges
- Help to implement OA
- Adjust to changes in the way you perform your duties

OA — The Challenge of the Future
- OA is revolutionizing the offices—three out of four office workers will have computers by 1990!
- Changes in the way secretaries and managers have worked together
- What OA means to you and your boss
- Productivity improvement

Technology Update — What's New in
- Word-processing systems
- Personal computers (PCs)
- Interfaces—OCRs, laser printers, phototypesetting
- Electronic mail and file
- Voice mail
- Teleconferencing

Your Boss May Use a Personal Computer To
- Perform math calculations on electronic spreadsheets
- Electronically access files from computerized databases
- Automatically create charts and graphs
- Type drafts of documents
- Electronically send and receive mail

If PCs Do So Much for Managers, What Will They Need Secretaries For?
- The most important work in the office
- Capitalizing on the changes
- Becoming an assistant to the boss
- Advancing to new careers

Is There a Personal Computer in Your Future?
- Assisting your boss with PC applications
- Which is better for your typing—a dedicated word processor or a PC?
- PCs at home

Communicating Electronically — Sending Messages in Seconds
- Communicating word processors and PCs
- Facsimile machines
- Electronic mail networks
- Electronic buildings—local area networks
- Work at home as a telecommuter

A Short Course in Computer Literacy — In Plain English!
- The computer process explained
- Hardware and software programs
- Bits, bytes, RAM, ROM, 8-bit, 16-bit, 32-bit
- Operating system—MS-DOS, CP/M, UNIX
- High resolution, pixels
- Modems, RS 232, 300 baud, 1200 baud
- Microchips, microprocessor, CPU
- Boards, ports, cards, expansion slots

Become An Innovator—Help Implement OA in Your Office. How To
- Identify needs
- Recommend and evaluate equipment
- Plan the change
- Recognize the importance of training
- Put your ideas in writing

Communicate and Relate to Others More Professionally. How To
- Build on your professionalism
- Resolve conflicts with better results
- Build confidence and develop assertiveness
- Understand psychological game players
- Communicate with peers and superiors more effectively

Managing Stress in an Automated Environment
- Are computers and word processors harmful to your health?
- Identifying stress
- Stress-coping skills
- Your stress management plan

Are You Ready for the Challenge of the Future?
- Setting goals—what's the next step for you?
- Mapping your journey to success
- The future looks bright!

DELIVERY SYSTEMS

What are the options for organizations desiring to offer office automation training to their employees? Many choices of delivery systems exist for office automation training with different advantages and disadvantages attached to each. Consequently, the best solution for office automation training often involves a combination of sources. Organizations mix and match delivery systems in order to meet all of their office automation training needs.

A survey by COMP-U-FAX, a computer trends reporting service, found most office employees were trained in-house (internally) using staff or vendor tutorials (instructions in print or on diskette).[4] In large organizations the source of the in-house training staff is either personnel from a separate training department or the **human resources department (HRD)** (formerly called personnel). These training areas are staffed with training specialists called trainers or internal consultants. Another source of in-house training staff would be office supervisors or experienced end users. These individuals provide employees at their workstations with instructions necessary to perform their job duties **(on-the-job training (OJT))**. Additional sources of training for office automation include contracts with external consultants, community colleges, or other educational organizations to provide employees with instruction. In organizations that maintain Information Centers (discussed in Chapter 2), training in office automation may be the responsibility of its support staff. Figure 16-4 illustrates some of the many sources of office automation training available.

TRAINING SPECIALIST VERSUS OFFICE SPECIALIST

One of the chief decisions that an organization has to make concerning office automation training is whether to use the services of a training specialist or a supervisor/experienced end user (office specialist). Training specialists, whether from within or outside the organization, should be expected to be experts in the design and delivery of training. The theoretical background of trainers would probably include the following:

1. *Psychology of learning.* This area includes such topics as how to motivate learners, how to provide for the individual differ-

---

4. Comp-U-Fax, "Survey Reports on PC-based Administrative Support Tasks," *Data Management* (May, 1987): 26.

Figure 16-4 **Sources of Office Automation Training**

Sources

In-house staff
Vendor tutorials
On-the-Job Training (OJT)
External consultants
Educational institutions/organizations
Information Center support staff

Source: Debra Haverson, ''How Today's Companies Approach OA Training: The Results of IWP's 'Training Services for Office Automation' Survey,'' (Willow Grove, Pa.: Association of Information Systems Professionals, 1983), p. 3.

ences among learners, how to reinforce or reward appropriate behavior, how to determine optimum practice time, and how to provide knowledge of results or feedback to learners.

2. *Andragogy*. **Andragogy** is the study of the adult learner. Trainers should know how to relate to adult learners and help them apply their past experiences to new learning situations. In addition, trainers should be able to help trainees feel comfortable in a training environment.

3. *Platform skills*. **Platform skills** involve teaching and communicating abilities. Trainers should be knowledgeable in the use of a variety of training methods, materials, and audiovisual aids.

Training specialists, on the other hand, may not be knowledgeable about office automation or office procedures. Many consulting firms, however, do employ specialists in these areas. Supervisors and experienced end users within a particular organization generally lack expertise in the discipline of training but are competent regarding office procedures and automated equipment. However, supervisors and experienced end users are busy with their own job responsibilities and may not welcome the extra work of training others or may not be suited to carry out this task. Frequently, the most knowledgeable person in the office is asked to train others, but this person may not have the necessary patience or may not be interested in working with novices. Another problem related to the use of supervisors is that because supervisors are responsible for performance appraisals of subordinates, their trainees might feel uncomfortable in a situation exposing their deficiencies.

Organizations that want to use supervisors and experienced end users should have them work together with an internal train-

Figure 16-5 · Trainers must be adept at communicating and teaching.

ing specialist, if available, or provide them with "train-the-trainer" training. Such classes are offered by professional training associations, private consulting firms, and some colleges and universities. Figure 16-6 illustrates an example of a train-the-trainer seminar for office automation trainers.

Figure 16-6 · Training the Trainer

DESCRIPTION

If you have corporate training responsibilities, this workshop gives you an opportunity to explore general training concepts (pedagogy) and to relate those concepts to the special training needs of users of microcomputers and word processors.

The workshop is organized around three major concepts: (1) Effective training programs include certain clearly defined elements; (2) each word processor or microcomputer makes special demands and offers corresponding opportunities; and (3) the trainer can develop an enhanced corporate role.

WHO SHOULD ATTEND

Any trainer, supervisor, or manager with responsibilities for planning, directing, or implementing training programs for microcomputers or word processors.

Figure 16-6 **Training the Trainer** *(continued)*

YOU LEARN HOW TO

- Define appropriate training goals for a specific system and organization
- Specify the best environment and resources to carry out defined training goals
- Understand and apply concepts of lesson plan, motivation, skill development, feedback, and evaluation
- Describe common elements of microcomputers and dedicated word processors and understand effects of the training situation
- Recognize special problems of trainees who lack technical backgrounds and provide valid training options for them
- Recommend goals, strategies, environments, and resources
- Identify additional corporate functions of the trainer
- Evaluate training techniques for occasional users, clerical and administrative staff, knowledge workers, and management

INSTRUCTOR

Paul A. Shapiro, Associate, R. N. Patterson and Associates, Inc.

COURSE OUTLINE

Background
- Training in the corporate environment
- Evolution of training
- Traditional values and resources
- Recent changes and demands
- Training configurations: self-training, tutorial, group
- Present status of corporate system and software training

Applying Training Principles
- Basic requirements for effective training
- Examples of program goals
- Training environments
- Resources: what and why
- Sample lesson plans
- Assessing motivation
- Teaching/learning strategies
- Feedback and evaluation

Microcomputers
- Basic concepts
- Small and large systems
- Peripherals

Figure 16-6   Training the Trainer *(continued)*

- Software: applications packages
- Microcomputers vs. word processors
- Levels of applied skills

Instructor-Student Interaction
- Setting priorities
- Classroom activities
- The matter of style
- Trainee education and experience
- Managers and professionals

Administering Training Programs
- Budgets—present and future
- Staff organization and responsibilities
- Enrollment: screening, registration, records
- Reporting to management

Equipment and Software Demonstrations
- Operating systems
- Basic functions
- Advanced functions
- Software options

Corporate Role of the Trainer
- Corporate perceptions
- Self-perceptions
- Relations with others
- Dealing with management
- Career paths
- Institutional values

INTERNAL VERSUS EXTERNAL TRAINING

Another decision for organizations involves the choice of internal or external training. One form of in-house training that eliminates some of the problems caused by the use of supervisors and experienced end users is that of vestibule training. **Vestibule training** usually is conducted by an office training specialist on an organization's premises but away from the actual job site of the trainee. Such training is designed to simulate on-the-job activities. The learning environment surrounding vestibule training is relatively free of job pressures, interruptions, and the frustration of trying to handle a regular work load while learning new skills. Vestibule training is relatively expensive for organizations because of the cost of the required physical training facility and the provision of an instructor, equipment, and materials. However, the organization is spared costly errors and the low productivity often incurred by inexperienced employees while learning on the job.

The most frequent choice by organizations for the training of their office employees, however, is not vestibule training but on-the-job training (OJT). Why is it so popular? The chief advantages of OJT are that each employee receives individual attention and coaching, and no special allocation of the organization's resources are required. Variations of OJT include cross training and job rotation. In **cross training,** employees are instructed in the job duties of other employees. Thus, these employees can serve as backup for employees who are absent from their jobs. **Job rotation** involves assigning an employee to work in a variety of departments or functional areas for a relatively short duration.

Despite the many advantages associated with internal training, external training can also be a valuable source of office automation training. External trainers can be specially contracted seminar leaders, private consultants, professors, or vendor representatives. The most common method of external office automation training has been the use of vendor training. Increasingly, however, vendor training is becoming a relic of the past. This change has occurred as equipment prices have gone down and the cost of training has gone up. Vendor training generally covers only basic operations and is short-term, lasting from one to five days. Such training may be administered at the vendor's training facilities or at the customer's location. When trainees complete this initial training period and attempt to apply their new skills to their job applications, they often meet with problems. The helpful trainer is gone, and the trainees become frustrated.

Even when trainees gain mastery of basic operations, they need advanced training to enable them to use the full range of features in their equipment. To assist trainees in making the transition from training to the job, many vendors provide a variety of services. Some of the services are free, some may be part of a prepaid service contract, and others may be offered on a pay-as-you-go basis. Typical services include such aids as hot lines, follow-up visits by market support representatives (MSRs), user newsletters, and participation in user groups.

Despite all of these forms of assistance, however, vendor training is equipment and operator oriented and usually directed toward generic functions rather than specific job applications within a particular organization. Consequently, such training cannot meet all of an organization's office automation training needs. Also, vendor training generally cannot supply training for all office personnel—operators, principals, and administrative support staff. Thus, organizations must pick and choose from a variety of delivery systems for office automation training.

TRAINING PROGRAMS

Individuals responsible for office automation training should be aware of concepts common to all types of training. These concepts involve knowledge of the when, what, and how of training. The "when" involves knowing when to apply the training solution to an organization's problems. The "what" involves determining what should constitute training program content. The "how" involves presentation skills, the selection of training strategies and media, the evaluation of training effectiveness, and the justification of training costs. Trainers need to understand these concepts and be able to apply them to the development of training programs for office automation.

NEEDS ASSESSMENTS

The most essential prerequisite to the administration of a training program is the needs assessment. A **needs assessment** is a diagnostic activity that allows training designers to become aware of problems in the organization that might be remedied by training. Some of the problems uncovered by a needs assessment will be **deficiencies in task execution** and cannot be corrected by training. Such problems mean that the employees have the knowledge and skill to perform their tasks but for various reasons are not performing them effectively. Examples include such cases as employees who perform poorly because of a lack of internal motivation or the lack of an adequate reward system in the organization.

Other problems revealed by a needs assessment, however, could be candidates for training solutions. These problems are called **deficiencies of skill** or **deficiencies of practice.** In these circumstances, training programs can aid employees in learning skills or acquiring knowledge to a sufficient degree so that they can meet the standards required for their job performance.

Methods of Needs Assessments. How is a needs assessment conducted? Several methods of needs assessment can be used by training designers to discover organizational problems with training implications. Some of these methods include the exit interview (questioning departing employees), critical incidents (reviewing events significantly affecting the organization), and performance appraisals (studying managerial evaluations of employees' work). However, a traditional approach that is commonly used involves questionnaires, interviews, and observation. All of the techniques for needs assessment can be used either singly or in combination with each other.

Questionnaires can be used to receive input about the training needs of office personnel and to provide information that could be helpful to the training designers in conducting interviews and in analyzing training needs. Training designers should interview all levels of employees affected by office automation—managers, professionals, operators, technical personnel, and administrative support staff. Time, budget constraints, and the number of office employees dictate whether all personnel or just a sample would be involved in these procedures.

Observations could be conducted either directly or indirectly. With direct observation the training designer would probe employees for information regarding the work being observed. Using indirect observation, a training designer might watch workers performing their tasks either with or without their knowledge. Another approach to indirect observation involves the examination of organizational records to determine training needs. For example, reviewing the production statistics of word processing employees might reveal several problem areas that could be improved with training. Other records that could reveal training needs include absenteeism, turnover, and filed grievances. A guide to help training designers inventory an organization's training needs for office automation is provided in Figure 16-7.

Figure 16-7 Assessing OA Training Needs

Use these questions to evaluate your organization's OA training needs:

1. What hardware and software are available today? What is likely to be available in the near future?
2. What are the specific capabilities of your OA system? Do they include word processing, list management, spreadsheets, electronic mail, remote database access, graphics, database creation and storage, and scheduling?
3. Who are your users? managers? professionals? secretarial staff?
4. Which of your users will be high-power users with the need for frequent, critical access to OA capabilities?
5. Which of your users will be low-power users with infrequent need to use system capabilities?
6. What attitudes toward OA and what expertise and experience in OA are common in the user community?
7. What types of operational training are available from your vendor?

Figure 16-7 **Assessing OA Training Needs** (continued)

8. Is there an internal training organization that can provide assistance? Is there an OA support group charged with training responsibilities?
9. Are there other resources, such as expert users of home personal computers or other OA office systems, who can provide assistance?
10. Are there any unique needs for training that require customized training assistance?

Source: Association of Information Systems Professionals Publications.

Levels of Needs Assessments. Whatever methods are used to determine training needs for office automation, the needs assessment should involve analysis at three levels—organizational, job or task, and individual. An explanation of each of these levels follows:

1. *Organizational analysis.* When training designers analyze organizations for an office automation needs assessment, their analysis must go beyond general knowledge of the organization's extent and level of office automation. In order to design an effective training program, both managers and trainers should have a clear, common understanding of the purpose and goals of office automation training. Managers who are unfamiliar with office automation could possess unrealistic expectations of its capabilities and put unreasonable demands on the support staff. Such demands create job pressures and a stressful office work environment. Those responsible for the development of training programs should take care to communicate to management the expected outcomes for an office automation training program.
2. *Job or task analysis.* If an organization's job descriptions and job specifications for each office position do not reflect the impact of office automation, a training designer will have to work closely with an office systems analyst or personnel specialist to match job requirements with an appropriate training design. Only with an understanding of how office automation affects the procedures of each office position can an effective training program be developed.
3. *Individual analysis.* Trainers should be able to identify which groups of employees or individuals need what training and at what level it should be provided. Such specific identification

will become even more necessary as increasing numbers of office employees become familiar with office automation in school and on the job.

Office Automation Training Needs. What kinds of results can be expected from a needs assessment for office automation training? Training needs in office automation can be classified into skill categories of human, conceptual, and technical. Human needs involve the ability to communicate and relate interpersonally. Conceptual needs involve the ability to deal with abstract ideas. Technical needs involve the ability to operate information processing hardware and software. Following the needs assessment for office automation training, a training designer must convert these identified needs into the actual content which will comprise a training program.

TRAINING CONTENT

The content of most office automation training programs has concentrated on technical training. Skills related to operations such as proofreading, spelling, and records or file management sometimes are included. For principals, technical training may involve instruction in the use of personal computers and dictation systems. Technical training does have its place, as it is necessary to operate automated equipment efficiently. However, when only technical training is offered to office employees, serious consequences can result. Technical training alone reflects an underestimation of the capabilities of office employees and can be self-defeating for an organization. When office employees lack depth of insight into the capabilities of office systems, little chance exists for their development of new applications and more productive procedures using the equipment. Technical training does contribute to employees' feelings of self-confidence and mastery over automated equipment. However, experts in office automation training usually recommend conceptual training as well as technical training, though they are divided over which should come first.

Conceptual training includes topics such as automation's effect on an employee's work role, organizational structure, procedures, and relationships. Other conceptual topics related to office automation could include time management, problem solving, performance appraisal, work-flow analysis, work-load distribution, and setting priorities. The human classification for office personnel training could include topics such as stress management, leadership styles, supervisory skills, interpersonal relations, and communication skills such as listening and speaking.

Because significant differences have been found in the training needs for the various levels of office personnel, content for office automation training programs should differ also. However, common elements of office automation could be expected to be present in training for all levels of office personnel, especially within a particular organization.

TRAINING STRATEGIES AND MEDIA

Once training content as a response to office automation training needs has been determined, the training designer next must decide upon training strategies and media. Training strategies involve methods of presentation, such as lecture, case study, role playing, and simulation. Training media include the materials and technology used to deliver training. Figure 16-8 lists types of media used for office automation training.

Figure 16-8   **Office Automation Training Media**

Print-Based Media	Technology-Based Media
	Audio- and videotapes
Vendor manuals	Computer-based training
Tutorials	Interactive video
Procedures manuals	Hypermedia
	Intelligent job aids
	Teletraining

PRINT-BASED MEDIA

Because most office employees receive their training in-house using manuals and tutorials, print-based media are of great importance. Printed instructions have an obvious advantage over oral directions as a training method. Of course, to be a helpful training aid, printed instructions must be accurate, current, and easy to understand.

Vendor Manuals and Tutorials.   Typically vendor manuals and tutorials are difficult for novice users to understand because of their technical language. Such media are written by programmers who generally do not understand a novice's anxieties and lack of technical background regarding a system. For example, novice users may be unable to use the index for lack of knowledge of the correct term under which a particular function might be listed.

Therefore, vendor manuals and tutorials usually are better suited for experienced users. Because of the difficulties associated with the use of vendor manuals and tutorials, office supervisors or trainers frequently assume the task of developing manuals, simplified and tailored for specific tasks within the organization.

Procedures Manuals.   A procedures manual contains written procedures custom created for a particular company. A procedure refers to a specific description of how a system operates and may involve a series of related actions necessary to accomplish the operation. Procedures manuals often form the basis for training current or new office employees and serve as a reference for infrequently performed or complex tasks. Because procedures manuals are paper based, they are convenient for office personnel to access and easy to distribute. With the advent of desktop publishing, procedures manuals can be professionally designed and produced in-house at relatively low cost.

Preparing Procedures Manuals.   Different procedures manuals may exist for different groups of employees. For example, word processing operators may use one manual while employees in the micrographics area might use another. The procedures to be included in a particular manual can be determined from the results of job or task analysis and input from the employees responsible for the performance of specific procedures.

Some basic guidelines for writing a procedures manual are listed below:

1. Identify what person or group is responsible for each task.
2. Identify when tasks are to start and stop.
3. Identify the forms to use, if required.
4. Identify each procedure to be performed.
5. Use headings and notations.
6. Number steps sequentially.
7. Subdivide the steps if necessary.
8. Use action verbs to initiate each step.
9. Include pictures, flow charts, examples, and samples, as appropriate.
10. Evaluate the procedures regularly.
11. Update the procedures when necessary.
12. Compile the procedures in a loose-leaf binder or other container allowing ease of maintenance.

TECHNOLOGY-BASED MEDIA

Technology is being increasingly incorporated into the development, delivery, and management of training. This infusion of technology into the instructional process has generated talk of electronic classrooms, the demise of the book, and the replacement of "live" instruction with electronic media. Although a total takeover by technology is perhaps as unlikely an occurrence as the totally paperless office, the trend toward the inclusion of technology into the training function is undeniable.

Audio- and Videotapes.   Audiotapes (sound only) or videotapes (picture and sound) sometimes accompany printed training materials. The use of audio- and videotapes personalizes the training and generally makes training more appealing to users. Audio- and videotapes bundled with printed training materials can speed and assist the learning process because trainees use more of their senses. In addition, the explanations and, in the case of video, demonstrations can add clarity to what might otherwise be a confusing passage in print.

Computer-Based Training.   The general term referring to the use of computer technology for instruction and monitoring of the training process is called **computer-based training (CBT).** When the computer is used specifically to present drill and practice exercises, tutorials, and simulations, the term **computer-assisted instruction (CAI)** is used. When the computer handles administrative tasks associated with the training function such as maintaining class rosters, class schedules, generating tests, scoring tests, and averaging grades, the term **computer-managed instruction (CMI)** is used. Computer-based training is commercially available for mainframe, minicomputer, and microcomputer systems. Most popular business software packages for microcomputers, for example, are supported by computer-based tutorials. According to the CRWTH Survey on End User Computing, CBT is currently being used in over half of the organizations surveyed (primarily FORTUNE 1000 companies).[5] Figure 16-9 illustrates this usage of CBT in large organizations.

The use of CBT offers trainees and organizations many benefits. The benefits of CBT reported primarily by FORTUNE 1000 companies and other large organizations in the CRWTH Survey on End User Computing are illustrated in Figure 16-10. One of the chief benefits of CBT is its ability to deliver individualized, self-paced instruction. If trainees do not understand a portion of a training program, they can repeat it without fear of embarrassment. Computer-based training is also timely in that it can be provided to trainees when needed instead of their waiting for

---

5.   "The Fourth Annual CRWTH Survey: Identifying New Trends and Directions in End User Computing," CRWTH Computer Courseware, Santa Monica, Calif., 1989: 13.

Figure 16-9 **Computer Based Training Usage**

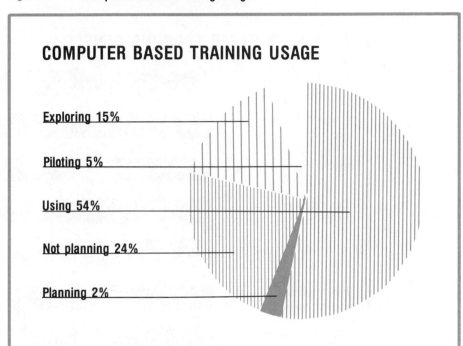

Source: The Fourth Annual CRWTH Survey: ''Identifying New Trends and Directions in End User Computing,'' CRWTH Computer Courseware, 2850 Ocean Park Blvd., Suite 200, Santa Monica, Calif., 1989, p. 13. Reproduced by permission.

classes to be scheduled. Trainees can make arrangements to work on the computer at their own convenience and, in some organizations, may even take computers home with them to learn in privacy. Ideally, the learning environment for computer-based training should be free of pressure from other employees or supervisors. For example, individual workstations enclosed with panels or a separate training facility can provide such relative isolation.

Organizations using computer-based training might save on labor costs because of the generally reduced need for "live" training. This possible advantage could become a disadvantage if organizations rely too heavily on technology to deliver training, thus dehumanizing the training process. Some organizations counteract this possibility by using the services of a trainer in conjunction with the technology. This trainer can provide trainees with emotional support, relieve fears about the use of the technology, and answer trainees' questions. In addition, trainers can be freed from routine training to provide training for specialized needs.

Figure 16-10   Computer Based Training Benefits

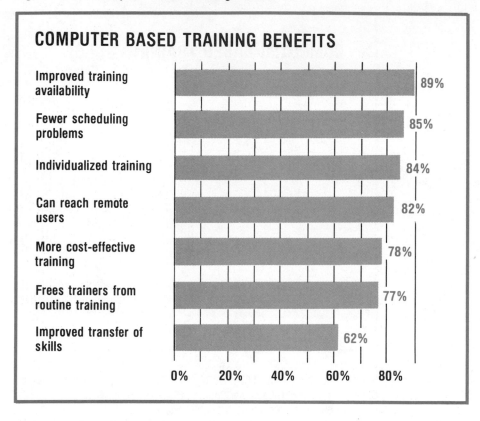

COMPUTER BASED TRAINING BENEFITS

- Improved training availability — 89%
- Fewer scheduling problems — 85%
- Individualized training — 84%
- Can reach remote users — 82%
- More cost-effective training — 78%
- Frees trainers from routine training — 77%
- Improved transfer of skills — 62%

0%   20%   40%   60%   80%

Source: The Fourth Annual CRWTH Survey: ''Identifying New Trends and Directions in End User Computing,'' CRWTH Computer Courseware, 2850 Ocean Park Blvd., Suite 200, Santa Monica, Calif., 1989, p. 13. Reproduced by permission.

Computer-based training can also be economically advantageous for organizations in that the cost of travel and other expenses associated with off-site training can be greatly diminished or even eliminated. Once a computer-based training program is operational, its repeated use becomes increasingly cost effective. If organizations use off-the-shelf software for training, the cost will be relatively low. Figure 16-11 illustrates the cost effectiveness of computer-based training compared to classes conducted by trainers and one-on-one employee training. If customized training is necessary, however, more expense will be involved.

Trainers requiring customized training programs can create their own computer-based training using authoring systems. **Authoring systems** are software programs that instruct the computer to display text, ask trainees questions, give trainees answers

Figure 16-11 A Comparison of Office Training Costs

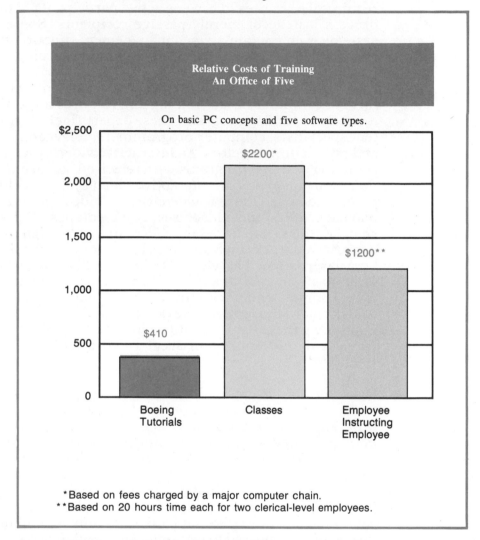

Relative Costs of Training
An Office of Five

On basic PC concepts and five software types.

*Based on fees charged by a major computer chain.
**Based on 20 hours time each for two clerical-level employees.

Source: Boeing Computer Services, Seattle, Washington

and feedback, and keep records of the trainees' progress. Both high-level and low-level authoring systems exist for trainers with various degrees of knowledge of computer programming. With authoring systems tutorial-type lessons can be created involving the use of matching, fill-in and multiple choice questions, and built-in branching. Branching refers to the presentation of alternate instruction to trainees based upon their responses to questions in the program. This dialogue format between computer and trainee is referred to as its interactive capability. The interaction requires the trainees to become active participants in the learning process instead of merely passive recipients. Some authoring systems even contain a video management function that allows the creation of interactive video training programs.

Interactive Video.   Interactive video represents an advanced form of computer-based training and requires a team of experts to create a training program. These experts include training content specialists, computer programmers, television technicians, and production directors. An **interactive video system** combines computer training programs with televised segments of instruction. Components of an interactive video system include a computer, video monitor, a videodisc or videotape player (video playback unit), and videodiscs or videotapes. Videodiscs are shiny platters that store both video and audio signals on 54,000 microscopic tracks etched in the surface of the disk that are read by a laser beam. The videodisc is virtually indestructible and offers faster access to any track on the disk compared to videotape. Training with interactive video presents trainees with sight, sound, color, and motion in text, video, audio, and graphics form. Combining these features into an interactive video system offers trainees the advantages of accelerated learning and increased retention.

Hypermedia.   Hypermedia refers to computerized-instruction tools, which can also be used for the development of training programs. **Hypermedia** tools allow users to explore topics by linking related segments of information from a database-like structure. This database can be a compendium of text, graphics, pictures, music, voice, and full-motion video. Hypermedia's capability to link such information is made possible by developments in **artificial intelligence (A.I.),** a field of study devoted to enabling computers to think like humans do. Human thinking is often associative as opposed to hierarchical (linear). In a free-association mode of thought, an individual moves spontaneously from one idea to the next according to the linkages in that person's thought patterns. In typical computer-based training programs, the authors establish the linkages for trainees with logical, sequentially developed programmed frames of instruction. With hypermedia tools trainees establish their own linkages by accessing so-called "stacks" of collected information. With hypermedia tools a user can query the program and receive a response at any point. Such systems have the capability to prescribe feedback to trainees based upon their infinite branching and database capabilities, often accessed from compact disk. Examples of hypermedia tools include Apple's HyperCard™ and IBM's Linkway™.

Intelligent Job Aids. Artificial intelligence is being increasingly embedded in many training media. The result has been the development of software programs called **expert systems,** which infuse "intelligence" into computer training; hence such terms as intelligent computer-assisted instruction (ICAI), intelligent interactive video (IVI), and intelligent job aids. One type of **intelligent job aid** could be likened to a computerized procedures manual in which the knowledge of "office experts" is captured and written into an expert system for reference by current and future office employees. Such systems provide an interactive, computerized database, which can provide answers to office workers' queries quickly without disrupting the work of others.

Teletraining. The use of telecommunications systems technology is becoming more common for training delivery. The application of teleconferencing tools to the training function is referred to as **teletraining.** A video teleconference allows trainees at geographically dispersed sites linked via satellite to view televised material on monitors while interacting with instructors over standard telephone lines. Organizations involved in teletraining can produce and transmit their own training programs. When the material to be presented is time-sensitive, and/or requires interaction between instructor and trainees, and involves delivery to participants at diverse, remote sites, teletraining can be a cost effective training medium.

In addition, companies engaged in teletraining can choose from thousands of hours of packaged programs delivered via satellite "universities." Such electronic educational organizations include The National Technological University, the Public Broadcasting Service's (PBS) National Narrowcast Service, and the Corporate Satellite Training Network. These organizations specialize in training and educational programming to serve the needs of adult workers. With the cost of a satellite dish or a trip to a location with a satellite dish (such as many hotel chains now have installed), companies can significantly augment their in-house training programs.[6]

SELECTION GUIDELINES

With so many training choices available, how can training designers determine which types of strategies and media are most suitable for office automation training? Fortunately, some guidelines exist to help trainers select appropriate training.

6. "BIG Teleconference Brings D.C. to Dallas," ASTD *National Report on Human Resources* (July/August, 1988): 2.

1. Strategies and media should facilitate the training program's objectives. For example, a lecture about operating instructions for a personal computer would not be as beneficial to operator-trainees as a demonstration followed by hands-on experience. Training designers should not allow the selection process to be unduly influenced by the newest or most novel training style or fad.

2. A variety of strategies and media should be included in a training program. Generally, the more the trainees' senses are stimulated by the training process, the more the trainees will remember. Learning specialists claim that people remember only 15–25 percent of what they hear, 45–75 percent of what they hear and see, and 70–90 percent if they hear, see, and do something in the learning process. Therefore, not only classroom lecture and printed materials are needed but also demonstrations, films, slides, cassette recordings, games, simulations, and hands-on computer training.

3. Training strategies and media should be investigated before they are selected. Personally contacting another trainer who has had experience with the media is perhaps one of the best ways to determine how effective an item might be for the needs of a particular organization. A film, for example, might appear to be excellent as described in a brochure but could be a disappointment when actually viewed. One reason for this problem is that films, especially on office automation, quickly become outdated. Another potential problem is that materials frequently appear in catalogs before actually being available for sale or rent. In other instances, a particular medium might be withdrawn from the market or repeatedly back ordered. Investigation of media is well worth the time and effort expended to prevent unnecessary expense or ineffective training.

4. The cost of a particular medium should be considered in relation to its usefulness and the total training budget. Media should not be assumed to be of excellent quality simply because of high cost.

5. Training strategies and media should be matched to the number, needs, and job level of personnel to be trained. For example, if a new product needs to be introduced to an organization's sales force dispersed across the country, teletraining could be the most efficient and cost effective media to select. If another training need called for sessions promoting teamwork among secretaries and managers, small, face-to-face groups of secretaries and managers would be appropriate. However, if a training program concerned specific job applications, then a small but homogeneous group would be more appropriate. Applying the same guideline to media, a film on office automation with highly technical language and content might be

inappropriate for secretaries and managers but fitting for information systems engineers.

6. The training strategies and media selected should be familiar to the training staff or provision should be made for the training of the trainers.

7. Before a training program authored in-house is presented for widespread use, it should be pilot tested.

TRAINING EVALUATION

Training programs for the automated office, like programs for any other training area, should be evaluated. Evaluation, however, is often the most neglected phase of the training cycle. Training programs can be evaluated at four stages:

1. *Reaction* — Often referred to as "smile" sheets, reaction involves a measure of trainee satisfaction with the training received. Assessing trainee reaction is the most common form of evaluation and is generally administered at the conclusion of the training program.

2. *Learning* — This stage of evaluation measures the effectiveness of the objectives of the training program involving knowledge, skills and/or attitudes. Such assessment can be administered before training to determine the entry level of trainee proficiency, during training to determine trainee progress, and after training to determine trainee achievement.

3. *Behavior* — How much and what type of change occurred on the job as a result of the training program can be gauged from a follow-up survey of both trainees and their supervisors.

4. *Results* — Such things as improved productivity, lower costs, and improved profits are the ultimate objectives of training programs. Post-training activity such as surveys, interviews, and examination of organizational data can provide such end result information to training designers.

Responses to the evaluation process allow designers of training programs to decide whether certain programs should be repeated or revised. In addition, evaluation can yield information for management regarding justification of programs. If management is not provided with the results of evaluation, withdrawal of support for the training program could be the result. Continued support from management is usually dependent upon effective evaluations of training programs.

TRAINING BENEFITS

What kinds of results from evaluations of office automation training programs are likely? Generally increases in skills and a

Figure 16-12 Computer-based
training is often offered in large
corporations.
International Business Machines

number of other less tangible benefits can be anticipated, such
as increases in job satisfaction and appreciation of the capabilities of office systems. In addition, the quantity and quality of
office automation training received by users can be expected to
positively affect users' perceptions regarding the quality of their
work environment.[7]

These improved job perceptions can benefit organizations in
the form of reductions in labor turnover, absenteeism, error rates,
transfer requests, and filed grievances (soft-dollar benefits). All
of these office automation training benefits could produce increases in productivity, ultimately affecting the organization's
bottom line (hard-dollar benefits). Today organizations need both

7. Donna Matherly, "Office Automation and Quality of Work Life: The Effects of Transition Variables on Employee Perceptions," *Office Systems Research Association Journal*,
Vol. 1, No. 2 (Spring, 1983): 72.

hard- and soft-dollar benefits to achieve the competitive edge necessary for success.

Unfortunately some of the less tangible soft-dollar benefits, such as enhanced employee appreciation for office automation, may go unnoticed by management because of the difficulty of measuring them. Traditional accounting procedures more easily evaluate the costs of a pretraining versus a posttraining bottom line or compare the costs of an in-house versus an off-site seminar. A somewhat nontraditional approach could compare the costs of developing a training program to the costs of not developing the training program. If financial gains were indicated because of the training program, it would appear to be justified. For example, low productivity might exist in a word processing department because of the lack of trained operators. This problem could be quantified and compared to the cost of developing an operator training program.

Another accounting procedure that could be used to evaluate an office automation training program is **return-on-investment (ROI)** analysis. With this procedure the total cost of the training program is calculated in relation to an assigned dollar value of the training benefit. This calculation results in a return on investment or ratio of dollars gained to dollars spent; for example:

$$ROI = Benefits/Cost \times 100\%$$

$$\$100,000/\$25,000 \times 100\% = 4.00 \times 100\% = 400\% \text{ or } 4.00{:}1$$

In this example, the ratio indicates that for every dollar spent the organization will realize $4 in benefits. Despite the difficulties in quantifying training programs, large numbers of organizations have accepted office automation training as justifiable.

WOHL'S BUSINESS PERSPECTIVE

Once we argued about whether computer literacy would become a requirement for office workers. As recently as the mid-1970's, only a few especially trained, skilled office workers actually used computers, acting as intermediaries for the rest of us.

Today, computer literacy is a business fact of life. The question isn't *whether* to train office workers in computer skills, it's *when, how,* and *how much.*

Too many office workers are made to feel incompetent about computing because the computer education, orientation, and training they receive is non-existent or inadequate. If computing is to be an important part of how we do office work, then investments in education, orientation, and training are not only a good idea, they're an absolute requirement!

Sometimes the mistake is simply to offer (or require) training without preceding it with the necessary education and orientation.

Education means learning about how computers are changing business environments and why this is an important opportunity to learn an exciting new skill.

Orientation is learning about how computers will be used in our business and how they may change the organization of our work or the work itself.

Training means learning what I will need to know when the computer arrives on my desk.

Timing is important, too. The best time for education and orientation are in order and separately, preferably a few months before training will occur. This gives time for information to be absorbed and discussed and questions to be asked and answered. Ideally, this interaction, over a period of weeks or months, should be built right into the pre-training cycle.

Training then occurs just before the equipment will arrive. A properly educated and oriented worker is ready, even eager, for training to begin. They will return to their newly equipped desk ready to try out their new skills. A few cautionary hints:

- Training is a job unto itself. Don't expect the worker to do his regular work or to use his new skill while the training cycle is in progress.

- Newly trained workers may be temporarily less productive rather than more productive. Be prepared to take up the slack—and be sure the professionals and managers that the newly trained workers support are also warned.

- No one remembers everything he just learned. And if he doesn't get to use it right away, it's even more easily forgotten. Try to teach skills in sections— basic first, advanced later—with the instant reinforcement of using the skill as soon as possible. Don't try to teach every worker everything; instead, emphasize spending time on job-specific skills.

It's good to keep in mind that no matter how user friendly computers become, workers will still need education, orientation, and training. We'll be able to do more sophisticated things with less training, but some training will always be with us.

SUMMARY

The American Society for Training and Development (ASTD) estimates that U.S. business spends $210 billion annually on formal and informal training. Among office personnel, most training has been directed toward management rather than the management support staff. However, with office automation as a driving force, organizations are extending training to all levels of office personnel. Traditionally, training is viewed as a function providing adults with opportunities for learning concepts, skills, or attitudes expected to improve job performance. A training model for the design of training programs includes the following: (1) identify training needs; (2) specify job content; (3) write training objectives; (4) determine training content; (5) select methods and media; (6) conduct training; (7) validate training; (8) modify or update training. The ARCS (attention, relevance, confidence, satisfaction) Model can be used by trainers to incorporate motivational strategies into the training process.

Organizational factors that affect training are the organization itself, its population, and its choice of training delivery systems. An organization that provides training for its employees demonstrates its philosophical and economic support for its human resources. The population of an organization especially affects office automation training because the number, type, and level of employee is a major consideration in the design of training programs. Organizations have many choices of sources for the delivery of office automation training, including in-house staff, vendor manuals and tutorials, on-the-job training, external consultants, contracts with educational institutions/organizations, and information center support staff. The training needs of office employees can be determined by conducting a needs assessment. A popular method of needs assessment involves the use of questionnaires, interviews, and observation. Office automation training needs can be classified as technical, conceptual, and human; but, typically, such training addresses only the technical level.

Training strategies include methods of presentation such as lectures and case studies, and training media include the materials and technologies used for delivering training. The types of media used for office automation training include print-based (vendor manuals, tutorials, and procedures manuals) and technology-based (audio- and videotapes, computer-based training, interactive video, hypermedia, intelligent job aids, and teletraining). In selecting training strategies and media, training designers should consider how well such methods and materials facilitate the learning process. Evaluation of training programs can be administered at four stages—reaction, learning, behavior, and results—and is recommended to secure the support of management. The benefits of office automation training are often soft-dollar benefits, but these benefits can lead to increases in productivity affecting the organization's bottom line (hard-dollar benefits). Soft-dollar benefits can be difficult to measure using traditional accounting procedures. However, quantification of training benefits is recommended with the use of such procedures as return-on-investment (ROI) analysis because of the need to provide cost justification to management.

KEY TERMS

training	deficiencies of skill
holistic training	deficiencies of practice
training model	computer-based
training objective	training (CBT)
ARCS Model	computer-assisted
human resources	instruction (CAI)
department (HRD)	computer-managed
on-the-job training (OJT)	instruction (CMI)
andragogy	authoring systems
platform skills	interactive video system
vestibule training	hypermedia
cross training	artificial intelligence
job rotation	expert systems
needs assessment	intelligent job aids
deficiencies in task	teletraining
execution	return on investment (ROI)

REVIEW QUESTIONS

1. How has office automation affected the development of training programs in organizations?

2. How can a knowledge of motivational strategies be useful to training designers? Give examples.

3. What organizational factors would be of critical importance to the development of an office automation training program?

4. How might training needs differ for office workers who are (a) entry level, (b) reentry level, (c) experienced users (d) principals, and (e) administrative-support staff? How can organizations meet these training needs for specific groups?

5. If you were designing an office automation training program, would you select a training specialist from the training department or an office specialist to conduct the training? Explain your reasons.

6. Describe your idea of an ideal office automation training program regarding delivery systems for a small office (1 to 10 support staff members); a midsized office (11–99 support staff members); and a large office (over 100 support staff members).

7. What concepts would most likely be the same in any office automation training program? How might these concepts differ in an organization?

8. Is a needs assessment for an office automation training program always necessary? Support your answer with specific cases.

9. Why should a training designer be knowledgeable concerning the preparation of procedures manuals?

10. Why would computer-based training for office automation be popular with trainees? With organizations? What precautions need to be taken with the use of this medium?

11. What could be the effect on an office automation training program if its overall evaluation were positive? Negative? If no evaluation were conducted at all?

12. What results might organizations expect from the soft-dollar benefits and hard-dollar benefits associated with office automation training programs?

13. Why is the justification of office automation training programs a problem? What means are available to trainers to deal with this problem?

CASE STUDY: THE CASE OF THE OVERBURDENED OFFICE SUPERVISOR

Sandra Sanchez is the office supervisor for a large automobile dealership. She has been with the company for over thirty years and prides herself in knowing everything about office procedures for an automobile dealership. Sandra supervises an office staff composed of fifteen secretaries, bookkeepers, and clerks. Sandra's duties as office supervisor include training the newly hired office workers using an on-the-job (OJT) approach.

Because of the dealership's recent expansion, an increased volume of paperwork has caused Sandra to request permission from management to hire an additional clerk. Instead, management responded by purchasing a microcomputer. Sandra's boss told her to learn how to operate the computer and then to train the other office workers in its use. No training other than a vendor manual came with the computer, although training was available on a fee-paid basis at the vendor's site. Sandra's boss assured her she would not need this instruction because the salesperson said the computer was user friendly. Sandra's boss expressed the hope that Sandra could have the new system up and running in a couple of weeks. The new system also included a software package designed especially for automobile dealerships. Sandra was told that this package was used widely in the area by other automobile dealerships.

Sandra was overwhelmed by the prospect of having to learn how to operate a computer, convert the dealership's office procedures to accommodate a software package, and train fifteen office workers in a few weeks. Although Sandra enjoyed her work, she gave serious thought to retirement. Nevertheless, she decided to accept her new challenge.

After the computer was installed in Sandra's office, she found it difficult to find the time to study the manual and work on the computer. One source of her frequent interruptions was Paul Bianco. Paul was a bright, young office worker who had been with the dealership less than a year. He told Sandra he had worked on a computer in school, enjoyed it, and hoped that he would have the opportunity to do so again. Paul even offered to help Sandra learn the new computer system. Sandra thanked Paul for his offer and pondered her situation.

QUESTIONS/ACTIVITIES

1. What are the organizational factors affecting the training function in this case?

2. Does Sandra have any options? If so, describe them.

3. What would you consider to be the best solution to Sandra's problem?

SUGGESTED READINGS

Arnall, Gail C. "Satellite Delivered Learning." *Training & Development Journal* (June, 1987): 90–94.

Brookfield, Stephen D. *Understanding and Facilitating Adult Learning*. San Francisco, Calif.: Jossey-Bass, 1986.

Casner-Lotto, Jill. *Successful Training Strategies*. San Francisco, Calif.: Jossey-Bass, 1988.

Eurich, Nell P. *Corporate Classrooms: The Learning Business*. Lawrenceville, N.J.: Princeton University Press, 1985.

Kirkpatrick, Donald L. *More Evaluating Training Programs*. Alexandria, Va.: American Society for Training and Development, 1988.

Robinson, John. "Beam Me Up, Scotty." *Training & Development Journal* (February, 1988): 46–48.

Rosnow, Jerome M. and Robert Zager. *Training — The Competitive Edge*. San Francisco, Calif.: Jossey-Bass, 1988.

Swanson, Richard A. and Deane B. Gradous. *Forecasting Financial Benefits of Human Resource Development*. San Francisco, Calif.: Jossey-Bass, 1988.

Wolman, Rebekah. "Is There A HyperCard In Your Future." *CBT Directions* (May/June, 1988): 20–25.

Zimmer, Markus B. "A Practical Guide to Videoconferencing." *Training & Development Journal* (May, 1988): 84–89.

PART 4

CHANGES AND CHALLENGES OF OFFICE AUTOMATION

CHAPTER 17

Human Factors in the Automated Office

OBJECTIVES

After studying this chapter, you should understand the following:

1. What constitutes the field of human factors
2. How human factors affect systems design
3. How the human mind acts as an information processing system
4. How human factors affect computer interfaces
5. The significance of the social context to organizations
6. Types of systems support
7. The role of peer support in the informal organization
8. The benefits of informal systems support to the organization
9. The necessity for management of informal systems support
10. How corporate climate influences informal systems support
11. The role of office politics in career success

This chapter focuses on the field of human factors as applied to the technical and social systems in organizations. As "high tech" increases in the work environment, a corresponding need arises for "high touch." Human factors play this important role in organizations today.

THE HUMAN FACTORS FIELD

Just what is meant by human factors? The term human factors is primarily found in North America, whereas almost everywhere else, the preferred designation is ergonomics. For all practical purposes the two terms are synonymous. Simply put, **human factors** concerns design for human use. A more complete definition is that the human factors field discovers and applies information about human abilities, limitations, and other characteristics to the design of tools, machines, systems, tasks, jobs, and environments for safe, comfortable, and effective human use. The field of human factors is multidisciplinary, drawing from engineering, anthropometry (a science dealing with measurements of the human body), psychology, and computer science. Human factors emerged as a field of study during World War II with emphasis on war-related designs, but today reference to ergonomics is common, for example, in advertisements ranging from automobiles to computers.[1]

The worldwide umbrella organization for human factors specialists is the International Ergonomics Association; however, in the U.S. the division of this society is called the Human Factors Society. The U.S. society supports several special interest groups (SIGs) such as computer systems, environmental design, and industry ergonomics and publishes the journal *Human Factors.* Other professional organizations in the U.S. dealing with human factors include the American Psychological Association (APA), the Institute of Electrical and Electronics Engineers (IEEE), and the Association for Computing Machinery (ACM).

Human factors specialists are largely employed in business and industry and colleges and universities. Other sources of employment for human factors specialists include the military, government, and self-employment as consultants. Employment opportunities for human factors specialists are growing as society increasingly expects developing technology to accommodate human needs.[2]

This societal expectation represents a change from the approach of the past when the implementation of automation was typically technology driven. This approach viewed the individual as more flexible than the technology, and the employee was ex-

1. Alphonse Chapanis, "Introduction to Human Factors Considerations in Systems Design," *Human Factors Considerations in Systems Design* (NASA Conference Proceedings 2246, 1982), 12.

2. Chapanis, pp. 20–23.

pected to change to accommodate it. With a **human factors approach** the human and technical systems are both subject to redesign. The result can be an organization with appropriate ergonomics and enriched jobs with optimal production and employee satisfaction and comfort.[3]

PHILOSOPHY AND OBJECTIVES OF HUMAN FACTORS

The philosophy of human factors is a simple one—to make designs to serve people. Such designs can be said to be user driven rather than technology driven. Such a philosophy provides for recognition of individual differences. The objectives of human factors are to enhance the effectiveness and efficiency of the work process and to enhance certain desirable human values such as improved safety, reduced fatigue and stress, increased comfort, greater user acceptance, increased job satisfaction, and improved quality of work life.[4] The study of human factors can be applied to many areas, such as building, office, and workstation design as presented in Chapter 10. This chapter moves beyond those commonly discussed aspects of ergonomics to provide a more global view of the socio-technical aspects of organizations.

HUMAN FACTORS IN SYSTEMS DESIGN

A consideration of human factors can improve the design of any system. The widespread use of computer-related technical systems in organizations today has benefited greatly from this application of human factors knowledge. Some of these contributions to systems design with special focus on computer systems are presented below:

1. *The establishment of user requirements.* This contribution of human factors is especially noticeable in the area of personal computer and workstation design. Here knowledge of individual differences in the physical and mental capabilities and limitations of users ranging from novice to expert and from generalist to specialist are incorporated into the design of computer systems.
2. *The development of systems design.* Human factors assists in the development of prototypes followed by testing and evalu-

---

3. Ann Majchrzak, *The Human Side of Factory Automation: Managerial and Human Resource Strategies for Making Automation Succeed* (San Francisco, Calif.: Jossey-Bass Publishers, 1988), 74.

4. Mark S. Sanders and Ernest J. McCormick, *Human Factors in Engineering and Design,* 6th ed. (New York: McGraw-Hill Book Co., 1987), 5.

ation in the systems design process. Computer and software vendors, for example, extensively test their new products in their laboratories before market release.

3. *The development of system documentation.* System documentation (written instructions) often is too technical or sketchily written to be helpful for the typical end user. With the application of human factors, more user-friendly system documentation can result. For example, on-line help may be programmed directly into the software for instant access eliminating the need for extensive searching in a thick user's manual.

4. *The establishment of personnel requirements.* In designing a system, consideration should be given to the number of workers required for its efficient and effective operation and to the skills required of the system operators. The criteria for staff selection, for example, could be established as a direct outgrowth of job and task design. Once workers are selected, training should be administered to ensure productive system operation. Various methods of instruction could then be used to accommodate individual differences in learning styles.

5. *Product testing.* This application of human factors consists of testing the product to see if it can do what it was designed to do. Such testing involves the use of human subjects before the product reaches the ultimate end user in the field. Vendors, for example, often use their own employees in their own offices to test the performance of new hardware and software products under normal office conditions.

6. *Installation and maintenance.* With the application of human factors to the installation process, user requirements can be accommodated instead of only technical requirements. For example, workstations can be situated for the convenience of the users rather than for the convenience of the cabling. In another example, diagnostic software assists in systems maintenance to help users determine the nature of a hardware problem and possible solutions.

7. *Evaluation.* Human factors can be applied to the evaluation process of systems design by on-going monitoring of problems encountered by users in the work environment. Such monitoring usually results in further improvements to the design.[5]

THE HUMAN-COMPUTER SYSTEM

Applying the study of human factors to systems design has resulted in the humanizing of technology. Interestingly, human

5. Chapanis, op. cit., 17–19.

factors specialists also study the human mind as a system. The likening of the human mind to an information processing system is referred to as the **Human Processor Model.** While initially this model may appear novel, the human mind, like the computer, is capable of receiving, storing, and transmitting information. These processing capabilities are controlled by the human's senses (e.g., vision, hearing, touching), memory, and cognitive (intellectual) powers. The user of a word processing program, for example, uses mental and visual capabilities to interpret instructions, formulate a sequence of commands, and physically communicate these commands to the computer.[6] Combining the information processing capabilities of the human and the computer yields a **human-computer system.** Figure 17-1 illustrates how the human-computer system interacts. As the figure shows, interaction occurs with the use of computer interfaces.

Figure 17-1   The Human-Computer System

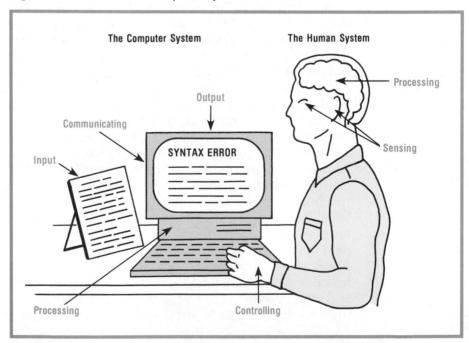

Source: Adapted from Mark S. Sanders and Ernest J. McCormick, *Human Factors in Engineering and Design*, 6th ed. (New York: McGraw-Hill, 1987), 13.

6.   Stuart K. Card, Thomas P. Moran, and Allen Newell, *The Psychology of Human-Computer Interaction* (Hillsdale, N.J.: Lawrence Erlbaum Associates, Publishers, 1983), 24.

THE HUMAN-COMPUTER INTERFACE

Rapidly becoming one of the most important topics of study in the field of human factors is the human-computer interface. The concept of the **human-computer interface** refers to the interaction of the human and computer systems based upon a given set of inputs to bring about a desired output. An interface refers to a point of interaction between two systems. Keyboards, visual screen displays, printers, and computer programs are all examples of human-computer interfaces. Human factors have significantly influenced the design of computer interfaces in such areas as the use of menus, icons, and function keys. (Attention to such physical properties of computer design has been addressed elsewhere in this text and is not the focus of this chapter.)

THE HUMAN-COMPUTER DIALOGUE

A key notion in the concept of the human-computer interface is that of the **human-computer communicative dialogue.** Communication is considered to be the proper term because both the user and the computer have access to a symbolic flow of information, which can affect the responses of each. As in conversation, both parties, user and computer, can interrupt, query, and correct the communication that flows between them.[7] This is a radical departure from the past when, for example, secretaries *operated* typewriters to accomplish a task; they did not *communicate* with typewriters. The interaction between the human-computer system, however, is not the only example of human factors in the socio-technical systems in organizations. Other systems are also involved.

ORGANIZATIONAL DESIGN

A helpful model for understanding how human factors affect the design of organizational systems is the **Open Systems Model** presented by Nadler and Tushman. (The open systems concept was first discussed in Chapter 2.) In this model the core of the organization is comprised of four components: the task, the individual, the formal organization, and the informal organization. These components are affected by inputs external to the organization, such as the environment. The interaction of the organizational systems results in outputs affecting the individual,

---

7. Card, Moran, and Newell, 4–7.

the group, and the total organization. Figure 17-2 illustrates the Open Systems Model for diagnosing organizational behavior.

Figure 17-2   **Open Systems Model for Diagnosing Organizational Behavior**

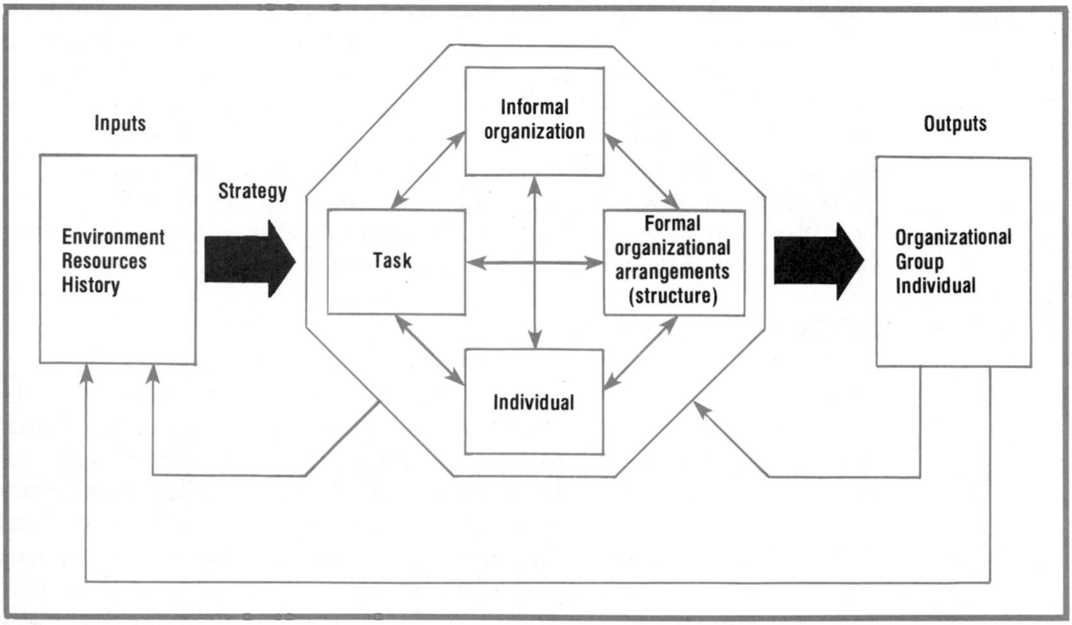

Source: D. A. Nadler and M. L. Tushman, "A Congruence Model for Diagnosing Organizational Behavior," in *Organizational Psychology*, 3rd ed., edited by David Kolb, Irwin Rubin, and James McIntyre (New York: Prentice-Hall, 1980), 451. Reprinted by permission.

All four organizational components can be affected by human factors. The task component involves the work of the organization, including its skill and knowledge demands. Human factors play an important role in task design, discussed elsewhere in this text. The individual component refers to the characteristics of individuals in the organization, including their knowledge and skills, needs and preferences, perceptions, and expectations. The field of human factors studies how these human qualities can affect the design of organizational systems. The formal organization includes its organizational structure and job designs. Human factors affect the formal organization in such areas as design of its organizational hierarchy and jobs; however, these topics are discussed elsewhere in this text and are not the focus of this chapter. The informal organization consists of arrangements such as leadership and influencing behavior, inter- and intragroup relations, and communication patterns. This chapter is concerned with the role of human factors in the informal organization with the focus of discussion on informal systems support and office politics.

According to Nadler and Tushman, the critical activity for an organization is recognizing the nature of the interaction of system components. The dynamics of the relationship between the components of the system is what contributes to organizational effectiveness. In addition, Nadler and Tushman caution that not only the dynamics need to be observed but also how well the components complement each other. For example, the needs of the individuals in the organization may not be met by its formal structure but by its informal structure.[8]

SOCIAL ERGONOMICS

The field of human factors is concerned with context as well as form. **Form** refers to aspects of design controlled by the designer, for example, screen displays. **Context** refers to the social system or surrounding environment (sometimes referred to as social ergonomics) into which systems design "fits." Both the formal and the informal structure of the organization would be included in its context.

In Chapter 2, discussion centered on the formal structure and how it affects the flow of authority. In this chapter emphasis is placed on the informal structure and how it affects the information flow and individual career success. The **information flow** is a comprehensive term representing the flow of information that takes place among the systems, documents, and users. The term "information flow" embraces information sources including manuals, other people, and various systems interfaces.[9]

Information received from the informal structure can be powerful in helping users learn about their systems and their organizations. For example, studies of office activities have reported that the informal social network in organizations serve important psychological functions for office employees such as providing companionship and emotional support. Of even more importance was the finding that informal social interaction is also crucial to the actual performance of office work itself.[10]

8.   Majchrzak, op. cit., 10–12.

9.   Donald A. Norman and Stephen W. Draper, editors, *User-Centered System Design: New Perspectives on Human-Computer Interaction* (Hillsdale, N.J.: Lawrence Erlbaum Associates, Publishers, 1986), 353.

10.   Liam J. Bannon, "Helping Users Help Each Other," in Donald A. Norman and Stephen W. Draper, editors, *User-Centered System Design: New Perspectives on Human-Computer Interaction* (Hillsdale, N.J.: Lawrence Erlbaum Associates, Publishers, 1986), 402.

Figure 17-3 Informal social networks at the office affect performance in positive ways.

SYSTEMS SUPPORT

The function of **systems support** in an organization refers to various forms of assistance, both human and electronic, available to users of systems. Systems support can be part of both the formal and the informal organization. An information center, for example, would generally be part of the formal organization and, as such, would be pictured on an organizational chart with its director. In this chapter the focus is on systems support in the informal organization. User-validated system documentation distributed through an electronic mail system or electronic bulletin board is an example of electronic support in the informal organization. An example of human support in the informal organization would be assistance provided by peers (individuals of the same organizational rank) who are not officially designated by their organization as in-house systems consultants. Even in organizations with formal systems support, as much as 80 percent of the total systems support received by users is still given by peers.[11]

11. Elliott Masie and Rebekah Wolman, *The Computer Training Handbook* (Raquette Lake, N.Y.: National Training & Computers Project, Sagamore Institute, 1988), 247.

PEER SUPPORT

People tend to prefer to ask other people for help. Reasons for this preference for human assistance are many. Formal training is often too generalized and not task related. Many manuals are too technical or otherwise unhelpful to users. Accumulating evidence indicates that users do not read manuals, no matter how well written. One study showed that several attempts to rewrite system documentation to improve clarity still failed to make an appreciable difference to users. Such a finding does not mean that written manuals, computer tutorials, or on-line help should be abandoned. The finding does suggest that options should be provided to users for locating systems information. Also the finding indicates that organizations need to become aware of the role of informal systems support and permit the organizational structure to accommodate such support.

When users turn to other people for systems support, whom do they seek? The people chosen most often are colleagues, people in close physical proximity to the user, and friends. The expertise of these peers lies not so much in their being able to solve any problem immediately but in their skill in data gathering and in their ability to exploit informational resources, such as manuals.

In an informal survey reported by Bannon, administrative and clerical interviewees all commented that their major source of information about computer systems was other users. The users reported acquiring this systems information by directly querying others and in casual encounters with peers in offices and other meeting places such as lounges and cafeterias. One new employee expressed the opinion that sharing an office with a more experienced computer user was the ideal environment for solving computer difficulties and picking up "over the shoulder" hints on computer use.[12]

However, users do not have to be "new" to an organization or even novice computer users to benefit from informal systems support. With the increasing complexity of computer systems, even experienced users can succumb to cognitive overload (inability to process mentally the deluge of available information), be subject to task uncertainty in particular applications, or have gaps in their knowledge of particular systems. In addition, the stress associated with the need for continuous learning of new or updated systems, all point to the obvious need for providing users with all the systems support they can get. As users develop proficiency in systems, their dependence on other people should

12.   Bannon, op. cit., 401–403.

decrease. Such systems sophistication can stem from a facility for searching manuals, interpreting program code, and learning from experimentation.[13]

User Selection of Peers.   Investigation has revealed why users prefer to use other people as their prime source of systems support. The particular person chosen by a user would be governed by circumstances and the personal weight that a user might attach to the following reasons:

1. Organizational Rank: (sometimes a user may be less inclined to ask a superior)
2. Technical Expertise: (local experts in various procedures and applications)
3. Sociability: (how approachable a person is)
4. Reciprocity: (favor giving and receiving status)
5. Accessibility: (physical proximity as same office, floor)
6. Availability: (how free or busy one is)
7. Organizational Role: (official status as in-house consultant)
8. Shared Experiences: (similarity in backgrounds)[14]

User Requests for Support.   When users need help, what information is usually requested? The following list cites the kinds of information that users typically seek:

1. File names
2. Little recipes (examples) for the key strokes to get some neat or useful effect
3. Getting into a system or subsystem
4. A minimum set of commands
5. Advanced commands
6. Where to get information
7. Efficiency—neater ways to do things
8. How things work
9. Strategies for combining system programs for user tasks
10. Recognizing information when it's there (e.g., learning to interpret screen prompts)
11. How to use information you have
12. How to recover from errors
13. What is commonly done on this system (i.e., standard user tasks and standard plans for accomplishing them)[15]

13.   Bannon, 404.
14.   Norman and Draper, op. cit., 354.
15.   John Seely Brown, "From Cognitive to Social Ergonomics and Beyond," in Donald A. Norman and Stephen W. Draper, editors, *User Centered System Design: New Perspectives on Human-Computer Interaction* (Hillsdale, N.J.: Lawrence Erlbaum Associates, Publishers, 1986), 472.

Benefits of Informal Systems Support.   Use of the social system as a means of informal systems support can be beneficial to organizations. A collaborative spirit can develop among employees that can foster teamwork. The mutual sharing of information by users builds a body of community systems knowledge. The conceptualization and verbalization by employees of systems knowledge serves to reinforce systems learning and often leads to a greater willingness on the part of employees to experiment with their systems. Some organizations, however, may fail to receive these benefits because their management does not recognize the potential value of the informal organization to systems support.

CORPORATE CLIMATE AND INFORMAL SYSTEMS SUPPORT

The corporate climate (discussed in Chapter 2) can encourage or discourage prevailing corporate attitudes toward informal systems support. The effectiveness of the human-computer system depends upon the interplay of the socio-technical systems. Employee behavior will be strongly affected by system synergy. An unfavorable corporate climate would be displayed when employees are reluctant to ask others for systems support, are deterred by management from using their systems more creatively, and are restricted by office layout from the informal exchange of systems knowledge. Such organizations will ultimately suffer from possibly inaccurate output, lost productivity, and lost opportunities to enhance employee morale and learning.

Why would any organization allow such an unfavorable corporate climate for informal systems support to exist? If the office environment is operating under a work measurement program, its employees may feel that time lost in casual conversation is lost money. Some managers may feel that, if a user's job description does not include systems support, the user is not performing the job properly and may penalize such behavior. Another possibility is that some managers may consider users incompetent who ask for systems help.

MANAGING INFORMAL SYSTEMS SUPPORT

Management should recognize that informal systems support needs to be monitored and managed. Systems support needs to be accurate and consistent with organizational standards. In addition, systems support should empower users; that is, work to achieve relatively independent users instead of encouraging dependency upon the local office "wizard." A management expectation of perfection in the systems knowledge of users is unrealistic. Management should realize that even experts must ask for help, continuously learn new systems, and engage in guessing. The "wizards," too, need to be supported with appropriate documentation to give to users and means to acquire support of their own for user problems that they are unable to handle.[16] If the corporate climate does not actively encourage informal systems support, then management can change the climate.

Managers can serve as change agents in their organizations. **Change agents** are persons who plan and conduct activities designed to bring about a modification of the environment. Change agents can alter the corporate climate through a planned process of change. Employees who have been discouraged from participating in informal systems support will need to be strongly motivated to change their behavior.

A model originally developed by psychologist Kurt Lewin could be adopted by managers desiring to effect change. This **Lewin Change Model**[17] suggests that the organization "unfreeze" the employees' current behavior. "Unfreezing" activity could involve a series of user meetings to share systems concerns. Next, users can be "moving forward" while their behavior is being modified (e.g., through formal training or redesigning the office layout to promote more casual peer interaction). The final stage of the model is to "refreeze" the organization into the new behavior. A "refreeze" activity could involve rewarding users for helping peers with their systems problems.

OFFICE POLITICS

One component of the informal organization that is deeply enmeshed in human factors is the political system. Out of this system arises the situation known as office politics. Office politics is ubiquitous in organizations and is generally a fact of corporate life. To believe that one can function in organizations and not encounter office politics is naive and unrealistic. An understanding of office politics is as vital to career success as one's knowledge of office systems.

Office politics involves an individual or group (often a clique) within an organization working against other individuals or group(s) in order to acquire power and status within that organization. At the core of understanding office politics is this

16. Masie and Wolman, loc. cit.
17. Kurt Lewin, *Field Theory and Social Science* (New York: Harper & Row, 1951).

fact: Individuals possess complex psychological needs such as self-esteem, power, and status which they need to maintain or enhance. Such needs permeate the human system of any organization. Corporate activity that is perceived by individuals as threatening to these needs can result in counter-behavior to mediate or reverse its effect.

TURF PROTECTION

One of the most common displays of office politics occurs as turf protection. **Turf protection** refers to the defense of a territory or domain that an individual perceives as one's own. For example, if a proposal is presented to merge office systems with data processing, the office systems manager would generally respond to the proposal with an arsenal of reasons for its defeat. Such resistance may occur even if the proposed merger is extremely logical and cost effective. Because the proposal would most likely reduce the status and power of the office systems manager while increasing these same qualities in the data processing manager, conflict can be expected. In such cases, office politics can become overtly ugly when an individual resorts to deliberately undermining another using legitimate or even illegitimate means to protect his or her own turf.

Office politics can also be displayed in subtle ways. For example, some individuals may resist sharing their knowledge because of their perceived need to guard their area of expertise.

Figure 17-4 An employee may protect his or her turf in various ways when threatened.

Such behavior could be explained by an assortment of fears. For example, these individuals may fear that if others understand their job operations, their procedures will be challenged, leading to changes in how they perform their work. Thoughts of change are disturbing and distressing to most people. Some systems professionals may be motivated by a need to keep their work shrouded in a veil of mystery and obfuscation, believing that secretive behavior enhances their status in the organization. Such individuals may even fear that they could lose their job if they shared job-related information with others.

POLITICAL RELATIONSHIPS

Another aspect of office politics is immersed in the area of political relationships. Smart office politics dictate that individuals who desire some action favorable to their own cause will engage in "politicking" in order to gain support for their cause. If other individuals disagree in a hostile fashion or otherwise seek to block the occurrence of such a cause, enmity may result. The reason for this is that some individuals perceive opposition to their beliefs or ideas as personal criticism.

Displays of political relationships are rampant within organizations. As stated in Chapter 2, the key power figures in an organization may not even be listed on the organizational chart. New employees can expect to be encircled by colleagues vying for their attention in order to assess their niche in the organizational ecosystem. Once assessed, efforts might be made by these office mates to use the newcomer to solidify or enhance their organizational status, garner favors, block rivals, or lobby for their causes.

POLITICAL SURVIVAL

How can one survive office politics? Become a master politician! While some might think of office politics as a "game" that they prefer not to play, the truth is that all organizational members by their very presence are in the game whether they like it or not. Remember that it is the quality of the interaction among the systems that determines organizational effectiveness. Office work is team work. A simple reliance upon your knowledge of office systems will not be enough for you to achieve career success. You must learn to "play ball" with all of your teammates.

How do you play the organization game? Learn as much as possible about your organization. Study the players. Align yourself with the winners. Avoid losers. Their constant whine of cynicism and negativism can work to erode the positive and professional attitude needed to achieve career success. Nonetheless, treat all teammates with respect and dignity. Observe what constitutes the "right moves" in the organization; so when the opportunity arises for your "big play," you will be ready. Express differences of opinion in a calm and nonthreatening way. Never harbor revenge or demonstrate ill feelings toward others because they disagree with you. How you respond to conflict will be closely observed by your teammates. The very individuals with whom you are in conflict today may be needed as your allies in the near future. If you desire career success, you cannot afford to alienate anyone— ever. By always behaving courteously and responsibly, you will earn the respect of your colleagues and can generally expect to reap the rewards of career success.[18]

WOHL'S BUSINESS PERSPECTIVE

The office of the future we read about in science fiction and see in futuristic movies seems peopled with robots and strange machines. But the office of the current and near future, the one we live and work in, is highly automated yet populated with ordinary human beings.

Humans and machines live together in today's office in an uneasy alliance. The humans are never quite sure what the machines want them to do—and the machines find the humans a somewhat unreliable source of information and direction!

Better times are coming.

The end of the eighties marked the end of the old-style computer interface. No longer will humans feel incompetent because they can't understand how to make their needs known to their computer partners. (And the computers will be a lot less frustrated, too). We'll substantially decrease all those frustrating exchanges where the computer hollers "Illegal Entry" or "Command Not Recognized" because the human and the computer are both more literate.

New-style computer interfaces understand that most humans aren't designed to memorize meaningless strings of characters. Instead humans will get to read from menus (lists) of English (or French or Japanese) words, offering meaningful alternatives, backed up by on-line help.

Users will have alternative ways of viewing their options. Some will choose to use simplified drawings, representing activities and sets of information. These "icons" permit the user to point at what he/she wants and select it. No memorization required here! Others will choose to use lists ordered by date, by name, or by type (letter? file folder? application program?).

18. Gerald L. Hershey, *Supervising Office Systems Personnel* (Englewood Cliffs, N.J.: Prentice-Hall, Inc., 1985), 61–66.

Better yet, cognitive psychology has shown interface designers how to order lists (and hone them down to size) so that a human brain-sized bundle of choices is all we get to see at one time. No more fifty-item menus or three-page directories or ten-page Help glossaries, without a clue as to how to proceed. Instead users will view a series of short lists, focusing in, closer and closer, until they reach the information they need.

Even better, a new level of human-computer interaction is beginning to appear. Based on Hypertext, it permits the human user to browse the computer for related information. Initially, relationships must be conveyed to the computer by another human. For instance, if I'm reading some history of the American Revolutionary War and I come upon George Washington, I could move to other references on George himself.

Eventually, the computer will be able to intuit information relationships based on rules (a kind of expert system). This referential use of Hypertext permits the human to see all of human knowledge (or at least the part of it accessible from his/her computer) as a kind of seamless, infinitely interrelated whole. Access at any point permits access to any related information. Users' computer workstations become Knowledge Navigators (Apple Computer's term), permitting them to freely negotiate the information cosmos.

SUMMARY

The field of human factors concerns design for human use. The formal definition of human factors states that the field discovers and applies information about human abilities, limitations, and other characteristics to the design of tools, machines, systems, tasks, jobs, and environments for safe, comfortable, and effective human use. The term human factors is preferred in North America, whereas the term ergonomics is preferred in the rest of the world. The terms, however, are considered to be synonymous. Human factors is a multidisciplinary field, drawing from engineering, anthropometry, psychology and computer science. The field of human factors is growing because of the changing expectations of society that design should accommodate the needs of people. Such design is said to be user driven rather than technology driven.

Human factors have assumed critical importance in systems design with the widespread use of computers. The contributions of human factors to systems design include the establishment of user requirements, the development of prototypes, system documentation, the establishment of personnel requirements, product testing, installation and maintenance, and evaluation.

Viewing the human mind as an information processing system is referred to as the human processor model. The combination of human-computer capabilities results in an interactive human-computer system. Such interaction, referred to as the human-computer communicative dialogue, occurs with the use of computer interfaces.

The open systems model of Nadler and Tushman presents the organization as comprising four components: task, individual, the formal organization, and the informal organization. The nature of the interaction of the system components determines the effectiveness of the organization.

Human factors is concerned with both form (design controlled by the designer) and context (social ergonomics) or social system of the organization. The informal structure of the organization affects the information flow that takes place among systems, documents, and users. The information flow includes all information resources, including manuals, systems, and people. The informal social network performs a critical function for employees, such as furnishing companionship and emotional support. In addition, informal social interaction is considered crucial to the actual performance of work.

Systems support can be formal or informal, electronic or human. Despite the availability of various means of systems support, people prefer to ask other people for help. Typically the people chosen are colleagues, people in close physical proximity to the user, and friends. The office environment should provide informal meeting places for users to share systems knowledge. Among the benefits to organizations from an informal support system are the development of a collaborative spirit, the building of a community body of systems knowledge, reinforcement of systems learning, and the development of a greater willingness by users to engage in experimentation. Management, however, needs to recognize that informal systems support needs to be monitored and managed in order to attain its benefits. If the corporate climate does not effectively encourage informal systems support, management can undertake a planned process of change involving "unfreezing," "moving forward," and "refreezing."

Office politics is an area deeply engrained in the human system of nearly every organization. Employees need to understand how to use the office political system in order to attain career success in their organizations.

KEY TERMS

human factors	Human Processor Model
human factors approach	human-computer system

human-computer interface	information flow
human-computer communicative dialogue	systems support
	change agent
Open Systems Model	Lewin Change Model
form	office politics
context	turf protection

REVIEW QUESTIONS

1. How does the technology driven approach to automation differ from the human factors approach?

2. Give five examples of the contributions of human factors to computer-systems design.

3. Why do human factors specialists consider the human mind to be an information processing system?

4. Explain the terms "form" and "context" as used by human factors specialists.

5. What is the role of the informal social network in the office?

6. Give an example of each: formal systems support, electronic systems support, informal systems support (nonelectronic).

7. How would you respond to an organization decision to discontinue purchase of systems manuals, videotapes, tutorials, and other learning aids because the office manager has just read that people are the major source of systems support for administrative and clerical employees?

8. What are the benefits to organizations of informal systems support?

9. Why would an office manager discourage informal systems support?

10. Do you feel it is necessary to play the organizational "game" in order to achieve career success? Defend your answer.

CASE STUDY: THE CASE OF THE SHATTERED DREAM

Ruby Singh, an Indian immigrant living in New York, was recently hired as an administrative assistant at the India Trading Company, an import-export firm with offices in the U.S. and Bombay. To Ruby, her new job seemed like a dream come true. She was delighted with the company's exotic, multicultural environment, her private office, and the prospects of using her computer experience in an organization serving both her old and new homelands. On Ruby's first day on the job, Mr. Raj, the company's office manager, commented that the India Trading Company had invested a "small fortune" in the new office systems to keep the company on the leading edge of technology. He also praised Ruby's systems background, expressing his high expectations of her and confidence that she would quickly "pick up" the necessary skills to operate the company's complex office systems. After Ruby completed her formal basic systems training, she received a vendor's systems manual to take back to her workstation.

Ruby served the administrative support needs of five principals. The diversity and specialized nature of her assignments frequently surpassed the limit of the knowledge she had acquired from her initial training. When Ruby encountered difficulty, she thumbed through the thick systems manual to locate the appropriate function. Ruby realized that searching the manual took time, but Gita, an office co-worker, confided in Ruby that Mr. Raj had terminated the employment of Ruby's predecessor for systems incompetence. Ruby felt that Mr. Raj would be disappointed in her if she asked questions, and she did not want to do anything that might negatively affect her first performance appraisal.

One morning soon after Ruby started her job, Mr. Raj asked her to process an intricate report he needed that afternoon. Scanning the report, Ruby realized that it would require the use of several functions with which she was unfamiliar. Ruby asked Gita how to handle the functions; however, Gita could not help her because she had no experience with this type of report. Gita, however, referred her to Mel Weinstein, the company's unofficial "office systems wizard." Mel did help Ruby with her problem, but Ruby noticed that Mel seemed rushed and uncomfortable while doing so. Ruby returned to her workstation, completed the report, and submitted it to Mr. Raj. Soon thereafter, Mr. Raj returned the report to Ruby with a note. Scrawled across the very section that had caused her difficulty, were the words, "Follow standard company procedures!" Ruby felt embarrassed and frustrated. She decided she had no alternative but to ask Mr. Raj for help. On the way to her manager's office, Ruby observed Mel being reprimanded by Mr. Raj for spending too much time away from his own work being a "computer tutor" for others. Ruby was stunned. Her dream job had turned into a nightmare.

QUESTIONS/ACTIVITIES

1. Describe the social context of the India Trading Company. What effect does this context appear to be having on (a) its employees and (b) the organization?

2. Describe a comprehensive plan of action that could be undertaken to improve the corporate climate at the India Trading Company.

SUGGESTED READINGS

Card, Stuart K., Thomas P. Moran, and Allen Newell. *The Psychology of Human-Computer Interaction.* Hillsdale, N.J.: Lawrence Erlbaum Associates, Publishers, 1983.

Christie, Bruce, editor. *Human Factors of Information Technology in the Of-*

fice. Chichester, England: John Wiley & Sons, 1985.

Cohen, Barbara G. F., editor. *Human Aspects in Office Automation.* Amsterdam, The Netherlands: Elsevier, 1984.

Galitz, Wilbert O. *Humanizing Office Automation.* Wellesley, Mass.: QED Information Sciences, Inc., 1984.

Hirschheim, R. A. *Office Automation: A Social and Organizational Perspective.* Chichester, England: John Wiley & Sons, 1985.

Karwowski, Waldemar, editor. *Trends in Ergonomics/Human Factors III.* Amsterdam, The Netherlands: North-Holland, 1986.

Long, Richard J. *New Office Information Technology: Human and Managerial Implications.* London, England: Croom Helm, 1987.

Miletich, Leo N. "A Business Bestiary." *Administrative Management* (April, 1988): 11–13.

Nickerson, Raymond S. *Using Computers: The Human Factors of Information Systems.* Cambridge, Mass.: MIT Press, 1986.

Norman, Donald A. and Stephen W. Draper, editors. *User Centered System Design: New Perspectives on Human-Computer Interaction.* Hillsdale, N.J.: Lawrence Erlbaum Associates, Publishers, 1986.

Salvendy, Gavriel, editor. *Handbook of Human Factors.* New York: John Wiley & Sons, 1987.

Sanders, Mark S. and Ernest J. McCormick. *Human Factors in Engineering and Design,* 6th ed. New York: McGraw-Hill, 1987.

Schneiderman, B. *Software Psychology: Human Factors in Computer and Information Systems.* Boston, Mass.: Little-Brown, 1980.

Walton, Richard E. "People Policies for the New Machines." *Harvard Business Review* (March–April, 1987): 98.

Zemke, Ron. "Sociotechnical Systems: Bringing People and Technology Together." *Training* (February, 1987): 47–49, 52, 57.

Handwritten notes at top of page:

Job ↑ trends

Human (Jobs)
- decreased work week
  (temporary)
- Job sharing
- Flextime
  - middle management
    will decrease
  - repetitive jobs
    will disappear.
  - Location

hardware
↓
3 yrs. diff.
like a new car

Software

CHAPTER 18

Future Systems Trends

OBJECTIVES

After studying this chapter, you should understand the following:

1. How futurists forecast change

2. How economic, political, social, and conceptual changes will affect organizations and offices

3. How information technology is affecting organizational structure and management

4. Job trends for office personnel

5. Primary trends affecting technological developments

6. The future hardware generation

7. The future software generation

8. A philosophy for the future

Predictions of the future have fascinated people down through the ages. The prophets and seers of yesterday have been replaced by the futurists of today. **Futurists** are individuals who forecast what will exist or happen in the future. Many changes are about to be unleashed upon society during the information age. While no one can predict with complete accuracy what these changes will be, methods for prediction have improved considerably from the days of the crystal ball or stargazing. For example, today futurists use methods such as trend analysis and visioning. **Trend analysis** is a forecasting method used to interpret developments in society's systems (social, economic, political, legal, ethical, and so on). **Visioning** refers to the process of foreseeing something not currently discernible. One way in which futurists use visioning is to identify future values to assist them in formulating relationships among society's systems. Both of these methods help futurists state the probable based upon assumptions of known facts and observations. Use of these forecasting methods yields "seeds of the future" from which futurists make predictions ranging from the plausible (telecommunications is to become the largest industry in the world) to the awesome (a permanently manned space outpost is to be established on Mars by 2030).

THE FUTURISTIC OFFICE

Some of the predictions made regarding the office of the future have been equally thought provoking. For example, some futurists claim that automation will lead to the death of the secretary and bring forth virtually peopleless office environments primarily inhabited by secretarial robots.

A more realistic portrayal of the office of the future includes people using integrated, computerized systems to perform organizational functions. This description does not include a physical location because of the impact of telecommunications. Growth of electronic mail, cellular phones, cellular radios (paging devices popularly known as beepers), portable telephones, and airfones (telephones used while in flight) enable office activities to happen almost anywhere. Another element missing from the description of the office of the future is a designated time period. This omission exists because the future is always tomorrow. What is considered today to be a state-of-the-art development can quickly become obsolete. As Figure 18-1 illustrates, visions of the office of the future continue to evolve with technology.

The effect of technological change is easily recognizable in the office environment. For example, newly purchased hardware and software become increasingly outdated with each introduction of updated equipment or software. Some say the office of the future exists now but that it is in its early developmental stages. Others claim that the office of the future always will be an elusive goal. Nevertheless, the destiny of the office has been forecasted by many futurists.

Futuristic thinking about the direction and extent of changes predicted to affect organizations and offices will be presented in this chapter using a sociotechnical systems approach. This approach, involving both human and technical considerations, is taken because the office of the future will not exist in a vacuum.

Figure 18-1 **Offices of the Future**

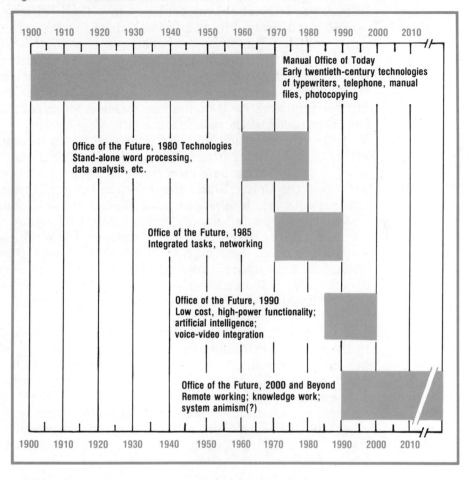

Source: V. Douglas Hines, *Office Automation: Tools and Methods for System Building* (New York: John Wiley & Sons), 449.

Broad trends emanating from the many facets of society need to be examined to help initiate an orderly preparation for change.

SOCIETAL TRENDS

The many changes predicted for the information age will influence the operation of organizations. These changes of an economic, political, social, and conceptual nature will impact on traditional organizational structure, work procedures, and forms of management.

Changes in the economy will affect all organizations because in order to survive they must be aware of and responsive to economic conditions. Fluctuations in the economy affect costs for rent, utilities, supplies, and labor. Increasingly organizations must be cognizant not only of conditions in the domestic economy but also among international economies. Such awareness is necessary because by the end of the century two hundred to three hundred multinational businesses (MNBs) are expected to account for 50 percent of the world's output.[1]

International trade, coupled with aggressive foreign marketing strategies, requires organizations to develop global consciousness in order to compete effectively in a world economy. Organizations in the United States must contend not only with traditional competitors, such as Japan and West Germany, but also with lesser developed nations in the Far East and Latin America, such as South Korea and Brazil. Such nations are working especially hard to increase their high-tech industrial bases. By making the transition to an information-based economy, nations are hopeful of creating increased economic opportunities for their populations.

The direction of a nation's economic development often is significantly affected by its political climate. The old Spanish proverb, *saber es poder* (knowledge is power), aptly applies to trends in the political economy. In the past, nations struggled to acquire power by becoming land-rich; today, the goal is to become information-rich. One futurist has said, "The trade wars of the past will become the information wars of the future."[2] Although information-based societies can be brought closer together because of the power of telecommunication, the danger of serious conflicts can also arise as the technology gap widens between the have and have-not nations.

In addition to economic and political changes, nations must gird themselves for coming changes in their social system. Social alienation, the erosion of traditional values, and loss of cultural cohesion may occur just as every infusion of information into a society in the past has produced a disruptive effect. For example, the invention of the printing press is credited not only with the spread of mass literacy but also for the profound social revolution that followed its introduction.[3] Such dangers for nations are far greater today because scientific and technical information now

1.   Harold Fearon *et al.*, "Management to the Year 2000," *Arizona Business*, Vol. 28, No. 4 (April, 1981): 10.

2.   Eugene Galenter, "Computers Will Unravel the Fabric of Our Social and Working Lives," *Words* (June-July, 1984): 20.

3.   Wilson P. Dizard, Jr., *The Coming Information Age: An Overview of Technology, Economics, and Politics* (New York: Longman, Inc., 1982), 150.

Figure 18-2 U.S. organizations must develop a global consciousness in order to compete effectively in a world economy.
Kentucky Fried Chicken

increases 13 percent annually, which means that it doubles every 5.5 years.[4] Such an increase is unprecedented for any age.

Another expected effect of an information-based society will be increases in white-collar crime. Such business crime is the fastest growing crime category in the United States and includes activities such as bank embezzlement with the use of computer programs, illegal access to data banks, and the theft and sale of confidential, computerized information. Computer-related crimes in the U.S. alone have been estimated at more than $500 million a year, and predictions are that this figure will rise to $1 billion a year by 1990 and beyond $3 billion a year by 2000. Computer crimes won't be the only concern of citizens of information-based societies. The expected increase in the use of electronic surveil-

4.   John Naisbitt, *Megatrends: Ten New Directions Transforming Our Lives* (New York: W. W. Norton & Co., Inc., 1984), 24.

lance and wiretapping devices will add realism to the fear of a society controlled by big brother, as depicted in Orwell's novel *1984.*[5] As troubling as these social problems might appear, even more far-reaching changes are predicted for the most basic of society's foundations—its conceptual base.

The very way people think about the world (this conceptual base) is slated to change during the information age. Ultimately this will amount to what has been called the most profound series of changes for civilization since the invention of agriculture. Concepts will be redefined and recharacterized for every aspect of society—including learning, shopping, traveling, healing, socializing, and working. All of these changes are of particular interest because of their implications for the future of organizations and the automated office.

ORGANIZATIONAL TRENDS

Organizations reflect their society. As the economic, political, social, and technical forces change society, so will organizations change. Past notions of how business should be conducted will be replaced by totally new concepts during the information age. Technology in the form of electronic mail and electronic fund transfer, for example, has already made obsolete the old adage that the check is in the mail. Other organizational change, however, evolving from far more subtle societal changes is supposedly destined to reshape the very character of U.S. corporate life.

In the past, corporations were loath to become involved in the private lives of their employees. In the future, according to predictions for the twenty-first century, corporations will become entwined in broad social issues such as education, child care, illiteracy, care of the elderly, broken homes, and teenage pregnancies. What is more, predictions are that organizations ignoring such involvement are doomed to failure. The major reason for this radical change in corporate behavior is because of demographics. Early in the twenty-first century the traditional labor pool of white male workers will shrink while the available labor supply will increasingly include women, blacks, Hispanics, and immigrants. Thus, organizations of the future, to insure themselves of a workforce, may be operating day-care centers and elementary schools, recruiting potential employees directly from high school with offers of college scholarships and jobs afterwards, and providing adult employees with daytime classes in

---

5.   Marvin Cetron and Thomas O'Toole, *Encounters with the Future: A Forecast of Life into the 21st Century* (New York: McGraw-Hill Book Company, 1982), 229–230.

remedial reading, mathematics, English as a second language, and courses in working in a culturally diverse environment.[6] Revolutionary changes such as these are already occurring in forward-thinking organizations. Undoubtedly, these changes, as well as many others still not foreseen, promise to make organizations of the future unique in the annals of corporate history.

THE INFORMATION INFRASTRUCTURE

Organizations are developing a new basic framework in their approach to operations called the **information infrastructure.** This new framework means that information is viewed not only as a strategic resource but also as a management strategy to enhance competitiveness. Examples of the latter include using computers for direct-line ordering systems for customers, instant access to company databases for traveling salespeople, and even the use of the "just-in-time" inventory delivery system. Therefore, the development of an information infrastructure implies the electronic linking of the organization to its suppliers, distributors, customers, and possibly government agencies. Such extensive, integrated networks will change the way businesses interrelate. Organizational benefits claimed from such information management methods include increased customer dependence, improved customer service, staff reduction, lowered production costs, and added value to products.

ALTERNATIVE ORGANIZATIONAL STRUCTURES

Changes are also forecast in traditional organizational structures because of the new role of information. Organizations are being urged to begin thinking in terms of the **"zero-based corporate structure"** just as accountants practice the concept of zero-based budgeting (ZBB). ZBB refers to examining all expenditures anew each budgetary period and justifying their existence instead of automatically adding or decreasing the previous period's figures to obtain the new budget. Therefore, the zero-based concept extended to corporate structure implies a possible total rebuilding of the organization's structure as organizational needs change.[7] This concept, applied to the automated office, was echoed by the internationally renowned management author/consultant, Peter Drucker, who stated, ". . . we have learned that installing new

---

6.   Amanda Bennett, "New Generation Asks More than its Elders of Corporate World," *The Wall Street Journal* (October 26, 1988): A1.

7.   David J. Baker, "Are We Doing the Best We Can With Our Office Systems?" *Administrative Management* (February, 1988): 18.

machinery in the office will not by itself result in more production or in lower costs. To be effective, office automation requires fairly radical changes in work flow, job design, job relationships, and staff. . . ."[8]

Some organizations are already moving away from assigning tasks by traditional work roles and functional divisions. Instead, work is being assigned according to the acceptance of expertise as a legitimate power base. Such change is reflected by the use of the matrix or multiple-reporting structures, project teams, task forces, and appointments of individuals as ad hoc liaisons. These alternative structures, referred to by various terms such as the **cluster organization,** the **network organization,** and **adhocracy,** are often only temporary, permitting more efficient matching of an organization's human resources to appropriate tasks. After these structures have accomplished their mission, they may be dismantled and permanently abandoned. Such alternative organizational structures are blurring the distinction between centralized and decentralized structures. The impact of information technology upon organizational structure appears to support the flexibility and responsiveness of a decentralized organization as well as the integratedness and control of a centralized organization. The end result is that technology is providing organizations with more fluid organizational forms.[9]

FORMS OF MANAGEMENT

Alternative organizational structures will require changes in forms of management. Traditional organizational design reinforces the division of labor whereby mid- and upper-level managers act as "guardians" of information, as distinguished from other staff. The spread of information technology throughout the organization makes it economically feasible to place more work-related knowhow and decision making directly at the operational level. Examples of such futuristic management include the autonomous work group and participative selection. In the **autonomous work group** employees who naturally work together, such as in a department, are given the authority to manage themselves through consensus decison making rather than by taking orders from an organizationally appointed manager. With **participative selection** employees nominate and then vote for the supervisor or manager whom they feel is best qualified to lead

8.   Peter Drucker, "Goodbye to the Old Personnel Department," *The Wall Street Journal* (May 22, 1986): 24.
9.   Lynda M. Applegate, James I. Cash, Jr., and D. Quinn Mills, "Information Technology and Tomorrow's Manager" *Harvard Business Review* (November-December, 1988): 129–130.

them. In addition, predictions are that in some organizations management will be a part-time activity that is routinely shared and rotated. Such management practices will erode the current, sharp distinctions between those who act and those who "manage."

The familiar managerial pyramid is predicted to become flattened in the future. Because of this compressed structure, organizational response to system changes can accelerate. The normal response time from invention to innovation can be a matter of weeks instead of months or years. Organizations will be able to move more quickly from problem identification to problem solution. Such swiftness of operation is being made possible by technological advancements.[10]

While managerial access to electronic devices for information processing and distribution can increase organizational productivity, it can also reduce the need for mid-level managers. Information technology, which once was viewed as a tool for organizational expansion, has become a tool for corporate downsizing and restructuring. On-line executive information systems can do the work of scores of analysts and mid-level managers whose work formerly involved the production of charts and graphs for communication to upper-level management. One estimate is that since 1979 organizations have shed more than one million managers and staff professionals. In addition, forecasts for the decade of the nineties continue to indicate more mergers, takeovers, and downsizing. The most vulnerable group for job displacement as a result of this corporate activity is the mid-level manager.[11] Managers, however, will not be the only members of the work force to experience change in the organizations of the future.

JOB TRENDS

Socioeconomic and technical forces are expected to impact dramatically on jobs. For example, the workweek is expected to be just 25 hours by the year 2000.[12] Jobs of a routine, repetitive nature are due to shrink or disappear. This trend might result in a shortage of jobs for office workers. For example, in 1980 there were 924,000 clerical workers in the insurance industry and 1.1 million in banking, but by the year 2000 forecasts call for 568,000 in insurance and 824,000 in banking.[13]

10. Harold Fearon et al., op. cit., 9.
11. Lynda M. Applegate, James I. Cash, Jr., and D. Quinn Mills, op. cit., 129.
12. Marvin Cetron and Thomas O'Toole, op. cit., 15.
13. Robert M. Mason, "Micros, White-Collar Workers & the Library," Library Journal (November 15, 1984): 2, 132.

Another future work concern involves the nature of workers. Office workers, in particular, compared to those in the past are more sophisticated, better educated, and possess diverse sets of work values. Organizations need to adjust their work systems to accommodate the expectations of this new class of workers. For example, managers may find that financial rewards will motivate some workers while others will desire to earn only enough to support the life-style they desire. Some office workers may expect increasing responsibilities and input into decision making as it affects their jobs; others will not. Some organizations claim that they cannot recruit office workers willing to fill less challenging clerical positions. A few organizations faced with this difficulty and other labor-related problems are resorting to a unique method of securing office employees.

Moving clerical jobs to places where willing workers are located has resulted in the trend called office sharing or offshore offices. Begun in the 1980s, **office sharing** involves the joint efforts of information service companies in lesser developed nations, such as Barbados and Jamaica. Countries are favored where labor costs are low and literacy rates are high. Such production sharing (a term first used in 1977 by the noted management author/consultant Peter Drucker) has become very common in industry and has potential for growth with several types of office work such as data entry and word processing.

Office sharing works like this: A U.S. organization sends source documents, such as mailing lists, usually by facsimile via satellite transmission (but in some cases by jet plane) to a remote site. The work is processed there and transmitted back, usually electronically, to the sending organization. By taking advantage of available technology and low production costs, organizations can become more competitive. Another positive result of office sharing is that it helps bridge the technology gap between industrialized and developing nations.[14] Office sharing is not expected to become a major work trend, but one futurist predicts that the office of the future will be staffed by a core group of full-time, on-site employees who will provide management with continuity and administrative support. The remaining members of the work force will consist of **networkers.** This group would be composed of loosely affiliated workers who rarely or never work on site. Such a work force would lead to radically reduced costs and could easily become feasible with the development of offshore

14.   Kevin P. Power, "Now We Can Move Office Work Offshore to Enhance Output," *The Wall Street Journal* (June 9, 1983): 30.

offices and some of the other equally interesting changes projected to affect office work in the future.[15]

Variations on the five-day, forty-hour workweek are becoming quite common. Such arrangements include permanent part-time and night work, free-lance work, temporary work, and sabbaticals. The latter is a relative newcomer to the business world but an old favorite of the academic community. **Business sabbaticals** involve paid periodic work leaves usually for executives. Rank-and-file employees often can obtain unpaid extended leaves of absence. Such leaves may become more popular if the predicted job shortages occur, as they can serve to stretch the amount of work available. In addition, such leaves enable employees to pursue personal goals related to their choice of life-style, such as education or travel.

Other relatively new work patterns include job sharing, flex-time, and telecommuting. With **job sharing** two people share a position title and salary. One person might work the morning hours and another the afternoon hours with an hour or so of overlap time to orient the incoming worker.

Flextime, begun in 1965, spread rapidly during the 1970s. With this arrangement, employees work during certain peak hours and have a choice regarding their arrival and departure times. For example, an employee might choose to work from 6 a.m. until 3 p.m. if the organization has peak hours (during which all employees must be present) from 10 a.m. until 2 p.m. An alternate plan of flextime allows the use of a shorter workweek but requires working more hours per day—for example, a four-day workweek of ten hours per day. Offering employees such flexibility in their working arrangements enlarges the recruiting options of organizations and enhances the job satisfaction of employees.

An additional work pattern, not yet popular but projected to grow, is **telecommuting.** This work-at-home plan also is referred to as the **electronic cottage.** This term updates the cottage industry concept of the early industrial age when workers, including women and children, performed factory work in their homes for piece-rate wages. Currently, less than 1 percent of the work force telecommutes, but within a few years that figure is expected to climb to 5 percent.

The process of telecommuting involves workers receiving their assignments over telephone lines connected to their home

15.   V. Douglas Hines, *Office Automation: Tools and Methods for System Building* (New York: John Wiley & Sons, 1985), 463.

computers. After processing, the work is returned electronically to their organizations. Many advantages exist for this emerging work pattern, both for individuals and for organizations.

Individuals such as the semiretired, the handicapped, and those with home obligations (such as care of children, the elderly, or the sick) have increased access to the job market. This same benefit from telecommuting also applies to organizations because their recruiting efforts can be expanded to include a larger geographic area and more diverse populations. Individual benefits also include savings in time and energy usually devoted to travel as well as savings in money spent on work clothing and transportation. Organizational savings would include the need for less work space, so rent and utilities as well as services to employees are reduced. However, one of the most important benefits from telecommuting for organizations will be increases in job productivity ranging from 10 to 100 percent. Such increases can result because home workers have more freedom to plan their work, resulting in greater job satisfaction. This job satisfaction also can be reflected in reductions in employee turnover and absenteeism as well as higher morale.

Disadvantages in telecommuting also exist for individuals and organizations, however. Distractions in the home could cause workers to miss deadlines if self-discipline and good time management are not practiced. Burn-out might overcome some individuals who compulsively overwork, while proximity to the refrigerator might cause others to gain weight. Some individuals may have difficulty in securing a quiet, comfortable work location.

Figure 18-3 Telecommuting enables the employee to work at home, transmitting and receiving organizational information and assignments.

However, the lack of social and professional interaction with fellow employees might prove to be the greatest disadvantage of all. Organizational difficulties include the selection of suitable candidates for home-based work, concern about security for work done at home, and managerial changes required for dealing with absentee workers.

Managers of telecommuters will have to be more concerned with worker output than with worker methods. Communication between telecommuters and managers will have to be of high quality in order to convey the organization's performance expectations. Equally important, managers must give telecommuters appropriate and frequent feedback regarding the nature of their work so that they will feel socially connected to their organizations. Otherwise, home workers might feel left out of the organizational milieu and become dissatisfied. To combat such possible feelings of social isolation, some organizations have home workers check-in occasionally or work on a rotating schedule between office and home. The existence of telecommuting is just one result of the many changes affecting office work. The effect of yet other technological developments promise to be equally innovative.

TECHNOLOGICAL TRENDS

The driving force behind most of the changes predicted for the information age is the computer. Its worldwide presence has become commonplace in homes and organizations of all sizes. Estimates are that there are about 45 million computers in the U.S. today.[16] Personal computers in 1988 in the U.S. alone numbered more than twenty-three million, with their ranks expected to increase by an addditional 20 to 25 percent each year.[17] Trends affecting the computer industry deserve close examination because its development is so critical to the automated office.

In writing about the future of the computer industry, analyst John Dvorak stated, "The present is the future." His pronouncement simply means that more of the same type of developments as in the past can be expected. He writes of technological advancements using terms that describe the same primary trends which he claims have always accompanied developing Western civilization: They will have more power and be less expensive, more reliable, and more comfortable. Also, in the case of computers,

16. Michael W. Miller, "A Brave New World: Streams of 1s and 0s," *The Wall Street Journal Centennial Edition* (June, 1989): A15.

17. Amy Wohl, Locknote Speech, Eighth Annual Conference of the Office Systems Research Association, Dallas, Tex., March 13, 1989.

he extends these trends to include "smaller" for physical size, "larger" for memory size, "faster" for speed, and "easier" for use. Dvorak believes these trends are a theme of the future and will continue forever. More significantly, he claims that the key to understanding the future of the computer industry is its movement toward the realization of this overriding trend: one person to one computer.[18]

Some individuals might even acquire more than one computer for use in the office, the home, and for travel. Other individuals might prefer to use a laptop computer that can be carried on the road and then plugged into a better screen and keyboard when used at home or at the office. Some futurists predict that by the mid-nineties people will walk around with a shirt-pocket computer with a gigabyte (one billion bytes, roughly equivalent to 700 books with an average of 400 pages, not counting pictures) of data. Such portable gigabytes of data are said to represent a paradigm (model) shift in thinking about information access, as people will have the advantage of an auxiliary memory with rapid access to specialized information. Such mass storage of data will be accomplished by developments in optical technology.[19] Many other equally interesting trends are predicted for computer hardware, especially those involving the ubiquitous personal computer.

HARDWARE

Smaller
Faster
Cheaper
Supercomputers
((Cray-NEC)
more powerful.
robots
multi tasking
multi processing
↳ use more than one processor

more than one task at a time

The microcomputer rapidly is becoming everybody's work tool. It is being heralded as the workstation of the future for all office personnel. Electric typewriters have become obsolete; the days of the stand-alone word processor are numbered as organizations increasingly turn to shared-logic systems or the versatile micro. These small but powerful computers can handle a multitude of office automation needs—word processing, spreadsheet, graphics, communication, as well as interfacing with larger computer systems. Indeed, the PC can almost single-handedly be considered the most important factor responsible for the growth and development of office automation.

The popularity of the microcomputer and its ever-increasing power and speed have caused some computer industry experts to predict the eventual obsolescence of the mainframe computer. However, other experts believe that the framework for future computing will more likely be **cooperative processing**—the fusion of mainframes and microcomputers into one system. The concept

18.   John C. Dvorak, ''Reflections on the Future,'' *InfoWorld* (February 18, 1985): 36.
19.   Kurt Sandholtz, ''You Ain't Seen Nothin' Yet,'' *The College Edition of the National Business Employment Weekly* (winter/spring, 1989): 5.

involves the execution of parts of an application on different linked machines for optimal job performance. The cooperative processing concept, first announced by IBM in the late eighties, seeks to promote consistency, commonality, and portability across a wide range of hardware and software architectures. IBM hopes to accomplish cooperative processing with the development of what the company refers to as **Systems Applications Architecture (SAA).** Although many office PCs are already wired to swap data with mainframes, the cooperative processing concept would make these links more intimate, meaning that the PCs and the mainframe would actually collaborate on problem solving.[20]

The reliance on computers by business for transaction processing has led to another burgeoning development—**Electronic Document Interchange (EDI).** The EDI concept involves a set of ANSI (American National Standards Institute)-based computer-to-computer communication standards that allow a number of business transactions such as ordering, shipping, billing, and paying to be electronically conducted between companies. The use of EDI can secure a competitive advantage for big and medium companies that electronically link up with their suppliers because it significantly facilitates the processing of business transactions.

Electronic document exchange has enormous implications for the automated office. No longer will clerks be needed to enter data or re-enter data several times for the same transactions. In addition, the company receiving the documents will be freed from entering the data into its system. The keying of data, however, is not the only clerical operation affected by EDI. The many manual tasks associated with document processing such as preparing documents for the mail, opening envelopes, and delivering and distributing the mail will disappear. The advantages of EDI include the elimination of paperwork, reduction of human error and data redundancy, and possibly significant cuts in the number of clerical workers needed for business transaction processing. The widespread growth of EDI in organizations will move the concept of the "paperless office," around since the 1950s, much closer to realization during the nineties.[21]

Another development targeted for much growth during the decade of the nineties is **Integrated Services Digital Network (ISDN).** ISDN provides the synergy so that both data and voice

20.   William A. Newman, "SAA: IBM's Commitment to the Future," *Information Executive*, Vol. 2, No. 1 (winter, 1989): 28.

21.   John Burch, "EDI: The Demise of Paper," *Information Executive*, Vol. 2, No. 1 (winter, 1989): 51–55.

technologies can be communicated over a single telephone line. Phone lines presently carry either voice or data, not both at once. In addition, ISDN will bring a ten-fold increase in data transmission speeds. For example, present telephone lines operate at 9600 baud; few modems operate faster than 2400 baud. ISDN can handle speeds of 64,000 baud.[22]

Major developments involving voice technology and the use of handwriting with PCs are also expected during the decade of the nineties. (Voice technology was discussed earlier in this text and will not be repeated here.) However, the implications of both voice and handwriting appear significant for the future of the automated office. Conversing with computers will become routine as office workers talk to them and they talk back. Computers incorporating voice technology will allow direct dictation and production of hard copy while bypassing the need for an intermediary—the typist. Some futurists think that the use of handwriting with PCs will have greater social and economic impact than the initial introduction of the PC. Several computer companies are trying to develop a new kind of portable computer that will appear less as a computer and more as an electronic notebook. Such a computer would contain a powerful microprocessor that would recognize handwriting, dispensing with the need for a keyboard. Writing to use a computer instead of typing would thus extend access to the power of computing to a far broader audience.[23]

An additional development being hailed as the "biggest revolution in the information revolution" is the use of multiprocessor computer systems. **Multiprocessing** (also called **parallel processing**) is characteristic of computers that rely on more than one central processing unit (CPU) for their brainpower. Computers in the past have used multiple processors; but usually one processor was "boss" and the others handled secondary operations such as doing the arithmetic, filing, and information retrieval. In the future as many as a million microprocessors may be used to perform computer operations.[24] These multiprocessor systems will characterize the next generation of so-called supercomputers.

Supercomputers are computers designed specifically to process vast numbers of repetitive calculations at tremendous speeds. The latest supercomputers increasingly utilize multiprocessors. For example, in 1989 the Cray 3 supercomputer had 16 proces-

22.   Kurt Sandholtz, *op. cit.*, 5, 18.

23.   John Markoff, "The Chip at 30: Potential Still Vast," *The New York Times* (September 14, 1988): D1.

24.   Richard Shaffer, "Commercial Use Approaching for Multiprocessor Computers," *The Wall Street Journal* (October 12, 1984): 27.

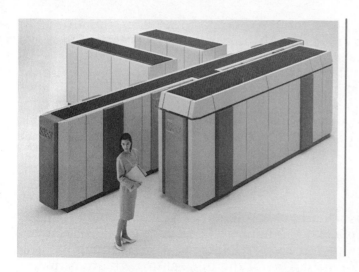

Figure 18-4 In 1989, the NEC Corporation of Japan introduced a new series of supercomputers capable of as many as 20 billion operations a second.
NEC Corporation

sors; the Cray 4 due in the early 1990s is scheduled to have 64 processors. Cray Research, Inc., the U.S. manufacturer of supercomputers, has 66 percent of the supercomputer world market and accounts for about two thirds of the world's 400 or so supercomputer installations. The NEC Corporation of Japan, however, in 1989 introduced a new series of supercomputers capable of performing as many as 20 billion operations a second, making these supercomputers eight times faster than their U.S. counterparts. By contrast, in 1989 the most advanced chips (Intel's 80486 and Motorola's 68040) operated at 15 and 17 MIPS (millions of instructions per second) respectively. However, computer scientists predict that in the future an ultracomputer will reach speeds of a trillion operations per second. Currently, the use for supercomputers has been primarily for research in such areas as the military, astrophysics, mineral exploration, and weather forecasting, but computer experts predict that a supercomputer will eventually be on every desktop. One reason preventing the proliferation of supercomputers is their cost, currently priced from $5 million to $23 million.[25]

Computer scientists also are busy working on another technological threshold: **computer-brain interfaces**. According to a report from the marketing research firm of International Resource Development, by the mid-1990s humans will be able to program a computer just by thinking. Electrodes will be attached to an individual's temple and neck while the computer deciphers the electromagnetic signals from the brain. These signals will then

25. Richard Gibson, ''Analysts Caution on NEC New Line of Supercomputer,'' *The Wall Street Journal* (April 11, 1989): B5.

be integrated with the human thought-processing signals stored in the computer's memory. Military personnel are using weapon-pointing systems now which read the movement of the pilot's eyes to control aircraft systems such as the wings and throttle. In the future this system may be augmented by sensors which will "read" the pilot's brain waves and convert them to air-craft movements. While these advancements in hardware appear quite remark-able, the software industry also will have its share of distinctive achievements.

SOFTWARE

OSI
ISDN
hardware
user friendly

The computer is usually championed as a productivity tool, yet software really makes it all happen. Thus, milestones in software development are just as important, if not more so, than those in hardware development. One of the biggest growth areas during the early nineties will be integrated office environments made possible by the linkage of hardware and software by global elec-tronic networks, such as ISDN. However, in order to achieve such integration, international standards need to be developed and adopted.

ANSI has produced a seven-layer standard termed the **Open Systems Interconnection (OSI) Reference Model.** X/Open is the independent international body responsible for establishing Open Systems standards. Such standards will eventually enable organizations to select the most appropriate hardware and soft-ware systems regardless of their source and without the con-straints of manufacturer-imposed standards. In the future the hope is that these and other OSI protocols being formulated will become international standards. Progress toward Open Systems became evident by the late eighties with over 100 leading soft-ware companies and 14 leading international system suppliers producing products conforming to OSI standards.

In addition to standardization, integration applied to both hardware and software appears to be a significant trend for the decade of the nineties. With the early integrated software pack-ages, the norm was to have one strong application such as a spreadsheet at the expense of "crippling" the power of the other applications. With the increasing power of PCs all the application capabilities of a software package can be equally strong. Some computer industry experts have even predicted the end of single application packages. Instead fully integrated packages are ex-pected to become the norm; for example, word processing, spread-sheet, database, graphics, and communication capabilities would be all bundled together.

Predictions are that such integrated packages will not only be convenient but also easy to use because of the direction toward

"applications interoperability." This term refers to the fact that all of the applications will have a similar "look and feel" made possible by the trend toward the use of graphical (icon-based) interfaces and the elimination of the need to learn additional formats for each application. Also, applications interoperability will provide users with easy transport of files within and between packages.

A change predicted to be of even more far-reaching significance for software users will be their ability to customize off-the-shelf packages. Even without knowledge of programming languages such as COBOL or PASCAL, users will be able to build programs. This trend, known as end user or **object-oriented programming** allows users to link building blocks of program code together in whatever pattern they desire. Such programming capability is consistent with the use of special purpose tools by programmers and nonprogrammers alike who need to tailor software applications to the particular demands of their work environment.[26]

Many such programming tools abound. For example, relational database management systems (DBMS) were considered important to software development because they facilitated the use of query and analysis tools for managers. Later **fourth generation languages (4GLs)** were hailed as a panacea to assist programmers and non-programmers in designing software. 4GLs consist of nonprocedural application generators, or very high-level languages unlike procedural languages such as COBOL and PASCAL. These third-generation languages told the computer how to do the job; nonprocedural languages refer to a small set of powerful commands that tell the computer simply what to do. Much software now comes equipped with built-in application generators. However, the latest set of tools receiving much attention from software developers is CASE technology. **CASE (Computer-Aided Software Engineering)** is the generic acronym for the many products, such as Index Technology's Excelerator, that automate the software application development process. CASE tools support not only programming but also system specification, design, testing, debugging, documentation, and maintenance.

The reason for all the interest in software development tools is to increase the productivity of the software development process. The many development tools and their accompanying procedures help reduce the application design backlog and enable the system development process to become more flexible, speedier, and responsive to users' needs. Users can engage in the prototyping of new software by offering iterative (repeated) feedback during

26. Kurt Sandholtz, *op. cit.*, 18.

the development process. Thus, users have the opportunity to see how the program will run before actual implementation. Automation of programming also benefits programmers because it eliminates much of the tedious and repetitive programming tasks associated with data entry and disk storage. However, although programming tools automate much of the application development process, software developers still need to understand the business problems and needs of users to be successful.[27] Software application development tools are an example of how automation can affect the organization for both DP and non-DP personnel. Although software application developments are impressive, other software developments of the more distant future will be even more innovative.

Major developments are expected to emerge from the so-called fifth generation during the 1990s. The **fifth generation** concept refers to an ambitious program being pursued vigorously by computer scientists (especially in Japan but also in the United States and European nations) to produce a totally new type of computer. The Japanese call these computers knowledge/information processing systems (**KIPS**). These machines will differ from previous computers in that they will be able to solve problems as humans do—by reasoning, making judgments, and learning. The authors of the popular book *The Fifth Generation* have said that these ". . . reasoning machines (represent) not just the second computer revolution but the important one."[28] Such revolutionary developments will come from software based on research in artificial intelligence (AI).

The most widely used application based on artificial intelligence is the expert system. An **expert system** is a computer program that emulates human thinking in a well-defined task. The human thinking is contained in a so-called knowledge base. This body of information on a particular topic is secured from experts by "knowledge engineers," who "mine" the experts' knowledge and write a computer program. The knowledge can be represented by if-then logic, script, or mathematical formulas. Users of the expert system can query the program, using language natural to the user, for example, conversational English. Such a capability is derived from the program's natural language processor. The expert system generates a response to the inquiry through the process of heuristics. Heuristics is a method of empirical thinking, using rules of thumb to produce a solution.[29]

27.   Esther Dyson, "Computers Programming Computers," *Forbes* (March 6, 1989), 137.

28.   Edward A. Feigenbaum and Pamela McCorduck, *The Fifth Generation* (Reading, Mass.: Addison-Wesley Publishing Company, 1983), 238.

29.   Laurence R. Paquette and Joseph L. Sardinas, "Productivity Tools: Past, Present, and Future," *Data Management* (June, 1985): 17.

The technology of expert systems is expected to make a major impact on homes and businesses during the 1990s. The Gartner Group estimates that U.S. sales of expert systems will hit the $300 million mark in 1992, up from $25 million in 1987, and that the U.S. market for AI equipment will climb to $1 billion by 1992. Currently expert systems are being widely embedded into existing hardware and software, used as "intelligent job aids" (Chapter 16 discusses the use of job aids in the office), and increasingly common as natural language front-ends to DBMS (database management systems).[30] AI, around since 1950, has become a commercial success during the decade of the eighties and promises even more far-reaching developments for the nineties. The interest and excitement that initially surrounded AI has now been transferred to neural networks.

A **neural network** is a computer system modeled roughly after the brain's web-like neuron structure. Neural networks are emerging as one of the most important technological advances of the nineties. Some computer experts feel that neural networks will revolutionize computing. The promise of neural networks lies in their ability to learn by example and to analyze incomplete, even inaccurate information, so-called fuzzy data, including spoken words and fingerprints. Neural networks require specialized hardware employing parallel processing capabilities. Neural networks excel in processing complex unstructured tasks requiring pattern matching, the process of associating certain data with certain properties or conditions. While conventional computer systems using expert systems can also analyze fuzzy data, such structured, rule-based systems stumble when the problem is too fuzzy, that is, involving too many rules with too many variations. Neural networks do not use rules but simply match unfamiliar patterns with the best approximation of them in their memories. Neural networks, however, cannot solve problems that conventional computers can, such as calculating numbers. For that reason neural network computers often work in conjunction with conventional computers. Examples of business applications for neural networks include reading handwritten numbers on checks, analyzing handwritten signatures on checks to detect forgeries, and assessing mortgage applications.[31]

The impact of these fifth-generation products on society is still a matter of speculation, but some basic effects such as the following are expected: (1) expansion of human intelligence; (2)

30. Jay Liebowitz, "Artificial Intelligence and the Corporate Environment," *Information Executive*, Vol. 2, No. 1 (winter, 1989): 56.

31. David Stipp, "Computer Researchers Find 'Neural Networks' Help Mimic the Brain," *The Wall Street Journal* (September 29, 1988): 1, 20.

coping difficulties with an extremely high information base; (3) improvements in human productivity; (4) natural language conversation with computers; and (5) development of multiple systems for business, consumer, and personal use for people to make the transition into a true information age environment.[32] Another fifth generation application of artificial intelligence with much potential for the future includes the use of robots.

Robotics as a fifth generation development has been targeted for tremendous growth. Predictions for the end of the century claim the three largest new industries will be robotics, genetic engineering, and telecommunications. Robots first were envisioned by the Czechoslovakian futuristic novelist/playwright, Karel Capek (1890–1938). He coined the word robot from the Czech noun for forced labor—"robota."

Robots of the future will be machines with sight, touch, and hearing and will have an advanced form of artificial intelligence for a brain. Because of robots, productivity can be increased and labor costs can be reduced since robots require no coffee breaks, lunch periods, sick days, or vacations. The impact of these uncomplaining "workers" has been projected to be enormous. In 1981 an estimated 14,000 robots populated the world. By the early 1990s this figure should reach 200,000 in the U.S. alone. By the turn of the century, robots are expected to replace 4.4 million workers. Currently, most robots are employed in factory work in activities such as painting, welding, grinding, lathing, and running drill presses. However, the true impact of the robot revolution is yet to come.

In addition to factory robots, the future should produce nuclear robots (to handle radioactive materials); mining robots (to work in dangerous and unhealthy mines); genetic robots (to handle germs in genetic engineering labs); underwater robots (to dive fathoms below the sea to locate oil and minerals); space robots (to explore the outer reaches of space); teacher robots (to instruct); playmate robots (to entertain); and domestic robots (to do housework).[33] Undoubtedly, the future also will see the use of office robots. The playwright Capek even included female stenographer robots in his future world. More recently a Japanese inventor has developed a robot that functions as an office receptionist. Currently, robots in offices have very limited uses, such as distributing mail and filing. However, managers in the future most likely will have to develop a plan to deal with this newest class of office workers.

---

    32.   Gary A. Berg, "The Future of Information Processing," *Business Education Forum Yearbook*, National Business Education Yearbook (Washington: National Business Education Association, 1985), 52.
    33.   Marvin Cetron and Thomas O'Toole, *op. cit.*, 233–250.

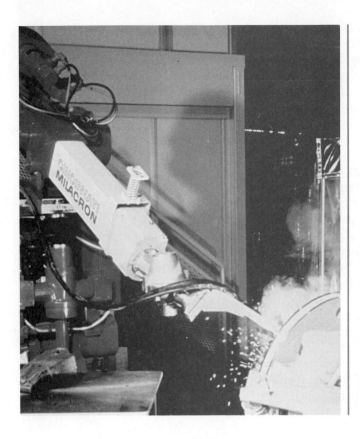

Figure 18-5 The development of robotics has been targeted for tremendous growth by the end of the century.
Cincinnati Milacron

EPILOG

Predictions such as those presented in this chapter are only extrapolations of what is currently known. The real future, no doubt, will contain surprises even for futurists. The only certain thing about the future is the element of continued change. A philosophy for the future might well be summed up by the systems concept of **dynamic equilibrium.** While seemingly a contradiction in terms, this concept means that the norm will be one of flux. Such conditions will produce difficult, trying times for both individuals and organizations as attempts are made to grapple with worldwide technical, socioeconomic, and political change. What the full consequences of all these changes will be no one really knows. For example, questions such as the following have yet to be answered:

How will organizations compete when all have access to powerful thinking machines? Will office personnel routinely labor at workstations in space? Will jobs be available to provide a livelihood for people as automation takes over more and more human tasks? Just how human will robots become? (One account of life in the future portrays humans selecting robots for mates because they can be programmed to their exact specifications.) With the availability of expert systems for homes and businesses, will people need or want to continue to learn? Questions such as these can be unsettling, but change always works to disturb the status quo.

The massive, monumental changes predicted to accompany the information age will affect every living creature on earth. The environment will be much more complex. Perhaps the only way to prepare for this future is to keep abreast of major trends and their impact upon society. In earlier times the "past was prologue." In other words, the wisdom of the ages could be counted upon to serve as guidelines for the future. However, that time may be gone forever.

Inhabitants of the post-industrial age must do what every age has done. Move forward bravely with the belief that tomorrow will bring a better world. And why should this not be so? Human beings are endowed by nature with an almost infinite capacity for growth and adaptation. Words of comfort and optimism for the transition to the information age are provided by the British philosopher Alfred North Whitehead: "It is the business of the future to be dangerous, and it is among the merits of science that it equips the future for its duties."

WOHL'S BUSINESS PERSPECTIVE

Once we added automation as an ingredient to the workplace, we tied ourselves to an ongoing need to predict and anticipate change. Too often, we spend months and years making technology decisions, securing their funding, and painfully installing them, only to find that they are obsolete just as we begin to use them!

This doesn't mean that our just-implemented system doesn't work. It does mean that we may not get an adequate payback on our investment, because we'll need to replace it sooner than planned. And it almost surely means that we'll be quickly disappointed by our inability to use seductive new software that requires more power or even an entirely new platform.

The trick to avoiding such disappointments and financial disasters (*you* try explaining to your management that the $5,000,000 they spent last year will need to be augmented by another (unplanned) $5,000,000 next year!) is looking ahead.

Some systems trends for the office are so nearly automatic that they need only be described. We have come to depend upon:

- Increases in computing power at roughly the same price level. This has permitted the power of a PC to grow more than fourfold while maintaining about the same price. New office workstations have street (discounted) prices of about $5,000 each. As workstations age, they become available at much lower prices (as little as $1,000 for a complete PC today), but this is always for aging technology and significantly less power than might currently be available.

- Decreases in size. Computer power not only increases, it also gets smaller. Today, we can store in a single chip more power than early personal computers put on an entire board—or early computers put in a large room. While there are some physical limits to how narrow a line can be—or how closely packed circuits can be placed onto chips—new technologies continue to emerge, assuring us that increasing miniaturization will continue. Very small versions of technology are usually more limited than their full-sized brothers and are often more expensive as well, but this can easily be justified for traveling workers.

It's important to remember that technology has a predictable aging cycle. When new computer technology enters the market it has power—but usually little software. About two years after its first shipment, volumes of software will appear. About six to twelve months later, the next round of technology starts. This means users who want to be toward the front of the technology curve expect to upgrade their hardware about every three to four years.

Most business buyers don't buy new technology at the very beginning of the hardware cycle since little software is available to exploit the power. A year or two later, it's much easier to make a rational business decision, buying software that matches the power of the hardware. (An exception might occur when a vendor figures out how to continue to run existing software on new hardware, offering benefits to the user that can't be obtained by continuing to use the older hardware platform.)

Smart business users know that it's a bad investment to buy technology at or after the end of its cycle. It still works. It's cheap. But it's unlikely to be durable or satisfying in running the good, new stuff. Bargains are nice, but wise buyers spend their dollars with a sharp look toward the future.

SUMMARY

Futurists are individuals who forecast what will exist or happen in the future using methods such as trend analysis and visioning. Often subject to such study is the concept of the office of the future.

Organizations need to consider the global effects of future economic, political, social, and conceptual changes. New roles for information will affect the organization's structure, work procedures, and forms of management. Because of the changes in employees' work expectations and values, organizations are responding with numerous alternative work systems, such as office sharing, job sharing, flextime, and telecommuting.

Technological developments for hardware will continue to be affected by the primary trends that have always accompanied the development of Western civilization. Hardware will be more powerful, less expensive, and more comfortable. More specifically, computers will be smaller in size but will have a larger memory and faster speed while being easier to use. The personal computer is considered to be the most important factor in the growth and development of office automation. Advancements in voice technology, handwriting with PCs, multiprocessing, and computer-brain interfaces all promise to have revolutionary input on the types of equipment used in the automated office.

Software application developments, such as object-oriented programming and CASE technology, are examples of how automation can increase organizational productivity for both DP and non-DP personnel. However, the fifth-generation developments of AI/expert systems and neural networks will be unprecedented because these systems will be capable of humanlike thinking. Currently, robots are used primarily for industrial applications, but future robots will have sight, touch, hearing, and artificial intelligence and are projected to displace millions of workers.

The transition to the information age can be characterized by the systems concept of "dynamic equilibrium." Although the full consequences of automation are unknown, human beings are capable of growth and adaptation and, hopefully, wisdom to use its power for a better future.

KEY TERMS

futurists
trend analysis
visioning
information infrastructure
zero-based corporate
   structure
cluster organization
network organization
adhocracy
autonomous work group
participative selection
office sharing

networkers
business sabbaticals
job sharing
flextime
telecommuting
electronic cottage
cooperative processing
Systems Applications
   Architecture (SAA)
Electronic Document
   Interchange (EDI)

Integrated Services Digital Network (ISDN)

multiprocessing

parallel processing

supercomputers

computer-brain interfaces

Open Systems Interconnection (OSI) Reference Model

applications interoperability

object-oriented programming

fourth generation languages (4GLs)

CASE (Computer-Aided Software Engineering)

fifth generation

expert system

neural network

dynamic equilibrium

REVIEW QUESTIONS

1. Do you believe that the office of the future exists now or that it will remain an elusive goal? Defend your position.

2. Why is the role of information of vital importance to the economic, political, and social future of nations?

3. How is information technology affecting organizational structure?

4. Do you think the forms of management in the future will be any different from the forms of management today? Why or why not?

5. Do you agree that the concept of office sharing has little chance of becoming a major work trend? Why or why not?

6. If given a job opportunity involving telecommuting, would you accept or not? What circumstances would affect your decision?

7. In view of the technological developments presented in this chapter, do you agree or disagree with the statement "the present is the future"?

8. How will the supercomputers of the future differ from the computers of the past?

9. How are software application developments contributing to both DP and non-DP personnel productivity?

10. What characteristics will make the computers of the fifth generation unique? What effect might this have?

11. Contrast a negative view of the future with a positive view. Which view do you believe will be realized?

CASE STUDY: THE CASE OF THE PIONEER OFFICE WORKER

The year is 2030. Dyan Carson hurriedly dressed for work in her small sleeping quarters, gulped her breakfast capsules, and then walked through the narrow corridor leading to her workstation. Easing into her ergonomically designed chair and checking her VDT controls, Dyan began another workday on Spaceship No. 1. Her chief office task consisted of processing all of the spaceship's supply requests by transmitting them to the planet earth. Dyan enjoyed her job and was proud of her role as one of the first civilian office workers to qualify for a regular spaceship assignment. After working twelve months in space, Dyan would be eligible for a one-month vacation on earth or on one of the other newly developed resort planets.

As Dyan monitored her controls, her thoughts turned to her plans for the evening. She considered attending the interterrestrial light show, or perhaps she and her boyfriend, John, would go for another space walk. But then she remembered that John was working the night shift this week. Dyan decided that probably she and her best girlfriend, April, would spend the evening watching satellite television. Occasionally Dyan grew earthsick for her family and friends, but she knew how proud they were of her pioneering spirit, which led her to become an office worker in space.

Pondering her future, Dyan wondered whether she and John would marry and take advantage of the government's spacesteading act and become permanent space colonists. That thought generally pleased Dyan, except for the constant threat of territorial space wars. Suddenly, Dyan was brought back to reality when her office supervisor walked in with additional orders to process.

QUESTIONS/ACTIVITIES

1. What do you believe the chances are for office personnel to work in space?

2. How might an office worker's life in space in 2030 differ from an office worker's life on earth today? How might they be similar?

3. Would you be willing to trade places with Dyan? Why or why not?

SUGGESTED READINGS

Applegate, Lynda M., James I. Cash, Jr., and D. Quinn Mills. "Information Technology and Tomorrow's Manager." *Harvard Business Review* (November-December, 1988): 128–136.

Holsapple, Clyde W. and Andrew B. Whinston. *Business Expert Systems.* Homewood, Ill.: Irwin, 1987.

Information Executive, Vol. 2, No. 1 (winter, 1989): 28–58. Special Section: Perspectives on the Future.

Inman, Thomas H. "The Future's Impact on Business Education." *Business Education Forum* (November, 1988): 5–6.

Kimmerling, George F. "The Future of HRD." *Training and Development Journal* (June, 1989): 46–55.

Kleinschrod, Walter A. *The Office of 1990: Strategies for Managing Office Automation.* Willow Grove, Pa.: Administrative Management Society Foundation, 1985.

Lippitt, Ronald, Paula Lugannani, and Edward Lindaman. *Futuring*. Reading, Mass.: Addison-Wesley Publishing Company, 1989.

Palmer, Janet. "Office Systems Offshore: A Field Research Report." Office Systems Research Association: *Proceedings of the Eighth Annual Office Systems Research Conference*, Dallas, Tex., March 11–13, 1989, 189–197.

Stewart, Hugh B. *Recollecting the Future: A View of Business, Technology, and Innovation in the Next 30 Years*. Homewood, Ill.: Dow-Jones-Irwin, 1989.

Outlook '89 and Beyond. Bethesda, Md.: The World Future Society.

Zuboff, Shoshana. *In the Age of the Smart Machine: The Future of Work and Power*. New York: Basic Books, Inc. 1988.

APPENDIX A

CASES FOR DECISION ASSISTANT SOFTWARE EXERCISES

ELECTRONIC FILING APPLICATION

The *Decision Assistant* software available to students who use this text provides five computer tools to analyze data extracted from these cases. The following quantitative and qualitative tools are available:

1. Multi-Attribute Scoring
2. Pro-Con Choice Analysis
3. Decision Tree
4. Goal Analysis
5. Project Planning Chart

The software includes a calculator and a memo pad, a simple word processor that can be used for typing reports involving the cases. Solutions can be printed and saved. Throughout the cases, you will be asked to save an analysis for later retrieval. This will prevent rekeying large amounts of data in subsequent analyses.

Each tool contains a brief tutorial that can be invoked by depressing ALT-I at any time while you are working in the tool. Instructors have more detailed documentation that describes the use of the tools; they are free to duplicate that documentation for students.

CASE 1—THE WARREN COMPANY AND SOFTWARE SELECTION

(For use with Chapter 5)

PREPARATION AND REVIEW

This case involves evaluation of microcomputer software. Review the portions of Chapter 5 that deal with the selection of software, especially Figure 5-2. Review the content of the Warren Company case at the end of Chapters 4 and 5. **Review the documentation (to be provided by the instructor) for using** DECISION ASSISTANT.

THE SITUATION

The Warren Company has completed its reorganization and has installed an information center with office systems analysts who help professionals and administrative support employees through out the organization to select hardware and software for their offices. One decision made in this process was to standardize word processing software throughout the firm. As a member of the software selection team, you are participating in this process.

The following material represents the software selection team's preliminary analysis of four powerful word processing packages. As a member of the project team, your job is to select a scheme to add some order to the selection process by quantifying the team's deliberations, using a quantitative model of some type. The Multi-Attribute Scoring Model will not only provide such a model; the software will also perform calculations quickly and enable the team to change the evaluations and quickly see the results.

The team has selected five criteria for use in the selection of a single word processing package for the firm. They have narrowed the choices to four popular packages. Table 1-1 identifies the criteria, the relative weights assigned to each criterion, and the team's evaluation of how well each package meets each of the five criteria.

Table 1-1 Evaluations for Four Word Processing Software Packages

| | CRITERIA | | | | |
	Features Included	Performance of Features	Documentation	Ease of Use	Tech. Support
WEIGHT	4	10	4	8	4
Brand A	90	80	60	88	80
Brand B	90	95	80	95	90
Brand C	100	80	80	85	60
Brand D	90	70	90	60	40

Note: The weight indicates the relative importance of each criterion (expressed on a scale of 10), compared to the importance of the other criteria.

BASIS FOR EVALUATIONS

The evaluations for each brand represent (on a scale of 1 to 100) the team's evaluation for each criterion. The following discussion interprets those evaluations.

Features.   Brand C has a superior screen image (the ability to show text very realistically as it will appear on the page). It offers a choice of keyed commands (typed on the keyboard) or function-key commands (invoked by depressing function keys or combinations such as ALT-F5). Because other features are almost identical, the other brands are rated equally.

Performance.   This evaluation involved many separate evaluations of features, but the team agreed that one package (Brand B) is superior. The basic editing features, the automatic reformatting, the spell checker, and the speed of performance influenced these ratings.

Ease of Use.   Since the team decided that most of the users would not have the patience to commit to memory the long lists of commands required for all of the packages, they rated a package highly if they considered its keyboard templates (a chart that fits next to the keys to indicate commands) easy to use and learn.

Documentation and Technical Support.   Documentation quality varied greatly. This evaluation presented a perplexing situation, because some of the best documentation accompanied software that was actually very difficult to learn. Sticking to their goal of applying the criteria individually, however, the team evaluated the documentation only. Even though technical support is very critical for a user working alone at home, support is not quite so critical for Warren Company, because they have a staff of very skilled advisers in the information center. However, they too need support at times. Support was evaluated by examining terms of warranty and upgrade provisions and by calling the toll-free support numbers. The number of answered calls, the quality of answers given, and the cooperation of support personnel affected these ratings. Brand D's support line was never answered. All of the efforts required multiple calls before receiving an answer.

THE SOLUTION TECHNIQUE

Use the Multi-Attribute Scoring Model in *Decision Assistant* by selecting F1 from the menu. After you have selected the tool, key ALT-I for instructions. Key the criteria labels, weights, and evaluations selected by the project team (Table 1-1). Enter abbreviated labels (for example, FEATRS for the Features Included Column) in the "choice factor labels" section on your screen. Use the arrow keys or Enter key to move from column to column.

"Importance weights" represent the weight for each criterion, and the "satisfaction scores" represent the evaluations of each product according to the individual criteria. Key ALT-D or ALT-G to display the score for each alternative. Use the Up and Down Arrow keys to locate a blank block and save your analysis to a file named CASE1A1. Print the analysis, interpret the results, and retrieve the file named MEMO from the memo pad to write a brief memo report to your superior. **(Note: The headings for the memo are included on the file named MEMO.)** The report should contain your interpretations and recommendations. Save your analysis in a file named CASE1R1.

WHAT IF

1. How would the choice be affected if the weight of the "List of Features" criterion were changed to 8 (the same as "Ease of Use")? Retrieve your analysis file (CASE1A1). Change the weight for "Features" to 8, leaving all other data the same as in Table 1-1, and use ALT-D or ALT-G to display the results. Print the results. Save this version of your analysis to a file named CASE1A2. (CASE1A1 will not be changed or erased). Use the memo pad to create a brief memo report that discusses the effect of changing the weight. Print the report. Save the report to a file named CASE1R2. (CASE1R1 will not be changed or erased).

2. Employees in the firm who already use one of these programs were asked to experiment with the other three packages and to complete evaluations (satisfaction scores). The result was an average of 86 for Brand A, 76 for Brand B, 80 for Brand C, and 60 for Brand D. Eliminate one of the criteria (your choice) used in Table 1-1, substituting in its place the employee evaluations above. Use either the same or a different weight. Retrieve CASE1A1 again and edit the chart to reflect these changes. Display the analysis. Save this version of your analysis in a file named CASE1A3. Print the analysis. How did this change affect the evaluation? Use the memo pad to write a brief explanation of the potential problem of substituting the evaluations of these employees for the criterion that you elected to eliminate. Save the memo to a file named CASE1R3. Print the report.

CASE 2—YOUNG-ART, INC. INVESTIGATES ELECTRONIC PUBLISHING

(For use with Chapter 6)

PREPARATION AND REVIEW

This case involves a decision about the production of documents for Young-Art, CPAs, a firm of certified public accountants. Review the portions of Chapter 6 that involve the advantages of using desktop publishing systems for the production of documents. Review the documentation provided by the instructor for using *Decision Assistant*.

THE SITUATION

As Administrative Manager for Young-Art, you must respond to the senior partners' request that you purchase a new copy machine (the current one is on its last legs) for the firm. They also want you to expand the project to include an investigation of the possibility of more in-house production of some of the documents now sent to local printers. Your investigation is to include a complete in-house desktop publishing system. This case deals with this portion of your assignment.

You have selected three alternatives and have investigated some of the costs associated with each:

1. Purchase a turnkey (complete, ready-to-operate) desktop publishing system, including hardware (computer, PostScript capable printer, etc.) and software. Cost: Approximately $12,000. Continue to use outside printers for some work ($4,000–$5,000 annual cost). Much of the printed work would be done from your camera-ready copy.
2. Continue the present arrangement which requires that virtually everything go to outside printers. Most in-house documents are produced on the copy machine, and some external documents are produced this way to save time. Correspondence and reports are typed on electronic typewriters. Annual printing bill $8,000–$10,000.
3. Purchase for one of the support employees a simple microcomputer, word processing software, and an inexpensive laser printer. This employee will create many documents as a central service and print documents created by other support employees. Complete as many reports and other documents as possible in-house. Approximate cost of hardware/software: $4,500. Estimated annual printing bill: $6,000–$8,000.

CRITERIA

You have concluded that the following criteria should influence your choice:

1. Cost of hardware/software. (medium importance)
2. Quality of documents produced. (maximum importance)
3. Turnaround time (time elapse between the decision to produce a document and the date the finished product is produced). (maximum importance)
4. Cost of producing documents on a daily basis. (medium-high importance)
5. Effect of the choice on firm's image. (maximum importance)
6. Cost of training support employees. (low importance)

THE SOLUTION TECHNIQUE

The Pro-Con Choice tool in *Decision Assistant* is designed to evaluate this type of situation. Select this tool from the *Decision Assistant* menu, and key ALT-I for instructions.

1. Enter abbreviated identification labels for each of the three alternatives. Use the following pro/con arguments and enter them into the system:

ALTERNATIVE NO. 1:   *Weight*

PRO: 1. Quality of output   _____

       2. Turnaround time   _____

       3. Positive image   _____

       4. Cost of everyday operation   _____

CON: 1. Cost of system   _____

       2. Cost of training   _____

ALTERNATIVE NO. 2:

PRO: 1. Quality of output   _____

       2. Cost of system (none)   _____

       3. Positive image   _____

       4. Cost of training (none)   _____

CON: 1. Turnaround time   _____

       2. Cost of everyday operation   _____

ALTERNATIVE NO. 3:

PRO: 1. Cost of system   _____

       2. Cost of everyday operation   _____

3. Cost of training _____

CON: 1. Quality of Output _____

2. Negative image _____

2. Select weights (1[n-]10) for each argument (weights indicate your evaluation of the strength or importance of the argument) and key them into the system. Remember to key ALT-A to advance after each alternative. You can achieve a comparison of alternatives and a weighting of criteria by varying the range. For example very important criteria might have a range of $+10$ to -10, and a criterion of medium importance might have a range of $+7$ to -7.

3. Key ALT-D or ALT-G to display a comparative list of alternatives. Locate the asterisk (*) to identify the relative position of the argument. Print the analysis. Save your analysis to a file named CASE2A1. Use the memo pad (beginning in a blank space on the MEMO File) to write a short report in which you evaluate the effectiveness of this process. How does the outcome compare to your "common sense" evaluation before you began the quantitative analysis? Save your report to a file named CASE2R1. Print the report.

WHAT IF

1. What would be the effect of altering the arguments so that you have the same number of pro-con arguments for each alternative? In other words, use only the two or three *major* arguments for each. Retrieve your CASE2A1 file. Make these alterations, adjust your weights if necessary, and observe the result. Save this version of the analysis to a file named CASE2A2. Use the memo pad to write a short analysis of the difference observed, if any. Save the memo to a file named CASE2R2. Print the report.

2. Assume that the senior partners are impressed with your analysis, but they want you to add another factor: "Effect on Competitiveness." Add this argument, placing it in the PRO column if you would consider it a positive argument or, in the CON column if you would consider it a negative argument. Display the analysis. Save the analysis to a file named CASE2A3. Compare the result of this analysis with your other two analyses in a brief memo. Save the memo to a file named CASE2R3. Print the report.

CASE 3—BROWN CORPORATION SELECTS AN INFORMATION MEDIUM

(For Use With Chapter 7)

PREPARATION AND REVIEW

Review the discussions of paper, micrographic, and electronic media in Chapter 7. Read the description of Brown Corporation in the case study at the end of Chapter 7.

THE SITUATION

Many of the paper records housed in the home office are hand-written forms from the retail outlets. Others are generated in regional warehouses, and a large portion comes from the firm's home-office computer center.

The volume of records is closely tied to the volume of sales and the number of retail outlets. Because of sensitive outlet-performance criteria, unprofitable outlets are closed quickly with little loss, because they are leased facilities. Likewise, new outlets are being opened at a rapid pace. The current document volume is 8,600,000 annually. As recently as five years ago, that volume was 5,000,000. If the firm grows at the same pace in the next five years, the volume could approach 12,000,000 documents. The firm is considering three alternatives:

1. The current paper-based system.
2. A computer-assisted retrieval micrographic systems.
3. An optical laser digital data disk system integrated with the firm's current office information system which operates on a series of local area networks. Because of the magnitude of this decision, all possible analyses are being made. Two tools from *Decision Assistant* will be used. They are the Pro-Con Choice tool and the Decision Tree tool.

THE SOLUTION TECHNIQUE

PART I. Decision Tree. First, use the following calculations (Table 3-1) of anticipated cost reduction (or increases) for the next five years for each alternative under three possible conditions: (1) the volume increases to 12,000,000 documents, (2) the volume remains at its current 8,600,000 documents, and (3) the volume declines to its previous level of 5,000,000 documents. Table 3-1 reveals the calculations for anticipated benefits (or losses) for each alternative, given the three different volume predictions. The table also gives the estimated probability that each condition will occur. Select the Decision Tree tool from *Decision Assistant*. Key the information from the table into the tool. The three volumn predictions represent alternatives "states of nature." The quantities represent dollars saved or lost over a five-year period. Use ALT-G to view the results. Save the results to a file named CASE3A1, and print the results.

Table 3-1 **Expected Benefits/Losses of Three Different Annual Volumes of Documents (Five-Year Totals)**

	VOLUME		
System	12,000,000	8,600,000	5,000,000
Film	600,000	110,000	120,000
Paper	−600,000	0	400,000
Optical Disk	635,000	110,000	100,000
Probability of Volume Occurrence	.60	.30	.10

After the completion of Part II, you will combine the two analyses and make observations, and write a report.

PART II. Pro-Con Choice Use the Pro-Con Choice tool from *Decision Assistant* (Key ALT-I for instructions) to examine the same three alternatives, using the following factors (arguments). You must decide whether each factor is an argument for the alternative or an argument against each alternative, and you must assign the weight of that argument (on a scale of 1–10). (You may wish to use a wide range of weights for very important criteria, as you did in the previous use of this tool.) To simplify the transfer to Pro-Con Choice, place a plus (+) by the pro weights and a minus (−) by the con weights. For the purpose of this analysis, *assume a high probability that volume will increase to the 12,000,000 document level.* Of course, your assignment of weights is subjective. In a real situation such as this, you would have quantitative data or managerial consensus to influence your choices.

Enter your pro and con arguments and their weights. Use ALT-G to view the results of your analysis. Save your analysis to a file named CASE3A2. Print both analyses, and use the memo pad to write a brief memo (saved to a file named CASE3R1) in which you compare the results of the two analyses. Do they lead you to the same conclusion? If not, is there a possibility that there is merit to both approaches?

Table 3-2 **Factors Affecting Choice of Information Storage Medium**

| | Medium | | |
Factors	Film	Paper	Optical Disk
System cost	_____	_____	_____
Effect on archival quality	_____	_____	_____
Office space consumed	_____	_____	_____
Speed, difficulty of info retrieval	_____	_____	_____
Continuous accessibility of info	_____	_____	_____
Support employee preference	_____	_____	_____
Knowledge worker preference	_____	_____	_____
Cost of day-to-day operations	_____	_____	_____
Reduce employee turnover	_____	_____	_____
Integration with other info systems	_____	_____	_____
Down-time interruptions	_____	_____	_____

WHAT IF

1. With the Decision Tree tool, retrieve File CASE3A1 and change the probability of occurrence for the 12,000,000 document volume to .75; the probability for remaining constant, to .15; and the probability of declining to 5,000,000, to .10. View the analysis and save a copy of this analysis to a file named CASE3A3; print the analysis. Use the memo pad to create a brief memo (CASE3R2) explaining how the change in probability affected the choice of alternatives.
2. Re-enter Pro-Con Choice and retrieve the CASE3A2 file. Reevaluate your arguments and weights, assuming that the volume of documents is likely to remain constant. Recalculate the analysis and save the results to a file named CASE3A4.

CASE 4—THE YAR CORPORATION'S TELECOMMUNICATION GOALS

(For use with Chapter 8)

THE SITUATION

In her attempt to improve data communication in the Finance Department at YAR Corporation (See Case Study in Chapter 8), Karen Lindblum, the department manager, caused corporate management to raise many questions. As a result, they delayed decisions until a set of "Telecommunication Goals" could be established. The goals would become the basis for telecommunication strategy—guidelines for the whole firm for the next few years. Gerald Fernicola, the recently appointed Manager of Office Systems, was asked to create a set of "rough draft" goals that a committee of top managers could consider. Fernicola produced the following goals. One is a general goal and the other three deal with more specific communication technology categories.

1. **General.** We want to use local area networks, voice recognition, voice mail, electronic mail, facsimile, cellular telephones, teleconferencing, fiber optics, and any other technology that will improve our firm whenever we can justify the cost.
2. **Voice Communication.** We want to be able to provide for adequate live and delayed telephone communication among employees and between employees and outsiders.
3. **Data and Text Communication.** We want individuals at their workstations to be able to file and retrieve program and text files and to send and receive documents that can be edited (contents changed) as well as those that merely communicate (contents cannot be changed).
4. **Image Communication.** We want to be able to create, transmit, file, and retrieve images of document pages, photographs, illustrations, and live or recorded full motion or frozen frame video.

As the chairperson of the committee that will revise and further develop these goals, you decide to use the criteria provided in the Goal Analysis tool from *Decision Assistant* to guide the committee's evaluation of the goals.

THE SOLUTION TECHNIQUE

Select the Goal Analysis tool from the *Decision Assistant* main menu and key ALT-I for instructions. Key in the four previously listed goals (in some cases, you may need to abbreviate the statement) and your evaluation of the goal statement's merits as measured by the criteria in the tool. A 5 indicates that a goal meets the criterion extremely well; a 1 indicates that the goal meets the criterion poorly or not at all. When the evaluation of each goal is complete, key ALT-G to display the evaluation of the goal. Save the analysis to a file named CASE4A1. Use the print option from the output menu to print the evaluation. Use the tool's recommendations and your own judgment to rewrite the goal statements. With the *Decision Assistant* memo pad, create a memo report that suggests a list of revised goals. Save this list to a file named CASE4R1.

WHAT IF

1. Assume that a top manager submits the following goal to be added to the list: **VOICE DATA INTEGRATION**
   YAR Corporation will work diligently toward integrating voice and data communication in the future.
      Analyze this goal using the Goal Analysis tool and draft a revised goal. Add it to the list already created, and print a new list. Save this version of your report to a file named CASE4R2.
2. Assume that top management accepts your five goals, as revised; but they also ask that a single goal statement that could serve as a foundation mission statement for telecommunication be written. Combine the major points (omitting any references to specific technologies) into such a single mission statement. Label this goal "Telecommunication Mission" and add it to the top of your list. Label the already created goals "Specific Goals." Print a final version of your report (CASE4R3) that contains this mission statement.

CASE 5 — STRATEGIC PLANNING AND WIDEWORLD INSURANCE

(For use with Chapters 11 and 13)

BACKGROUND AND PREPARATION

This case involves office systems planning and implementation, the subject of Chapters 11, 12, and 13 in the text. After your study of Chapter 11, complete the first part of this case. Part II should be completed after the study of Chapter 13.

THE SITUATION

You are a member of an office systems project team for the home office of WideWorld Insurance. The home office occupies

16 floors of a major office tower and employs more than twenty-four hundred persons who work in the headquarters tower.

Multiple mainframe computers and extensive office automation hardware are already being used by the firm. However, there has been no real effort to coordinate or train end users or to integrate the technologies they use with other information systems. There is virtually no electronic communication or filing except for terminals that provide access to the mainframe computer for some professionals.

The office systems team will establish office systems technology (a term they have substituted for the original "office automation" label) goals, conduct studies of existing systems and procedures, and recommend new or revised systems for the firm.

THE SOLUTION TECHNIQUES—PART I:

(To be completed with the study of Chapter 11)

Establish a set of goal statements for WideWorld that would incorporate the anticipated integration of office technologies. The following statements roughly indicate management philosophy and understanding of possible technologies.

The goals should incorporate computer-based technology that will support all employees, regardless of level or location, who work in an office environment. The firm's management is committed to an environment that will allow necessary communication among workers (including information sharing) and with other groups and systems where a need can be justified. They appear willing to consider proposals that are within "reasonable" budgetary commitments.

Consider whether the following specific technologies should be mentioned in these goals: word processing, data processing/personal computing/financial analysis, electronic file storage and retrieval, electronic file sharing, peripheral sharing, electronic and voice mail, reprographics, desktop publishing, document management, presentation graphics, database management systems, electronic document storage and retrieval, computer-assisted micrographics, integrated office systems, voice technology, telephony, graphics, and image management packages. The goal statements should reflect management's desire to increase managerial staff and administrative support employee productivity and to remain competitive in the industry.

Use the Goal Analysis tool from *Decision Assistant* to evaluate your list of goals. Print the initial statements and their evaluations. Save the analysis to a file named CASE5A1. Then use memo pad to rewrite the list according to the reactions of Goal Analysis. Save your revised report to a file named CASE5R1.

PART II. The Solution Techniques   (To be completed with the study of Chapter 13)

At its first meeting, the project team concludes that its first task is to project a plan for the project. They are able to identify 20 specific project activities that fall into three phases: strategic planning, analysis and design, and implementation.

The team is able to identify several sets of activities that can be performed concurrently by subgroups of the team; other activities must be performed individually. They have determined that each individual activity and each group of concurrent activities must be completed before the next activity can begin, so a critical path determination is necessary for planning.

Examine the activities and use the Project Planning tool in *Decision Assistant* to create a critical path and to chart the schedule for the project. You will need to select a short phrase (25 characters or less) to represent each activity and designate the previous activities that must be completed before this activity begins (called predecessor codes in the instructions). For example, Activity A must be completed before Activity B begins, and Activities E, F, and G must be completed before Activity H begins.

The number in parentheses following each activity in the list below is the team's estimate of the time that will be consumed by the completion of each task (in weeks).

Strategic Planning Phase Activities
A. Organize team and plan project schedule. (1)
B. Conduct organizational analysis and write report. (4)
C. Conduct office systems study. (6)
D. Complete strategic plan and incorporate it into organization's strategic plan. (2)

Analysis and Design Phase Activities
Three concurrent activities:
E. Gather data about the costs and capabilities of the technologies on the "potential technology list" generated by the office systems study, conduct cost-benefit analyses, and report the results. (6)
F. Conduct detailed analyses of the work performed by potential users and project future needs (including the need to communicate with others inside and outside the organization) and report the results. (6)

G. Research the human-factor elements of office automation (reviews of current literature and interviews with representatives from other organizations that have already implemented office technologies) and identify human factors that should influence system design and technology selection. (2)

H. Identify the target units (individuals, departments, divisions, branches, etc.) for initial installation and determine the "technology list" that the organization will make available (broad hardware, applications software, and communication capabilities that would make up a "shopping list" for each unit). (1)

I. Design the systems that incorporate needed technologies and meet the human-factor needs of the users—systems that contain system functions and features necessary for current needs and reasonable future growth. (6)

Implementation Activities

Three concurrent activities:

J. Secure commitment for financial resources for the specific design. (2)

K. Establish office systems policies (responsibility for coordination, staffing, relationships among users and staff, etc.)

L. Create an implementation schedule that projects the remainder of the project.

Two concurrent activities:

For participating individuals, departments, and divisions,

M. Identify hardware functions and features necessary to deliver the technologies on the technology list and determine the cost range and the hardware requirements necessary to deliver these tools. (3)

N. Identify software functions and features necessary to deliver technologies on the technology list and determine cost range, documentation quality, and training requirements. (3)

Two concurrent activities:

O. Prepare and distribute requests for proposals (RFPs). (5)

P. Visit specimen installations in other organizations and gather data about implementation problems and information obtained through follow-up analyses. (5)

Two concurrent activities:

Q. Evaluate vendor proposals, select vendor(s), and negotiate purchase and/or lease contracts. (2)

R. Orient, educate, and train users. (2)

Two concurrent activities:

S. Install systems in targeted offices. (1)

T. Activate user support system, initiate follow-up analyses, and begin planning future installations. (1)

When the data are entered, key ALT-D or ALT-G to display the Project Planning Chart. Save the analysis to your disk in a file named CASE5A2. Print the chart. Use the chart (which resembles a Gantt chart) to prepare a calendar (assume that Day One was the first Monday in February of the current year). Use the memo pad to create a memo in which you outline the dates for each phase and assign calendar dates for the beginning of each activity. Save your report to a file named CASE5R2.

WHAT IF

1. Assume that one month into the project the team decides that many of the projected timeframes are unrealistic and that all remaining activities should be reevaluated. The project is already two weeks behind schedule. Retrieve the file CASE5A2, reevaluate the remaining activities and change any that you think are unrealistic or out of sequence. If you conclude that they are correct, leave them as they are. When you save the file this time, use the file name CASE5A3. Print the analysis.
2. Assume that an emergency during the week preceding the scheduled beginning of Activities J-K-L will prevent the subgroup assigned to complete Activity L from doing that work. Instead, all the work in these three activities will need to be done by the other two sub- groups. Retrieve CASE5A3, determine the effect of the emergency, correct the timeframes and predecessor codes to a file named CASE5A4. Print the analysis. Using the memo pad, create a report (File name CASE5R3) that explains the delay and revises the calendar of activities.

CASE 6 — VENDOR SELECTION AT STANFORD CORPORATION

PREPARATION AND REVIEW

Review the portions of Chapter 13 that deal with vendor selection and the portions of Chapter 12 that deal with vendor negotiations. These materials will be helpful in making the decisions necessary in this case.

THE SITUATION

You are the Manager of End User Computing at Stanford Corporation, where you are about to begin the installation phase of an office automation project that will provide microcomputer workstations for several dozen employees. The office automation project team has selected three or four computer types that will be made available to employees, depending upon their needs. However, they intend to purchase all workstations from one vendor to take advantage of volume discounts on hardware and maintenance costs and, they hope, to receive better service from the vendor. Four vendors are currently being considered. Brief descriptions of these vendors are as follows:

Vendor A: a local retail computer store operating under a franchise that includes franchises in most cities in the country with a population of 50,000 or more. This vendor holds dealerships for multiple microcomputer manufacturers and most of the popular software houses. The store has a maintenance staff in the store and access to manufacturer-sanctioned service outlets in nearby cities. You would be required to take units to the store for maintenance. There is no guaranteed limit on downtime, but this vendor has a good reputation for service.

Vendor B: a local retail outlet of a manufacturer-owned chain with one or more outlets in most major cities in the country. This outlet sells only its own brand of hardware but is a dealer for major software packages. A local maintenance person handles minor repairs; the firm's service center in a nearby city handles major repairs. Customers bring units to the store for maintenance. This dealer also has a good reputation for quick turnaround time on maintenance, although the contract specifies no specific time.

Vendor C: a microcomputer manufacturer selling through its local sales representative. Since this manufacturer is also one of the country's largest manufacturers of mainframe computers and minicomputers, they have an extensive maintenance staff in the city where you are located. Additional maintenance staff persons are available in nearby cities. The warranty provides for on-site, next-day service; but this firm sometimes is able to provide same-day service for minor problems.

Vendor D: a manufacturer who sells its product by telephone, this vendor operates in another state but maintains telephone help lines and a network of service center agreements that promise next-day service. The maintenance contract provides for next-day, on-site service. Minor problems are handled by telephone.

The following chart summarizes the team's findings regarding the cost of the 286-based computers they have selected as the basic workstation for most employees, as well as their evaluation of other factors.

Table 6-1 Evaluation of Four Microcomputers with 286-chip CPUs

Computer Cost	Maintenance Cost—YR 1	Maintenance Cost—YR 2+	Service Reputation	Training?	Training Cost	Stability Rating
A $3,700	None	$210	Good	Yes	$50 hr*	Good
B $2,700	Parts only	$180	Good	Yes	$45 hr*	Good
C $4,000	$30	$120	Excellent	No	na	Excellent
D $3,000	None	$200	Fair	No	na	Fair

THE SOLUTION TECHNIQUE

Your team must choose one of the vendors from the four final candidates. Select the Multi-Attribute Scoring tool from the *Decision Assistant* software. After selecting this tool, key ALT-I for instructions. Your team decides that the following five choice factors (criteria) should influence your decision:

1. Cost of Hardware
2. Quality of Available Maintenance
3. Cost of Maintenance
4. Vendor Reputation and Stability
5. Cost and Availability of Training

Make the decisions and key in the results necessary to complete the following:

(a) Assign importance weights for the five choice factors (criteria); each should be weighted from one to ten. These weights should indicate the importance of that factor to the decision, relative to the other factors. Assign the same number to two factors that you believe should carry equal weight in the decision. The most important choice factor should receive the highest rating.

(b) Rate each of the four vendors on a scale of 0-100 for each factor. The vendor that best provides for the factor should receive the highest rating; the vendor that least provides for the factor should receive the lowest rating, and so on.

When you have completed keying the weights and evaluations, key ALT-D to display the weighted scores. Save your chart in a file named CASE6A1. Print the chart. The alternative with the highest score is considered the most attractive.

WHAT IF

1. Assume that, through further analysis and discussion, your team decides that one of the choice factors that you used (the

one to which you assigned the lowest weight) probably should not be used at all, because the low-satisfaction scores assigned to that factor could have influenced the decision too much. Retrieve File CASE6A1; eliminate the lowest-weight factor, reassign weights if necessary, and display new scores. Print the new table, and save the second analysis under the name CASE6A2. In a memo report (CASE6R1), compare the two analyses.

2. If time and resources permit (and at the discretion of your instructor), select a microcomputer workstation that you believe to be adequate for an environment that you have in mind, gather data to evaluate the workstation using the criteria in this case, assign weights and evaluations, and calculate a new chart of weighted evaluations.

APPENDIX B

CALCULATIONS OF COSTS IN A BEFORE/AFTER EXPERIMENT

ELECTRONIC FILING APPLICATION

The following calculations demonstrate one method of calculating the records management costs before and after installation of electronic filing. The task involves retrieval of a paper file needed to answer a telephone caller's query and the time required to refile the folder. The pilot system involves an electronic management system which would permit the employee to retrieve the information via an electronic workstation with access to stored digitized images of documents. The statistics are fictitious; they are presented as an example of the observations and calculations that might be made to collect such data.

The data represent five employees observed on "typical" days. Employees accumulate files and refile them at the end of the day.

Summary Data:

Average travel time from workstation to files and return	.330 min.
Average time to retrieve file	.083 min.
Total travel and retrieval time	.413 min.
Average time to refile one file or document	.150 min.

Calculations for typical day using traditional paper files:

Employee	No. Calls	Retrieval Time N × .413	End-of-Day Refile (N × .15) + .33	Total
1	9	3.72	1.68	5.40
2	11	4.54	1.98	6.52
3	13	5.37	2.28	7.65
4	7	2.89	1.38	4.27
5	6	2.48	1.23	3.71
Totals	46	19.00	8.55	27.55

Average time per call = (27.55 min. ÷ 46 calls) = .6 min. per call

Hours consumed = 27.55 min. ÷ 60 = .46 hrs. ÷ 5 = .092 hrs. per employee

Calculations for typical day using electronic image management system:

Average time to retrieve index code	.083 min.
Average time to key index code	.041 min.
Average wait time for information display	.079 min.
Average time per call	.203 min.

.203 × 9.2 (average no. of calls) =
1.867 min. ÷ 60 = .031 hrs. per employee

Cost/Benefit Analysis:

	Time	Wage	Employees	Wage	Days	Cost
Old method:	.092	5.78	24 ×	.532 ×	260	= 3,319.68
New method:	.031	5.78	24 ×	.179 ×	260	= 1,116.96

Annual Savings $2,202.72

Productivity Improvement:

New Method Time		**Old Method Time**	**Increased Productivity**
.031 hrs.	÷	.092 = 33.70%	100% − 33.70% = 66.30%

Cost Improvement:

	Old Method	**New Method**
Cost of Labor	$ 3,319.68	$1,116.96
Cost of Floor Space:		
676 sq. ft. × $16	10,816.00	
200 sq. ft. × $16		3,200.00
	$14,135.68	$4,316.96

New Method Cost		**Old Method Cost**	**Cost Reduction**
$4,316.96	÷	$14,135.68 = 31%	100% − 31% = 69%

The cost of the systems and the effectiveness benefits would need to be weighed against these savings to determine whether or not the system is worth the cost. If the volume of calls were greater or if the quality of service is greatly improved, the savings is within a range that would make the change desirable.

APPENDIX C

EXAMPLE OF A TIME STANDARD CALCULATION

Activity: Keyboard a double-spaced report from a handwritten rough draft.

Task	Date	Line Count	Total Time*	Time per line
Initial keyboarding (3 observations)	10-19-87	260	60.67	.23
	10-20-87	203	45.11	.22
	10-23-87	189	41.34	.22
KEYBOARD TOTALS		652	147.12	.23
Proof and edit entire report (3 observations)	10-19-87	260	24.07	
	10-20-87	203	17.78	
	10-23-87	189	17.50	
PROOF AND EDIT TOTALS		652	59.35	.09
KEYBOARD, PROOF, AND EDIT TOTALS		652	206.47	.32

*Time is calculated in minutes.

Data for Standards Calculation:

652 lines ÷ 54 lines per page = 12.07 pages
147.12 minutes of keyboarding time ÷ 60 min. = 2.45 hours
 59.35 minutes of proof and edit time ÷ 60 min. = .99 hours
206.47 minutes of total time ÷ 60 min. = 3.44 hours

Standards:

Keyboarding: 4.43 lines/min. (652 ÷ 147.12)
                      4.93 pages/hr. (12.07 ÷ 2.45)

Proof and edit: 10.99 lines/min. (652 ÷ 59.35)
                                      12.19 pages/hr. (12.07 ÷ .99)

Keyboard, proof, and edit: 3.16 lines/min. (652 ÷ 206.47)
                                      3.51 pages/hr. (12.07 ÷ 3.44)

GLOSSARY

A

access floor A raised floor in areas with a heavy concentration of information processing hardware. Movable floor sections allow access to cables and power supplies.

acoustical hood A sound-deadening cover for noisy machines.

adhocracy A practice of assigning tasks according to the skills of the individual—not according to job title.

administrative support (1) Work done by an employee who supports a knowledge worker (executive, manager, or professional staff person); work such as clerical, secretarial, or any assistance-type activity; (2) the nontyping secretarial function, particularly in an environment where the word processing function is separated from other secretarial functions; and (3) a family of software that enables knowledge workers to perform office automation tasks for themselves.

administrative value In records/information management, the value of information that enables management to make effective decisions.

advanced comfort systems An environmental control system that allows workers to maintain control over their workstation environmental elements (temperature, air flow, lighting).

airfones Telephone systems that provide service to airborne participants.

ambient lighting The surrounding light condition provided for a work area.

analog computer A computer that works directly with physical quantities such as weight, voltage, and speed or other continuously supplied transmissions.

analog transmission Transmission of information in a continuous signal, such as in voice transmission over telephone links or continuous data supplied to analog computers.

analyst In information systems, an employee who plans, develops, evaluates, and implements systems for an organization's information needs.

andragogy The study of the adult learner.

androgyny The study of male and female characteristics in the behavior of people in general—the concept suggests that all humans have representative characteristics of both sexes.

aperture card Paper cards containing "windows" (openings) over which microfilm images are mounted and through which the images are viewed when magnified. The card may also contain a machine-readable identification code.

application generators Programming software that generates applications programs.

applications interoperability A capability of applications software making possible easy movement from one application function to another without noticeable difference to the user; having a standard "look and feel."

applications program A set of instructions to a computer that instructs the central processing unit to carry out specific information processing tasks such as accounting functions or word processing.

architecture The structure of the software and hardware devices that make up an information processing system.

archival value For records/information management, the value or potential value of records or information for historical or scholarly research in the future.

ARCS Model A model for employee training—attention, relevance, confidence, and satisfaction are the objectives of a training experience.

asynchronous mode Information transmission mode that communicates each character, one at a time, separated by start and stop signals (start, character, stop).

arithmetic/logic unit (ALU) The portion of a computer's central processing unit that performs calculations.

artificial intelligence A group of computer programs in the expert systems category of fifth-generation language programs which includes a knowledge base, a driver program, an explanation program, and a knowledge refining program.

assessment center An in-house center for evaluating job applicants' performances on a variety of activities that simulate a job.

authoring system Computer software that enables trainers to create software that instructs the computer to display text or graphics, ask questions, give responses to trainees' answers, evaluate progress, and keep records of trainees' progress.

automatic typewriter A typewriter that has keys which are activated by holes in a cylinder or punched paper tape.

automation Any augmentation of the physical and mental capabilities of individuals by technology.

B

backup (1) The concept that members of administrative support teams will assist each other during times of unbalanced work loads; (2) systems and/or procedures developed to provide duplicate information in the event of an equipment or power failure.

baseband A telecommunication link that uses the whole link for one transmission at a time (may transmit it multiple signals alternately).

BASIC Beginners' all-purpose instruction code, a high-level computer programming language used for writing microcomputer applications programs.

batch office A subcategory of a type I office in which the activity switches among multiple routine tasks (usually automated). Work may be governed by strict guidelines. A "batch" of processing related to one task is likely to be completed before switching to another task.

batch processing A technique for processing information with computers. Programs and data to be processed are loaded into computers in batches (usually in a mainframe computer facility). The output is returned to the user, who has no access to the system.

baud rate A measure of data transmission speed over telecommunication links in bits of information per second.

benchmark position The work of an employee considered to be an average, well-trained worker. Such positions are used for measurement when time standards or productivity standards are being established.

bilateral mobility Job change involving job rotation or an extended temporary change from one job to another.

bit In data structures, one binary digit or one item of information recorded as an "on" or an "off" condition.

branching A technique used to produce computer/assisted instruction experiences that provide alternate instructions to trainees based upon learners responses to questions in the program. Example: An accurate response would cue the program to move to the next item in the sequence; an inaccurate response would cue the program to repeat a previously covered sequence.

broadband A telecommunication link that can be divided into channels for transmitting multiple signals simultaneously.

bubble memory An internal memory system for a computer's central processing unit that is nonvolatile. It stores information as "bubbles" on tiny crystal sheets, consumes very little space, and is not erased when the power supply is disrupted.

buffer zone In office design, a flexible space available for future expansion.

bus The internal mechanism in a computer that controls communication of information among the central processor, memory units, and peripheral equipment.

bus topology A local area network topology that features a single length of cable or other communication link along which nodes are installed without a central server or controller.

business sabbatical Paid, periodic work leaves, usually for executives.

byte In data structures, a group of bits that make up a character of information (a digit or an alphabetic character) that is recognized by the computer as a unit.

C

CAI (Computer-assisted instruction) Computer-based training that involves use of the computer as the presentation medium.

career The sequence of jobs held during one's work life.

career development program A formal system for assisting employees in planning careers.

career mobility Movement in one's career that may involve advancement (upward mobility) or lateral movement. It may involve change in employer as well as job.

career planning Conducting a self-assessment, engaging in job exploration, and setting career goals.

career stages The phases of career development: apprenticeship, self-dependence, mentor, and senior management.

career temp Employees of temporary service agencies who work full time for the agency.

career tracks A path of employment experiences that leads to advancement.

CASE (Computer Aided Software Engineering) Software systems that automate the software applications development process.

cathode ray tube (CRT) An electronic TV-like screen for displaying information in a computer system (used for viewing input to the system and the system's output).

CBT (Computer-Based Training) The use of computer technology for instruction and monitoring of the training process.

CDROM (Compact Disk Read Only Memory) An optical storage medium that holds information signals recorded and read by laser beams; a disk about five inches in diameter, named for the audio compact disk of about the same size; contain permanent recordings—cannot be erased—of the write once, read many times variety.

cellular radio A wireless communication system that broadcasts voice communication within designated areas or activates a "beeper" device to cue a participant to call a message service.

centralized design An organizational design representing authority concentrated at the top-management level and flowing downward to the ranks.

centralized plan A plan for providing all the needed administrative support from one physical location.

central processing unit (CPU) The component of a computer system which manipulates information according to a program.

central voice processing unit A computer that controls voice input, storage, and output for voice mail and other voice communication management.

certification A formal process for designating distinctive achievement and experience in a career field.

change agent Persons who plan and conduct activities designed to bring about a modification of the environment or organizational climate.

channel For information processing systems, the path between one component and another over which data travels.

chip An integrated circuit etched on a tiny piece of silicon or geranium.

CIO (Chief Information Officer) An officer who is responsible for office automation, computer resources, records management, telecommunications, and all the other information needs of an organization.

clipart Collections of graphic design files; as used in electronic office systems, usually refers to electronic files of such designs.

closed system An organization which operates without consideration of its external environment.

cluster organization The practice of assigning tasks to temporary groups, influenced by the skill of the group—

not the permanent job titles of the individuals.

coaxial cable A telecommunication link consisting of a cable containing a center wire surrounded by plastic sheathing. The sheathed wire is surrounded by a braided wire sleeve.

COBOL (Common Business-Oriented Language) A popular computer language made up of English-like words and used mostly for business information processing applications programs.

communication The transmission of information.

communication effectiveness A measure of the quality of communication—the degree to which information is understood by the receiver and applied as intended by the sender.

communication efficiency The maintenance of communication costs at reasonable levels and the expenditure of resources compared to the number of messages communicated or the number of recipients of a message.

communication link The pathway or route over which signals travel from one information processing or transmission component to another. It may be a hard (physical) link, such as a wire or cable, an airwave link, an optical (light-beam) link, or any combination of these.

comparable worth An issue regarding the wage gap between males and females performing the same jobs and, particularly, the comparison of the overall compensation for male-dominated jobs and that of female-dominated jobs requiring similar levels of preparation.

compensation administration A program for administering pay and employee benefits.

computer A system of interconnected components which electronically process (calculate, correlate, select, and compile) information according to a set of instructions and which possesses the capacity for storing information.

computer-assisted retrieval (CAR) A computer-stored index to records and information that indicates a particular record's location (such as a microfilm cartridge number and image number) or the computer-directed retrieval of document images held in micrographic form.

computer auditing (1) Using the computer as a tool for auditing information resources, (2) the periodic examination of computers and the systems they operate.

computer-assisted instruction (CAI) The use of the computer to present drill and practice exercises, tutorials, and simulations in a training environment.

computer-based training The use of computer technology for instruction and monitoring of the training process.

computer-brain interface Interfaces (via electrodes attached to the temples of human beings) between the human brain and computers, allowing electro-magnetic signals to pass from the human brain to the computer. Expected development would enable an individual to program a computer through thought processes by the mid-1990s.

computer-managed instruction The use of a computer to handle administrative tasks associated with the training function, such as maintaining class rosters and schedules, generating tests, scoring tests, and maintaining grades.

computer crime The illegal access to computer information systems, manipulation of information in a manner that provides unwarranted gains to the perpetrator, or vandalism or sabotage of hardware or software systems.

computer output microfilm (COM) Microfilm containing computer-generated images either from a laser imaging process or a photographic process capturing cathode ray tube display images.

computer virus A computer program that may be attached to electronic files or public domain software. Programs are usually written to be triggered by some event or condition; this may lead to uncontrolled files reproduction or information destruction.

computerized branch exchange (CBX) An automatic switching system (a computer manages the switching) for voice and data communication signals. Signals are converted to digital signals for switching and back to analog signals for transmission.

computer operator An employee who operates computers, computer peripherals, and data-entry equipment.

concurrent logic system An information processing system featuring a central processing unit that can be used concurrently by multiple terminals to process a variety of applications.

conflict resolution The process of seeking solutions to conflict among employees.

consultant In-house employees or externally engaged specialists who conduct feasibility studies, make recommendations to management, direct the implementation of systems, and may serve as advisers to designers, software developers, or manufacturers of office equipment or furnishings.

context In social ergonomics, refers to the social system or surrounding environment into which systems designs fit.

continuous speaker-dependent recognition (CSDR) A voice recognition technology that allows the speaker to use a continuous stream of words in a normal conversational pattern, with no special or awkward pronunciations or pauses. The system will respond to prerecorded vocabulary which appears in a "stream."

cooperative processing The fusion of mainframe and microcomputer processing into one system, involving parts of the execution of applications on one central processor and parts on another processor, perhaps without the knowledge of the user.

copier A document-reproduction device that replicates document images by either a heat or an electrostatic process—also called a photocopier.

corporation An organization that is a legal entity, having a "life" independent of its owners.

cost-benefit analysis Projected costs and anticipated benefits from proposed changes.

CP/M A control program for microprocessors; a microcomputer operating system.

CPS (Characters Per Second) A measurement of printer speed.

critical record Records that could be damaging to the organization or to an individual if they fell into the wrong hands.

cross training Training received by administrative support employees for the performance of tasks not normally included in their work loads enabling team members to fill in for each other during emergencies.

cryoelectronic storage A highly sensitive electronic information storage medium that is kept at zero degrees centigrade or lower to improve storage performance of the medium.

cursor A location symbol on a computer's display screen, indicates the position of the next information entered.

custom office Subcategory of a type I office which is equipped to handle events individually because of special handling or unique characteristics of tasks and may involve standard procedures applied according to need of individual events.

D

data Raw facts, symbols, letters, numbers; in automated systems, information that is statistical, financial, or quantitative in nature; plural of datum.

database Any collection of related information. The term is frequently used to refer to electronic data files housed within the organization or those housed externally and accessed on a fee basis.

database machine A computer dedicated to the management of an electronic database.

database management system (DBMS) Computer software that manages the creation and use of an electronic database.

data communication Transmission of digital code representing quantitative information over communication links (sometimes used synonymously with telecommunication).

data people Category of individuals who prefer jobs that emphasize details and the planning, organizing, and analyzing of information.

data processing Support system associated with large-volume processing of raw quantitative and factual information into useful information after it has been calculated, compiled, sorted, and formatted.

decentralized administrative support plan A plan for dispersing administrative support employees physically throughout the facilities occupied by the knowledge workers served by the support employees.

decentralized design Organizational design represented by dispersed policy making, planning, and decision making throughout the organization.

decentralized plan A plan that locates administrative support employees in the functional units they support in close proximity to the principals they support.

decibel A unit of measurement for the intensity of sound. (The difference between the decibels of two sounds is equal to 10 times the common logarithm of the ratio of their power levels.)

decision support Support provided for knowledge workers to assist their information retrieval and processing and application of technology for this purpose. Examples: retrieve information from files, plan and track projects, perform calculations, and prepare graphics.

decision support system (DSS) (1) A family of computer software that provides decision support capabilities for knowledge workers and may be applied to budget allocations, personnel assignments, market or production planning, projections of revenue, and the calculation of profit margins. (2) Large-scale organization-wide decision modeling systems that may be referred to as management information systems (MIS) and depend upon corporate databases for information that is plugged into the system.

dedicated computer A computer employed for a single activity.

dedicated word processor A stand-alone system employing computer technology to perform word processing applications but not other information processing applications.

deficiencies in task execution An employee productivity deficiency that is not related to knowledge or skills required to perform tasks and which cannot be corrected by training.

deficiencies of practice An employee productivity deficiency that involves inadequate opportunity to apply a skill that has been learned. Training can provide such practice.

deficiencies of skill An employee productivity deficiency involving a lack of skill. Such deficiencies may be corrected by training.

delivery system The source of training: supervisor of an employee, in-house training department or training specialist, outside agency, or educational institution.

demotion Job change involving "downward" movement to a job with less responsibility.

demountable wall A movable, upholstered wall that screens work areas in open-plan offices and reduces the noise level, and can be easily moved to rearrange the office space.

desktop publishing A collection of software, computer, and printer technology for producing near-professional quality documents. These systems are capable of page design, type font and size selection, and the incorporation of graphic elements into pages of text.

digital branch exchange (DBX) May be called "digital PBX." A telephone switching system using telephones with microprocessor chips that convert voice signals to digital signals which are switched and routed by computer and reversed to analog signals by another chip on the receiving end of the link.

digital computer One that processes digits (quantitative information) or alphanumeric information recorded in digital code.

digital image processing A process that uses electronic scanning equipment to digitally store document images, including text and graphics. The text of such images cannot be manipulated in the manner that text stored in a character-based system can be edited.

digital image processor Hardware capable of scanning documents with a laser beam, converting their images to digitized code for storage in any electronic storage medium.

digital speech compression A feature of digitized voice storage that removes extraneous components (pauses or sighs) from the storage to consume less storage space.

digital transmission The transmission of information in intermittent signals over communication links which permits multiple transmissions on the same link simultaneously.

disaster backup service A range of disaster recovery services provided by firms specializing in aiding organizations that are affected by natural or other disasters and may include complete office facilities, computer systems, and the staff needed to keep a firm operating while facilities are being restored.

disk drive A computer peripheral that writes information to a storage medium and reads information from such media. In some cases, such as the CDROM optical medium, the peripheral reads prerecorded information but does not write new information.

diskette system A device for storing digital information in electronic code on disk-shaped recording media. Popular sizes are 8-inch, 3½-inch, and 5¼-inch diameters. The medium is flexible and is sometimes referred to as a floppy disk.

disk library A device for storing optical disks and retrieving information stored on the disks. See also jukebox.

disk operating system (DOS) A computer operating system recorded on magnetic disks and transferred to the computer's memory for directing the applications programs.

distributed data processing The distribution of computer power throughout an organization either by installing remote, independently operating computer systems or the distribution of computing power and file access from a mainframe computer to users over communication links.

dithering A process used to scan and reproduce graphic images, producing a variety of shades of gray for enhanced reproduction.

division of labor The subdivision of tasks among workers.

document A recording of graphic and/or textual information (traditionally, a paper record) which may have evidentiary value if it is maintained in the original format or a legally acceptable reproduction of the original format.

documentary value In records/information management, the value of information that provides proof of past events or conditions.

dot-matrix printer A printer that creates text when steel pins are triggered by computer signals within a matrix. Characters are formed when the pins strike the paper through an inked ribbon.

dots per inch (DPI) The measure of image resolution or density produced by image scanners and reproduced by printers.

download To transfer software or information from one information processing component to another over a communication link.

draft mode The mode in which a printer operates when it is printing at maximum speed. The quality of output is legible but inferior to other modes.

duplex A telecommunication transmission path that carries a two-way information flow.

Dvorak keyboard The simplified keyboard arrangement devised by August Dvorak in the 1930s.

dynamic equilibrium A philosophical description of the technological future which describes the norm as a state of flux.

E

EEOC (Equal Employment Opportunity Commission) An agency of the U.S. federal government that oversees employment practices attempting to prevent identified discriminatory practices in staffing.

effectiveness benefit A real or anticipated benefit resulting from a change; a benefit that represents improved quality of productivity.

efficiency benefit A real or anticipated benefit resulting from a change; a benefit that can be quantified and identified through reduced expenditures or increased revenues.

electromyographic (emg) bio-feedback The warning signals that come from system that signals the presence of muscle tension. Audible sounds from a lightweight headset warn the employee to correct posture or change positions.

electronic blackboard An information transmission device that captures an image of information that has been written by hand on a chalkboard-sized frame and transmits the image to remote display screens using a telecommunication link.

electronic cottage See *telecommuting.*

electronic document interchange (EDI) A concept of information exchange using communication standards that allow electronic documents for a number of routine business transactions to be electronically transmitted among firms.

electronic file Any collection of information recorded in digitized code that can be read, stored, and retrieved by a computer.

electronic mail A communication system involving the transmission of text over communication links from one electronic workstation to another (screen to screen) and may feature "electronic mailboxes" for storing incoming and outgoing messages for later delivery. (Some vendors refer to voice mail systems as electronic mail.)

electronic printer A nonimpact printer that uses a light source to reflect character and graphic images through a series of mirrors using electrostatic processes to create images on paper. See also *intelligent printer, laser printer* and *xerographic printer.*

electronic publishing The earliest use of this term applied to the use of computers in the printing industry, e. g., electronic typesetting. Now the term is sometimes used synonymously with *desktop publishing.*

electronic workstation A workstation or system capable of processing information independently, accessing remote databases and mainframe computers, and retrieving a variety of software.

employee performance appraisal A combination of formal evaluation, day-to-day informal evaluation, and future performance planning for employees.

employee turnover ratio The portion of the work force replaced each year.

encryption An information security system that garbles information during transmission but decodes it when it is received by a system or a system component operated by a person with the correct decoder key.

end-user computing The phase of office automation involving distributed information processing capabilities for individuals at their workstations with application of computer power by administrative support employees, managers, executives, and professional staff members.

ENIAC (Electronic Numerical Integrator And Computer) The first true computer developed at the University of Pennsylvania by Dr. John W. Mauchly and J. Presper Eckert, Jr. and operated with 18,000 vacuum tubes.

ergonomics The study of the interaction between people and their work environments.

executive office A subcategory of the type II office created for an organization's high-level officials. Systems involve communication (face-to-face meetings, telecommunication, written communication) and complex, loose procedures.

expert system A set of computer programs in the fifth-generation language category, an expert system consists of these parts: a knowledge base, a driver program, an explanation program, a knowledge refining program, and a natural language processor. (The first four parts comprise what is known as artificial intelligence.)

F

facsimile A document image transmission device involving a scanning process and a communication link (frequently an ordinary telephone line). Documents are produced a line at a time at a remote receiver.

fault tolerant Information system hardware and software capabilities that allow systems to continue to operate during an equipment malfunction and involve backup systems, emergency power supplies, power distribution systems, and self-diagnostic maintenance aids.

feedback In organizational systems theory, reaction to systems output; in communication, a response or observed reaction; in training, a reaction to a training experience, trainees' reactions to a trainer, or trainers' evaluations of trainees' accomplishments.

fiber-optic cable Telecommunication link made from tiny strands of glass over which laser beams carry information signals. Multiple strands usually make up one cable.

fiber optics The application of laser light beams as the medium for information transmission—beams are transmitted over tiny continuous glass rods.

fifth generation Applied to information processing software, refers to software combinations that enable computers to solve problems as humans do—by reasoning, making judgments, and learning; also called knowledge/information processing systems (KIPS).

file A collection of related information treated as a unit which may be recorded on electronic, micrographic, or paper media.

file integrity Quality of a group of related information (documents, files, etc.) can be kept together for reference purposes. Order and sequence may be considered characteristics of file integrity.

file procedure Steps involved in electronic records management of electronic files, for example, a sequence of commands to organize, view, retrieve, delete, and combine files.

financial analysis software Any applications software product that supports financial analysis through simplification of calculations and application of models to financial situations; frequently used to refer to spreadsheet software.

first-line supervisor The supervisor of operative employees; the first level of management in an organizational hierarchy.

flextime A work arrangement wherein employees work during certain peak hours but have a choice regarding arrival and departure times.

flicker The slight movements of displayed characters on a video display screen which can result in operator eyestrain.

floppy disk An electronic information storage medium constructed from flexible disks encased in plastic jackets. Popular disks have either 8-inch, 5¼-inch, or 3½-inch diameters.

flow office A subcategory of the type I office which involves one main procedure executed repeatedly. Examples include a hotel reservation office and a credit office in a retail store.

font A complete set of typefaces in a single type style, including alphabetic characters, numeric characters, and related symbols such as punctuation marks.

form (in social ergonomics) Aspects of system design affecting the people who work with systems and controlled by the designer, such as the user interface or other screen displays.

form (in records management) A document—paper or electronic—containing fixed data plus prompts and space for insertion of variable data into records.

footcandle A measure of the quantity of light in a particular location—technically, the quantity of light produced by the flame of one candle at a distance of one foot.

formal structure For organizations, that structure depicted on the organizational chart which indicates who is responsible for various functions.

fourth generation languages (4GLs) A category of computer languages that are nonprocedural programs (they use simple commands to tell the computer what to do) for developing application programs needed by an individual who may not be familiar with programming languages.

frozen video A category of video transmission used in teleconferencing applications to create frequently updated still-screen images. (Transmission involves a series of still pictures—not a motion video.)

full duplex A telecommunication transmission path that per its simultaneous two-way information flow.

full motion video Video transmissions or recordings that depict full, natural motion of subjects—as opposed to frozen video that transmits "still" pictures of subjects.

futurism The study of the future using organized processes such as trend analysis and visioning.

futurist One who attempts to forecast what will exist or happen in the time yet to come.

G

general-purpose computer A computer that can be programmed to perform a wide variety of information processing tasks.

generation A time span during which similar technologies are applied. For computers, a time during which a particular technology is used for the manufacture of hardware.

gigabyte One billion bytes.

global consciousness An awareness of conditions, particularly markets and productivity efforts, on a worldwide scope.

graphics Charts, graphs, or illustrations; in information processing, graphic representation of quantitative information; a category of computer software designed to create graphic illustrations.

gray scale A process used to electronically scan and reproduce graphic images in a desktop publishing or printing system. The result is a variety of shades of gray to enhance the reproduction of photographic materials.

groupware Software designed for collaborative use by multiple users.

H

hacker A computer buff who is an expert at data communication and information system access. This term may be used to describe the innocent pilferage of information systems or intentional criminal acts by those who intend to secure financial gain for themselves or classified (confidential) information.

half duplex A telecommunication transmission path that per its two-way flow of information but in only one direction at a time.

hard disk Electronic information storage medium constructed of rigid disks coated with a magnetic recording medium similar to that used in audio recording media and flexible disks.

hard-dollar benefit Direct benefits from change measurable in dollars; an efficiency benefit that is realized immediately.

heating recovery system A system for capturing and using otherwise wasted heat in a building.

heuristics A method of empirical thinking employed by computer programs with artificial intelligence to solve problems using rules of thumb.

hierarchical database A database holding information in related collections as it is stored using a multilayered or "tree" effect.

high-speed transmission Sometimes applied to information transmission speeds of 4800 baud or more; however, steadily increasing transmission speeds render the term useless.

holistic training An approach to training that affects the individual not only as an employee but as a whole person.

horizontal mobility Job change from one career path to another but between jobs at similar levels.

human-computer communicative dialogue An exchange of information between a person and a computer whereby the person and the computer have access to a symbolic flow of information and each party has the ability to interrupt, query, and correct the communication flowing between them.

human-computer interface The interaction of humans and computer systems based upon a given set of inputs to bring about a desired output; the point of interaction; examples: screen displays and keyboards.

human-computer system The combined information processing capabilities of humans and computers.

human factors The discovery and application of information about human abilities, limitations, and other characteristics to the design of tools, machines, systems, tasks jobs, and environments for safe, comfortable, and effective human use. See *ergonomics*.

human factors approach An approach to technological systems design approach that gives equal consideration to the human and technical effects of systems design; in some cases, greater consideration to the human conditions may be given; in office systems, referred to as user-driven design.

human factors engineering The incorporation of physical and psychosocial needs of users into the design of physical office environments.

human processor model The likening of the human mind to an information processing system.

human resources department The organizational unit responsible for employee recruitment, hiring, training, compensation, appraisal, and employee benefits programs.

human resources development (HRD) A name frequently applied to the department within an organization responsible for staffing, training, and employee benefits. Formerly these departments were called personnel departments.

hybrid approach In office design, encompasses both open and closed spaces with easy and economical convertibility.

hypermedia Computerized instruction tools that can be used for the development of training programs; permit users to explore topics by linking related segments of information from a database-like collection of information.

hypertext A system of information storage that permits retrieval from multiple locations within the information collection of textual and graphic information about related topics; system permits linkages of a nature described by the user for a particular use.

icons Graphic representations of computer commands, some of which can be activated by touching them on a display screen, moving a cursor to them with the aid of a "mouse," or pointing a light pen to the image on the screen.

image An information processing system or an information category that deals with the replication of documents or other information media into filmed or electronic media so that exact reproductions of originals can be viewed or committed to paper.

impact printer The computer peripheral that creates text or graphics on paper with a mechanism that makes physical contact with paper.

implementation A broad range of organizational activity including organizational assessment, problem identification, strategic planning for the future, installation of changes represented by long-range strategy, and integration of changes into existing structures. In office systems literature, the term may be used to indicate only the installation of technologies.

implementation team For office systems technologies, a team of people who plan the implementation of office automation throughout an organization with representatives from all information processing activities within the organization.

informal structure For organizations, those self-grouped individuals who communicate with each other, form loyalties to each other, and function outside the formal structure.

information That knowledge which informs or has the capacity to inform the recipient.

information age The era that began in the mid 1950s in which major attention shifted from industrial development to information management, from the blue-collar work force to the white-collar work force.

information center A central facility or service within organizations for providing end users with advice, training, and support for developing their own applications of information technology.

information industries Those involved with the processing and distribution of information through hardware manufacture or software development; marketing hardware, software or systems; or offering information services.

information infrastructure An organizational structure based on information as a method of management as well as a strategic resource and a tool for management support.

information interviews An interview conducted in the process of gathering information as in a job exploration process.

information life cycle The stages through which information passes from creation to manipulation to distribution to storage/retrieval and, finally, to disposition—destruction or permanent preservation.

information management software A category of computer applications software (a database) that allows creation, editing, addition, deletion, and manipulation of internal organizational files.

information manipulation Processing raw information or in some way changing existing information.

information overload Too much information for effective use or application in a particular environment.

information processing cycle The input, processing, storage, output, and communication (distribution) of information.

information resources The information holdings and information-handling tools and systems within or available to an organization.

information resource A collection of potentially useful information held by an organization which may be held in a variety of forms (e.g., paper, micrographic, or electronic media).

information resources management Management of the collections of information resources within an organization in a systematic manner and with the objective of providing information to those who need it in the form in which it is needed and when it is needed. The term may also refer to the treatment of all of an organization's information resources as an economic resource with identifiable value.

information system A system for creating, communicating, storing, and retricving information.

infrared transmission An optical telecommunication link involving transmission of signals on infrared light beams.

ink-jet printer A nonimpact printer that creates character and graphic images on paper by spraying fast-drying ink onto paper in a dot matrix.

input In organizational systems theory, any force that affects the organization; in information processing, information entering a system or a category of computer components designed to accept information for processing.

instructor A title for an educator, trainer, or entry-level position for college or university teachers.

integrated office system The concept of linking separate information systems into a single system. Examples include data processing, word processing, and records management systems that are interconnected and available to large numbers of employees whose electronic workstations are connected by a network or other communication link.

integrated services digital networks (ISDN) Giant timesharing networks to information processing services offering multiple service subscriptions and telecommunication opportunities on a wide area basis.

integrated software A collection of computer applications programmed into a single software package.

integrated source graphics (ISG) The integration (combination) of filmed images and digital code on a single medium.

integrity A quality of information collections which relates to the extent to which a collection of information remains intact over time or the extent to which related information can be physically housed together.

intelligent A descriptor for equipment which has the capacity to select, compare, calculate, and display information. This capacity may be provided by a microprocessor.

intelligent building A building with computers installed to regulate building services and utilities (climate control, elevator services, security, and light control).

intelligent character recognition (ICR) The capability of a text scanner that can recognize and electronically input virtually any type size or shape.

intelligent copier See *intelligent printer.*

intelligent job aids The infusion of expert systems technologies into training media.

intelligent printer A machine that has the capacity to replicate (copy) existing documents (called direct copy process) as well as the capability to for alphabetic, numeric, and graphic images from digital information received from a computer.

interactive A characteristic of computer-assisted instruction software that describes the capability of the program to involve the learner in the process and requires learner responses—not passive participation—in the presentation of materials.

interactive design Repetitive designing process permitted by applications generators which is used to test software applications before the software is implemented.

interactive video system The combination of computer training programs with full motion video instruction. The system combines textual screen image instruction and video presentations.

interactive videodisc system A computer-assisted instruction system that combines computer training with motion video pictures in an interactive format. For portions of the training experience, the learner may be reacting to text on the screen while other sequences may involve watching video materials; however, all of the material is stored on a videodisk.

interface (1) A physical device that connects information processing components and transmits information from one to the other; (2) protocols under which physical interfaces operate.

interview guide Document with questions and spaces for recording answers during a face-to-face interview which is used during office systems analysis to assure uniformity of data gathered throughout the organization.

ion-deposition printer A nonimpact printer that creates text and graphics by depositing ions (electronically charged particles) on an electrostatic field created by signals from a computer. An image is first created on a drum and then transferred to paper.

J

job A set of tasks related to a particular employment position.

job analysis The process of collecting data about job content and analyzing the nature of the functions, duties, tasks, and responsibilities that comprise a specific job. The analysis involves carefully planned data gathering.

job description A document that details the nature of a job (the results of a job analysis).

job evaluation The process of placing a monetary worth on a particular job.

job fair An event in a public place that brings together employer representatives and individuals seeking employment.

job rotation A training experience that involves moving an employee from one job assignment to another for brief periods, and frequently involves a variety of departments and functional areas.

job sharing Dividing a job into segments (usually two) staffed by different people. Together, two persons fill one job with each person working a different portion of the workday.

job specification A document that specifies minimum and desirable qualifications for the person who will hold a particular job.

jukebox A device for storing optical disks and accessing information contained on the disks.

K

kerning The production of typeset or printed characters that extend into the "space" belonging to the next character.

key (information security) A feature of an information security system that uses a protected and discriminately distributed code to "unscramble" encrypted information. The key is applied at the receiving end of a data transmission.

KIPS (Knowledge/Information Processing System) A computer system in the fifth generation software concept. The term was coined by Japanese developers of expert systems designed to engage in reasoning activities to solve problems as humans do.

knowledge worker Managers, executives, and professional staff employees who work with information and make decisions.

L

laser-beam transmission An optical communication link that transmits signals on laser beams for short distances.

LCS printer A page printer that creates characters on paper without physical impact or ribbons.

leading The space between the baselines of two lines of print.

LED Light emitting diode.

legal value In information resources management, the value created by a government's requirement that information (records) be maintained, preserved, or protected.

letter-quality printer Any printer that creates text that is equal or similar in quality to that created by shaped-character type fonts. Some printers in this category may actually form the characters by dot-matrix or nonimpact devices that produce high-quality print.

letterpress A printing press using raised molded characters and ink to print images on paper.

Lewin Change Model A process for changing employee behavior by first "unfreezing" current behavior, behavior modification, and "refreezing" the new behavior.

librarian One who specializes in the management of information collections. Duties include classification, housing, circulating, and protecting information media and the management of other personnel.

line office Subcategory of a type II office, a fairly complex job involving lower and middle line managers with 20–30 percent of time devoted to desk work and heavy communication involvement.

line position A job in the organization's formal structure that represents responsibility for personnel and processes directly related to the purpose of the organization's existence.

local area network (LAN) A communication link among multiple information processing components within a relatively small geographical area (technically, confined to the premises of the owner) that may require special computer (servers) to manage the flow of information and network software. See also bus topology, ring topology, and star topology.

lumens A measure of the flow of light.

M

machine language A set of symbols that computers recognize.

mainframe computer Large, centralized, high-capacity, expensive computer systems. The term came into popular use to distinguish between these systems and smaller computer systems called minicomputers and microcomputers.

management by objectives (MBO) A goal-oriented planning and appraisal system that emphasizes written goals, superior-subordinate agreement on goals and scheduled subordinate-superior reviews of accomplishments. The goals are behavior oriented and measurable or identifiable when accomplished.

management information system (MIS) The application of large, mainframe computer systems and concentration on transaction information processing to produce information reports based upon past activity for management use in guiding the organization (concentrates on standardized reporting on a regular basis).

Mark I The digital computer developed by Professor Howard Aiken of Harvard University and built by IBM in the 1940s. It was controlled by electro-mechanical relays and performed about three additions per second.

mass storage Large-capacity electronic information capabilities. Sometimes used to refer to external storage devices because of the unlimited capacity of this method of storing information.

mastering The production of a "master" copy of a videodisk or optical disk from which duplicates of the disk are produced.

matrix design An organizational design concept based on the concept of project management. Work of the organization is carried out by groups responsible for the completion of a particular job.

matrix plan A combination of centralized and decentralized administrative support services.

MC/ST (Magnetic Card Selectric Typewriter) A machine introduced by IBM in 1969 used for text editing and storage. Editing and storage capabilities were similar to the earlier MT/ST, but the MC/ST used a magnetic "card" (magnetic recording medium the size of an 80-column data processing card) as the recording medium.

media conversion The process of transforming information stored in one medium or format to another medium or format. Examples include transforming magnetic tape to computer output microfilm; a magnetic disk configured in the format for one information processing system to that configured for another; and text on paper to digital code through the OCR technique.

medium In information management, the vehicle for holding information. The three major categories of information media are paper, film, and electronically produced media (magnetic and optical technologies).

megabyte (MB) A measure of computer memory or the capacity of storage media. One megabyte equals 1,048,576 bytes and is popularly referred to as a million bytes or 1,000 K bytes.

mentor A superior or experienced peer, usually within an organization, who assumes professional interest in another person's career development and acts in an advisory capacity.

menu In information systems, a "help" feature consisting of a list of options available to the user. Functions are initiated by viewing the menu of options and selecting one of them with a command.

method In procedures analysis or work measurement applications, a subdivision of a procedure or one step in a multistep procedure.

methods time measurement (MTM) The measurement of time consumed in performing each method in a procedure. Repeated measurements are averages to determine a "standard" time quantity for the performance of that method.

microcomputer A small computer, as measured by RAM capacity, operating speed, and physical size. Recent developments have made the distinction between "large" microcomputers and "small" minicomputers difficult.

microcomputer processor unit (MPU) The central processing unit for a microcomputer.

microfiche A micrographic film category containing a matrix of document images usually cut into 4 x 6-inch pieces of transparent film from 105mm rolls of film.

microfilm jacket A device for storing microfilm images constructed of transparent plastic sleeves into which strips of microfilm images are inserted.

micrographics The field of information management involving the creation of filmed, miniaturized information images (usually transparent photographs of document images) but also includes computer-manipulated data collections and X-ray images.

micro-opaque A paper micrographic image medium. Images are produced as miniature photographs (printed on paper) of document images and the paper photographic image is illuminated and magnified for reading.

microwave transmission An airway communication link that transmits signals over relatively short distances in a straight line using microwaves.

minicomputer A computer system, usually smaller in capacity, processing speed, and physical size than a mainframe computer but larger (as determined by the same characteristics) than a microcomputer.

mixed process The combination of administrative support and word processing functions into the jobs of secretaries, usually in a decentralized pattern.

MNB (Multinational business) A business that operates facilities or markets products or services in many nations.

modeling A technique for predicting the future by making computer analyses that incorporate past quantitative information and expected future conditions.

modem External computer peripheral that communicates information from one system to another by converting information signals from digital to analog format for transmission over ordinary telephone lines.

MSDOS (Microsoft Disk Operating System) a microcomputer operating system software package developed for the IBM personal computer and compatible systems.

MT/ST (Magnetic Tape Selectric Typewriter) A stand-alone word processor introduced in 1964 by IBM, activated by magnetic code recorded on reels of magnetic tape and used to edit and repetitively type text.

multiplexer A telecommunication device that combines multiple transmission signals into one analog signal for transmission over ordinary telephone lines.

multiprocessing Application of computer power from more than one central processing unit to the information processing tasks of multiple users.

muscle loading A condition of muscular strain and fatigue caused by the effect of gravity on the human body when it remains in a fixed position for a long period of time.

N

natural language One set of computer programs in the category of artificial intelligence languages, these programs feature the conversion of human language to machine language and simplify custom application of computer programs.

natural language processor An element of an expert system (computer program) enabling the user to apply conversational English to communicate with a computer instead of the traditional formal commands required for such communication.

near letter quality A printer quality that approaches the quality of a typewriter.

needs assessment A diagnostic activity that allows trainers to become aware of problems in the organization that might be remedied by training.

network A system of communication links for moving electronic data from one information processing device or storage medium to another.

network organization Organizational units formed for temporary or ad hoc assignments because of the relationships or skills among the individuals—not because of the job titles of the individuals.

networking Computer: The process of connecting information processing devices by a communication link that enables the exchange of information among all devices connected to the network. Human: The process of forming connections with other people who are helpful in career development and professional learning.

neural network A computer system modeled roughly after the human brain's web-like neuron structure; systems learn by example, analyze incomplete and inaccurate information; examples: reading finger-prints, handwritten signatures, handwritten numerals.

node Intersections along the communication link that serves as a network which per its the connection of an information processing or transmitting device to the network.

nonexempt employee A category of employees for whom employers must meet wage and hour restrictions. Managerial employees are exempt from such restrictions.

nonimpact printer A computer peripheral that creates text or graphics on paper by a process that does not involve printer parts that physically strike the paper. Examples include ink-jet and laser printers.

nonprocedural language A computer language that consists of a small set of powerful commands that simply tell the computer what to do, as opposed to procedural languages that tell the computer how to do it; less complicated than procedural languages and may be used by persons with relatively little programming experience.

O

objectivity A term used to describe the characteristic of a test that allows different people to grade the test and reach the same score.

object-oriented programming Programming that will customize software by connecting blocks of program code in a pattern to accomplish a special task.

office An organizational support system made up of people, processes, and technologies for processing and communicating information needed to perform the organization's basic functions. The concept, which developed during the late nineteenth century, originally referred to a physical place as well as the human and technical systems operating in that physical place. Office automation has rendered that definition somewhat archaic.

office automation The concept of the interaction of people in office environments using technology to support the processing and communication of information needed to meet the organization's basic goals.

office automation software A category of integrated computer software containing a variety of office automation capabilities in a single software package.

office landscaping The use of open spaces for office design; *landscaping* as a descriptor for such processes refers to the extensive use of plants in open-design offices.

office marriage The traditional boss-secretary team involving one support person for each executive.

office of the future A concept envisioned in the 1970s that predicted office environments similar to current concepts of integrated office systems and electronic workstations whereby communication and information storage and retrieval functions would take place electronically without paper documents.

office politics The existence of an individual or a group within an organization working against other individuals or groups in order to acquire power and status within that organization.

office procedure A task that is performed within an office environment.

office sharing The use of satellite tele-communication links to employ the services of office workers in other countries, particularly the lesser developed nations where labor costs are low (also referred to as "offshore offices").

office systems analyst A specialized information systems analyst who works with the office automation needs of an organization and develops plans for information systems implementation.

office systems study The process of identifying existing office systems, particularly those associated with information processing and communication within an organization. For organizations that do not use information technologies to manage office systems, the study will identify units with potential for improvement of productivity through the application of such technologies.

office systems team The group selected to analyze organizational needs for office systems, plan a strategy for satisfying such needs, design systems, install systems, and evaluate systems.

off-line storage Electronic information storage on a medium outside the computer's central processing unit which requires operator intervention to access the information.

offset A duplication process that produces multiple paper copies of information created on a master original. More sophisticated applications of the process are called "offset printing."

offset lithography A sophisticated offset duplication process used for printing artwork and four-color business publications.

OJT (On-The-Job Training) The training provided employees who begin to perform job routines during the learning process.

on-line Descriptor for an information processing configuration permitting a computer to access information without manual loading of that information into the system.

open plan A concept of office design based on the idea of fostering the free flow of information which features office spaces with few partitions and workstations divided by partitions, screens, and plants.

open system An organizational system which is influenced in its operations by the external environment.

Open Systems Interconnection (OSI) Reference Model A seven-layered system of standards or protocols for information processing systems with the goal of interchangeable information, regardless of manufacturer, without restraint of proprietary protocols or operating standards.

Open Systems Model The Nadler and Tushman model for understanding how human factors affect the design of organizational systems; views organizations as four components: task, individual, formal organization, and informal organization.

operating environment software Software that functions "between" the operating system and the applications package to instruct the computer's handling of information storage and retrieval to simplify such processes for the user; combined with "friendly" user interfaces, such software eliminates the need for users to remember details involved in entering applications and storing files.

operating system Computer programs that control the computer and direct the processing of information required to perform an applications program.

operational value In records/information management, the value of information that supports or documents routine activities of the organization.

operative Workers at the basic or fundamental level within an organization who may be referred to as "nonexempt" employees; they are among the employees to whom employers must pay the minimum wage and satisfy other requirements.

optical character recognition (OCR) A process performed when computers recognize printed, typewritten, coded, or specially lettered handwritten characters, converting them to electronic data that the computer can process.

optical disk A medium for storing digitized code created by laser beams, it was developed for storing the huge amounts of code necessary to store digitized document images.

organizational climate The perceived characteristics present in the work environment.

organizational fit The degree to which an individual matches the values, traditions, and behaviors of other individuals in an organization.

organizational profile A subsection of a strategic plan that identifies the organization's objectives, goals, and overall mission; its strengths, weaknesses, and limitations; and its projected directions while concentrating on the present status of the organization.

orientation (employee) For new employees, the routines associated with introduction to the organization, the working environment, organizational policy and procedure, and peers.

output In organizational systems theory, the end result of processing the systems' input; in information processing, the processed information that comes from the system or that category of computer peripherals that produce processed information.

P

paraprofessional Work similar to that of a principal but performed by a person at a lower level, usually by an individual without the full credentials of the principal. For example, a legal paraprofessional performs tasks for an attorney.

people people A category of individuals who prefer jobs that require a high degree of social interaction.

peripheral An accessory hardware piece connected to a computer's central processing unit.

personal computer A small, general-purpose computer used by one individual which sometimes serves as an electronic workstation connected to a large system in addition to operating independently.

personal development A planned activity that enables employees to maintain effective performance and productivity levels; training and skills updating activity.

personal support A category of computer applications software that allows users to organize time, keep track of appointments, schedule activities, keep track of events that must transpire before projects can move from one stage to another, and provide other personal reminders and records.

personnel management The field of management charged with the fundamental responsibility for recruiting, hiring, training, compensating, developing, and caring for the general welfare of employees.

photocomposition A word processing-like computer application that creates high-quality text (in a virtually unlimited range of font styles and type sizes) and graphics suitable for printing applications; output of this process is "master" copy for offset printing processes.

pica In printing terminology, one-sixth of a horizontal inch or 12 points; in typewriter terminology, a size of type and spacing arrangement that creates 10 characters per inch (See *pitch*.).

pilot An experimental or trial application of a concept; for office systems, the installation of a technology in a single department, allowing observations in that department to affect the nature of the installations in other departments. Similar to prototype installations, but larger in scale.

pitch A measure of type size and typewriter spacing systems that indicates the number of characters per inch. For example, 10 pitch = 10 cpi, 12-pitch = 12 cpi, and 15 pitch = 15 cpi.

planetary camera A microfilm camera mounted above a plane or bed where documents are placed for photographing.

platform skills In training, the communication skills of the trainer; oral communication skills; the ability to organize presentations and to incorporate learning mate-

rials, audio-visual aids, and a variety of training methods.

point A measure of type size, 1/72 of one inch.

PostScript language A computer and printer language designed for page description tasks, developed by Adobe Systems; the language controls the appearance of type, making possible the manipulation of type size and other features.

primary system In organizational systems, a subsystem directly related to the purpose(s) for which the organization exists. An example is the production system for a manufacturing organization.

print-wheel printer An impact printer that creates text using the impact of shaped characters on the ends of a wheel with petal-like devices — one for each character; it is frequently referred to as a "daisy wheel" or "letter-quality" printer.

priority basis In administrative support services, the scheme for determining the sequence in which tasks are performed by support employees.

private branch exchange (PBX) An automatic switching system accepting and transmitting analog signals.

procedural language High-level, machine independent programming languages designed to specifically tell the computer how to process each step in a sequence of instructions.

procedure A subdivision of a system; a standardized routine for carrying out one of the activities that make up a system.

procedures analyst A position title for one who conducts detailed analysis of standard procedures and writes descriptive procedures statements, usually for inclusion in a procedures manual or a general office manual.

procedures audit   An examination of all standard procedures used by an organization to accomplish standardized tasks.

processing   In organizational systems theory, any transformation of systems input; in information processing, the manipulation of information or a category of computer components designed to manipulate information.

productivity   The value of measurable output by an individual or a group of individuals compared to the value of input. Examples are goods produced in an hour of an employee's time that consume a given quantity of raw materials or the value of services provided in a given amount of time.

professional office   A subcategory of type II office—offices of nonline managers or executives. Examples include legal staff, architectural staff, and planners. About 40 percent of a professional's time is devoted to "desk work," the communication component varies, and administrative-secretarial support varies (but is likely to be limited).

program   In information processing, a set of instructions that tell a computer how to perform an information processing task. See also *applications program, operating system,* and *system software.*

programmer   One who writes detailed instruction code that lists in logical order the steps the computer must follow to perform a task.

programming language   A set of symbols or instructions (words, phrases, or codes) to which computers will react.

proportional spacing   A typewriter or printer spacing capability that designates space for a character based upon the width of that character, rather than devoting a standard spacing to every character.

protocol   A set of conventions or guidelines that governs the for at, electrical conditions, and transmission speeds of electronic information transmission.

prototype   A small-scale, experimental, or trial application of a concept; for office systems, a small-scale use of an office technology to evaluate its effectiveness or the product of a particular vendor.

prototyping   The trial application of software prior to implementation.

punched card   A paper card into which holes are punched according to a code to represent information and which is used as an information input medium. Many information processing systems input information directly to the system without the necessity of this medium.

Q

qualitative benefit   A benefit resulting from a change that improves the quality of performance of employees and systems or the quality of a product or service of an organizational unit, though not a measurable benefit.

quality circle (QC)   A type of employee group that strives for improvements in efficiency and effectiveness in the work environment and in the productivity of the groups and features regular meetings and statistical analysis of productivity.

QWERTY keyboard The traditional keyboard for typewriters and information processing components which follows the arrangement of keys developed for the Sholes typewriter in 1868.

QWL benefit A benefit derived from a system that involves improvement of the quality of work life for employees who work with that system.

query system In information systems, a feature that involves questions posed to the user by the system; decision support systems and project planning systems employ this technique.

R

raceway A channel fitted in the bottom or middle of a wall panel or divider in an open office for the distribution of electricity and information communication cables to workstations.

radio wave transmission An airwave telecommunication link that uses Federal Communication Commission identified radio frequencies over which business information may be transmitted.

random access The capacity of an information processing system to go directly to desired information without "reading" through long lists of data to discover the desired information.

random access memory (RAM) An internal computer storage device that accepts programs and files necessary to operate an applications program; access is random and new information may be added until the memory capacity is reached.

read only memory (ROM) The internal storage memory in a computer's central processing unit. Information contained in this memory is permanently installed by the computer manufacturer and can be accessed randomly to assist in various operational details.

record A collection of information or that which informs or has the potential to inform, regardless of medium-recorded information that has value.

records life cycle The stages in the existence of recorded information: creation, distribution, maintenance, storage, disposition, and preservation.

records maintenance The holding of information with a potential for active use so that it can be easily and quickly retrieved and the procedures, personnel, systems, and equipment necessary to accomplish this goal.

records management The support system that manages the creation, distribution, maintenance, retrieval, disposition, and protection of information resources in electronic, film, or paper media and the management of technologies and personnel required to accomplish these tasks.

records retention schedule A listing of every record that exists within an organization, along with the duration of that record's retention in each stage of the information resources life cycle: active use, inactive storage, archival (or date of destruction if not archived).

records storage   The phase of the information life cycle after the information has passed the potential for active use; for tangible records, their removal from high-use records collections and storage in an inactive records collection.

relational database   A database holding information in tables; output is related by commands that pull related information from the tables and compile it in the desired format.

reliability   In testing, the characteristic of a test that produces consistent results on multiple applications.

repetitive strain injury   Injuries caused by repeated, forceful motions; examples: wrist injury and neck strain.

reprographics   Support system involving technology, personnel, and processes for reproducing textual or graphic information through a variety of techniques. Examples are duplicating, printing, and reproduction of micro-filmed information media.

research and technical writer   A job title for one who specializes in the research and writing of books, manuals, directives, newsletters, training materials, descriptive literature, and any documentation that accompanies hardware or software.

resume   A document that describes the educational and work experiences, personal characteristics, and special interests of an individual who seeks employment (also referred to as a personal data sheet).

ring topology   A local area network topology involving an arrangement of nodes along an unbroken circular communication link.

robot   A computer-operated device with sensors that read input signals or environmental conditions and react accordingly. It may have the ability to "see" objects, detect "touch" sensations, hear, and think with the aid of a form of artificial intelligence software.

ROI (Return On Investment)   The cost of an activity, system, or procedure is compared with the dollar value of that activity, system, or procedure. It may be expressed as a ratio. For example, 4:1 = four dollars in benefits for each dollar of investment.

roll film   A micrographic film category involving continuous document or other images on a roll of transparent film.

rotary camera   A microfilm camera through which documents are rotated for photographing; most rotary cameras film both sides of a document simultaneously.

RPG (Report Programming Generator)   A popular business information systems program language for writing applications programs.

S

sabbatical   Paid work leave, usually for executives only, for development activity, study or research away from the job.

self-assessment   The stage in the career planning process that involves self-evaluation of aptitudes, interests, values, and skills.

shared logic system An information processing system featuring a dedicated central processing unit and provision for multiple terminals. An example is a word processor with multiple terminals for creating documents.

shrinkwrap agreement An agreement which appears on the plastic wrapping for software packages. The software developer who wishes to consider payment for software to be a lease agreement (not an outright purchase) indicates that breaking the wrap and using the software constitutes agreement to such a plan.

simplex A telecommunication path carrying information in one direction only.

social system In organizational systems, the pattern of human behaviors among the people who comprise an organization. It is influenced by social forces such as employee needs, values, motivations, attitudes, and expectations.

sociotechnical approach In office automation, an approach that considers the behavioral as well as the technical aspects of office automation.

soft-dollar benefit Measurable dollar benefits that result from a change but that are not immediately realized; an efficiency benefit resulting in an indirect or long-term dollar saving.

software Usually a set of computer programs used for information processing applications or program preparation. See also *applications program, operating system*, and *system software*.

software house A firm that employs programmers, develops and tests computer programs, and markets the programs to the public.

software on a chip A computer program that has been recorded in a microchip.

solar lighting Sunlight supplement to artificial lighting.

speaker-dependent recognition (SDR) A voice-recognition technology that allows identified users to record a vocabulary of words that the system will recognize and respond to. Vocabulary is prerecorded and stored in the system and input must be pronounced clearly and slowly.

speaker-independent recognition (SIR) A voice-recognition technology that involves voice input with equipment that recognizes words within a limited vocabulary without the necessity for equipment "training" through prerecorded vocabulary.

speaker verification A voice-recognition technology that matches speakers' unique voice patterns to stored patterns for security purposes; a no-match prevents entry to the system.

speech synthesis A computer system that creates audio responses representing stored information. Responses resemble the human voice, but signals are not recorded human voice signals; they are computer-generated sounds.

spreadsheet A category of computer applications software used for financial analysis allowing users to work with extensive screen worksheets of quantitative information and built-in formulas that allow users to plug in data to observe the results of "what-if" situations.

staff position A position that has responsibility for special functions that support the main functions. Examples include legal, accounting, engineering, and other positions that assist line positions.

stand-alone system An independently functioning computer system or other information processing system that does not communicate with any other system.

standard commands A user interface (system capability) that enables a user to use one language or set of commands to control computer operations. Examples include saving a file or transferring a file. Many applications programs use different commands to perform similar tasks.

standardized test A test that has been subjected to reliability and validity measures (an employment test, for example).

standard office time data Published standards that identify the time consumed by small elements of tasks. Standards are applied to identified task elements to create a standard time for completing the entire task.

standard operating procedure The collection of procedures for an organization, usually written descriptions of procedures which may be bound in a collection of written procedures for a whole organization or some unit of that organization.

star topology A local area network topology requiring devices located at nodes along the network to communicate with each other via links to a central controlling device.

step-and-repeat camera A camera used to photograph documents and record images in a matrix pattern on film that will later be sliced into microfiche units.

storage medium A tangible device on which information is recorded electronically. Examples include magnetic tapes, magnetic disks, and optical disks.

stored program The concept of creating computer instructions (programs) as coded numbers and storing them in the computer's memory, it was first applied with the EDVAC (electronic discrete variable automatic computer).

strategic plan The document that outlines implementation.

strategic planning A long-range, holistic approach to planning for organizations; planning with a vision and foresight that enables planners to include evolving conditions and to predict future needs.

stress A pattern of physiological, psychological, and behavioral responses to environmental demands that exceed an individual's capacity to cope.

subsystem An element, subdivision, or subgroup of a system.

supercomputer A computer designed specifically to process vast numbers of repetitive calculations at very rapid speeds.

support staff Those workers who manipulate or provide information for knowledge workers and have responsibility for routine administrative tasks and decision making. Examples include executive secretaries, word processing specialists, data-entry operators, bookkeepers, and clerks.

support system In organizational systems, a subsystem that exists to assist the primary systems in achieving their objectives. Examples are a personnel (or HRD) department, word processing and administrative support centers, and an MIS department.

synchronous mode Information transmission mode that communicates groups of characters a block at a time with control characters before and after each block; requires clock-synchronized sending and receiving equipment.

synergy The concept that a group generally accomplishes more work and achieves better results than individuals working independently.

system A set of related elements that interact with each other to achieve a purpose.

systems analysis The process of breaking apart and examining descriptive data about a system.

systems applications architecture (SAA) The IBM version of a cooperative processing (fusion of mainframes and personal computers) plan for mainframe/personal computer linkages in a manner that is more sophisticated than direct links or telephone-line link.

systems approach An approach to visualizing, developing, and managing a family of related activities that work together in concert to achieve goals and objectives; in office automation, people, equipment, and procedures functioning interdependently.

systems design For office systems, the creation of systems that employ technology to enhance knowledge worker and support worker productivity and communication, without sacrificing the human factors or the quality of work life for users.

systems furniture Modular, interchangeable components for designing workstations to fit the needs of both systems and people.

systems model A conceptual representation of a system usually depicted by graphic representations that label ingredients of the system and depict the nature of their interaction.

system prompt Cues to users of computer systems, such as requests for the name of a file to be retrieved or a request for a password for security clearance.

system software A set of programs that directs the functions of a computer as it performs applications (also called an operating system).

T

task lighting Light provided for a specific workstation as a supplement to ambient lighting.

task seating Office seating designed for those who perform a particular specialized task such as keyboarding.

taxonomy A system for categorizing or classifying phenomena.

team approach In a centralized administrative support plan, a work group or team of principals and support employees.

technical system For organizations, an element needed to accomplish objectives — one that goes beyond the human and social elements. Examples include physical facilities, technology, organizational structure, and standardized procedures.

technophobia Fear of technology.

technostress A condition resulting from the inability of an individual or organization to adapt to the introduction and operation of new technology.

telecommunications Transmission of information over communications links using a variety of transmission methods or the professional discipline involving hardware, systems, and personnel for communicating information (voice, data, text, image) from one device to another and from one location to another.

telecommuting A work-at-home arrangement (or arrangement to work at some location other than the traditional work-place), often referred to as the "electronic cottage," for people whose primary job activities take place at an electronic workstation. The workstation is installed in the employee's home and connected by a telecommunication link (hotels may also provide such facilities).

teletraining The application of teleconferencing tools to the training function using video teleconference transmissions.

teleconferencing A telecommunication system combining various information transmission devices. Full teleconferencing involves full motion video, voice, data, graphics, and facsimile transmitted simultaneously from two or more locations.

temporary employment A firm that provides the services of an employee on a temporary basis,

usually to fill the position of an employee who is unable to perform in the usual capacity.

termination The permanent dismissal of an employee from employment.

territoriality A psychological need of humans to establish spaces to call their own.

test reliability Characteristic of a test that gives consistent results.

test validity Characteristic of a test that measures that which it was designed to measure.

test objectivity Characteristic of a test that can be graded without scorer bias affecting the result.

text Written information in the form of words, sentences, and paragraphs which may be recorded and transmitted in a variety of media.

Theory X Label for a leadership style which assumes that workers are lazy, that they are motivated only by pay or fear, and that the leader must be autocratic to get results.

Theory Y Label for a leadership style of a manager who assumes that the worker wants to work, will accept responsibility, strives to produce good things, and can be trusted to participate in the job effort.

Theory Z A combination of Japanese and American leadership styles and organizational philosophy. Factors influencing this style are long-term employment, decision making by group consensus, infrequent employee promotions, less specialized career paths, and holistic concern for people.

things people A category of individuals who prefer jobs that involve the manipulation of machines or working with tangible objects.

tight building syndrome The absence of fresh air in tightly constructed buildings.

time standard The quantity of time consumed by a given productive effort which may be reversed to express the productivity accomplished in a specified time period.

time study See *methods time measurement.*

toner A thick substance used in printers and copiers; electrostatic images on paper draw toner to the paper where it is affixed by heat to form images.

transmission mode In telecommunication, nature of signals representing characters and indicators which tell receiving equipment where the signals for each character begin and end.

transmission path In telecommunication, direction of flow and the condition or absence thereof for simultaneous flow in two directions on one communication link.

topology The configuration of lines and nodes in an information network. See also bus, ring, and star topologies.

turf protection Behaviors of individuals and groups who wish to prevent erosion of responsibility or authority by the transfer of authority, responsibility, or personnel to other portions of the organization or the elimination of tasks performed.

trainee One who is being trained.

trainer The specialist who directs the training experience or the title of a human resource development spe-

cialist who plans and organizes all training efforts for an organization.

training Educational experiences that provide the opportunity for learning concepts, skills, or attitudes and usually associated with improvement of employee performance.

training medium Any teaching material or technology used to deliver training (such as printed material, class room experience, or computer software).

training model A guide to the development of the training program; components specify the events and the sequence of events in a training cycle.

training objective A detailed statement about a training experience such as what the employee must learn, the resources that will be provided, the constraints that affect the process, and the standards of performance expected at the completion of the experience.

training strategies Methods of presentation for training experiences (for example, lecture, case study, role playing, and simulation).

trend analysis Forecasting method used to analyze and interpret patterns in society's systems (social, economic, political, legal, ethical, etc.) and to project them into the future.

twisted pair wire A telecommunication line composed of two wires (the type of wiring used in ordinary telephone wiring).

type I office An office in which the processed information is of a fairly routine nature (examples are correspondence, business forms, scheduled reports and other documents, and routine clerical procedures such as filing).

type II office An office in which knowledge work predominates (examples are nonroutine or customized activity involving problem solving or decision making at a nonclerical level).

U

UNIVAC The first commercially developed digital computer installed at General Electric Appliance Park in Louisville, Kentucky and built by Remington Rand.

UNIX A computer operating system developed by Bell Laboratories.

updatable microfilm A microfilm medium onto which documents are created by either an electrostatic or a heat transfer process; the microfiche-sized film may be reinserted into the camera for adding additional images until the film is filled. Some systems permit obliteration of images and their replacement with new images.

user-driven system A philosophical approach to office automation that stresses the end user as the primary consideration in selecting technologies—the technology is considered secondary.

user group Individuals who use one manufacturer's hardware and form an association or society to share information about developments and applications for that system. Such groups are popular among both business and personal users of computing equipment. (The term also refers to groups that use a common technology—not necessarily one manufacturer's equipment.)

user interface Information system capability allowing individuals to perform information processing functions from a single software package (includes standard commands, menu structures, system prompts, and file procedures).

user liaison An information systems specialist who acts as an in-house consultant, helping others in the organization with their computer hardware and software needs.

utility Computer programs that may be considered part of the operating system collection and permit users to carry out "housekeeping" chores such as copying files and formatting blank disks.

V

validity Characteristic of a test that it measures what it is intended to measure.

value added A term associated with productivity measurement which concentrates on the value added to productivity by a quantifiable effort. Also portion of profit that is represented by a particular effort to produce more or to maintain production but do so at a lower cost.

value-added benefit The combined, long-range effect of efficiency and effectiveness benefits brought about by changes in organizational structure or processes. For office systems, these benefits are represented by improved organizational performance because of the existence and effective functioning of such systems.

value-added network (VAN) A public long-distance network for information transmission (added services include electronic mail, access to public databases, and syndicated databases).

value-added vendor For information systems, one who buys hardware components from original equipment manufacturers and resells the components along with software as systems designed for their customers' particular needs.

vendor training Training experiences provided by the seller of systems hardware.

vertical market software Computer applications software developed for highly specialized applications, such as accounting for a medical office or a database for a law firm.

vertical mobility Job changes involving "upward" movement to jobs with increased responsibility.

vestibule training In-house training provided for employees before they begin a job. This type of training may simulate on-the-job activities but is conducted away from the workstation in a classroom or other training facility.

video The portion of image technology that involves either moving or still television pictures, live transmission, or recorded images (may be combined with audio signals).

video display screen The computer peripheral that displays program or file content on a screen such as a cathode ray tube or a liquid crystal display.

visioning An attempt to identify future values by formulating relationships among society's past and present systems.

vital records Records that are so critical to the daily operation of an organization that their destruction could threaten the continued existence of the organization.

voice communication In information systems, any communication process involving the human voice.

voice key software Software to sequence computer keystrokes and associate them with spoken vocabulary or user-given voice commands instead of keyboard commands.

voice mail A system for storing and forwarding voice messages to specified recipients or lists of recipients and receiving incoming messages that are stored in "electronic mailboxes." See also electronic mail and voice store and forward.

voice recognition technology An information-input technology for computer systems that converts the human voice to digital form for processing by computers.

voice response Audible voice output from an information processing system that has accepted and stored the human voice in digitized format. (Output carries the inflection and intonation of the original speaker.)

voice store and forward A voice mail feature which converts an oral message to digital form, stores the message, dials the recipient's number, delivers the oral message, and records a signal for the sender that the message has been delivered.

W

wage gap The difference in typical pay between two groups of workers (frequently applied to male-female pay differentials).

white-collar crime Acts engaged in by white-collar employees (for example, illegal manipulation of funds, illegal manipulation or disposal of information, or personal gain from illegally obtained information).

white-collar labor sector Executives, managers, professional staff, administrative support employees, and other nonindustrial or nonproduction jobs.

white-collar productivity The productivity of executives, managers, and professional staff persons.

white sound Continuous, artificially produced background sounds that mask distracting noises in a work environment.

windowing A feature of computer software that allows the user to view multiple files on subdivisions of the display screen simultaneously.

word In data structures, a set of characters of information "housed" at one location in a computer's memory.

word processing A support system involving the use of technology to support the creation, editing, and manipulation of text in the communication process.

workbench Software development systems in the fourth generation language category that enable the user to generate software. (This includes design, logic generation, testing, and documenting the software being developed).

work measurement Quantifying the volume of productivity in a working environment through physical counts or other volume measures.

work simplification A formal effort to examine and eliminate negative factors affecting work procedures by reducing the time consumed during tasks through improving

the work environment, changing the sequence of procedures, or eliminating delays.

work specialization Limiting the nature of work done by an individual to enable the development of greater skill in a specific work area.

WYSIWYG (What You See Is What You Get) The quality of the screen image for desktop publishing systems; images approximate the type style and proportion when printed.

Z

zero-based corporate structure The possibility of total rebuilding of an organization's structure as organizational needs changed.

zoning A technique for building climate control that allows temperature variations in one area without affecting the temperature in another area.

INDEX